BASICS OF SOCIAL RESEARCH

QUALITATIVE AND QUANTITATIVE APPROACHES

THIRD CANADIAN EDITION

W. LAWRENCE NEUMAN
UNIVERSITY OF WISCONSIN-WHITEWATER

KAREN ROBSON
YORK UNIVERSITY

Toronto

Editor-in-Chief: Michelle Sartor
Acquisitions Editor: Matthew Christian
Sponsoring Editor: Joel Gladstone
Marketing Manager: Lisa Gillis
Project Manager: Andrea Falkenberg
Developmental Editor: Patti Sayle
Media Content Developer: Marisa D'Andrea
Media Content Editor: Rachel Stuckey
Media Producer: Bogdan Kosenko
Production Services: Aptara
Permissions Project Manager: Daniela Glass
Photo Permissions Research: Stephen Merland, PreMedia Global
Text Permissions Research: Anna Waluk, Electronic Publishing Services
Cover Designer: Suzanne Behnke
Cover Image: David P. Lewis/Shutterstock

---

10 9 8 7 6 5 4 3 2 1 CKV

Library and Archives Canada Cataloguing in Publication

Neuman, William Lawrence, 1950-, author
Basics of social research / W. Lawrence Neuman, Karen Robson.—Third Canadian edition.

Includes bibliographical references and index.
ISBN 978-0-205-92790-6 (pbk.)

1. Sociology—Research—Methodology—Textbooks. 2. Social sciences—Research—Methodology—Textbooks. I. Robson, Karen, 1973-, author II. Title.

HM571.N49 2014 301.072 C2013-906530-X

ISBN 13: 978-0-205-92790-6
ISBN 10: 0-205-92790-4

Brief Contents

Table of Contents

Preface

Many students approach a first course on social research with anxiety and trepidation. Some of them associate the course with mathematics and statistics, which they may have had an unpleasant experience with; some may have struggled in natural science courses that used experiments; and some do not know what to expect from a course in social research and believe it is beyond them and only for advanced, very smart scholars. Many students delay taking the required "methods" course until the last semester of their degree—although the course is often meant to be taken in the second year of study. Indeed, courses in research methods often carry the unfortunate reputation that they are difficult or boring. As university professors who have considerable experience teaching these courses, the authors are well aware of the inherent challenges of convincing students that the study of methods can be enjoyable!

Basics of Social Research introduces you to social research and presents "what researchers do and why" in a nonthreatening manner that captures both the excitement and the importance of doing "real" research. Once you overcome any anxiety and recognize what research is actually about, you will probably find it fascinating. A course in social research methodology differs from most other social science courses. Most courses examine content topics such as inequality, crime, racial divisions, gender relations, urban society, and so forth. A methodology course is relevant, as it prepares you to think more systematically about content and also reveals how content findings are created. That is, this social research method teaches you how the knowledge in social sciences comes into being.

This book aims to make the information it presents easy to understand and accessible, but that does not mean that it is simplistic. Indeed, proper research is a serious activity, and often how well a study was conducted can have real consequences on many outcomes, including how policies and laws are put in place. An underlying goal of this book is to show you how social research has very real applications in real life—it is not just a topic you are forced to learn for your degree requirements. It is something that you can take with you as a skill and be critical of what the media are telling you about results from the "latest poll." Just as the actual daily work of a nurse, social worker, police officer, teacher, physician, or counsellor often involves serious issues that have real implications for people's lives, so does social research.

Basics of Social Research has three goals. First, it seeks to show you that social research is simultaneously an important enterprise and one that is not beyond you—you *can* understand it. And it can even be interesting and fun. Second, it uses many examples from "real research" in published Canadian studies to show you the origins of the findings and information found in textbooks or in the media. Finally, it gives you a foundation for further learning about research and shows you that this activity requires dedication, creativity, and mature judgment.

This book is a shortened version of a larger, in-depth textbook on social research that one of the authors (Neuman) first wrote about 20 years ago and that has been updated many times since then. It was written to provide an uncomplicated introduction to social research for students with a limited background in research.

Like most written works, this book, too, reflects its authors. From the beginning, we have been firmly committed to the value of both quantitative and qualitative approaches to research. We believe that each approach offers a distinct as well as a complementary perspective to understanding the social world and that both approaches are equally important and necessary.

NEW IN THE THIRD CANADIAN EDITION

This new edition has been thoroughly updated and revised for the Canadian market. Key revisions to the content include the following:

- Updated Canadian information and examples throughout
- More detailed content on the components of social theory and the introduction of newer types of social theory (Chapter 3)
- New content on the importance of proper source citation and the steps to proper paraphrasing of research literature (Chapter 4)
- More detailed and simplified explanation of the standard deviation and its applications (Chapter 11)
- Expanded content on the steps of how to do a discourse analysis (Chapter 14)
- A *new* appendix entitled "Doing a Research Project" provides students with the skills and tools needed to design, complete, and write up a research project.

There are a number of new features that help make the text more student friendly:

- Learning objectives listed at the start of each chapter
- Chapter summaries at the end of each chapter

- Checklists to aid in the comprehension of subject matter
- New boxed features on a social research and the internet

STUDENT SUPPLEMENTS

MySearchLab with eText (www.mysearchlab.com) A passcode-protected website that provides engaging experiences that personalize learning, MySearchLab contains an eText that is just like the printed text. Students can highlight and add notes to the eText online or download it to an iPad or Android tablet. MySearchLab also offers self-grading practice quizzes, discipline-specific media and readings, access to a variety of academic journals, and Associated Press news feeds, along with a wide range of writing, grammar, and research tools to help hone writing and research skills.

CourseSmart for Students CourseSmart goes beyond traditional expectations—providing instant, online access to the textbooks and course materials you need at an average savings of 60 percent. With instant access from any computer and the ability to search your text, you'll find the content you need quickly, no matter where you are. And with online tools like highlighting and note-taking, you can save time and study efficiently. See all the benefits at www.coursesmart.com/students.

INSTRUCTOR SUPPLEMENTS

The following instructor supplements are available for download from a password-protected section of Pearson Canada's online catalogue (www.pearsoned.ca/highered). Navigate to your book's catalogue page to view a list of supplements that are available. See your local sales representative for details and access.

- **Instructor's Manual:** This manual includes chapter-by-chapter learning objectives and classifies the test bank questions by topic, objective, and skill.
- **Test Item File:** This test bank in Microsoft Word includes approximately 800 questions, including essay, multiple-choice, and definition questions. These questions are also available in MyTest format (see below).
- **Image Library:** All the figures in the text are provided in electronic format, for use in PowerPoint slides, handouts, or other presentations.

MyTest MyTest from Pearson Canada is a powerful assessment-generation program that helps instructors easily create and print quizzes, tests, exams, as well as homework or practice handouts. Questions and tests can all be authored online, allowing instructors ultimate flexibility and the ability to efficiently manage assessments at anytime, from anywhere. MyTest for *Basics of Social Research*, Third Canadian Edition, includes approximately 800 questions in essay, multiple-choice, and definition formats.

Technology Specialists Pearson's Technology Specialists work with faculty and campus course designers to ensure that Pearson technology products, assessment tools, and online course materials are tailored to meet your specific needs. This highly qualified team is dedicated to helping schools take full advantage of a wide range of educational resources by assisting in the integration of a variety of instructional materials and media formats. Your local Pearson Canada sales representative can provide you with more details on this service program.

CourseSmart for Instructors CourseSmart goes beyond traditional expectations—providing instant, online access to textbooks and course materials at a lower cost for students. And even as students save money, you can save time and hassle with a digital eTextbook that allows you to search for the most relevant content at the very moment you need it. Whether it's evaluating textbooks or creating lecture notes to help students with difficult concepts, CourseSmart can make life a little easier. Find out how when you visit www.coursesmart.com/instructors.

Pearson Custom Library For enrollments of at least 25 students, you can create your own textbook by choosing the chapters that best suit your own course needs. To begin building your custom text, visit www.pearsoncustomlibrary.com. You may also work with a dedicated Pearson Custom editor to create your ideal text—publishing your own original content or mixing and matching Pearson content. Contact your local Pearson Representative to get started.

peerScholar Firmly grounded in published research, peerScholar is a powerful online pedagogical tool that helps develop your students' critical and creative thinking skills. peerScholar facilitates this through the process of creation, evaluation and reflection. Working in stages, students begin by submitting a written assignment. peerScholar then circulates their work for others to review, a process that can be anonymous or not depending on your preference. Students receive peer feedback and evaluations immediately, reinforcing their learning and driving the development of higher-order thinking skills. Students can then resubmit revised work, again depending on your preference. Contact your Pearson Representative to learn more about peerScholar and the research behind it.

Acknowledgments

Karen Robson would like to thank Patti Sayle and Leanne Rancourt for their assistance in the production of this manuscript. I would also like thank my undergraduate students in Soci 2030 who help bring this material to life with their willingness to plunge into this topic and understand how the knowledge in social sciences comes into being. Without my undergraduate teaching, I would not have the motivation to keep this material as fresh and relevant to everyday lives as I hope it is.

Finally, I wish to thank the reviewers for their very helpful suggestions, the majority of which have been incorporated into the text. Reviewers who contributed to the third Canadian edition include the following:

Joanne Clarke, Wilfrid Laurier University
Said Ahmed Aboubacar, Concordia University
Tracy Supruniuk, York University
Ruben Zaiotti, Dalhousie University
Eric Fong, University of Toronto
Lyne Marie Larocque, Vanier College, CEGEP
Bruce Hardy, Douglas College
Kevin Gosine, Brock University
Michael Seredycz, Grant MacEwan University

—Karen Robson

Chapter 1

Doing Social Research

Photo Credit: iQoncept/Fotolia/LLC

LEARNING OBJECTIVES

After reading this chapter, you will be able to

LO 1 Explain why knowledge of social research methods is a useful "everyday" skill to have.

LO 2 Identify and define the six sources of knowledge.

LO 3 Explain what is meant by the *scientific community*.

LO 4 Describe the general steps in the research process.

LO 5 Explain the three major purposes of social research.

LO 6 Compare the two major time dimensions in social research.

LO 7 Explain the difference between qualitative and quantitative approaches.

LO 8 Identify the main qualitative and quantitative data collection approaches.

INTRODUCTION

You are probably reading this textbook because you are enrolled in a social research methods course in the social sciences, social work, education, or a similar discipline. As teachers of this subject, the authors know that this is not a course that students approach with enthusiasm and excitement. In fact, most students dread it and often put off taking it for as long as possible. Others enter the classroom with gritted teeth, expecting to be barraged with boring information and complicated statistics.

As teachers of social research methods, we believe that this topic is the most interesting and most exciting topic in our fields. No, we are not delusional! The fact of the matter is that social research affects many aspects of our everyday lived experiences. Educators, government officials, business managers, human service providers, and health care professionals regularly use social research methods to guide their policies and practices. People use the findings from social research to reduce crime, improve public health, sell products, or just understand aspects of their lives. Reports of research findings, especially those that are "shocking," appear on news programs, in the print media, and on the internet. Most importantly, however, because the results of research are discussed in the popular media, understanding how researchers arrived at their findings can make you an informed consumer of research. The knowledge and skills you will acquire from this book and a course on research methods is a *practical* skill that you can use in your everyday life as a consumer and informed citizen. It is not just some course-specific information that has no applicability in the "real world." The skills you can obtain from understanding social research methods are perhaps one of the most real-world applicable skill sets you will ever receive for distinguishing good information from false information.

LO 1 Explain why knowledge of social research methods is a useful "everyday" skill to have.

WHY DO SOCIAL RESEARCH?

People conduct social research to learn something new about the social world; to carefully document guesses, hunches, or beliefs about it; or to refine their understanding of how the social world works. A researcher combines theories or ideas with facts in a careful, systematic way. He or she learns to organize and plan carefully and creatively and to select the appropriate technique to address a specific kind of question. A researcher must treat the people in a study in ethical and moral ways. In addition, a researcher must fully and clearly communicate the results of a study to others.

social research: A process in which a researcher combines a set of principles, outlooks, and ideas with a collection of specific practices, techniques, and strategies to produce knowledge.

Social research is a process in which people combine a set of principles, outlooks, and ideas (i.e., methodology) with a collection of specific practices, techniques, and strategies (i.e., a method of inquiry) to produce knowledge. It is a challenging process of discovery that requires persistence, personal integrity, tolerance for ambiguity, interaction with others, and commitment to doing quality work.

Reading this book cannot transform you into an expert researcher, but it can teach you to be a better consumer of research results, help you to understand how the research enterprise works, and prepare you to conduct small research projects. It will also make you a better consumer of research, someone who is able to identify "good" research practices and critically assess whether the shocking finding reported on the news this morning is an outcome of sound research design. After studying this book, you will be aware of what research can and cannot do and why properly conducted research is important.

LO 2 Identify and define the six sources of knowledge.

ALTERNATIVES TO SOCIAL RESEARCH

Most of what you know about the social world is not based on doing social research. You probably learned most of your knowledge about the social world by using an alternative to social research, based on what your parents and other people (e.g., friends, teachers) have told you. You also have knowledge based on your personal experiences, the books and magazines you have read, and the movies and television shows you have watched. You may also use plain old "common sense."

More than just a collection of techniques, social research is a process for producing knowledge. It is a more structured, organized, and systematic process than the alternatives that most of us use in daily life. Knowledge from the alternatives is often correct, but knowledge based on research is more likely to be accurate and have fewer errors. Although research does not always produce perfect knowledge, compared with the alternatives it is much less likely to be flawed. Let us review the alternatives before examining social research.

Authority

You have acquired knowledge from parents, teachers, and experts as well as from books, television, and other media. When you accept something as true because someone in a position of authority says it is true or because it is in an authoritative publication, you are relying on authority as a basis for knowledge. Relying on the wisdom of authorities is a quick, simple, and cheap way to learn something. Authorities often spend time and effort to gain knowledge, and you can benefit from their experience and work.

There are also limitations to relying on authority. First, it is easy to overestimate the expertise of other people. You may assume that they are right when they are not. History is full of past experts whom we now see as being misinformed. For example, some "experts" of the past measured intelligence by counting bumps on the skull; other "experts" used bloodletting to try to cure diseases. Their errors seem obvious now, but can you be certain that today's experts will not become tomorrow's fools? Second, authorities may not agree, and all authorities may not be equally dependable. Whom should we believe if authorities disagree? Third, authorities may speak on fields they know little about, or they may be plain wrong. An expert who is very informed about one area may use his or her authority in an unrelated area. Also, using the halo effect (discussed later), expertise in one area may spill over illegitimately to be authority in a totally different area. Have you ever seen television commercials in which an athlete uses his or her fame as authority to convince you to buy a product? We need to ask: Who is, or is not, an authority?

An additional issue is the misuse of authority. Sometimes organizations or individuals give an appearance of authority so they can convince others to agree to something that they might not otherwise. For example, the Fraser Institute, a "free market" conservative advocacy group funded by major corporations, published a book in 1999 entitled *Passive Smoke: The EPA's Betrayal of Science and Policy*. The book, authored by John Luik and Gio Batta Gori of the Fraser Institute, claimed that the breadth of previous evidence on the dangers of secondhand smoke was based on "junk" research. Nowhere, however, were the authors' long-standing affiliations with the tobacco industry mentioned as obvious conflicts of interest. More recently, another independent research group (C.D. Howe Institute, 2010) published findings that advocated for privatized garbage collection because it would save municipalities money. A major funder of this study was the Ontario Waste Management Association (a private-sector lobby group)—a clear stakeholder in the recommendations put forward by the researchers (Sheuer, 2011).

A related situation occurs when a person with little training and expertise is named as a "senior fellow" or "adjunct scholar" in a private "think tank" with an impressive name, such as the Centre for the Study of X or the Institute on Y Research. Some think tanks are legitimate research centres, but many are mere fronts created by wealthy special-interest groups to engage in advocacy politics. Think tanks can make someone a "scholar" to facilitate the mass media's acceptance of the person as an authority on an issue. In reality, the person may not have any expertise.[1]

Too much reliance on authorities can be dangerous to a democratic society. Experts may promote ideas that strengthen their own power and position. When we accept the authority of experts but do not know how the experts arrived at their knowledge we lose the ability to evaluate what the experts say.

Tradition

People sometimes rely on tradition for knowledge. Tradition is a special case of authority—the authority of the past. Tradition means you accept something as being true because "it's the way things have always been." Many people believe that children who are raised at home by their mothers grow up to be better adjusted and have fewer personal problems than those raised in other settings. People "know" this, but how did they learn it? Most accept it because they believe (rightly or wrongly) that it was true in the past or is the way things have always been done. Some traditional social knowledge begins as simple prejudice. You might rely on tradition without being fully aware of it when you believe such things as "People from 'that' neigbourhood will never amount to anything" or "You can never trust that type of person" or "That's the way men (or women) are." Even if traditional knowledge was once true, it can become distorted as it is passed on, and soon it is no longer true.

Common Sense

You know a lot about the social world from your everyday reasoning or common sense. You rely on what everyone knows and what "just makes sense." For example, it "just makes sense" that murder rates are higher in nations that do not have the death penalty because people are less likely to kill if they face execution for doing so. This and other widely held common sense beliefs—such as that poor youth are more likely to commit deviant acts than those from the middle class, or that most Catholics do not use birth control—are false.

Common sense is valuable in daily living, but it allows logical fallacies to slip into thinking. For example, the so-called gambler's fallacy is, "If I have a long string of losses playing a lottery, the next time I play my chances of winning will be better." In terms of probability and the facts, this is false. Also, common sense contains contradictory ideas that often go unnoticed because people use the ideas at different times, such as "opposites attract" and "birds of a feather flock together." Common sense can originate in tradition. It is useful and sometimes correct, but it also contains errors, misinformation, contradiction, and prejudice.

Media Myths

Television shows, movies, and newspaper and magazine articles are important sources of information. For example, most people have no contact with criminals but learn about crime by watching television shows and movies and by reading newspapers. However, the television portrayals of crime (and of many other things) do not accurately reflect social reality. The writers who create or "adapt" images from life for television shows and movie scripts distort reality, either out of ignorance or because they rely on authority, tradition, and common sense. Their primary goal is to entertain, not to represent reality accurately. Although many journalists try to present a realistic picture of the world, they must write stories in short periods with limited information and within editorial guidelines.

Unfortunately, the media tend to perpetuate the myths of a culture, as do some bloggers and individuals on social networking tools such as Twitter, Tumblr, and reddit. And because what bloggers and other social media users post is very current, people often mistake the information on such sites for fact, when it is often just opinion. For example, the media purport that most Canadians who receive welfare are single mothers (in reality, single and childless men are the largest group of recipients), that most people who are mentally ill are violent and dangerous (only a small percentage actually are), or that extreme weather is evidence that climate change is a hoax (when, in fact, this supports the climate change arguments). Also, mass media "hype" can create the perception of a problem being a major one (see Box 1.1). People are misled by visual images more easily than by other forms of "lying"; this means that stories or stereotypes that appear in film and on television can have a powerful effect.

Box 1.1 In the News

Is the Vaccine Panic a Media Myth?

Canadians hear a lot about the importance of getting vaccinated. They must make decisions about vaccinating themselves against seasonal flu and new "pandemic" strains (e.g., H1N1). Many must also make decisions about vaccinating their children against potentially life-threatening illnesses.

Parents obviously only want to have such injections administered to their children if they are proven to be safe. In the past few years, a purported link between childhood vaccinations—particularly the vaccine for measles, mumps, and rubella (known as MMR)—and childhood autism has come into the media spotlight. Measles, mumps, and rubella are potentially life-threatening illnesses that strike in childhood. This rumour about the supposed link between the vaccine and autism has surfaced time and time again in the media across the United Kingdom, the United States, and Canada. Even *The Oprah Winfrey Show* gave a platform to celebrities to voice their opinions that the MMR vaccine causes autism.

What caused this media myth to start? A paper by Wakefield and colleagues, originally published in 1998 in the prestigious British medical journal *The Lancet*, argued that they found a link between the MMR vaccine and later bowel disease and autism in children. Since then, the paper has been officially retracted and shown to be extremely flawed. For one, the study's findings relied on a very small biased sample of 12 children. Subsequent studies, all of which were much larger (in the thousands) and had much more rigorous research designs, have failed to show any link between the MMR vaccination and autism.*

While the Wakefield paper was retracted, this was not done until several years after the original publication date. Although Wakefield was stripped of his licence to practise medicine in Britain in 2010 and later evidence from the *British Medical Journal* has accused Wakefield of outright research fraud (Godlee, Smith, & Marcovitch, 2011), public confidence in vaccines had been severely damaged in the media frenzy that followed the publicity surrounding the original flawed research paper. In fact, the myth still exists that there is a link between vaccinations and autism, and this myth continues to be perpetuated by influential celebrities.

*See Murch, S. H., Anthony, A., Casson, D. H., et al. (2004). Retraction of an interpretation. *Lancet, 363*(9411), 750.

Competing interests use the media to win public support.[2] Public relations campaigns try to alter public opinion about scientific findings, making it difficult for the public to judge research findings. For example, a large majority of scientific research supports the theory on global warming (i.e., pollutants from industrialization and massive deforestation are raising Earth's temperature and will cause dramatic climate change and bring about environmental disasters). But the media give equal attention to a few dissenters who question global warming, creating the impression in the public mind that "no one really knows" or that scientists are undecided about the issue of climate change. Media sources do not mention that the dissenters represent less than 2 percent of all scientists or that most dissenting studies are paid for by heavily polluting industries. Industries also spend millions of dollars to publicize the negative findings because their goal is to deflect growing criticism and delay environmental regulations, not to advance knowledge.

Newspapers offer horoscopes, and television programs and movies report on supernatural powers, ESP (extrasensory perception), UFOs (unidentified flying objects), and angels or ghosts. Although no scientific evidence exists for such phenomena, between 20 and 50 percent of the Canadian public accepts them as true, and the percentage holding such beliefs has been growing over time as the entertainment media give the phenomena more prominence.[3]

Personal Experience

If something happens to you, if you personally see it or experience it, you accept it as true. Personal experience, or "seeing is believing," has a strong impact and is a powerful source of knowledge. Unfortunately, personal experience can lead you astray. What appears true may actually be due to a slight error or distortion in judgment. The power of immediacy and direct personal contact is very strong. In spite of knowing this, many people believe what they see or personally experience rather than what very carefully designed research has discovered.

The four errors of personal experience—overgeneralization, selective observation, premature closure, and the halo effect—reinforce each other and can occur in other areas, as well. They are a basis for misleading people through propaganda, cons or fraud, magic, stereotyping, and some advertising.

overgeneralization: An error that people often make when using personal experience as an alternative to science for acquiring knowledge. It occurs when some evidence supports a belief, but a person falsely assumes that it applies to many other situations, too.

The first and most common problem is **overgeneralization**. It occurs when some evidence supports your belief, but you falsely assume that it also applies to many other situations. Limited generalization may be appropriate; under certain conditions, a small amount of evidence can explain a larger situation. The problem is that many people generalize far beyond limited evidence. For example, over the years the authors of this text have known a number of blind people. All of them have been very friendly. Can the authors then conclude that all blind people are friendly? Do the six or so people with whom they happened to have personal experience represent all blind people?

selective observation: The tendency to take notice of certain people or events based on past experience or attitudes.

The second error, **selective observation**, occurs when you take special notice of some people or events and tend to seek out evidence that confirms what you already believe and to ignore contradictory information. People often focus on or observe particular cases or situations, especially when they fit preconceived ideas. We are sensitive to features that confirm what we think but ignore features that contradict our ideas. Psychologists have found that people tend to "seek out" and distort their memories to make them more consistent with what they already think.[4]

premature closure: An error that is often made when using personal experience as an alternative to science for acquiring knowledge. It occurs when a person feels he or she has the answers and does not need to listen, seek information, or raise questions any longer.

A third error is premature closure, which often operates with and reinforces the first two errors. **Premature closure** occurs when you feel you have the answer and do not need to listen, seek information, or raise questions any longer. Unfortunately, most of us are a little lazy or get a little sloppy. We take a few pieces of evidence or look at events for a short while and then think we have it figured out. We look for evidence to confirm or reject an idea and stop when a small amount of evidence is present. We jump to conclusions. For example, we want to learn whether people in a particular town support Mary Smith or Juan Sanchez for mayor. We ask 20 people; 16 say they favour Mary, 2 are undecided, and only 2 favour Juan, so we stop there and believe Mary will win on the basis of a small sampling of town residents.

halo effect: An error often made when people use personal experience as an alternative to science for acquiring knowledge. It occurs when a person overgeneralizes from what he or she accepts as being highly positive or prestigious and lets its strong reputation or prestige "rub off" onto other areas.

The fourth common error is the **halo effect**, which occurs when we overgeneralize from what we accept as being highly positive or prestigious and let its strong reputation or prestige "rub off" onto other areas. For example, you pick up a report by a person from a prestigious university—say, McGill or the University of Toronto. You assume that the author is smart and talented and that the report will be excellent. You do not make this assumption about a report by someone from an unknown university or college. Under the halo effect, you form an opinion and prejudge the report and may not approach it by considering its own merits alone.

HOW SCIENCE WORKS

Although social research builds on some aspects of alternative ways of developing knowledge, it is science that distinguishes social research. Social research involves thinking scientifically about questions about the social world and following scientific processes. This suggests that we examine the meaning of science and how it works.

Science

The term *science* conjures up an image of test tubes, computers, and people in white lab coats. These outward trappings are a part of science, especially natural science (i.e., astronomy, biology, chemistry, geology, and physics), which deals with the physical and material world (e.g., planets, plants, chemicals, rocks, electricity). The social sciences—such as anthropology, psychology, political science, and sociology—involve the study of people,

Table 1.1 Sources of Knowledge

Example Issue	**How safe are vaccinations for children?**
Authority	Doctors say that vaccinations are safe and that they are rigorously tested before they are administered to the public. My doctor says they are safe, too.
Tradition	Vaccines have been around since the 18th century and have served to eradicate many devastating diseases.
Common Sense	Pharmaceutical companies spend a lot of money on developing vaccines, so vaccines must be safe.
Media Myth	I heard a celebrity say that some vaccines are dangerous. The newspapers are suggesting that many other people may feel the same way.
Personal Experience	My mother had me and my siblings vaccinated, and we are all fine.
Scientific	The study linking MMR to autism has been retracted because it was severely flawed, and several other studies have since shown absolutely no linkage between the vaccine and developing autism.

their beliefs, behaviour, interaction, institutions, and so forth. Fewer people associate these disciplines with the word *science*. Science is a social institution and a means of producing knowledge. Not everyone is well informed about science.

Scientists gather data using specialized techniques and use the data to support or reject theories. **Data** are the empirical evidence or information that one gathers carefully according to rules or procedures. Data can be **quantitative** (i.e., expressed as numbers) or **qualitative** (i.e., expressed as words, visual images, sounds, or objects). **Empirical evidence** refers to observations that people experience through the senses—touch, sight, hearing, smell, and taste. This confuses some people, because researchers cannot use their senses to directly observe many aspects of the social world they seek answers about (e.g., intelligence, attitudes, opinions, feelings, emotions, power, authority).

The various ways in which acquiring knowledge might address the topic of the safety of vaccinations are shown in Table 1.1.

data: The *empirical evidence* or information that a person gathers carefully according to established rules or procedures; it can be qualitative or quantitative.

quantitative data: Information in the form of numbers.

qualitative data: Information in the form of words, pictures, sounds, visual images, or objects.

empirical evidence: The observations that people experience through their senses—touch, sight, hearing, smell, and taste; these can be direct or indirect.

The Scientific Community

LO 3 Explain what is meant by the *scientific community*.

Science comes to life through the operation of the scientific community, which sustains the assumptions, attitudes, and techniques of science. The **scientific community** is a collection of people who practise science and a set of norms, behaviours, and attitudes that bind them together. It is a professional community—a group of interacting people who share ethical principles, beliefs and values, techniques and training, and career paths. For the most part, the scientific community includes both the natural and social sciences.

scientific community: A collection of people who share a system of rules and attitudes that sustain the process of producing scientific knowledge.

Many people outside the core scientific community use scientific research techniques. A range of practitioners and technicians apply research techniques that scientists developed and refined. Many use the research techniques (e.g., a survey) without possessing a deep knowledge of scientific research. Yet anyone who uses the techniques or results of science can do so better if they also understand the principles and processes of the scientific community.

At the core of the scientific community are researchers who conduct studies on a full-time or part-time basis, usually with the help of assistants. Many research assistants are graduate students, and some are undergraduates. Working as a research assistant gives most young scientists a real grasp on the details of doing research. Universities employ most members of the scientific community's core. Some scientists work for the government (such as for Statistics Canada) or for private industry (such as for Ipsos Canada, Gallup, Pollara, and Environics). Most, however, work at the approximately 200 research universities and institutes located mostly in the advanced, industrialized countries. Thus, the scientific community is scattered geographically, but its members tend to work together in small clusters.

How big is the scientific community? A discipline such as sociology may have about 8000 active researchers worldwide. Most researchers complete only two or three studies in their careers, whereas a small number of highly active researchers conduct a large number of studies. In a specialty or topic area (e.g., the study of at-risk youth, social movements, divorce), only about 100 researchers are very active and conduct most research studies. Although research results represent what humanity knows and have a major impact on the lives of millions of people, only a small number of people are actually producing most new scientific knowledge.

THE SCIENTIFIC METHOD AND ATTITUDE

scientific method: The process of creating new knowledge using the ideas, techniques, and rules of the *scientific community.*

You have probably heard of the scientific method, and you may be wondering how it relates to all of this. The **scientific method** is not one single thing: It refers to the ideas, rules, techniques, and approaches that the scientific community uses. The method arises from a loose agreement within the community of scientists. It includes a way of looking at the world that places a high value on professionalism, craftsmanship, ethical integrity, creativity, rigorous standards, and diligence. It also includes strong professional norms, such as honesty and uprightness in doing research, openness about how a study is conducted, and a focus on the merits of the research itself and not on any characteristics of the individuals who conducted the research.

Journal Articles in Science

Consider what happens once a researcher finishes a study. First, he or she writes a detailed description of the study and the results as a research report or a paper using a special format. Often, he or she also gives an oral presentation of the paper before other researchers at a conference or a meeting of a professional association and seeks feedback. Next, the researcher sends the manuscript to the editor of a scholarly journal. This editor, a respected researcher chosen by other scientists to oversee the journal, removes any identifying information of the author and sends the article to several reviewers. The reviewers are respected scientists who have conducted studies in the same specialty area or topic. The reviewers do not know who conducted the study, and the author of the paper does not know who the reviewers are—this process is called a *blind* review. This reinforces the scientific principle of judging a study on its merits alone. Reviewers evaluate the research based on its clarity, originality, standards of good research methods, and advancing knowledge. They return their evaluations to the editor; the editor, on the basis of the reviews, may decide to reject the paper, ask the author to revise and resubmit it, or accept it for publication. It is a very careful, cautious method to ensure quality control.

The scholarly journals that are highly respected and regularly read by most researchers in a field receive many more papers than they can publish. They accept only 10 to 15 percent of submitted manuscripts. Thus, several experienced researchers screen a journal article on its merits alone, and publication represents the scientific community's tentative acceptance of the study as a valid contribution to knowledge. Unlike the authors of articles in popular magazines found at newsstands, scientists are not paid for publishing in scholarly journals. In fact, they may have to pay a small fee to help defray costs just to have their papers considered. Researchers are happy to make their research available to their peers (i.e., other scientists and researchers) through scholarly journals. The article communicates the results of a study to which a researcher might have devoted years of his or her life, and it is the means by which a researcher gains respect and visibility among professional peers. Publishing in academic journals is also an important part of the careers of many scientists, as their careers and contributions to their disciplines are often assessed through the scholarly articles they have published. Likewise, reviewers are not paid for their work; they consider it an honour to be asked to conduct peer reviews and to carry out one of the responsibilities of being part of the scientific community.

You may never publish an article in a scholarly journal, but you will probably read many such articles. It is important to understand that they are a vital component in the system of scientific research. Researchers regularly read what appears in the journals to learn about new research findings and the methods used to conduct a study. Eventually, the new knowledge is used in textbooks, news reports, or public talks.

STEPS IN THE RESEARCH PROCESS

LO 4 Describe the general steps in the research process.

Social research proceeds in a sequence of steps. Although various approaches to research suggest slightly different steps, most studies follow the seven steps discussed here.

Experimental Methods Explained

To begin the process, you select a *topic*—a general area of study or issue, such as domestic abuse, homelessness, or powerful corporate elites. But a topic is too broad for conducting a study—this makes the next step crucial. You must then narrow down the topic, or *focus* the topic into a specific research question for a study (e.g., "Are people who marry at a younger age more likely to physically abuse a spouse under conditions of high stress than those who marry at an older age?"). As you learn about a topic and narrow the focus, you should review past research, or the literature, on a topic or question. You also want to develop a possible answer, or hypothesis, so theory can be important at this stage.

Research Methodology

After specifying a research question, you have to develop a highly detailed plan on how you will carry out the study. This third step requires that you decide on the many practical details of doing the research (e.g., whether to use a survey or qualitative observation in the field, how many subjects to use). It is only after completing the design stage that you are ready to *collect* the data or evidence (e.g., ask people the questions, record answers). Once you have gathered the data carefully, your next step is to *analyze* the data. This will help you see any patterns and give meaning to, or *interpret*, the data (e.g., "People who marry young and grew up in families with abuse have higher rates of physical domestic abuse than those with different family histories.").

Finally, you must *inform others* by writing a report that describes the study's background, how you conducted it, and what you discovered. The seven-step process shown in Figure 1.1

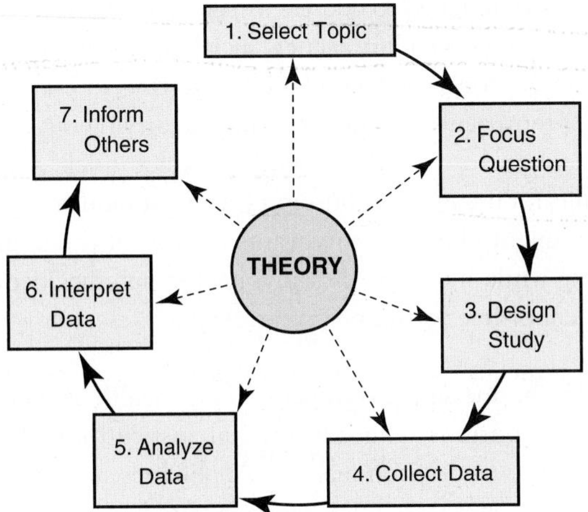

Figure 1.1 Steps in the Research Process

is oversimplified. In practice, you will rarely complete one step totally and then leave it behind to move to the next step. Rather, the process is an interactive one in which the steps blend into each other. What you do in a later step may stimulate you to reconsider and slightly adjust your thinking in a previous one. The seven steps are for one research project; it is one cycle of going through the steps in a single study on a specific topic.

USE OF RESEARCH

For over a century, science has had two wings: Some researchers adopt a detached, purely scientific, and academic orientation; others are more activist, pragmatic, and interventionist oriented. This is not a rigid separation. Researchers in the two wings cooperate and maintain friendly relationships. Some individuals move from one wing to another at different stages in their careers. In simple terms, some researchers concentrate on advancing general knowledge over the long term, whereas others conduct studies to solve specific, immediate problems. Those who concentrate on examining the fundamental nature of social reality are engaged in basic research.

Academic Research

academic social research: Research designed to advance fundamental knowledge about the social world.

Academic social research advances fundamental knowledge about the social world. Academic researchers focus on testing theories that explain how the social world operates, what makes things happen, why social relations are a certain way, and why society changes. Academic research is the source of most new scientific ideas and ways of thinking about the world. Many laypersons criticize basic research, asking "What good is it?" and consider it to be a waste of time and money. Although academic research often lacks a practical application in the short term, it provides a foundation for knowledge in a specific discipline that may advance understanding in many policy areas, problems, or areas of study. Academic research is the source of most of the tools, methods, theories, and ideas used by applied researchers to analyze underlying causes of people's actions or thinking. It provides the major breakthroughs that significantly advance knowledge; it is the painstaking study of broad questions that has the potential to shift how we think about a wide range of issues. It may have an impact for the next 50 or 100 years. Often, the applications of academic research appear many years or decades later. Practical applications may be apparent only after many accumulated advances in academic knowledge that build over a long period.

Applied Research

applied social research: Research that attempts to solve a concrete problem or address a specific policy question and that has a direct, practical application.

Applied social research is designed to address a specific concern or to offer solutions to a problem identified by an employer, club, agency, social movement, or organization. Applied social researchers are rarely concerned with building, testing, or connecting to a larger theory; developing a long-term general understanding; or carrying out a large-scale investigation that might span years. Instead, they usually conduct quick, small-scale studies that provide practical results for use in the short term (i.e., next month or next year). For example, the student government of a university wants to know if the number of students who are arrested for driving while intoxicated or involved in auto accidents will decline if the university sponsors alcohol-free parties next year. Applied research would be most applicable for this situation.

People employed in businesses, government offices, health care facilities, social service agencies, political organizations, and educational institutions often conduct applied research and use the results in decision making. Applied research affects decisions such as the following: Should an agency start a new program to reduce the wait time before a client receives benefits? Should a police force adopt a new type of response to reduce spousal abuse? Should a political candidate emphasize his or her stand on the environment instead of the economy? Should a company market a skin care product to mature adults and not to teenagers?

While the *scientific community* is the primary consumer of academic research, the consumers of applied research findings are *practitioners* (e.g., teachers, counsellors, social workers) or *decision makers* (e.g., managers, agency administrators, public officials). Often, in applied research, someone other than the researcher who conducted the study uses the results.

Applied research results are less likely to enter the public domain in publications and may be available only to a few decision makers or practitioners. This means that applied research findings often are not widely disseminated and that well-qualified researchers rarely get to judge the quality of applied studies.

The decision makers who use the results of an applied study may or may not use them wisely. Sometimes, despite serious problems with a study's methodology and cautions from the researchers, politicians use results to justify cutting programs they dislike or to advance programs they favour. Also, because applied research often has immediate implications or involves controversial issues, it often generates conflict. In 2002, the *Toronto Star*, working with a York University psychology professor, published an analysis of a database containing police-related incidents. The results supported the idea that the Toronto police engaged in racial profiling—that is, they stopped Black people more often for no other reason than that they were Black. The research was met with extreme hostility, and the newspaper was sued by the police union. The Toronto Police Service then commissioned an independent review of the *Toronto Star*'s analysis, which was undertaken by a criminal lawyer and a University of Toronto sociology professor, who came up with different results that found no evidence of racial profiling. Who is correct? The debate over the extent of racial profiling in Canadian policing continues to be a very controversial topic in the news and among Canadian academics.[5]

Applied and basic researchers adopt different orientations toward research methodology (see Table 1.2). Academic researchers emphasize high methodological standards and try to conduct near-perfect research. Applied researchers must make more tradeoffs. They may compromise scientific rigour to get quick, usable results, but compromise is never an excuse for sloppy research. Applied researchers try to squeeze research into the

Table 1.2 Academic and Applied Social Research Compared

Academic	Applied
1. Research is intellectually stimulating and judgments are by other social scientists.	1. Research is part of a job and is assessed by funders who may be outside the disciplines of social science and not scientists themselves.
2. Research topics are selected based upon intellectual interests.	2. Topics for research are selected based upon problems identified by funders.
3. Research is judged on the basis of high scientific standards.	3. The scientific standards of the research can vary.
4. The primary concern is with the internal logic and rigour of research design.	4. The primary concern is with the ability to generalize findings to areas of interest to funders.
5. The major objective is to contribute to basic theoretical knowledge.	5. The major objective is to have action-orientated objectives for results.
6. Research is considered successful when it appears in peer-reviewed scientific publication.	6. Research is considered successful when findings are used to inform policy or practice.

Source: Based on Freeman, H., & Rossi, P. H. (1984). Furthering the applied side of sociology. *American Sociological Review, 49*, 571–580

constraints of an applied setting and balance rigour against practical needs. Such balancing requires an in-depth knowledge of research and an awareness of the consequences of compromising standards.

Types of Applied Research

There are many specific types of applied research. Here you will learn about three major types: evaluation, action, and social impact assessment.

evaluation research study: A type of *applied social research* in which one tries to determine how well a program or policy is working or reaching its goals and objectives.

Evaluation Research Study

An **evaluation research study** is applied research designed to find out whether a program, a new way of doing something, a marketing campaign, a policy, and so forth is effective—in other words, "Does it work?" The most common type of applied research is evaluation research. This type of research is widely used in large bureaucratic organizations (e.g., businesses, schools, hospitals, government, large nonprofit agencies) to demonstrate the effectiveness of what they are doing. An evaluation researcher does not use techniques different from those of other social researchers. The difference lies in the fact that decision makers, who may not be researchers themselves, narrowly define the scope and purpose of the research, with the objective of using results in a practical situation.[6]

Evaluation research questions might include the following: Do blended learning classes improve learning better than lecture-only classes? Does a law-enforcement program of mandatory arrest reduce youth offences? Does a flextime program increase employee productivity? Evaluation researchers measure the effectiveness of a program, policy, or way of doing something. Practitioners involved in a policy or program may conduct evaluation research for their own information or at the request of outside decision makers. The decision makers may place limits on the research by fixing boundaries on what can be studied and by predetermining the outcome of interest. This often creates ethical dilemmas for researchers.

Evaluation research has several limitations: The reports of research rarely go through a peer review process, raw data are seldom publicly available, and the focus is narrowed to select only the inputs and outputs of a program that have a direct effect on people's lives. In addition, decision makers may selectively use or ignore evaluation findings.

action research: A type of *applied social research* in which a researcher treats knowledge as a form of power and abolishes the division between creating knowledge and using knowledge to engage in political action.

Action Research Study

Action research is applied research that treats knowledge as a form of power and abolishes the division between creating knowledge and using knowledge to engage in political action. There are several types of action research, but most share five characteristics: (1) the people being studied actively participate in the research process; (2) the research incorporates ordinary or popular knowledge; (3) the research focuses on issues of power; (4) the research seeks to raise consciousness or increase awareness of issues; and (5) the research is tied directly to a plan or program of political action. Action research tends to be associated with a social movement, political cause, or advocacy for an issue. It can be conducted to advance a range of political positions. Some action research has an insurgent orientation with goals of empowering the powerless, fighting oppression and injustice, and reducing inequality. Wealthy and powerful groups or organizations also sponsor and conduct action research to defend their status, position, and privileges in society.

social impact assessment (SIA): A type of *applied social research* in which a researcher estimates the likely consequences or outcome of a planned intervention or intentional change to occur in the future.

Social Impact Assessment Research Study

A researcher who conducts **social impact assessment (SIA)** research estimates the likely consequences of a planned intervention or intentional change to occur in the future. It may be part of a larger environmental impact statement required by government agencies and used for planning and making choices among alternative policies. The researcher forecasts how aspects of the social environment may change and suggests ways to mitigate changes likely to be adverse from the point of view of an affected population. *Impacts* are the difference between a future with the

Box 1.2 Concepts in Action

The Social Impact of Gambling

Many forms of legal gambling have expanded rapidly across Canada in recent decades. In Alberta, video lottery terminals (VLTs) were introduced into drinking establishments and electronic slot machines were allowed in casinos and racetracks in the early 1990s. Gaming revenue rose from $225 million per year in 1992 to $1545 million in 2003.[7] Provincial politicians sought new sources of revenue without raising taxes and wanted to promote economic development. The gambling industry promised the government new jobs, economic revitalization, and a "cut" in the huge flow of money from gambling. This looked ideal to the politicians: They could help create jobs, strengthen the local economy, and get revenue without raising taxes.

While the boost to Alberta's economy was remarkable, the provincial economic benefits derived from gambling revenue did not come without a cost. The problem of compulsive gambling has increased, particularly among youth and Aboriginal populations (Smith & Wynne, 2002). Compulsive gamblers have low work productivity, devastate their families, and often turn to crime.

Were such social results predictable? Yes, if the officials had first conducted high-quality social impact assessment research. This is rare, however. Officials often accept extravagant claims made by special-interest industry advocates who promise the illusion of getting something for next to nothing. Also, some officials are ignorant or distrustful of social research. More recently, since the global economic crisis that began in 2008, governments are increasingly looking at potential sources of revenue. In many provinces, gambling revenue is being hailed by politicians as the panacea to many provincial and municipal revenue problems.

Williams, Rehm, and Stevens (2011) have recently conducted a thorough review of social impact assessments on gambling in Canada. They found that the impacts of gambling are mixed and differ depending on the type of gambling that is taking place. In general, economic impacts of gambling do indeed lead to increased government revenues, which result in increased public services. However, there is also consistent evidence that the social impacts tend to be an increase in problem gambling, a small increase in crime, and an increase in socio-economic inequality.

project or policy and that without the project or policy. For example, the SIA might estimate the ability of a local hospital to respond to an earthquake, determine how housing availability for older adults will change if a major new highway is built, or assess the impact on university admissions if students receive interest-free loans. Researchers who conduct SIAs often examine a range of social outcomes and work in an interdisciplinary research team to estimate them. The outcomes include measuring "quality of life" issues, such as access to health care, illegal drug and alcohol use, employment opportunities, schooling quality, teen pregnancy rates, commuting time and traffic congestion, availability of parks and recreation facilities, shopping choices, viable cultural institutions, crime rates, interracial tensions, or social isolation. See Box 1.2 for an example of social impact assessment.

PURPOSE OF A STUDY

LO 5 Explain the three major purposes of social research.

If you asked someone why he or she was conducting a study, you might get a range of responses: "My boss told me to"; "It was a class assignment"; "I was curious"; "My roommate thought it would be a good idea." There are almost as many reasons to do research as there are researchers. Yet the purposes of social research may be organized into three groups based on what the researcher is trying to accomplish: explore a new topic, describe a social phenomenon, or explain why something occurs. Studies may have multiple purposes (e.g., both to explore and to describe), but one of three major purposes is usually dominant (see Box 1.3).

Exploration

Perhaps you have explored a new topic or issue to learn about it. If the issue was new or no researchers had written about it, you began at the beginning. In **exploratory research**, a researcher examines a new area to formulate precise questions that he or she can address in future research. Exploratory research may be the first stage in a sequence of studies. A researcher may need to conduct an exploratory study to know enough to design and execute

exploratory research: Research into an area that has not been studied and in which a researcher wants to develop initial ideas and a more focused research question.

Box 1.3 Making It Practical

Purposes of Research

Exploration

- Become familiar with the basic facts, setting, and concerns
- Create a general mental picture of conditions
- Formulate and focus questions for future research
- Generate new ideas, conjectures, or hypotheses
- Determine the feasibility of conducting research
- Develop techniques for measuring and locating future data

Description

- Provide a detailed, highly accurate picture
- Locate new data that contradict past data
- Create a set of categories or classify types
- Clarify a sequence of steps or stages
- Document a causal process or mechanism
- Report on the background or context of a situation

Explanation

- Test a theory's predictions
- Elaborate and refine a theory's explanation
- Extend a theory to new issues or topics
- Support or refute an explanation or prediction
- Link issues or topics with a general principle
- Determine which of several explanations is best

a second, more systematic and extensive, study. It addresses the "What?" question: "What is this social activity really about?" See Box 1.4 for an example of exploratory research.

Sociological Perspective on Gender

Exploratory researchers tend to use qualitative data and not be committed to a specific theory or research question. Exploratory research rarely yields definitive answers. If you conduct an exploratory study, you may get frustrated and feel it is difficult because there are few guidelines to follow. Everything is potentially important, the steps are not well defined, and the direction of inquiry changes frequently. You need to be creative, open-minded, and flexible; adopt an investigative stance; and explore all sources of information.

Description

descriptive research: Research in which one "paints a picture" with words or numbers, presents a profile, outlines stages, or classifies types.

You may have a more highly developed idea about a social phenomenon and want to describe it. **Descriptive research** presents a picture of the specific details of a situation, social setting, or relationship. Descriptive research focuses on "How?" and "Who?" questions: "How did it happen?" "Who is involved?" A great deal of social research is descriptive. Descriptive researchers use most data-gathering techniques—surveys, field research, content analysis, and historical research—but experimental research is less often used. Much of the social research found in scholarly journals or used for making policy decisions is descriptive.

Descriptive and exploratory research often blur together in practice. In descriptive research, a researcher begins with a well-defined subject and conducts a study to describe it

Box 1.4 Concepts in Action

Sexual Minority Refugees to Canada

Lee and Brotman (2011) undertook an exploratory study to examine the migration experiences of sexual minority refugees to Canada. The authors studied individuals who came to Canada as refugees (i.e., those who left their countries of origin due to fear of being persecuted) because of their sexual orientation (i.e., gay, lesbian, transgendered). The research is considered exploratory because there is a limited body of research on this particular group of refugees, particularly in Canada. The authors were exploring a previously under-researched topic and hoping to contribute to a new body of knowledge around sexual minority refugees.

Qualitative interviews were undertaken with sexual minority refugees in Montreal and Toronto—14 were done in each city. The interviewees came from countries within the Caribbean and Latin America, Asia, Africa, and the Middle East. The researchers found evidence of racism and heterosexism within Canadian refugee policies and practices, which served to traumatize sexual minorities, often labelling them as "bogus" refugee claimants.

Box 1.5 Concepts in Action

Undergraduate Students Who Are Parents

Van Rhijn, Smit Quosai, and Lero (2011) undertook a descriptive study to understand the characteristics of undergraduate students in Canada who are also parents. Using two Statistics Canada data sets—the Labour Force Survey and the Survey of Labour and Income Dynamics—the authors created a profile of undergraduate students who were also raising children. They found increasing enrolment of "parent students" over the past 30 years, with this group more likely to enrol in college programs than university degree programs. Parent students were also more likely to study part time compared to nonparent students and were, unsurprisingly, considerably older on average than their nonparent colleagues. Student parents were also found to be disproportionately female and married and were less likely to hold jobs compared to nonparents.

accurately; the outcome is a detailed picture of the subject. The results may indicate the percentage of people who hold a particular view or engage in specific behaviours—for example, that 8 percent of parents physically or sexually abuse their children. A descriptive study presents a picture of types of people or of social activities. See Box 1.5 for an example of descriptive research.

Explanation

When you encounter an issue that is well recognized and has already been described, you might begin to wonder why things are the way they are. **Explanatory research** identifies the sources of social behaviours, beliefs, conditions, and events; it documents causes, tests theories, and provides reasons. It builds on exploratory and descriptive research. For example, an exploratory study discovers a trend in lower rates of marriage; a descriptive researcher documents that 10 percent of couples living together are not married and describes the kinds of men and women who are most frequently in these relationships; the explanatory researcher focuses on why certain couples are choosing cohabitation over marriage. See Box 1.6 for an example of explanatory research.

explanatory research: Research that focuses on why events occur or tries to test and build social theory.

TIME DIMENSION IN RESEARCH

LO 6 Compare the two major time dimensions in social research.

An awareness of how a study uses the time dimension will help you read or conduct research. This is because different research questions or issues incorporate time differently. Some studies give a snapshot of a single, fixed point in time and allow you to analyze it in detail

Box 1.6 Concepts in Action

Why Are Immigrant Youth More Likely to Drop Out of School?

Anisef and colleagues (2010) were interested in finding out more about the possible reasons behind the higher dropout rates of immigrant teens that have been observed in Toronto and other major urban centres. They note that previous research has found that immigrant youth's decision to leave school has been highly associated with social class, country of origin, age at arrival, and generational status. Using quantitative data from the Toronto District School Board, the researchers tested two theories. The first was assimilation theory, which suggests that the longer an immigrant has been in the host country, the more he or she will "behave" as a native born—in this case, the more likely he or she is to stay in school. They also tested segmented assimilation theory, which states that different paths of assimilation characterize different ethnic groups. Some groups "assimilate" in the sense that they become more like members of the host society, while others experience severe economic hardship and have significant downward social mobility.

The findings revealed support for segmented assimilation theory insofar as ethnic groups that experienced a disproportionate amount of poverty (e.g., Caribbean and Latin American immigrants) were more likely to drop out of high school than other ethnic groups (e.g., European, East Asian, South Asian).

CROSS-SECTIONAL: Observe a collection of people at one time.

TIME SERIES: Observe different people at multiple times.

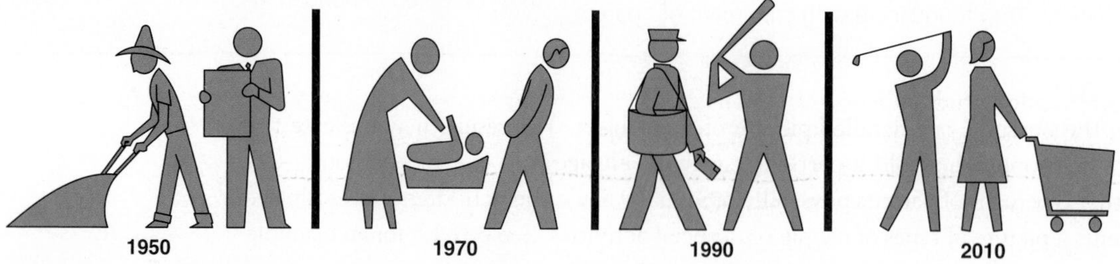

PANEL: Observe the same people at two or more times.

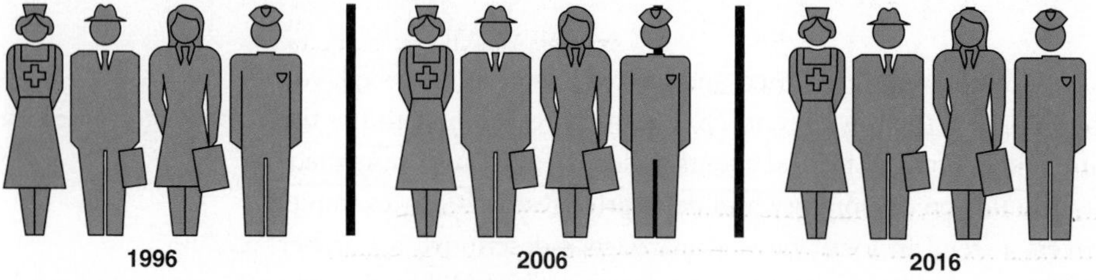

COHORT: Observe people who shared an experience at two or more times.

CASE STUDY: Observe a small set intensely across time.

Figure 1.2 The Time Dimension in Social Research

(cross-sectional). Other studies provide a moving picture that lets you follow events, people, or social relations over several points in time (longitudinal). Quantitative studies generally look at many cases, people, or units and measure limited features about them in the form of numbers. By contrast, a qualitative study usually involves qualitative data and examines many diverse features of a small number of cases across either a short or long time period (see Figure 1.2).

Cross-Sectional Research

Most social research studies are cross-sectional: They examine a single point in time or take a one-time snapshot approach. **Cross-sectional research** is usually the simplest and least costly alternative. Its disadvantage is that it cannot capture social processes or change. Cross-sectional research can be exploratory, descriptive, or explanatory, but it is most consistent with a descriptive approach to research. For example, the exploratory study by Veenstra (2007) about the relationship between social class and sports knowledge and participation was based on quantitative survey data from residents of British Columbia.

cross-sectional research: Research in which a researcher examines a single point in time or takes a one-time snapshot approach.

Longitudinal Research

Researchers using **longitudinal research** examine features of people or other units at more than one time. It is usually more complex and costly than cross-sectional research, but it is also more powerful and informative. Descriptive and explanatory researchers use longitudinal approaches. Let us now look at the three main types of longitudinal research: time series, panel, and cohort.

longitudinal research: Research in which the researcher examines the features of people or other units at multiple points in time.

Time-Series Study A **time-series study** gathers the same type of information across two or more periods. Researchers can observe stability or change in the features of the units or can track conditions over time. The specific individuals may change, but the overall pattern is clear. For example, every year since 1985 Statistics Canada has been gathering data on social trends in the Canadian population using the General Social Survey (GSS). Each year for the GSS, Statistics Canada collects information from several thousand people age 15 years and older living in private households. The focus of the questions changes annually with each "cycle," with these topic cycles being repeated every few years. For example, the focus of the survey in 1986 was "Time Use," and this topic was again repeated in 1992, 1998, and 2005. Collecting data across several points in time can show us how trends in social life change. In this particular example, it was possible to see the changes in how the average person spends his or her time. Researchers found that the average time it took for people in 1992 to get from their residence to their place of work was 54 minutes. By 2005, this had risen to 63 minutes. If you multiply this by the number of days that people work during the year, this amounts to an additional 12 full days of commuting per year.[8]

time-series study: Any research that takes place over time in which different people or cases may be looked at in each time period.

Panel Study The **panel study** is a powerful type of longitudinal research in which the researcher observes the same people, group, or organization across multiple time points. It is more difficult to conduct than time-series research and is very costly—tracking people over time is often difficult because some people die or cannot be located. Nevertheless, the results of a well-designed panel study are very valuable. Even short-term panel studies can clearly show the impact of an event. For example, Statistics Canada annually interviews about 30 000 individuals about their work patterns and labour market activity for the Survey of Labour and Income Dynamics. Because the study design uses panels, the same individuals are followed up with over time and data are gathered from the same individuals at more than one point in time. Researchers using this rich data source have been able to examine many topics about the labour market experiences of Canadians, including, for example, the labour market transition patterns of immigrant-born and refugee-born youth and how these differ from those of Canadian-born youth (Wilkinson, 2008).

panel study: A powerful type of *longitudinal research* in which a researcher observes exactly the same people, group, or organization across multiple time points.

Cohort Study A **cohort study** is a special type of panel study that focuses on the same people over time who share a similar life experience in a specified period. Commonly used cohorts include all people born in the same year (called *birth cohorts*), all people hired at the same time, and all people who graduate in a given year. Canadian sociologist Harvey Krahn (n.d.) has been conducting a cohort study since 1985, when he surveyed individuals in Alberta who were just graduating high school. This group of individuals were known as

cohort study: A type of *longitudinal research* in which a researcher focuses on a category of people who share a similar life experience in a specified period.

"Generation X" and had left high school during a time of great economic uncertainty. Krahn and his colleagues have periodically re-interviewed this cohort over the past 26 years, following their postsecondary choices and work transitions.

case-study research: Research, usually qualitative, on one or a small number of cases in which a researcher carefully examines a large number of details about each case.

Case Studies In **case-study research**, a researcher examines, in depth, many features of a few cases over a duration of time with very detailed, varied, and extensive data, often in a qualitative form. The researcher carefully selects a few key cases to illustrate and study an issue in detail and considers the specific context of each case. This contrasts with other longitudinal studies (panel, cohort, time series) in which the researcher gathers data on many units or cases, then looks for general patterns in the mass of numbers. The major distinguishing feature of a case study is that it involves detailed study of a small number of cases.

LO 7 Explain the difference between qualitative and quantitative approaches.

QUANTITATIVE AND QUALITATIVE APPROACHES

Social researchers collect data using one or more specific techniques. This section gives a brief overview of the major techniques. In later chapters, you will read about these techniques in detail and learn how to use them. Some techniques are more effective when addressing specific kinds of questions or topics. It takes skill, practice, and creativity to match a research question to an appropriate data collection technique.

Graphing Data

There are two major approaches or orientations to social research methods: qualitative and quantitative. You may have heard your professors or teaching assistants talking about whether they are qualitative or quantitative researchers. Quantitative research is associated with data collection techniques that include experiments, surveys, and the analysis of existing statistics, while qualitative data collection techniques include qualitative interviews, focus groups, field research, and historical research.

Apart from the actual data collection techniques, however, there are different theoretical and even philosophical differences between the qualitative and quantitative approaches. These differences will be elaborated upon later in this book, but briefly, quantitative research tends to try to use statistical analytic techniques to analyze large data sets and make generalized statements about social life. Usually, quantitative researchers are testing hypotheses and believe that social science should study its subjects in a similar manner to that practised by natural scientists. In contrast, qualitative researchers tend to study smaller groups and often believe that the study of people requires specialized techniques that allow researchers to understand and properly interpret the meanings behind their subjects' words and actions. In the next sections we briefly introduce the more frequently used quantitative and qualitative data collection techniques

LO 8 Identify the main qualitative and quantitative data collection approaches.

Quantitative Data Collection Techniques

Techniques for quantitative data collection include experiments, surveys, content analysis, and existing statistics.

experimental research: Research in which one intervenes or does something to one group of people but not to another and then compares the results of the two groups.

Experiments **Experimental research** closely follows the logic and principles found in natural science research: Researchers create situations and examine their effects on participants. A researcher conducts experiments in laboratories or in real life with a relatively small number of people and a well-focused research question. Experiments are most effective for explanatory research. In the typical experiment, the researcher divides the people being studied into two or more groups, then treats both groups identically except that one group is given a condition the researcher is interested in: the "treatment." The researcher measures the reactions of both groups precisely. By controlling the setting for both groups and giving only one group the treatment, the researcher can conclude that any differences in the reactions of the groups are due to the treatment alone.

Discussion of Methodology

Surveys **Survey research** is done by asking people questions using a written questionnaire (mailed or handed to people) or during an interview and then recording answers. The researcher manipulates no situation or condition; he or she simply asks many people numerous questions in a short period. Typically, he or she then summarizes answers to questions in percentages, tables, or graphs. Researchers use survey techniques in descriptive or explanatory research. Surveys give the researcher a picture of what many people think or report doing. Survey researchers often use a sample or a smaller group of selected people (e.g., 150 students) but generalize results to a larger group (e.g., 5000 students) from which the smaller group was selected. Survey research is widely used in many fields.

survey research: A quantitative social research technique in which one systematically asks many people the same questions and then records and analyzes their answers.

Content Analysis A **content analysis** is a technique for examining information, or content, in written or symbolic material (e.g., pictures, movies, song lyrics). In content analysis, a researcher first identifies a body of material to analyze (e.g., books, newspapers, films) and then creates a system for recording specific aspects of it. The system might include counting how often certain words or themes occur. Finally, the researcher records what was found in the material. He or she often measures information in the content as numbers and presents it as tables or graphs. This technique lets a researcher discover features in the content of large amounts of material that might otherwise go unnoticed. Researchers can use content analysis for exploratory and explanatory research, but primarily it is used for descriptive research.

content analysis: Research in which one examines patterns of symbolic meaning within written text, audio, visual, or other communication medium.

Existing Statistics In **existing statistics research**, a researcher locates previously collected information, often in the form of government reports or previously conducted surveys, then reorganizes or combines the information in new ways to address a research question. Locating sources can be time consuming, so the researcher needs to consider carefully the meaning of what he or she finds. Frequently, a researcher does not know whether the information of interest is available when he or she begins a study. Sometimes, the existing quantitative information consists of stored surveys or other data that a researcher reexamines using various statistical procedures. Existing statistics research can be used for exploratory, descriptive, or explanatory purposes, but it is most frequently used for descriptive research.

existing statistics research: Research in which one examines numerical information from government documents or official reports to address new research questions.

Qualitative Data Collection Techniques

When Can We Use Qualitative Methods?

Social Psychology Methods for Sociology

Techniques for qualitative data collection include qualitative interviews, focus groups, field research, and historical research.

Qualitative Interviews Researchers conduct **qualitative interviews** with a selection of people to gain an in-depth understanding of the meaning of a social phenomenon to a group of people. A researcher conducting qualitative interviews will choose a research topic and then select a fairly small group of individuals with whom to explore this topic (usually less than 30 individuals). Researchers using this technique will get data that are highly detailed and express the unique and comprehensive perspectives of the individuals who were interviewed. Qualitative interviewing is often used for exploratory and descriptive studies.

qualitative interview: A one-on-one interview between a researcher and an interviewee that is usually semi-structured and open ended.

Focus Groups **Focus groups** are like qualitative interviews but they are conducted in a group. A group of around five to seven individuals is given a topic to discuss, and data about the research question are derived from this group discussion. Like qualitative interviewing, focus group research is used mostly for exploratory and descriptive studies.

focus group: A type of group interview in which an interviewer poses questions to the group and answers are given in an open discussion among the group members.

Field Research Most field researchers conduct case studies looking at a small group of people over a length of time (e.g., weeks, months, years). A person involved in **field research** begins with a loosely formulated idea or topic, selects a social group or natural setting for study, gains access and adopts a social role in the setting, and observes in detail.

field research: A type of qualitative research in which a researcher directly observes the people being studied in a natural setting for an extended period. Often, the researcher combines intense observation with participation in the people's social activities.

Box 1.7 Focus

Quantitative and Qualitative Data Collection Techniques

Quantitative	Qualitative
Experiments	Qualitative Interviews
Surveys	Focus Groups
Content Analysis	Field Research
Existing Statistics	Historical Research
	Content Analysis

Field Research

After leaving the field site, the researcher carefully rereads the notes and prepares written reports. Field research is used most often for exploratory and descriptive studies; it is rarely used for explanatory research.

historical research: Research in which one examines different cultures or periods to better understand the social world.

Historical Research **Historical research** examines aspects of social life in a past historical era or across different cultures. Researchers who use this technique may focus on one historical period or several, compare one or more cultures, or mix historical periods and cultures. Like field research, a researcher combines theory building/testing with data collection and begins with a loosely formulated question that is refined during the research process. Researchers often gather a wide array of evidence, including existing statistics and documents (e.g., novels, official reports, books, newspapers, diaries, photographs, and maps) for study. In addition, they may make direct observations and conduct interviews. Historical research can be exploratory, descriptive, or explanatory and can blend types.

The Promise and Pitfalls of Going into the Field

Document Research

Content Analysis While content analysis was described in the previous section as being a quantitative data collection technique, it can also be qualitative in nature. While content can be analyzed quantitatively (e.g., by counting instances of observing a certain type of image or message), it can also be done in a more qualitative manner, such as by exploring implied meanings and discourses. These distinctions will be made clearer in the sections of this book that deal with both quantitative and qualitative content analysis.

Box 1.7 summarizes the quantitative and qualitative data collection techniques, and Box 1.8 discusses the internet as a tool for social research.

Box 1.8 Social Research and the Internet

The internet is a useful tool for spreading information, and the dissemination of social research is no exception. There are many websites that report on the findings of social research. Universities and other research organizations use the internet to publicize their findings and to reach a wider audience. Statistics Canada, for example, has a Twitter feed and a Facebook page to publicize its research and resources and to interact with researchers. Other research organizations have also created similar social media presences.

But what about using the internet as a tool for social research? More resources are becoming available that allow researchers to remotely explore data online. Statistics Canada has statistical tables available on a wide variety of topics for researchers to use, for example. Other international organizations, such as the World Bank (www.worldbank.org) and the Organisation for Economic Co-operation and Development (www.oecd.org), offer a variety of data, reports, and tables on a number of socio-economic factors for a wide variety of countries. The World Bank's Open Data Initiative provides the public with data on over 200 countries (http://data.worldbank.org), while the OECD site allows researchers to remotely create customized statistical tables for their personalized use (www.oecd.org/statistics).

Box 1.8 (continued)

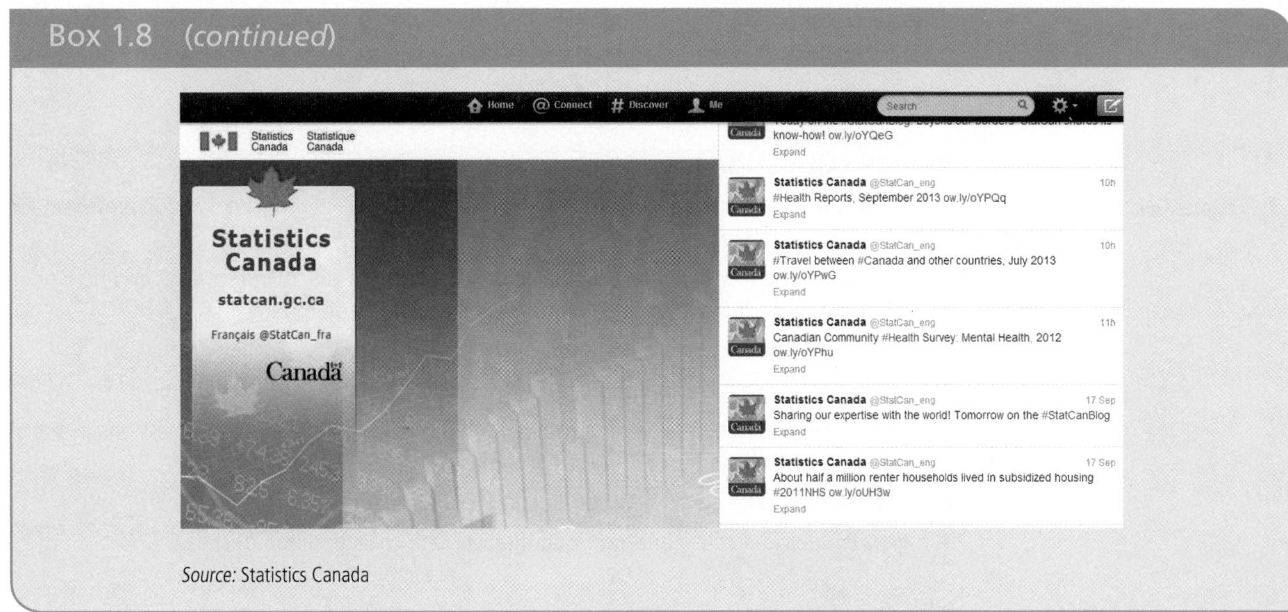

Source: Statistics Canada

CHAPTER SUMMARY

This chapter gave you an overview of social research. We began by explaining why social research methods are an important skill to have not only for success in your coursework, but also for being a discerning consumer of research. Research findings are everywhere; a day does not go by without a story about a new finding of what "causes" poverty or what food has been found to "cause" or to "prevent" cancer or heart disease. With the information that is provided in this book, you will be able to assess the merits and flaws of such studies and thus the validity of their claims. This has far-reaching benefits beyond the classroom.

You saw how social research differs from the ordinary ways of learning/knowing about the social world, and six forms of knowledge were presented to you as ways that we can know things about the social world. Scientific knowledge was presented as the form of knowledge that is preferred when doing research as it is based on scientific methods and rigour. Characteristics of scientific knowledge and the scientific community were also presented. Within the scientific community, the importance of the "blind review" of academic journal articles was described to demonstrate how academic research comes into being and the rigorous quality controls that are put into place along the way by the scientific community.

Various steps in the research process were outlined in this chapter. Later in this book, all of these steps will be explicated upon in some detail as each step is fundamental in the process of conducting social research. We also introduced the two major types of social research: academic and applied. Many of the differences between the two types were highlighted, and three specific applied research approaches were also introduced.

Social research is motivated by a researcher's purpose, or the nature of his or her research question. Three different (and sometimes overlapping) purposes were introduced. Time is also a major factor in social research, and we described how studies can either be a "one off" examination of a social phenomenon (cross-sectional) or span large time periods (longitudinal). Various types of longitudinal approaches were described.

Social research is often divided into two broad approaches: quantitative and qualitative. This division is characterized by different philosophies about the nature and purpose of research, which naturally extends to the types of research techniques used by researchers. You were introduced to the various types of quantitative and qualitative research data collection techniques, all of which will be fully explored in later chapters of this book. In the next chapter, you will learn how theory and research methods work together and about several types of theory.

Review Questions

Chapter Quiz

1. Identify and define the six sources of knowledge. Why is scientific knowledge preferred for answering social research questions?
2. Explain what is meant by the scientific community. What is a "blind review" and how does it contribute to the knowledge created in the scientific community?
3. Identify and describe the seven steps in the research process.
4. Explain the three major purposes of social research.
5. Explain the difference between cross-sectional and longitudinal time dimensions in social research. Define the four different types of longitudinal designs.
6. Explain three differences between qualitative and quantitative social research.
7. Identify four qualitative and four quantitative data collection approaches.

Exercises

Research Activity

1. Find a recent news item (from your local newspaper or a national paper like the *Globe and Mail*) that discusses recent research findings. What does the report describe as being the major finding of the research? Does the news item give any indication of exactly how the research was conducted? If so, what does it say? Can you tell what data collection method was used in the study? Was it a longitudinal study or a cross-sectional study? What are the implications of the findings of the study?
2. Go to the Statistics Canada website (www.statcan.gc.ca) and find three studies that have been conducted by this agency. Identify the data collection techniques used and the time dimension of the research.
3. Again, on the Statistics Canada website, look at a recent issue of *The Daily* that deals with social research. What is the name of the study on which the findings are based? Is there any implication for social policy in the findings reported in this issue of *The Daily*?
4. Using EBSCO's ContentSelect, search within the *Canadian Review of Sociology* for articles on a topic that interests you. Your search should reveal at least five sources. Make a chart with four columns: Citation Information of Study, Qualitative or Quantitative, Data Collection Technique, and Time Dimension. Fill in this information for your five studies. Most likely you will have to look at the methods section of these articles to find this information.
5. Using Google, find either a social impact assessment or evaluation study that has recently been undertaken in Canada (within the past five years). What was the study trying to determine? What were the main findings?

Chapter 2

Theory and Social Research

Photo Credit: vlorzor/Fotolia/LLC

LEARNING OBJECTIVES

After reading this chapter, you will be able to

LO 1 Explain how theory is closely linked to social research methods.

LO 2 Explain what is meant by levels of theory.

LO 3 Define empirical generalization.

LO 4 Define agency and structure.

LO 5 Explain what is meant by ontology and epistemology as they apply to the approach a researcher takes to social research.

LO 6 Compare the positivist and interpretivist paradigms.

LO 7 Differentiate between inductive and deductive approaches to theory.

LO 8 Define causality and its three criteria.

INTRODUCTION

As with social research methods, students often are required to complete a course (or more) in theory to fulfill their degree requirements. Sometimes students ask why they have to take both theory and methods? Why is it mandatory?

What is the Importance of Sociological Theory to an Understanding of Society and Social Behaviour?

Theory has a core role in research and is a necessary tool for the researcher. In simple terms, researchers interweave a story about the operation of the social world (the theory) with what they observe when they examine it systematically (the data). Theory and methods are the backbone of the social sciences. One cannot practise the social sciences without a mastery of both.

People who seek absolute, fixed answers for a specific individual or a particular one-time event may be frustrated with science and social theories. To avoid frustration, it is wise to keep in mind three things about how social scientific theories work. First, social theories explain recurring patterns, not unique or one-time events. For example, they are not good for explaining why terrorists decided to attack New York City's World Trade Center on September 11, 2001, but they can explain patterns, such as the conditions that generally lead to increased levels of fear and "spin-off" terrorist groups such as the Toronto 18. Second, social theories are explanations for aggregates, not particular individuals. **Aggregates** are collections of many individuals, cases, or other units (e.g., businesses, schools, families, clubs, cities, nations). A social theory can rarely explain why your sister decided to get a degree in nursing rather than engineering, but it can explain why generally more females than males choose nursing over engineering. Third, social theories state a probability, chance, or tendency for events to occur, rather than stating that one event must absolutely follow another. For example, instead of stating that someone who was abused as a child will always later abuse his or her own children, a theory might state that someone who experiences abuse during his or her childhood is *more likely to* or is *at a higher risk to* become an abusive parent as an adult. Likewise, it might state that people who did not experience childhood abuse might become abusive parents, but they are *less likely to* than someone who has experienced abuse as a child.

aggregate: Collection of many individuals, cases, or other units.

WHAT IS THEORY?

LO 1 Explain how theory is closely linked to social research methods.

social theory: A system of interconnected abstractions or ideas that condenses and organizes knowledge about the social world.

Social theory can be defined as a system of interconnected abstractions or ideas that condenses and organizes knowledge about the social world. It is a compact way to think of the social world. People are always creating new theories about how the world works.

Some people confuse the history of social thought, or what great thinkers said, with social theory. You may have heard the saying "I think, therefore I am," which is attributed to Descartes, a French philosopher from the seventeenth century. Or you may have heard quotes from Gandhi, Confucius, Aristotle, or some other great thinker of the past. The ideas associated with these great thinkers are different from social theory. The classical social theorists (e.g., Marx, Weber, and Durkheim) played an important role in generating innovative ideas about the workings of social life in particular. They developed original theories about how society was organized and functioned that laid the foundation for subsequent generations of social researchers. Great thinkers, in contrast, are often associated with a particular issue (often political) or topic (e.g., a branch of philosophy). Social theorists, on the other hand, create explanations about the workings of society and the interactions between members of social groups. As social scientists, we study classical theorists because they provided the foundations of our understanding of the social world. Many of their contributions are still valid, even though today's society is much different than when they were writing (the late 1800s and early 1900s). There are also new generations of social theorists who have made important contributions to our understanding of social life.

At times, people confuse theory with a "hunch," or speculative guessing. They may say, "It's only a theory," or ask, "What's your theory about it?" This lax use of the term *theory* causes confusion. Such guessing differs from a serious social theory that has been carefully built and debated over many years by dozens of researchers who found support for the theory's key parts in repeated empirical tests. A related confusion is when what people consider to be a "fact" (i.e., light a match in a gasoline vapour–filled room and the room will explode) is what scientists call a theory (i.e., a theory of how combining certain quantities of particular chemicals with oxygen and a certain level of heat is likely to produce the outcome of explosive force). People use simple theories without making them explicit or labelling them as such. For example, newspaper articles or television reports on social issues usually have unstated social theories embedded within them. A news report on the difficulty of implementing a charter school will contain an implicit theory about education and pedagogy. Likewise, political leaders frequently express social theories when they discuss public issues. Politicians who claim that inadequate education causes poverty or that a decline in traditional moral values causes higher crime rates are expressing theories (ideological stances on political issues are really just theories that individuals adhere to). Compared with the theories of social scientists, such laypersons' theories are less systematic, less well formulated, and harder to test with empirical evidence.

The Big Picture: Sociological Theory and Research

Almost all research involves some theory, so the question is not so much *whether* you should use theory as *how* you should use it and *which* theory is most appropriate for your research.

macrosocial theory: Social theories and explanations about abstract, large-scale, and broad-scope aspects of social reality, such as social change in major institutions (e.g., the family, education) in a whole nation across several decades.

LEVELS OF THEORY

LO 2 Explain what is meant by levels of theory.

Social theories can be divided into three broad groupings by the level of social reality they deal with. Some theories focus on individuals while others focus on entire societies. A **macrosocial theory** is one that focuses on society at the level of social structures and populations. Macrosocial theories focus on society as a whole on a large scale. Their focus on structure means that they explain social life at high levels of abstraction. The social structures of interest to macro theorists can refer to societies, cities, nations, and populations in general. Families and cultures can be studied within a macro sociological framework, but only in the context of the larger social structures in which they are found. A **microsocial theory**, in contrast, is focused on individuals and individual action.

microsocial theory: Social theories and explanations about the concrete, small-scale, and narrow level of reality, such as face-to-face interaction in small groups during a two-month period.

Mesosocial theory occupies a position between the micro and the macro. While a microsociological approach focuses on individuals and a macrosciological approach focuses on the grand processes of social order, **mesosocial theory** directs its attention to the rule of social organizations and social institutions in society. See Box 2.1 for a discussion of levels of theory in two Canadian research studies.

mesosocial theory: Social theories and explanations about the middle level of social reality between a broad and narrow scope, such as the development and operation of social organizations, communities, or social movements over a five-year period.

Box 2.1 Concepts in Action

Levels of Theory in Two Canadian Studies

Researchers generally start out with theories that frame their orientations toward the social processes they wish to study. In the examples below, the authors were motivated to answer questions that focused on large social processes in society (macro processes), and therefore the initial point of departure was from a macrosociological perspective.

Nakhaie and Brym. Nakhaie and Brym (2011) studied the political affiliations of Canadian university professors. Drawing from conflict theory (as well as other theories), the authors tested whether university professors would be more left-leaning because of the culture of their profession being critical of the social order. They also considered class-based theories, suggesting that professors might actually be more right-leaning because of their position as "elites." The authors analyzed data from a national survey of Canadian university professors and found that the political leanings of professors depended on a variety of factors, including the "eliteness" of the university where they worked, their gender, and their academic discipline.

Conflict theory is a traditional sociological approach rooted in Marxism that holds that capitalism separates individuals into distinct classes that are in opposition to one another. Major institutions operate in ways that contain or suppress the activities of nondominant groups in society, especially if they challenge or threaten the established socio-economic hierarchy. Each class has its own fairly homogeneous set of ideologies that are the result of their common interests.

Funk and Kobayashi. Studies by Funk (2010, 2012) and Funk and Kobayashi (2009) have focused on the motivations and experiences of individuals engaged in caring for older family members—mostly parents. The authors approached their research question using a well-established macrosocial theory that posits that the care of older adults in Western

Box 2.1 (*continued*)

society is characterized by a range of choices available to individuals because of improved services for the aged and changing norms surrounding elder care, such that caring for older family members is seen as "voluntary." On the other hand, elder care may be understood as an overarching system of obligation that requires family members, particularly women, to care for aging parents. The authors argue that these two perspectives are often approached as though they were polar opposites (i.e., "choice" versus "obligation") but they should be understood in tandem as they both contribute to how families make decisions about elder care.

The theory proposed by Funk and Kobayashi (2009) is macrosocial in nature because it is a theory of filial care that applies to an entire society. Structural functionalism is a traditional sociological theoretical approach rooted in the work of Durkheim that holds that processes of industrialization and urbanization change human society from a traditional to modern form. In this process of modernization, social institutions and practices evolve. The evolution includes those that fill the social system's basic needs, socialize people to cultural values, and regulate social behaviour. Institutions that filled needs and maintained the social system in a traditional society (such as the traditional family structure) are superseded by modern ones (such as new family forms and responsibilities).

LO 3 Define empirical generalization.

EMPIRICAL GENERALIZATIONS AND MIDDLE RANGE THEORY

empirical generalization: A quasi-theoretical statement that summarizes findings or regularities in *empirical evidence*. It uses few, if any, abstract concepts and only makes a statement about a recurring pattern that researchers observe.

middle-range theory: A theory that focuses on specific aspects of social life and sociological topics that can be tested with empirical hypotheses.

Empirical generalizations are not theories but are derived from theories and offer a simple statement about a pattern or generalization among two or more concrete concepts that are very close to empirical reality—for example, "More men than women choose engineering as a university major." This summarizes a pattern between gender and choice of major. It is easy to test or observe. It is called a *generalization* because the pattern operates across many periods and social contexts.

Middle-range theories are slightly more abstract than empirical generalizations. **Middle-range theory** does not try to bridge the micro–macro divide, but instead offers theories about limited aspects of social life. Rather than having theories about all aspects of social life (such as the grand theories associated with the macrosocial approach), middle-range theorists focus on specific aspects of social life that they can test with empirical hypotheses (Merton, 1967). See Box 2.2 for a discussion of how Nakhaie and Brym (2011) and Funk

Box 2.2 Concepts in Action

Middle Range Substantive Theory and Empirical Generalization in Two Canadian Studies

Although influenced by macrosociological ideas about the nature of society, the authors of the two studies introduced earlier in this chapter actually test middle-range theories that are more specific to their research topics. They also translate these middle-range theories to narrowly focused empirical generalizations that they can test with their data.

Middle-Range Substantive Theory

Nakhaie and Brym. Neo-Marxists argue that intellectuals, such as university professors, while coming from a variety of class backgrounds, form a specific occupational group. As such, these individuals have similar interests, which suggests there should be class uniformity among professors.

Funk and Kobayashi. Families have historically always provided the majority of care for older adults. Within the North American culture, however, there is a range of choices for how to deal with care for older adults. Children have the choice to care for their aging parents or use formal care arrangements.

Empirical Generalization

Nakhaie and Brym. Canadian professors are part of a class system, but the relationships among the professors of employment, gender, area of study, and ethnoreligious background account more for professors' political affiliations than class alone.

Funk and Kobayashi. Providing care to older adults is not such a cut-and-dried issue of choice or obligation, but instead hinges on several factors. Caregivers are constrained by their own resources and social supports, which they must negotiate in tandem with feelings of obligation, guilt, and helplessness.

and Kobayashi (2009) moved from macrosocial theory to middle-range theories and empirical generalizations.

THE PARTS OF THEORY

LO 4 Define agency and structure.

All theories contain concepts, and concepts are the building blocks of theory.[1] A **concept** is an idea expressed as a symbol or in words. Natural science concepts are often expressed in symbolic forms, such as Greek letters (e.g., Σ) or formulas (e.g., $s = d/t$, where s = speed, d = distance, t = time). Most social science concepts are expressed as words.

concept: An idea expressed as a symbol or in words.

Everyday culture is filled with concepts, but many have vague and unclear definitions. Likewise, the values and experiences of people in a culture may limit everyday concepts, which are often rooted in misconceptions or myth. Social scientists borrow concepts from everyday culture, but they refine these concepts and add new ones. Many concepts—such as *sexism*, *lifestyle*, *peer group*, *urban sprawl*, and *social class*—began as precise, technical concepts in social theory but have diffused into the larger culture and become less precise.

We create concepts from personal experience, creative thought, or observation. The classical theorists originated many concepts. Examples include *family system*, *gender role*, *socialization*, *self-worth*, *frustration*, and *displaced aggression*. Nakhaie and Brym (2011), for example, used various concepts in their study of the attitudes of Canadian professors, including race, region, academic rank, and field of specialization.

Researchers define scientific concepts more precisely than the concepts we use in daily discourse. Social theory requires that concepts be well defined; the definition helps link theory with research. A valuable goal of exploratory research, and of most good research, is to clarify and refine concepts. Weak, contradictory, or unclear definitions of concepts restrict the advancement of knowledge.

Sociology on the Job: Sociological Theory and Research

Concept Clusters

Concepts are rarely used in isolation. Rather, they form interconnected groups, or **concept clusters**. This is true for concepts in everyday language as well as for concepts in social theory. Theories contain collections of associated concepts that are consistent and mutually reinforcing. Together, they form a web of meaning. For example, if we want to discuss a concept like *urban decay*, we will need a set of associated concepts (e.g., *urban expansion*, *economic growth*, *urbanization*, *suburbs*, *downtown*, *revitalization*, and *mass transit*). In their study of the attitudes of Canadian professors, Nakhaie and Brym (2011) also used concept clusters in their understanding of the ideological orientations of professors. Their general concept of ideological orientations had a set of associated concepts: support for economic equality, support for unions, support for gender equality, and support for racial/ethnic equality. In other words, the authors were interested in the general idea of political ideology, but found that this concept could be broken down into various aspects (i.e., clusters) of ideology pertaining to specific topics.

concept cluster: A collection of interrelated ideas that share common *assumptions*, belong to the same larger *social theory*, and refer to one another.

Assumptions

Theories contain built-in **assumptions**, statements about the nature of things that are not observable or testable. We accept them as a necessary starting point. Concepts and theories build on assumptions about the nature of human beings, social reality, or a particular phenomenon. Assumptions often remain hidden or unstated. One way for a researcher to deepen his or her understanding of a concept is to identify the assumptions on which it is based.

assumption: A part of a social theory that is not tested but acts as a starting point or basic belief about the world. These are necessary to make other theoretical statements and to build *social theory*.

The assumptions that a theory has are manifold, but we will examine three different types of assumptions that are inherent to all social theories: their emphasis on agency or structure, and their epistemological and ontological orientations.

agency: Refers to the individual's ability to act and make independent choices.

structure: Refers to aspects of the social landscape that appear to limit or influence the choices made by individuals.

Agency and Structure What is more important in explaining social life—individuals or the social structures around them? This is the question at the heart of what is known as the debate between the primacy of *agency* or *structure*. **Agency** refers to the individual's ability to act and make independent choices, while **structure** refers to aspects of the social landscape that appear to limit or influence the choices made by individuals. What takes priority then—individual autonomy or socialization? Of course this question is not quickly resolvable and is of central concern to social theory. Some theorists emphasize the importance of individual experience, therefore favouring agency. Other theorists view society as a large functional organism, therefore favouring structure.

The debate in social theory isn't simply what is more important—the individual or social structures. If agency and structure are so distinct, what is it that ties the individual to society? Society is more than a bunch of individuals; there is something larger at work that makes it a *society*. Structural functionalists and conflict theorists emphasize how social structures determine social life and that individual actions can really be reinterpreted as the outcomes of structural forces. So while people may seem to have made decisions to act in certain ways (i.e., get a specific job, take a specific course), it was really the larger forces of society (structure) that constrained their choices in such a way that this was the only decision they could have reached. Microsociological theorists like symbolic interactionists, in contrast, focus on the subjective meaning of social life and how this is responsible for creating individuals' social worlds. Much work in social theory has focused on how to reconcile the structure and agency debate by theorizing about how individuals are connected to society.

LO 5 Explain what is meant by ontology and epistemology as they apply to the approach a researcher takes to social research.

Ontology and Epistemology There are two major philosophical assumptions about the nature of social research from which social researchers approach their work. These are largely taken-for-granted viewpoints that scientists have in their minds as they are conducting their research. One has to do with the nature of reality itself and appropriate ways to research it, while the other relates to the relationship that the researcher has with his or her subject matter. The terms for these assumptions about social life are ontology and epistemology, respectively.

ontology: A branch of philosophy that considers the way we understand the nature of reality.

epistemology: A branch of philosophy that studies knowledge, including how we pursue knowledge.

positivism: The philosophical orientation that the social world should be studied in a similar manner to the natural world.

interpretivism: The philosophical orientation that the study of society requires research techniques specific to understanding the interpretation of meaning.

paradigm: A general organizing framework for *social theory* and empirical research. It includes basic *assumptions*, major questions to be answered, models of good research practice and theory, and methods for finding the answers to questions.

Ontology, as it relates to social theory, has to do with how we understand the nature of reality. Ontological studies are a huge branch of philosophy, and so the discussion here really only scratches the surface of the scholarship that has been carried out in social theory. Essentially, however, there are two polar opposites of thinking about ontology. One view is that there is an objective social reality that exists "out there" that is the same for everyone and that is ours to discover. On the opposite side of the spectrum is subjectivity—that social reality is constructed by individuals and that it is unique for everyone.

Epistemology is a closely related topic, and within the context of sociological theory and research it refers to the techniques by which we study the social world. On the one hand is **positivism**, which is the belief that the social world should be studied in a similar manner to the scientific world. Positivist researchers advocate the use of statistics, surveys, and experiments. On the other hand is **interpretivism**, which understands society as fundamentally different from the topics of the natural sciences and argues that it is wholly inappropriate to study society in similar manners. Rather, interpretivists advocate for research techniques that involve understanding how individuals interpret the social world around them, usually focusing on qualitative methods.

Ontological and epistemological assumptions are at the core of the central differences between the two major paradigms in the social sciences, which we now turn to.

LO 6 Compare the positivist and interpretivist paradigms.

TWO MAJOR PARADIGMS

About 45 years ago, a now famous philosopher of science, Thomas Kuhn, argued that how science develops in a specific field across time is based on researchers sharing a general approach, or paradigm. A **paradigm** is an integrated set of assumptions, beliefs, models of doing good research, and techniques for gathering and analyzing data. It organizes core ideas, theoretical frameworks, and research methods. Kuhn observed that scientific fields tend to be held together around a paradigm for a long period. Very few researchers question the paradigm, and most focus on operating within its general boundaries to accumulate new knowledge. On rare occasions in history, intellectual difficulties increase, unexpected issues grow, and troubling concerns over proper methods multiply. Slowly, the members of a scientific field come to see things differently and switch to a new paradigm. Once the new paradigm becomes fully established and widely adopted, the process of accumulating knowledge begins anew.

Kuhn's explanation covered how most sciences operate most of the time, but some fields operate with multiple or competing paradigms. This is the case in several of the social sciences. This situation greatly bothers some social scientists, and they believe having multiple paradigms hinders the growth of knowledge. They see multiple paradigms as a sign of the immaturity or underdevelopment of the "science" in the social sciences. Some believe all social science researchers should embrace a single paradigm and stop using alternatives to it.

Other social scientists accept the coexistence of multiple paradigms. They recognize that this can be confusing and often makes communication difficult among those who use different approaches. Despite this, they argue that each social science paradigm provides important kinds of knowledge and insights, so to drop one would limit what we can learn about the social world. These social scientists note that no one definitely can say which approach is "best" or even whether it is necessary or highly desirable to have only one paradigm. So, instead of closing off an approach that offers innovative ways to study social life and gain insight into human behaviour, they argue for keeping a diversity of approaches.

In this section, we will look at two fundamental paradigms or approaches used in social science. Each approach has been around for over 150 years and is used by many highly respected professional researchers. These approaches are unequal in terms of the number of followers, quantity of new studies, and types of issues addressed. Often, people who strongly adhere to one approach disagree with researchers who use the other approach, or see the other approach as being less valuable or less "scientific" than their approach. Although adherents to each approach may use various research techniques, theories, and theoretical frameworks, researchers who adopt one approach tend to favour certain research techniques, theories, or theoretical frameworks over others. The two approaches we will discuss are the positivist and interpretive approaches; each has internal divisions, offshoots, and extensions, but the information presented below contains the core ideas of each approach.

Positivist Approach

Positivism is the most widely practised social science approach, especially in North America. *Positivism* sees social science research as fundamentally the same as natural science research; it assumes that social reality is made up of objective facts that value-free researchers can precisely measure and that statistics can be used to test causal theories. Large-scale bureaucratic agencies, companies, and many people in the general public favour a positivist approach because it emphasizes getting objective measures of "hard facts" in the form of numbers.

Positivists put great value on the principle of replication, even if only a few studies are replicated. **Replication** occurs when researchers or others repeat the basics of a study and get identical or very similar findings. Positivists emphasize replication as the ultimate test of knowledge. This is because they believe that different observers looking at the same facts will get the same results if they carefully specify their ideas, precisely measure the facts, and follow the standards of objective research. When many studies by independent researchers yield similar findings, confidence grows that we accurately captured the workings of social reality, and therefore scientific knowledge increases.

replication: The principle that researchers must be able to repeat scientific findings in multiple studies to have a high level of confidence that the findings are true.

If a researcher repeats a study and does not get similar findings, one or more of five possibilities may be occurring: (1) The initial study was an unusual fluke or based on a misguided understanding of the social world; (2) important conditions were present in the initial study, but no one was aware of their significance so they were not specified; (3) the initial study, or the repetition of it, was sloppy—it did not include careful, precise measures; (4) the initial study, or the repetition of it, was improperly conducted—researchers failed to closely follow the highest standards for procedures and techniques, or failed to be completely objective; or (5) the repeated study was an unusual fluke.

nomothetic: An approach based on laws or one that operates according to a system of laws.

The positivist approach is **nomothetic**, which means explanations use law or law-like principles. Positivists may use inductive and deductive inquiry, but the ideal is to develop a general causal law or principle, then use logical deduction to specify how it operates in concrete situations. Next, the researcher empirically tests outcomes predicted by the principle in concrete settings using precise measures. In this way, a general law or principle covers many specific situations. For example, a general principle says that when two social groups are unequal and compete for scarce resources, in-group feelings and hostility toward the other group intensify, and the competing groups are likely to engage in conflict. The principle applies to sports teams, countries, ethnic groups, families, or other social groupings. A researcher might deduce that in cities with high levels of interracial inequality, when jobs become scarcer and thereby economic competition increases, each group will express greater hostility toward the other racial groups and intergroup conflict (e.g., riots, demonstrations, violent attacks) will increase.

The vast majority of positivist studies are quantitative, and positivists generally see the experiment as the ideal means of doing research. Positivist researchers also use other quantitative research techniques, such as surveys or existing statistics, but tend to see them as approximations of the experiment for situations where an experiment is impossible. Positivist researchers advocate value-free science, seek precise quantitative measures, test causal theories with statistics, and believe in the importance of replicating studies.

Interpretive Approach

The interpretive approach is also scientific, but it defines the idea of "scientific" differently from positivism. Unlike the positivist approach, interpretive researchers say that human social life is qualitatively different from other things studied by science. This means that social scientists cannot just borrow the principles of science from the natural sciences. Instead, they believe it is necessary to create a special type of science, one based on the uniqueness of humans and that can really capture human social life.

Most researchers who use an interpretive approach adopt a version of the constructionist view of social reality. This view holds that human social life is based less on objective, hard, factual reality than on the ideas, beliefs, and perceptions that people hold about reality. In other words, people socially interact and respond based as much, if not more, on what they believe to be real as on what is objectively real. This means that social scientists will be able to understand social life only if they study how people go about constructing social reality. As people grow up, interact, and live their daily lives, they continuously create ideas, relationships, symbols, and roles that they consider to be meaningful or important. These include things such as intimate emotional attachments, religious or moral ideals, patriotic values, racial–ethnic or gender differences, and artistic expressions. Rarely do people relate to the objective facts of reality directly; instead, they do so through the filter of these socially constructed beliefs and perceptions. What positivists and many other people view to be objective facts (e.g., a person's height), interpretive researchers say are only at the trivial surface level of social life. Or the "facts" are images/categories that humans created (i.e., I am two metres tall), and we "forget" that people originated the images/categories but now treat them as being separate from people and objectively real.

Interpretive researchers are skeptical of the positivist attempts to produce precise quantitative measures of objective facts. This is because they view social reality as very fluid. For most humans, social reality is largely the shifting perceptions that they are constantly constructing, testing, reinforcing, or changing and that have become embedded in social traditions or institutions. For this reason, interpretive researchers tend to trust and favour qualitative data. They believe that qualitative data can more accurately capture the fluid processes of social reality. In addition, they favour interpretive over causal forms of theory.

Interpretive researchers are not likely to adopt a nomothetic approach but, instead, favour an idiographic form of explanation and use inductive reasoning. **Idiographic** literally means "specific description" and refers to explaining an aspect of the social world by offering a highly detailed picture or description of a specific social setting, process, or type of relationship. For example, qualitative researchers do not see replication as the ultimate test of knowledge. Instead, they emphasize *verstehen*, or empathetic understanding. ***Verstehen*** is the desire of a researcher to get inside the worldview of those he or she is studying and accurately represent how the people being studied see the world, feel about it, and act in it. In other words, the best test of good social knowledge is not replication, but whether the researcher can demonstrate that he or she really captured the inner world and personal perspective of the people studied.

idiographic: An approach that focuses on creating detailed descriptions of specific events in particular time periods and settings. It rarely goes beyond *empirical generalizations* to abstract social theory or causal laws.

***verstehen*:** A German word that translates as "understanding"; specifically, it means an empathic understanding of another's worldview.

Figure 2.1 illustrates how the various terms discussed so far are related to each other. Although there are exceptions, microsocial theory, which focuses on individuals, tends to emphasize agency over structure. Researchers who have this perspective tend to focus on the interactions of individuals, and they tend to have an interpretivist epistemology and an ontological orientation that is focused on the subjective meanings that individuals attribute to their actions. In contrast, macrosocial theorists focus on social structures and tend to have a positivist orientation in which they try to apply the techniques of the natural sciences to the study of society. They believe that there is an objective reality out there that social scientists are able to study in an objective manner.

The way that the terms have somewhat dichotomized themselves into two extremes also relates to the types of techniques that are used by researchers. On the left-hand side of the continuum lies researchers who stress the importance of subjective meaning and tend to focus on interpretivism and microsocial theory. These researchers are much more likely to use qualitative research methods like field research and semi-structured interviews. On the other side of the continuum are researchers who are more likely to be focused on macrosociological

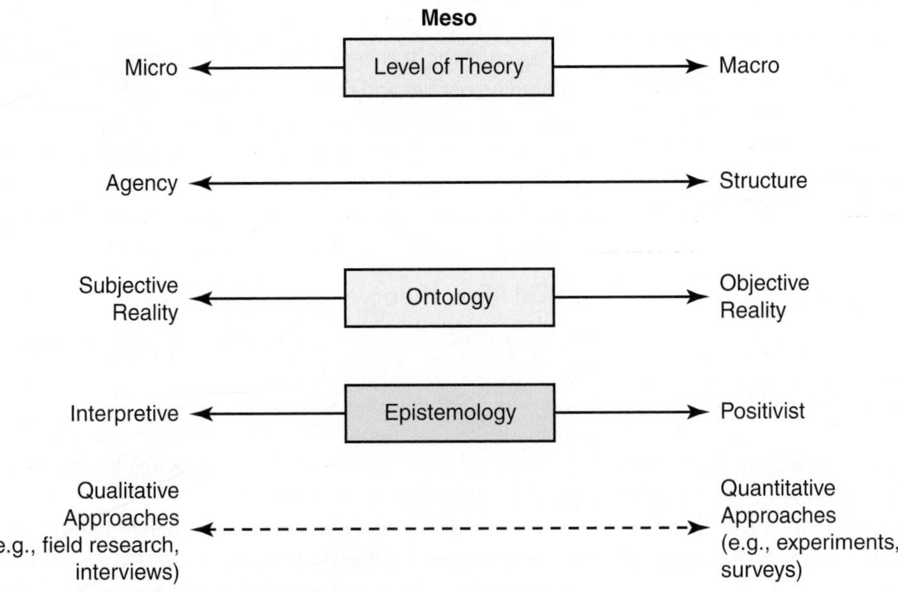

Figure 2.1 Aspects and Assumptions of Theory

The Basics: Sociological Theory and Research

Functionalism

issues and believe in exploring social research questions in a similar manner to researchers of the "hard" or natural sciences. Such researchers are more likely to employ the use of surveys and experiments in their work.

MAJOR THEORETICAL FRAMEWORKS

Income Inequality

Why We Still Need Booster Shots of Feminism

Questions and Debates in the Field of Race and Ethnicity

White Privilege in the U.S.

Sociology and other social sciences have several major theoretical frameworks.[2] The frameworks are orientations, or sweeping ways of looking at the social world. They provide collections of assumptions, concepts, and forms of explanation. Frameworks include many formal or substantive theories (e.g., theories of crime, theories of family). Thus, there can be a structural functional theory, an exchange theory, and a conflict theory of family. Theories within the same framework share assumptions and major concepts. Some frameworks are oriented more to the micro-level, while others focus on more macro-level phenomena. Box 2.3 shows three major traditional frameworks (structural functionalism, symbolic interaction, and conflict theory) and two more recent frameworks in sociology (critical feminism and critical race theory) and briefly describes the key concepts and assumptions of each. Box 2.4 tells you how you can learn more about these theories on the internet.

Box 2.3 Focus

Major Traditional Theoretical Frameworks in Sociology

Structural Functionalism

Major Concepts. System, equilibrium, dysfunction, social cohesion
Key Assumptions. Society is a system of interdependent parts that is in equilibrium or in balance. Over time, society has evolved from a simple to a complex type that has highly specialized parts. The parts of society fulfill different needs or functions of the social system. A basic consensus on values or a value system holds society together.
Level of Theorizing. Macro
Major Theorists. Emile Durkheim, Talcott Parsons

Symbolic Interactionism

Major Concepts. Self, reference group, role-playing, perception
Key Assumptions. People transmit and receive symbolic communication when they socially interact. People create perceptions of each other and social settings. People largely act on their perceptions. How people think about themselves and others is based on their interactions.
Level of Theorizing. Micro
Major Theorists. George Herbert Mead, Erving Goffman

Conflict Theory

Major Concepts. Power, exploitation, struggle, inequality, alienation
Key Assumptions. Society is made up of groups that have opposing interests. Coercion and attempts to gain power are ever-present aspects of human relations. Those in power attempt to hold on to their power by spreading myths or by using violence if necessary.
Level of Theorizing. Macro
Major Theorists. Karl Marx, Max Weber, Erik Olin Wright

Major Recent Theoretical Frameworks in Sociology

Critical feminism and critical race theory are orientations that have received much attention in recent social research. These perspectives highlight how gender and race (and class, often in unison) work together to produce structured inequalities in various aspects of social life. These theories are attributable to numerous authors and therefore their classification into micro- and macrosocial theories is not as clear-cut since they discuss structural inequalities but often at a small-scale level.

Critical Feminism

Major Concepts. Gender, inequality, discourse, power
Key Assumptions. It is imperative to understand the meaning surrounding gender and how power relations play themselves out in subtle ways in various aspects of social inequality.
Level of Theorizing. Micro, meso, macro (depending on the specific orientation of the theorist)
Major Theorists. Varied, but includes Judith Butler, Dorothy Smith

Critical Race Theory

Major Concepts. Race, inequality, racialization, stratification
Key Assumptions. Race is embedded in various aspects of social life. Inequalities experienced in society cannot be explained solely by theories of class or gender—race and the experience of being racialized also contributes to stratification in many aspects of social life.
Level of Theorizing. Micro, meso, macro (depending on the specific orientation of the theorist)
Major Theorists. Gloria Ladson-Billings, bell hooks

Box 2.4 Social Research and the Internet

There are numerous theories about social life that exist in the social sciences. Some have been introduced in this chapter—structural functionalism, conflict theory, symbolic interaction, critical feminism, and critical race theory. This, however, is just scratching the surface of the myriad theories that have been developed in the social sciences. You will likely cover a broad range of classical and contemporary social theorists in the course of your studies.

One way of exploring various theoretical orientations that you might be interested in incorporating into your research is by visiting Sociosite (www.sociosite.net). Sociosite is a free sociological resource that has been online since 1996. It is run by Dutch scholars at the University of Amsterdam. Among the many resources available to users, there is a comprehensive listing of "Sociological Theories and Perspectives" with links to various websites on a wide spectrum of sociological theorists and terminology.

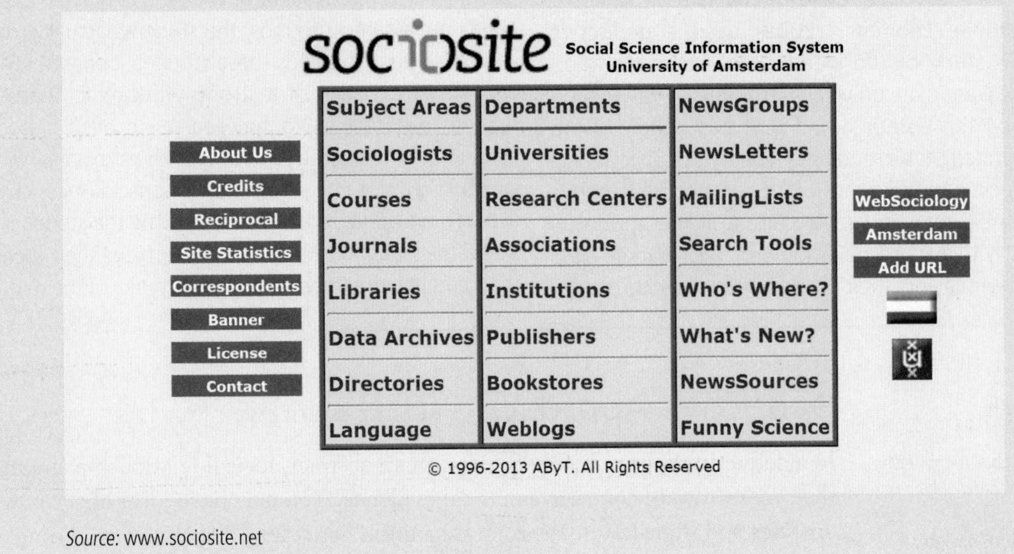

Source: www.sociosite.net

DIRECTION OF THEORIZING

LO 7 Differentiate between inductive and deductive approaches to theory.

Researchers approach the building and testing of theory from two directions. Some begin with abstract thinking; they logically connect the ideas in theory to concrete evidence and then test the ideas against the evidence. Others begin with specific observations of empirical evidence; on the basis of the evidence they generalize and build toward increasingly abstract ideas. In practice, most researchers are flexible and use both approaches at various points in a study (see Figure 2.2).

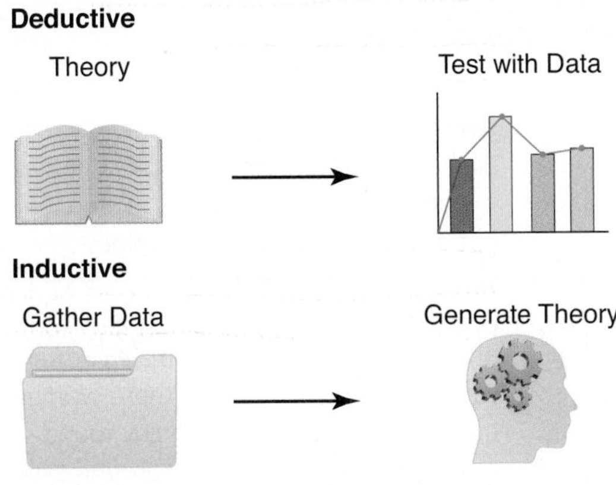

Figure 2.2 Direction of Theorizing

Box 2.5 Concepts in Action

Examples of Deductive Approaches

The deductive approach to theorizing is most commonly associated with quantitative research. Nakhaie and Brym (2011) tested conflict theory and other theories using quantitative data on Canadian university professors. They started with theories that they were interested in testing and then tested them using data—a classic deductive approach.

While the deductive approach is typically associated with quantitative research methods, sometimes researchers using qualitative techniques may also use this approach to theorizing. For example, Lehmann (2009) used a deductive approach in a study of the identities of first-generation working-class Canadian university students. Drawing on conflict theory, the author noted that past studies from Canada, the United States, and Britain showed that students from working-class backgrounds often had trouble integrating into the intellectual and social culture of the university, often having to mimic the behaviours of their middle-class peers and downplaying their working-class backgrounds. The author deductively reasoned that the students from working-class backgrounds would constantly have to negotiate their identities and overcome barriers in an institution that typically services the middle class.

To test the theory, Lehmann interviewed first-generation working-class students at a large Ontario university. The researcher interviewed the students twice, where possible: once when they were starting their university careers (i.e., in their first year) and again in the second year of their studies. Data revealed that instead of rejecting characteristics of their working-class backgrounds, the students actually used them as strategies to succeed. These students benefited from their class-instilled values of a strong work ethic, maturity, and real-life experiences to succeed in an alien class culture. Lehmann further argued that the views expressed by these students did not characterize class consciousness. They were actually individualized attitudes used by the students to transcend their class backgrounds and achieve their dreams (and their parents' dreams) of joining the ranks of the middle class.

deductive approach: An approach to inquiry or social theory in which one begins with abstract ideas and principles then works toward concrete, *empirical evidence* to test the ideas.

Deductive Approach

In a **deductive approach**, you begin with an abstract, logical relationship among concepts, then move toward concrete empirical evidence. You may have ideas about how the world operates and want to test these ideas against "hard data." Deductive reasoning is all about testing theories with data—usually statistical data—as Box 2.5 demonstrates.

inductive approach: An approach to inquiry or social theory in which one begins with concrete empirical details then works toward abstract ideas or general principles.

grounded theory: Social theory that is rooted in observations of specific, concrete details.

Inductive Approach

If you use an **inductive approach**, you begin with detailed observations of the world and move toward more abstract generalizations and ideas. When you begin, you may have only a topic and a few vague concepts. As you observe, you refine the concepts, develop empirical generalizations, and identify preliminary relationships. You build the theory from the ground up. Box 2.6 provides an example of the inductive approach. Many researchers who adopt an inductive approach use **grounded theory**, where a researcher builds ideas and

Box 2.6 Concepts in Action

Inductive Theorizing in Practice

Inductive approaches to theorizing are largely associated with the qualitative approaches to doing research. Inductive approaches to theorizing first gather data and then attempt to create a theory from the data.

For example, Malacrida (2007) used a microsocial theory about mothers with disabilities and the difficulties they face balancing their own dependency with the nurturance their children require. Malacrida interviewed 43 mothers with disabilities in Alberta using qualitative, semi-structured, open-ended interviews. The theory, derived inductively from the data, stated that these mothers faced several challenges living up to the normative standard of being a good mother. They indicated that they often felt judged because their style of parenting could not be the same as that of someone without any disability. Their challenges stemmed from both private and public spheres. They faced numerous problems securing housing that was disability accessible, and they often had to rely heavily on male partners, which made them vulnerable to abuse. While these women experienced many hardships and challenges, many found strength in networks of support that they created around them.

Box 2.7 Focus

What Is Grounded Theory?

Grounded theory is a widely used approach in qualitative research. It is not the only approach, and it is not used by all qualitative researchers. Grounded theory is "a qualitative research method that uses a systematic set of procedures to develop an inductively derived theory about a phenomenon" (Strauss & Corbin, 1990, p. 24). Its purpose is to build a theory that is faithful to the evidence. It is a method for discovering new theory. In it, the researcher compares unlike phenomena with a view toward learning similarities. He or she sees micro-level events as the foundation for a more macro-level explanation. Grounded theory shares several goals with more positivist-oriented theory. It seeks theory that is comparable with the evidence, precise and rigorous, capable of replication, and generalizable. A grounded theory approach pursues generalizations by making comparisons across social situations.

Qualitative researchers use alternatives to grounded theory. Some qualitative researchers offer an in-depth depiction that is true to an informant's worldview. They excavate a single social situation to elucidate the micro processes that sustain stable social interaction. The goal of other researchers is to provide an exact depiction of events or a setting. They analyze specific events or settings to gain insight into the larger dynamics of a society. Still other researchers apply an existing theory to analyze specific settings that they have placed in a macro-level historical context. They show connections among micro-level events and between micro-level situations and larger social forces for the purpose of reconstructing the theory and informing social action.

theoretical generalizations based on closely examining and creatively thinking about the data (see Box 2.7).

EXPLAINING RELATIONSHIPS IN SOCIAL RESEARCH

LO 8 Define causality and its three criteria.

A theory's primary purpose is to explain. Many people confuse prediction with explanation. There are two meanings or uses of the term *explanation*. Researchers focus on *theoretical explanation*, a logical argument that tells why something occurs and how concepts are connected. It refers to a general rule or principle. The second type of explanation, *ordinary explanation*, makes something clear or describes something in a way that illustrates it and makes it intelligible. For example, a good teacher "explains" in the ordinary sense. The two types of explanation can blend together. This occurs when a researcher explains (i.e., makes intelligible) his or her explanation (i.e., a logical argument involving theory).

prediction: A statement about something that is likely to occur in the future.

Prediction is a statement that something will occur. It is easier to predict than to explain, and an explanation has more logical power than a prediction because good explanations also predict. An explanation rarely predicts more than one outcome, but the same outcome may be predicted by opposing explanations. Although it is less powerful than explanation, many people are entranced by the dramatic visibility of a prediction.

A gambling example illustrates the difference between explanation and prediction. If you enter a casino and consistently and accurately predict the next card to appear or the next number on a roulette wheel, it will be sensational. You may win a lot of money, at least until the casino officials realize you are always winning and expel you! Yet your method of making the predictions is more interesting than the fact that you can do so. Telling us what you do to predict the next card is more fascinating than being able to predict.

Here is another example. You know that the sun "rises" each morning. You can predict that at some time, every morning, whether or not clouds obscure it, the sun will rise. But why is this so? One explanation is that the Great Turtle carries the sun across the sky on its back. Another explanation is that a god sets his arrow ablaze, which appears to us as the sun, and shoots it across the sky. Few people today believe these ancient explanations. The explanation you probably accept involves a theory about the rotation of Earth and the position of the sun, the star of our solar system. In this explanation, the sun only appears to rise. The sun does not move; its apparent movement depends on Earth's rotation. We are on a planet that both spins on its axis and orbits around a star millions of miles away in space.

All three explanations make the same prediction: The sun rises each morning. As you can see, a weak explanation can produce an accurate prediction. A good explanation depends on a well-developed theory and is confirmed in research by empirical observations.

Causal Explanation

causal explanation: A statement in social theory about why events occur that is expressed in terms of causes and effects. They correspond to associations in the empirical world.

Causal explanation, the most common type of explanation, is used when the relationship is one of cause and effect. We use it all the time in everyday language, which tends to be sloppy and ambiguous. What do we mean when we say *cause?* For example, you may say that poverty causes crime or that looseness in morals causes an increase in divorce. But this does not tell how or why the causal process works. Researchers try to be more precise and exact when discussing causal relations.

Philosophers have long debated the idea of cause. Some people argue that causality occurs in the empirical world, but that it cannot be proven. Causality is "out there" in objective reality, and researchers can only try to find evidence for it. Others argue that causality is only an idea that exists in the human mind—a mental construction, not something "real" in the world. This second position holds that causality is only a convenient means of thinking about the world. Without entering into the lengthy philosophical debate, many researchers pursue causal relationships.

You need three things to establish causality: temporal order, association, and the elimination of plausible alternatives. An implicit fourth condition is an assumption that a causal relationship makes sense or fits with broader assumptions or a theoretical framework. Let's examine the three basic conditions.

temporal order: In establishing causation, the cause must come before the effect.

Temporal order

The **temporal order** condition means that a cause must come before an effect. This common sense assumption establishes the direction of causality: from the cause toward the effect. You may ask, "How can the cause come after what it is to affect?" It cannot, but temporal order is only one of the conditions needed for causality. Temporal order is necessary but not sufficient to infer causality. Sometimes people make the mistake of talking about "cause" on the basis of temporal order alone. For example, a professional baseball player pitches no-hit games when he kisses his wife just before a game. The kissing occurred before the no-hit games. Does that mean the kissing is the cause of the pitching performance? It is very unlikely. As another example, race riots occurred in four separate U.S. cities in 1968, one day after an intense wave of sunspots. The temporal ordering does not establish a causal link between sunspots and race riots. After all, all prior human history occurred before some specific event. The temporal order condition simply eliminates from consideration potential causes that occurred later in time.

It is not always easy to establish temporal order. With cross-sectional research temporal order is tricky. For example, a researcher finds that people who have a lot of education are also less prejudiced than others. Does more education cause a reduction in prejudice? Or do highly prejudiced people avoid education or lack the motivation, self-discipline, and intelligence needed to succeed in school? Here is another example: The students who get high grades in our classes say we are excellent teachers. Does getting high grades make them happy, so they return the favour by saying we are excellent teachers (i.e., high grades cause a positive evaluation)? Or are we both doing a great job, so students study hard and learn a lot, which the grades reflect (i.e., their learning causes them to get high grades)? It is a chicken-and-egg problem. To resolve it, a researcher needs to bring in other information or design research to test for the temporal order.

Simple causal relations are unidirectional, operating in a single direction from the cause to the effect. Most studies examine unidirectional relations. More complex theories specify reciprocal-effect causal relations—that is, a mutual causal relationship or simultaneous causality. For example, studying a lot causes a student to get good grades, but getting good grades also motivates the student to continue to study. Theories often have reciprocal

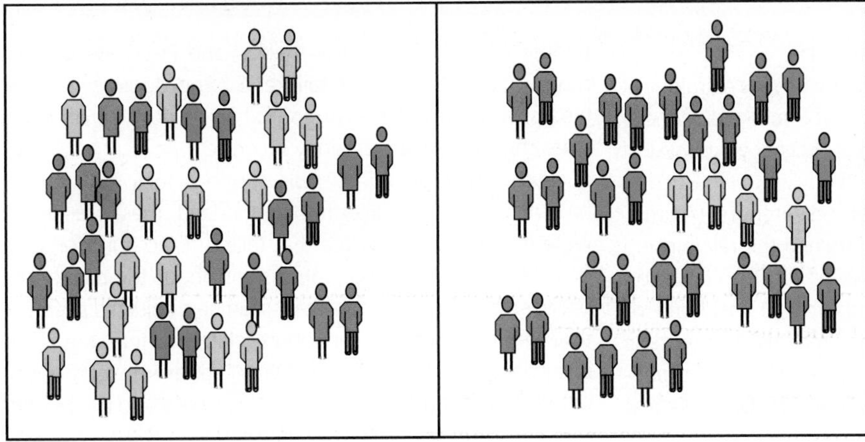

Figure 2.3 Association of Income and Race

or feedback relationships, but these are difficult to test. Some researchers call unidirectional relations *nonrecursive* and reciprocal-effect relations *recursive*.

Association A researcher also needs an **association** for causality. Two phenomena are associated if they occur together in a patterned way or appear to act together. People sometimes confuse correlation with association. *Correlation* has a specific technical meaning, whereas *association* is a more general idea. A correlation coefficient is a statistical measure that indicates the amount of association, but there are many ways to measure association. For example, Figure 2.3 shows 38 people from a lower-income neighbourhood and 35 people from an upper-income neighbourhood. Can you see an association between race and income level?

association: A co-occurrence of two events, factors, characteristics, or activities such that when one happens, the other is likely to occur as well. Many statistics measure this.

Correlations Do Not Show Causation

Cause, Effect and Correlation

People mistake association for causality more than they confuse it with temporal order. For example, a student gets high grades on the exams he takes on Fridays but low grades on those he takes on Mondays. There is an association between the day of the week and the exam grade, but it does not mean that the day of the week caused the exam grade. Instead, the reason was that he worked 20 hours each weekend and was very tired on Mondays. If a researcher cannot find an association, a causal relationship is unlikely. This is why researchers attempt to find correlations and other measures of association. Yet a researcher can often find an association without causality. The association eliminates potential causes that are not associated, but it cannot definitely identify a cause. It is a necessary but not a sufficient condition. In other words, you need it for causality, but it is not enough alone.

An association does not have to be perfect (i.e., every time one variable is present the other is also present) to show causality. In the example involving exam grades and days of the week, there is an association if on 10 Fridays the student got seven A's, two B's, and one C, whereas his exam grades on 10 Mondays were six D's, two C's, and two B's. An association exists, but the days of the week and the exam grades are not perfectly associated. The race and income-level association shown in Figure 2.3 is also an imperfect association.

Eliminating Alternatives *Eliminating alternatives* means that a researcher interested in causality needs to show that the effect is due to the causal variable and not to something else (see Box 2.8). It is also called *no spuriousness* because an apparent causal relationship that is actually due to an alternative but unrecognized cause is called a spurious relationship, which is discussed in Chapter 4 (see Box 2.9).

Researchers can observe temporal order and associations, but they cannot observe the elimination of alternatives. They can only demonstrate it indirectly. Eliminating alternatives is an ideal, because eliminating all possible alternatives is impossible. A researcher tries to eliminate major alternative explanations in two ways: through built-in design controls and by

Box 2.8 Concepts in Action

Learning to See Causal Relations

Do you read your horoscope? How many of your astrological sign's characteristics do you have? Do you take special note of your horoscope when considering aspects of your physical health?

A group of Canadian medical researchers (Austin, Mamdani, Juurlink, & Hux, 2006) examined the relationship between astrological sign and diagnoses for hospitalization using health administration records for all residents of Ontario alongside hospital admissions records. The authors found many sign-specific diagnoses. For example, Aries people were more likely to have intestinal infections, Taurus people had more fractured necks, and Pisces people had more instances of heart failure. So the doctors had two pieces of information: astrological sign and type of illness. Does this prove that astrology is correct?

You must consider possible spurious factors when you hear research results like this. And indeed, these researchers were trying to demonstrate that failure to account for spurious factors leads to poor conclusions about the relationship between two factors. After the researchers adjusted the statistical results to account for cohort-related factors, the results disappeared, thus revealing any apparent relationship between astrological sign and specific illnesses to be spurious.

measuring potential hidden causes. Experimental researchers build controls into the study design itself to eliminate alternative causes. They isolate an experimental situation from the influence of all variables except the main causal variable.

Researchers also try to eliminate alternatives by measuring possible alternative causes. This is common in survey research and is called *controlling for* another variable. Researchers use statistical techniques to learn whether the causal variable or something else operates on the effect variable.

Causal explanations are usually presented in a linear form; that is, they state cause and effect in a straight line: *A* causes *B*, *B* causes *C*, *C* causes *D*, etc.

The study by Nakhaie and Brym (2011) on Canadian professors discussed earlier used a causal explanation: It said that characteristics of professors (cause) led to political affiliations (effect).

Box 2.9 In the News

Flawed Research Leads to Flawed Public Policy

You may think that all this talk of causality only relates to academics, but the reality is that a lot of government policies and laws are based on the outcomes of social science research. And if that research is flawed it can lead to flawed public policy.

For example, in 2008 a study was completed on the effectiveness of French immersion programs in New Brunswick (Croll & Lee, 2008), Canada's only officially bilingual province. Such programs have English speakers conduct the majority of their classes at school in French, starting in elementary school or earlier, depending on the particular program. The study's authors made numerous suggestions, which included the elimination of Early French Immersion, a program in which children are immersed in French-language instruction from as early as Grade 1.

The report and its recommendations made headlines across the province and across the country. Parents of children in French immersion were furious, as was to be expected. The study attracted the attention of many researchers as well, who questioned the causal arguments being made in the report, stating that the statistical analyses were deeply flawed.

The study's authors argued that one shortcoming of the Early French Immersion program was that a very small number of its students achieved Advanced Oral Proficiency in Grade 12. This is troubling, considering that children who have been educated in French for many years should have an excellent command of the language! The authors, however, failed to consider that young people who had been in French immersion might be less likely to enrol in Grade 12 French classes, which is where such a test would have been administered. Critics argued that assuming writing this test was the same as having proficiency in the language was a serious flaw—the possibility that having enough proficiency as to not want to take Grade 12 French was not considered.

Despite an outcry from academics and a review of the research by an ombudsperson, the minister of education announced that Early French Immersion would be eliminated in 2008. Further protests by parent groups, however, led to a decision by the government to overhaul the curriculum of the French programs, focusing on improving them instead of eliminating them.

We can restate the logic in a deductive causal form: If the proposition is true, then we observe certain things in the empirical evidence. Good causal explanations identify a causal relationship and specify a causal mechanism. A simple causal explanation is X causes Y, or Y occurs because of X, where X and Y are concepts (e.g., early marriage and divorce). Some researchers state causality in a predictive form: If X occurs, then Y follows. Causality can be stated in many ways: X leads to Y, X produces Y, X influences Y, X is related to Y, the greater X the higher Y.

Here is a simple causal theory: A rise in unemployment causes an increase in child abuse. The subject to be explained is an increase in the occurrence of child abuse. What explains it is a rise in unemployment. We "explain" the increase in child abuse by identifying its cause. A complete explanation also requires elaborating the causal mechanism. One theory says that when people lose their jobs they feel a loss of self-worth. Once they lose self-worth, they become easily frustrated, upset, and angry. Frustrated people often express their anger by directing violence toward those they have close personal contact with (e.g., friends, spouse, children). This is especially true if they do not understand the source of the anger or cannot direct it toward its true cause (e.g., an employer, government policy, or "economic forces").

The unemployment and child abuse example illustrates a chain of causes and a causal mechanism. Researchers can test different parts of the chain. They might test whether unemployment rates and child abuse occur together, or whether frustrated people become violent toward the people close to them. A typical research strategy is to divide a larger theory into parts and test various relationships against the data.

Relationships between variables can be positive or negative. Researchers imply a positive relationship if they say nothing. A **positive relationship** means that a higher value on the causal variable goes with a higher value on the effect variable. For example, the more education a person has, the longer his or her life expectancy is. A **negative relationship** means that a higher value on the causal variable goes with a lower value on the effect variable. For example, the more frequently a couple attends religious services, the lower the spouses' chances of divorcing each other. In diagrams, a plus sign (+) signifies a positive relationship and a negative sign (−) signifies a negative relationship. Figure 2.4 illustrates positive and negative correlations.

positive relationship: An *association* between two variables such that as values on one increase, values on the other also increase.

negative relationship: An *association* between two variables such that as values on one variable increase, values on the other variable fall or decrease.

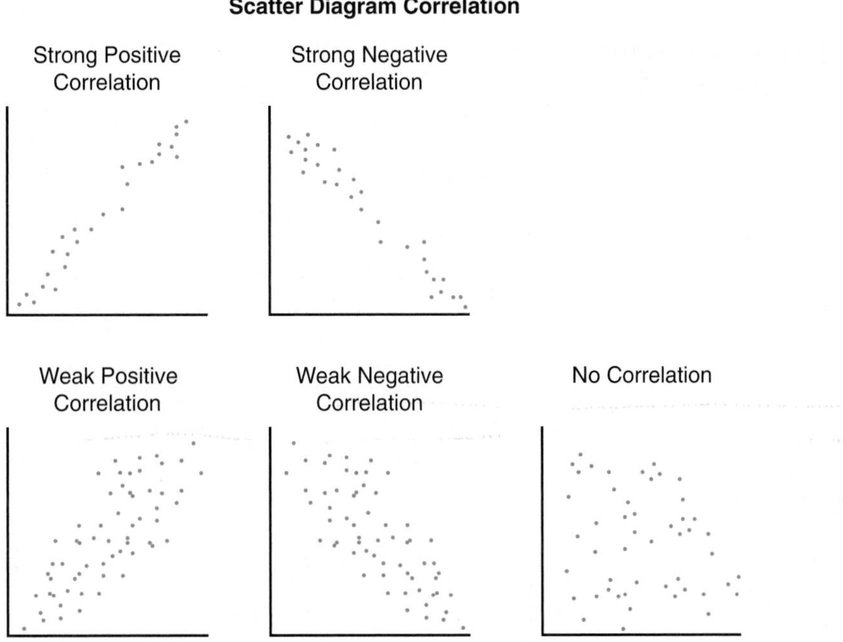

Figure 2.4 Positive and Negative Associations

Glossary Flashcards

CHAPTER SUMMARY

In this chapter, you learned about social theory—its parts, purposes, and types. We began by discussing the different levels of theory: macro, micro, and meso. The level of theory is related to whether it is focused on society as a whole, individual interactions, or somewhere in between, such as social structures and institutions. Researchers typically choose to test middle-range theories that are more specific and closely linked to the particular social phenomenon they are interested in exploring. They are then able to move to empirical generalizations that summarize the particular relationships that they believe to exist in the social world.

Theories consist of parts that are called concepts. Essentially, theories comprise numerous concepts that are all linked together. Concepts represent the various ideas about social life that a researcher wishes to study. In addition, theories also have inherent assumptions. Theories tend to either emphasize individual action and choice (i.e., agency) or structural constraints (i.e., structure). Many theories can be divided into micro and macro camps, which emphasize the individual or social structures, respectively.

Along with an emphasis on the individual or society, theories also have inherent assumptions about the nature of reality (ontology) and the relationship of the researcher to what he or she is studying (epistemology). These assumptions also translate into the two major paradigms in the social sciences: positivism and interpretivism. The former emphasizes the study of the social sciences in a scientific and objective manner, with a search for causal relationships using an extension of the techniques used in the natural sciences. The latter instead begins with the underlying assumption of a need to understand the subjective lived experiences of individuals using techniques that are more appropriate for this mode of inquiry.

The two possible directions of theorizing were also discussed. The deductive approach begins with a theory and then tests it using empirical data. In contrast, the inductive approach begins with data and then searches for a theory to emerge from the data. The inductive approach is often characterized by grounded theory.

Causal explanation was then explored. Social research is concerned with the discovery of causal relationships between concepts, although the ways to achieve this end are varied. In order to demonstrate that there is a cause-and-effect relationship between two concepts, there are three criteria that must be satisfied: temporal ordering, association, and elimination of alternatives.

Review Questions

Chapter Quiz

1. Explain why theory is closely related to social research methods.
2. Identify and define the three different levels of theory.
3. What is meant by empirical generalization? How is it related to middle-range theory?
4. What is the difference between agency and structure? Give an example of a theory that emphasizes each.
5. Define what is meant by ontology and epistemology as they pertain to social research methods. Explain how these two terms are related to the two major paradigms in the social sciences.
6. Differentiate between inductive and deductive approaches to theory.
7. What is meant by causality? What are the three criteria of causality?

Exercises

Research Activity

1. Using EBSCO's ContentSelect, search within the *Canadian Review of Sociology* for an article on a topic that interests you. Make sure that the article is not a "review article" and that the author engages in some sort of data analysis. After choosing your article, figure out what kind of approach to theorizing the author is using (deductive or inductive). How do you know? What kind of theory is the author using? At what level of theory has the author theorized?

2. Using EBSCO's ContentSelect, search within the *Canadian Journal of Sociology* for an article on a topic that examines some aspect of ethnicity or race. What theory is being used by the researcher? How does the author go from "theoretical framework" to "middle-range substantive theory" to "empirical generalization"?
3. Look through the past few days of news stories in the *Globe and Mail* for any headlines about new scientific findings. Pick one of these stories. From what the journalist has written, is the new scientific finding causal? If so, what is the cause (*X*) and what is the effect (*Y*)? If it is a correlation, explain the association. Can you think of any spurious relationships that may be affecting the relationship between the two factors under discussion?

MySearchLab

Visit MySearchLab, where you'll find thousands of full-text articles from academic journals and help with the research and writing process. Access the eText within MySearchLab to take self-grading practice tests and view a variety of multimedia resources.

Chapter 3

Ethics in Social Research

Photo Credit: Yale University Archives/From the film Obedience ©1968 by Stanley Milgram, copyright renewed 1993 by Alexandra Milgram and distributed by Penn State Media Sales. Permission granted by Alexandra Milgram.

LEARNING OBJECTIVES

After reading this chapter, you will be able to

LO 1 Explain why it is important to be ethical in research.

LO 2 Define scientific misconduct, research fraud, and plagiarism.

LO 3 Describe power relations in social research.

LO 4 Identify major ethical issues involving research with human participants.

LO 5 Differentiate between voluntary and informed consent.

LO 6 Explain special considerations that need to be made when working with special populations.

LO 7 Define privacy, anonymity, and confidentiality.

LO 8 Explain ethical issues that are specific to research involving sponsors.

INTRODUCTION

The pause that refreshes your ethics

Ethics include the concerns, dilemmas, and conflicts that arise over the proper way to conduct research. Ethics help to define what is or is not legitimate to do, or what "moral" research procedures involve. This is not as simple as it may seem, because there are few ethical absolutes and only agreed-upon broad principles. These principles require judgment in their application, and some may conflict with others in practice. Many ethical issues ask you to balance two values: the pursuit of knowledge and the rights of research participants or others in society. Social researchers balance potential benefits (such as advancing the understanding of social life, improving decision making, or helping research participants) against potential costs (such as loss of dignity, self-esteem, privacy, or democratic freedoms). Social researchers confront many ethical dilemmas and must decide how to act. They have a moral, professional obligation to be ethical, even if research participants are unaware of or unconcerned about ethics.

Many areas of professional practice have ethical standards (e.g., journalists, police departments, business corporations), but the ethical standards for doing social research are often stricter. To do professional social research, you must both know the proper research techniques (e.g., sampling, data collection) and be sensitive to ethical concerns. This is not always easy. For centuries, moral, legal, and political philosophers have debated the ethical issues researchers regularly face.

It is difficult to fully appreciate the ethical dilemmas experienced by researchers until you actually begin to do research, but waiting until the middle of a study is too late. You need to prepare yourself ahead of time and consider ethical concerns as you design a study so that you can build sound ethical practices into a study's design. In addition, by developing sensitivity to ethical issues you will be alert to potential ethical concerns that can arise as you make decisions while conducting a study. Also, an ethical awareness will help you better understand the overall research process.

Ethics begin and end with you, the individual social researcher. A researcher's strong personal moral code is the best defence against unethical behaviour. Before, during, and after conducting a study, a researcher has opportunities to, and *should*, reflect on the ethics of research actions and consult his or her conscience. Ultimately, ethical research depends on the integrity of the individual researcher.

Why Be Ethical?

LO 1 Explain why it is important to be ethical in research.

Given that most people who conduct social research are genuinely concerned about others, you might ask why any researcher would ever act in an ethically irresponsible manner. Apart from the rare disturbed individual, most unethical behaviour by researchers is due to a lack of awareness and to pressures on researchers to take ethical shortcuts. Researchers face pressures to build a career, publish new findings, advance knowledge, gain prestige, impress family and friends, hold on to a job, and so forth. Being ethical almost always means that the research will take longer to complete, cost more money, be more complicated, and be more likely to produce ambiguous results. Moreover, there are many opportunities in research to act unethically, the odds of getting caught are small, and written ethical standards are in the form of vague, loose principles.

The ethical researcher gets few rewards and wins no praise. The unethical researcher, if caught, faces public humiliation, a ruined career, and possible legal action. The best preparation for ethical behaviour is to internalize a sensitivity to ethical concerns, to adopt a serious professional role, and to interact regularly with other researchers. Moreover, the scientific community demands ethical behaviour without exceptions.

LO 2 Define scientific misconduct, research fraud, and plagiarism.

Scientific Misconduct The research community and agencies that fund research particularly oppose a type of unethical behaviour called scientific misconduct, which includes research fraud and plagiarism.

Scientific misconduct occurs when a researcher falsifies or distorts the data or the methods of data collection, or plagiarizes the work of others. It also includes significant, unjustified departures from the generally accepted scientific practices for doing and reporting on research.

scientific misconduct: When someone engages in *research fraud, plagiarism,* or other unethical conduct that significantly deviates from the accepted practice for conducting and reporting research within the *scientific community.*

Box 3.1 In the News

Accusations of Scientific Misconduct

A high-profile case of suspected research fraud made media headlines and became the subject of a three-part special on CBC's *The National* in 2006. Dr. Ranjit Chandra, a world-renowned researcher in nutrition and immunology at Memorial University, Newfoundland, held several large industry-sourced research grants and was twice nominated for a Nobel Prize. His career was on a stellar trajectory until allegations of research fraud began to surface.

The first allegation that something was amiss with Chandra's research arose in the early 1990s. One of his research associates, a nurse-researcher at Janeway Hospital, had been put in charge of recruiting newborns to take part in a study on whether infant formula could reduce allergies. She was to find more than 200 newborns who had parents with allergies and who resided in St. John's. Suspicion arose when, despite the fact that the nurse had not even completed recruiting the infants for the study, Chandra published a research paper on the outcomes of the study, finding that formula was able to reduce allergies—specifically, formula that was made by a major funder of his research (Nestlé Company). She decided to report this to the university administration. An inquiry by the university was not successful as Chandra could not produce the data under question; he stated that it had been stolen, even suggesting that the nurse had stolen it.

Then, in 2001, the *British Medical Journal* (*BMJ*) contacted Memorial University with concerns over some statistical findings that Chandra had reported in a research article. Chandra had apparently made some striking findings about how seniors' memories were affected by taking a multivitamin—the same multivitamin for which he held a patent. Months passed after Chandra was requested to provide the data and Chandra failed to comply; again, he said that his data had been lost. It should be noted that although *BMJ* did not publish this article, Chandra went on to publish the research in 2001 in another journal, *Nutrition*, which retracted the article in 2005, citing Chandra's conflict of financial interests (i.e., Chandra owned the patent of the supplement) and suspicious data among the reasons for retracting.

While Memorial University followed procedures for investigating the allegations made against Chandra, no disciplinary action against him was ever taken. Chandra retired from the university in 2002 and moved out of the country.

research fraud: A type of unethical behaviour in which a researcher fakes or invents data that he or she did not really collect or fails to honestly and fully report how he or she conducted a study.

Research fraud occurs when a researcher fakes or invents data that he or she did not really collect or fails to honestly and fully report how he or she conducted a study. Though rare, it is considered a very serious violation. The most famous case of research fraud was that of Sir Cyril Burt, the father of British educational psychology. Burt died in 1971 as an esteemed researcher who was famous for his studies on twins, which showed a genetic basis for intelligence. In 1976, however, it was discovered that he had falsified data and the names of his coauthors. Unfortunately, the scientific community had been misled for nearly 30 years.[1] Box 3.1 presents a recent Canadian case of scientific misconduct.

plagiarism: A type of unethical behaviour in which one uses the writings or ideas of another without giving proper credit. It is "stealing ideas."

Plagiarism occurs when a researcher "steals" the ideas or writings of another or uses them without citing the source. Plagiarism includes stealing the work of another researcher, an assistant, or a student and misrepresenting it as one's own. This is a serious breach of ethical standards. Plagiarism by students is just as unethical as when it is done by research professionals, and it can have serious consequences. An undergraduate student at Memorial University was recently accused of child abuse when she failed to reference an account of a juvenile sex offender who abused children in the offender's care. A graphic description of the abuse, which was added as an appendix to her research paper, had been copied word for word out of a textbook. The student failed to reference the source, however, and the professor marking her paper thought that it was the student's personal account of abusing children. The professor then contacted Child Protection Services, which resulted in a 12-year battle for this student to clear her name.[2]

Unethical but Legal

Behaviour may be unethical but legal (i.e., not break any law). A plagiarism case illustrates the distinction between legal and ethical behaviours. The American Sociological Association documented that a 1988 book by a dean from Eastern New Mexico University contained large sections of a 1978 dissertation that a sociology professor at Tufts University

LEGAL	ETHICAL	
	Yes	*No*
Yes	Moral and Legal	Legal but Immoral
No	Illegal but Moral	Immoral and Illegal

Figure 3.1 Typology of Legal and Moral Actions in Social Research

had written but that it did not have any footnotes. Copying the dissertation was not *illegal*; it did not violate copyright law because the sociologist's dissertation did not have a copyright filed with the U.S. government. Nevertheless, it was clearly *unethical* according to standards of professional behaviour.[3] (See Figure 3.1 for the relations between legal and moral actions.)

Power Relations

LO 3 Describe power relations in social research.

A professional researcher and the research participants or employee-assistants are in a relationship of unequal power and trust. An experimenter, survey director, or research investigator has power over participants and assistants, and in turn they trust his or her judgment and authority. The researcher's credentials, training, and professional role and the place of science in modern society legitimate the power and make it into a form of expert authority. Some ethical issues involve an abuse of power and trust. A researcher's authority to conduct social research and to earn the trust of others is always accompanied by an immutable ethical responsibility to guide, protect, and oversee the interests of the people being studied.

When looking for ethical guidance, researchers are not alone. They can turn to a number of resources: professional colleagues, ethical advisory committees, institutional review boards or human subjects committees at a college or institution (discussed later), codes of ethics by professional associations (discussed later in this chapter), and writings on ethics in research. The larger research community firmly supports and upholds ethical behaviour, even if an individual researcher is ultimately responsible to do what is ethical in specific situations.

ETHICAL ISSUES INVOLVING RESEARCH PARTICIPANTS

LO 4 Identify major ethical issues involving research with human participants.

Have you ever been a participant in a research study? If so, how were you treated? More attention is focused on the possible negative effects of research on those being studied than on any other ethical issue, beginning with concerns about biomedical research. Acting ethically requires a researcher to balance the value of the advancement of knowledge against the value of noninterference in the lives of others. Either extreme causes problems. Giving research participants absolute rights of noninterference could make empirical research impossible, but giving researchers absolute rights of inquiry could nullify participants' basic human rights. The moral question becomes this: When, if ever, are researchers justified in risking physical harm or injury to those being studied, causing them great embarrassment or inconvenience, violating their privacy, or frightening them?

The law and codes of ethics recognize some clear prohibitions: Never cause unnecessary or irreversible harm to subjects; secure prior voluntary consent, when possible; and never unnecessarily humiliate and degrade subjects or release harmful information about specific individuals that was collected for research purposes. In other words, you should always show respect for the research participant. These are minimal standards and are subject to interpretation (e.g., What does *unnecessary* mean in a specific situation?).

Origins of Research Participant Protection

Concern over the treatment of research participants arose after the revelation of gross violations of basic human rights in the name of science. The most notorious violations were "medical experiments" conducted on Jews and others in Nazi Germany and similar "medical experiments" to test biological weapons by Japan in the 1940s. In these experiments, terrible tortures were committed. For example, people were placed in freezing water to see how long it took them to die, purposely starved to death, or intentionally infected with horrible diseases, and limbs were severed from children and transplanted onto others.[4]

Such human rights violations did not occur only in the distant past. In 1997, as a result of a famous case of unethical research known as the Tuskegee syphilis experiment (also called *bad blood*), the president of the United States admitted wrongdoing and formally apologized to the participant victims. Until the 1970s, when a newspaper report caused the scandal to erupt, the U.S. Public Health Service had been sponsoring a study in which poor, uneducated Black men in Alabama suffered and died of untreated syphilis while researchers studied the severe physical disabilities that appear in advanced stages of the disease. The unethical study began in 1929, before penicillin was available to treat the disease, but it continued long after treatment had become available. Despite their unethical treatment of the subjects, the researchers were able to continue to publish their results for 40 years. The study ended in 1972, but a formal apology took another 25 years to materialize.[5]

Unfortunately, the bad blood scandal is not unique. During the 1950s, the U.S. government periodically compromised ethical research principles for military and political goals, including within Canadian research institutions. From 1957 to 1964, experiments using the psychedelic drug lysergic acid diethylamide (LSD, or "acid" as it is commonly known) were conducted at the Allan Memorial Institute in Montreal. The experiments were tied to a larger U.S. Central Intelligence Agency (CIA) project (Project MKULTRA) that aimed to learn how drugs can be used to control people's minds. The CIA research undertaken at the Allan Memorial Institute focused on the use of LSD for mind control and for correcting schizophrenia. Today, researchers widely recognize these to be violations of two fundamental ethical principles: Avoid physical harm, and obtain informed consent.[6]

Physical Harm, Psychological Abuse, and Legal Jeopardy

The Promise and Pitfalls of Going Into the Field

Social research can harm a research participant in several ways—physically, psychologically, and legally—as well as harm a person's career, reputation, or income. Different types of harm are more likely in certain types of research (e.g., in experiments versus field research). It is a researcher's responsibility to be aware of all types of potential harm and to take specific actions to minimize the risk to participants at all times.

Physical Harm Physical harm is rare. Even in biomedical research, where the intervention into a person's life is much greater, only 3 to 5 percent of studies involved any person who suffered any harm.[7] A straightforward ethical principle is that researchers should never cause physical harm. An ethical researcher anticipates risks before beginning a study, including basic safety concerns (e.g., safe buildings, furniture, and equipment). This means that he or she screens out high-risk subjects (e.g., those with histories of heart conditions, mental breakdown, or seizures) if great stress is involved and anticipates possible sources of injury or physical attacks on research participants or assistants. The researcher accepts moral and legal responsibility for injury from participation in research and terminates a project immediately if he or she can no longer fully guarantee the physical safety of the people involved (see the Zimbardo study in Box 3.2).

Box 3.2 Concepts in Action

Three Cases of Ethical Controversy

Stanley Milgram's *obedience study* (1963, 1965, 1974) attempted to discover how the horrors of the Holocaust under the Nazis could have occurred by examining the strength of social pressure to obey authority. After signing "informed consent forms," subjects were assigned, in rigged random selection, to be a "teacher" while a confederate of the researcher was the "pupil." The teacher was to test the pupil's memory of word lists and increase the electric shock level if the pupil made mistakes. The pupil was located in a nearby room, so the teacher could hear but not see the pupil. The shock apparatus was clearly labelled with increasing voltage. As the pupil made mistakes and the teacher turned switches, the pupil also made noises as if in severe pain. The researcher was present and made comments such as "You must go on" to the teacher. Milgram reported, "Subjects were observed to sweat, tremble, stutter, bite their lips, groan, and dig their fingernails into their flesh. These were characteristic rather than exceptional responses to the experiment" (1963, p. 375). The percentage of subjects who would shock to dangerous levels was dramatically higher than expected. Ethical concerns arose over the use of deception and the extreme emotional stress experienced by subjects.

In Laud Humphreys's (1975) *tearoom trade study* (a study of male homosexual encounters in public restrooms), about 100 men were observed engaging in sexual acts as Humphreys pretended to be a "watchqueen" (a voyeur and lookout). Subjects were followed to their cars, and their licence plate numbers were secretly recorded. Names and addresses were obtained from police registers by Humphreys posing as a market researcher. One year later, in disguise, Humphreys used a deceptive story about a health survey to interview the subjects in their homes. Humphreys was careful to keep names in safety deposit boxes, and identifiers with subject names were burned. He significantly advanced knowledge of homosexuals who frequent "tearooms" and overturned previous false beliefs about them. There has been controversy over the study, however: The subjects never consented; deception was used; and the names could have been used to blackmail subjects, to end marriages, or to initiate criminal prosecution.

In Philip Zimbardo's *prison experiment* (Zimbardo, 1972, 1973; Zimbardo et al., 1973, 1974), male students were divided into two role-playing groups: guards and prisoners. Before the experiment, volunteer students were given personality tests, and only those in the "normal" range were chosen. Volunteers signed up for two weeks, and "prisoners" were told that they would be under surveillance and would have some civil rights suspended, but that no physical abuse would be allowed. In a simulated prison in the basement of a Stanford University building, prisoners were deindividualized (dressed in standard uniforms and called only by their numbers) and guards were militarized (with uniforms, nightsticks, and reflective sunglasses). Guards were told to maintain a reasonable degree of order and served eight-hour shifts, while prisoners were locked up all 24 hours a day. Unexpectedly, the volunteers became too caught up in their roles. Prisoners became passive and disorganized, while guards became aggressive, arbitrary, and dehumanizing. By the sixth day, Zimbardo called off the experiment for ethical reasons. The risk of permanent psychological harm, and even physical harm, was too great.

Psychological Abuse, Stress, or Loss of Self-Esteem The risk of physical harm is rare, but social researchers may place people in highly stressful, embarrassing, anxiety-producing, or unpleasant situations. Researchers want to learn about people's responses in real-life, high-anxiety-producing situations, so they might place subjects in realistic situations of psychological discomfort or stress. Is it unethical to cause discomfort? The ethics of the famous Milgram obedience study are still debated (see Box 3.2). Some say that the precautions taken and the knowledge gained outweighed the stress and potential psychological harm that subjects experienced. Others believe that the extreme stress and the risk of permanent harm were too great. Such an experiment could not be conducted today because of heightened sensitivity to the ethical issues involved.

Social researchers have created high levels of anxiety or discomfort. They have exposed participants to gruesome photos; misled male students into believing that they have strong feminine personality traits or lied to students that they have failed; created situations of high fear (e.g., releasing smoke into a locked room); asked participants to harm others; placed people in situations where they face social pressure to deny their convictions; and had participants lie, cheat, or steal.[8] Researchers who study helping behaviour often place participants in emergency situations to see whether they will lend assistance. For example, Piliavin and associates (1969) studied helping behaviour in subways by having someone pretend to collapse on the floor. In the field experiment, the riders in the subway car were unaware of the experiment and did not volunteer to participate in it but were nonetheless exposed to this stressful experience.

Only highly experienced researchers should consider conducting a study that purposely induces great stress or anxiety in research participants, and they must take all necessary precautions before inducing anxiety or discomfort. The researchers should consult with others who have conducted similar studies and with mental health professionals as they plan the study. They should screen out high-risk populations (e.g., those with emotional or cardiac problems) and arrange for emergency interventions or termination of the research if dangerous situations arise. They must always obtain written informed consent (discussed later) before the research, and they must debrief subjects immediately afterward (i.e., explain any deception and what actually happened in the study). Researchers should never create *unnecessary* stress (i.e., beyond the minimal amount needed to create the desired effect) or stress that lacks a very clear, legitimate research purpose. Knowing what constitutes a "minimal amount" of stress comes only with experience. It is better to begin with too little stress, risking a finding of no effect, than to create too much stress. It is always wise to work in collaboration with other researchers when the risk to participants is high, because the involvement of several ethically sensitive researchers reduces the chances of making an ethical misjudgment.

Research that induces great stress and anxiety in participants also carries the danger that experimenters will develop a callous or manipulative attitude toward others. Some researchers have reported feeling guilt and regret after conducting experiments that caused psychological harm to subjects. Experiments that place subjects in anxiety-producing situations may produce significant personal discomfort for the ethical researcher as well.

Legal Harm A researcher is responsible for protecting research participants from increased risk of arrest. If participation in research increases the risk of arrest, few individuals will trust researchers or be willing to participate in future research. Potential legal harm is one criticism of Humphreys's 1975 tearoom trade study (see Box 3.2).

A related ethical issue arises when a researcher learns of illegal activity when collecting data. A researcher must weigh the value of protecting the researcher–subject relationship and the benefits to future researchers against potential serious harm to innocent people. The researcher bears the cost of his or her judgment. For example, in his field research on police, Van Maanen (1988, pp. 114–115) reported witnessing police beatings, illegal acts, and irregular procedures but said, "On and following these troublesome incidents, I followed police custom: I kept my mouth shut." Is this ethical? While the researcher was able to maintain his relationship with the police, he did nothing while illegal acts occurred. This is just one case where the ethical responsibilities of the researcher are not clear-cut.

Field researchers in particular can face difficult ethical decisions. For example, when studying a mental institution, Taylor (1987) discovered the mistreatment and abuse of inmates by the staff. He had two choices: (1) Abandon the study and call for an immediate investigation, or (2) keep quiet and continue with the study for several months, publicize the findings afterward, and then become an advocate to end the abuse. After weighing the situation, he followed the latter course and is now an activist for the rights of inmates in mental institutions.

In some studies, observing illegal behaviour may be central to the research project. If a researcher covertly observes and records illegal behaviour, then supplies the information to law-enforcement authorities, he or she is violating ethical standards regarding research participants and is undermining future social research. At the same time, a researcher who fails to report illegal behaviour is indirectly permitting criminal behaviour. He or she could be charged as an accessory to a crime. It should be noted that all Canadians, including researchers, are legally required to report any cases of abuse involving children.

Other Harm to Participants

Research participants may face other types of harm. For example, a survey interview may create anxiety and discomfort if it asks people to recall unpleasant or traumatic events. An ethical researcher must be sensitive to any harm to participants, consider precautions, and weigh potential harm against potential benefits.

Another type of harm is a negative impact on the careers, reputations, or incomes of research participants. For example, a researcher conducts a survey of employees and concludes that the supervisor's performance is poor. As a consequence, the supervisor loses her job. Or a researcher studies homeless people living on the street. The findings show that many engage in petty illegal acts to get food. As a consequence, a city government "cracks down" on the petty illegal acts and the homeless people can no longer eat. What is the researcher's responsibility? The ethical researcher considers the consequences of research for those being studied. The general goal is not to cause any harm simply because someone was a research participant. However, there is no set answer to such questions. A researcher must evaluate each case, weigh potential harm against potential benefits, and bear the responsibility for the decision.

Maximizing Benefit

On the flipside of minimizing harm is the principle of maximizing benefit. In Canada, the *Tri-Council Policy Statement on the Ethical Conduct for Research Involving Humans* (discussed in more detail later) specifies that researchers have a duty to maximize the benefits that their research has on others. Some research involving humans, such as that in social work, education, and health care, can produce clear benefits to the research subjects themselves. The benefits of most social science research, however, would be for society as a whole and for the advancement of knowledge.

Deception and Consent

LO 5 Differentiate between voluntary and informed consent.

Has anyone ever told you a half-truth or a lie to get you to do something? How did you feel about it? Social researchers follow the ethical **principle of voluntary consent**: Never force anyone to participate in research, and do not lie to anyone unless it is necessary and the only way to accomplish a legitimate research purpose. Those who participate in social research should explicitly agree to participate. A person's right not to participate can be a critical issue whenever the researcher uses deception, disguises the research, or uses covert research methods.

principle of voluntary consent: An ethical principle of social research that people should never participate in research unless they first explicitly agree to do so.

Social researchers sometimes deceive or lie to participants in field and experimental research. A researcher might misrepresent his or her actions or true intentions for legitimate methodological reasons. For example, if participants knew the true purpose they might modify their behaviour, making it impossible to learn about their real behaviour. Another situation occurs when access to a research site would be impossible if the researcher told the truth. Deception is never preferable, however, if the researcher can accomplish the same thing without using deception.

Experimental researchers often deceive subjects to prevent them from learning the hypothesis being tested and to reduce "reactive effects" (see Chapter 9). Deception is acceptable only if a researcher can show that it has a clear, specific methodological purpose, and even then the researcher should use it only to the minimal degree necessary. Researchers who use deception should always obtain informed consent, never misrepresent risks, and always explain the actual conditions to participants afterward. You might ask: How can a researcher obtain prior informed consent and still use deception? He or she can describe the basic procedures involved and conceal only specific information about hypotheses being tested.

Sometimes field researchers use covert observation to gain entry to field research settings. In covert observation, the people who are being studied are not aware that they are being studied. This is different from overt observation, where researchers openly reveal themselves as persons conducting research to the people they are studying (this is covered more in Chapter 13). In studies of cults, small extremist political sects, illegal or deviant behaviour, or behaviour in a large public area, it may be impossible to conduct research if a researcher announces and discloses her or his true purpose. But if a covert stance is not essential, a researcher should not use it. If he or she does not know whether covert access is necessary, then a strategy of gradual disclosure may be best. When in doubt, it is best to err in the direction of disclosing one's true identity and purpose. Covert research remains controversial, and many researchers feel that all covert research is unethical. Even those who accept covert research as ethical in certain situations say that it should be used only when overt observation is impossible. Whenever possible, the researcher should inform participants of the observation immediately afterward and give them an opportunity to express concerns.

Deception and covert research may increase mistrust and cynicism and may diminish public respect for social research. Misrepresentation in field research is analogous to being an undercover agent or government informer in nondemocratic societies. The use of deception has a long-term negative effect: It increases distrust among people who are frequently studied and makes doing social research more difficult in the long term.

Informed Consent A fundamental ethical principle of social research is this: Never coerce anyone into participating; participation *must* be voluntary at all times. Permission alone is not enough. People need to know what they are being asked to participate in so that they can make an informed decision. Participants can become aware of their rights and what they are getting involved in when they read and sign a statement giving **informed consent**—an agreement by participants stating that they are willing to be in a study after they know something about what the research procedure will involve.

informed consent: An agreement by participants stating that they are willing to be in a study after they learn something about what the research procedure will involve.

Governments vary in the requirement for informed consent. The Canadian federal government does not require informed consent in all research involving human subjects, although there is a strong recommendation that informed consent be received. The *Tri-Council Policy Statement* does consider research situations where obtaining informed consent may be problematic. Nevertheless, researchers should get written informed consent unless there are good reasons for not obtaining it (e.g., covert field research, use of secondary data) as judged by a research ethics board (REB).

Informed consent statements provide specific information (see Box 3.3). A general statement about the kinds of procedures or questions involved and the uses of the data is sufficient for informed consent. Studies suggest that participants who receive a full informed consent statement do not respond differently from those who do not. If anything, people who refuse to sign such a statement are more likely to guess or answer "no response" to questions.

Box 3.3 Making It Practical

Informed Consent

Informed consent statements contain the following:

1. A brief description of the purpose and procedure of the research, including the expected duration of the study
2. A statement of any risks or discomfort associated with participation
3. A guarantee of anonymity and the confidentiality of records
4. The identification of the researcher and of where to receive information about subjects' rights or questions about the study
5. A statement that participation is completely voluntary and can be terminated at any time without penalty
6. A statement of alternative procedures that may be used
7. A statement of any benefits or compensation provided to subjects and the number of subjects involved
8. An offer to provide a summary of findings

It is unethical to coerce people to participate, including offering them special benefits that they cannot otherwise attain. For example, it is unethical for a commanding officer to order a soldier to participate in a study, for a professor to require a student to be a research subject to pass a course, or for an employer to expect an employee to complete a survey as a condition of continued employment. It is unethical even if someone other than the researcher (e.g., an employer) coerces people (e.g., employees) to participate in research.

Full disclosure with the researcher's identification helps to protect research participants against fraudulent research and to protect legitimate researchers. Informed consent lessens the chance that a con artist in the guise of a researcher will defraud or abuse subjects. It also reduces the chance that someone will use a bogus identity to market products or obtain personal information on people for unethical purposes.

Legally, a signed informed consent statement is optional for most survey, field, and secondary data research, but it is often mandatory for qualitative interviews and experimental research. Informed consent is impossible to obtain in existing statistics and documentary research. The general rule is this: The greater the risk of potential harm to research participants, the greater is the need to obtain a written informed consent statement from them. In sum, there are many sound reasons to get informed consent and few reasons not to get it. See Box 3.4 for a discussion of informed consent and social research on the internet.

Box 3.4 Social Research and the Internet

Online Research and Ethics

In the past decade, the internet has not only improved researchers' access to data through high-speed connections to remote sources, but has also increasingly served as the mechanism through which data are collected as well as the subject of data collection itself. Numerous studies have been completed using web materials and online communities. The ethical issues in online research are complex because they ask new questions about the boundaries between public and private life. Is everything that is viewable on the internet "public" and therefore requires no consent from participating users?

Canada's *Tri-Council Policy Statement on the Ethical Conduct for Research Involving Humans* states that

> [r]esearch that is non-intrusive, and does not involve direct interaction between the researcher and individuals through the Internet, also does not require REB review. Cyber-material such as documents, records, performances, online archival materials or published third party interviews to which the public is given uncontrolled access on the Internet for which there is no expectation of privacy is considered to be publicly available information. Exemption from REB review is based on the information being accessible in the public domain, and that the individuals to whom the information refers have no reasonable expectation of privacy.
>
> However, there are situations where REB review is required. There are publicly accessible digital sites where there is a reasonable expectation of privacy. When accessing identifiable information in publicly accessible digital sites, such as Internet chat rooms and self-help groups with restricted membership, the privacy expectation of contributors to these sites is much higher. (Canadian Institutes of Health Research, Natural Sciences and Engineering Research Council of Canada, & Social Sciences and Humanities Research Council of Canada, 2010, p. 140)

Note that an important distinction is made in the *Tri-Council Policy Statement*: If no interaction is occurring between the researcher and the individuals, no ethics clearance is required. If researchers are interacting with internet community members, particularly in areas of restricted access, research ethics approval is required. This means that it will be necessary for researchers to obtain informed consent from the people on which they wish to do research.

In her study of online eating disorder (pro-ED) communities, Whitehead (2010) did not undergo ethics review:

> All the data (written material and photographs) gathered for the present case study is—or was at the time of the study—publicly available on the Internet. I did not become a member of any of the websites nor did I announce my presence to the community . . . I only analyzed information that was publicly available online and was not under any expectation of privacy . . . On the websites I visited, the statements, narratives, photos, and opinions of the members were under no expectation of privacy and were thus treated as public information. In fact, numerous sites I visited were personal homepages of women involved in the Pro-ED community designed specifically for public viewing. Some sites had private chatrooms and message boards which I did not enter, nor did I participate in any communication that was assumed to be private." (p. 601)

If Whitehead had engaged in private communications through emailing individuals or participating in private chat rooms and wished to use the exchanges in her research, she would have needed to obtain research ethics approval and gain the informed consent of the individuals with whom she was corresponding.

LO 6 Explain special considerations that need to be made when working with special populations.

SPECIAL POPULATIONS AND NEW INEQUALITIES

Some populations are unique in that efforts to "enforce" the practice of obtaining informed consent by obtaining written consent, for example, can actually work to discourage the participants from participating. It simply is not the case that everyone sees these efforts to protect research participants as respectful safeguards. People may be offended to be asked to sign a form, for example, as it may represent something "too formal" or suggest that their word is not good enough.

The *Tri-Council Policy Statement* specifies that researchers must have respect for vulnerable persons. Some populations or groups of research participants are not capable of giving true voluntary informed consent. **Special populations** include those who may be more susceptible to possible abuse by researchers given their (1) limited mental capacity, (2) subservient power position in a potential research study, or (3) history of oppression and exploitation. Students, prison inmates, employees, military personnel, the homeless, welfare recipients, children, or the developmentally disabled may not be fully capable of making a decision, or they may agree to participate only because they see their participation as a means of obtaining a desired good—such as teacher approval, early parole, promotions, or additional services.

special populations: People who lack the necessary cognitive competency to give real informed consent, people in a weak position who might compromise their freedom to refuse to participate in a study, or groups who have been historically exploited and oppressed.

It is unethical to involve such vulnerable people (e.g., children, the mentally disabled) in research unless a researcher meets two minimal conditions: (1) a legal guardian grants written permission, and (2) the researcher follows all standard ethical principles to protect the participant from harm. For example, a researcher wants to conduct a survey of high school students to learn about their sexual behaviour and drug/alcohol use. If the survey is conducted on school property, school officials must give official permission. For any research participant who is a legal minor (usually less than 18 years old), written parental permission is needed. It is best to ask permission from each student as well. See Box 3.5 for a discussion of ethical considerations around doing research on Aboriginal peoples—a population that has been historically oppressed and exploited in Canada.

The use of coercion to participate can be a tricky issue, and it depends on the specifics of a situation. For example, a convicted criminal faces the choice between imprisonment and participation in an experimental rehabilitation program. The convicted criminal may not believe in the benefits of the program, but the researcher may believe that it will help the criminal. This is a case of coercion. A researcher must honestly judge whether the benefits to the criminal and to society greatly outweigh the ethical prohibition on coercion. This is risky. History shows many cases in which a researcher believed he or she was doing something "for the good of" someone in a powerless position (e.g., prisoners, students, homosexuals), but it turned out that the "good" actually was for the researcher or a powerful organization in society, and it did more harm than good to the research participant.

Today, it is unlikely that individuals will be coerced into participating in research; however, there are still cases where people may be implicitly coerced. Undergraduate students who are asked to participate in research in classes may feel obligated to participate because they want a good grade. Prisoners or people in institutions may feel that they would receive better treatment if they participated in research studies or, conversely, they may feel that if they did not participate they would receive worse treatment.

You may have been in a social science class in which a teacher required you to participate as a subject in a research project. This is a special case of coercion and is usually ethical. Teachers have made three arguments in favour of requiring student participation: (1) It would be difficult and prohibitively expensive to get participants otherwise, (2) the knowledge created from research with students serving as subjects benefits future students and society, and (3) students will learn more about research by experiencing it directly in a realistic research setting. Of the three arguments, only the third justifies limited coercion. This limited coercion is acceptable only as long as it meets three conditions: (1) It is

Box 3.5 Making It Practical

Special Populations: The Case of Aboriginal Peoples in Canada

Aboriginal peoples in Canada (which refers to all First Nations, Métis, and Inuit peoples) have a marked history of colonization in Canada, the practices of which have severely compromised their ability to uphold their traditions and cultural practices. Much social research has been conducted "on" Aboriginal peoples in Canada, and until recently this practice of "studying" Aboriginal peoples was undertaken without much critical discussion by research ethics boards.

Recall from Chapter 2 that one of the major assumptions of social science is the positivist epistemological view. This is the view that society can and should be studied in a manner similar to the "hard sciences" by objective, value-free scientists. This view is a prevailing orientation that originated from Western Europe and continues to be a dominant cultural view that characterizes Western science. In stark contrast to this worldview is that which characterizes many Aboriginal cultures in Canada. Brant Castellano (2004) quotes Leroy Little Bear, who describes the clash between Western scientific and Aboriginal worldviews as "jagged worldviews colliding" (p. 103), which aptly describes the striking contrast between positivist scientific thought and Aboriginal philosophies.

There have been many decades of research on Aboriginal peoples in Canada, which has been characterized as researchers "parachuting" into Indigenous communities (often without obtaining consent), collecting data, and leaving, frequently without sharing with findings with the very community they were studying (Brant Catellano, 2004; Castleden, Garvin, & Huu-ay-aht First Nation, 2008). As a result, there is a feeling of great skepticism of the benefits of research by many Aboriginal communities; they feel they have been "researched to death" without any benefits having been experienced by their communities, a phenomenon that has been called **research fatigue** (National Aboriginal Health Organization, 2005).

The historical imbalance of power between Aboriginals and non-Aboriginals in Canada has crept into the research process, and as such recent attention has been given to developing culturally appropriate research techniques. One major aspect of such an approach is the idea of *ownership*. Rather than simply being a "subject" of research with little or no community benefits, techniques that involve the community in all aspects of study design, data collection, analysis, and policy implications are advocated, thereby giving Aboriginal communities ownership of the research process and outcomes. Rather than being people who are researched, culturally appropriate research techniques demand that Aboriginal communities be involved in all aspects of the research to maximize the benefits to the community. In addition, such techniques also reduce the power imbalances between the researcher and subject because such an approach requires the researcher to relinquish control over decision making (Castleden, Garvin, and Huu-ay-aht First Nation, 2008). Techniques that permit this sort of power sharing are often called *community-based participatory research* and are discussed in more detail in Chapter 13.

In 2008, the Government of Canada issued new protocols on research involving human subjects (*Tri-Council Policy Statement on the Ethical Conduct for Research Involving Humans*) to add a new section specifically directed at research involving Aboriginal peoples (Chapter 9 of the report: Research Involving Aboriginal Peoples). The protocols require community engagement in the research practice, respect for community governing authorities, respect for traditional knowledge, and demonstration of mutual benefit of the research. Many research ethics boards have also adjusted their membership to include Aboriginals or created REBs that are specific to research with Aboriginals so that decisions regarding the ethics of research involving Aboriginal people can be assessed more closely in accordance to the principles of the *Tri-Council Policy Statement*.

attached to a clear educational objective, (2) the students have a choice between research experience or an alternative activity, and (3) all other ethical principles of research are being followed. Researchers must be aware of the power differentials between themselves and the people they are studying when they are seeking voluntary participation from potential research subjects.

research fatigue: The perception by a community that has been extensively researched that they have experienced no measurable gains from participating in the research and are therefore uninterested in further participation.

PRIVACY, ANONYMITY, AND CONFIDENTIALITY

LO 7 Define privacy, anonymity, and confidentiality.

How would you feel if private details about your personal life were shared with the public without your knowledge? Because social researchers sometimes invade the privacy of subjects to study social behaviour, they must take several precautions to protect research participants' privacy.

Privacy

Survey researchers invade a person's privacy when they probe into beliefs, backgrounds, and behaviours in a way that reveals intimate private details. Experimental researchers sometimes use two-way mirrors or hidden microphones to "spy" on subjects. Even if people know they are being studied, they are unaware of what the experimenter is looking for. Field researchers may observe private aspects of behaviour or eavesdrop on conversations.

In field research, privacy may be violated without advance warning. When Humphreys (1975) served as a "watchqueen" in a public restroom where homosexual contacts took place, he observed very private behaviour without informing the subjects. When Piliavin and colleagues (1969) had people pretend to collapse on subways to study helping behaviour, those in the subway car had the privacy of their ride violated. People have been studied in public places (e.g., in waiting rooms, on streets, in classrooms), but some "public" places are more private than others (consider, for example, the use of periscopes to observe people who believed they were alone in a public toilet stall).

Eavesdropping on conversations and observing people in quasi-private areas raises ethical concerns. To be ethical, a researcher violates privacy only to the minimal degree, as necessary, and only for legitimate research purposes. In addition, he or she takes steps to protect the information about participants obtained from public disclosure.

Anonymity

anonymity: Research participants remain anonymous or nameless.

Researchers protect privacy by not disclosing a participant's identity after information is gathered. This takes two forms, both of which require separating an individual's identity from his or her responses: anonymity and confidentiality. **Anonymity** means that people remain anonymous or nameless. For example, a field researcher provides a social picture of a particular individual but gives a fictitious name and location and alters some characteristics. The subject's identity is protected, and the individual remains unknown or anonymous. Survey and experimental researchers discard the names or addresses of subjects as soon as possible and refer to participants only by a code number to protect anonymity. There are some cases where keeping participants' names is necessary. If a researcher uses a mail survey and includes a code on the questionnaire to determine which respondents failed to respond, he or she is not keeping respondents anonymous during that phase of the study. In panel studies, researchers track the same individuals over time, so they do not uphold participant anonymity within the study. Likewise, historical researchers use specific names in historical or documentary research. They may do so if the original information was from public sources; if the sources were not publicly available, a researcher must obtain written permission from the owner of the documents to use specific names.

It is difficult to protect research participant anonymity. In one study about a fictitious town, "Springdale," in *Small Town in Mass Society* (Vidich & Bensman, 1968), it was easy to identify the town and specific individuals in it. Town residents became upset about how the researchers portrayed them and staged a parade mocking the researchers. People often recognize the towns studied in community research. Yet, if a researcher protects the identities of individuals with fictitious information, the gap between what was studied and what is reported to others raises questions about what was found and what was made up. A researcher may breach a promise of anonymity unknowingly in small samples. For example, let us say you conduct a survey of 100 university students and ask many questions on a questionnaire, including age, sex, religion, and hometown. The sample contains one 22-year-old Jewish male born in Stratford, Ontario. With this information, you could find out who the specific individual is and how he answered very personal questions, even though his name was not directly recorded on the questionnaire.

Confidentiality

Even if a researcher cannot protect anonymity, he or she should protect participant confidentiality. Anonymity means protecting the identity of specific individuals from becoming known. **Confidentiality** can include information with participant names attached, but the researcher holds it in confidence or keeps it secret from public disclosure. The researcher releases data in a way that does not permit linking specific individuals to responses and presents it publicly only in an aggregate form (e.g., as percentages or statistical means).

confidentiality: Information has participant names attached, but the researcher holds it in confidence or keeps it secret from the public.

A researcher can provide anonymity without confidentiality or vice versa, although they usually go together. Anonymity without confidentiality occurs if all the details about a specific individual are made public but the individual's name is withheld. Confidentiality without anonymity occurs if detailed information is not made public, but a researcher privately links individual names to specific responses.

In 1917, the Statistics Act was passed in Canada, which gave the Canadian government the right "to collect, compile, analyze, abstract, and publish statistical information relating to the commercial, industrial, financial, social, economic, and general activities and conditions of the people." In addition to the rights of Statistics Canada to collect information on the public, the Statistics Act also established the legal obligation of the agency to protect the confidentiality of research subjects such that information will never be made public that could identify them.[9]

In 1999, the chief statistician at Statistics Canada refused to hand over control of the 1901 Historic Census records to the National Archives of Canada because it was assumed that a promise of "perpetual confidentiality" was made to census respondents in 1901. Some people argued that the records should be destroyed to protect the privacy of respondents, while other people felt that destroying these census records would be a senseless waste of valuable historical data. After investigation by an expert panel, however, census data was eventually handed over to the National Archives and can be examined online and in person at the Archives in Ottawa. A revised section of the Statistics Act from 2005 now allows census information to be publicly released after 92 years.[10]

In other situations, other principles may take precedence over protecting research participant confidentiality. For example, when studying patients in a mental hospital, a researcher discovers that a patient is preparing to kill an attendant. The researcher must weigh the benefit of confidentiality against the potential harm to the attendant. Each situation must be considered on its own merits (see Box 3.6).

Box 3.6 In the News

The Case of Russell Ogden

Social researchers can pay high personal costs for being ethical. Russell Ogden, a master's degree criminology student at Simon Fraser University, became the first (and so far only) Canadian researcher to receive a subpoena and be asked to reveal the identities of his research participants. Ogden had been studying assisted suicide during the time when Sue Rodriguez, a British Columbia woman dying of amyotrophic lateral sclerosis (ALS, or Lou Gehrig's disease), was bringing the "right to die" debate all the way to the Supreme Court of Canada. She died in 1994, and that same year the Vancouver coroner subpoenaed Ogden and asked him to identify two of his research participants who may have witnessed an assisted suicide and therefore would be possible murder suspects under Canadian law. Ogden refused to provide the information, even under threat of contempt of court and prison time, as he had guaranteed confidentiality to his research participants. The judge at the coroner's inquest ruled that Ogden was in a position of privilege and did not have to reveal his sources to the coroner.[11]

Ogden's research made headlines again[12] in 2008 and 2009 when Kwantlen University College, his current employer, denied Ogden permission to pursue additional research on assisted suicides. For his research, Ogden had proposed to be present at and observe assisted suicides of the terminally ill. Kwantlen University College did not want to be implicated in endorsing a researcher's presence during an illegal act. The research itself had been approved by the university research ethics board in 2005; it was the university administration that ordered him to stop in 2008. The case was brought to the attention of the Canadian Association of University Teachers for possibly putting the academic freedom of Ogden at risk. In early 2009, Ogden was permitted to continue the research that was originally approved by Kwantlen University College.

A special concern with anonymity and confidentiality arises when a researcher studies "captive" populations (e.g., students, prisoners, employees, patients, soldiers). Gatekeepers, or those in positions of authority, may restrict access unless they receive information on subjects. For example, a researcher studies drug use and sexual activity among high school students. School authorities agree to cooperate under two conditions: (1) Students need parental permission to participate, and (2) school officials get the names of all drug users and sexually active students to assist the students with counselling and to inform the students' parents. An ethical researcher will refuse to continue rather than meet the second condition. Even though the officials claim to have the participants' best interests in mind, the privacy of participants will be violated and they could be in legal harm as a result of disclosure. If the school officials really want to assist the students and not use researchers as spies, they could develop an outreach program of their own.

Privacy, Anonymity, and Confidentiality in Online Research

The issues relating to privacy, anonymity, and confidentiality apply to all forms of research, including those that occur online. The waters become quite a bit murkier, however, in the area of online research. We can probably agree that observational research that takes place in a shopping mall or busy urban street is "public" and ethically sound, but does this realm also include all information that can be obtained online (Bos et al., 2009)? In an online setting, where does the distinction between "private" and "public" lie?

Research ethics boards (REBs) have guidelines to follow as per the *Tri-Council Policy Statement* (discussed in Box 3.4). Many researchers, however, are encountering new and unique problems with online research, especially as digital cultures become more and more researched. In the event of disasters, for example, is it necessary to obtain REB approval (which can sometimes be rather time consuming) before studying the online response on Twitter or similar social media sites? Can such phenomena even be studied given such requirements? Is it necessary—or even possible—to uphold anonymity for individuals with very prominent online presences, such as a Twitter user with thousands of followers? At this point in social research, there is no "set standard" across nations in terms of how such ethical dilemmas are addressed in social research, unlike the other much more clear-cut ethical issues discussed earlier (such as physical and psychological harm). From a social research methods perspective, this murkiness is likely to play itself out in a variety of interesting cases in the near future.

RESPECT FOR HUMAN DIGNITY

While numerous principles of ethical research have been identified above, the basic principle of modern research ethics and the basis for the aforementioned ethical principles is nested in the "cardinal" principle of *respect for human dignity*. It is this principle—which endeavours to safeguard the multifaceted interests of the person—that guides the ethical standards by which scientists must undertake research in Canada.

Mandated Protections of Research Participants

Many governments have regulations and guidelines to protect research participants and their rights. In Canada, these guidelines are found in the rules and regulations issued by the Interagency Advisory Panel on Research Ethics (PRE). This panel comprises experts from three Canadian research agencies: (1) the Social Sciences and Humanities Research Council (SSHRC), (2) the Canadian Institutes of Health Research (CIHR), and (3) the Natural

Sciences and Engineering Research Council (NSERC). From this panel, the *Tri-Council Policy Statement on the Ethical Conduct for Research Involving Humans* was born. This code began development in 1994 but was not implemented until 1998.

ETHICS AND THE SCIENTIFIC COMMUNITY

The Canadian Sociological Association (CSA) and the American Sociology Association (ASA) set the standards for ethics codes within North American sociology. These discipline-based codes of ethics emerged in the early 1970s. Prior to the early 1990s, the CSA referred to the ASA code, after which it decided to create its own code. The standards of these professional organizations were implemented by the universities within individual departments, although the application was not uniform. The Social Sciences and Humanities Research Council then developed a code of ethics for the social sciences and made adherence to these guidelines mandatory for the receipt of funding. The *Tri-Council Policy Statement* was implemented in 1998 with the idea that it would be a single, standardized policy that would be applicable to all research in Canada, which would be preferable to the numerous codes of ethics created by various professional organizations and funding agencies.

In Canada, researchers wishing to use human subjects in their studies must write a proposal about their research detailing how and why human subjects will be used and safeguards that will be put in place to guarantee that the ethical principles outlined above are adhered to, which is then vetted by the *research ethics board* at their home university.

Physicians, attorneys, family counsellors, social workers, and other professionals have a *code of ethics* and peer review boards or licensing regulations. The codes formalize professional standards and provide guidance when questions arise in practice. Professional social science associations have codes of ethics that identify proper and improper behaviour. They represent a consensus of professionals on ethics. All researchers may not agree on all ethical issues, and ethical rules are subject to interpretation, but researchers are expected to uphold ethical standards as part of their membership in a professional community.

The origins of codes of research ethics can be traced to the Nuremberg Code adopted during the Nuremberg Military Tribunal on Nazi war crimes held by the Allied Powers immediately after World War II. The code, developed as a response to the cruelty of concentration camp experiments, outlines ethical principles and rights of human subjects, including the following:

- Voluntary consent
- Avoidance of unnecessary physical and mental suffering
- Avoidance of any experiment where death or disabling injury is likely
- Termination of research if its continuation is likely to cause injury, disability, or death
- Conduct of experiments by highly qualified people using the highest levels of skill and care
- Results that are aimed at the good of society and that are unattainable by any other method

The principles in the Nuremberg Code dealt with the treatment of human subjects and focused on medical experimentation, but they became the basis for the ethical codes in social research as well. Similar codes of human rights, such as the 1948 Universal Declaration of Human Rights by the United Nations and the 1964 Declaration of Helsinki by the World Medical Association, also have implications for social researchers. Box 3.7 lists some of the basic principles of ethical social research.

give a realistic appraisal of what can be accomplished for a given level of funding. The issue of limits is common in contract research, when a firm or government agency asks for work on a particular research project. There is often a tradeoff between quality and cost. Moreover, once the research begins, a researcher may need to redesign the project, or costs may be higher than expected. The contract procedure makes midstream changes difficult. A researcher may find that he or she is forced by the contract to use research procedures or methods that are less than ideal. The researcher then confronts a dilemma: Complete the contract and do low-quality research, or fail to fulfill the contract and lose money and future jobs.

A researcher should refuse to continue a study if he or she cannot uphold generally accepted standards of research. If a sponsor demands a biased sample or leading survey questions, the ethical researcher should refuse to cooperate. If a legitimate study shows a sponsor's pet idea or project to be a disaster, a researcher may anticipate the end of employment or pressure to violate professional research standards. In the long run, the sponsor, the researcher, the scientific community, and society in general are harmed by the violation of sound research practice. The researcher has to decide whether he or she is a "hired hand" who always gives the sponsors what they want, even if it is ethically wrong, or a professional who is obligated to teach, guide, or even oppose sponsors in the service of higher moral principles.

A researcher should ask: Why would sponsors want the social research conducted if they are not interested in using the findings or in the truth? The answer is that some sponsors are not interested in the truth and have no respect for the scientific process. They see social research only as a "cover" to legitimate a decision or practice that they plan to carry out, and use research only to justify their action or deflect criticism. They abuse the researcher's professional status and undermine the integrity of science to advance their own narrow goals. They are being deceitful by trying to "cash in" on social research's reputation for honesty. When such a situation occurs, an ethical researcher has a moral responsibility to expose and stop the abuse.

Suppressing Findings

What happens if you conduct a study and the findings make the sponsor look bad, so the sponsor does not want to release the results? Government agencies may suppress scientific information that contradicts official policy or embarrasses high-ranking officials. Social researchers who are employed by government agencies and who make information public experience retaliation. In 2000, David Healy was to take up a position at the University of Toronto's Centre for Addiction and Mental Health (CAMH). The British researcher was becoming known for his research that claimed that the antidepressant drug Prozac was associated with suicide attempts and estimated that a quarter of a million people worldwide had attempted suicide while on Prozac. Prior to taking up his appointment, Healy was invited to speak at a two-day conference at CAMH, where his lecture included references to his findings on the association between Prozac and suicide attempts. After this talk, however, Healy's job offer was withdrawn. The reason he was given was that he was a poor fit for CAMH because his approach was not "compatible" with the goals of the organization. An uproar was created in the scientific community when it was revealed that Eli Lilly, manufacturers of the drug Prozac, were major funders of CAMH. The University of Toronto denied that there was any connection between Eli Lilly and the withdrawal of the job offer. Healy filed a lawsuit against the University of Toronto in 2001, and the case was eventually settled out of court.[14]

In sponsored research, a researcher can negotiate conditions for releasing findings *prior to beginning* the study and sign a contract to that effect. It may be unwise to conduct the study without such a guarantee, although competing researchers who have fewer ethical scruples may do so. Alternatively, a researcher can accept the sponsor's criticism and hostility and release the findings over the sponsor's objections. Most researchers prefer the first choice, since the second one may scare away future sponsors.

Box 3.9 Making It Practical

Funding for Research in Canada

In Canada, most social science research is funded through the Social Sciences and Humanities Research Council (SSHRC), which is a federal government–based granting agency. Two other federal granting agencies are the Canadian Institutes of Health Research (CIHR), which funds health and medical research, and the Natural Sciences and Engineering Research Council (NSERC).

Among these three councils, there is considerable discrepancy in the amount of funds that are allocated for research funding. For 2011–2012, the SSHRC had a budget of $332.4 million, while comparable figures for the CIHR and the NSERC were around $1 billion each. Each year in the social sciences, professors and graduate students put in applications, proposals, and budgets to the SSHRC. In 2011–2012, about 33 percent of applicants received funding. Nineteen members of the council are responsible for reporting to the Minister of Industry, who then reports to Parliament.

While most of the social sciences funding in Canada is granted through the SSHRC, there is an increasing trend to look to private or corporate sources of funding in all areas of research, especially if a researcher is not successful at obtaining government-based funds. If you think about the types of topics that many sociologists are interested in studying, such as those who critique the corporate sector (i.e., its employment and business practices) and globalization, many areas of social science research stand a much smaller chance of obtaining private sources of funding.

Social researchers sometimes self-censor or delay the release of findings. They do this to protect the identity of informants, to maintain access to their research sites, to hold on to their jobs, or to protect their personal safety or that of family members.[15] This is a less disturbing type of censorship because it is not imposed by an outside power. It is done by someone who is close to the research and who is knowledgeable about possible consequences. Researchers shoulder the ultimate responsibility for their research. Often they can draw on many different resources, but they face many competing pressures as well.

Concealing the True Sponsor

Is it ethical to keep the identity of a sponsor a secret? For example, an abortion clinic funds a study on members of religious groups who oppose abortion, but it tells the researcher not to reveal to participants information about who is funding the study. The researcher must weigh the ethical rule that it is usually best to reveal a sponsor's identity to participants against the sponsor's desire for confidentiality and the reduced cooperation of participants in the study. In general, an ethical researcher will tell the subjects who is sponsoring the study unless there is a strong methodological reason for not doing so. When reporting or publishing results, the ethical mandate is very clear: A researcher must always reveal the sponsor who provides funds for a study. In Canada, most funding for university-based social science research comes from the Social Sciences and Humanities Research Council of Canada (see Box 3.9).

POLITICS OF RESEARCH

Ethics largely address the moral concerns and standards of professional conduct in research that are under the researcher's control. Political concerns also affect social research, but many of these considerations are beyond the control of researchers. The politics of research usually involves actions by organized advocacy groups, powerful interests in society, governments, or politicians trying to restrict or control the direction of social research. Historically, the political influence over social research has included preventing researchers from conducting a study, cutting off or redirecting funds for research, harassing individual researchers, censoring the release of research findings, and using social research as a cover or guise for covert government intelligence/military actions.

Most users of political or financial influence to control social research share a desire to limit knowledge creation or restrict the autonomous scientific investigation of controversial topics. Attempts at control seem motivated by a fear that researchers might discover something damaging if they have freedom of inquiry. This shows that free scientific inquiry is connected to fundamental political ideals of open public debate, democracy, and freedom of expression.

The attempts to block and to steer social research have three main causes. First, some people defend or advance positions and knowledge that originate in deeply held ideological, political, or religious beliefs, and they fear that social researchers might produce knowledge that contradicts them. Second, powerful interests want to protect or advance their political/financial position and fear social researchers might yield findings showing that their actions are harmful to the public or some sectors of society. And third, some people in society do not respect the ideal of science to pursue truth and knowledge and instead view scientific research only as a means for advancing private interests.

CHAPTER SUMMARY

This chapter began by asking the question of why researchers should be ethical. Scientific misconduct, which includes research fraud and plagiarism, was then discussed. Social researchers, by nature of their position as experts and researchers, are often in relationships of unequal power with their research subjects. It is because of this imbalance in power that measures must be taken to protect the individuals who are being researched so that their rights are not compromised.

Several ethical issues that pertain to using human research participants were then discussed. The obligations of the researcher to not cause physical, psychological, or legal harm to those he or she is researching were highlighted. The principles of obtaining voluntary and informed consent from your research participants was also explained. Circumstances around the topic of dealing with special populations were considered, particularly the case of individuals who are vulnerable or have been oppressed through racism and colonization.

The chapter then moved on to the efforts that researchers must make to protect the rights and identities of the people they are researching through ensuring anonymity and confidentiality. Social researchers must ensure participant privacy because they are, due to the nature of their topics of inquiry, very likely to uncover sensitive information. They must not reveal the identities of their participants or reveal information that could identify them.

The scientific community has ethical guidelines in place to govern the behaviour of its members. All institutes of higher learning in Canada are obliged to follow the *Tri-Council Policy Statement* when it comes to doing research that involves human subjects. The funding of research is often provided by the Tri-Council in Canada, although private and corporate sponsoring of research also occurs. There are ethical issues that are particular to situations relating to the sponsors of research (i.e., those who are paying for the research), particularly if they attempt to suppress or influence the findings of researchers. Finally, the relationship between political ideology and research was briefly discussed, highlighting the reasons that individuals may have for trying to block or steer the course of particular research agendas.

Review Questions

1. Why it is important to be ethical in research? Give three reasons.
2. Define scientific misconduct, research fraud, and plagiarism.
3. Describe the balance of power in social research and why it is an ethical concern.
4. Identify four ethical concerns around research that involves human subjects and define them.
5. Differentiate between voluntary and informed consent.

6. Define special populations and explain the considerations that need to be made when working with such groups.
7. Define privacy, anonymity, and confidentiality.
8. Explain three ethical issues that are specific to research involving sponsors.

Exercises

1. Go to your university or college's website and find its official documents on the research ethics policies surrounding the use of human participants in research. Find passages that specifically relate to the ideas of informed consent, confidentiality, and risk. Summarize what you found in one or two paragraphs. Research Activity
2. Find the forms on your university or college's website that you would have to fill out if you wanted to do a study of your own using human participants. Thinking of a study you might like to do, fill out these forms. Which parts of the forms are most difficult to complete?
3. With regard to the story of Dr. Chandra discussed in Box 3.1, how many ethical concerns discussed in this chapter can be applied there?
4. Type "research fraud" or "scientific misconduct" into Google News and examine the first three stories that come up. Summarize the issue being dealt with in each of the stories. What types of ethical violations are being discussed? What academic disciplines do your stories cover? What are the major problems being discussed by the journalists?
5. Type "research ethics and developing countries" into Google Scholar and see what articles come up. Pick two that you will locate and read in their entirety. While this chapter's topic was ethics in social research, what do these articles tell you about ethical issues that have emerged in biomedical research?

Chapter 4

Reviewing the Scholarly Literature and Planning a Study

Photo Credit: James Woodson/Photodisc/Getty Images

LEARNING OBJECTIVES

After reading this chapter, you will be able to

- LO 1 Explain the purpose of the literature review in the larger context of a research study.
- LO 2 Describe how to conduct a systematic review of the literature.
- LO 3 Differentiate between an annotated bibliography and a literature review.
- LO 4 Explain how the internet can assist you with doing research for your literature review.
- LO 5 Explain which internet resources are not suitable for your scholarly review of the literature.

INTRODUCTION

In this chapter, we discuss how to organize and synthesize the findings of previous research. You may wonder why this important—after all, if you are going to do a study you will have your own results, right? Reading the "literature," or the collection of studies already published on a topic, serves several important functions. First, it helps you narrow down a broad topic by showing you how others conducted their studies. Previous studies give you a model of how narrowly focused a research question should be, what kinds of study designs others

Box 4.1 Making It Practical

Goals of a Literature Review

1. *To demonstrate familiarity with a body of knowledge and establish credibility.* A review tells a reader that the researcher knows the research in an area and knows the major issues. A good review increases a reader's confidence in the researcher's professional competence, ability, and background.
2. *To show the path of prior research and how a current project is linked to it.* A review outlines the direction of research on a question and shows the development of knowledge. A good review places a research project in a context and demonstrates its relevance by making connections to a body of knowledge.
3. *To integrate and summarize what is known in an area.* A review pulls together and synthesizes different results. A good review points out areas where prior studies agree, where they disagree, and where major questions remain. It collects what is known up to a point in time and indicates the direction for future research.
4. *To learn from others and stimulate new ideas.* A review tells what others have found so that a researcher can benefit from the efforts of others. A good review identifies blind alleys (underexamined topics) and suggests hypotheses for replication. It divulges procedures, techniques, and research designs worth copying so that a researcher can better focus his or her hypotheses and gain new insights.

have used, and how the parts of a study fit together. Second, it informs you about the "state of knowledge" on a topic. From the studies of others, you can learn the key ideas, terms, and issues that surround a topic. You should consider replicating, testing, or extending what others already found. Third, the literature often stimulates your creativity and curiosity. Finally, even if you never get to conduct or publish your own research study, a published study offers you an example of what the final report on a study looks like—its major parts, its form, and its style of writing. This reason is more practical; just as attentively reading a lot of top-quality writing can help you improve your own writing skills, reading many reports of good-quality social research enables you to better grasp the elements that go into conducting a research study.

Locating Relevant Sources

LO 1 Explain the purpose of the literature review in the larger context of a research study.

It is best to be organized and not haphazard as you locate and read the scholarly or academic literature on a topic and associated research questions. Also, it is wise to plan to prepare a written literature review. There are many specialized types of reviews, but in general a **literature review** is a carefully crafted summary of the recent studies conducted on a topic that includes key findings and methods researchers used, while making sure to document the sources.

literature review: A systematic examination of previously published studies on a research question, issue, or method that a researcher undertakes and integrates together to prepare for conducting a study or to bring together and summarize the "state of the field."

Reviews vary in scope and depth. Different kinds of reviews are stronger at fulfilling one or another of four goals (see Box 4.1). It may take a researcher over a year to complete an extensive professional summary review of all the literature on a broad question. The same researcher might complete a highly focused review in a very specialized area in a few weeks. When beginning a review, a researcher decides on a topic, how much depth to go into, and the kind of review to conduct.

HOW TO FIND RESEARCH LITERATURE

Researchers present reports of their research projects in several written forms: books, periodicals, dissertations, government documents, or policy reports. They also present them as papers at the meetings of professional societies, but for the most part you can find them only in a college or university library. This section briefly discusses each type of research literature and gives you a simple road map on how to access them.

Books

There are many different types of books. Our concern here is with those books containing reports of original research or collections of research articles. Libraries shelve these books and assign call numbers to them, as they do with other types of books. You can find citation information on them (e.g., title, author, publisher) in the library's catalogue system. The best first place to search for books that are relevant to your topic is your library's electronic catalogue. Your school's librarians likely organize regular sessions for students on how to conduct library searches and even how to do literature reviews; if this is completely new to you, it is a very good idea to sign up for these tutorials, which will give you the skills to work more efficiently. Your library's catalogue will have resources for searching the titles held by the library and resources for searching for articles within *scholarly journals* (more below). Searching the catalogue by *keywords*—or a selection of words relevant to your research topic—will provide you with books that are related to your search.

Locating original research articles in books can be difficult because there is no single source listing them. Two types of books contain collections of articles or research reports. The first is designed for teaching purposes. Such books, called *readers*, may include original research reports. Usually, articles on a topic from scholarly journals are gathered and edited to be easier for nonspecialists to read and understand. The second type of collection is designed for scholars and may gather journal articles or may contain original research or theoretical essays on a specific topic. Some collections contain articles from journals that are difficult to locate; they may include original research reports organized around a specialized topic. The table of contents lists the titles and authors. Libraries shelve these collections with other books, and some library catalogue systems include the table of contents. Increasingly, many new books are becoming available as electronic books through the library, which you can download from anywhere you have an internet connection.

Periodicals

It is easy for someone preparing a first literature review to be confused about the many types of periodicals. With skill, you will be able to distinguish among scholarly academic journals and the other various types of periodicals. Peer-reviewed, empirical research findings appear in a complete form only in the scholarly academic journals, although articles in the other types of periodicals occasionally talk about findings published elsewhere.

Scholarly Journals The primary type of periodical to use for a literature review is the scholarly journal, which is filled with peer-reviewed reports of research (e.g., *Canadian Review of Sociology*, *Canadian Journal of Sociology*, *American Sociological Review*, *American Journal of Sociology*, *Canadian Journal of Criminology and Criminal Justice*, and *European Sociological Review*). One rarely finds them outside of college and university libraries. Recall from Chapter 1 that researchers disseminate findings of new studies in scholarly journals.

Some scholarly journals are specialized. Instead of reports of research studies, they have only book reviews that provide commentary and evaluations on a book (e.g., *Contemporary Sociology*), or they contain only literature review essays (e.g., *Annual Review of Sociology*, *Annual Review of Psychology*, and *Annual Review of Anthropology*) in which researchers provide a "state of the field" essay for others. Publications that specialize in literature reviews can be helpful if an article was recently published on a specific topic of interest. Many other scholarly journals have a mix of articles that include literature reviews, book reviews, reports on research studies, and theoretical essays.

No simple solution or "seal of approval" distinguishes a scholarly journal (the kind of publication on which to build a serious literature review from other periodicals) or instantly distinguishes the report on a research study from other types of articles. One needs to develop judgment or ask experienced researchers or professional librarians. Nonetheless, distinguishing among types of publications is essential to build on a body of research. One of the best ways to learn how to do this is by reading many articles in scholarly journals.

The number of journals varies by field. Psychology has over 400 journals, whereas sociology has about 250 scholarly journals, political science and communication have slightly fewer than sociology, anthropology/archeology and social work have about 100 each, urban studies and women's studies have about 50 each, and there are about a dozen journals in criminology. Each publishes from a few dozen to over 100 articles a year.

Obviously it would be very time consuming to search through all the journals for articles related to your research topic. More efficient searching can be accomplished by using one of your library's social science databases that will search several journal titles by a list of keywords that you specify. In the social sciences, popular databases include *Sociological Abstracts*, *Web of Science*, and *Social Sciences Abstracts*. *Sociological Abstracts*, for example, will search around 2500 journals in the field of sociology based on the keywords that you enter. You can even narrow the search criteria to specific ranges of years (i.e., the past decade) if you find your search is returning too many articles. Figure 4.1 shows you one database, *Sociological Abstracts*, and the search results it provided for the keywords "teenage motherhood." The first study listed is from 1980 and was published in the *American Sociological Review*. The results indicate that 159 articles were found using these keywords. To narrow our results, we may want to use "advanced search" options and narrow the date to the past 20 years, or add additional keywords, such as "educational attainment" or "socio-economic outcomes," depending on the specific topic area we were interested in. In the second search, the term "educational attainment" was added and results were limited to those published in the past 20 years. As you can see, there were much fewer matches—this time only eight.

Nearly all scholarly journals may be viewed in electronic format these days as many libraries have been moving away from print subscriptions to electronic versions. Sometimes

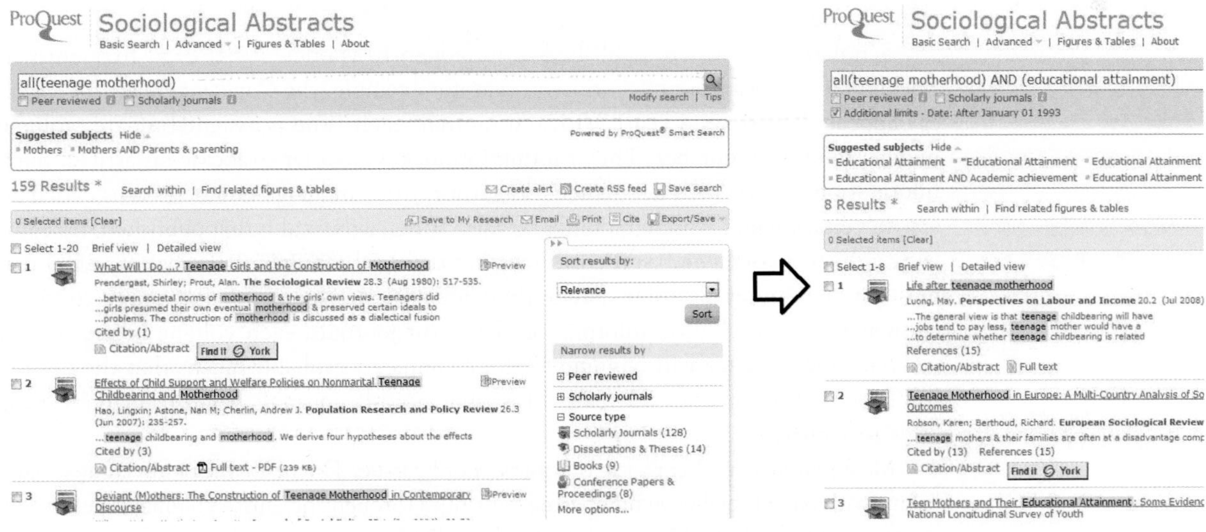

Figure 4.1 Sample Search for Scholarly Articles in *Sociological Abstracts*

Source: http://www.proquest.com. Printed with permission of ProQuest.

online versions are limited to selected years and to libraries that pay special subscription fees. These subscription fees are very expensive, so not all universities and colleges will have subscriptions to all the journals you might be interested in accessing. Indeed, the recent economic crisis of 2008 has resulted in smaller operating budgets for many libraries. Individuals without access to postsecondary libraries or located in developing countries will often not be able to access the majority of the most highly regarded journals in their field because of restricted access to those affiliated with institutions that pay high subscription fees. Recent protests by academics occurred in 2012 (mostly in the United Kingdom) about the high cost of journal subscriptions and the lack of access to research findings for individuals who are not affiliated with postsecondary institutions that can afford the high subscription rates;[1] these researchers are essentially prevented from reading scientific articles blocked behind "pay walls."

As a result of this action and cost-cutting measures, increased attention is being paid to *open access journals* that do not require readers to pay to access content, but instead may recoup their fees by having authors pay administrative costs to publish within them (although this may be waived for authors from developing countries). There are thousands of open access journals that can be searched for using the Directory of Open Access Journals (www.doaj.org). At the time of writing, the traditional "prestige" associated with publishing in an open access journal has been debated, with more scholars in the health and natural sciences adapting to the open access model because quick and broad dissemination of research findings to a wider readership has been strongly emphasized. Also at the time of writing, the Directory of Open Access Journals listed 322 social science journals, which include non-English publications. All open access journals listed in the directory are peer reviewed (discussed below) or exercise quality control through editorial boards.

Once you locate a scholarly journal that reports on social science research studies, you need to make sure that a particular article presents the results of a study, since the journal may have other types of articles. It is easier to identify quantitative studies because they usually have a methods or data section and charts, statistical formulas, and tables of numbers. Qualitative research articles are more difficult to identify, and many students confuse them with theoretical essays, literature review articles, idea-discussion essays, policy recommendations, book reviews, and legal case analyses. To distinguish among these types of reports requires a good grasp of the varieties of research as well as experience in reading many articles.

Scholarly journals are published as infrequently as once a year or as frequently as weekly. Most appear four to six times a year; for example, the *Canadian Review of Sociology* appears four times a year. Within a journal, each issue is assigned a date, volume number, and issue number. This information makes it easier to locate an article. Such information—along with details such as author, title, and page number(s)—is called an article's **citation** and is used in bibliographies. When a journal is first published, it begins with volume 1, number 1 and continues increasing the numbers thereafter. Although most journals follow a similar system, there are enough exceptions that you have to pay close attention to citation information. For most journals, each volume is one year. If you see a journal issue with volume 52, for example, it probably means that the journal has been in existence for 52 years. Most, but not all, journals begin their publishing cycle in January.

citation: Details of a scholarly journal article's location that help people find it quickly.

Most journals number pages by volume, not by issue. The first issue of a volume usually begins with page 1, and page numbering continues through the entire volume; for example, the first page of volume 52, issue 4, may be page 547. Most journals have an index for each volume and a table of contents for each issue that lists the title, the author's or authors' names, and the page on which the article begins. Issues contain as few as 1 or 2 articles or as many as 50. Most have 8 to 18 articles, which may be 5 to 50 pages long. The articles

Box 4.2 Concepts in Action

Meta-Analysis: The Effects of Lone Parenthood on Children

There have been volumes of research on the effects of lone parenthood on children, published in various countries at various times. Sometimes we hear about findings suggesting that children raised by lone parents suffer a host of disadvantages, including poverty and psychological distress. Other times we might hear that children raised in lone parent families do just fine compared with those raised in "intact" families. How can we find out what the general average finding is from the vast majority of reports out there? One technique is with the meta-analysis.

A very thorough overview of the impact of lone parenthood on child well-being has recently been undertaken by Chapple (2009), who employed a meta-analysis of 122 studies from a cross-section of OECD countries (excluding the United States). After statistically analyzing the results of the 122 studies, Chapple found that the overall effect of lone parenting on child well-being was, indeed, negative but that this effect was very small.

often have **abstracts**, short summaries on the first page of the article or grouped together at the beginning of the issue.

abstract: A term with two meanings in literature reviews: a short summary of a scholarly journal article that usually appears at its beginning, and a reference tool for locating scholarly journal articles.

A particularly useful journal article that you might find on your topic is a meta-analysis. A **meta-analysis** is a study undertaken by a researcher in which he or she analyzes the results from all the available studies on a given topic. It is like a statistical review of the literature in which the researcher looks at all the previous research findings on a topic to examine overall statistical trends when all the studies are combined together (see Box 4.2).

meta-analysis: A quantitative overview of existing evidence on a particular topic.

Other Types of Periodicals Mass-market publications (e.g., *Maclean's*, *Time Canada*, *L'actualité*, *The Economist*, and *The Walrus*) are sold at newsstands and are designed to provide the general public with news, opinion, and entertainment. A researcher might occasionally use them as a source on current events, but they do not provide full reports of research studies in the form needed to prepare a literature review.

Popularized social science magazines and professional publications (e.g., *Society* and *Psychology Today*) are sometimes peer reviewed. Their purpose is to provide the interested, educated lay public with a simplified version of findings or a commentary. However, they are not meant to be an outlet for original research findings. At best, popularized social science magazines can supplement other sources in a literature review.

It is harder to recognize serious opinion magazines (e.g., *Inroads*, *Dissent*, and *Canadian Dimension*). Larger bookstores in major cities sell them. Leading scholars often write articles for opinion magazines about topics on which they may also conduct empirical research (e.g., welfare reform, prison expansion, voter turnout). They differ in purpose, look, and scope from scholarly journals of social science research findings. The publications are an arena where intellectuals debate current issues, not where researchers present findings of their studies to the broader scientific community.

Dissertations

All graduate students who receive the Ph.D are required to complete a work of original research, which they write up as a dissertation thesis. The dissertation is bound and placed on the shelves in the library of the university that granted the Ph.D. About half of all dissertations are eventually published as books or articles. Because dissertations report on original research, they can be valuable sources of information. Some students who receive a master's degree conduct original research and write a master's thesis, although they can be much more difficult to locate than unpublished dissertations.

Specialized indexes list dissertations completed by students at accredited universities. For example, *Dissertation Abstracts International* lists dissertations with their authors, titles, and universities. This index is organized by topic and contains an abstract of each dissertation. You can borrow most dissertations via interlibrary loan from the degree-granting university if the university permits this.

Government Documents

The federal government of Canada, the governments of other nations, provincial or state-level governments, the United Nations, and other international agencies like the World Bank all sponsor studies and publish reports of the research. Many university libraries have these documents in their holdings, usually in a special "government documents" section. Most university libraries hold only the most frequently requested documents and reports.

Policy Reports

A researcher conducting a thorough review of the literature will examine papers and reports from research institutes and policy centres (e.g., Canadian Research Institute for Social Policy, Canada West Foundation, Caledon Institute of Social Policy), which are difficult for all but the trained specialist to obtain. Some major research libraries purchase these and place them on shelves along with books. The only way to be sure of what has been published is to inquire directly with the institute or centre. Often these organizations have lists of publications on their websites.

CITATION STYLES

Citations are useful for two purposes: locating a source and referencing it properly. An article's citation is the key to locating it and referencing it properly in your list of sources at the end of your literature review. Sometimes it won't be possible to just click on a link and have the article open directly from a database—you will either need to physically locate it in the library or navigate to it manually through your library's electronic resources. Suppose you want to read the study by Malacrida on mothers with disabilities in Chapter 2. Its citation is as follows: Malacrida, C. (2007). Negotiating the dependency/nurturance tightrope: Dilemmas of motherhood and disability. *Canadian Review of Sociology*, 46(3), 235–252.

This tells you that you can find the article in an issue of *Canadian Review of Sociology* published in 2007. The citation also gives the volume number (46) and issue (3), as well as the page numbers, 235 to 252. Therefore, you would search for "Canadian Review of Sociology" in your library catalogue, connect to the online resource (assuming your library subscribes to this service), or write down the call number and go to the place in your library's stacks where this journal is stored. Then you would go to those volumes published in 2007, select volume 46, issue 3, and then go to page 235 (or click on the hyperlink from your electronic database).

There are many ways to cite the literature that have been developed by scholarly organizations and publishers. Formats for citing literature in the text itself vary, with the internal citation format of using an author's last name and date of publication in parentheses being very popular. The full citation appears in a separate bibliography or reference section. There are many styles for full citations of journal articles, with books and other types of works each having a separate style. When citing articles, it is best to check with an instructor, journal, or other outlet for the desired format. Almost all include the names of authors, article title, journal name, and volume and page numbers. Figure 4.2 illustrates the most common types of referencing styles for the social sciences in Canada.

The oldest journal of sociology in Canada, *Canadian Review of Sociology*, includes a report by Martin Cooke on how lone mothers in Canada use social assistance payments. It appears on pages 179 to 206 of the August 2009 issue (number 3) of the journal, which begins counting issues in February. It is in volume 46, or the journal's 46th year.

If you are talking about this source or giving information provided by this author you will need to cite the article within your literature review. Three very popular styles are those of the *American Sociological Review (ASR)*, *American Psychological Association (APA)*, and *Modern Language Association (MLA)*. Even though the first two are "American" styles, they are very much the convention in Canadian sociology and psychology as well. Depending on the style that you are using, it will follow a certain format. This type of citation is called an "in-text citation" and is used by the ASR and APA styles. The following styles are very similar, with the major difference being that APA requires a comma between the author and year. MLA, in contrast, requires that a page number, rather than the year, be reported.

ASR style

Previous Canadian research has found that marital history is a strong indicator of single mothers receiving social assistance (Cooke 2009).

APA style

Previous Canadian research has found that marital history is a strong indicator of single mothers receiving social assistance (Cooke, 2009).

MLA

Previous Canadian research has found that marital history is a strong indicator of single mothers receiving social assistance (Cooke 179).

If you were directly quoting the authors (which you should do only sparingly!), here is what your in-text citation would look like:

ASR style

According to Cooke, "lone mothers' education and labour force experience were less important predictors for their duration on social assistance than their previous marital history" (2009: 179).

APA style

According to Cooke (2009), "lone mothers' education and labour force experience were less important predictors for their duration on social assistance than their previous marital history" (p. 179).

MLA

According to Cooke, "lone mothers' education and labour force experience were less important predictors for their duration on social assistance than their previous marital history" (179).

Here are ways to cite the article in the list of references at the end of your literature review or report:

ASR Style

Cooke, Martin. 2009. "A Welfare Trap? The Duration and Dynamics of Social Assistance Use Among Lone Mothers in Canada." *Canadian Review of Sociology* 46 (3): 179–206.

APA Style

Cooke, M. (2009). A welfare trap? The duration and dynamics of social assistance use among lone mothers in Canada. *Canadian Review of Sociology*, *46*(3), 179–206.

MLA Style

Cooke, Martin. "A Welfare Trap? The Duration and Dynamics of Social Assistance Use Among Lone Mothers in Canada." *Canadian Review of Sociology*, 46.3. (2009): 179–206. Print.

Figure 4.2 Different Reference Citations for a Journal Article

If you are working on a research paper that requires several sources, you should be aware that there are also software programs (e.g., Endnote) and online bibliographic managers (e.g., RefWorks) that can help you organize your literature and can convert your entire bibliography from one citation style to another with the click of a button. Many colleges and universities have subscriptions to these services. Check with a librarian at your college or university for more information about what is available to you. Another way of getting your citations into the proper style is by using free online citation tools like Easy Bib (www.easybib.com), Son of Citation Machine (citationmachine.net), or Bib Me (www.bibme.org). It should be noted, however, that not all web citation tools can create citations in all styles, although APA and MLA are usually supported.

LO 2 Describe how to conduct a systematic review of the literature.

HOW TO CONDUCT A SYSTEMATIC LITERATURE REVIEW

Define and Refine a Topic

Just as a researcher must plan and clearly define a topic and research question when beginning a research project, you need to begin a literature review with a clearly defined, well-focused research question and a plan. A good review topic should be as focused as a research question. For example, "divorce" or "crime" is much too broad. A more appropriate review topic might be "the stability of families with stepchildren" or "economic inequality and crime rates across nations." If you conduct a context review for a research project, it should be slightly broader than the specific research question being tested. Often, a researcher will not finalize a specific research question for a study until he or she has reviewed the literature. The review helps bring greater focus to the research question.

Design a Search Strategy

After choosing a focused research question for the review, the next step is to plan a search strategy. The reviewer needs to decide on the type of review, its extensiveness, and the types of materials to include. The key is to be careful, systematic, and organized. Set parameters on your search: how much time you will devote to it, how far back in time you will look, the minimum number of research reports you will examine, how many libraries you will visit, and so forth.

Also, decide how to record the bibliographic citation for each reference you find and how to take notes (e.g., in a notebook, on 3″ by 5″ cards, in a document or spreadsheet file on your computer). Develop a schedule, because several sessions of searching are usually necessary. You should begin a file folder or computer file in which you can place possible sources and ideas for new sources. As the review proceeds, it should become more focused.

Locate Research Reports

Locating research reports depends on the type of report or "outlet" of research being searched. As a general rule, use multiple search strategies to counteract the limitations of a single search method. To be thorough, you will not want to limit yourself to one database—use several. You will likely encounter many of the same articles by using multiple databases, but you will also find that one database may pick up a valuable research article that others did not.

Taking Notes

As you gather the relevant research literature, it is easy to feel overwhelmed by the quantity of information, so you need a system for taking notes. The old-fashioned approach is to write notes onto index cards. You then shift and sort the note cards, place them in piles, and so forth as you look for connections among them or develop an outline for a report or paper. This method still works. Today, however, most people use word-processing software and gather photocopies or electronic versions of many articles.

As you discover sources, it is a good idea to create two kinds of files for your note cards or computer documents: a Source File and a Content File. Record all bibliographic information for each source in the Source File, even though you may not use some; you can later remove them. Do not forget anything in a complete bibliographic citation, such as a page number or the name of the second author—you will regret it later. It is far easier to remove a source you do not use than to try to locate bibliographic information later for a source you discover that you need or from which you forgot one detail.

We recommend creating two kinds of Source Files, or dividing a master file into two parts: Have File and Potential File. The Have File is for sources that you have found and for which you have already taken content notes. The Potential File is for leads and possible new sources that you have yet to track down or read. You can add to the Potential File anytime you come across a new source or find a promising lead in the bibliography of something you read. Toward the end of writing a report, the Potential File will disappear while the Have File will become your bibliography.

Your note cards or computer documents go into the Content File. This file contains substantive information of interest from a source, usually its major findings, details of methodology, definitions of concepts, or interesting quotations. If you directly quote from a source or want to take some specific information from a source, you need to record the specific page number(s) on which the quotation appears. Link the files by putting key source information, such as author and date, on each content file.

What to Record You will find it much easier to take all notes on the same type and size of paper or card, rather than having some notes on sheets of paper, others on cards, and so on. Researchers have to decide what to record about an article, book, or other source. It is better to err in the direction of recording too much rather than too little. In general, record the hypotheses tested, how major concepts were measured, the main findings, the basic design of the research, the group or sample used, and ideas for future study. It is wise to examine the report's list of references, too, and note sources that you can add to your search. Box 4.3 suggests some guidelines to keep in mind as you read journal articles so that you benefit the most from the time you spend researching your topic.

Photocopying or downloading all relevant articles or reports will save you time recording notes and will ensure that you will have an entire report. Also, you can make notes on the photocopy. There are several warnings about this practice. First, photocopying can be expensive for a large literature search. Second, be aware of and observe copyright laws; Canadian copyright laws permit photocopying for personal research use. Third, remember to record or photocopy the entire article, including all citation information. It should be noted that many of these articles are available as downloadable files (usually PDFs), so if you can read on-screen you can save a lot of paper. Whatever format you decide to use, however, unless you highlight carefully or take good notes, you may have to reread the entire article later.

Organize Your Notes After gathering a large number of references and notes, you need an organizing scheme. One approach is to group studies or specific findings by skimming

Box 4.3 Making It Practical

How to Read Journal Articles

1. Read with a clear purpose or goal in mind. Are you reading for basic knowledge or to apply it to a specific question?
2. Skim the article before reading it all. What can you learn from the title, abstract, summary and conclusions, and headings? What are the topic, major findings, method, and main conclusion?
3. Consider your own orientation. What is your bias toward the topic, the method, the publication source, and so on that may colour your reading?
4. Marshal external knowledge. What do you already know about the topic and the methods used? How credible is the publication source?
5. Evaluate as you read the article. What errors are present? Do findings follow the data? Is the article consistent with the assumptions of the approach it takes?
6. Summarize information as an abstract with the topic, the methods used, and the findings. Assess the factual accuracy of findings and write down questions about the article.

Source: Adapted from Katzer, J., Cook, K. H., & Crouch, W. W. (1991). *Evaluating information: A guide for users of social science research* (3rd ed., pp. 199–207). New York, NY: McGraw-Hill.

notes and creating a mental map of how they fit together. Try several organizing schemes before settling on a final one. Organizing is a skill that improves with practice. For example, place notes into piles representing common themes, or draw charts comparing what different reports state about the same question, noting agreements and disagreements. You may also find it helpful to organize the citations in a spreadsheet, grouping them by common findings.

In the process of organizing your notes, you will find that some references and notes do not fit and should be discarded as irrelevant. Also, you may discover gaps or areas and topics that are relevant but that you did not examine. This necessitates additional searches for literature.

There are many organizing schemes. The best one depends on the purpose of the review. Usually, it is best to organize reports around a specific research question or around core common findings of a field and the main hypotheses tested. You may find it helpful to start with an annotated bibliography first (discussed shortly) to help you more easily organize the findings of the many sources upon which you are drawing.

Writing the Review

A literature review requires planning and good, clear writing, which requires a lot of rewriting. This step is often merged with organizing your notes. All the rules of good writing (e.g., clear organizational structure, an introduction and conclusion, transitions between sections) apply to writing a literature review. Keep your purposes in mind when you write, and communicate clearly and effectively.

To prepare a good review, read articles and other literature critically. Recall that skepticism is a norm of science. You should not accept what is written simply because it has been published. Question what you read and evaluate it. The first hurdle to overcome is thinking something must be perfect just because it has been published.

Critically reading research reports requires skills that take time and practice to develop. Despite a peer review procedure and high rejection rates, errors and sloppy logic slip in. Read carefully to see whether the introduction and title really fit with the rest of the article. Sometimes the title, abstract, or introduction is misleading. It may not fully explain the research project's method and results. Be prepared to read the article more than once.

LO 3 Differentiate between an annotated bibliography and a literature review.

annotated bibliography: A list of sources pertaining to a specific topic, which includes full citation information, a summary of the article (including research methods employed) and its findings, as well as evaluative comments about the quality of the research.

Synthesize An author should communicate a review's purpose to the reader by its organization. The wrong way to write a review is to list a series of research reports with a summary of the findings of each. This is more like an **annotated bibliography**, which is different from a literature review. Writing your notes in the style of an annotated bibliography is a good first step in a literature review, but remember: It is a first step. Box 4.4 shows you the style of an annotated bibliography.

The right way to write a review is to organize common findings or arguments together. The key to a good review is to organize the findings and research approaches by their commonalities and discuss them together (i.e., synthesize) where possible. This is a challenging task, and the first few times you do a literature review you will likely find the task of synthesizing to be quite difficult.

Avoid Over-quoting Another common beginner's error in literature reviews is over-quoting. As a general rule of thumb, one should never quote unless the ideas are so profound that the writer cannot rephrase (and then cite) them. Many novices' attempts at literature reviews often resemble a series of quotes strung together. Again, the idea is to synthesize findings and use your own words as much as possible. Paraphrasing is a valuable skill to acquire because it helps you resist the urge to quote too much and requires you to develop a deeper comprehension of the materials you are reading. See Table 4.1 for hints on how to effectively paraphrase.

Box 4.4 Making It Practical

Writing an Annotated Bibliography

Here are annotated bibliography entries for three journal articles on the topic of teenage parenthood. The annotated bibliography lists the citation information (done here in APA style), a summary of the article, and comments about the findings and research quality.

1. Robson, K., & Pevalin, D. (2008). Gender differences in the predictors and socio-economic outcomes of young parenthood. *Research in Social Stratification and Mobility, 25*(3), 205–218.

In this article, the authors examine how gender affects the different antecedents and life outcomes of young parents. The authors examine longitudinal cohort data from Britain. They find that young parents are more likely to come from single-parent households and to have had teenage mothers themselves. They also find a range of negative later-life socio-economic outcomes associated with teen parenting, including poverty.

This article uses somewhat advanced statistics to test what would happen if young people who were at risk of a teen pregnancy actually did not have a baby compared with those who did. The authors compare those who aborted or miscarried as teens with those who had a baby as teens, finding that the outcomes were not much different. They conclude that outcomes were determined more by social background characteristics, like class, than by whether a teen had a baby. This is a rather complicated analysis, but it seems to point to the finding that social class plays a bigger part in later-life socio-economic outcomes than does being a teen mother.

2. Robson, K., & Berthoud, R. (2006). Age at first birth and disadvantage among ethnic groups in Britain. *Ethnic and Racial Studies, 29*(1), 153–172.

The authors start with the findings of other studies that suggest three things: (1) Poverty is associated with being a teenage mother, (2) many immigrant groups experience poverty, and (3) many ethnic minority groups have teenage births. They test the hypothesis that teenage births in ethnic minorities contribute to their experience of poverty. Using several years of data from the UK Labour Force Survey, they find that while ethnic minorities experience disproportionate rates of poverty in the UK, this is not further exacerbated by a teen birth. The ethnic minority groups' experience of poverty is found to be linked to lack of employment. The authors argue that family formation theories suggest that the cultures of these ethnic groups, such as Bangladeshis, are more supportive of early births and provide forms of social support that are not found in white British culture.

This article rationalizes the findings in a theory of social stigma surrounding family structure norms in different ethnic groups. The authors look at Pakistanis, Bangladeshis, Indians, whites, Black Caribbeans, and Black Africans. The study is not able to differentiate between "ethnic" whites, such as those from Southern and Eastern Europe, which may be problematic as "white" as a heterogeneous group. Also, they cannot test their theory on Asian groups such as the Chinese because the numbers in the sample were not large enough.

3. Robson, K., & Berthoud, R. (2003). Teenage motherhood in Europe: A multi-country analysis of socioeconomic outcomes. *European Sociological Review, 19*(5), 451–466.

The authors argue that there are several studies about the outcomes of teen motherhood in the United States and the UK, but little is known about how young motherhood affects the later-life outcomes of those in other European countries. The authors use survey data from 13 countries in Europe and find that the range of outcomes differs greatly by country. The authors theorize that family formation norms in the countries may help explain the differences that are observed among the countries. In the Nordic countries, risk of poverty is highest because the norm for young people is to delay family formation until education is completed. In the Southern European countries, the risk of negative outcomes is the least because of the role of extended families for support in these countries.

The article uses an interesting theory of "stigma" to help explain why mothers in various countries have such vast differences in the outcomes they experience after a teenage birth. The article talks about only 13 of the first members of the European Union, though, so there is no information on later ascension states, such as those in Eastern Europe. They also are not able to test how social class of family of origin affects later-life outcomes.

The Difference Between a Good Review and a Bad Review

LO 4 Explain how the internet can assist you with doing research for your literature review.

LO 5 Explain which internet resources are not suitable for your scholarly review of the literature.

Box 4.5 shows two examples of excerpts from a literature review. The first is done poorly. It fails to synthesize and quotes where quotations are not necessary (and it even quotes improperly!). The writer just (poorly) summarizes the three articles and does not link them together in any way. In the second, better example, the findings are grouped by similarity, and the differences between the articles are highlighted. The common theoretical ground of two of the studies is also pointed out.

Table 4.1 Seven Steps to Effective Paraphrasing

1. Reread the original passage several times until you understand its full meaning.
2. Without looking at the original source, rewrite the material in your own words.
3. Make some notes under your paraphrase to remind you later how you imagine you will use the paraphrased material.
4. Check your version with the original source to ensure that your paraphrase is consistent with the meaning conveyed in the original. It is not enough to simply shuffle some words around.
5. Use quotation marks to identify any unique terms you have borrowed exactly from the source.
6. Record the source (including the page) on your note card so that you can credit it easily if you decide to incorporate the material into your paper.
7. Be sure to express to your reader where your paraphrase ends and where your original ideas begin. This should be done through proper citation. You must properly cite information you have paraphrased from other sources.

Source: Adapted from Paraphrase: Write it in Your Own Words, Purdue Owl Online Writing Lab and http://wps.prenhall.com/hss_understand_plagiarism_1/0,6622,427107-,00.html

It should be noted that length does not determine a good literature review. Sometimes students think that if they fill more pages, the review will be better, or the grader will not notice that it is poorly written or researched. The example of the bad review in Box 4.5 is longer than the better review. An effectively organized review most often results in a shorter page count.

On a final note, the internet has changed the way many researchers (and students) research and write a literature review. Box 4.6 outlines the impact this medium has had.

Box 4.5 Making It Practical

Examples of Reviews and Common Mistakes

Typically, a literature review is just that—it reviews the literature on a given topic. For simplicity's sake, however, we are going to show you part of a literature review that is based on the three articles discussed in the annotated bibliography example in Box 4.4. The first example is riddled with common mistakes that novice reviewers typically make.

Example of a Poorly Written Review

According to Robson and Pevalin (2007), teenage mothers in the UK come from disadvantaged social origins. "Our findings confirm much of the previous research demonstrating that young parents tend to come from poorer socioeconomic backgrounds, 'broken homes,' larger families, and themselves have mothers whose first birth was at a young age" (p. 215). The mothers also experience poverty later in life.

Robson and Berthoud (2003) found that young mothers experienced poverty in many European countries. There was a difference among countries they said was due to norms in family formation.

Robson and Berthoud (2006) found that ethnic minorities in the UK were at a higher risk of poverty because they had less of a chance of being employed and not because of teenage births. They state that some ethnic groups may have social norms in the community that help young mothers. "The high rates of unemployment and poverty among Pakistani and Bangladeshi families will not be impacted by reducing the number of women who have a birth at an early age" (pp. 170–171). Therefore, just because a person has a baby when they are young does not mean they will be poor.

Example of a Better Review

Teenage mothers experience a range of socio-economic disadvantages in the UK (Robson & Pevalin, 2007) and across Europe (Robson & Berthoud, 2003). Evidence points to a cycle of poverty being rooted in social class, with teenage mothers being more likely to come from poor backgrounds themselves (Robson & Pevalin, 2007).

Interestingly, some research has pointed to the importance of other background characteristics in determining the outcomes associated with early pregnancies. Robson and Pevalin (2007) show that social class of origin is more important than a teen pregnancy in predicting later-life poverty. Robson and Berthoud (2006) show that, while some ethnic minorities in Britain have a high rate of poverty, teen pregnancy does not contribute to this. A theory of family formation (Robson & Berthoud, 2003, 2006) suggests that the severity of risks associated with an early pregnancy has much to do with the norms surrounding family formation in particular ethnic and cultural groups in society.

Box 4.6 Social Research and the Internet

The internet has been a mixed blessing for social research, but it has not proven to be the panacea that some people first thought it might be. It provides new and important ways to find information, but it remains to be just one tool among others. It can make some specific pieces of information accessible very quickly. The internet is, however, best thought of as a supplement rather than as a replacement for traditional library research. There is an upside and a downside to using the internet for social research.

The Upside

The internet is easy, fast, and cheap, and it allows people to find source material from almost anywhere, given the increasing availability of WiFi technology. The internet does not close; it operates 24 hours a day, seven days a week. More and more information is available on the internet, particularly as databases and libraries have started to store electronic versions of journal articles—often exclusively, so that the print subscriptions are no longer maintained. Many universities and colleges are creating apps so that users can login to the university library resources using their smartphones and do research "on the go."

The internet is the provider of a wide range of information sources, with some in formats that are dynamic and interesting. Unlike traditional academic journals and sources, which use straight black-and-white text, the internet is capable of much, much more. Using the internet, authors and other originators of information can be creative in their presentations. Many websites, home pages, and other internet resource pages have useful links that can call up information from related sites or sources with the click of a button. This connects people to more information and provides instant access to cross-referenced material. Links make it easy to embed one source within a network of related sources.

The internet speeds up the flow of information around the globe and has a "democratizing" effect. It provides rapid transmission of information (e.g., text, news, data, and photographs) across long distances and international borders. Instead of waiting a week for a report or having to send a request for a foreign publication and wait a month for it to be delivered, researchers often receive the information in seconds at no cost. In addition, it is possible to email and correspond directly with researchers in your field and to obtain research-related materials directly from the researcher.

The Downside

There is no quality control over what gets put on the internet. People can publish whatever they like on webpages and blogs—there is no guarantee that any of it is factual. Unlike in standard academic publications, there is no peer review process or editorial review. Anyone can put almost anything on a website. It may be poor quality, undocumented, highly biased, totally fabricated, or just plain fraudulent. Once a person finds material, the real work is to distinguish the trash from the valid information. Even the contents of "reputable" sites can be questionable. For example, many students wonder if they can use Wikipedia as a source in their essays, but it is possible for users to change the content of Wikipedia articles. While the site is an interesting resource for a multitude of topics, it should *not* be used as a replacement for library books and journal articles. Wikipedia entries can, however, often point you to legitimate sources, such as journal articles. Cite those when writing a report—never cite Wikipedia! Also, it is easy to copy, modify or distort, then reproduce copies of a source. For example, a person could alter a text passage or a photo image, then create a new webpage to disseminate the false information. This raises issues about copyright protection and the authenticity of source material.

Many excellent sources and some of the most important resource materials (research studies and data) for social research are not available on the internet (e.g., *Sociological Abstracts*, GSS data files, and recent journal articles). Much information is available only through special subscription services, which can be expensive. Contrary to popular belief, the internet has not made all information free and accessible to everyone. Often, what is free is limited, and fuller information is available only to those who pay.

Finding sources on the internet can be very difficult and time consuming. Most search engines simply look for specific words in a short description of the webpage. This description may not reveal the full content of the source, just as a title does not fully tell you what a book or article is about. In addition, search engines often come up with tens of thousands of sources, far too many for anyone to examine. The ones at the "top" may be there because they were recently added to the internet or because their short description had several versions of the search word. The best or most relevant source might be buried as the 150th item found in a search. Also, you must often wade through a lot of commercials and advertisements to locate "real" information.

It is not easy to locate specific source materials. Also, different search engines can produce very different results. Google is the most widely used search engine, but you should also try Google Scholar, which is the equivalent for academic purposes. Once you locate citations of articles that may be useful, however, it will likely be necessary for you to log in to your institution's library resources and locate the journal article through the electronic resources available there; Google Scholar just points you to the right citation—it does not give you access to subscription services.

Internet sources can be unstable and difficult to document. After you conduct a search on the internet and locate webpages with information, it is important to note the specific URL (universal resource locator, or web address). This address refers to an electronic file sitting on a server somewhere. If the

Box 4.6 (*continued*)

file is moved, it may not be at the same address two months later. Unlike a journal article that will be stored on a shelf, on microfiche, or electronically in a database in hundreds of libraries for many decades to come, available for anyone to read, webpages can quickly vanish. This means it may not be possible to check someone's web references easily, verify a quotation in a document, or go back to original materials and read them for ideas or to build on them.

There are few rules for locating the best sites on the internet— ones that have useful and truthful information. Sources that originate at universities, research institutes, or government agencies usually are more trustworthy for research purposes than individual home pages, sites of unspecified origin or location, or sites sponsored by a commercial organization or political/social issue advocacy group. In addition to moving or disappearing, many webpages or sources fail to provide complete information to make citation easy. Better sources provide fuller or more complete information about the author, date, location, and so on.

CHAPTER SUMMARY

✓ Glossary Flashcards

In this chapter, you encountered the groundwork needed to begin a study. We have discussed the steps required to undertake a literature review and made some suggestions to help you organize the masses of information that you will encounter when collecting previous research on your chosen topic. It was explained that a literature review is a necessary step in the research process in order to familiarize yourself with the previous work done on your topic of interest. We have also covered the different formats in which previous research can appear, including journal articles, books, and government documents, and we have discussed the various ways in which these resources can be searched using the resources available from your library. We also explained the various citation styles available and what the different parts of a citation tell you. Different stages of doing the library research for your literature review were also explained, with techniques on how to organize your searches and resulting articles in a manner that allows you to organize your newly amassed information in a systematic manner.

Common newbie pitfalls in writing the literature review were discussed and illustrated, with particular emphasis on failure to synthesize and over-quoting. The purpose of the literature review is to synthesize the research in your topic area. The differences between an annotated bibliography and a literature review were noted as well.

The internet as a source of information has been addressed, and while it does not replace visiting libraries, sources on the internet can point you to important research findings and allow you online access to electronically held journal articles. In the next chapter, we go on to examine issues surrounding the design of both qualitative and quantitative studies.

Review Questions

1. Explain four goals of the literature review in the larger context of a research study.
2. Describe four major steps in the process of conducting a systematic review of the literature.
3. Explain two differences between an annotated bibliography and a literature review.
4. Describe the ways that the internet can assist you with doing research for your literature review.
5. Identify three internet resources that are not suitable for your scholarly review of the literature.

Exercises

1. Think of a topic that interests you. Some ideas are "divorce and child well-being," "ethnic differences in earnings," and "gender differences in academic achievement." Using

EBSCO's ContentSelect, find five journal articles published within the past five years about your topic.

a. Make a list of the citations from the article you found in two of the forms discussed in the chapter (i.e., ASR, APA, and MLA). Write a paragraph on the differences in style.
b. Read each article carefully and write detailed notes. From your rough notes, make a chart or a spreadsheet, noting the similarities and differences in the findings of the articles.
c. Create an annotated bibliography of your set of five articles. Use the examples given in this chapter as a guideline on how this should be done.
d. Create an excerpt from a literature review with these five articles. Be sure to synthesize the findings as well as highlight differences where they exist. Use the example given earlier in this chapter as a guideline on how this should be done.

2. Using Google, search for a topic that may be examined through social research (e.g., crime rates in Canada, single motherhood, same-sex marriage) and look at the first 10 entries that appear from your search. Which—if any—of these would be appropriate for you to cite in a research paper? Provide a rationale for each.
3. Repeat the search from Exercise 2 in Google Scholar. Which of the items from your search results would you be able to use for a research paper? Why?

Chapter 5
Designing a Study

Photo Credit: huaxiadragon/Fotolia LLC

LEARNING OBJECTIVES

After reading this chapter, you will be able to

LO 1 Explain the difference between linear and nonlinear paths.

LO 2 Differentiate between preplanned and emergent research questions.

LO 3 Identify the major differences between qualitative and quantitative research design practices.

LO 4 Explain what a variable is, as well as its attributes.

LO 5 Distinguish between independent, dependent, and intervening variables.

LO 6 Describe the major characteristics of a hypothesis.

LO 7 Differentiate between units and levels of analysis.

LO 8 Explain the five different types of errors of explanation.

INTRODUCTION

In earlier chapters, you learned about the main principles and types of social research, how researchers use theory in a study, the place of ethics in social research, and the process of the literature review. You are now ready to get into the specifics of how to go about designing a study. In this chapter, we will continue to elaborate upon how the qualitative and quantitative approaches to research are different. These differences in orientation result in differences in how such studies are typically designed.

QUALITATIVE AND QUANTITATIVE ORIENTATIONS TOWARD RESEARCH

LO 1 Explain the difference between linear and nonlinear paths.

As highlighted in the previous chapters thus far, qualitative research and quantitative research differ in many ways, but they complement each other as well. All social researchers systematically collect and analyze empirical data and carefully examine the patterns in them to understand and explain social life. One of the differences between the two styles comes from the nature of the data. *Soft data*—in the form of impressions, words, sentences, photos, symbols, and so forth—dictate different research strategies and data collection techniques than *hard data*, which are in the form of numbers. As noted in Chapter 2, another difference is that qualitative and quantitative researchers often hold different assumptions about social life and have different objectives. These differences can make tools used by the other style inappropriate or irrelevant. People who judge qualitative research by standards of quantitative research are often disappointed, and vice versa. It is best to appreciate the strengths each style offers.

Experimental Methods Explained

Qualitative vs. Quantitative Research

To appreciate those strengths, it is important to understand the distinct orientations of researchers. *Qualitative* researchers often rely on interpretive social science, follow a nonlinear research path, and speak a language of "cases and contexts." They emphasize conducting detailed examinations of cases that arise in the natural flow of social life. They usually try to present authentic interpretations that are sensitive to specific social–historical contexts.

Research Methodology

When Can We Use Qualitative Methods?

Almost all *quantitative* researchers rely on a positivist approach to social science. They follow a linear research path, speak a language of "variables and hypotheses," and emphasize precisely measuring variables and testing hypotheses that are linked to general causal explanations.

Researchers who use one style alone do not always communicate well with those using the other, but the languages and orientations of the styles are mutually intelligible. It takes time and effort to understand both styles and to see how they can be complementary.

Linear and Nonlinear Paths

Researchers follow a path when conducting research. The path is a metaphor for the sequence of things to do: what is finished first or where a researcher has been, and what comes next or where he or she is going. The path may be well worn and marked with signposts where many other researchers have trodden. Alternatively, it may be a new path into unknown territory where few others have gone and without signs marking the direction forward. Figure 5.1 illustrates the two general types of paths researchers can follow.

In general, quantitative researchers follow a more linear path than do qualitative researchers. A **linear research path** follows a fixed sequence of steps; it is like a staircase leading in one clear direction. It is a way of thinking and a way of looking at issues—the direct, narrow, straight path that is most common in Western European and North American culture.

linear research path: Research that proceeds in a clear, logical, step-by-step straight line. It is more characteristic of a quantitative than a qualitative approach to social research.

Qualitative research is more nonlinear and cyclical. Rather than moving in a straight line, a **nonlinear research path** makes successive passes through steps, sometimes moving backward and sideways before moving on. It is more of a spiral, moving slowly upward but not directly. With each cycle or repetition, a researcher collects new data and gains new insights.

nonlinear research path: Research that proceeds in a circular, back-and-forth manner. It is more characteristic of a qualitative than a quantitative style to social research.

People who are used to the direct, linear approach may be impatient with a less direct cyclical path. From a strict linear perspective, a cyclical path looks inefficient and sloppy. But the diffuse cyclical approach is not merely disorganized, undefined chaos. It can be highly effective for creating a feeling for the whole, for discerning subtle shades of meaning, for pulling together divergent information, and for switching perspectives. It is not an excuse for doing poor-quality research, and it has its own discipline and rigour. It borrows devices from the humanities (e.g., metaphor, analogy, theme, motif, and irony) and is

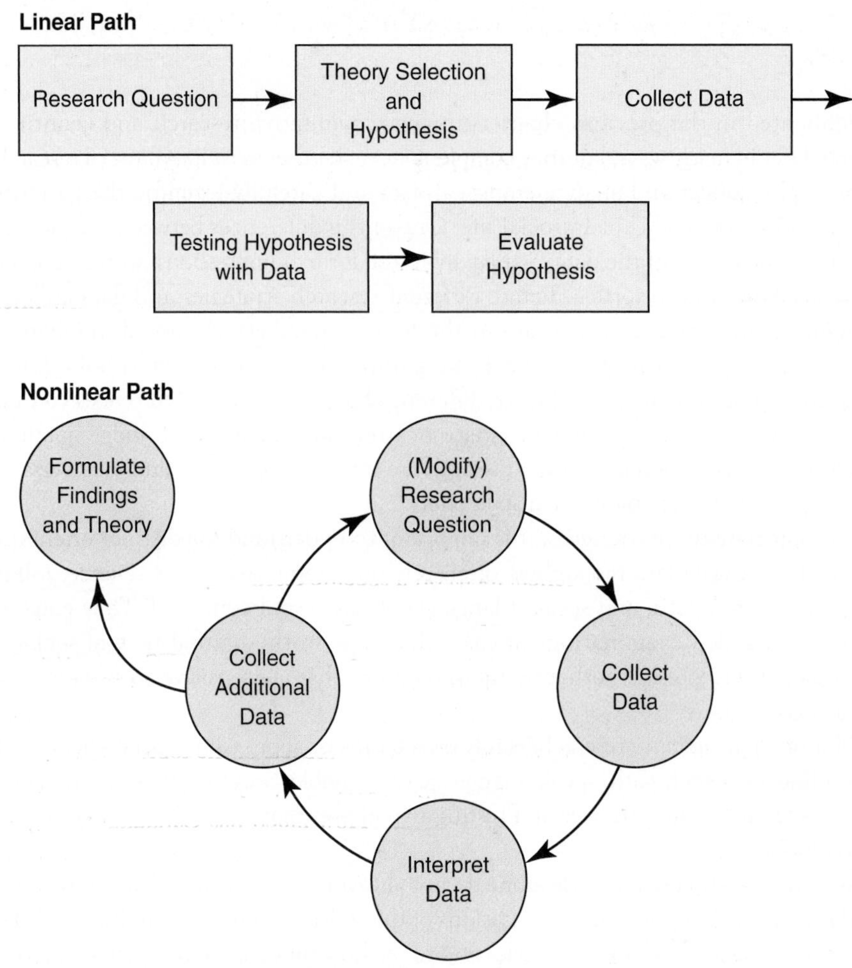

Figure 5.1 Linear and Nonlinear Paths of Conducting Research

oriented toward constructing meaning. A cyclical path is suited for tasks such as translating languages, where delicate shades of meaning, subtle connotations, or contextual distinctions can be important.

LO 2 Differentiate between preplanned and emergent research questions.

Preplanned and Emergent Research Questions

Your first step when beginning a research project is to select a topic. There is no formula for this task. Whether you are an experienced researcher or a novice, the best guide is to conduct research on something that interests you.

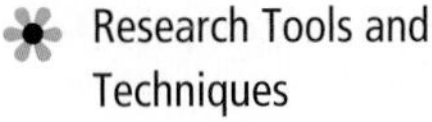

Research Tools and Techniques

Judith Stacey: Qualitative Methods in Research

All research begins with a topic, but a topic is only a starting point that researchers must narrow into a focused research question. Qualitative and quantitative researchers tend to adopt different approaches to this task. Qualitative researchers often begin with very general research questions and the specific topic emerges slowly during the study. The researchers often combine focusing on a specific question with the process of deciding the details of study design that occurs while they are gathering data. By contrast, quantitative researchers narrow a topic into a focused question as a discrete planning step before they finalize the study design. They use it as a step in the process of developing a testable hypothesis (to be discussed later) and to guide the study design before they collect any data.

The qualitative research style is flexible and encourages slowly focusing the topic throughout a study. In contrast to quantitative research, only a small amount of topic narrowing occurs in an early research planning stage, and most of the narrowing occurs after a researcher has begun to collect data.

The qualitative researcher begins data gathering with a general topic and notions of what will be relevant. Focusing and refining continues after he or she has gathered some of the data and started preliminary analysis. Qualitative researchers use early data collection to guide how they adjust and sharpen the research question(s) because they rarely know the most important issues or questions until after they become fully immersed in the data. Developing a focused research question is a part of the data collection process, during which the researcher actively reflects on and develops preliminary interpretations. The qualitative researcher is open to unanticipated data and constantly reevaluates the focus early in a study. He or she is prepared to change the direction of research and follow new lines of evidence.

Typical research questions for qualitative researchers include the following: How did a certain condition or social situation originate? How is the condition/situation maintained over time? What are the processes by which a condition/situation changes, develops, or operates? Another type of question tries to confirm existing beliefs or assumptions. A further type of question tries to discover new ideas.

Research projects are designed around research problems or questions. Before designing a project, quantitative researchers focus on a specific research problem within a broad topic. For example, your personal experience might suggest a study of immigrants. "Immigrants" is a topic, not a research question or a problem. In any large library, you will find hundreds of books and thousands of articles written by sociologists, historians, economists, management officials, political scientists, and others on the subject of immigrants and immigration. The books and articles focus on different aspects of the topic and adopt many perspectives on it. Before proceeding to design a research project, you must narrow and focus the topic. An example research question is, "How much has Canadian immigration policy contributed to racial inequality by creating barriers to skilled jobs for immigrants?"

Data analysis: Crime Study

When starting research on a topic, ask yourself, "What is it about the topic that is of greatest interest?" For a topic about which you know little, first get background knowledge by reading about it. Research questions refer to the relationships among a small number of variables. Identify a limited number of variables and specify the relationships among them.

A research question has one or a small number of causal relationships. Box 5.1 lists some ways to focus a topic into a research question. For example, the question, "What causes divorce?" is not a good research question. A better research question is, "Is age at

Box 5.1 Making It Practical

Narrowing a Topic into a Research Question

- *Examine the literature.* Published, peer reviewed journal articles are an excellent source of ideas for research questions. They are usually at an appropriate level of specificity and suggest research questions that focus on the following:
  a. Replicate a previous research project exactly or with slight variations.
  b. Explore unexpected findings discovered in previous research.
  c. Follow suggestions an author gives for future research at the end of an article.
  d. Extend an existing explanation or theory to a new topic or setting.
  e. Challenge findings or attempt to refute a relationship.
  f. Specify the intervening process and consider linking relations.
- *Talk over your ideas with others.*
  a. Ask people who are knowledgeable about the topic for questions about it that they have thought of.
  b. Seek out those who hold opinions that differ from yours on the topic and discuss possible research questions with them.
- *Apply your topic to a specific context.*
  a. Focus the topic onto a specific historical or other period.
  b. Narrow the topic to a specific society or geographical unit.
  c. Consider which subgroups or categories of people/units are involved and whether there are differences among them.
- *Define the aim or desired outcome of the study.*
  a. Will the research question be for an exploratory, explanatory, or descriptive study?
  b. Will the study involve applied or basic research?

marriage associated with divorce?" The second question suggests two variables: age at marriage and divorce.

When refining a topic into a research question and designing a research project, you also need to consider practical limitations. Designing a perfect research project is an interesting academic exercise, but if you expect to carry it out, practical limitations will have an impact on its design.

Major limitations include time, costs, access to resources, approval by authorities, ethical concerns, and expertise. If you have ten hours a week for five weeks to conduct a research project but the answer to a research question will take five years to discover, reformulate the research question more narrowly. Estimating the amount of time required to answer a research question is difficult. The research question specified, the research technique used, and the type of data collected all play significant roles. Experienced researchers are the best source of good estimates.

Cost is another limitation. As with time, there are inventive ways to answer a question within limitations, but it may be impossible to answer some questions because of the expense involved. For example, a research question about the attitudes of all sports fans toward their team mascot can be answered only with a great investment of time and money. Narrowing the research question to how students at two different schools feel about their team mascots might make it more manageable.

Access to resources is a common limitation. Resources can include the expertise of others, special equipment, or information. For example, a research question about burglary rates and family income in many different nations is almost impossible to answer because information on burglary and income is not collected or available for most countries. Some questions require the approval of authorities (e.g., to see medical records) or involve violating basic ethical principles (e.g., causing serious physical harm to a person to see how the person reacts). The expertise or background of the researcher is also a limitation. Answering some research questions involves the use of data collection techniques, statistical methods, knowledge of a foreign language, or other skills that the researcher may not have. Unless the researcher can acquire the necessary training or can pay for another person's services, the research question may not be practical.

In summary, qualitative and quantitative researchers have much in common, but the researchers often differ on design issues, such as taking a linear or nonlinear research path and developing a research question (see Table 5.1). In addition, researchers tend to adopt a different language and approach to study design, which we will consider next.

Table 5.1 Quantitative Research versus Qualitative Research

Quantitative Research	Qualitative Research
Tests hypothesis that the researcher poses.	Captures and discovers meaning once the researcher becomes immersed in the data.
Concepts are in the form of distinct variables.	Concepts are in the form of themes, motifs, generalizations, and taxonomies.
Measures are systematically created before data collection and are standardized.	Measures are created in an *ad hoc* manner and are often specific to the individual setting or researcher.
Data are in the form of numbers from precise measurement.	Data are in the form of words and images from documents, observations, and transcripts.
Theory is largely causal and is deductive.	Theory can be causal or noncausal and is often inductive.
Procedures are standard, and replication is assumed.	Research procedures are particular, and replication is very rare.

QUALITATIVE DESIGN ISSUES

LO 3 Identify the major differences between qualitative and quantitative research design practices.

The Language of Cases and Contexts

Qualitative researchers use a language of cases and contexts, examine social processes and cases in their social context, and look at interpretations or the creation of meaning in specific settings. They try to look at social life from multiple points of view and explain how people construct identities. Only rarely do they use variables or test hypotheses or try to convert social life into numbers.

Qualitative researchers see most areas and activities of social life as being intrinsically qualitative. To them, qualitative data are not imprecise or deficient—they are highly meaningful. Instead of trying to convert social life into variables or numbers, qualitative researchers borrow ideas from the people they study and place them within the context of a natural setting. They examine motifs, themes, distinctions, and ideas instead of variables, and they often adopt the inductive approach of *grounded theory*.

Some people believe that qualitative data are "soft," intangible, and immaterial; such data are so fuzzy and elusive that researchers cannot really capture them. This is not necessarily the case. Qualitative data are scientific. They involve documenting real events, recording what people say (with words, gestures, and tone), observing specific behaviours, studying written documents, and examining visual images. These are all concrete aspects of the world. For example, some qualitative researchers take and closely scrutinize photos or videotapes of people or social events. This evidence is just as "hard" and physical as that used by quantitative researchers to measure attitudes, social pressure, intelligence, and the like.

Grounded Theory

A qualitative researcher develops theory during the data collection process. This more inductive method means that theory is built from data or grounded in data. Moreover, conceptualization and operationalization occur simultaneously with data collection and preliminary data analysis. This makes qualitative research flexible and allows data and theory to interact. Qualitative researchers remain open to the unexpected, are willing to change the direction or focus of a research project, and may abandon their original research question in the middle of a project.

A qualitative researcher builds theory by making comparisons. For example, when a researcher observes an event (e.g., a police officer confronting a speeding motorist), he or she immediately ponders questions and looks for similarities and differences. When watching a police officer stop a speeder, a qualitative researcher might ask, "Does the police officer always radio in the car's licence plate number before proceeding? After radioing the car's location, does the officer sometimes ask the motorist to get out of the car but at other times casually walk up to the car and talk to the seated driver?" When data collection and theorizing are interspersed, theoretical questions arise that suggest future observations, so new data are tailored to answer theoretical questions that came from thinking about previous data. While grounded theory is a widely used approach in qualitative research, it is not used by all qualitative researchers.

The Context Is Critical

Qualitative researchers emphasize the social context for understanding the social world. They hold that the meaning of a social action or statement depends, in an important way, on the context in which it appears. When a researcher removes an event, social action, answer to a question, or conversation from the social context in which it appears, or ignores the context, social meaning and significance are distorted.

Attention to social context means that a qualitative researcher notes what came before or what surrounds the focus of study. It also implies that the same events or behaviours can have different meanings in different cultures or historical eras. For example, instead of ignoring the context and counting votes across time or cultures, a qualitative researcher asks, "What does voting mean in the context?" He or she may treat the same behaviour (e.g., voting for a prime minister) differently depending on the social context in which it occurs. Qualitative researchers place parts of social life into a larger whole; otherwise, the meaning of the part may be lost.

The Case and the Process

In quantitative research, cases are usually the same as a unit of analysis, or the unit on which variables are measured (discussed later). Quantitative researchers typically measure variables of their hypotheses across many cases. For example, if a researcher conducts a survey of 450 individuals, each individual is a case, or unit, on which the researcher measures variables. Qualitative researchers tend to use a "case-oriented approach [that] places cases, not variables, center stage" (Ragin, 1992, p. 5). They examine a wide variety of aspects of one or a few cases. Their analyses emphasize contingencies in "messy" natural settings (i.e., the co-occurrence of many specific factors and events in one place and time). Explanations or interpretations are complex and may be in the form of an unfolding plot or a narrative story about particular people or specific events. Rich detail and astute insight into the cases replace the sophisticated statistical analysis of precise measures across a huge number of units or cases found in quantitative research.

The passage of time is integral to qualitative research. Qualitative researchers look at the sequence of events and pay attention to what happens first, second, third, and so on. Because qualitative researchers examine the same case or set of cases over time, they can see an issue evolve, a conflict emerge, or a social relationship develop. The researcher can detect process and causal relations.

In historical research, the passage of time may involve years or decades. In field research, the passage of time is shorter. Nevertheless, in both, a researcher notes what is occurring at different points in time and recognizes that *when* something occurs is often important.

Interpretation

The word *interpretation* means assigning significance or a coherent meaning to something. Quantitative and qualitative researchers both interpret data, but they do so in different ways. A quantitative researcher gives meaning by rearranging, examining, and discussing the numbers by using charts and statistics to explain how patterns in the data relate to the research question. A qualitative researcher gives meaning by rearranging, examining, and discussing textual or visual data in a way that conveys an authentic voice, or that remains true to the original people and situations that he or she studied.

Instead of relying on charts, statistics, and displays of numbers, qualitative researchers put a greater emphasis on interpreting the data. Their data are often "richer" or more complex and full of meaning. The qualitative researcher interprets to "translate" or make the originally gathered data understandable to other people.

LO 4 Explain what a variable is, as well as its attributes.

QUANTITATIVE DESIGN ISSUES

The Language of Variables and Hypotheses

variable: A concept or its *empirical* measure that can take on multiple values.

Variation and Variables The variable is a central idea in quantitative research. Simply defined, a **variable** is a concept that varies. Quantitative research uses a language of variables and relationships among variables.

In Chapter 2, you learned about concepts. Concepts are used in qualitative and quantitative research to represent major components of what researchers are interested in studying. In quantitative research, concepts are converted into variables that represent the concepts. Variables take on two or more values—the core of the word *variable* is "vary," so there must be more than one value in a variable. Once you begin to look for them, you will see variables everywhere. Marital status is a variable: It can take on the values of never married, single, cohabiting, married, separated, divorced, or widowed. Type of crime committed is a variable: It can take on the values of robbery, burglary, theft, murder, and so forth. Family income is a variable: It can take on values from zero to billions of dollars. A person's attitude toward abortion is a variable: It can range from strongly favouring legal abortion to strongly condemning abortion.

The values or the categories of a variable are its **attributes**. It is easy to confuse variables with attributes. Variables and attributes are related, but they have distinct purposes. The confusion arises because the attribute of one variable can itself become a separate variable with a slight change in definition. The distinction is between concepts themselves that vary and conditions within concepts that vary. For example, "male" is not a variable; it describes a category of gender and is an attribute of the variable "gender." Yet a related idea, "degree of masculinity," is a variable. It describes the intensity or strength of attachment to attitudes, beliefs, and behaviours associated with the concept of *masculine* within a culture. "Married" is not a variable; it is an attribute of the variable "marital status." Related ideas such as "number of years married" or "depth of commitment to a marriage" are variables. Likewise, "robbery" is not a variable; it is an attribute of the variable "type of crime." "Number of robberies," "robbery rate," "amount taken during a robbery," and "type of robbery" are all variables because they vary or take on a range of values.

attributes: The categories or levels of a *variable.*

Quantitative researchers redefine concepts of interest into the language of variables. As the examples of variables and attributes illustrate, slight changes in definition change a nonvariable concept into a variable concept. As you saw in Chapter 2, concepts are the building blocks of theory; they organize thinking about the social world. Clear concepts with careful definitions are essential in theory.

Types of Variables Researchers who focus on causal relations usually begin with an effect and then search for its causes. Variables are classified into three basic types, depending on their locations in a causal relationship. The cause variable, or the one that identifies forces or conditions that act on something else, is the **independent variable.** Independent variables are often denoted by X (often with subscripts) by quantitative researchers. The variable that is the effect or is the result or outcome of another variable is the **dependent variable** and is often denoted by Y by quantitative researchers. The independent variable is "independent of" prior causes that act on it, whereas the dependent variable "depends on" the cause.

LO 5 Distinguish between independent, dependent, and intervening variables.

independent variable: The first variable that causes or produces the effect in a *causal explanation.*

dependent variable: The effect variable that is last and results from the causal variable(s) in a *causal explanation.* Also the variable that is measured in the *pretest* and *post-test* and that is the result of the *treatment* in *experimental research.*

It is not always easy to determine whether a variable is independent or dependent. Two questions help you identify the independent variable: (1) Does it come before other variables in time? (Independent variables come before any other type.) (2) If the variables occur at the same time, does the author suggest that one variable has an impact on another variable? (Independent variables affect or have an impact on other variables.) Research topics are often phrased in terms of the dependent variables because dependent variables are the phenomenon to be explained. For example, suppose a researcher examines the reasons for an increase in the crime rate in Calgary, Alberta; the dependent variable is the crime rate.

A basic causal relationship requires only an independent and a dependent variable. A third type of variable, the **intervening variable,** appears in more complex causal relations. It comes between the independent and dependent variables and shows the link or mechanism between them. Advances in knowledge depend not only on documenting cause-and-effect

intervening variable: A variable that is between the initial causal variable and the final effect variable in a *causal explanation.*

Basic Causal Relationship

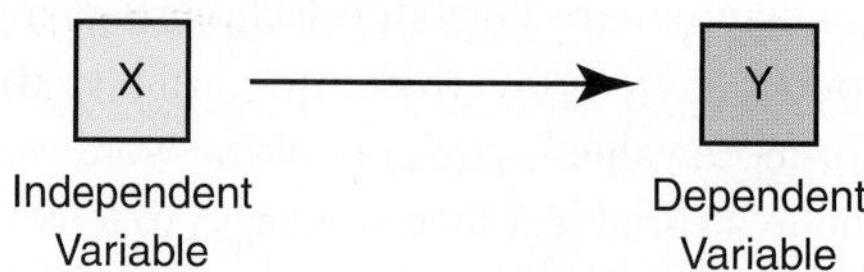

Causal Relationship with an Intervening Variable

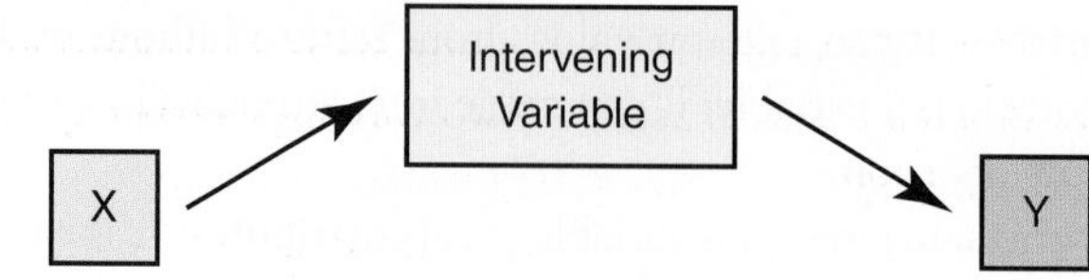

Figure 5.2 Causal Relationships

relationships but also on specifying the mechanisms that account for the causal relation. In a sense, the intervening variable acts as a dependent variable with respect to the independent variable and acts as an independent variable toward the dependent variable. You will see intervening variables also referred to as *mediators*. See Figure 5.2 for illustrations of both basic and more complex causal relations.

For example, French sociologist Émile Durkheim (1951) developed a theory of suicide that specified a causal relationship between marital status and suicide rates. Durkheim found evidence that married people are less likely to commit suicide than are single people. He believed that married people have greater social integration (i.e., feelings of belonging to a group or family). He thought that a major cause of one type of suicide was that people lacked a sense of belonging to a group. Thus, his theory can be restated as a three-variable relationship: marital status (independent variable) causes the degree of social integration (intervening variable), which affects suicide (dependent variable). Specifying the chain of causality makes the linkages in a theory clearer and helps a researcher test complex explanations.

Simple theories have one dependent variable and one independent variable, whereas complex theories can contain dozens of variables with multiple independent, intervening, and dependent variables. For example, a theory of criminal behaviour (dependent variable) identifies four independent variables: an individual's economic hardship, opportunities to commit crime easily, membership in a deviant subgroup of society that does not disapprove of crime, and lack of punishment for criminal acts. A multi-cause explanation usually specifies the independent variable that has the greatest causal effect.

A complex theoretical explanation contains a string of multiple intervening variables that are linked together. For example, family disruption causes lower self-esteem among children, which causes depression, which causes getting poor grades in school, which causes reduced prospects for a good job, which cause a lower adult income. The chain of variables is family disruption (independent), childhood self-esteem (intervening), depression (intervening), grades in school (intervening), job prospects (intervening), adult income (dependent).

Two theories on the same topic may have different independent variables or predict different independent variables to be important. In addition, theories may agree about the independent and dependent variables but differ on the intervening variable or causal mechanism. For example, two theories say that family disruption causes lower adult income, but for different reasons. One theory holds that disruption encourages children to join deviant peer groups that are not socialized to norms of work and thrift. Another emphasizes the impact of the disruption on childhood depression and poor academic performance, which directly affect job performance later in life.

A single research project usually tests only a small part of a causal chain. For example, a research project examining six variables may take the six from a large, complex theory with two dozen variables. Explicit links to a larger theory strengthen and clarify a research project. This applies especially for explanatory basic research, which is the model for most quantitative research.

Causal Theory and Hypotheses

LO 6 Describe the major characteristics of a hypothesis.

hypothesis: The statement from a *causal explanation* or a *proposition* that has at least one *independent* and one *dependent variable,* but it has yet to be empirically tested.

Cause, Effect, and Correlation

The Hypothesis and Causality A **hypothesis** is a proposition to be tested or a tentative statement of a relationship between two variables. Hypotheses are guesses about how the social world works; they are stated in a value-neutral form.

A causal hypothesis has five characteristics (see Box 5.2). The first two characteristics define the minimum elements of a hypothesis. The third restates the hypothesis. For example, the hypothesis that attending religious services reduces the probability of divorce can be restated as a prediction: Couples who attend religious services frequently have a lower divorce rate than do couples who rarely attend religious services. The prediction can be tested against empirical evidence. The fourth characteristic states that the hypothesis should be logically tied to a research question and to a theory. Researchers test hypotheses to answer the research question or to find empirical support for a theory. The last characteristic requires that a researcher use empirical data to test the hypothesis. Statements that are necessarily true as a result of logic or questions that are impossible to answer through empirical observation (e.g., "What is the meaning of life?" "Is there a God?") cannot be scientific hypotheses.

Testing and Refining Hypotheses Knowledge rarely advances on the basis of one test of a single hypothesis. In fact, it is easy to get a distorted picture of the research process by focusing on a single research project that tests one hypothesis. Knowledge develops over time as researchers throughout the scientific community test many hypotheses. Knowledge grows from shifting and winnowing through many hypotheses. Each hypothesis represents an explanation of a dependent variable. If the evidence fails to support some hypotheses, they are gradually eliminated from consideration. Those that receive support remain in contention. Theorists and researchers constantly create new hypotheses to challenge those that have received support.

Scientists are a skeptical group; support for a hypothesis in one research project is not sufficient for them to accept it. The positivist principle of replication says that a hypothesis needs several tests with consistent and repeated support to gain broad acceptance. Another way to strengthen confidence in a hypothesis is to test related causal linkages in the theory from which it comes.

Types of Hypotheses Hypotheses are links in a theoretical causal chain and can take several forms. Researchers use them to test the direction and strength of a relationship between variables. When a hypothesis defeats its competitors or offers alternative explanations

Box 5.2 Focus

Five Characteristics of Causal Hypotheses

1. It has at least two variables.
2. It expresses a causal (cause-and-effect) relationship between the variables.
3. It can be expressed as a prediction or an expected future outcome.
4. It is logically linked to a research question and a theory.
5. It is falsifiable; that is, it is capable of being tested against empirical evidence and shown to be true or false.

for a causal relation, it indirectly lends support to the researcher's explanation. A curious aspect of hypothesis testing is that researchers treat evidence that supports a hypothesis differently from evidence that opposes it. They give negative evidence more importance. The idea that negative evidence is critical when evaluating a hypothesis comes from the *logic of disconfirming hypotheses*.[1] It is associated with Karl Popper's idea of falsification and with the use of null hypotheses (see later in this section).

A hypothesis is never proven, but it can be disproven. A researcher with supporting evidence can say only that the hypothesis remains a possibility or that it is still in the running. Negative evidence is more significant because the hypothesis becomes "tarnished" or "soiled" if the evidence fails to support it. This is because a hypothesis makes predictions. Negative and disconfirming evidence shows that the predictions are wrong. Positive or confirming evidence for a hypothesis is less critical because alternative hypotheses may make the same prediction. A researcher who finds confirming evidence for a prediction may not elevate one explanation over its alternatives.

For example, a man stands on a street corner with an umbrella and claims that his umbrella protects him from falling elephants. His hypothesis that the umbrella provides protection has supporting evidence: He has not had a single elephant fall on him in all the time he has had his umbrella open. Yet such supportive evidence is weak; it also is consistent with an alternative hypothesis—that elephants do not fall from the sky. Both predict that the man will be safe from falling elephants. Negative evidence for the hypothesis—the one elephant that falls on him and his umbrella, crushing both—would destroy the hypothesis for good.

null hypothesis: A *hypothesis* that says there is no relationship or *association* between two variables, or no effect.

alternative hypothesis: A *hypothesis* paired with a *null hypothesis* stating that the *independent variable* has an effect on a *dependent variable.*

Researchers test hypotheses in two ways: a straightforward way and a null hypothesis way. Many quantitative researchers, especially experimenters, frame hypotheses in terms of a **null hypothesis** based on the logic of the disconfirming hypotheses. They test hypotheses by looking for evidence that will allow them to accept or reject the null hypothesis. Most people talk about a hypothesis as a way to predict a relationship. The null hypothesis does the opposite; it predicts no relationship. For example, Sarah believes that students who live on campus in residence get higher grades than do students who live off campus and commute. Her null hypothesis is that there is no relationship between residence and grades. Researchers use the null hypothesis with a corresponding **alternative hypothesis** or experimental hypothesis. The alternative hypothesis says that a relationship exists. Sarah's alternative hypothesis is that living in residence has a positive effect on grades.

For most people, the null hypothesis approach is a backward way of hypothesis testing. Null hypothesis thinking rests on the assumption that researchers try to discover a relationship, so hypothesis testing should be designed to make finding a relationship more demanding. A researcher who uses the null hypothesis approach only directly tests the null hypothesis. If evidence supports or leads the researcher to accept the null hypothesis, he or she concludes that the tested relationship does not exist. This implies that the alternative hypothesis is false. On the other hand, if the researcher can find evidence to reject the null hypothesis, then the alternative hypotheses remain a possibility. The researcher cannot prove the alternative; rather, by testing the null hypotheses, he or she keeps the alternative hypotheses in contention. When null hypothesis testing is added to confirming evidence, the argument for an alternative hypothesis can grow stronger over time.

Many people find the null hypothesis to be confusing. Another way to think of it is that the scientific community is extremely cautious. It prefers to consider a causal relationship to be false until mountains of evidence show it to be true. This is similar to the legal idea—found in countries such as Canada, the United Kingdom, and the United States—of a person being innocent until proven guilty. A researcher assumes, or acts as if, the null hypothesis is correct until *reasonable doubt* suggests otherwise. Researchers who use a null hypothesis generally use it with specific statistical tests (e.g., *t*-test or *F*-test). Thus, a researcher may say there is reasonable doubt in a null hypothesis if a statistical test suggests that the odds of its being false are 99 in 100. This is what a researcher means when he or she says that statistical tests allow him or her to "reject the null hypothesis at the 0.01 level of significance."

Aspects of Explanation

LO 7 Differentiate between units and levels of analysis.

Clarity About Units and Levels of Analysis It is easy to become confused at first about the ideas of units and levels of analysis. Nevertheless, they are important for clearly thinking through and planning a research project. All studies have both units and levels of analysis, but few researchers explicitly identify them as such. The units and levels of analysis are restricted by the topic and the research question.

A **level of analysis** is the level of social reality to which theoretical explanations refer. The level of social reality varies on a continuum from micro-level (e.g., small groups or individual processes) to macro-level (e.g., civilizations or structural aspects of society). The level includes a mix of the number of people, the amount of space, the scope of the activity, and the length of time. For example, an extreme micro-level analysis can involve a few seconds of interaction between two people in the same small room. An extreme macro-level analysis can involve billions of people on several continents across centuries. Most social research uses a level of analysis that lies somewhere between these extremes.

level of analysis: A way to talk about the scope of a *social theory, causal explanation, proposition, hypothesis,* or theoretical statement. The range of phenomena it covers, or to which it applies, goes from social psychological (micro-level) to organizational (meso-level) to large-scale social structure (macro-level).

The level of analysis delimits the kinds of assumptions, concepts, and theories that a researcher uses. For example, if we want to study the topic of dating among university students, we can use a micro-level analysis and develop an explanation that uses concepts such as interpersonal contact, mutual friendships, and common interests. We may think that students are likely to date someone with whom they have had personal contact in a class, share friends in common, and share common interests. The topic and focus fit with a micro-level explanation because they are targeted at the level of face-to-face interaction among individuals. Another example topic is how inequality affects the forms of violent behaviour in a society. Here, we chose a more macro-level explanation because of the topic and the level of social reality at which it operates. We are interested in the degree of inequality (e.g., the distribution of wealth, property, income, and other resources) throughout a society and in patterns of societal violence (e.g., aggression against other societies, sexual assault, feuds between families). The topic and research question suggest macro-level concepts and theories.

The **unit of analysis** refers to the type of unit a researcher uses when measuring. Common units in sociology are the individual, the group (e.g., family, friendship group), the organization (e.g., corporation, university), the social category (e.g., social class, gender, race), the social institution (e.g., religion, education, the family), and the society (e.g., a nation, a tribe). Although the individual is the most commonly used unit of analysis, it is by no means the only one. Different theories emphasize one or another unit of analysis, and different research techniques are associated with specific units of analysis. For example, the individual is usually the unit of analysis in survey and experimental research.

unit of analysis: The kind of empirical case or unit that a researcher observes, measures, and analyzes in a study.

As an example, the individual is the unit of analysis in a survey in which 150 students are asked to rate their favourite professional athlete. The individual is the unit because each individual student's response is recorded. On the other hand, a study that compares the amount of money different universities spend on their athletic programs would use the organization (the university) as the unit of analysis because the spending by universities is being compared and each university's spending is recorded.

Researchers also use units of analysis other than individuals, groups, organizations, social categories, institutions, and societies. For example, a researcher wants to determine whether the speeches of two candidates for leader of the Conservative Party of Canada contain specific themes. The researcher uses content analysis and measures the themes in each speech of the candidates. Here, the speech is the unit of analysis. Geographic units of analysis are also used. A researcher interested in determining whether cities that have a high number of teenagers also have a high rate of vandalism would use the city as the unit of analysis. This is because the researcher measures the percentage of teenagers in each city and the amount of vandalism for each city.

The units of analysis determine how a researcher measures variables or themes. They also correspond loosely to the level of analysis in an explanation. Thus, social–psychological or micro-levels of analysis fit with the individual as a unit of analysis, whereas macro-levels of analysis fit with the social category or institution as a unit. Theories and explanations at the micro-level generally refer to features of individuals or interactions among individuals. Those at the macro-level refer to social forces operating across a society or relations among major parts of a society as a whole.

Researchers use levels and units of analysis to design research projects, and being aware of them helps researchers avoid logical errors. For example, a study that examines whether universities in Western provinces spend more on their student union activities than do universities in Eastern provinces implies that a researcher gathers information on spending by university and the location of each university. The unit of analysis—the organization, or specifically the university—flows from the research problem and tells the researcher to collect data from each university.

Researchers choose among different units or levels of analysis for similar topics or research questions. For example, a researcher could conduct a project on the topic of patriarchy and violence with society as the unit of analysis for the research question "Are patriarchal societies more violent?" He or she would collect data on societies and classify each society by its degree of patriarchy and its level of violence. On the other hand, if the research question was "Is the degree of patriarchy within a family associated with violence against a spouse?" the unit of analysis could be the group or the family, and a more micro-level of analysis would be appropriate. The researcher could collect data on families by measuring the degree of patriarchy within different families and the level of violence between spouses in these families. The same topic can be addressed with different levels and units of analysis, because patriarchy can be a variable that describes an entire society or it can describe social relations within one family. Likewise, violence can be defined as general behaviour across a society or as the interpersonal actions of one spouse toward the other.

LO 8 Explain the five different types of errors of explanation.

ecological fallacy: Something that appears to be a *causal explanation* but is not. It occurs because of a confusion about *units of analysis.* A researcher has *empirical evidence* about an *association* for large-scale units or huge aggregates but *overgeneralizes* to make theoretical statements about an *association* among small-scale units or individuals.

Ecological Fallacy The **ecological fallacy** arises from a mismatch of units of analysis. It refers to a poor fit between the units for which a researcher has empirical evidence and the units about which he or she wants to make statements. It is due to imprecise reasoning and generalizing beyond what the evidence warrants. Ecological fallacy occurs when a researcher gathers data at a *higher* or an *aggregated* unit of analysis but wants to make a statement about a *lower* or *disaggregated* unit. It is a fallacy because what happens in one unit of analysis does not always hold for a different unit of analysis. Thus, if a researcher gathers data for large aggregates (e.g., organizations, entire countries) and then draws conclusions about the behaviour of individuals from those data, he or she is committing the ecological fallacy. You can avoid this error by ensuring that the unit of analysis you use in an explanation is the same as or very close to the unit on which you collect data (see Box 5.3).

Example Tomsville and Joansville each have about 45 000 people living in them. Tomsville has a high percentage of upper-income people. Over half of the households in the town have family incomes of over $200 000. The town also has more motorcycles registered in it than any other town of its size. The town of Joansville has many poor people. Half of its households live below the poverty line. It also has fewer motorcycles registered in it than any other town its size. But it is a *fallacy* to say, on the basis of this information alone, that rich people are more likely to own motorcycles or that the evidence shows a relationship between family income and motorcycle ownership. The reason is that we do

Box 5.3 Concepts in Action

The Ecological Fallacy

Researchers have criticized the famous study *Suicide* ([1897] 1951) by Émile Durkheim for the ecological fallacy of treating group data as though they were individual-level data. In the study, Durkheim compared the suicide rates of Protestant and Catholic districts in 19th-century Western Europe and explained observed differences as being due to differences between people's beliefs and practices in the two religions. He said that Protestants had a higher suicide rate than did Catholics because they were more individualistic and had lower social integration. Durkheim and early researchers only had data by district. Since people tended to reside with others of the same religion, Durkheim used group-level data (i.e., region) for individuals.

Later researchers (van Poppel & Day, 1996) reexamined 19th-century suicide rates using individual-level data that they discovered for some areas. They compared the death records and looked at the official reason of death and at religion, but their results differed from Durkheim's. Apparently, local officials at that time recorded deaths differently for people of different religions. They recorded "unspecified" as a reason for death far more often for Catholics because of a strong moral prohibition against suicide among Catholics. Durkheim's larger theory may be correct, yet the evidence he had to test it was weak because he used data aggregated at the group level while trying to explain the actions of individuals.

not know which families in Tomsville or Joansville own motorcycles. We only know about the two variables—average income and number of motorcycles—for the towns as a whole. The unit of analysis for observing variables is the town as a whole. Perhaps all of the low- and middle-income families in Tomsville belong to a motorcycle club, and not a single upper-income family does. Or perhaps one rich family and five poor ones in Joansville each own motorcycles. In order to make a statement about the relationship between family ownership of motorcycles and family income, we have to collect information on families, not on towns as a whole.

Reductionism Another problem involving mismatched units of analysis and imprecise reasoning about evidence is **reductionism**, also called the *fallacy of nonequivalence* (see Box 5.4). This error occurs when a researcher explains macro-level events but has evidence only about specific individuals. It occurs when a researcher observes a *lower* or *disaggregated* unit of analysis but makes statements about the operations of *higher* or *aggregated* units. It is a mirror image of the mismatch error in the ecological fallacy. A researcher who has data on how individuals behave but makes statements about the dynamics of macro-level units is committing the error of reductionism. It occurs because it is often easier to get data on concrete individuals. Also, the operation of macro-level units is more abstract and nebulous. As with the ecological fallacy, you can avoid this error by ensuring that the unit of analysis in your explanation is very close to the one for which you have evidence.

reductionism: Something that appears to be a *causal explanation* but is not, because of a confusion about *units of analysis*. A researcher has *empirical evidence* for an *association* at the level of individual behaviour or very small-scale units but *overgeneralizes* to make theoretical statements about very large-scale units.

Researchers who fail to think precisely about the units of analysis and those who do not couple data with theory are likely to commit the ecological fallacy or reductionism. They may make mistakes about the data appropriate for a research question, or they may seriously overgeneralize from the data.

You can make assumptions about units of analysis other than the ones you study empirically. Thus, research on individuals rests on assumptions that individuals act within a set of social institutions. Research on social institutions is based on assumptions about individual behaviour. We know that many micro-level units form macro-level units. The danger is that it is easy to slide into using the causes or behaviour of micro units, such as individuals, to explain the actions of macro units, such as social institutions. What happens among units at one level does not necessarily hold for different units of analysis. Sociology is a discipline that rests on the fundamental belief that a distinct level of social reality exists beyond the individual. Explanations of this level require data and theory that go beyond the individual alone. The causes, forces, structures, or processes that exist among macro units cannot be reduced to individual behaviour.

Box 5.4 Concepts in Action

Error of Reductionism

Suppose you pick up a book and read the following:

> Canadian employer–employee relations changed dramatically during the Winnipeg General Strike of 1919. The walkout of approximately 35 000 workers in May of 1919 resulted in greatly improved working conditions for Canadians, which had been previously characterized as dismal and dangerous and marked by an absence of labour regulations. The federal election of 1921 saw a defeat of the Conservative Party, and the newly elected Liberal government introduced extensive labour reforms. This was the result of the vision, dedication, and actions of Canada's pioneering socialist leader, James Shaver Woodsworth.

This says: dependent variable = major change in labour relations after World War I; independent variable = Woodsworth's vision and actions.

If you know much about the labour movement, you see a problem: The labour movement and its successes are attributed to a single individual. Yes, one individual can make a difference and helps build and guide a movement, but the movement is missing. The idea of a social–political movement as a causal force is reduced to its major leader; the distinct social phenomenon—a movement—is obscured. Lost are the actions of thousands of people (marches, imprisonment, speeches, rioting, etc.) involved in advancing a shared goal and the responses to them. The movement's ideology, popular mobilization, politics, organization, and strategy are absent. Related macro-level historical events and trends that may also have influenced the movement (e.g., Canadian soldiers returning from World War I with little prospects, poor working conditions, the Bolshevik Revolution in Russia) are ignored.

This error is not unique to historical explanations. Many people think only in terms of individual actions and have an individualist bias, sometimes called *methodological individualism*. This is especially true in the extremely individualistic North American culture. The error is that it disregards units of analysis or forces beyond the individual. The *error of reductionism* shifts explanation to a much lower unit of analysis. One could continue to reduce from an individual's behaviour, to biological processes in a person, to micro-level neurochemical activities, to the subatomic level.

Most people live in "social worlds" focused on local, immediate settings and their interactions with a small set of others, so their everyday sense of reality encourages seeing social trends or events as individual actions or psychological processes. Often, they become blind to more abstract, macro-level entities—social forces, processes, organizations, institutions, movements, or structures. The idea that all social actions cannot be reduced to individuals alone is the core of sociology. In his classic work *Suicide*, Émile Durkheim was one of the first researchers to fight methodological individualism and demonstrate that that larger, unrecognized social forces explain even highly individual, private actions.

Example Why did World War I occur? You may have heard that it was because a Serbian shot an archduke in the Austro-Hungarian Empire in 1914. This is reductionism. Yes, the assassination was a factor, but the macro-political event between nations—war—cannot be reduced to the specific act of one individual. If it could, we could also say that the war occurred because the assassin's alarm clock worked and woke him up that morning. If it had not worked, there would have been no assassination, so the alarm clock caused the war! The event, World War I, was much more complex and was due to many social, political, and economic forces that came together at a point in history. The actions of specific individuals had a role, but only a minor one compared with these macro forces. Individuals affect events, which eventually, in combination with larger-scale social forces and organizations, affect others and move nations, but individual actions alone are not the cause. Thus, it is likely that a war would have broken out at about that time even if the assassination had not occurred.

Spuriousness As introduced in Chapter 2, part of the process of demonstrating causality requires eliminating alternatives. In other words, researchers must eliminate possible spurious factors that contribute to an apparent causal relationship. To call a relationship between variables *spurious* means that it is false, a mirage. Researchers get excited if they think they have found a spurious relationship because they can show that what appears on the surface is false and a more complex relation exists. Any association between two variables might be spurious, so researchers are cautious when they discover that two variables are associated; upon further investigation, the association may not be the basis for a causal relationship. It may be an illusion, just like the mirage that resembles a pool of water on a road during a hot day.

Spuriousness occurs when two variables are associated but are not causally related because an unseen third factor is the real cause (see Box 5.5 for a special case of spuriousness). The unseen third or other variable is the cause of both the independent and the dependent variable in the apparent but illusionary relationship and accounts for the observed association. In terms of conditions for causality, the unseen factor is a more powerful alternative explanation.

spuriousness: A statement that appears to be a *causal explanation* but is not, because of a hidden, unmeasured, or initially unseen variable. The unseen variable comes earlier in the temporal order, and it has a causal impact on what was initially posited to be the *independent variable* as well as the *dependent variable*.

You now understand that you should be wary of correlations or associations, but how can you tell whether a relationship is spurious, and how do you find out what the mysterious third factor is? You will need to use statistical techniques (discussed later in this book) to test whether an association is spurious. To use them, you need a theory or at least a guess about possible third factors. Actually, spuriousness is based on common sense logic that you already use. For example, you already know that there is an association between the use of air conditioners and ice cream cone consumption. If you measured the number of air conditioners in use and the number of ice cream cones sold for each day, you would find a strong correlation, with more cones sold on the days when more air conditioners are in use. But you know that eating ice cream cones does not cause people to turn on air conditioners. Instead, both variables are caused by a

Correlations Do Not Show Causation

Simpson's paradox: An error in explanation where apparent differences between groups tend to reverse or disappear when groups are combined.

Box 5.5 Concepts in Action

Spuriousness Seen in Sentencing

A special type of spurious relationship is known as **Simpson's paradox**. This refers to the apparent peculiar situation where differences between groups tend to disappear or even reverse when the groups are combined.

For example, Latimer and Foss (2005) found that Aboriginal youth in five Canadian cities, when sentenced to custody under the Young Offenders Act, tended to receive longer sentences than non-Aboriginals. Doob and Sprott (2007) argued that this study failed to factor in important jurisdictional differences—namely, that in two of the cities under consideration (Halifax and Toronto) there were relatively small numbers of Aboriginal cases to analyze compared with the other cities in the sample (Edmonton, Winnipeg, and Vancouver). Latimer and Foss failed to make the distinction among the cities and combined (or "pooled") the data into one large analysis of Aboriginals and non-Aboriginals. This was problematic because cities with very few sentences of Aboriginals were treated in the same way as cities with many more sentences of Aboriginals. Doob and Sprott showed that when different jurisdictions were accounted for there was no difference in the sentencing of Aboriginals and non-Aboriginals, although both groups tended to receive longer sentences in Edmonton and Vancouver.

Using illustrative data, Doob and Sprott showed how the "pooled" data could be deceiving. In the Total (pooled) line, Aboriginals appear to be more likely to receive long sentences (70 percent compared with 45 percent of non-Aboriginals). But when we look across cities (instead of at the pooled totals), we can see that non-Aboriginals are more likely to receive long sentences: 85 percent in City A and 35 percent in City B. This reflects the problem of pooling data and treating the populations across City A and City B as though they were comparable.

Hypothetical Data: Number receiving long sentences/Number sentenced (% receiving long sentences)

	Aboriginal	**Non-Aboriginal**	**Total**
City A	64/80 (80%)	17/20 (85%)	81/100 (81%)
City B	6/20 (30%)	28/80 (35%)	34/100 (34%)
Total (pooled)	70/100 (70%)	45/100 (45%)	115/200 (57.5%)

Source: Doob, A. N., & Sprott, J. B. (2007). The sentencing of Aboriginal and non-Aboriginal youth: Understanding local variation. *Canadian Journal of Criminology and Criminal Justice, 49*(1), 109–123. Reprinted with permission from University of Toronto Press (www.utpjournals.com)

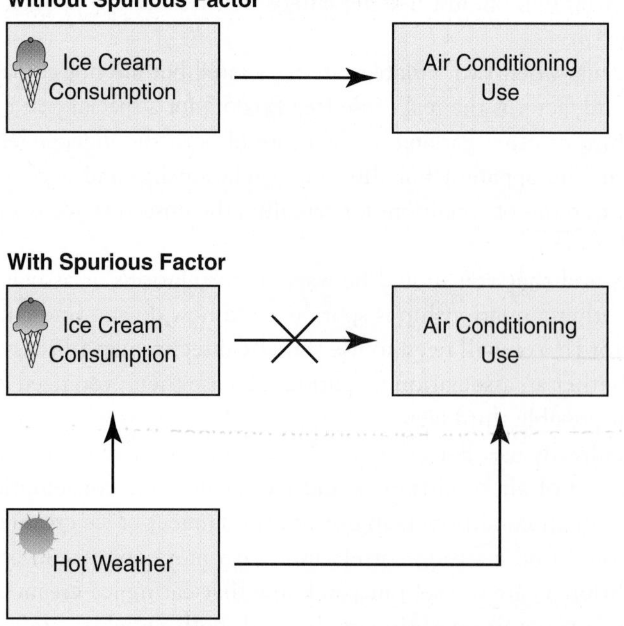

Figure 5.3 Illustration of a Spurious Relationship

third factor: hot days (see Figure 5.3). You could verify the same thing through statistics by measuring the daily temperature as well as ice cream consumption and air conditioner use. In social research, opposing theories help people figure out which third factors are relevant for many topics (e.g., the causes of crime or the reasons for war or child abuse).

Example 1 Some people argue that taking illegal drugs causes suicide, school dropouts, and violent acts. Advocates of the "drugs are the problem" position point to the positive correlations between taking drugs and being suicidal, dropping out of school, and engaging in violence. They argue that ending drug use will greatly reduce suicide, dropouts, and violence. Others argue that many people turn to drugs because of their emotional problems or high levels of disorder of their communities (e.g., high unemployment, unstable families, high crime, few community services, lack of civility). The people with emotional problems or who live in disordered communities are also more likely to commit suicide, drop out, and engage in violence. This means that reducing emotional problems and community disorder will cause illegal drug use, dropping out, suicide, and violence all to decline greatly. Reducing drug use alone will have only a limited effect because it ignores the root causes. The "drugs are the problem" argument is spurious because the initial relationship between taking illegal drugs and the problems is misleading. The emotional problems and community disorder are the true and often unseen causal variables.

Example 2 In the United States and Canada, we observe an empirical association between students being classified in a non-White racial category and scoring lower on academic tests (compared with students classified in a White category). The relationship between racial classification and test scores is illusionary because a powerful and little-recognized variable is the true cause of both the racial classification and the test scores (see Figure 5.4). In this case, the true cause operates directly on the independent variable (racial classification) but indirectly through an intervening process on the dependent variable (test scores). A belief system that is based on classifying people as belonging to racial groups and assigning great significance to

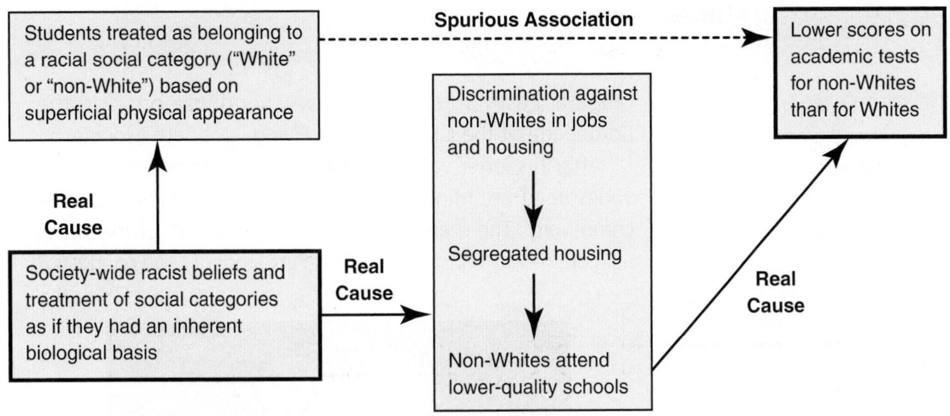

Figure 5.4 Example of a Spurious Relationship between Belonging to a Non-White "Race" and Getting Low Academic Test Scores

superficial physical appearance, such as skin colour, is the basis of what people call "race," which can often better be thought of instead as a "cultural category."[2] Such a belief system also is the basis for prejudice and discriminatory behaviour. In such a situation, people are seen as belonging to different races and are treated differently because of it, such as having different job opportunities and housing choices. People in some racial categories who are discriminated against find limitations in their housing choices. This means they get separated or grouped together in undesirable areas based on their skin colour. Poor housing gets combined with unequal schooling, such that the lowest-quality schools are located in areas with the least desirable housing. Since the relationship between school quality and test scores is very strong, students from families living in less desirable housing areas with low-quality schools get lower test scores.

Tautology and Teleology The next two errors in explanation are not unique to social research, but nonetheless are important to avoid when making any type of argument. **Tautology** refers to circular reasoning and can often be detected when the first half of a sentence appears to be a rephrasing of the second half of the sentence. For example, the statement, "People are poor because they have little money" initially seems like a cause-and-effect argument with the cause being "poverty" and the outcome being "no money." But obviously, these two things—being poor and having little money—are the same thing.

tautology: An error in explanation that rests on circular reasoning.

Photo Credit: xkcd.com

Teleology refers to an argument that explains the cause–effect relationship as one that fulfills a function or ultimate purpose. Many times, functionalist arguments may fall into this category, particularly if the explanation for the existence of a social phenomenon rests

teleology: An error in explanation that relies on the fulfillment of an ultimate purpose.

Box 5.6 In the News

Pastafarians versus Intelligent Design

In recent years, various interest groups have urged schools to teach intelligent design theory alongside evolution theory in North American classrooms. Intelligent design theory has its fundamental roots in creationism but is somewhat distinctive in that it provides what its proponents regard as evidence for a divine intelligence being the cause of the existence of the universe, arguing that the complexity of the universe points to the necessity of its having been crafted by a deliberate designer.

In 2005, the Kansas State Department of Education legislated that intelligent design theory be taught alongside and with equal weighting to evolution theory, which sparked the outrage of Bobby Henderson.

His response was to write an open letter to the education board, proposing evidence of a religion that parodied the major arguments of intelligent design, but whose creator was a deity who resembled spaghetti and meatballs. He named this the Church of the Flying Spaghetti Monster. He called for this religion to be taught in the classroom alongside intelligent design theory. He further argued that since intelligent design theory gave only ambiguous references to the identity of the intelligent designer, it was conceivable that a multitude of entities could fulfill this role, including the Flying Spaghetti Monster. He named the followers of this religion Pastafarians. (See www.venganza.org for the homepage of the Church of the Flying Spaghetti Monster.)

After his letter was published on the internet, it received widespread attention and much support from the scientific community. There are thousands of "followers" of this mock religion, mostly consisting of university students and scientists.[3]

Photo Credit: Ivan Nikulin/Shutterstock

solely on the argument that it fulfills some purpose (e.g., "Religion exists because it fulfills a purpose in society."). See Box 5.6 for a response by scientists to the teleological groundings of intelligent design.

Table 5.2 provides a review of the major errors in causal explanation. We can now turn from errors to other issues involving hypotheses.

Table 5.2 Summary of Errors in Explanation

Type of Error	Short Definition	Example
Ecological Fallacy	The empirical observations are at too high a level for the causal relationship that is stated.	Toronto has a high crime rate. Joan lives in Toronto. Therefore, she probably stole my watch.
Reductionism	The empirical observations are at too low a level for the causal relationship that is stated.	Because Steven lost his job and did not buy a new car, the country entered a long economic recession.
Spuriousness	An unseen third variable is the actual cause of both the independent and dependent variables.	Hair length is associated with TV programs. People with short hair prefer watching football; people with long hair prefer romance stories. (*Unseen:* Gender)
Tautology	Circular reasoning where the second part of a statement is rephrased to repeat the first.	Obesity is the result of being overweight.
Teleology	A cause is described as fulfilling some kind of ultimate purpose.	Women get paid less than men are because that is the way it is supposed to be.

Box 5.7 Making It Practical

Examples of Bad and Good Research Questions

Bad Research Questions

Not Empirically Testable, Nonscientific Questions

- Should abortion be legal?
- Is it right to have capital punishment?

General Topics, Not Research Questions

- Treatment of alcohol and drug abuse
- Sexuality and aging

Set of Variables, Not Questions

- Capital punishment and racial discrimination
- Urban decay and gangs

Too Vague, Ambiguous

- Do the police affect delinquency?
- What can be done to prevent child abuse?

Need to Be Still More Specific

- Has the incidence of child abuse risen?
- How does poverty affect children?
- What problems do children who grow up in poverty experience that others do not?

Good Research Questions

Exploratory Questions

- Has the actual incidence of child abuse changed in Nova Scotia in the past 10 years?

Descriptive Questions

- Is child abuse, violent or sexual, more common in families that have experienced a divorce than in intact, never-divorced families?
- Are the children raised in poor households more likely to have medical, learning, and social–emotional adjustment difficulties than children who are not poor?

Explanatory Questions

- Does the emotional instability created by experiencing a divorce increase the chances that divorced parents will physically abuse their children?
- Is a lack of sufficient funds for preventive treatment a major cause of more serious medical problems among children raised in families in poverty?

From the Research Question to Hypotheses

It is difficult to move from a broad topic to hypotheses, but the leap from a well-formulated research question to hypotheses is a short one. Hints about hypotheses are embedded within a good research question. In addition, hypotheses are tentative answers to research questions (see Box 5.7).

Consider an example research question: "Is age at marriage associated with divorce?" The question contains two variables: "age at marriage" and "divorce." To develop a hypothesis, a researcher asks, "Which is the independent variable?" The independent variable is "age at marriage" because marriage must logically precede divorce. The researcher also asks, "What is the direction of the relationship?" The hypothesis could be, "The lower the age at the time of marriage, the greater are the chances that the marriage will end in divorce." This hypothesis answers the research question and makes a prediction. Note that the research question can be reformulated and better focused now: "Are couples who marry younger more likely to divorce?"

Several hypotheses can be developed for one research question. Another hypothesis from the same research question is, "The smaller the difference between the ages of the marriage partners at the time of marriage, the less likely it is that the marriage will end in divorce." In this case, the variable "age at marriage" is specified differently.

Glossary Flashcards

Hypotheses can specify that a relationship holds under some conditions but not others. For example, a hypothesis states, "The lower the age of the partners at time of marriage, the greater are the chances that the marriage will end in divorce, unless it is a marriage between members of a tightly knit traditional religious community in which early marriage is the norm."

Formulating a research question and a hypothesis does not have to proceed in fixed stages. A researcher can formulate a tentative research question and then develop possible hypotheses; the hypotheses then help the researcher state the research question more precisely. The process is interactive and involves creativity.

You may be wondering, "Where does theory fit into the process of moving from a topic to a hypothesis I can test?" Recall from Chapter 2 that theory takes many forms. Researchers use general theoretical issues as a source of topics. Theories provide concepts that researchers turn into variables as well as the reasoning or mechanism that helps researchers connect variables to form a research question. A hypothesis can both answer a research question and be an untested proposition from a theory. Researchers can express a hypothesis at an abstract, conceptual level or restate it in a more concrete, measurable form.

CHAPTER SUMMARY

In this chapter, you encountered the groundwork needed to begin designing a study. You saw how differences in the qualitative and quantitative styles or approaches to social research direct a researcher to prepare for a study differently. All social researchers narrow their topic into a more specific, focused research question. The styles of research suggest a different form and sequence of decisions, and different answers to when and how to focus the research. The style that a researcher uses will depend on the topic he or she selects, the researcher's purpose and intended use of study results, the orientation toward social science that he or she adopts, and the individual researcher's own assumptions and beliefs.

Quantitative researchers take a linear path and emphasize objectivity. They are more likely to use explicit, standardized procedures and a causal explanation. Their language of variables and hypotheses is found across many other areas of science. The process is often deductive with a sequence of discrete steps that precede data collection: Narrow the topic to a more focused question, transform nebulous theoretical concepts into more exact variables, and develop one or more hypotheses to test. In actual practice, researchers move back and forth, but the general process flows in a single, linear direction. In addition, quantitative researchers take special care to avoid logical errors in hypothesis development and causal explanation.

Qualitative researchers follow a nonlinear path and emphasize becoming intimate with the details of a natural setting or a particular cultural–historical context. They use fewer standardized procedures or explicit steps and often devise on-the-spot techniques for one situation or study. Their language of cases and contexts directs them to conduct detailed investigations of particular cases or processes in their search for authenticity. They rarely separate planning and design decisions into a distinct pre–data collection stage, but continue to develop the study design throughout early data collection. In fact, the more inductive qualitative style encourages a slow, flexible evolution toward a specific focus based on a researcher's ongoing learning from the data. Grounded theory emerges from the researcher's continuous reflections on the data.

The quantitative language of variables and hypotheses was also explored, with discussion of variables and their attributes. The role of variables in demonstrating causality was described, as was the use of intervening variables in more complex causal models. Variables are important components of hypothesis testing. The null and alternative hypotheses were identified as the two major aspects of positivist hypothesis testing.

Next, the difference between level of analysis and unit of analysis was explained, with the former being much more closely tied to the "level" of theory to which the research corresponded and the latter being closely tied to the actual individual "things" that the researcher was soliciting information from (e.g. individuals, organizations, cities).

Errors in explanation can be a result of mismatching units of analysis within a study, which is the case of the errors called the ecological fallacy and reductionism. In the former, individuals make observations at an aggregated unit of analysis and then erroneously make assumptions at an individual level of analysis. In the case of reductionism, the error occurs in the opposite manner: Observations about an individual are used to make assumptions about larger aggregates, like society. Spuriousness is also an error of explanation that fails to consider additional causal factors that may eliminate perceived associations between two variables. Tautology and teleology were also considered as additional errors in explanation that were not necessarily empirically based, but still major mistakes in logic nonetheless.

Review Questions

Chapter Quiz

1. What is meant by a linear path and a nonlinear path? Which path is characteristic of quantitative research and which is characteristic of qualitative research?
2. Identify five major differences between qualitative and quantitative research design practices.
3. What is a variable? What is meant by a variable's attributes?
4. Define and give examples of independent, dependent, and intervening variables.
5. List the five major characteristics of a hypothesis.
6. What is meant by level of analysis? What is meant by unit of analysis?
7. Name and define the five different types of errors of explanation.

Exercises

Using EBSCO's ContentSelect, find three quantitative sociology articles and three qualitative sociology articles published within the past five years on the topics of your choice.

Research Activity

1. For the quantitative articles, fill in a chart that has the following information for each of the articles (an example is provided to help get you started):

	Article 1	**Article 2**	**Article 3**
Citation and Title (APA format style)	Cooke, M. (2009). A welfare trap? The duration and dynamics of social assistance use among lone mothers in Canada. *Canadian Review of Sociology, 46*(3), 179–206.		
Methodological Technique	Secondary data analysis		
Topic	Duration of social assistance use among single mothers		
Research Question	What factors contribute to the duration of social assistance use among single mothers?		
Main Hypothesis Tested	Previous marital history will impact social assistance use.		
Main Independent Variable(s)	Previous marital status of single mother		
Main Dependent Variable(s)	Social assistance use		
Unit of Analysis	Individuals		
Specific Units in the Study	Single mothers		

2. For the qualitative articles, fill in a chart that has the following information for each of the articles:

	Article 1	Article 2	Article 3
Study Citation (APA format style)	Funk, L. (2010). Prioritizing parental autonomy: Adult children's accounts of feeling responsible and supporting aging parents. *Journal of Aging Studies, 24*(1), 57–64.		
Methodological Technique	Qualitative interviews		
Topic	Feelings of responsibility that adult children have around the care of their aging parents		
Research Question	How do adult children negotiate the care needs of their aging parents?		
Grounded Theory	Adult children must balance responsibility and parental autonomy in making decisions about their parents' care needs.		
Social Process	Caregivers are constrained by their own resources and social supports, which they must negotiate in tandem with feelings of obligation, guilt, and helplessness.		
Social Context or Field Site	Canadian adults with aging parents who have care requirements.		

3. How do your two research articles (either qualitative or quantitative) deal with potential errors in explanation? Explain how the authors address such potential problems. Are there any potential errors in explanation that they may have overlooked? Discuss.

Chapter 6
Qualitative and Quantitative Measurement

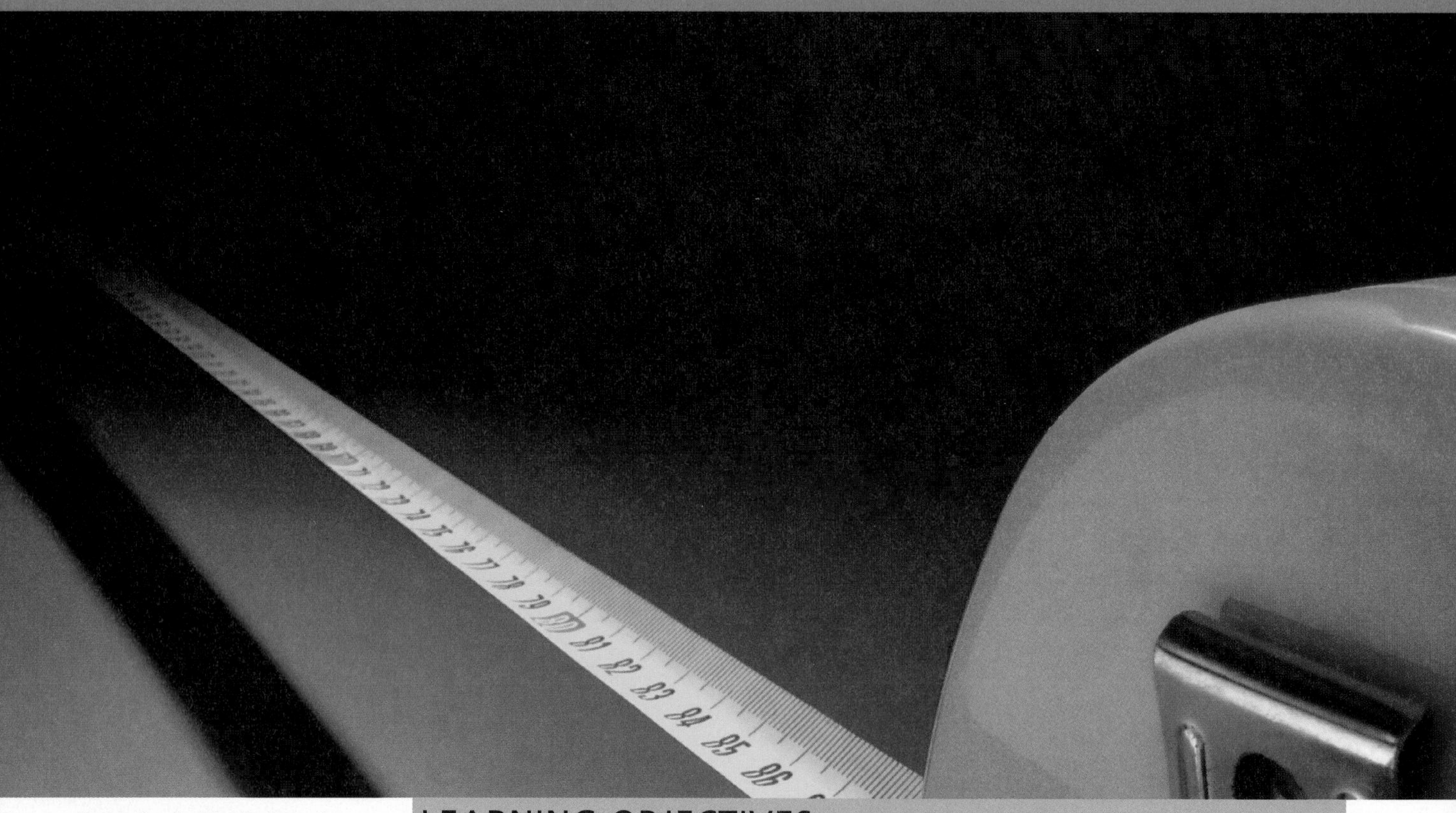

Photo Credit: Martin Green/ Fotolia/LLC

LEARNING OBJECTIVES

After reading this chapter, you will be able to

LO 1 Define conceptualization and operationalization.

LO 2 Demonstrate how to work through the process of abstract concept to a concrete measure.

LO 3 Explain how conceptualization and operationalization are different in qualitative and quantitative work.

LO 4 Define reliability and validity.

LO 5 Explain the ways that reliability can be improved.

LO 6 Identify the four major ways of establishing measurement validity.

LO 7 Explain how reliability and validity are approached in qualitative research.

LO 8 Define and give examples of the four levels of measurement.

LO 9 Differentiate between the different ways of creating scales and indices.

INTRODUCTION

You have probably heard of various "indicators" of social phenomena discussed in the news or the classroom, such as the unemployment rate or the poverty line (or low income cut-off, as it is commonly referred to in Canada). When social researchers test a hypothesis, evaluate an explanation, provide empirical support for a theory, or systematically study an applied issue or some area of the social world, they measure concepts and variables.

Recall from Chapter 2 that a *concept* refers to an idea expressed as a symbol or in words. Unemployment rates and poverty indicators are ways of measuring specific concepts of interest. How social researchers measure the numerous concepts of interest to social research—such as poverty, unemployment, crime, intelligence, self-esteem, political power, alienation, or racial prejudice—is the focus of this chapter.

Previous chapters have outlined the fundamental differences between the approaches of qualitative and quantitative research. These differences also extend to issues of measurement. It should come as no surprise that quantitative researchers are far more concerned about details around measurement issues than qualitative researchers. Quantitative researchers treat measurement as a distinct step in the research process that occurs prior to data collection and have developed special terminology and techniques for it. Using a deductive approach, they begin with a concept and then create empirical measures that precisely and accurately capture the concept in a form that can be expressed numerically.

Using Multiple Data Sets

Qualitative researchers approach measurement very differently. They develop ways to capture and express variable and nonvariable concepts using various alternatives to numbers. They often take an inductive approach, so they measure features of social life as part of a process that integrates creating new concepts or theories with measurement.

Judith Stacey: Qualitative Methods in Research

How people conceptualize and operationalize variables can significantly affect social issues beyond concerns of research methodology. For example, psychologists debate the meaning and measurement of intelligence. Most intelligence tests that people use in schools and on job applications measure only analytical reasoning (i.e., one's capacity to think abstractly and to infer logically). Yet, many argue that there are other types of intelligence in addition to analytical intelligence. Some say that there is practical and creative intelligence. Others suggest more types, such as social–interpersonal, emotional, body–kinesthetic, musical, or spatial. If people narrowly limit measurement to one type even though there are many forms of intelligence, it seriously restricts how schools identify and nurture learning; how larger society evaluates, promotes, and recognizes the contributions of people; and how a society values diverse human abilities.

Likewise, different policymakers and researchers conceptualize and thus measure poverty differently. How poverty is measured will determine whether people get assistance from numerous social programs (e.g., subsidized housing, health care, child care). For example, some say that people are poor only if they cannot afford the food required to prevent malnutrition. Others say that people are poor if they have an annual income that is less than one-half of the average (median) income. Still others say that people are poor if they earn below a "living wage" based on a judgment about the income needed to meet minimal community standards of health, safety, and decency in hygiene, housing, clothing, diet, transportation, and so forth. Statistics Canada assesses poverty by using a "low income cut-off" (LICO), which is a complicated measure that is based on family size and geographic location. A person or family is said to be in poverty if their family income is below the LICO for their family size and geographic location.[1] Decisions about how to conceptualize and measure a variable—poverty—can greatly influence the daily living conditions of millions of people.

WHY MEASURE?

We use many different measures in our daily lives. For example, you might have recently used a bathroom scale to find out how well your new workout regimen or celebrity diet is shaping up. You might check a thermometer to decide how warmly to dress. If you drive a car, you will be aware of the gas gauge to make sure you have enough fuel to get to where you want to go. And while you are driving, you will be mindful of the speedometer to make sure you do not get a ticket. It is possible that before 9:00 a.m. you may have already measured weight, temperature, gasoline volume, and speed—all measures about the physical world. Such precise, well-developed measures are fundamental in the natural sciences.

We also measure the nonphysical world in everyday life, but usually in less exact terms. We are measuring when we say that a restaurant is excellent, that Alain is really smart, that Eloise has a negative attitude toward life, that Johnson is really prejudiced, or that the movie last night had a lot of violence in it. However, such everyday judgments as "really prejudiced" or "a lot of violence" are imprecise.

Measurement also extends our senses. The astronomer or biologist uses the telescope or the microscope to extend natural vision. In contrast to our senses, scientific measurement is more sensitive, varies less with the specific observer, and yields more exact information. You recognize that a thermometer gives more specific, precise information about temperature than touch can. Likewise, a good bathroom scale gives you more specific, constant, and precise information about the weight of a five-year-old girl than you get by lifting her and calling her "heavy" or "light." Social measures provide information about social reality.

In addition, measurement helps people observe what is otherwise invisible. It lets us observe things that were once unseen and unknown but were predicted by theory.

Before you can measure, you need a clear idea about what you are interested in. For example, you cannot see or feel magnetism with your natural senses. Magnetism comes from a theory about the physical world. You observe its effects indirectly; for instance, metal flecks move near a magnet. The magnet allows you to "see" or measure the magnetic fields. Natural scientists have invented thousands of measures to "see" very tiny things (molecules or insect organs) or very large things (huge geological land masses or planets) that are not observable through ordinary senses. In addition, researchers are constantly creating new measures.

Some of the things a social researcher is interested in measuring are easy to see (e.g., age, sex, skin colour), but most cannot be directly observed (e.g., attitudes, ideology, divorce rates, deviance, sex roles). Even things that are "easy to see" are open to interpretation, however. What one researcher sees as "old," another might see as "elderly," and another might see as "middle-aged." What if someone is prematurely grey? Another example is the "easy to see" characteristic of skin colour. One person might see someone as being "Black," but would this person be "Afro-Caribbean" to someone else, or "West Indian" to another person?

Like the natural scientist who invents indirect measures of the "invisible" objects and forces of the physical world, the social researcher devises measures for difficult-to-observe aspects of the social world. In Box 6.1 we discuss a particular instance of trying to get a precise measure of a sociological concept—social class.

LO 1 Define conceptualization and operationalization.

LO 2 Demonstrate how to work through the process of abstract concept to a concrete measure.

QUANTITATIVE AND QUALITATIVE MEASUREMENT

Both qualitative and quantitative researchers use careful, systematic methods to gather high-quality data. Yet differences in the styles of research and the types of data mean that they approach the measurement process differently. Designing precise ways to measure

Box 6.1 Focus

Precise Measurement of Fuzzy Concepts? Measuring Social Class

If you ask a Canadian what class he or she comes from, most likely the response will be "middle." Class membership is not as much of an identity characteristic in Canada as it is in other countries, like the United Kingdom.[2] Sociologically speaking, however, social background has been shown to affect a variety of life outcomes, like educational attainment, family size, and occupation. Our socio-economic origins, or our class, is therefore a significant predictor of what sociologists call "life chances," or our prospects in the social and economic world. As such, the concept of class has been an important one in social science research.

But how do we measure class? What does the concept of class entail? Class is just one of the many "fuzzy concepts" that social scientists try to measure as precisely as possible. If you think about how you would measure the concept of social class, you might think that income would be a good way of measuring it, or perhaps occupation. But there are problems with these operationalizations. Income, for example, does not include people who do not have a wage, such as students or those who work within the home. Does this mean that they have no social class? Or does it mean they have the lowest social class, even if the student's parents are very wealthy or the homemaker is married to a millionaire?

These problems have no easy answer and have actually resulted in a variety of competing operationalizations within social science, each of which has its own strengths and weaknesses. Canadian sociologists have contributed to this debate with their own measurement techniques. The Pineo-Porter scale and the Blishen scale are two operationalizations of social class that are widely used in Canada.

The Pineo–Porter scale (Pineo & Porter, 1967) is an occupational prestige scale. Occupational prestige is based on the assumption that there are certain social standings attributed to various occupations. In order to derive an occupational prestige scale, data are gathered on what individuals think about the social standing of certain occupations—so they are given a list of occupations and asked to rank their social standing. The Blishen scale (Blishen, 1967), in contrast, is a socio-economic index of occupations that takes occupation, education, and earnings into account in its operationalization. In addition to these established measures, other researchers prefer to use parents' education to operationalize the idea of social origins. Clearly, there is no perfect way to operationalize this difficult concept.

But social class is not the only concept that is difficult to measure. Think about the range of topics that social scientists are interested in—such as happiness, job satisfaction, or social attitudes. There are no objectively correct ways to operationalize these and the many concepts that we might be interested in studying. It is important, however, to recognize that no measure will be ideal and that we need to critically evaluate the decisions that we (and others) make in this regard.

variables is a vital step in planning a study for quantitative researchers. Qualitative researchers use a wider variety of techniques to measure. The two approaches to measurement have three distinctions.

Qualitative vs. Quantitative Research

One difference between the two styles involves timing. Quantitative researchers think about variables and convert them into specific actions during a planning stage that occurs before and is separate from gathering or analyzing data. Measurement for qualitative researchers occurs during the data collection process.

A second difference involves the data themselves. Quantitative researchers develop techniques that can produce quantitative data (i.e., data in the form of numbers). Thus, the researcher moves from abstract ideas to specific data collection techniques to precise numerical information produced by the techniques. The numerical information is an empirical representation of the abstract ideas. Data for qualitative researchers sometimes are in the form of numbers; more often, they include written or spoken words, actions, sounds, symbols, physical objects, or visual images (e.g., maps, photographs, videos). The qualitative researcher does not convert all observation into a single medium such as numbers. Instead, he or she develops many flexible, ongoing processes to measure the data that leave them in various shapes, sizes, and forms.

All researchers combine ideas and data to analyze the social world. In both research styles, data are empirical representations of concepts, and measurement links data to concepts. A third difference is how the two styles make such linkages. Quantitative researchers contemplate and reflect on concepts before they gather any data. They construct measurement techniques that bridge concepts and data. Qualitative researchers also reflect on ideas

Table 6.1 Key Differences between Quantitative and Qualitative Measurement

Issue	Quantitative	Qualitative
Timing	Occurs before data are collected	Occurs during data collection
Nature of data	Data and measurements are numeric	Data and measurements are more abstract
Linkage of data to concepts	Quantitative measurement bridges concepts and data	Ways of measuring concepts developed in the process of data collection in response to what they encounter

before data collection, but they develop many, if not most, of their concepts during data collection. The qualitative researcher reexamines and reflects on the data and concepts simultaneously and interactively. Researchers start gathering data and creating ways to measure those data based on what they encounter. As they gather data, they reflect on the process and develop new ideas. The main differences between the quantitative and qualitative approaches to measurement are summarized in Table 6.1.

PARTS OF THE MEASUREMENT PROCESS

When a researcher measures, he or she takes a concept and develops a measure (i.e., a technique, a process, a procedure) by which he or she can observe the idea empirically. As discussed earlier, quantitative researchers primarily follow a deductive route. They begin with the abstract idea, follow with a measurement procedure, and end with empirical data that represent the ideas. Qualitative researchers primarily follow an inductive route. They begin with empirical data, follow with abstract ideas, relate ideas and data, and end with a mixture of ideas and data. In reality, the process is more interactive in both styles of research. As a quantitative researcher develops measures, the constructs become refined and clearer, and as the researcher applies the measures to gather data, he or she often adjusts the measurement technique. As a qualitative researcher gathers data, he or she uses some pre-existing ideas to assist in data collection and will then mix old and new ideas that are developed from the data.

conceptualization: The process of developing clear, rigorous, systematic *conceptual definitions* for abstract ideas or concepts.

conceptual definition: A careful, systematic definition of a construct that is explicitly written to clarify one's thinking. It is often linked to other concepts or theoretical statements.

Both qualitative and quantitative researchers use two processes: conceptualization and operationalization in measurement. **Conceptualization** is the process of taking a concept and refining it by giving it a conceptual or theoretical definition. A **conceptual definition** is a definition in abstract, theoretical terms. There is no magical way to turn a construct into a precise conceptual definition. It involves thinking carefully, observing directly, consulting with others, reading what others have said, and trying possible definitions.

How might you develop a conceptual definition of the construct *prejudice*? When beginning to develop a conceptual definition, researchers often rely on multiple sources—personal experience and deep thinking, discussions with other people, and the existing scholarly literature. You might reflect on what you know about prejudice, ask others what they think about it, and go to the library and look up its many definitions. As you gather definitions, the core idea should get clearer, but you have many definitions and need to sort them out. Most definitions state that prejudice is an attitude about another group and involves a prejudgment, or judging prior to getting specific information.

As you think about the concept, note that all the definitions refer to prejudice as an attitude, and usually it is an attitude about the members of another group. There are many forms of prejudice, but most are negative views about people of a different racial–ethnic group. Prejudice could be about other kinds of groups (e.g., people of a particular religion, of a different physical stature, or from a certain region), but it is always about a collectivity to which one does not belong. Many concepts have multiple dimensions or types, so you should consider whether there can be different types of prejudice—racial prejudice, religious prejudice, age prejudice, gender prejudice, nation prejudice, and so forth.

You also need to consider the units of analysis that best fit your definition of the concept. Prejudice is an attitude. Individuals hold and express attitudes, but so might groups (e.g., families, clubs, churches, companies, media outlets). You need to decide, "Do I want my definition of prejudice to include only the attitudes of individuals, or should it include attitudes held by groups, organizations, and institutions as well?" Can you say, "The school or newspaper was prejudiced?" You also must distinguish your construct from closely related ones. For example, you must ask, "How is prejudice similar to or different from ideas such as discrimination, stereotyping, or racism?"

Conceptualization is the process of thinking through the meaning of a concept. At this stage, let's say you believe that *prejudice* means an inflexible negative attitude that an individual holds and is directed toward a race or ethnic group that is an out-group. It can, but does not always, lead to behaviour such as treating people unequally (i.e., discrimination), and it generally relies on a person's stereotypes of out-group members. Thus, your initial thought, "Prejudice is a negative feeling," has become a precisely defined concept. Even with all your conceptualization, you need to be even more specific. For example, if prejudice is a negative attitude about a race or an ethnic group of which one is not a member, you need to consider the meaning of *race* or *ethnic group*. You should not assume everyone sees racial–ethnic categories the same. Likewise, is it possible to have a positive prejudgment, and if so, is that a kind of prejudice? The main point is that conceptualization requires that you become very clear and state what you mean explicitly for others to see.

Sex Segregation in the U.S. Labor Force

Operationalization links a conceptual definition to a specific set of measurement techniques or procedures, the concept's **operational definition** (i.e., a definition in terms of the specific operations of actions a researcher carries out). An operational definition could be a survey questionnaire, a method of observing events in a field setting, a way to measure symbolic content in the mass media, or any process carried out by the researcher that reflects, documents, or represents the abstract construct as it is expressed in the conceptual definition.

operationalization: The process of moving from the *conceptual definition* of a *concept* to a set of specific activities or measures that allow a researcher to observe it empirically (i.e., its *operational definition*).

operational definition: The definition of a variable in terms of the specific activities to measure or indicate it with *empirical evidence*.

There are usually multiple ways to measure a concept. Some are better or worse and more or less practical than others. The key is to fit your measure to your specific conceptual definition, to the practical constraints within which you must operate (e.g., time, money, available subjects), and to the research techniques you know or can learn. You can develop a new measure from scratch, or it can be a measure that is already being used by other researchers (see Boxes 6.2 and 6.3).

Box 6.2 Making It Practical

Five Guidelines for Coming up with a Measure

1. *Remember the conceptual definition.* The underlying principle for any measure is to match it to the specific conceptual definition of the concept that will be used in the study.
2. *Keep an open mind.* Do not get locked into a single measure or type of measure. Be creative and constantly look for better measures.
3. *Borrow from others.* Do not be afraid to borrow from other researchers, as long as credit is given. Good ideas for measures can be found in other studies or modified from other measures.
4. *Anticipate difficulties.* Logical and practical problems often arise when trying to measure variables of interest. Sometimes a problem can be anticipated and avoided with careful forethought and planning.
5. *Do not forget your units of analysis.* Your measure should fit with the units of analysis of the study and permit you to generalize to the universe of interest.

Operationalization links the language of theory with the language of empirical measures. Theory is full of abstract concepts, assumptions, relationships, definitions, and causality. Empirical measures describe how people concretely measure specific variables. They refer to specific operations or things people use to indicate the presence of a construct that exists in observable reality.

LO 3 Explain how conceptualization and operationalization are different in qualitative and quantitative work.

Quantitative Conceptualization and Operationalization

The measurement process for quantitative research is a straightforward sequence: first conceptualization, then operationalization, and finally application of the operational definition or measuring to collect the data. Quantitative researchers have developed several ways to rigorously link abstract ideas to measurement procedures that will produce precise quantitative information about empirical reality.

Box 6.3 Social Research and the Internet

In Box 6.2, it was suggested that you consider "borrowing" measurements from others. This is very sage advice and could save you considerable amounts of time. Questions from well-established and reputable studies have the advantage that they have been tested on large samples and have been shown to have demonstrated properties of validity and reliability (discussed later in this chapter).

But where can you see examples of such operationalizations? A resource that archives questions from a host of large-scale surveys in the United Kingdom and beyond is called the "Survey Question Bank," which can be accessed at http://surveynet.ac.uk/sqb. The Survey Question Bank is searchable by question text, which generally can be interpreted as "concept." In the example below, we searched for questions containing text on social class, which produced 18 hits. We can now examine the different questions and see if any of them seem suitable for our particular research needs (i.e., if they match our conceptual definition).

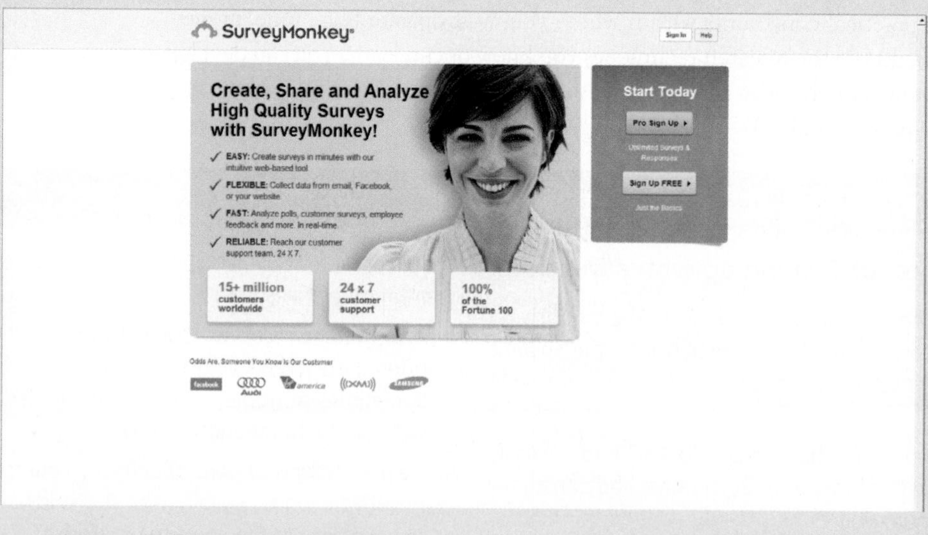

Source: Used with permission of SurveyMonkey.

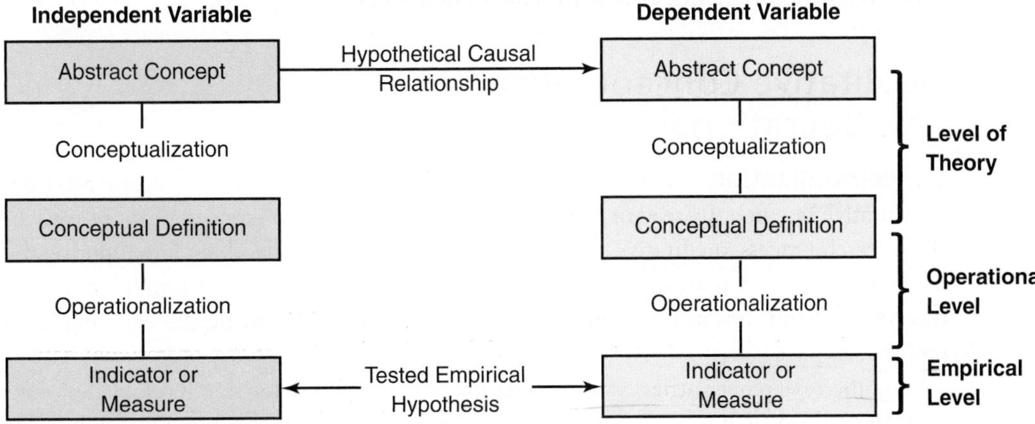

Figure 6.1 Conceptualization and Operationalization

Figure 6.1 illustrates the measurement process for two variables that are linked together in a theory and a hypothesis. There are three levels to consider: conceptual, operational, and empirical. At the most abstract level, the researcher is interested in the causal relationship between two concepts, or a **conceptual hypothesis**. At the level of operational definitions, the researcher is interested in testing an **empirical hypothesis** to determine the degree of association between indicators. This is the level at which correlations, statistics, questionnaires, and the like are used. The third level is the concrete empirical world. If the operational indicators of variables (e.g., questionnaires) are logically linked to a concept (e.g., racial discrimination), they will capture what happens in the empirical social world and relate it to the conceptual level.

conceptual hypothesis: A type of *hypothesis* in which the researcher expresses variables in abstract, conceptual terms and expresses the relationship among variables in a theoretical way.

empirical hypothesis: A type of *hypothesis* in which the researcher expresses variables in specific terms and expresses the *association* among the measured indicators of observable, *empirical evidence.*

The measurement process links together the three levels, moving deductively from the abstract to the concrete. A researcher first conceptualizes a variable, giving it a clear conceptual definition. Next, he or she operationalizes it by developing an operational definition or set of indicators for it. Last, he or she applies the indicators in the empirical world. The links from abstract concepts to empirical reality allow the researcher to test empirical hypotheses. Those tests are logically linked back to a conceptual hypothesis and causal relations in the world of theory.

A hypothesis has at least two variables, and the processes of conceptualization and operationalization are necessary for each variable. In the preceding example, prejudice is not a hypothesis—it is one variable. It could be a dependent variable caused by something else, or it could be an independent variable causing something else. It depends on the theoretical explanation.

Let's consider an example of conceptualizing and operationalizing variables. A study of refugee resettlement in Canada by Lamba (2003) examined recent refugees' use of their social networks in the quality of their resulting jobs. This study is an explanatory study with two main variables in a causal hypothesis. The researchers began with the *conceptual hypothesis:* The social networks of recent refugees affect their quality of employment in Canada. They *conceptualized* the *independent variable*, social networks, and defined it as the size of the refugees' formal and informal networks. The researchers *conceptualized* the dependent variable, job quality, and defined it as how desirable the refugee's job was. The researchers *operationalized* the independent variable by asking refugees about the extent of their familial and extra-familial social networks. They *operationalized* the dependent variable by creating an index of job quality, which included the status of the job, if it was permanent or temporary, and if the individual refugee's educational qualifications matched those required by the position. They then tested the *empirical hypothesis*: The greater the social networks of recent immigrants, the more likely they are to have higher-quality jobs.

Qualitative Conceptualization and Operationalization

Conceptualization The conceptualization process in qualitative research differs from quantitative research. Instead of refining abstract ideas into theoretical definitions early in the research process, qualitative researchers refine rudimentary "working ideas" during the data collection and analysis process. Conceptualization is a process of forming coherent theoretical definitions as one struggles to "make sense of" or organize the data and one's preliminary ideas.

As the researcher gathers and analyzes qualitative data, he or she develops new concepts, formulates definitions for the concepts, and considers relationships among the concepts. Eventually, he or she links concepts to one another to create theoretical relationships that may or may not be causal. Qualitative researchers form the concepts as they examine their qualitative data (i.e., field notes, photos and maps, historical documents). Often, this involves a researcher asking theoretical questions about the data (e.g., "Is this a case of class conflict? What is the sequence of events and could it be different? Why did this happen here and not somewhere else?").

A qualitative researcher conceptualizes by developing clear, explicit definitions of constructs. The definitions are somewhat abstract and linked to other ideas, but usually they are also closely tied to specific data and can be expressed in the words and concrete actions of the people being studied. In qualitative research, conceptualization is largely determined by the data.

Operationalization The operationalization process for qualitative research significantly differs from that in quantitative research and often precedes conceptualization. A researcher forms conceptual definitions out of rudimentary "working ideas" that he or she used while making observations or gathering data. Instead of turning refined conceptual definitions into a set of measurement operations, a qualitative researcher operationalizes by describing how specific observations and thoughts about the data contributed to working ideas that are the basis of conceptual definitions and theoretical concepts.

Operationalization in qualitative research is an after-the-fact description more than a before-the-fact preplanned technique. Almost in a reverse of the quantitative process, data gathering occurs with or prior to full operationalization.

Just as quantitative operationalization deviates from a rigid deductive process, the process followed by qualitative researchers is one of mutual interaction. The researcher draws on ideas from beyond the data of a specific research setting. Qualitative operationalization describes how the researcher collects data, but it includes the researcher's use of pre-existing techniques and concepts that were blended with those that emerged during the data collection process. In qualitative research, ideas and evidence are mutually interdependent.

We now turn to an example of qualitative operationalization in a study of exotic dancers in Canada (Lewis, 2006). It is a descriptive study that developed three main constructs: reciprocity, power, and autonomy. The researcher began with an interest in the social organization of the exotic dancing club, particularly on how the dynamics of power relations functioned among the various types of workers in these clubs. The researcher's *empirical data* consisted of field observation data and interviewer data. After several visits to these clubs and interviewing 30 individuals who worked in them, Lewis *operationalized* the data by developing working ideas and concepts from an inductive examination of the data. Lewis discovered that like other service-sector workers, the dancers used a variety of techniques to enhance their autonomy. The dancers also exhibited various forms of resistance that operated within what she referred to as an "informal economy of favours." The operationalization moved inductively from observation and interviews to creating working ideas based on what the researcher found in the data. Lewis *conceptualized* her working ideas into the abstract concept "informal economy of favours." She saw that strip club workers had created a power structure around themselves that operated on "favours" with each other and that this system allowed them to have power and autonomy that they otherwise would not have.

RELIABILITY AND VALIDITY

LO 4 Define reliability and validity.

Reliability and validity are central issues in all measurement. Both concern how concrete measures are connected to concepts. Reliability and validity are salient because concepts in social theory are often ambiguous, diffuse, and not directly observable. Perfect reliability and validity are virtually impossible to achieve. Rather, they are ideals researchers strive for.

All social researchers want their measures to be reliable and valid. Both ideas are important in establishing the truthfulness, credibility, or believability of findings. Both terms also have multiple meanings. Here, they refer to related, desirable aspects of measurement. It is also important to remember that the terms reliability and validity have their own definitions within your own vocabulary; these words have very specific meanings within the context of social research methods. *Be careful not to confuse your "everyday" definitions of reliability and validity with those that are specific to the issue of concept measurement.*

Reliability means dependability or consistency. It suggests that the same thing will be repeated or recur under identical or very similar conditions. The opposite of reliability is a measurement that yields erratic, unstable, or inconsistent results.

reliability: The dependability or consistency of the measure of a variable.

Validity suggests truthfulness and refers to the match between a concept, or the way a researcher conceptualizes the idea in a conceptual definition, and a measure. It refers to how well an idea about reality "fits" with actual reality. The absence of validity occurs if there is poor fit between the constructs a researcher uses to describe, theorize, or analyze the social world and what actually occurs in the social world. In simple terms, validity addresses the question of how well the social reality being measured through research matches with the constructs researchers use to understand it.

validity: A term meaning "truth" that can be applied to the logical tightness of *experimental design*, the ability to generalize findings outside a study, the quality of measurement, and the proper use of procedures.

Qualitative and quantitative researchers want reliable and valid measurement, but beyond an agreement on the basic ideas at a general level, each style sees the specifics of reliability and validity in the research process differently.

Reliability and Validity in Quantitative Research

Reliability As just stated, reliability means dependability. It means that the numerical results produced by an indicator do not vary because of characteristics of the measurement process or measurement instrument itself. For example, you get on your bathroom scale and read your weight. You get off and get on again and again. You have a reliable scale if it gives you the same weight each time—assuming, of course, that you are not eating, drinking, changing clothing, and so forth in between measurements. An unreliable scale will register different weights each time, even though your "true" weight does not change. Another example is a car's speedometer. If you are driving at a constant slow speed on a level surface but the speedometer needle jumps from one end to the other, the speedometer is not a reliable indicator of how fast you are travelling.

How to Improve Reliability It is rare to have perfect reliability. However, there are four ways to increase the reliability of measures: (1) clear conceptualization; (2) use a precise level of measurement; (3) use multiple indicators; and (4) use pilot tests.

LO 5 Explain the ways that reliability can be improved.

Clear Conceptualization Reliability increases when a single concept or subdimension of a concept is measured. This means developing unambiguous, clear theoretical definitions. Concepts should be specified to eliminate "noise" (i.e., distracting or interfering information) from other concepts. Each measure should indicate one and only one concept. Otherwise, it is impossible to determine which concept is being "indicated." For example, the indicator of a pure chemical compound is more reliable than one in which the chemical is mixed with other material or dirt. In the latter case, it is difficult to separate the "noise" of other material from the pure chemical.

Increase the Level of Measurement Levels of measurement are discussed later in this chapter. Indicators at higher or more precise levels of measurement are more likely to be reliable than less precise measures because the latter pick up less detailed information. If more specific information is measured, then it is less likely that anything other than the concept will be captured. The general principle is this: Try to measure at the most precise level possible. However, it is more difficult to measure at higher levels of measurement. For example, if you have a choice of measuring prejudice as either high or low, or in 10 categories from extremely low to extremely high, it would be better to measure it in 10 refined categories.

multiple indicators: Many procedures or instruments that indicate or provide evidence of the presence or level of a variable using *empirical evidence*. Researchers use the combination of several indicators together to measure a variable.

Use Multiple Indicators of a Variable A third way to increase reliability is to use **multiple indicators** because two (or more) indicators of the same concept are better than one. Figure 6.2 illustrates the use of multiple indicators in hypothesis testing. Three indicators of the one independent variable concept are combined into an overall measure, A, and two indicators of a dependent variable are combined into a single measure, *B*.

For example, let's say you create three indicators of the variable racial–ethnic prejudice. Your first indicator is an attitude question on a survey. You ask research participants their beliefs and feelings about many different racial and ethnic groups. For a second indicator, you observe research participants from various races and ethnic groups interacting together over the course of three days. You look for those who regularly either (1) avoid eye contact, appear to be tense, and sound cool and distant; or (2) make eye contact, appear relaxed, and sound warm and friendly as they interact with people of their same racial–ethnic group or a different one. Finally, you create an experiment. You ask research participants to read the grade transcripts, résumés, and interview reports on 30 applicants for five jobs—youth volunteer coordinator, office manager, janitor, clothing store clerk, and advertising account executive. The applicants have many qualifications, but you secretly manipulate their racial or ethnic group to see whether a research participant decides on the best applicant for the jobs based on an applicant's race and ethnicity.

Multiple indicators let a researcher take measurements from a wider range of the content of a conceptual definition. Different aspects of the concept can be measured, each with

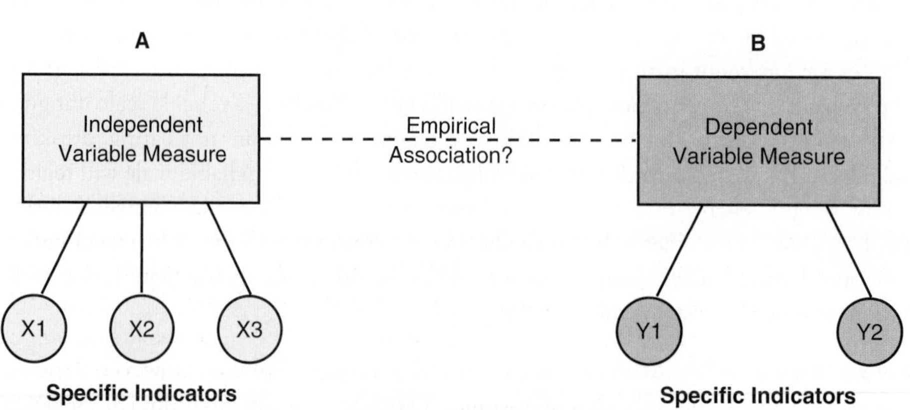

Figure 6.2 Measurement Using Multiple Indicators

its own indicator. Also, one indicator (e.g., one question on a questionnaire) may be imperfect, but several measures are less likely to have the same (systematic) error. Multiple indicator measures tend to be more stable than measures with one item.

Use Pretests, Pilot Studies, and Replication Reliability can be improved by using a pretest or *pilot* version of a measure first. Develop one or more draft or preliminary versions of a measure and try them before applying the final version in a hypothesis-testing situation. This takes more time and effort.

The principle of using pilot tests extends to replicating the measures other researchers have used. For example, you can search the literature and find measures of prejudice from past research. You may want to build on and use a previous measure if it is a good one (citing the source, of course). In addition, you may want to add new indicators and compare them to the previous measure.

Validity

Validity is an overused term. Sometimes it is used to mean "true" or "correct." There are several general types of validity. Here, we are concerned with *measurement validity*, although there are also several types of measurement validity. Nonmeasurement types of validity are discussed later in the book.

When a researcher says that an indicator is valid, it is valid for a particular purpose and definition. The same indicator can be valid for one purpose (i.e., a research question with units of analysis and universe) but less valid for others. For example, the measure of prejudice discussed here might be valid for measuring prejudice among teachers but invalid for measuring the prejudice of police officers.

At its core, **measurement validity** refers to how well the conceptual and operational definitions mesh with each other. The better the fit, the greater the measurement validity. Validity is more difficult to achieve than reliability. We cannot have absolute confidence about validity, but some measures are *more valid* than others. For example, IQ tests are a more valid measurement of intelligence than hair colour. The reason we can never achieve absolute validity is that concepts are abstract ideas, whereas indicators refer to concrete observation. This is the gap between our mental pictures about the world and the specific things we do at particular times and places. Validity is part of a dynamic process that grows by accumulating evidence over time, and without it all measurement becomes meaningless.

measurement validity: How well an empirical indicator and the *conceptual definition* of the concept that the indicator is supposed to measure "fit" together.

Types of Measurement Validity

LO 6 Identify the four major ways of establishing measurement validity.

Face Validity The most basic kind of validity and easiest to achieve is **face validity**. It is a judgment by the scientific community that the indicator really measures the concept. It addresses the questions, "On the face of it, do people believe that the definition and method of measurement fit? Does it look about right?" It is a consensus method of measurement validity. Recall that in the scientific community, aspects of research are scrutinized by others.

face validity: A type of *measurement validity* in which an indicator "makes sense" as a measure of a construct in the judgment of others, especially those in the scientific community.

Content Validity **Content validity** is a special type of face validity. It addresses the question, "Is the full content of a definition represented in a measure?" A conceptual definition holds ideas; it is a "space" containing ideas and concepts. Measures should sample or represent all ideas or areas in the conceptual space. Content validity involves three steps: First, specify the content in a concept's definition; next, sample from all areas of the definition; finally, develop an indicator that taps all of the parts of the definition.

content validity: *Measurement validity* that requires that a measure represent all the aspects of the *conceptual definition* of a construct.

An example of content validity is our definition of *feminism* as a person's commitment to a set of beliefs creating full equality between men and women in areas of the arts, intellectual pursuits, family, work, politics, and authority relations. We create a measure of feminism in which we ask two survey questions: (1) "Should men and women get equal pay for equal work?" and (2) "Should men and women share household tasks?" Our measure has low content validity because the two questions ask only about pay and household tasks.

They ignore many other areas (intellectual pursuits, politics, authority relations, and other aspects of work and family life). For a content-valid measure, we must either expand the measure or narrow the definition.

criterion validity: *Measurement validity* that relies on some independent, outside verification.

Criterion Validity Criterion validity uses some standard or criterion to indicate a construct accurately. The validity of an indicator is verified by comparing it with another measure of the same concept that is widely accepted. There are two subtypes of this kind of validity: concurrent and predictive.

concurrent validity: *Measurement validity* that relies on a pre-existing and already accepted measure to verify the indicator of a concept.

To have **concurrent validity**, an indicator must be associated with a pre-existing indicator that is judged to be valid (i.e., it has face validity). For example, you create a new test to measure intelligence. For it to be concurrently valid, it should be highly associated with existing IQ tests (assuming the same definition of intelligence is used). This means that most people who score high on the old measure should also score high on the new one, and vice versa. The two measures may not be perfectly associated, but if they measure the same or a similar concept, it is logical for them to yield similar results.

predictive validity: *Measurement validity* that relies on the occurrence of a future event or behaviour that is logically consistent to verify the indicator of a concept.

Criterion validity whereby an indicator predicts future events that are logically related to a concept is called **predictive validity**. It cannot be used for all measures. The measure and the action predicted must be distinct from but indicate the same concept. Predictive measurement validity should not be confused with prediction in hypothesis testing, where one variable predicts a different variable in the future. For example, the Law School Admission Test (LSAT), which many undergraduate students take, measures scholastic aptitude—the ability of a student to perform in law school. If the LSAT has high predictive validity, then students who get high LSAT scores will subsequently do well in law school. If students with high scores perform the same as students with average or low scores, then the LSAT has low predictive validity.

Another way to test predictive validity is to select a group of people who have specific characteristics and predict how they will score (very high or very low) compared with the construct. For example, you may have a measure of political conservatism. You would predict that members of conservative groups (e.g., Canadian National Taxpayers Coalition, REAL Women of Canada, Canada Family Action Coalition) will score high on it, whereas members of liberal groups (e.g., Ontario Coalition Against Poverty, Greenpeace, Democracy Watch) will score low. You therefore "validate" the measure with the groups—that is, you pilot-test it by using it on members of the groups. It can then be used as a measure of political conservatism for the general public. Table 6.2 provides a summary of the types of measurement validity.

LO 7 Explain how reliability and validity are approached in qualitative research.

Reliability and Validity in Qualitative Research

Most qualitative researchers accept the principles of reliability and validity but use the terms infrequently because of their close association with quantitative measurement. In addition, qualitative researchers apply the principles differently in practice.

Table 6.2 Summary of Measurement Validity Types

Validity (True Measure)
Face—in the judgment of others
Content—captures the entire meaning
Criterion—agrees with an external source
• Concurrent—agrees with a pre-existing measure
• Predictive—agrees with future behaviour

Reliability *Reliability* means dependability or consistency. Qualitative researchers use a variety of techniques (e.g., interviews, participation, photographs, document studies) to record their observations consistently. Qualitative researchers want to be consistent (i.e., not vacillating and erratic) in how they make observations over time, similar to the idea of reliability. One difficulty is that they often study processes that are not stable over time. Moreover, they emphasize the value of a changing or developing interaction between the researcher and what he or she studies.

Qualitative researchers believe that the subject matter and a researcher's relationship with it should be a growing, evolving process. The metaphor for the changing relationship between a researcher and the data is one of a living organism (e.g., a plant) that naturally matures. Most qualitative researchers resist the quantitative approach to reliability, which they see as a cold, fixed mechanical instrument that one repeatedly injects into or applies to some static, lifeless material.

Qualitative researchers consider a range of data sources and employ multiple measurement methods. They accept that different researchers or researchers using alternative measures will get distinctive results. This is because qualitative researchers see data collection as an interactive process in which particular researchers operate in an evolving setting, and the setting's context dictates using a unique mix of measures that cannot be repeated. The diverse measures and interactions with different researchers are beneficial because they can illuminate different facets or dimensions of a subject matter. Many qualitative researchers question the quantitative researcher's quest for standard, fixed measures. They fear that such measures ignore the benefits of having a variety of researchers with many approaches and may neglect key aspects of diversity that exist in the social world.

Validity *Validity* means truthfulness. It refers to the bridge between a concept and the data. Qualitative researchers are more interested in authenticity than validity. *Authenticity* means giving a fair, honest, and balanced account of social life from the viewpoint of someone who lives it every day. Qualitative researchers are less concerned with trying to match an abstract concept to empirical data and more concerned with giving a candid portrayal of social life that is true to the experiences of the people being studied. Most qualitative researchers concentrate on ways to capture an inside view and provide a detailed account of how those being studied feel about and understand events.

Qualitative researchers have developed several methods that serve as substitutes for the quantitative approach to validity. These emphasize conveying the insider's view to others. Historical researchers use internal and external criticisms to determine whether the evidence they have is real. Qualitative researchers adhere to the core principle of validity, to be truthful (i.e., avoid false or distorted accounts). They try to create a tight fit between their understanding, ideas, and statements about the social world and what is actually occurring in it.

To assess the "truth value" and applicability of qualitative researchers' claims, Lincoln and Guba (1985) have suggested that similar yet distinct notions of "validity" be used, which they call *credibility* and *transferability* (see Box 6.4).

The Relationship between Reliability and Validity

Reliability is necessary for validity and is easier to achieve than validity. Although reliability is necessary to have a valid measure of a concept, it does not guarantee that a measure will be valid; it is not a sufficient condition for validity. A measure can produce the same result over and over (i.e., it has reliability), but what it measures may not match the definition of the concept (i.e., validity).

A measure can be reliable but invalid. For example, you can get on a scale and get weighed. The weight registered by the scale is the same each time you get on and off. But then you go to another scale—an "official" one that measures true weight—and it says that

Box 6.4 Making It Practical

How Are Reliability and Validity Comparable in Qualitative and Quantitative Research?

According to Lincoln and Guba (1985), reliability in qualitative research focuses on the issue of how consistent the data are. While we cannot replicate qualitative studies in the same way that we can in quantitative projects, we can assess how "trustworthy" the data are. Lincoln and Guba suggest that rather than using the same definitions of reliability that are attributed to quantitative research, the term *dependability* be used to assess how consistent the data are. We can check for dependability by making the data, document, and interview notes available to other researchers to see if they would have come up with similar conclusions.

Similarly, assessing the internal and external validity in qualitative studies must be done in a manner that is more suited to these techniques. Internal and external validity are concerned with upholding the truth value and the applicability of the research findings. Lincoln and Guba suggest that to ensure trustworthiness in qualitative research, the corresponding principles of credibility and transferability be applied. *Credibility* means very much what the word suggests: Does this sound right? We can check for credibility in a variety of ways, such as spending as much time as possible in the research setting, using a variety of research techniques (called triangulation, which is covered in a later chapter), and asking those we are studying what they think about our interpretations. *Transferability*, like external validity, concerns the extent to which our findings are applicable beyond our immediate research setting. We can increase the transferability of our findings by using as much rich description in our qualitative data as possible, such that judgments about the transferability of the study can be made by other researchers. We can maximize the transferability of our qualitative research by choosing subjects and locations that differ (which pertains to issues of sampling, covered in a later chapter).

Using Lincoln and Guba's (1985) Notions of Trustworthiness

Aspect of Research	Quantitative	Qualitative
Consistency	Reliability	Dependability
Truth Value	Internal Validity	Credibility
Applicability	External Validity	Transferability

your weight is twice as much as the original scale reported. The first scale yielded reliable (i.e., dependable and consistent) results, but it did not give a valid measure of your weight.

A diagram might help you see the relationship between reliability and validity. Figure 6.3 illustrates the relationship between the concepts by using the analogy of a target. The bull's-eye represents a fit between a measure and the definition of the construct.

Validity and reliability are usually complementary concepts, but in some situations they conflict with each other. Sometimes as validity increases, reliability is more difficult to attain, and vice versa. This occurs when the concept has a highly abstract and not easily observable definition. Reliability is easiest to achieve when the measure is precise and observable. Thus, there is a strain between the true essence of the highly abstract concept and measuring it in a concrete manner. For example, "alienation" is a very abstract, highly subjective construct, often defined as a deep inner sense of loss of one's humanity that diffuses across many aspects of one's life (e.g., social relations, sense of self, orientation toward nature). Highly precise questions in a questionnaire give reliable measures, but there is a danger of losing the subjective essence of the concept.

Other Uses of the Terms *Reliability* and *Validity*

Many words have multiple definitions, including *reliability* and *validity*. This creates confusion unless we distinguish among alternative uses of the same word.

Reliability We use *reliability* in everyday language. A reliable person is one who is dependable, stable, and responsible; a reliable car is dependable and trustworthy. This means the person responds in similar, predictable ways at different times and under different

A Bull's-Eye = A Perfect Measure

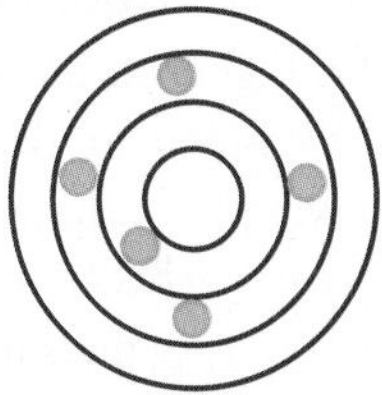

Low Reliability
and Low Validity

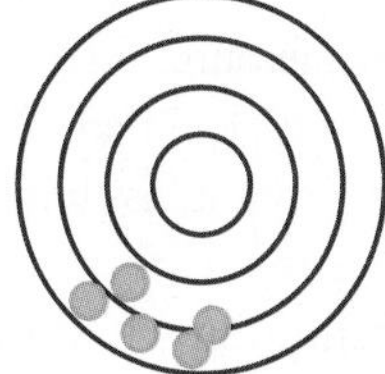

High Reliability
but Low Validity

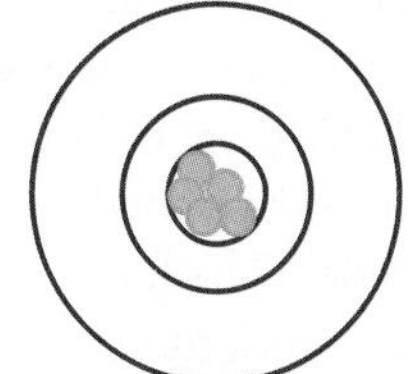

High Reliability
and High Validity

Figure 6.3 Illustration of the Relationship between Reliability and Validity

Source: Adapted from Babbie, E. (1995). *The practice of social research* (7th ed.). Belmont, CA: Wadsworth.

conditions; the same can be said for the car. In addition to measurement reliability, researchers sometimes say a study or its results are reliable. By this they mean that the method of conducting a study or the results from it can be reproduced or replicated by other researchers.

Internal Validity **Internal validity** means that there are no errors internal to the design of the research project. It is used primarily in experimental research to talk about possible errors or alternative explanations of results that arise despite attempts to institute controls. High internal validity means there are few such errors; low internal validity means that such errors are likely.

internal validity: The ability of experimenters to strengthen a *causal explanation's* logical rigour by eliminating potential alternative explanations for an *association* between the *treatment* and the *dependent variable* through an *experimental design.*

External Validity **External validity** is used primarily in experimental research. It is the ability to generalize findings from a specific setting and small group to a broad range of settings and people. It addresses the question, "If something happens in a laboratory or among a particular group of subjects (e.g., university students), can the findings be generalized to the 'real' (nonlaboratory) world or to the general public (nonstudents)?" High external validity means that the results can be generalized to many situations and many groups of people; low external validity means that the results apply only to a very specific setting.

external validity: The ability to generalize from *experimental research* to settings or people that differ from the specific conditions of the study.

Statistical Validity **Statistical validity** means that the correct statistical procedure is chosen and its assumptions are fully met. Different statistical tests or procedures are appropriate for different conditions, which are discussed in textbooks that describe the statistical procedures.

statistical validity: This is achieved when an appropriate statistical procedure is selected and the assumptions of the procedure are fully met.

Measures of Central Tendency: Mean, Median, Mode

All statistics are based on assumptions about the mathematical properties of the numbers being used. A statistic will be invalid and its results nonsense if the major assumptions are violated. For example, to compute an average (actually the mean, which is discussed in a later chapter), one cannot use information at the nominal level of measurement (discussed later in this chapter). For example, suppose we measure the race of a class of students. We give each race a number: White = 1, Black = 2, Asian = 3, Others = 4. It makes no sense to say that the "mean" race of a class of students is 1.9 (almost Black?). This is a misuse of the statistical procedure, and the results are invalid even if the computation is correct. The degree to which statistical assumptions can be violated or bent (the technical term is *robustness*) is a topic in which professional statisticians take great interest.

A GUIDE TO QUANTITATIVE MEASUREMENT

LO 8 Define and give examples of the four levels of measurement.

Thus far, you have learned about the principles of measurement, including the principles of reliability and validity. Quantitative researchers have developed ideas and specialized measures to help them in the process of creating operational definitions that will be reliable and valid measures and yield numerical data for their variable constructs.

Levels of Measurement

levels of measurement: A system that organizes the information in the measurement of variables into four general levels, from the *nominal level* to the *ratio level.*

Levels of measurement is an abstract but important and widely used idea. Basically, it says that some ways in which a researcher measures a concept are at a higher or more refined level, and others are crude or less precisely specified. The level of measurement depends on the way in which a concept is defined—that is, assumptions about whether it has particular characteristics. The level of measurement affects the kinds of indicators chosen and is tied to basic assumptions in a concept's definition. How a researcher conceptualizes a variable limits the levels of measurement that he or she can use and has implications for how measurement and statistical analysis can proceed.

continuous variables: Variables measured on a continuum in which an infinite number of finer gradations between variable *attributes* are possible.

discrete variables: Variables in which the *attributes* can be measured only with a limited number of distinct, separate categories.

Continuous and Discrete Variables

Variables can be thought of as being either continuous or discrete. **Continuous variables** have an infinite number of values or attributes that flow along a continuum. The values can be divided into many smaller increments; in mathematical theory, there is an infinite number of increments. Examples of continuous variables include temperature, age, income, crime rate, and amount of schooling. **Discrete variables** have a relatively fixed set of separate values or variable attributes. Instead of a smooth continuum of values, discrete variables contain distinct categories. Examples of discrete variables include gender (male or female), religion (Christian, Jewish, Muslim, Buddhist, atheist, other), and marital status (never married, married, common law, divorced or separated, widowed). Whether a variable is continuous or discrete affects its level of measurement.

Four Levels of Measurement

Precision and Levels

The idea of levels of measurement expands on the difference between continuous and discrete variables and organizes types of variables for their use in statistics. The four levels of measurement categorize the degree of precision of measurement.

Deciding on the appropriate level of measurement for a construct often creates confusion. The appropriate level of measurement for a variable depends on two things: (1) how a concept is defined and (2) the type of indicator or measurement that a researcher uses.

The concept itself limits the level of precision. That is, the way a researcher defines a concept can limit how precisely it can be measured. For example, some of the variables listed earlier as continuous can be reconceptualized as discrete. Temperature can be a continuous variable (e.g., degrees, fractions of degrees), or it can be crudely measured with discrete categories (e.g., hot or cold). Likewise, age can be continuous (how old a person is in years, months, days, hours, and minutes) or treated as discrete categories (infancy, childhood, adolescence, young adulthood, middle age, old age). Yet most discrete variables cannot be conceptualized as continuous variables. For example, sex, religion, and marital status cannot be conceptualized as continuous; however, related concepts *can* be conceptualized as continuous (e.g., femininity, degree of religiousness, commitment to a marital relationship).

The level of measurement limits the statistical measures that can be used. A wide range of powerful statistical procedures are available for the higher levels of measurement, but the types of statistics that can be used with the lowest levels are very limited.

There is a practical reason to conceptualize and measure variables at higher levels of measurement. You can change higher levels of measurement to lower levels, but the reverse is not true. In other words, it is possible to measure a concept very precisely, gather very specific information, and then ignore some of the precision. But it is not possible to measure a concept with less precision or with less specific information and then make it more precise later.

nominal measures: The lowest, least precise *level of measurement* for which there is only a difference in type among the categories of a variable.

ordinal measures: A *level of measurement* that identifies a difference among categories of a variable and allows the categories to be rank ordered.

Distinguishing among the Four Levels

The four levels from lowest precision to greatest or highest precision are nominal, ordinal, interval, and ratio. Each level gives a different type of information (see Table 6.3). **Nominal measures** indicate only that there is a difference among categories (e.g., religion: Christian, Jewish, Muslim; racial heritage: African, Asian, Hispanic, other). **Ordinal measures** indicate a difference *plus* the categories can be

Table 6.3 Characteristics of the Four Levels of Measurement

Level	Different Categories	Ranked	Categories Measured	True Zero
Nominal	Yes			
Ordinal	Yes	Yes		
Interval	Yes	Yes	Yes	
Ratio	Yes	Yes	Yes	Yes

ordered or ranked (e.g., letter grades: A, B, C, D, F; opinion measures: Strongly Agree, Agree, Disagree, Strongly Disagree). **Interval measures** indicate everything the first two do *and* can specify the amount of distance between categories (e.g., Fahrenheit or Celsius temperature: 5°, 45°, 90°; IQ scores: 95, 110, 125). Arbitrary zeros may be used in interval measures; they are just there to help keep score. **Ratio measures** do everything all the other levels do *plus* there is a true zero, which makes it possible to state relations in terms of proportion or ratios (e.g., money income: $10, $100, $500; years of formal schooling: one year, 10 years, 13 years).

interval measures: A *level of measurement* that identifies differences among variable *attributes,* ranks, and categories and that measures distance between categories, but there is no true zero.

ratio measures: The highest, most precise *level of measurement* for which variable *attributes* can be rank ordered, the distance between the *attributes* precisely measured, and an absolute zero exists.

In most practical situations, the distinction between interval and ratio levels makes little difference. The arbitrary zeros of some interval measures can be confusing. For example, a rise in temperature from 30 to 60 degrees is not really a doubling of the temperature, even though the numbers double, because zero degrees is not the absence of all heat.

Discrete variables are nominal and ordinal, whereas continuous variables can be measured at the interval or ratio level. A ratio-level measure can be turned into an interval, ordinal, or nominal level. The interval level can always be turned into an ordinal or nominal level, but the process does not work in the opposite way!

In general, use at least five ordinal categories and obtain many observations. This is because the distortion created by collapsing a continuous construct into a smaller number of ordered categories is minimized as the number of categories and the number of observations increase. Examples of the four levels of measurement are shown in Table 6.4.

Table 6.4 Example of Levels of Measurement

Variable (Level of Measurement)	How the Variable Is Measured
Religion (nominal)	Different religious denominations (Jewish, Islamic, Christian) are not ranked, just different.
Attendance (ordinal)	"How often do you attend religious services? (0) Never, (1) less than once a year, (2) several times a year, (3) about once a month, (4) two or three times a month, or (5) several times a week?" This might have been measured at a ratio level if the exact number of times a person attended was asked instead.
IQ Score (interval)	Most intelligence tests are organized with 100 as average, middle, or normal. Scores higher or lower indicate distance from the average. Someone with a score of 115 has somewhat above average measured intelligence for people who took the test, while 90 is slightly below. Scores of below 65 or above 140 are rare.
Age (ratio)	Age is measured by years of age. There is a true zero (birth). Note that a 40-year-old is twice as old as a 20-year-old.

Specialized Measures: Scales and Indices

Researchers have created thousands of different scales and indices to measure social variables. For example, scales and indices have been developed to measure the degree of formalization in bureaucratic organizations, the prestige of occupations, the adjustment of people to marriage, the intensity of group interaction, the level of social activity in a community, and the level of socio-economic development of a nation. We cannot discuss the thousands of scales and indices. Instead, we will focus on principles of scale and index construction and explore some major types.

Violent Crime Rates and Four Measures of Serious Violent Crime

Data Analysis: Crime Study

Keep two things in mind. First, virtually every social phenomenon can be measured. Some concepts can be measured directly and produce precise numerical values (e.g., family income). Other concepts require the use of "proxies" that indirectly measure a variable and may not be as precise (e.g., predisposition to commit a crime). Second, a lot can be learned from measures used by other researchers. You are fortunate to have the work of thousands of researchers to draw on, so it is not always necessary to start from scratch. You can use a past scale or index, or you can modify it for your own purposes.

Indices and Scales You might find the terms *index* and *scale* confusing because they are often used interchangeably. One researcher's scale is another's index. Both produce ordinal- or interval-level measures of a variable. To add to the confusion, scale and index techniques can be combined in one measure. Scales and indices give a researcher more information about variables and make it possible to assess the quality of measurement. Scales and indices increase reliability and validity, and they aid in data reduction; that is, they condense and simplify the information that is collected (see Box 6.5).

Mutually Exclusive and Exhaustive Attributes Before discussing scales and indices, it is important to review features of good measurement. The attributes of all measures, including nominal-level measures, should be mutually exclusive and exhaustive.

mutually exclusive attributes: The principle that response categories in a *scale* or other measure should be organized so that a person's responses fit into only one category (i.e., categories should not overlap).

Mutually exclusive attributes means that an individual or case fits into one and only one attribute of a variable. For example, a variable measuring type of religion—with the attributes Christian, non-Christian, and Jewish—is not mutually exclusive. Judaism is both a non-Christian religion and a Jewish religion, so a Jewish person fits into both the non-Christian and the Jewish categories. Likewise, a variable measuring type of city, with the attributes port city, provincial capital, and major highway exit, lacks mutually exclusive attributes. One city could be all three (a port provincial capital with a major highway exit), any one of the three, or none of the three.

exhaustive attributes: The principle that response categories in a *scale* or other measure should provide a category for all possible responses (i.e., every possible response fits into some category).

Exhaustive attributes means that all cases fit into one of the attributes of a variable. When measuring religion, a measure with the attributes Catholic, Protestant, and Jewish is not exhaustive. The individual who is a Buddhist, a Muslim, or an agnostic does not fit anywhere. The attributes should be developed so that every possible situation is covered.

Box 6.5 Making It Practical

Scales and Indices: Are They Different?

For most purposes, you can treat scales and indices as interchangeable. Social researchers do not use a consistent nomenclature to distinguish between them.

A *scale* is a measure in which a researcher captures the intensity, direction, level, or potency of a variable construct. It arranges responses or observations on a continuum. A scale can use a single indicator or multiple indicators. Most are at the ordinal level of measurement.

An *index* is a measure in which a researcher adds or combines several distinct indicators of a construct into a single score. This composite score is often a simple sum of the multiple indicators. Indices are often measured at the interval or ratio level.

Researchers sometimes combine the features of scales and indices into a single measure. This is common when a researcher has several indicators that are scales (i.e., that measure intensity or direction). He or she then adds these indicators together to yield a single score, thereby creating an index.

For example, Christian, Jewish, Muslim, Buddhist, Agnostic, Atheist, or Other is an exhaustive and mutually exclusive set of attributes.

Unidimensionality In addition to being mutually exclusive and exhaustive, scales and indices should also be unidimensional or one-dimensional. **Unidimensionality** means that all the items in a scale or index fit together, or measure a single concept. Unidimensionality was suggested in discussions of content and concurrent validity. Unidimensionality says that if you combine several specific pieces of information into a single score or measure, all the pieces measure the same thing.

unidimensionality: The principle that when using *multiple indicators* to measure a construct, all the indicators should consistently fit together and indicate a single construct.

There is an apparent contradiction between using a scale or index to combine parts or subparts of a concept into one measure and the criterion of unidimensionality. It is only an apparent contradiction, however, because concepts are theoretically defined at different levels of abstraction. General, higher-level, or more abstract concepts can be defined as containing several subparts. Each subdimension is a part of the concept's overall content.

For example, we define the concept "feminist ideology" as a general ideology about gender. Feminist ideology is a highly abstract and general concept. It includes specific beliefs and attitudes toward social, economic, political, family, and sexual relations. The ideology's five belief areas are parts of the single general concept. The parts are mutually reinforcing and together form a system of beliefs about the dignity, strength, and power of women.

If feminist ideology is unidimensional, then there is a unified belief system that varies from very anti-feminist to very pro-feminist. We can test the validity of the measure that includes multiple indicators that tap the concept's subparts. If one belief area (e.g., sexual relations) is consistently distinct from the other areas in empirical tests, then we question its unidimensionality.

It is easy to become confused: A specific measure can be an indicator of a unidimensional concept in one situation and indicate a part of a different concept in another situation. This is possible because concepts can be used at different levels of abstraction. For example, a person's attitude toward gender equality with regard to pay is more specific and less abstract than feminist ideology (i.e., beliefs about gender relations throughout society). An attitude toward equal pay can be both a unidimensional concept in its own right *and* a subpart of the more general and abstract unidimensional concept *ideology toward gender relations*.

INDEX CONSTRUCTION

LO 9 Differentiate between the different ways of creating scales and indices.

The Purpose

You hear about indices all the time. For example, Canadian newspapers report the consumer price index (CPI). The CPI, which is a measure of inflation, is created by totalling the cost of buying a list of goods and services (e.g., food, rent, and utilities) and comparing the total with the cost of buying the same list in the previous year. The consumer price index has been used by Statistics Canada since 1914; wage increases, union contracts, and social program payments are based on it. An **index** is a combination of items into a single numerical score. Various components or subparts of a construct are each measured, then combined into one measure.

index: The summing or combining of many separate measures of a construct or variable.

There are many types of indices. For example, if you take an exam with 25 questions, the total number of questions correct is a kind of index. It is a composite measure in which each question measures a small piece of knowledge, and all the questions scored correct or incorrect are totalled to produce a single measure. Indices measure the most desirable place to live (based on unemployment, commuting time, crime rate, recreation opportunities, weather, etc.), the degree of crime (based on combining the occurrence of different specific crimes), the mental health of a person (based on the person's adjustment in various areas of life), and the like. Box 6.6 illustrates the uncomplicated nature of indices by having you use one.

Box 6.6 Using an Index

One way to demonstrate that indices are not very complicated is to use one. Answer "yes" or "no" to the seven questions below on the characteristics of the four occupations listed. Score each answer 1 for yes and 0 for no.

Total the seven answers for each of the four occupations. Which had the highest and which had the lowest score? The seven questions represent an operational definition of the construct *good occupation*. Each question represents a subpart of a theoretical definition. A different theoretical definition would result in different questions, perhaps more than seven.

	Long-distance truck driver	Medical doctor	Accountant	Telephone operator
1. Does it pay a good salary?	❑	❑	❑	❑
2. Is the job secure from layoffs or unemployment?	❑	❑	❑	❑
3. Is the work interesting and challenging?	❑	❑	❑	❑
4. Are its working conditions (e.g., hours, safety, time on the road) good?	❑	❑	❑	❑
5. Are there opportunities for career advancement and promotion?	❑	❑	❑	❑
6. Is it prestigious or looked up to by others?	❑	❑	❑	❑
7. Does it permit self-direction and the freedom to make decisions?	❑	❑	❑	❑

Creating indices is so easy that it is important to be careful that every item in the index has face validity. Items without face validity should be excluded. Each part of the concept should be measured with at least one indicator. Of course, it is better to measure the parts of a concept with multiple indicators.

Weighting

An important issue in index construction is whether to weight items. Unless it is otherwise stated, assume that an index is unweighted. Likewise, unless you have a good theoretical reason for assigning different weights, use equal weights. An *unweighted index* gives all items equal weight. It involves adding up the items without modification, as if each were multiplied by 1 (or −1 for items that are negative).

In a weighted index, a researcher values or weights some items more than others. The size of weights can come from theoretical assumptions, the theoretical definition, or a statistical technique such as factor analysis. Weighting changes the theoretical definition of the construct.

Weighting can produce different index scores, but in most cases weighted and unweighted indices yield similar results. Researchers are concerned with the relationship between variables, and weighted and unweighted indices usually give similar results.

Missing Data

Missing data can be a serious problem when constructing an index. Validity and reliability are threatened whenever data for some cases are missing. For example, we construct an index of the degree of societal development in 1975 for 50 nations. The index contains four items: (1) life expectancy, (2) percentage of homes with indoor plumbing, (3) percentage of population that is literate, and (4) number of telephones per 100 people. We locate a source of United Nations statistics for our information. The values for Belgium are 68 + 87 + 97 + 28; for Turkey, the scores are 55 + 36 + 49 + 3; for Finland, however, we discover that literacy data are unavailable. We check other sources of information, but none has the data because they were not collected. What are the consequences of this? Finland would end up getting a zero for literacy, which would reduce its overall index score.

Rates and Standardization

You have heard of crime rates, rates of population growth, or the unemployment rate. Some indices and single-indicator measures are expressed as rates. Rates involve standardizing the value of an item to make comparisons possible. The items in an index frequently need to be standardized before they can be combined.

standardization: The procedure to statistically adjust measures to permit making an honest comparison by giving a common basis to measures of different units.

Standardization involves selecting a base and dividing a raw measure by the base. For example, City A had 10 murders and City B had 30 murders in the same year. In order to compare murders in the two cities, the raw number of murders needs to be standardized by the city's population. If the cities are the same size, City B is more dangerous. But City B may be safer if it is much larger. For example, if City A has 100 000 people and City B has 600 000, then the murder rate per 100 000 is 10 for City A and 5 for City B.

Standardization makes it possible to compare different units on a common base. The process of standardization, also called *norming,* removes the effect of relevant but different characteristics to make the important differences visible. For example, there are two classes of students. An art class has 12 smokers, and a biology class has 22 smokers. A researcher can compare the rate or incidence of smokers by standardizing the number of smokers by the size of the classes. The art class has 32 students, and the biology class has 143 students. One method of standardization that you already know is the use of percentages, whereby measures are standardized to a common base of 100. In terms of percentages, it is easy to see that the art class has more than twice the rate of smokers (37.5 percent) than the biology class has (15.4 percent).

A critical question in standardization is deciding what base to use. In the examples given, how did we know to use city size or class size as the base? The choice is not always obvious; it depends on the theoretical definition of a concept.

Different bases can produce different rates. For example, the unemployment rate can be defined as the number of people in the workforce who are out of work. The overall unemployment rate is calculated as follows:

$$\text{Unemployment rate} = \frac{\text{Number of unemployed people}}{\text{Total number of people working}}$$

We can divide the total population into subgroups to get rates for subgroups in the population, such as Canadian-born males, foreign-born males, foreign-born males between the ages of 18 and 28, or people with university degrees. Rates for these subgroups may be more relevant to the theoretical definition or research problem. For example, a researcher believes that unemployment is an experience that affects an entire household or family and that the base should be households, not individuals. The rate will then look like this:

$$\text{New unemployment rate} = \frac{\text{Number of households with at least one unemployed person}}{\text{Total number of households}}$$

Different conceptualizations suggest different bases and different ways to standardize. When combining several items into an index, it is best to standardize items on a common base (see Box 6.7).

Box 6.7 In the News

Standardization and the Real Winners at the Olympics

Canada won the most gold medals—a total of 14—at the 2010 Winter Olympics in Vancouver. This is the most gold medals ever won by a single nation in the history of the Winter Olympics. Canada was followed by Germany (with 10 gold medals) and then the United States and Norway (both with 9 gold medals). China, Korea, and Switzerland tied for fourth place by winning 6 gold medals.

However, this way of reporting "winning" fails to *standardize* the outcome (i.e., number of gold medals won). Of course, countries with larger populations do well in one-on-one competition among all nations. To see what really happened, one can standardize on a base of the population. Standardization yields a more accurate picture by adjusting the results as if the nations had equal populations.

We will standardize the results to show the number of medals per 10 million effective population. For example, based on Canada's population of 34 million in 2010, we will divide by 10 million, and divide again by the total number of gold medals won. Standardizing the results shows that Norway, with just over 5 million citizens, proportionately won the most gold; this small country won 9 gold medals, which, when standardized to account for its small population, works out to an effective 18.5 gold medals! Canada falls to fifth place with 4.1 medals per 10 million people. Adjusted for population size, Germany falls toward the bottom of the rankings, as it appeared to be a leader only because of its population size. The United States and China are not even in the top 10 after standardization!

Gold Medal-Winning Countries at the 2010 Winter Olympics in Vancouver

Unstandardized Rank			**Standardized Rank**		
Rank	*Country*	*Total*	*Rank*	*Country*	*Population**
1	Canada	14	1	Norway	18.5
2	Germany	10	2	Switzerland	7.7
3	United States	9	3	Sweden	5.4
3	Norway	9	4	Austria	4.8
4	China	6	5	Canada	4.1
4	Korea	6	6	Netherlands	2.4
4	Switzerland	6	7	Czech Republic	1.9
5	Sweden	5	8	Slovakia	1.8
6	Netherlands	4	9	Germany	1.2
6	Austria	4	10	Korea	1.2

Note: *Population is gold medals per 10 million people.

Sources: Population Reference Bureau, www.prb.org, and Vancouver Winter Olympics, www.vancouver2010.org

SCALES

The Purpose

scale: A type of *quantitative data* measure often used in *survey research* that captures the intensity, direction, level, or potency of a variable construct along a continuum. Most are at the *ordinal level* of measurement.

A **scale**, like an index, is an ordinal, interval, or ratio measure of a variable expressed as a numerical score. Scales are common in situations where a researcher wants to measure how an individual feels or thinks about something.

Scales are used for two related purposes. First, scales help in the conceptualization and operationalization processes. Scales show the fit between a set of indicators and a single construct. For example, a researcher believes that there is a single ideological dimension that underlies people's judgments about specific policies (e.g., housing, education, foreign affairs). Scaling can help determine whether a single construct—for instance, "conservative/liberal ideology"—underlies the positions people take on specific policies. Second, scaling produces quantitative measures and can be used with other variables to test

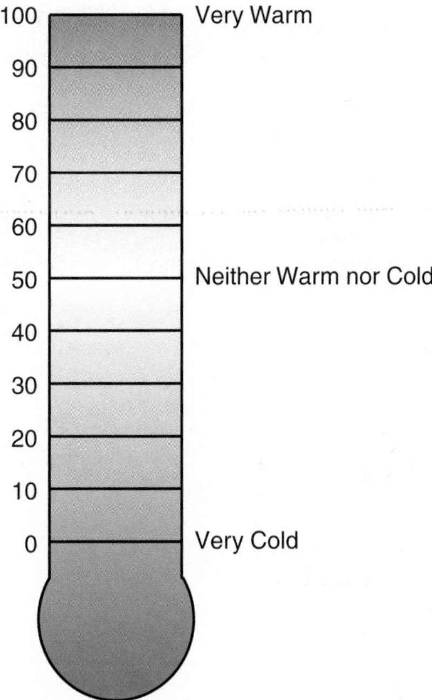

Figure 6.4 "Feeling Thermometer" Graphic Rating Scale

hypotheses. This second purpose of scaling is our primary focus because it involves the scale as a tool for measuring a variable.

Logic of Scaling

As stated before, scaling is based on the idea of measuring the intensity or strength of a variable. Graphic rating scales are an elementary form of scaling. People indicate a rating by checking a point on a line that runs from one extreme to another. This type of scale is easy to construct and use. It conveys the idea of a continuum, and assigning numbers helps people think about quantities. Scales assume that people with the same subjective feeling mark the graphic scale at the same place.

Figure 6.4 is an example of a "feeling thermometer" scale that is used to find out how people feel about various groups in society (e.g., Greenpeace, political parties, labour unions, physicians). This type of measure has been used by political scientists in Canada to examine attitudes toward political candidates, social groups, and issues.[3]

Commonly Used Scales

Likert Scale You have probably used **Likert scales**; they are widely used and very common in survey research. They were developed in the 1930s by American psychologist Rensis Likert to provide an ordinal-level measure of a person's attitude. Likert scales usually ask people to indicate whether they agree or disagree with a statement. Other modifications are possible: People might be asked whether they approve or disapprove of something, or whether they believe something is "almost always true." Box 6.8 presents several examples of Likert scales.

Likert scale: A *scale* often used in *survey research* in which people express attitudes or other responses in terms of several *ordinal-level* categories (e.g., agree, disagree) that are ranked along a continuum.

Likert scales need a minimum of two categories, such as "agree" and "disagree." Using only two choices creates a crude measure and forces distinctions into only two categories. It is usually better to use four to eight categories. A researcher can combine or collapse categories after the data are collected, but data collected with crude categories cannot be made more precise later.

Box 6.8 Focus

Examples of Types of Likert Scales

Items from the Rosenberg Self-Esteem Scale

	Strongly Agree	Agree	Strongly Disagree	Disagree
1. All in all, I am inclined to feel that I am a failure.*				
2. I am able to do things as well as most other people.				
3. I take a positive attitude toward myself.				
4. I feel I have a number of good qualities.				
5. I feel I do not have much to be proud of.*				

*Items are reverse scored.

A Student Evaluation of Instruction Scale

Overall, I rate the quality of instruction in this course as:

Excellent	Good	Average	Fair	Poor

A Market Research Mouthwash Rating Scale

Brand	Dislike Completely	Dislike Somewhat	Dislike a Little	Like a Little	Like Somewhat	Like Completely
X	______	______	______	______	______	______
Y	______	______	______	______	______	______

Work Group Supervisor Scale

My supervisor:

	Never	Seldom	Sometimes	Often	Always
Lets members know what is expected of them	1	2	3	4	5
Is friendly and approachable	1	2	3	4	5
Treats all unit members as equals	1	2	3	4	5

You can increase the number of categories at the end of a scale by adding "strongly agree," "somewhat agree," "very strongly agree," and so forth. Keep the number of choices to eight or nine at most. More distinctions than that are probably not meaningful, and people will become confused. The choices should be evenly balanced (e.g., balance "strongly agree" and "agree" with "strongly disagree" and "disagree").

Researchers have debated about whether to offer a neutral category (e.g., "don't know," "undecided," "no opinion") in addition to the directional categories (e.g., "disagree," "agree"). A neutral category implies an odd number of categories.

A researcher can combine several Likert scale questions into a composite index if they all measure a single construct. Consider the Social Dominance Index that van Laar and colleagues (2005) used in their study of racial–ethnic attitudes among university roommates (see Box 6.9). As part of a larger survey, they asked four questions about group inequality. The answer to each question was a seven-point Likert scale with choices from "Strongly Disagree"

Box 6.9 Concepts in Action

Creating Indices

Example 1

In a study of university roommates and racial–ethnic groups, van Laar and colleagues (2005) measured social dominance (i.e., a feeling that groups are fundamentally unequal) with the following four-item index that used a Likert scale, from 1 (Strongly Disagree) to 7 (Strongly Agree).

1. It is probably a good thing that certain groups are at the top and other groups are at the bottom.
2. Inferior groups should stay in their place.
3. We should do all we can to equalize the conditions of different groups.*
4. We should increase social equality.*

*NOTE: This item was reverse scored.

The scores for the Likert responses (1 to 7) for items 1 to 4 were added to yield an index that ranged from 4 to 28 for each respondent. They report a Cronbach's alpha for this index as 0.74.[4]

Example 2

In a study of perceptions of police misconduct, Weitzer and Tuch (2004) measured a respondent's experiences with police by asking seven questions that had "yes" or "no" answers to create two composite indices. The index for vicarious experiences was the sum of items 2, 4, and 6, with "yes" scored as 1 and "no" scored as zero. An index of personal experience was the sum of answers to items 1, 3, 5, and 7, with "yes" scored as 1 and "no" scored as zero.

1. Have you ever been stopped by police on the street without a good reason?
2. Has anyone else in your household been stopped by police on the street without a good reason?
3. Have the police ever used insulting language toward you?
4. Have the police ever used insulting language toward anyone else in your household?
5. Have the police ever used excessive force against you?
6. Have the police ever used excessive force against anyone else in your household?
7. Have you ever seen a police officer engage in any corrupt activities (such as taking bribes or involvement in drug trade)?

Weitzer and Tuch (2004) report a Cronbach's alpha for the personal experiences as 0.78 and for vicarious experience as 0.86.

to "Strongly Agree." They created the index by adding the answers for each student to create scores that ranged from 4 to 28. Note that they worded the fourth question in a reverse direction from the other questions. The reason for switching directions in this way is to avoid the problem of the *response set*. The response set, also called *response style* and *response bias*, is the tendency of some people to answer a large number of items in the same way (usually agreeing) out of laziness or a psychological predisposition. For example, if items are worded so that saying "strongly agree" always indicates self-esteem, we would not know whether a person who always strongly agreed had high self-esteem or simply had a tendency to agree with questions. The person might be answering "strongly agree" out of habit or a tendency to agree. Researchers word statements in alternative directions so that anyone who agrees all the time appears to answer inconsistently or to have contradictory opinions.

Researchers often combine many Likert-scaled attitude indicators into an index. The scale and indices have properties that are associated with improving reliability and validity. An index uses multiple indicators, which improves reliability. The use of multiple indicators that measure several aspects of a construct or opinion improves content validity. Finally, the index scores give a more precise quantitative measure of a person's opinion. For example, each person's opinion can be measured with a number from 10 to 40, instead of in four categories: "strongly agree," "agree," "disagree," "strongly disagree."

Instead of scoring Likert items, as in the previous example, the scores 2, 1, +1, +2 could be used. This scoring has an advantage in that a zero implies neutrality or complete ambiguity, whereas a high negative number means an attitude that opposes the opinion represented by a high positive number.

The numbers assigned to the response categories are arbitrary. Remember that the use of a zero does not give the scale or index a ratio level of measurement. Likert scale measures are at the ordinal level of measurement because responses indicate a ranking only. Instead of 1 to 4 or 2 to +2, the numbers 100, 70, 50, and 5 would have worked just as well. Also, do not be fooled into thinking that the distances between the ordinal categories are intervals just because numbers are assigned. Although the number system has nice mathematical properties, the numbers are used for convenience only. The fundamental measurement is only ordinal. To elaborate, on a four-point Likert scale you cannot argue that the "distance" between "strongly agree" and "agree" is exactly same as the "distance" between "agree" and "disagree." They may be the same in terms of distances on paper in the scale, but the feelings that they are meant to represent cannot be discussed in such a manner.

The simplicity and ease of use of the Likert scale is its real strength. When several items are combined, more comprehensive multiple indicator measurement is possible. The scale has two limitations: Different combinations of several scale items can result in the same overall score or result, and the response set is a potential shortcoming.

semantic differential: A *scale* in which people are presented with a topic or object and a list of many polar opposite adjectives or adverbs. They are to indicate their feelings by marking one of several spaces between two adjectives or adverbs.

Semantic Differential

Semantic differential provides an indirect measure of how a person feels about a concept, object, or other person. The technique measures subjective feelings toward something by using adjectives. This is because people communicate evaluations through adjectives in spoken and written language. Because most adjectives have polar opposites (e.g., *light/dark, hard/soft, slow/fast*), it uses polar opposite adjectives to create a rating measure or scale. The semantic differential captures the connotations associated with whatever is being evaluated and provides an indirect measure of it.

The semantic differential has been used for many purposes. In marketing research, it tells how consumers feel about a product; political advisers use it to discover what voters think about a candidate or issue; and therapists use it to determine how a client perceives himself or herself (see Box 6.10).

To use the semantic differential, a researcher presents subjects with a list of paired opposite adjectives with a continuum of 7 to 11 points between them. The subjects mark the spot on the continuum between the adjectives that expresses their feelings. The adjectives can be very diverse and should be well mixed (e.g., positive items should not be located mostly on either the right or the left side). Studies of a wide variety of adjectives in English found that they fall into three major classes of meaning: evaluation *(good–bad)*, potency *(strong–weak)*, and activity *(active–passive)*. Of the three classes of meaning, evaluation is usually the most significant. The analysis of results is difficult, and a researcher needs to use statistical procedures to analyze a subject's feelings toward the concept.

Results from a semantic differential tell a researcher how one person perceives different concepts or how different people view the same concept. For example, political analysts might discover that young voters perceive their candidate as traditional, weak, and slow, and as halfway between good and bad. Older adult voters perceive the candidate as leaning toward strong, fast, and good, and as halfway between traditional and modern.

Box 6.10 Concepts in Action

Using the Semantic Differential

As part of her undergraduate thesis, Hawkes studied attitudes toward women with tattoos using the semantic differential (Hawkes, Senn, & Thorn, 2004). The researchers had 268 students at a medium-sized Canadian university complete a semantic differential form in response to several scenarios about a 22-year-old female university student with a tattoo. They had five scenarios in which they varied the size of the tattoo (small versus large) and whether or not it was visible, and one scenario with no details about the tattoo. The authors also varied features of the scenario: overweight or not; part-time job at restaurant, clothing store, or grocery store; boyfriend or not; average grades or failing grades. They used a semantic differential with 22 adjective pairs. They also had participants complete two scales: a feminist and women's movement scale and a neosexism scale. The semantic differential terms were selected to indicate three factors: evaluative, activity, and potency (strong/weak). Based on statistical analysis, three adjectives were dropped. The 19 items used are listed below. Among other findings, the authors found that there were more negative feelings toward a woman with a visible tattoo.

Box 1.3 *(continued)*

Good	_____	_____	_____	_____	_____	_____	_____	Bad*
Beautiful	_____	_____	_____	_____	_____	_____	_____	Ugly
Clean	_____	_____	_____	_____	_____	_____	_____	Dirty
Kind	_____	_____	_____	_____	_____	_____	_____	Cruel*
Rich	_____	_____	_____	_____	_____	_____	_____	Poor*
Honest	_____	_____	_____	_____	_____	_____	_____	Dishonest*
Pleasant	_____	_____	_____	_____	_____	_____	_____	Unpleasant*
Successful	_____	_____	_____	_____	_____	_____	_____	Unsuccessful
Reputable	_____	_____	_____	_____	_____	_____	_____	Disreputable
Safe	_____	_____	_____	_____	_____	_____	_____	Dangerous
Gentle	_____	_____	_____	_____	_____	_____	_____	Violent*
Feminine	_____	_____	_____	_____	_____	_____	_____	Masculine
Weak	_____	_____	_____	_____	_____	_____	_____	Powerful*
Passive	_____	_____	_____	_____	_____	_____	_____	Active*
Cautious	_____	_____	_____	_____	_____	_____	_____	Rash*
Soft	_____	_____	_____	_____	_____	_____	_____	Hard
Weak	_____	_____	_____	_____	_____	_____	_____	Strong
Mild	_____	_____	_____	_____	_____	_____	_____	Intense
Delicate	_____	_____	_____	_____	_____	_____	_____	Rugged*

*These items were presented in reverse order.

CHAPTER SUMMARY

Glossary Flashcards

In this chapter, you learned about the principles and processes of measurement in quantitative and qualitative research. All researchers conceptualize—or refine and clarify their ideas into conceptual definitions. All researchers operationalize—or develop a set of techniques or processes that will link their conceptual definitions to empirical reality. Qualitative and quantitative researchers, however, differ in how they approach these processes. The quantitative researcher takes a more deductive path, whereas the qualitative researcher takes a more inductive path. The goal remains the same, however: to establish unambiguous links between a researcher's abstract ideas and empirical data.

You also learned about the principles of reliability and validity. Reliability refers to the dependability or consistency of a measure; validity refers to its truthfulness, or how well a construct indicator and data for it fit together. Quantitative and qualitative styles of research significantly diverge in how they understand these principles. Nonetheless, both quantitative and qualitative researchers try to measure in a consistent way, and both seek a tight fit between the abstract ideas they use to understand the social world and what occurs in the actual, empirical social world. Alternative criteria for assessing the properties of reliability and validity of qualitative data and studies were also considered. It was discussed that many of the criteria of reliability and validity that quantitative researchers are concerned with can be argued to be inappropriate standards by which to judge qualitative research. Instead, the principles associated with Lincoln and Guba's (1985) notion of trustworthiness were introduced.

With regard to quantitative measurement, a number of terms were also introduced. First, levels of measurement were discussed, going from the least precise (nominal) to the most precise (interval/ratio). Examples of each level of measurement were given and it was described how various concepts can be measured at several different levels of measurement, but that the most detail is retained at the interval/ratio level. All indicators of concepts need to be measured in such a way that their categories are mutually exclusive (i.e., the categories do not overlap) and exhaustive (i.e., there is a potential response for anyone who answers the question).

Indices and scales were discussed as common ways that quantitative researchers measure various concepts that are relevant to social science research. The importance of standardization was also considered insofar as it makes rates across groups or categories (e.g., countries or provinces) of interest truly comparable.

Review Questions

Chapter Quiz

1. Define conceptualization and operationalization.
2. Using Figure 6.1 as a guide, explain the three levels of moving from conceptualization to operationalization.
3. Explain three ways that conceptualization and operationalization are different in qualitative and quantitative work.
4. Define reliability and validity.
5. Explain the four ways that reliability can be improved.
6. Identify and define the four major ways of establishing measurement validity.
7. Explain what is meant by mutually exclusive and exhaustive attributes.
8. Define trustworthiness and explain how it applies to the assessment of qualitative research.
9. Define and give examples of the four levels of measurement.
10. What is a Likert scale? How are scales and indices different?

Exercises

 Research Activities

1. Think of the concept of income and educational attainment. Create these variables at the nominal, ordinal, and interval/ratio levels of measurement. Be sure to include the survey question that would be asked to a respondent as well as the response categories. Comment on the amount of detail a researcher would lose moving from the highest level of measurement to the lowest level of measurement.
2. Using EBSCO's ContentSelect, find two quantitative sociology articles that use a scale or index as part of their methodology. Describe the scale or index. What concept was it measuring? How was it created? Did the authors use the scale or index as a dependent or independent variable?
3. Using EBSCO's ContentSelect, find a quantitative sociology article that addresses the idea of reliability or validity. What type of reliability or validity does the author talk about? How does he or she address it?

MySearchLab

Visit MySearchLab, where you'll find thousands of full-text articles from academic journals and help with the research and writing process. Access the eText within MySearchLab to take self-grading practice tests and view a variety of multimedia resources.

Chapter 7
Qualitative and Quantitative Sampling

Photo Credit: Dreamstime

LEARNING OBJECTIVES

After reading this chapter, you will be able to

LO 1 Define nonprobability sampling.

LO 2 Explain the various types of nonprobability sampling.

LO 3 Define probability sampling.

LO 4 Explain the different terminologies associated with probability sampling.

LO 5 Explain why randomness is important in sampling and how randomness is related to the margin of error.

LO 6 Explain the various types of probability sampling.

LO 7 Explain the relationship between samples and drawing inferences.

INTRODUCTION

Qualitative and quantitative researchers approach sampling differently. Most discussions of sampling come from researchers who use the quantitative style. Their primary goal is to get a representative **sample**, or a small collection of units or cases from a much larger collection or population, such that the researcher can study the smaller group and produce accurate generalizations about the larger group. They tend to use sampling based on theories of probability from mathematics (called probability sampling).

sample: A smaller set of cases a researcher selects from a larger pool and generalizes to the *population*.

Box 7.1 In the News

The Canadian Census Controversy

In the summer of 2010, the Conservative government announced that there would be changes to how the 2011 Canadian Census was conducted. For the past 35 years, in addition to the standard "short form" comprising about 10 questions, the Canadian Census has included the "long form," which was administered to 20 percent of Canadians. The long form contained around 40 additional questions, ranging from ethnic and religious identity to how much time people spent in unpaid work (e.g., caring for the elderly).

The Conservative government argued that these data could be collected through a *voluntary* household survey. Industry Minister Tony Clement argued that a primary reason for eliminating the long form was to protect Canadians from fear of being jailed or fined (as everyone is required by law to complete the Census), although there is no evidence that anyone has ever been prosecuted under this law.

Statistics Canada's chief statistician, Munir Sheikh, resigned from his post on July 21, 2010, out of protest that the quality of data that Statistics Canada was being asked to collect through a *voluntary* survey logically could not replace the mandatory 20 percent sample of the Canadian population. Even though the voluntary form would be sent to one-third of Canadian households, prior research shows that such voluntary surveys are much less likely to be returned by ethnic, linguistic, and economic minorities—the very groups that social policy researchers who use these data are trying to help. In other words, the data would not be representative of the Canadian population because of poor *response rates*. There is the very real concern that the people who are not filling out the survey are systematically different from the target population, a phenomenon known as *nonresponse bias*. It could be the case that people who do answer the survey are more fluent in English or French, are more personally interested in surveys, or are less busy than those who do not. The result of nonresponse bias is that a sample is not representative of its target population, making generalizations from the data produced from such samples questionable.

census: An attempt to count everyone in a target population.

Discussion of Methodology

Research Methodology

Researchers have two motivations for using probability or random sampling. The first motivation is saving time and cost. If sampling is properly conducted, results from a sample may yield results at one-thousandth of the cost and time. For example, instead of gathering data from 20 million people, a researcher may draw a sample of 2000; the data from those 2000 are equal for most purposes to the data from all 20 million. The second purpose of probability sampling is accuracy. The results of a well-designed, carefully executed probability sample will produce results that are equally as accurate as trying to reach every single person in the whole population. A **census** is an attempt to count everyone in the target population. National censuses take place in Canada every five years, with the next one to occur in May of 2015 (see Box 7.1).

Qualitative researchers focus less on a sample's representativeness or on detailed techniques for drawing a probability sample. Instead, they focus on how the sample or small collection of cases, units, or activities illuminates key features of social life. The purpose of sampling is to collect cases, events, or actions that clarify and deepen understanding. Qualitative researchers' concern is to find cases that will enhance what the researchers learn about the processes of social life in a specific context. For this reason, qualitative researchers tend toward a second type of sampling: nonprobability sampling.

LO 1 Define nonprobability sampling.

NONPROBABILITY SAMPLING

nonrandom sample: A type of *sample* in which the *sampling elements* are selected using something other than a mathematically random process.

Qualitative researchers rarely draw a representative sample from a huge number of cases to intensely study the sampled cases—which is the goal in quantitative research. Instead, they use nonprobability or **nonrandom samples**. This means they rarely determine the sample size in advance and have limited knowledge about the larger group or population from which the sample is taken. Unlike the quantitative researcher, who uses a preplanned approach based on mathematical theory, the qualitative researcher selects cases gradually, with the specific content of a case determining whether it is chosen. Table 7.1 shows a variety of nonprobability sampling techniques.

Table 7.1 Types of Nonprobability Samples

Type of Sample	Principle
Haphazard	Get any cases in any manner that is convenient.
Quota	Get a preset number of cases in each of several predetermined categories that will reflect the diversity of the population, using haphazard methods.
Purposive	Get all possible cases that fit particular criteria, using various methods.
Snowball	Get cases using referrals from one or a few cases, and then referrals from those cases, and so forth.
Sequential	Get cases until there is no additional information or new characteristics (often used with other sampling methods).

Haphazard, Accidental, or Convenience Sampling

LO 2 Define nonprobability sampling.

haphazard sampling: A type of *nonrandom sample* in which the researcher selects anyone he or she happens to come across.

Haphazard sampling can produce ineffective, highly unrepresentative samples and is not recommended. When a researcher haphazardly selects cases that are convenient, he or she can easily get a sample that seriously misrepresents the population. Such samples are cheap and quick; however, the systematic errors that easily occur make them worse than no sample at all. The person-on-the-street interview conducted by television programs is an example of a haphazard sample. Television interviewers go out on the street with camera and microphone to talk to a few people who are convenient to interview. The people walking past a television studio in the middle of the day do not represent everyone (e.g., homemakers, people in rural areas). Likewise, television interviewers often select people who look "normal" to them and avoid people who are unattractive, poor, very old, or inarticulate.

Another example of a haphazard sample is that of television shows or websites that ask people to phone in or to vote on topics online. Not everyone watches the show or looks at these websites, has an interest in the topic, or will take the time to vote by phone or online. Some people will, and the number who do so may seem large (e.g., 5000), but the sample cannot be used to generalize accurately to the population. Such haphazard samples may have entertainment value, but they can give a distorted view and seriously misrepresent the population.

Quota Sampling

quota sampling: A type of *nonrandom sample* in which the researcher first identifies general categories into which cases or people will be selected, then he or she selects a predetermined number of cases in each category.

Quota sampling is an improvement over haphazard sampling. In quota sampling, a researcher first identifies relevant categories of people (e.g., male and female; under age 30, ages 30 to 60, over age 60), then decides how many to get in each category. Thus, the number of people in various categories of the sample is fixed. For example, a researcher decides to select five males and five females under age 30, 10 males and 10 females aged 30 to 60, and five males and five females over age 60 for a 40-person sample. It is difficult to represent all population characteristics accurately (see Figure 7.1).

Quota sampling is an improvement over haphazard sampling because the researcher can ensure that some differences are in the sample; in haphazard sampling, all those interviewed might be of the same age, sex, or race. But once the quota sampler fixes the categories and number of cases in each category, he or she uses haphazard sampling. For example, the researcher interviews the first five males under age 30 he or she encounters, even if all five just walked out of the campaign headquarters of a political candidate. Not only is misrepresentation possible because haphazard sampling is used within the categories, but nothing prevents the researcher from selecting people who "act friendly" or who want to be interviewed.

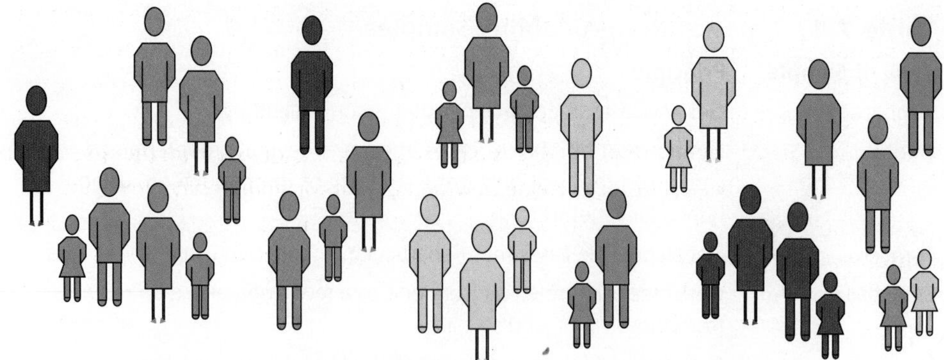
Of 32 adults and children in the street scene, select 10 for the sample:

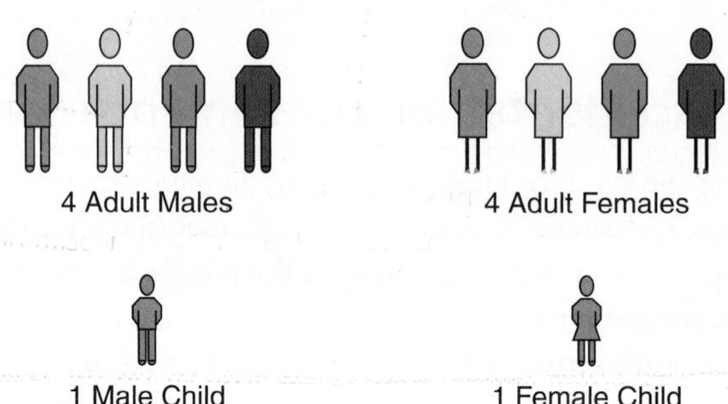

Figure 7.1 Quota Sampling

Purposive Sampling

purposive sampling: A type of *nonrandom sample* in which the researcher uses a wide range of methods to locate all possible cases of a highly specific and difficult-to-reach *population*.

Purposive sampling is used in situations in which an expert uses judgment in selecting cases with a specific purpose in mind. It is inappropriate if it is used to pick the "average housewife" or the "typical school." With purposive sampling, the researcher never knows whether the cases selected represent the population. It is often used in exploratory research or in field research.

Purposive sampling is appropriate in three situations. First, a researcher uses it to select unique cases that are especially informative. For example, a researcher wants to use content analysis to study magazines to find cultural themes. He or she selects a specific popular women's magazine to study because it is trend setting.

Second, a researcher may use purposive sampling to select members of a difficult-to-reach, specialized population (see "Hidden Populations" later in this chapter). For example, the researcher wants to study sex workers. It is impossible to list all sex workers and sample randomly from the list. Instead, he or she uses subjective information (e.g., locations where sex workers solicit, social groups with whom sex workers associate) and experts (e.g., police who work on vice units, other sex workers) to identify a "sample" of sex workers for inclusion in the research project. The researcher uses many different methods to identify the cases, because his or her goal is to locate as many cases as possible.

Third, purposive sampling occurs when a researcher wants to identify particular types of cases for in-depth investigation. The purpose is less to generalize to a larger population than it is to gain a deeper understanding of types.

deviant case sampling: A type of *nonrandom sample* in which a researcher selects unusual or nonconforming cases purposely as a way to provide greater insight into social processes or a setting; especially used by qualitative researchers.

A special case of purposive sampling is known as **deviant case sampling**, in which a researcher seeks cases that differ from the dominant pattern or that differ from the predominant characteristics of other cases. Like purposive sampling, a researcher uses a variety of techniques to locate cases with specific characteristics. Deviant case sampling is a special type of purposive sampling in that the goal is to locate a collection of unusual, different, or peculiar cases that are not representative of the whole. The deviant cases are selected because they are unusual, and a researcher hopes to learn more about social life by considering cases that fall outside the general pattern or by including what is beyond the main flow of events.

When Can We Use Qualitative Methods?

For example, a researcher is interested in studying high school dropouts. Let's say that previous research suggested that the majority of dropouts come from families that have low income, are single-parent or unstable, have been geographically mobile, and are racial minorities. The family environment is one in which parents or siblings have low education or are themselves dropouts. A researcher using deviant case sampling would seek majority-group dropouts who are from stable two-parent, upper-middle-income families who are geographically stable and well educated.

Snowball Sampling

Snowball sampling (also called *network, chain referral,* or *reputational sampling*) is a method for identifying and sampling (or selecting) the cases in a network. It is based on an analogy to a snowball, which begins small but becomes larger as it is rolled and picks up additional snow. Snowball sampling is a multistage technique. It begins with one or a few people or cases and spreads out on the basis of links to the initial cases.

snowball sampling: A type of *non-random sample* in which the researcher begins with one case then, based on information about interrelationships from that case, identifies other cases, and then repeats the process again and again.

One use of snowball sampling is to sample a network. Social researchers are often interested in an interconnected network of people or organizations. The network could be scientists around the world investigating the same problem, elites of a medium-sized city, members of an organized crime family, individuals who sit on the boards of directors of major banks and corporations, or people on a university campus who have had sexual relations with each other. The crucial feature is that each person or unit is connected with another through a direct or indirect linkage. This does not mean that each person directly knows, interacts with, or is influenced by every other person in the network; rather, it means that, taken as a whole, with direct and indirect links, they are within an interconnected web of linkages.

Researchers represent such a network by drawing a **sociogram**—a diagram of circles connected with lines. For example, Sally and Tim do not know each other directly, but each has a good friend in common, Susan, so they have an indirect connection. All three are part of the same friendship network. The circles represent each person or case, and the lines represent friendship or other linkages (see Figure 7.2).

sociogram: A diagram or "map" that shows the network of social relationships, influence patterns, or communication paths among a group of people or units.

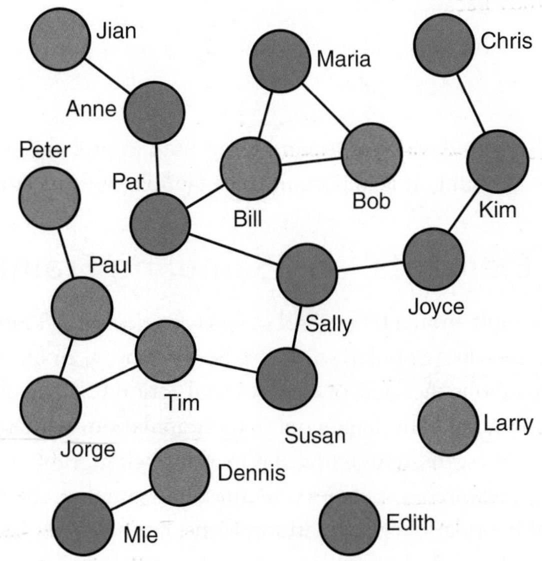

Figure 7.2 Sociogram of Friendship Relations

Researchers also use snowball sampling in combination with purposive sampling, as in the case of Albanese (2006) in a qualitative study of women in Quebec whose children were in provincial child care. The Quebec policy to provide low-cost child care to families changed in 2000 to create a network of child care centres that provided out-of-school care to 0- to 12-year-olds. Albanese was interested in studying the social and economic impact of the low-cost child care program in the community and within domestic family relations. She focused on a small, economically hard-hit community comprising two towns near the Ontario–Quebec border. First, she used snowball sampling to identify mothers who used the child care program. Her snowball sample began asking mothers for the names of other mothers in the area who used the daycare program and the names of the care providers they used. She then asked those women to refer her to others in a similar situation, and asked those respondents to refer her to still others. She identified 16 mothers who used the child care program and 17 child care providers and conducted in-depth, open-ended interviews about their experiences and opinions of the program.

Sequential Sampling

sequential sampling: A type of *nonrandom sample* in which a researcher tries to find as many relevant cases as possible until there is no new information or diversity from the cases.

Sequential sampling is similar to purposive sampling with one difference. In purposive sampling, the researcher tries to find as many relevant cases as possible until time, financial resources, or his or her energy is exhausted; the goal is to get every possible case. In sequential sampling, a researcher continues to gather cases until the amount of new information or diversity of cases is filled. In economic terms, information is gathered until the marginal utility, or incremental benefit for additional cases, levels off or drops significantly. It requires that a researcher continuously evaluate all the collected cases. For example, a researcher locates and plans in-depth interviews with 60 widows over 70 years old who have been living without a spouse for 10 or more years. Depending on the researcher's purposes, getting an additional 20 widows whose life experiences, social backgrounds, and worldviews differ little from the first 60 may be unnecessary.

theoretical sampling: An iterative sampling technique associated with the *grounded theory* approach in which the sample size is determined when the data reach *theoretical saturation.*

theoretical saturation: A term associated with the *grounded theory* approach that refers to the point at which no new themes emerge from the data and sampling is considered complete.

Related to sequential sampling is the concept of *theoretical sampling*, which is a sampling concept that is tied to grounded theory, which was discussed in Chapters 2 and 5. With grounded theory, the theory emerges from the data and we don't know how many cases we will need in our study beforehand. Researchers who use grounded theory techniques often employ **theoretical sampling**, which means that they continue to collect data until no new information emerges. Researchers refer to this point as **theoretical saturation**.

LO 3 Define probability sampling.

LO 4 Explain the different terminologies associated with probability sampling.

PROBABILITY SAMPLING

A specialized vocabulary has developed around terms used in probability sampling. Before examining probability sampling, it is important to be familiar with its language.

Populations, Elements, and Sampling Frames

sampling element: The name for a case or single unit to be selected.

population: The name for the large general group of many cases from which a researcher draws a *sample* and which is usually stated in theoretical terms.

A researcher draws a sample from a larger pool of cases, or *elements*. A **sampling element** is the unit of analysis or case in a population. It can be a person, a group, an organization, a written document or symbolic message, or even a social action (e.g., an arrest, a divorce, or a kiss) that is being measured. The large pool is the **population**, which has an important role in sampling. Sometimes, the term *universe* is used interchangeably with *population*. To define the population, a researcher specifies the unit being sampled, the geographical location, and the temporal boundaries of populations. Consider the examples of populations in Box 7.2. All the examples include the elements to be sampled (e.g., people, businesses, hospital admissions, commercials) and geographical and time boundaries.

Box 7.2 Making It Practical

Examples of Populations

1. All persons aged 16 or older living in Regina on December 2, 2013, who were not incarcerated in prison, asylums, and similar institutions
2. All business establishments employing more than 100 persons in Ontario that operated in the month of July 2012
3. All admissions to public or private hospitals in the province of Alberta between August 1, 2010, and August 1, 2012
4. All television commercials aired between 7:00 a.m. and 11:00 p.m. Eastern Standard Time on three major Canadian networks between November 1 and November 25, 2012
5. All currently practising physicians in Canada who received medical degrees between January 1, 1960, and the present
6. All male heroin addicts in the Vancouver, British Columbia, or Seattle, Washington, metropolitan areas during 2012

A researcher begins with an idea of the population (e.g., all people in a city) but defines it more precisely. The term **target population** refers to the specific pool of cases that he or she wants to study. The ratio of the size of the sample to the size of the target population is the **sampling ratio**. For example, the population has 50 000 people, and a researcher draws a sample of 150 from it. Thus, the sampling ratio is 150/50 000 = 0.003, or 0.3 percent. If the population is 500 and the researcher samples 100, then the sampling ratio is 100/500 = 0.20, or 20 percent.

target population: The name for the large general group of many cases from which a *sample* is drawn and which is specified in very concrete terms.

sampling ratio: The number of cases in the *sample* divided by the number of cases in the *population* or the *sampling frame*, or the proportion of the *population* in the *sample*.

A population is an abstract concept. How can population be an abstract concept when there are a given number of people at a certain time? Except for specific small populations, one can never truly freeze a population to measure it. For example, in a city at any given moment, some people are dying, some are boarding or getting off airplanes, and some are in cars driving across city boundaries. The researcher must decide exactly whom to count. Should he or she count a city resident who happens to be on vacation when the time is fixed? What about the tourist staying at a hotel in the city when the time is fixed? Should he or she count adults, children, people in jails, or those in hospitals? A population—even that of all those over the age of 18 years in the city limits of St. John's, Newfoundland, at 12:01 a.m. on March 1, 2013—is an abstract concept. It exists in the mind but is impossible to pinpoint concretely.

Because a population is an abstract concept, except for small specialized populations (e.g., all the students in a classroom), a researcher needs to estimate the population. As an abstract concept, the population needs an operational definition. This process is similar to developing operational definitions for constructs that are measured.

A researcher operationalizes a population by developing a specific list that closely approximates all the elements in the population. This list is a **sampling frame**. He or she can choose from many types of sampling frames: telephone directories, tax records, driver's licence records, and so on. Listing the elements in a population sounds simple, but it is often difficult because there may be no good list of elements in a population, or the list that does exist is not available to the researcher (i.e., lists held by government agencies).

sampling frame: A list of cases in a *population*, or the best approximation of it.

A good sampling frame is crucial to good sampling. A mismatch between the sampling frame and the conceptually defined population can be a major source of error. Just as a mismatch between the theoretical and operational definitions of a variable creates invalid measurement, so too does a mismatch between the sampling frame and the population, which causes invalid sampling. Researchers try to minimize mismatches. For example, you would like to sample all people in a region of Canada, so you decide to get a list of everyone with a driver's licence. But some people do not have a driver's licence, and the lists of those with a licence, even if updated regularly, quickly go out of date. Next, you try income tax records. But not everyone pays taxes; some people cheat and do not pay, others have no income and do not have to file, some have died or have not begun to pay taxes, and still

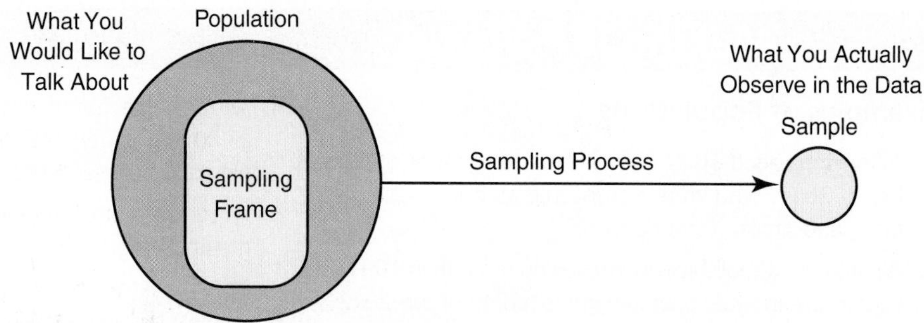

Figure 7.3 A Model of the Logic of Sampling

others have entered or left the area since the last time taxes were due. You try telephone directories, but they are not much better; some people are not listed in a telephone directory, many people now only use cellphones and don't have a landline, some people have unlisted numbers, and others have recently moved. With a few exceptions (e.g., a list of all students enrolled at a university), sampling frames are almost always inaccurate. A sampling frame can include some of those outside the target population (e.g., a telephone directory that lists people who have moved away) or might omit some of those inside it (e.g., those without a landline telephone).

parameter: A characteristic of the entire *population* that is estimated from a *sample*.

statistic: A numerical estimate of a *population parameter* computed from a *sample*.

Any characteristic of a population (e.g., the percentage of city residents who smoke cigarettes, the average height of all women over the age of 21, the percentage of people who believe in UFOs) is a population **parameter**. It is the true characteristic of the population. Parameters are determined when all elements in a population are measured. The parameter is never known with absolute accuracy for large populations (e.g., an entire nation), so researchers must estimate it on the basis of samples. They use information from the sample, called a **statistic**, to estimate population parameters (see Figure 7.3). You can remember these easily because parameters relate to populations (both starting with a *P*) and statistics relate to samples (both starting with an *S*)!

A famous case in the history of sampling illustrates the limitations of the technique. The *Literary Digest*, a major American magazine, sent postcards to people before the 1920, 1924, 1928, and 1932 U.S. presidential elections. The magazine took the names for the sample from automobile registrations and telephone directories—the sampling frame. People returned the postcards indicating whom they would vote for. The magazine correctly predicted all four election outcomes. The magazine's success with predictions was well known, and in 1936 it increased the sample to 10 million. The magazine predicted a huge victory for Alf Landon over Franklin D. Roosevelt. But the *Literary Digest* was wrong: Franklin D. Roosevelt won by a landslide.

The prediction was wrong for several reasons, but the most important was mistakes in sampling. Although the magazine sampled a large number of people, its sampling frame did not accurately represent the target population (i.e., all voters). It excluded people without telephones or automobiles, which was a sizable percentage of the population in 1936, during the worst of the Great Depression of the 1930s. The frame excluded as much as 65 percent of the population and a segment of the voting population (lower income) that tended to favour Roosevelt. The magazine had been accurate in earlier elections because people with higher and lower incomes did not differ in how they voted. Also, during elections before the Depression more lower-income people could afford to have telephones and automobiles.

You can learn two important lessons from the *Literary Digest* mistake. First, the sampling frame is crucial. Second, the size of a sample is less important than whether or not it accurately represents the population. A representative sample of 2500 can give more accurate predictions about a population than a nonrepresentative sample of 1 million or even 10 million.

Box 7.3 Making It Practical

It's Not So Random

A word on language: The term *random* has become a common word in everyday language, where it is used to describe an odd or unusual event or something that the speaker thinks is strange (e.g., "That's so random!" in the cartoon above). When you are speaking of samples and statistics, however, random has a *very precise* meaning. It means that the odds of that sample or sample statistic having been produced can be calculated into a probability. Do not confuse the slang version of *random* with the statistical meaning of *random*—they have very different and even opposing meanings!

"Ha-ha, that's so random."

Photo Credit: Original Artist/CSL, CartoonStock Ltd

Why Random?

LO5 Explain why randomness is important in sampling and how randomness is related to the margin of error.

The area of applied mathematics called probability theory relies on random processes. The word *random* has a special meaning in mathematics (see Box 7.3). It refers to a process that generates a mathematically random result: that is, the selection process operates in a truly random method (i.e., no pattern), and a researcher can calculate the probability of outcomes. In a true random process, each element has an equal probability of being selected.

Probability samples that rely on random processes require more work than nonrandom ones. A researcher must identify specific sampling elements (e.g., individuals) to include in the sample. For example, if conducting a telephone survey, the researcher needs to try to reach the specific sampled person by calling back four or five times to get an accurate random sample.

Random samples are most likely to yield a sample that truly represents the population. In addition, random sampling lets a researcher statistically calculate the relationship between the sample and the population—that is, the size of the **sampling error**. A nonstatistical definition of the sampling error is the deviation between sample results and a population parameter caused by random processes. This is related to an idea called the **margin of error** (see Box 7.4), which is an estimate about the amount of sampling error that exists in a survey's results.

sampling error: How much a *sample* deviates from being representative of the *population.*

margin of error: An estimate about the amount of *sampling error* that exists in a survey's results.

A **random sample** is based on a great deal of sophisticated mathematics. This chapter focuses on the fundamentals of how sampling works, the difference between good and bad samples, how to draw a sample, and basic principles of sampling in social research. This does not mean that random sampling is unimportant, but it is essential to first master the fundamentals. If you plan to pursue a career using quantitative research, you should get more statistical background than space permits here.

random sample: A type of *sample* in which the researcher uses a *random-number table* or similar mathematical random process so that each *sampling element* in the *population* will have an equal probability of being selected.

LO6 Explain the various types of probability sampling.

Types of Probability Samples

Simple Random The simple random sample is both the easiest random sample to understand and the one on which other types are modelled. In **simple random sampling,** a researcher develops an accurate sampling frame, selects elements from the sampling frame according to a mathematically random procedure, then locates the exact element that was selected for inclusion in the sample.

simple random sampling: A type of *random sample* in which a researcher creates a *sampling frame* and uses a pure random process to select cases. Each *sampling element* in the *population* will have an equal probability of being selected.

Box 7.4 In the News

What Is the Margin of Error?

You have probably heard a news announcer, after talking about the results of a poll, state that the margin of error was "plus or minus" some percentage points "19 times out of 20." Or perhaps you've seen a similar phrase written at the end of a newspaper article that is reporting on some kind of poll result. What does it mean?

A poll conducted shortly after the 2010 Winter Olympics in Canada by Ipsos Reid found that two-thirds of Quebecers and 80 percent of all Canadians would consider themselves "Canadian nationalists," which was a sharp rise from the results of an identical poll taken a year previously, where the corresponding figures were 48 percent and 72 percent, respectively. Thus, it seems like the success of Canada at the Olympics managed to drum up Canadian nationalism, particularly in French Canada. We are also told in the news story that "The margin of error was 3.1 percent, 19 times out of 20."

Simply put, this means that the figures of 66 percent of Quebecers and 80 percent of Canadians reportedly calling themselves Canadian nationalists would likely be more in the region of 62.9 to 69.1 percent (66 − 3.1 and 66 + 3.1) for Quebecers and 76.9 to 83.1 percent (80 − 3.1 and 80 + 3.1) for all Canadians if we took additional random samples of the Canadian population. One random sample was actually taken for the study, which is always subject to some kind of sampling error. If we were to do 18 more random samples, we would find that the percentages of Quebecers and Canadians in general saying they considered themselves Canadian nationalists would fit in the range of answers plus or minus 3.1 percentage points of the figure that was already obtained. And this would occur in 19 of 20 samples. One time out of 20, we would expect results that fell outside of this range due to chance alone.

Source: Iype, M. (2010, March 8). Canadian unity in 'sweet spot' thanks to Olympic afterglow: Pollster. *Vancouver Sun.* Retrieved from www.vancouversun.com/sports/2010wintergames/Canadian+unity+sweet+spot+thanks+Olympics/2654061/story.html

random-number table: A list of numbers that has no pattern in it and that is used to create a random process for selecting cases and other randomization purposes.

After numbering all elements in a sampling frame, a researcher uses a list of random numbers (see Box 7.5) to decide which elements to select. He or she needs as many random numbers as there are elements to be sampled; for example, for a sample of 100, 100 random numbers are needed. The researcher can get random numbers from a **random-number table**, a table of numbers chosen in a mathematically random way. Random-number tables are available in most statistics and research methods books. The numbers are generated by a pure random process so that any number has an equal probability of appearing in any position. Computer programs can also produce lists of random numbers.

You may ask, "Once I select an element from the sampling frame, do I then return it to the sampling frame or do I keep it separate?" The common answer is that it is not returned. Unrestricted random sampling is random sampling with replacement—that is, replacing an element after sampling it so it can be selected again. In simple random sampling without replacement, the researcher ignores elements already selected into the sample.

The logic of simple random sampling can be illustrated with an example. You have a large university campus with 30 000 students. It would be very expensive and time consuming to survey every student on campus. You want to know the gender and age composition of the student body. You don't have to survey everyone to get an estimate of the proportion of females to males or the average age. You can take a random sample and get reasonable estimations of the population parameters.

The 30 000 students are your population, and the parameters you want to estimate are the proportion of males/females and the average age of undergraduate students. You randomly select 30 students by their student ID numbers (a 0.1 percent sample) using a random sample generator on your statistical software program. Now you have a random sample of students you can administer a survey to. Count the number of males and females in your sample to estimate the percentage of males versus females in the population. This is a lot easier than counting all 30 000 students. Let's say that your sample has 15 males and 15 females.

Box 7.5 Social Research and the Internet

There are various free online services that can help you pick random numbers if you do not have access to statistical software and find the idea of a random-number table a bit too "old fashioned" or cumbersome. The aptly named website www.random.org has a variety of resources for social researchers as well as links to dozens of free tools that will help you pick any random number between two integers, randomize lists that you already have, and even more fully explain the definition and principles of randomness.

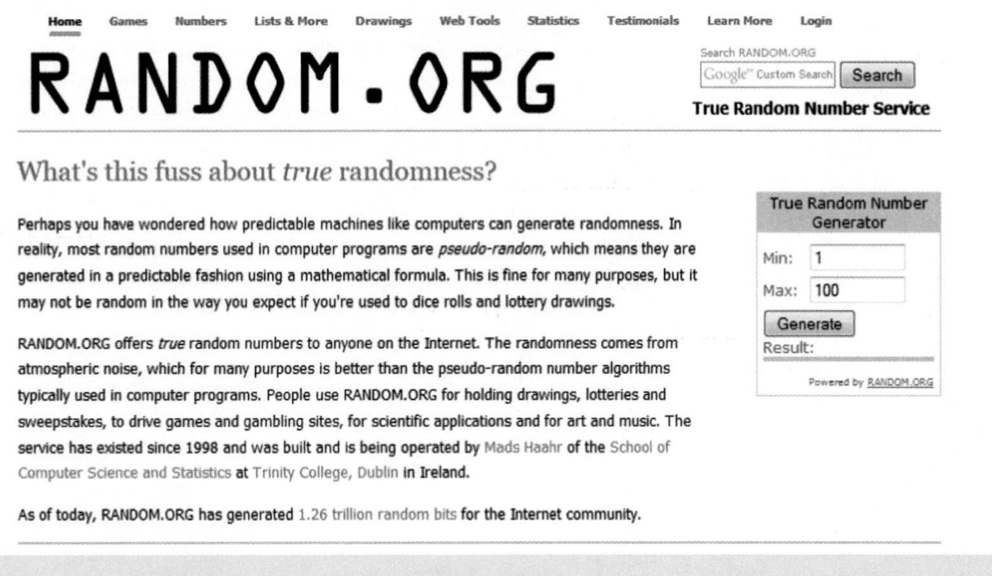

Home Games Numbers Lists & More Drawings Web Tools Statistics Testimonials Learn More Login
RANDOM.ORG
Search RANDOM.ORG
Search
True Random Number Service
What's this fuss about true randomness?
Perhaps you have wondered how predictable machines like computers can generate randomness. In reality, most random numbers used in computer programs are pseudo-random, which means they are generated in a predictable fashion using a mathematical formula. This is fine for many purposes, but it may not be random in the way you expect if you're used to dice rolls and lottery drawings.
RANDOM.ORG offers true random numbers to anyone on the Internet. The randomness comes from atmospheric noise, which for many purposes is better than the pseudo-random number algorithms typically used in computer programs. People use RANDOM.ORG for holding drawings, lotteries and sweepstakes, to drive games and gambling sites, for scientific applications and for art and music. The service has existed since 1998 and was built and is being operated by Mads Haahr of the School of Computer Science and Statistics at Trinity College, Dublin in Ireland.
As of today, RANDOM.ORG has generated 1.26 trillion random bits for the Internet community.
True Random Number Generator
Min: 1
Max: 100
Generate
Result:
Powered by RANDOM.ORG

Source: www.random.org. Printed with permission.

Does this mean that the population parameter is 50 percent female? Maybe, maybe not. Because of random chance, your specific sample might be off. You can check your results by drawing a second random sample of 30 students. On the second try, your sample has 17 males and 13 females. Now you have a problem. Which is correct? How good is this random sampling business if different samples from the same population can yield different results? Let's say you repeat the procedure over and over until you have drawn 100 different samples of 30 samples. The results of your 100 different samples reveal a clear pattern (see Table 7.2). The most common mix of males and females is 50/50. Samples that are close to that split are more frequent than those with more uneven splits. The population parameter appears to be 50 percent female and 50 percent male.

Table 7.2 represents a special statistical feature called the **sampling distribution**. In the second part of the table we have graphed the numbers of females in each of our 100 samples. You can see that the resulting shape is one that resembles a normal curve. In other words, the more samples we take, the more likely we are to get an estimate of the true population parameter. In a handful of cases we got samples that were way off—with 22 females or 8 females, for example. However, the middle of the sampling distribution contains the greatest number of cases. In our random selection of 100 samples of 30, an equal number of males and females was observed the most—22 times. And estimates around those similar figures, such as 14 or 16 females, were observed rather frequently as well.

sampling distribution: A distribution created by drawing many *random samples* from the same *population.*

We can also do this type of illustration with a continuous variable like age. In Table 7.2, sex was used as an example of a nominal variable, with the sample averages represented as proportions (e.g., half or 15/30 respondents were female). In your first random sample of 30 students, you could calculate the average age of students by adding up all the ages and dividing by 30, finding that the average is 20.44 years. Again, this does not necessarily mean that the average age of students in your population is 20.44 years of age.

Table 7.2 Example of Sampling Distribution

Males	Females	Number of Samples
22	8	1
21	9	1
20	10	2
19	11	4
18	12	5
17	13	9
16	14	16
15	15	22
14	16	15
13	17	10
12	18	8
11	19	4
10	20	2
9	21	1
	Total	100

Number of male and female students who were randomly drawn from a population of 30 000 students with 30 drawn each time, repeated 100 times for 100 independent random samples.

Number of Samples

22								*							
21								*							
20								*							
19								*							
18								*							
17								*							
16							*	*							
15							*	*	*						
14							*	*	*						
13							*	*	*						
12							*	*	*						
11							*	*	*						
10							*	*	*	*					
9						*	*	*	*	*					
8						*	*	*	*	*	*				
7						*	*	*	*	*	*				
6						*	*	*	*	*	*				
5					*	*	*	*	*	*	*				
4				*	*	*	*	*	*	*	*	*			
3				*	*	*	*	*	*	*	*	*			
2			*	*	*	*	*	*	*	*	*	*	*		
1	*	*	*	*	*	*	*	*	*	*	*	*	*	*	*
	22	21	20	19	18	17	16	15	14	13	12	11	10	9	8

Number of Females in a Sample

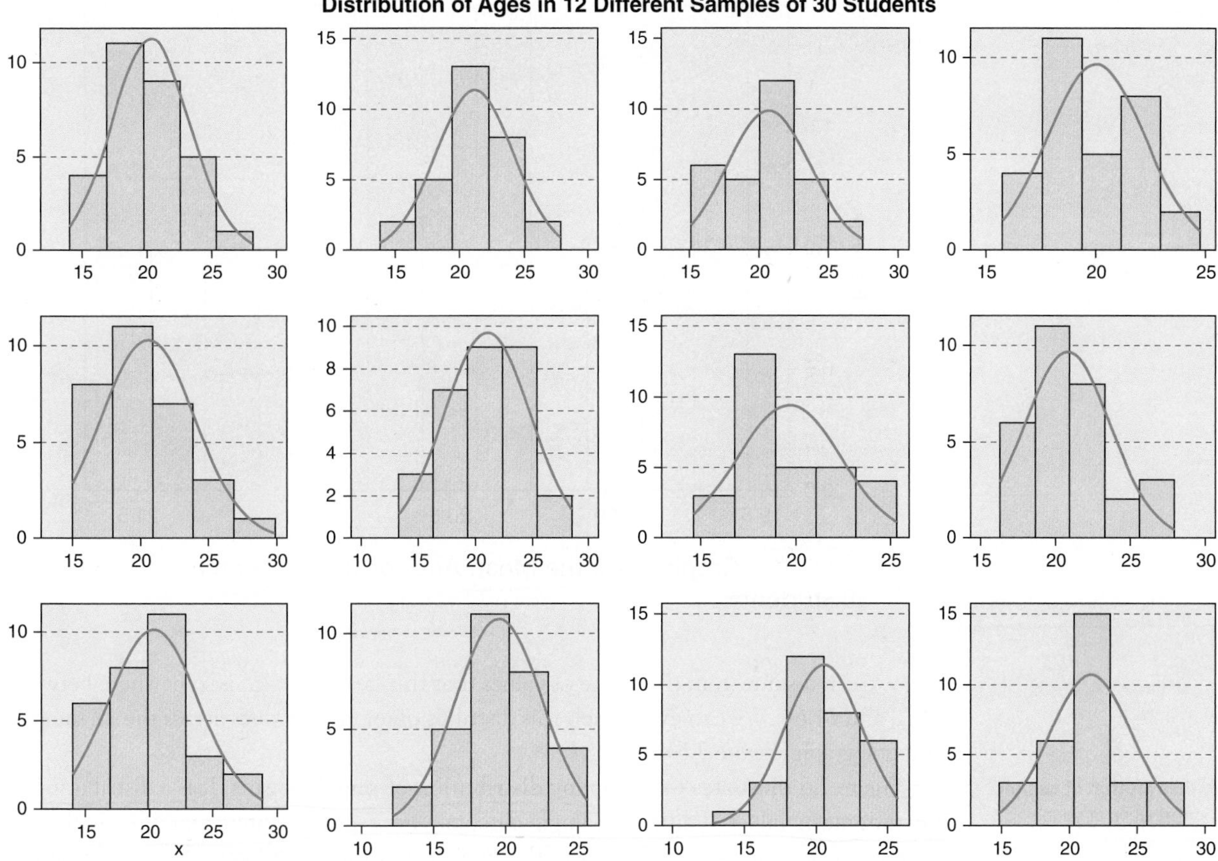

Figure 7.4 Distributions of Ages in 12 Different Samples of 30 Students

Because of random chance, your specific sample might be "off." You can check your results by sampling another 30 students. On the second try, your average age is 19.63. By way of example, we repeat the procedure over and over until we have drawn 12 different samples of 30 students each. The results of the 12 different samples reveals an average that ranges from 19.70 to 21.63, summarized below in Figure 7.4. The graphs of the 12 different distributions of age across each of the samples shows that each sample revealed slightly different information on age.

Sample	Age
1	21.63
2	20.38
3	21.16
4	20.71
5	20.01
6	20.53
7	21.05
8	19.70
9	20.80
10	20.27
11	19.55
12	20.61

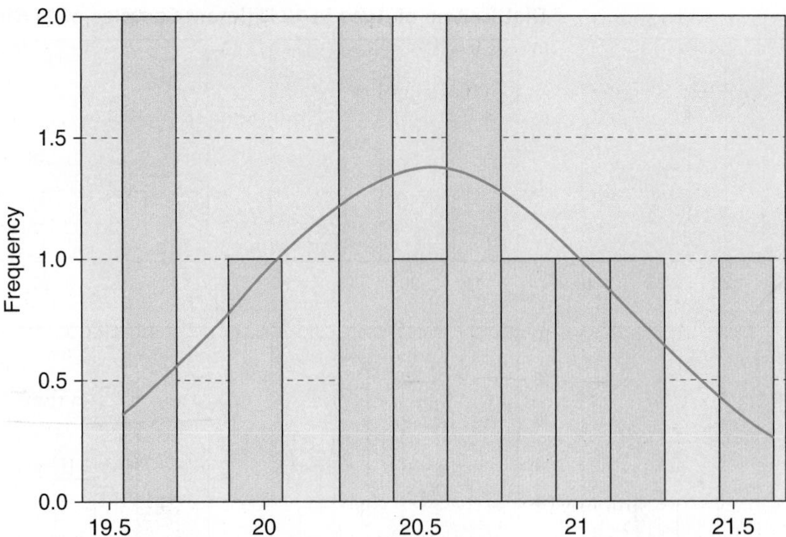

Figure 7.5 Graph of All the Mean Ages of the 12 Samples of 30 Students

We can assume from this range of values that the "real" average is somewhere between 19.70 and 21.64. We can even graph this distribution of mean values across the 12 samples into one graph (Figure 7.5).

sampling distribution of sample means: A distribution of sample means created by drawing many *random samples* from the same *population.*

Figure 7.5 illustrates the **sampling distribution of sample means.** It is a distribution of different mean values of different sample outcomes from many separate random samples. As more random samples are taken from the population, the more likely the distribution of sample means represents a normal distribution. This tendency toward shaping a normal distribution is illustrated in Figure 7.6, where the mean age of 100 different random samples of 30 students are plotted.

This tendency toward a normal distribution of the sample mean will appear if the sample size is 100 instead of 30; if the population has 100 000 students or 10 million students instead of 30 000; and if the population is cats, automobiles, or hospitals instead of students. In fact, the pattern will become clearer as more and more independent random samples are

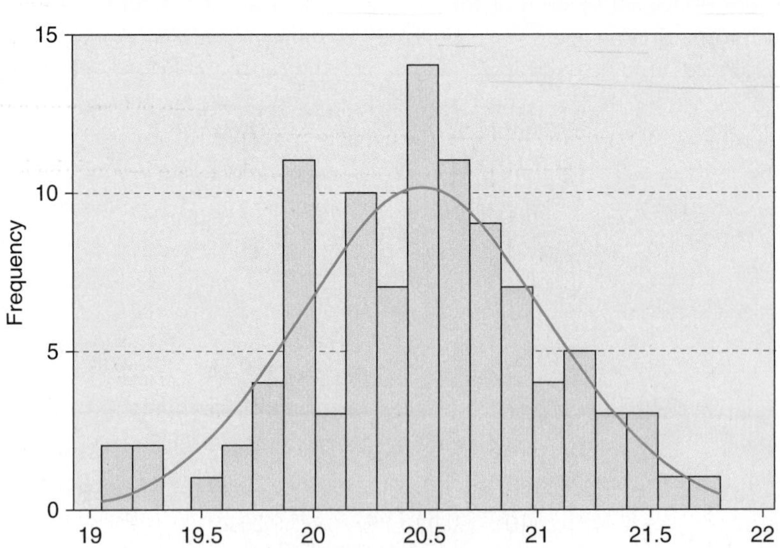

Figure 7.6 Graph of All the Mean Ages of 100 Samples of 30 Students

drawn from the population. The sampling distribution of the mean demonstrates how the average of a value across a sample behaves if we repeated the process of producing data and computing summary statistics many, many times.

The pattern in the sampling distribution of sample means suggests that over many separate samples, the true population parameter is more common than any other result. At the middle of the distribution, the mean age most frequently observed is 20.5 years. Many samples deviate from the population parameter by various amounts—some by very little (near the centre of the distribution) to others that are more anomalous (toward the extreme ends of the distribution). When many different random samples are plotted, as in Figure 7.6, then the sampling distribution of sample means looks like a normal or bell-shaped curve. Such a curve is theoretically important and is used throughout statistical science.

The **central limit theorem** is a mathematic principle that tells us that as the number of different random samples in a sampling distribution increases toward infinity, the pattern of sample means and the population parameter become more predictable. With a huge number of random samples, the sampling distribution forms a normal curve and the midpoint of the curve approaches the population parameter. In the illustrations above, we can see how the distribution of sample means moves into a normal curve-like pattern after we draw numerous samples.

central limit theorem: A law-like mathematical relationship stating that whenever many *random samples* are drawn from a *population* and plotted, a *normal distribution* is formed, and the centre of such a distribution for a variable is equal to its *population parameter.*

Perhaps you want only one sample because you do not have the time or energy to draw many different samples. You are not alone. A researcher rarely draws many samples. He or she usually draws only one random sample, but the central limit theorem lets him or her generalize from one sample to the population. The theorem is about many samples, but it lets the researcher calculate the probability of a particular sample's being off from the population parameter. In other words, these principles allow a researcher to estimate how likely it is that his or her sample is representative of the true population parameter.

Random sampling does not guarantee that every random sample perfectly represents the population. You can see in the distribution of sample means above that some of the samples produced sample means that were way off in the "tails" of the distribution—a considerable distance from the mean. Most random samples, however, will be close to the population most of the time, and researchers can calculate the probability of a particular sample being inaccurate. A researcher estimates the chance that a particular sample is off or unrepresentative (i.e., the size of the sampling error) by using information from the sample to estimate the sampling distribution. He or she combines this information with knowledge of the central limit theorem to construct confidence intervals.

The **confidence interval** is a relatively simple but powerful idea related to the idea of margin of error discussed above. A confidence interval is a range around a specific point used to estimate a population parameter. A range is used because the statistics of random processes do not let a researcher predict an exact point, but they let the researcher say with a high level of confidence (e.g., 95 percent) that the true population parameter lies within a certain range.

confidence interval: A range of values, usually a little higher and lower than a specific value found in a *sample,* within which a researcher has a specified and high degree of confidence that the *population parameter* lies.

The calculations for sampling errors or confidence intervals are beyond the level of this discussion, but they are based on the idea of the sampling distribution that lets a researcher calculate the sampling error and confidence interval. For example, you cannot say, "There are precisely 2500 red marbles in the jar based on a random sample." However, you can say, "I am 95 percent certain that the population parameter lies between 2450 and 2550." You can combine characteristics of the sample (e.g., its size, the variation in it) with the central limit theorem to predict specific ranges around the parameter with a great deal of confidence.

systematic sampling: A type of *random sample* in which a researcher selects every *k*th (e.g., 12th) case in the *sampling frame* using a *sampling interval.*

sampling interval: The inverse of the *sampling ratio,* which is used in *systematic sampling* to select cases. The sampling interval (i.e., 1 in *k*, where *k* is some number) tells the researcher how to select elements from a *sampling frame* by skipping elements in the frame before selecting one for the sample.

Systematic Sampling **Systematic sampling** is simple random sampling with a shortcut for random selection. Again, the first step is to number each element in the sampling frame. Instead of using a list of random numbers, a researcher calculates a sampling interval, and the interval becomes his or her quasi-random selection method. The **sampling interval** (i.e., 1 in k, where k is some number) tells the researcher how to select elements from a sampling frame by skipping elements in the frame before selecting one for the sample.

Box 7.6 In the News

Canadian University Rankings

You've probably heard about Canadian university rankings in the news, in magazines, or while talking with your classmates. You have probably been interested to know where your university or college "ranks" in Canada. But how are these rankings arrived at?

The most popular ranking is provided every year by *Maclean's* magazine, which has been doing this ranking annually since 1990. Universities would compile data for the *Maclean's* study, which includes various statistics on enrolment, tuition, and other administrative items. In 2006, however, more than 20 universities (including some of the largest in Canada, such as the University of Toronto, the University of Alberta, and McMaster University), being dismayed by the methodology used to compile the rankings, refused to participate in *Maclean's* ranking exercise. The refusal on the part of these universities required *Maclean's* to compile the data itself from publicly available sources. In some cases, the magazine filed requests under provincial freedom of information acts. In many rankings now, *Maclean's* relies on two data surveys—the National Survey of Student Engagement, and the Canadian University Survey Consortium—to produce a series of rankings of student experience and quality of education. It should be understood that *Maclean's* doesn't actually administer these surveys—often the university commissions and uses these surveys for budgeting and related purposes—and *Maclean's* uses some of the data that are contained in these surveys to compile its rankings. Not all universities and colleges participate in these surveys every year, either.

Another source of rankings comes from the *Globe and Mail*'s annual Canadian University Report. The results from the *Globe* survey sound rather impressive, with a sample of around 42 000 undergraduates across Canada. But how did they recruit these 42 000 students? The sampling frame is derived from university students who used the studentawards.com student aid website. In order to be part of the study, students had to have been registered users of this website. How many eligible students are actually part of this online facility is not known. Furthermore, the survey is conducted over the web using email invitations. The pros and cons of online surveys are discussed in the next chapter.

Sources: Keller, T., & Farran, S. (2009, February 4). University students grade their schools. *Maclean's*. Retrieved from http://oncampus.macleans.ca/education/2009/02/04/university-students-grade-their-schools/2/; Beck, S. (Ed.). (2010). *Canadian university report.* Insert to the *Globe and Mail.*

For instance, let's say that you want to sample 300 names from 900. After a random starting point, you select every third name of the 900 to get a sample of 300. The sampling interval is 3. Sampling intervals are easy to compute. You need the sample size and the population size (or sampling frame size as a best estimate). You can think of the sampling interval as the inverse of the sampling ratio. The sampling ratio for 300 names out of 900 is 300/900 = 0.333 = 33.3 percent. The sampling interval is 900/300 = 3.

There are many ways to handle the data compiled using sampling techniques, but not all methods inspire the same degree of confidence, as is shown in Box 7.6.

In most cases, a simple random sample and a systematic sample yield equivalent results. One important situation in which systematic sampling cannot be substituted for simple random sampling occurs when the elements in a sample are organized in some kind of cycle or pattern. For example, a researcher's sampling frame is organized by married couples with the male first and the female second (see Table 7.3). Such a pattern gives the researcher an unrepresentative sample if systematic sampling is used. His or her systematic sample can be nonrepresentative and include only wives because of how the cases are organized. When his or her sample frame is organized as couples, even-numbered sampling intervals result in samples with all husbands or all wives.

Box 7.7 illustrates simple random sampling and systematic sampling. Notice that different names were drawn in each sample. For example, H. Adams appears in both samples, but C. Droullard is only in the simple random sample. This is because it is rare for any two random samples to be identical. The sampling frame contains 20 males and 20 females (gender is in parentheses after each name). The simple random sample yielded three males and seven females, and the systematic sample yielded five males and five females. Does this mean that systematic sampling is more accurate? No. To check this, draw a new

Table 7.3 Problems with Systematic Sampling of Cyclical Data

Case	
1	Husband
2[a]	Wife
3	Husband
4	Wife
5	Husband
6[a]	Wife
7	Husband
8	Wife
9	Husband
10[a]	Wife

Random start = 2; Sampling interval = 4.

[a] Selected into sample.

Box 7.7 Making It Practical

How to Draw Simple Random and Systematic Samples

1. Number each case in the sampling frame in sequence. The list of 40 names is in alphabetical order, numbered from 1 to 40.
2. Decide on a sample size. We will draw two 25 percent (10 name) samples.
3. For a *simple random sample*, locate a random-number table (see excerpt). Before using the random-number table, count the largest number of digits needed for the sample (e.g., with 40 names, two digits are needed; for 100 to 999, three digits; for 1000 to 9999, four digits). Begin anywhere on the random number table (we will begin in the upper left) and take a set of digits (we will take the last two). Mark the number on the sampling frame that corresponds to the chosen random number to indicate that the case is in the sample. If the number is too large (over 40), ignore it. If the number appears more than once (10 and 21 occurred twice in the example), ignore the second occurrence. Continue until the number of cases in the sample (10 in our example) is reached.
4. For a *systematic sample*, begin with a random start. The easiest way to do this is to point blindly at the random-number table then take the closest number that appears on the sampling frame. In the example, 18 was chosen. Start with the random number, then count the sampling interval, or 4 in our example, to come to the first number. Mark it, and then count the sampling interval for the next number. Continue to the end of the list. Continue counting the sampling interval as if the beginning of the list was attached to the end of the list (like a circle). Keep counting until ending close to the start, or on the start if the sampling interval divides evenly into the total of the sampling frame.

No.	Name (Gender)	Simple Random	Systematic	No.	Name (Gender)	Simple Random	Systematic
01	Abrams, J. (M)			11	Droullard, C. (M)	Yes	
02	Adams, H. (F)	Yes		12	Durette, R. (F)		
03	Anderson, H. (M)			13	Elsnau, K. (F)	Yes	
04	Arminond, L. (M)			14	Falconer, T. (M)		Yes (9)
05	Boorstein, A. (M)			15	Fuerstenberg, J. (M)		
06	Breitsprecher, P. (M)	Yes	Yes (7)	16	Fulton, P. (F)		
07	Brown, D. (F)			17	Gnewuch, S. (F)		
08	Cattelino, J. (F)			18	Green, C. (M)	START, Yes (10)	
09	Cidoni, S. (M)	Yes*		19	Goodwanda, T. (F)	Yes	
10	Davis, L. (F)	Yes*	Yes (8)	20	Harris, B. (M)		

(continued)

Box 7.7 (continued)

No.	Name (Gender)	Simple Random	Systematic	No.	Name (Gender)	Simple Random	Systematic
21	Hjelmhaug, N. (M)	Yes*		31	Lee, R. (F)		
22	Huang, J. (F)	Yes	Yes (1)	32	Ling, C. (M)		
23	Ivono, V. (F)			33	McKinnon, K. (F)		
24	Jaquees, J. (M)			34	Min, H. (F)	Yes	Yes (4)
25	Johnson, A. (F)			35	Moini, A. (F)		
26	Kennedy, M. (F)	Yes (2)		36	Navarre, H. (M)		
27	Koschoreck, L. (F)			37	O'Sullivan, C. (M)		
28	Koykkar, J. (M)			38	Oh, J. (M)	Yes (5)	
29	Kozlowski, C. (F)	Yes		39	Olson, J. (M)		
30	Laurent, J. (M)	Yes (3)		40	Ortiz y Garcia, L. (F)		

Excerpt From a Random-Number Table (for Simple Random Sample)

15010	18590	00102	42210	94174	22099
90122	38221	21529	00013	04734	60457
67256	13887	94119	11077	01061	27779
13761	23390	12947	21280	44506	36457
81994	66611	16597	44457	07621	51949
79180	25992	46178	23992	62108	43232

*Numbers that appeared twice in random numbers selected.

sample using different random numbers: Try taking the first two digits and beginning at the end (e.g., 11 from 11921, then 43 from 43232). Also draw a new systematic sample with a different random start. The last time the random start was 18. Try a random start of 11. What did you find? How many of each sex were included in your revised samples?

stratified sampling: A type of *random sample* in which the researcher first identifies a set of *mutually exclusive* and *exhaustive* categories, then uses a random selection method to select cases for each category.

Stratified Sampling In **stratified sampling,** a researcher first divides the population into subpopulations (strata) on the basis of supplementary information. After dividing the population into strata, the researcher draws a random sample from each subpopulation. He or she can sample randomly within strata using simple random or systematic sampling. In stratified sampling, the researcher controls the relative size of each stratum rather than letting random processes control it. This guarantees representativeness or fixes the proportion of different strata within a sample. Of course, the necessary supplemental information about strata is not always available.

In general, stratified sampling produces samples that are more representative of the population than simple random sampling if the stratum information is accurate. A simple example illustrates why this is so. Imagine a population that is 51 percent female and 49 percent male; the population parameter is a sex ratio of 51 to 49. With stratified sampling, a researcher draws random samples among females and among males so that the sample contains a 51 to 49 percent sex ratio. If the researcher had used simple random sampling, it would be possible for a random sample to be off from the true sex ratio in the population. Thus, he or she makes fewer errors representing the population and has a smaller sampling error with stratified sampling.

Researchers use stratified sampling when a stratum of interest is a small percentage of a population and random processes could miss the stratum by chance. For example, a

Box 7.8 Concepts in Action

Illustration of Stratified Sampling

In some situations, a researcher wants the proportion of a stratum or subgroup to differ from its true proportion in the population. For example, the 1996 General Social Survey oversampled senior citizens, particularly in the province of Quebec. This oversampling was undertaken so that in-depth analyses of the opinions and experiences of seniors could be studied. A random sample of the Canadian population would yield relatively few seniors. Statistics Canada and the Quebec Institute of Statistics conducted a separate sample of seniors to increase the total number to 1250 sampled nationally and 700 sampled from the province of Quebec. The researcher who wants to use the entire sample (not just seniors but all people in the study) must adjust it to reduce the number of sampled seniors before generalizing to the Canadian population. Many other studies intentionally oversample ethnic minorities, particularly if the desired outcome of the study is to investigate topics particularly relevant to this group in Canada. Disproportionate sampling helps the researcher who wants to focus on issues most relevant to a subpopulation.

The table that follows gives the example of 100 staff at General Hospital, stratified by position. The simple random sample over-represents nurses, nursing assistants, and medical technicians, but under-represents administrators, staff physicians, maintenance staff, and cleaning staff. The stratified sample gives an accurate representation of each type of position.

Sample of 100 Staff of General Hospital, Stratified by Position

	Population		Simple Random Sample	Stratified Sample	Errors Compared to the Population
Position	*N*	*Percent*	*n*	*n*	
Administrators	15	2.88	1	3	−2
Staff physicians	25	4.81	2	5	−3
Intern physicians	25	4.81	6	5	+1
Registered nurses	100	19.23	22	19	+3
Nurse assistants	100	19.23	21	19	+2
Medical technicians	75	14.42	9	14	+5
Orderlies	50	9.62	8	10	−2
Clerks	75	14.42	5	14	+1
Maintenance staff	30	5.77	3	6	−3
Cleaning staff	25	4.81	3	5	−2
Total	520	100.00	100	100	

Randomly select 3 of 15 administrators, 5 of 25 staff physicians, and so on.

Note: Traditionally, *N* symbolizes the number in the population and *n* represents the number in the sample.

researcher draws a sample of 200 from 20 000 university students. He or she gets information from the university registrar indicating that 2 percent of the 20 000 students, or 400, are divorced women with children under the age of five. This group is important to include in the sample. There would be four such students (2 percent of 200) in a representative sample, but the researcher could miss them by chance in one simple random sample. With stratified sampling, he or she obtains a list of the 400 such students from the registrar and randomly selects four from it. This guarantees that the sample represents the population with regard to the important stratum (see Box 7.8).

In special situations, a researcher may want the proportion of a stratum in a sample to differ from its true proportion in the population. For example, the population contains 0.5 percent Aleuts, but the researcher wants to examine Aleuts in particular. He or she oversamples so that Aleuts make up 10 percent of the sample. With this type of disproportionate stratified sample, the researcher cannot generalize directly from the sample to the population without special adjustments.

cluster sampling: A type of *random sample* that uses multiple stages and is often used to cover wide geographic areas in which aggregated units are randomly selected; *samples* are then drawn from the sampled aggregated units, or clusters.

Cluster Sampling

Cluster sampling addresses two problems that occur when researchers lack a good sampling frame for a dispersed population and the cost to reach a sampled element is very high. For example, there is no single list of all automobile mechanics in North America. Even if a researcher got an accurate sampling frame, reaching the sampled mechanics, who are geographically spread out, would cost too much. Instead of using a single sampling frame, researchers use a sampling design that involves multiple stages and clusters.

A *cluster* is a unit that contains final sampling elements but can be treated temporarily as a sampling element itself. A researcher first samples clusters, each of which contains elements, and then draws a second sample from within the clusters selected in the first stage of sampling. In other words, the researcher randomly samples clusters, then randomly samples elements from within the selected clusters. This has a big practical advantage: He or she can create a good sampling frame of clusters even if it is impossible to create one for sampling elements. Once the researcher gets a sample of clusters, creating a sampling frame for elements within each cluster becomes more manageable. A second advantage for geographically dispersed populations is that elements within each cluster are physically closer to one another. This may produce a savings in locating or reaching each element.

A researcher draws several samples in stages in cluster sampling. In a three-stage sample, Stage 1 is random sampling of big clusters; Stage 2 is random sampling of small clusters within each selected big cluster; and Stage 3 is sampling of elements from within the sampled small clusters. For example, a researcher wants a sample of individuals from Mapleville. First, he or she randomly samples city blocks, then households within blocks, and then individuals within households (see Box 7.9). Although there is no accurate list of all residents of Mapleville, there is an accurate list of blocks in the city. After selecting a random sample of blocks, the researcher counts all households on the selected blocks to create a sample frame for each block. He or she then uses the list of households to draw a random sample at the stage of sampling households. Finally, the researcher chooses a specific individual within each sampled household.

Cluster sampling is usually less expensive than simple random sampling, but it is less accurate. Each stage in cluster sampling introduces sampling errors. This means a multistage cluster sample has more sampling errors than a one-stage random sample.

A researcher who uses cluster sampling must decide on the number of clusters and the number of elements within each cluster. For example, in a two-stage cluster sample of 240 people from Mapleville, the researcher could randomly select 120 clusters and select two elements from each, or randomly select two clusters and select 120 elements in each. Which is best? The general answer is that a design with more clusters is better. This is because elements within clusters (e.g., people living on the same block) tend to be similar to each other (e.g., people on the same block tend to be more alike than those on different blocks). If few clusters are chosen, many similar elements could be selected, which would be less representative of the total population. For example, the researcher could select two blocks with relatively wealthy people and draw 120 people from each. This would be less representative than a sample with 120 different city blocks and two individuals chosen from each.

When a researcher samples from a large geographical area and must travel to each element, cluster sampling significantly reduces travel costs. As usual, there is a tradeoff between accuracy and cost. For example, Alan, Ricardo, and Barbara each plan to visit and personally interview a sample of 1500 students who represent the population of all college and university students in North America. Alan obtains an accurate sampling frame of all students and uses simple random sampling. He travels to 1000 different locations to interview one or two students at each. Ricardo draws a random sample of three universities from

Box 7.9 Making It Practical

Illustration of Cluster Sampling

Goal: Draw a random sample of 240 people in Mapleville.

Step 1: Mapleville has 55 districts. Randomly select six districts.

1 2 3* 4 5 6 7 8 9 10 11 12 13 14 15* 16 17 18 19 20 21 22 23 24 25 26 27* 28 29 30 31* 32 33 34 35 36 37 38 39 40* 41 42 43 44 45 46 47 48 49 50 51 52 53 54* 55

* = Randomly selected.

Step 2: Divide the selected districts into blocks. Each district contains 20 blocks. Randomly select four blocks from each district.

Example of District 3 (selected in Step 1):

Block 4 contains a mix of single-family homes, duplexes, and four-unit apartment buildings. It is bounded by Oak Street, River Road, South Avenue, and Greenview Drive. There are 45 households on the block. Randomly select 10 households from the 45.

1 2 3 4* 5 6 7 8 9 10* 11 12 13* 14 15 16 17* 18 19 20

* = Randomly selected.

Step 3: Divide blocks into households. Randomly select households.

Example of Block 4 of District 3 (selected in Step 2):

1 #1 Oak Street
2 #3 Oak Street
3* #5 Oak Street
4 "
5 "
6 "
7 #7 Oak Street
8 "
9* #150 River Road
10* "
11 "
12 "
13 #152 River Road
14 "
15 "
16 "
17* #154 River Road
18 #156 River Road
19* #158 River Road
20* "
21 #13 South Avenue
22 "
23 #11 South Avenue
24 #9 South Avenue
25 #7 South Avenue
26 #5 South Avenue
27 #3 South Avenue
28 #1 South Avenue
29* "
30 #152 Greenview Drive
31* "
32* "
33 "
34 #156 Greenview Drive
35* "
36 "
37 "
38 "
39 #158 Greenview Drive
40 "
41 "
42 "
43 #160 Greenview Drive
44 "
45 "

* = Randomly selected.

Step 4: Select a respondent from within each household.

Summary of cluster sampling:

1 person randomly selected per household
10 households randomly selected per block
4 blocks randomly selected per district
6 districts randomly selected in the city
1 × 10 × 4 × 6 = 240 people in sample

a list of all 3000 universities and colleges, then visits the three and selects 500 students from each. Barbara draws a random sample of 300 universities and colleges. She visits the 300 and selects five students at each. If travel costs average $250 per location, Alan's travel bill is $250 000, Ricardo's is $750, and Barbara's is $75 000. Alan's sample is highly accurate, but Barbara's is only slightly less accurate for one-third the cost. Ricardo's sample is the cheapest, but it is not representative at all.

Probability Proportionate to Size (PPS) There are two methods of cluster sampling. The method just described is proportionate or unweighted cluster sampling. It is proportionate because the size of each cluster (or number of elements at each stage) is the same. The more common situation is for the cluster groups to be of different sizes. When this is the case, the researcher must adjust the probability or sampling ratio at various stages in sampling.

The foregoing cluster sampling example with Alan, Barbara, and Ricardo illustrates the problem with unweighted cluster sampling. Barbara drew a simple random sample of 300 colleges and universities from a list of all 3000, but she made a mistake (unless every institution has an identical number of students). Her method gave each institution an equal chance of being selected—a 300/3000 or 10 percent chance. But colleges and universities have different numbers of students, so each student does not have an equal chance to end up in her sample.

Barbara listed every college and university and sampled from the list. A large university with 40 000 students and a small college with 400 students had an equal chance of being selected. But if she chose the large university, the chance of a given student at that college being selected was 5 in 40 000 (5/40 000 = 0.0125 percent), whereas a student at the small college had a 5 in 400 (5/400 = 1.25 percent) chance of being selected. The small-college student was 100 times more likely to be in her sample. The total probability of being selected for a student from the large university was 0.125 percent (10 × 0.0125), while it was 12.5 percent (10 × 1.25) for the small-college student. Barbara violated a principle of random sampling—that each element has an equal chance to be selected into the sample.

probability proportionate to size (PPS): An adjustment made in *cluster sampling* when each cluster does not have the same number of *sampling elements*.

If Barbara uses **probability proportionate to size (PPS)** and samples correctly, then each final sampling element or student will have an equal probability of being selected. She does this by adjusting the chances of selecting a college in the first stage of sampling. She must give large colleges with more students a greater chance of being selected and small colleges a smaller chance. She adjusts the probability of selecting a college on the basis of the proportion of all students in the population who attend it. Thus, a college with 40 000 students will be 100 times more likely to be selected than one with 400 students. (See Box 7.10 for another example.)

random-digit dialing (RDD): A method of randomly selecting cases for telephone interviews that uses all possible telephone numbers as a *sampling frame*.

Random-Digit Dialing **Random-digit dialing (RDD)** is a special sampling technique used in research projects in which the general public is interviewed by telephone. It differs from the traditional method of sampling for telephone interviews because a published telephone directory is not the sampling frame.

Box 7.10 Concepts in Action

Complex Sampling

The Programme for International Student Assessment (PISA) is a study of 15-year-olds in industrialized countries organized by the Organisation for Economic Co-operation and Development (OECD). The study's mandate is to examine how students nearing the end of compulsory schooling are faring in terms of the skills and knowledge they possess that are required for full participation in society. The study has been conducted every three years since 2000, with the most recent taking place in 2012.

Because the study covers students in several countries, the sampling procedure is complex by definition. Each year a growing number of countries participate. In 2000, 43 countries participated, while in 2012 this number had grown to 67.

Each country uses a two-stage sample of schools and students. First, the school sample is stratified by geographic and school characteristics. The schools themselves are selected with probability proportional to size (PPS). After the schools are selected, the students within the schools need to be sampled. A systematic sample of 35 students is done within each school.

In April and May 2012, around 22 000 students from 1000 schools across Canada participated in the 2009 cycle of PISA. The OECD only required that 150 schools be sampled, but the Canadian researchers in charge of the survey in Canada targeted many more to ensure that each province and official language system would be represented in sufficient numbers.

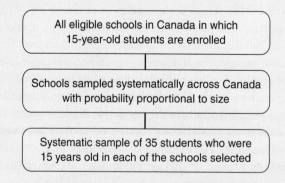

All eligible schools in Canada in which 15-year-old students are enrolled

↓

Schools sampled systematically across Canada with probability proportional to size

↓

Systematic sample of 35 students who were 15 years old in each of the schools selected

Source: Bussière, P., Knighton, T., & Pennock, D. (2007). *Measuring up: Canadian results of the OECD PISA study. The performance of Canada's youth in science, reading and mathematics—2006 first results for Canadians aged 15.* Canada: Human Resource and Skills Development Canada and Council of Ministers of Education.

Three kinds of people are missed when the sampling frame is a telephone directory: people without landline telephones, people who have recently moved, and people with unlisted numbers. Those without phones (e.g., the poor, the uneducated, and transients, but also the growing number of people who only use cellphones) are missed in any telephone interview study, but the proportion of the general public with a telephone is nearly 95 percent in advanced industrialized nations. As the percentage of the public with telephones has increased, the percentage with unlisted numbers has also grown. Several kinds of people have unlisted numbers: people who want to avoid collection agencies; the very wealthy; and those who want privacy and want to avoid obscene calls, salespeople, and prank calls. In some urban areas, the percentage of unlisted numbers is as high as 50 percent. In addition, people change their residences, so directories that are published annually or less often have numbers for people who have left and do not list those who have recently moved into an area. Also, directories do not list cellphone numbers. A researcher using RDD randomly selects telephone numbers, thereby avoiding the problems of telephone directories. The population is telephone numbers, not people with telephones. Random-digit dialing is not difficult, but it takes time and can frustrate the person doing the calling.

Here is how RDD works in Canada. Telephone numbers have three parts: a three-digit area code, a three-digit exchange number or central office code, and a four-digit number. For example, the area code for Edmonton, Alberta, is 780, and there are many exchanges within the area code (e.g., 433, 468, 467); but not all of the 999 possible three-digit exchanges (from 001 to 999) are active. Likewise, not all of the 9999 possible four-digit numbers in an exchange (from 0000 to 9999) are being used. Some numbers are reserved for future expansion, are disconnected, or are temporarily withdrawn after someone moves. Thus, a possible Canadian telephone number consists of an active area code, an active exchange number, and a four-digit number in an exchange.

In RDD, a researcher identifies active area codes and exchanges, then randomly selects four-digit numbers. A problem is that the researcher can select any number in an exchange. This means that some selected numbers are out of service, disconnected, pay phones, or numbers for businesses; only some numbers are what the researcher wants—working residential phone numbers. Until the researcher calls, it is not possible to know whether the number is a working residential number. This means spending a lot of time getting numbers that are disconnected, for businesses, and so forth.

Remember that the sampling element in RDD is the phone number, not the person or the household. Several families or individuals can share the same phone number, and in other situations each person may have a separate phone number or more than one phone number. This means that after a working residential phone is reached, a second stage of sampling is necessary, within-household sampling, to select the person to be interviewed.

Hidden Populations

In contrast to sampling the general population or visible and accessible people, sampling **hidden populations** (i.e., people who engage in concealed activities) is a recurrent issue in the studies of deviant or stigmatized behaviour. It illustrates the creative application of sampling principles, mixing qualitative and quantitative styles of research and often using nonprobability techniques. Examples of hidden populations include illegal drug users, sex workers, people with HIV/AIDS, and homeless people.

hidden populations: People who engage in clandestine, deviant, or concealed activities and who are difficult to locate and study.

Pearce and colleagues (2008) described how they were able to access the hidden population of young Aboriginals who used injection and noninjection drugs in two Canadian cities. They partnered with health care providers and community outreach centres, where staff at these facilities would give information about the researchers' study to individuals who fit the description of the desired sample (young Aboriginal drug users). Information

Table 7.4 Types of Probability Samples

Type of Sample	Technique
Simple Random	Create a sampling frame for all cases, then select cases using a purely random process (e.g., random-number table or computer program).
Stratified	Create a sampling frame for each of several categories of cases, draw a random sample from each category, then combine the samples.
Systematic	Create a sampling frame, calculate the sampling interval 1/*k*, choose a random starting place, and then take every 1/*k* case.
Cluster	Create a sampling frame for larger cluster units, draw a random sample of the cluster units, create a sampling frame for cases within each selected cluster unit, then draw a random sample of cases, and so forth.

about the study was also passed along through word of mouth. Through these techniques, the researchers managed to find 543 individuals to participate in their study.

Similarly, Manzoni and associates (2006) were interested in studying property crime among opiate drug users outside of treatment in five Canadian cities. Since there is no official sampling frame of illegal opiate drug users, this population was studied using snowball sampling techniques. The participants were recruited through outreach centres, through advertisements, and by posting notices in local social and health agencies. The researcher was able to recruit 677 participants, with each interviewed drug-using participant being paid $20 for an interview.

You are now familiar with several major types of probability samples (see Table 7.4) and the supplementary techniques used with them (e.g., PPS, within-household sampling, and RDD) that may be appropriate. In addition, you have seen how researchers combine nonprobability and probability sampling for special situations, such as hidden populations. Next, we turn to determining a sample size for probability samples.

How Large Should a Sample Be?

Students and new researchers often ask, "How large does my sample have to be?" The best answer is, "It depends." It depends on the kind of data analysis the researcher plans, on how accurate the sample has to be for the researcher's purposes, and on population characteristics. As you have seen, a large sample size alone does not guarantee a representative sample. A large sample without random sampling or with a poor sampling frame is less representative than a smaller one with random sampling and an excellent sampling frame. Good samples for qualitative purposes can be very small.

The question of sample size can be addressed in two ways. One is to make assumptions about the population and use statistical equations about random sampling processes. The calculation of sample size by this method requires a statistical discussion that is beyond the level of this text. The researcher must make assumptions about the degree of confidence (or number of errors) that is acceptable and the degree of variation in the population.

A second and more frequently used method is a rule of thumb—a conventional or commonly accepted amount. Researchers use it because they rarely have the information required for the statistical method and because it provides sample sizes close to those of the statistical method. Rules of thumb are not arbitrary but are based on past experience with samples that have met the requirements of the statistical method.

One principle of sample sizes is this: The smaller the population, the bigger the sampling ratio has to be for an accurate sample (i.e., one with a high probability of yielding the same results as the entire population). Larger populations permit smaller sampling ratios for equally good samples. This is because as the population size grows, the returns in accuracy for sample size shrink.

For small populations (under 1000), a researcher needs a large sampling ratio (about 30 percent); a sample size of about 300 is required for a high degree of accuracy. For moderately large populations (10 000), a smaller sampling ratio (about 10 percent) is needed to be equally accurate, or a sample size of around 1000. For large populations (over 150 000), smaller sampling ratios (1 percent) are possible, and samples of about 1500 can be very accurate. To sample from very large populations (over 10 million), one can achieve accuracy using tiny sampling ratios (0.025 percent) or samples of about 2500. The size of the population ceases to be relevant once the sampling ratio is very small, and samples of about 2500 are as accurate for populations of 200 million as for populations of 10 million. These are approximate sizes, and practical limitations (e.g., cost) also play a role in a researcher's decision.

A related principle is that for small samples, small increases in sample size produce big gains in accuracy. Equal increases in sample size produce more of an increase in accuracy for small than for large samples.

A researcher's decision about the best sample size depends on three things: (1) the degree of accuracy required, (2) the degree of variability or diversity in the population, and (3) the number of different variables examined simultaneously in data analysis. Everything else being equal, larger samples are needed if one wants high accuracy, if the population has a great deal of variability or heterogeneity, or if one wants to examine many variables in the data analysis simultaneously. Smaller samples are sufficient when less accuracy is acceptable, when the population is homogeneous, or when only a few variables are examined at a time.

The analysis of data on subgroups also affects a researcher's decision about sample size. If the researcher wants to analyze subgroups in the population, he or she needs a larger sample. For example, I want to analyze four variables for males between the ages of 30 and 40 years old. If this sample is of the general public, then only a small proportion (e.g., 10 percent) of sample cases will be males in that age group. A rule of thumb is to have about 50 cases for each subgroup to be analyzed. Thus, if I want to analyze a group that is only 10 percent of the population, then I should have 10 × 50 or 500 cases in the sample to be sure I get enough for the subgroup analysis.

Drawing Inferences

LO 7 Explain the relationship between samples and drawing inferences.

A researcher samples so that he or she can draw inferences from the sample to the population. In fact, a subfield of statistical data analysis that concerns drawing accurate inferences is called **inferential statistics**. The researcher directly observes variables using units in the sample. The sample stands for or represents the population. Researchers are not interested in samples in themselves; they want to infer to the population. Thus, a gap exists between what the researcher concretely has (a sample) and what is of real interest (a population) (see Figure 7.7).

inferential statistics: A branch of applied mathematics or statistics based on a *random sample*. It lets a researcher make precise statements about the level of confidence he or she has in the results of a *sample* being equal to the *population parameter*.

In the last chapter, you saw how the logic of measurement could be stated in terms of a gap between abstract concepts and concrete indicators. Measures of concrete, observable data are approximations for abstract concepts. Researchers use the approximations to estimate what is of real interest (i.e., concepts and causal laws). Conceptualization and operationalization bridge the gap in measurement just as the use of sampling frames, the sampling process, and inference bridges the gap in sampling.

StatsCan: Doing Secondary Analysis on Census Data

Researchers put the logic of sampling and the logic of measurement together by directly observing measures of constructs and empirical relationships in samples (see Figure 7.7). They infer or generalize from what they can observe empirically in samples to the abstract causal laws and concepts in the population.

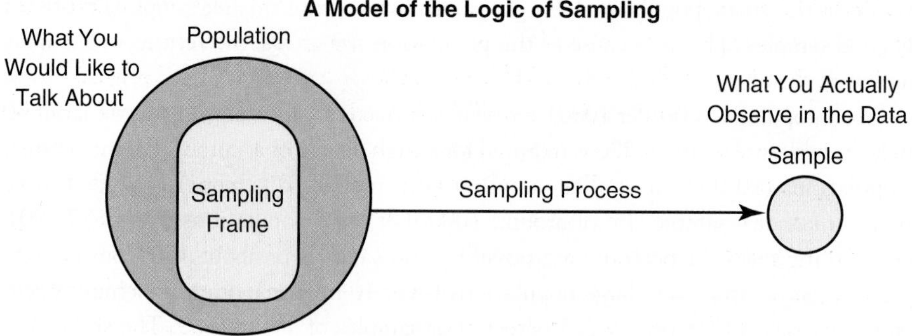

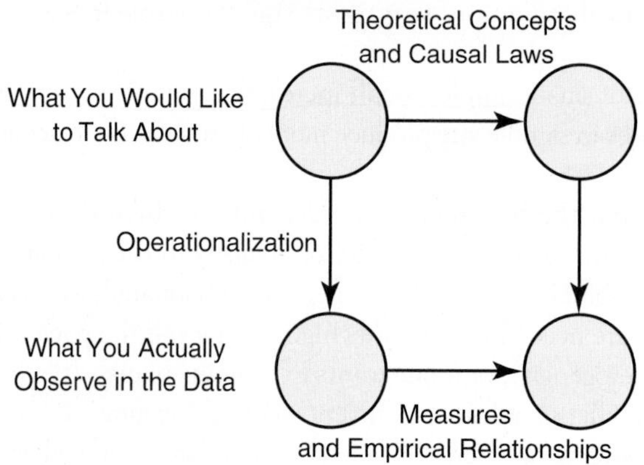

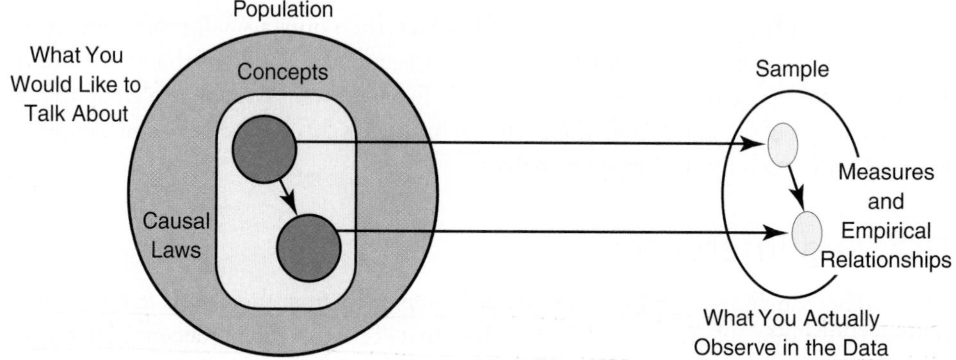

Figure 7.7 Model of the Logic of Sampling and of Measurement

Validity and sampling error have similar functions, as can be illustrated by the analogy between the logic of sampling and the logic of measurement—that is, between what is observed and what is discussed. In measurement, a researcher wants valid indicators of concepts—that is, concrete indicators that accurately represent abstract concepts. In sampling, he or she wants samples that have little sampling error—concrete collections of cases that accurately represent unseen and abstract populations. A valid measure deviates little from the concept it represents. A sample with little sampling error permits estimates that deviate little from population parameters.

Researchers try to reduce sampling errors. The calculation of the sampling error is not presented here, but it is based on two factors: the sample size and the amount of diversity in the sample. Everything else being equal, the larger the sample size, the smaller the sampling error. Likewise, the greater the homogeneity (or the less the diversity) in a sample, the smaller its sampling error.

Sampling error is also related to confidence intervals. If two samples are identical except that one is larger, the one with more cases will have a smaller sampling error and narrower confidence intervals. Likewise, if two samples are identical except that the cases in one are more similar to each other, the one with greater homogeneity will have a smaller sampling error and narrower confidence intervals. A narrow confidence interval means more precise estimates of the population parameter for a given level of confidence. For example, a researcher wants to estimate average annual family income. He or she has two samples. Sample 1 gives a confidence interval of $30 000 to $36 000 around the estimated population parameter of $33 000 for an 80 percent level of confidence. For a 95 percent level of confidence, the range is $23 000 to $43 000. A sample with a smaller sampling error (because it is larger or is more homogeneous) might give a $30 000 to $36 000 range for a 95 percent confidence level.

CHAPTER SUMMARY

Glossary Flashcards

In this chapter, you learned about sampling. Sampling is widely used in social research. You learned about both nonprobability and probability sampling. Five different types of nonprobability sampling were covered: haphazard, quota, purposive, snowball, and sequential. The advantages and disadvantages of each were discussed before moving on to probability sampling.

In general, probability sampling is preferred by quantitative researchers because it produces a sample that represents the population and enables the researcher to use powerful statistical techniques. The principles of probability sampling rest on the statistical principle of randomness, which was discussed as being a very precise term that allows researchers to predict the likelihood of obtaining their observed results. Various other important terms related to probability sampling were also introduced, including the sampling element, population, target population, sampling ratio, and sampling frame. Understanding how these terms are related to the principles of probability sampling are of key importance.

In addition to simple random sampling, you learned about systematic, stratified, and cluster sampling. Although this book does not cover the statistical theory used in random sampling, from the discussion of sampling error, sampling distributions, the central limit theorem, and sample size it should be clear that random sampling produces more accurate and precise sampling. It is because of the underlying principles of probability sampling that researchers are able to sample from large populations and make accurate inferences. The more technical body of work responsible for estimating relationships in samples and generalizing these findings to the general population is called inferential statistics.

Review Questions

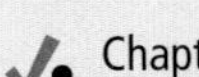 Chapter Quiz

1. Define what is meant by the family of sampling techniques called "nonprobability sampling."
2. Identify the five types of nonprobability sampling and explain their main principles.
3. Define probability sampling.
4. Explain what is meant by a population, a sampling element, a target population, a sampling frame, and a sampling ratio.
5. Explain how simple random sampling is undertaken.
6. Identify the three additional types of probability sampling techniques covered in this chapter and explain how they are different from simple random sampling.
7. Explain what is meant by a sampling distribution and a sampling distribution of sample means.
8. Define the margin of error and confidence interval.
9. Explain the relationship between samples and drawing inferences.

Exercises

Research Activities

1. Using EBSCO's ContentSelect, find three quantitative sociology articles and three qualitative sociology articles published within the past five years on topics of your choice. For each of the articles, identify the sampling technique used by the authors of the articles. Report the sample sizes for each of the studies.
2. On Google News, identify a recent Canadian news story that reports the results of a poll and includes a statement about the margin of error. What are the main findings of the study? Interpret the results as they relate to the margin of error.
3. Using EBSCO's ContentSelect, identify a study that uses a multistage sampling technique. Explain the different stages employed in the sample design.
4. Using EBSCO's ContentSelect, find a study that examines a hidden population. How did the researchers go about obtaining their sample?

MySearchLab

Visit MySearchLab, where you'll find thousands of full-text articles from academic journals and help with the research and writing process. Access the eText within MySearchLab to take self-grading practice tests and view a variety of multimedia resources.

Chapter 8
Survey Research

Photo Credit: George Doyle/Stockbyte/Thinkstock

LEARNING OBJECTIVES

After reading this chapter, you should be able to

LO 1 Explain the steps involved in conducting a survey.
LO 2 Describe the principles of good question writing.
LO 3 Give examples of the different types of survey questions that are used.
LO 4 Explain the advantages and disadvantages of open and closed questions.
LO 5 Identify major questionnaire design issues.
LO 6 Describe the major types of surveys and identify their advantages and disadvantages.
LO 7 Explain the differences between ordinary conversation and a structured survey interview.
LO 8 Describe the role of the interviewer.

INTRODUCTION

Research Methodology

The survey is the most widely used data-gathering technique in social research, and it is used in many other fields, as well. In fact, surveys are almost too popular. People sometimes say, "Do a survey" to get information about the social world, when they should be asking, "What is the most appropriate data collection technique?" Despite the popularity of surveys, it is easy to conduct a survey that yields misleading or worthless results. Good surveys require thought and effort. In this chapter, you will learn the main ingredients of good survey research, as well as the limitations of the survey method.

Research Questions Appropriate for a Survey

Survey research developed within the positivist approach to social science. The survey asks many people (called *respondents*) about their beliefs, opinions, characteristics, and past or present behaviour.

Surveys are appropriate for research questions about self-reported beliefs or behaviours. They are strongest when the answers people give to questions measure variables. Researchers usually ask about many things at one time in surveys, measure many variables (often with multiple indicators), and test several hypotheses in a single survey.

Although the categories overlap, the following can be asked in a survey:

1. *Behaviour*. How frequently do you go to art galleries? Did you vote in the last city election? When did you last visit a close relative?
2. *Attitudes/beliefs/opinions*. What kind of job do you think the mayor is doing? Do you think other people say many negative things about you when you are not there? What is the biggest problem facing Canada these days?
3. *Characteristics*. Are you married, cohabiting, single, divorced, separated, or widowed? Do you belong to a union? What is your age?
4. *Expectations*. Do you plan to enrol in a degree program in the next 12 months? How much schooling do you think your child will get? Do you think the population in your town or city will grow, shrink, or stay the same?
5. *Self-classification*. Do you consider yourself to be liberal, moderate, or conservative? Into which social class would you put your family?
6. *Knowledge*. Who was elected prime minister in the last election? About what percentage of the people in this city are non-White? Is it legal to be in possession of small amounts of marijuana in this country?

Researchers warn against using surveys to ask "why" questions (e.g., "Why do you think crime occurs?"). "Why" questions are appropriate, however, if a researcher wants to discover a respondent's subjective understanding or informal theory (i.e., the respondent's own view of "why" he or she acts in a certain way). Because few respondents are fully aware of the causal factors that shape their beliefs or behaviour, such questions are not a substitute for the researcher developing a consistent causal theory of his or her own that builds on the existing scientific literature.

Survey of U.S. Troops

An important limitation of survey research is that it provides data only of what a person or organization says, and this may differ from what he or she actually does. This was illustrated by Rubenson and associates (2007). These researchers found that 83 percent of people responding to the Canadian election survey said that they had voted in the 2000 federal election. The actual official voter turnout, however, was substantially lower—approximately 61 percent. In other words, 83 percent of people *said* they voted, but only about 61 percent *actually did*.

THE LOGIC OF SURVEY RESEARCH

LO 1 Explain the steps involved in conducting a survey.

What Is a Survey?

Survey researchers sample many respondents who answer *the same questions, in the same order, in the same way*. They measure many variables, test multiple hypotheses, and infer temporal order from questions about past behaviour, experiences, or characteristics. For example, years of schooling or a respondent's race exist prior to current attitudes. An association among variables is measured with statistical techniques. Survey researchers think of alternative explanations when planning a survey, measure variables that represent alternative explanations (i.e., control variables), then statistically examine their effects to rule out alternative explanations.

Survey research is often called *correlational*. Survey researchers use questions as control variables to approximate the rigorous test for causality that experimenters achieve with their physical control over temporal order and alternative explanations. In other words, control variables are other characteristics that the researcher accounts for so as to minimize the possibility of spuriousness.

Steps in Conducting a Survey

The survey researcher follows a deductive approach. He or she begins with a theoretical or applied research problem and ends with empirical measurement and data analysis. Once a researcher decides that the survey is an appropriate method, basic steps in a research project can be divided into the substeps outlined in Figure 8.1.

In the first phase, the researcher develops an instrument—a survey questionnaire or interview schedule—that he or she uses to measure variables. Respondents read the questions themselves and mark answers on a *questionnaire*. An **interview schedule** is a set of questions read to the respondent by an interviewer, who also records responses. To simplify the discussion, we will use only the term *questionnaire*.

interview schedule: The name of a survey research questionnaire when a telephone or face-to-face interview is used.

A survey researcher conceptualizes and operationalizes variables as questions. He or she writes and rewrites questions for clarity and completeness and organizes questions on the questionnaire based on the research question, the respondents, and the type of survey. (The types of surveys are discussed later.)

When preparing a questionnaire, the researcher thinks ahead to how he or she will record and organize data for analysis. He or she pilot-tests the questionnaire with a small set of respondents similar to those in the final survey. If interviewers are used, the researcher trains them with the questionnaire. He or she asks respondents in the pilot test whether the questions were clear and explores their interpretations to see if his or her intended meaning was clear. The researcher also draws the sample during this phase.

After the planning phase, the researcher is ready to collect data. This phase is usually shorter than the planning phase. He or she locates sampled respondents in person, by telephone, email, or by postal mail. Respondents are given information and instructions on completing the questionnaire or interview. The questions follow, and there is a simple question and answer pattern. The researcher accurately records answers or responses immediately after they are given. After all respondents complete the questionnaire and are thanked, he or she organizes the data and prepares them for statistical analysis.

Survey research can be complex and expensive, and it can involve coordinating many people and steps. The administration of survey research requires organization and accurate record keeping. The researcher keeps track of each respondent, questionnaire, and interviewer; for example, he or she gives each sampled respondent an identification number, which also appears on the questionnaire. He or she then checks completed questionnaires against a list of sampled respondents. Next, the researcher reviews responses on individual questionnaires, stores original questionnaires, and transfers information from questionnaires to a format for statistical analysis. Meticulous bookkeeping and labelling are essential. Otherwise, the researcher may find that valuable data and effort are lost through sloppiness.

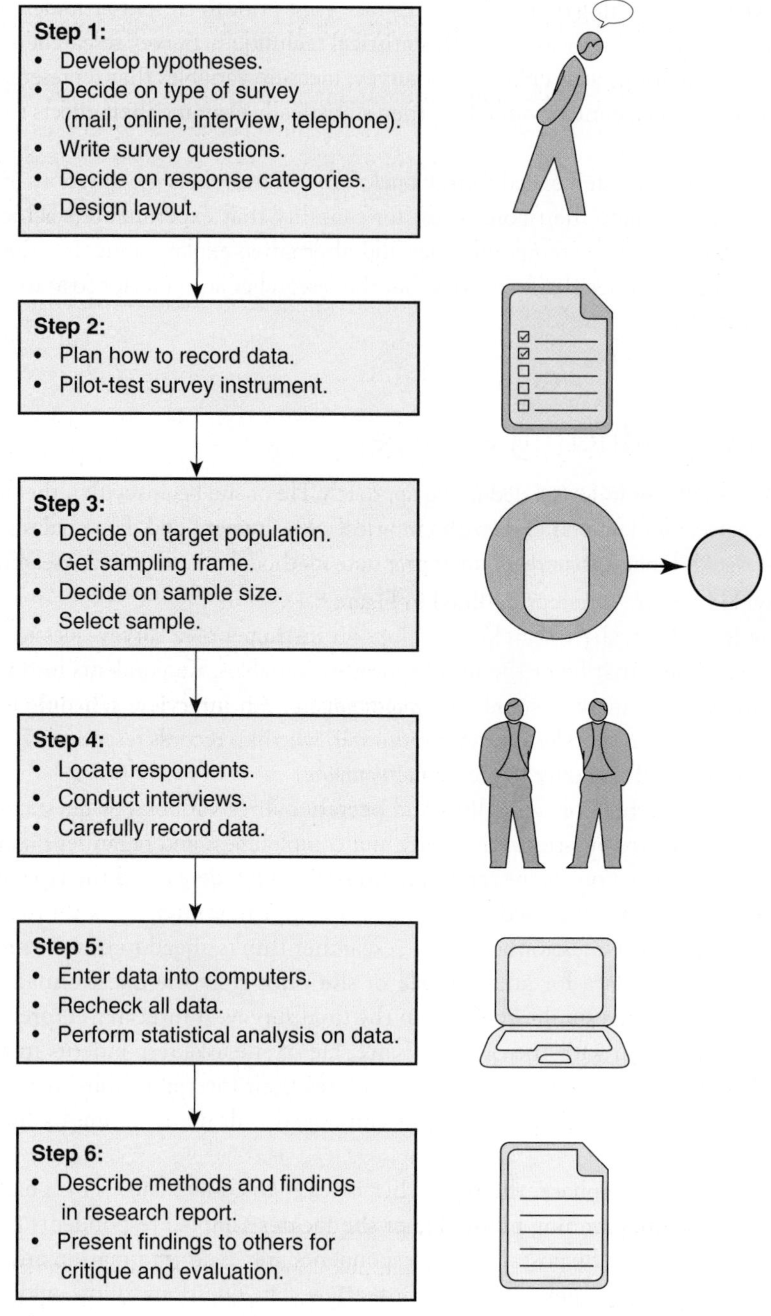

Step 1:
• Develop hypotheses.
• Decide on type of survey (mail, online, interview, telephone).
• Write survey questions.
• Decide on response categories.
• Design layout.
Step 2:
• Plan how to record data.
• Pilot-test survey instrument.
Step 3:
• Decide on target population.
• Get sampling frame.
• Decide on sample size.
• Select sample.
Step 4:
• Locate respondents.
• Conduct interviews.
• Carefully record data.
Step 5:
• Enter data into computers.
• Recheck all data.
• Perform statistical analysis on data.
Step 6:
• Describe methods and findings in research report.
• Present findings to others for critique and evaluation.

Figure 8.1 Steps in the Process of Survey Research

LO 2 Describe the principles of good question writing.

CONSTRUCTING THE QUESTIONNAIRE

Principles of Good Question Writing

A good questionnaire forms an integrated whole. The researcher weaves questions together so that they flow smoothly. He or she includes introductory remarks and instructions for clarification and measures each variable with one or more survey questions.

There are three principles for effective survey questions: Keep it clear, keep it simple, and keep the respondent's perspective in mind. Good survey questions give the researcher valid and reliable measures. They also help respondents feel that they understand the question and that their answers are meaningful. Questions that do not mesh with a respondent's viewpoint or that respondents find confusing are not good measures. Survey researchers must exercise extra care if their respondents are heterogeneous or come from different life situations than their own.

Researchers face a dilemma. They want all respondents to hear exactly the same questions, but will the questions be equally clear, relevant, and meaningful to all respondents? If respondents have diverse backgrounds and frames of reference, the same wording may not have the same meaning. Yet tailoring question wording to each respondent makes comparisons almost impossible. A researcher would not know whether the wording of the question or the differences in respondents accounted for different answers.

Sense and Nonsense about Surveys

Question writing is more of an art than a science. It takes skill, practice, patience, and creativity. The principles of question writing are illustrated in the following 12 things to avoid when writing survey questions. The list does not include every possible error, only the more frequent problems.

1. *Avoid jargon, slang, and abbreviations*. Jargon and technical terms come in many forms: Plumbers talk about *snakes*, lawyers about a contract of *uberrima fides*, psychologists about the *Oedipus complex*. Slang is a kind of jargon within a subculture—for example, marijuana smokers talk about a *spliff* and snowboarders talk about a *fakie*. Also avoid abbreviations. *NATO* usually means North Atlantic Treaty Organization, but for a particular respondent it might mean something else (National Auto Tourism Organization, Native Alaskan Trade Orbit, or North African Tea Office). Avoid slang and jargon unless a specialized population is being surveyed. Target the vocabulary and grammar to the respondents sampled. For the general public, this is the language used on television or in the newspaper (about a Grade 8 reading vocabulary).
2. *Avoid ambiguity, confusion, and vagueness*. Ambiguity and vagueness plague most question writers. A researcher might make implicit assumptions without thinking of the respondents. For example, the question, "What is your income?" could mean weekly, monthly, or annual; family or personal; before taxes or after taxes; for this year or last year; from salary or from all sources. The confusion causes inconsistencies in how different respondents assign meaning to and answer the question. The researcher who wants before-tax annual family income for last year must explicitly ask for it.[1]

   Another source of ambiguity is the use of indefinite words or response categories. For example, an answer to the question, "Do you jog regularly? Yes/No" hinges on the meaning of the word *regularly*. Some respondents may define *regularly* as every day, others as once a week. To reduce respondent confusion and get more information, be specific—ask whether a person jogs "about once a day," "a few times a week," "once a week," and so on. (See Box 8.1 on improving questions.)
3. *Avoid emotional language*. Words have implicit connotative as well as explicit denotative meanings. Words with strong emotional connotations can colour how respondents hear and answer survey questions.

   Use neutral language. Avoid words with emotional "baggage," because respondents may react to the emotionally laden words rather than to the issue. For example, the question, "What do you think about a policy to pay murderous terrorists who threaten to steal the freedoms of peace-loving people?" is full of emotional words (*murderous*, *freedoms*, *steal*, and *peace*).
4. *Avoid prestige bias*. Titles or positions in society (e.g., prime minister, expert) carry prestige or status. Issues linked to people with high social status can influence how respondents hear and answer survey questions, resulting in **prestige bias**. Avoid associating a statement with a prestigious person or group. Respondents may answer on the basis of their feelings toward the person or group rather than addressing the issue. For example, saying, "Most doctors say that cigarette smoke causes lung disease for those near a smoker. Do you agree?" affects people who want to agree with doctors. Likewise, a question such as, "Do you support the prime minister's policy regarding Syria?" will be

prestige bias: A problem in *survey research* question writing that occurs when a highly respected group or individual is linked to one of the answers.

Box 8.1 Making It Practical

Improving Unclear Questions

Here are three survey questions written by experienced professional researchers. They revised the original wording after a pilot test revealed that 15 percent of respondents asked for clarification or gave inadequate answers (e.g., "don't know"). As you can see, question wording is an art that may improve with practice, patience, and pilot testing.

Original Question	Problem	Revised Question
Do you exercise or play sports regularly?	What counts as exercise? What is meant by "regularly"?	How often per week do you do any sports, physical activities, or exercise, including walking?
What is the average number of days each week you have butter?	Does margarine count as butter?	The next question is just about butter—not including margarine.
[Following a question on eggs] What is the number of servings in a typical day?	How many eggs is a serving? What is a typical day?	On days when you eat eggs, how many eggs do you usually have?

Source: Fowler, F. J. (1992). How unclear terms affect survey data. *Public Opinion Quarterly, 56*, 218–231. Adapted with permission from Oxford University Press.

answered by respondents who have never heard of Syria on the basis of their view of the prime minister.

double-barrelled question: A problem in *survey research* question wording that occurs when two ideas are combined into one question and it is unclear whether the answer is for the combination of both or one or the other question.

5. *Avoid double-barrelled questions*. Make each question about one and only one topic. A **double-barrelled question** consists of two or more questions joined together. It makes a respondent's answer ambiguous. For example, if asked, "Does your employer have pension and health insurance benefits?" an employee with only health insurance benefits might answer either yes or no. The response has an ambiguous meaning, and the researcher cannot be certain of the respondent's intention. A researcher who wants to ask about the joint occurrence of two things—for example, an employer with both health insurance and pension benefits—should ask two separate questions.
6. *Do not confuse beliefs with reality*. Do not confuse what a respondent believes with what you, the researcher, measure. A respondent may think that a relationship exists between two variables, but this is not an empirical measurement of variables in a relationship. For example, a researcher wants to find out if students rate teachers higher who tell many jokes in class. The two variables are "teacher tells jokes" and "rating the teacher." The *wrong* way to approach the issue is to ask students, "Do you rate a teacher higher if the teacher tells many jokes?" This measures whether or not students *believe* that they rate teachers based on joke telling; it does not measure the empirical relationship. The *correct* way is to ask two separate empirically based questions: "How do you rate this teacher?" and "How many jokes does the teacher tell in an average class?" Then the researcher can examine answers to the two questions to determine if there is an association between them. People's beliefs about a relationship among variables are distinct from an actual empirical relationship.

leading (or loaded) question: A question that leads the respondent to choose one response over another by its wording.

7. *Avoid leading questions*. Make respondents feel that all responses are legitimate. Do not let them become aware of an answer that the researcher wants. A **leading (or loaded) question** is one that leads the respondent to choose one response over another by its wording. There are many kinds of leading questions. For example, the question, "You don't smoke, do you?" leads respondents to state that they do not smoke.

   Loaded questions can be stated to get either positive or negative answers. For example, "Should the mayor spend even more tax money trying to keep the streets in top shape?" leads respondents to disagree, whereas "Should the mayor fix the pot-holed and dangerous streets in our city?" is loaded for agreement.

8. *Avoid asking questions that are beyond respondents' capabilities.* Asking something that few respondents know frustrates respondents and produces poor-quality responses. Respondents cannot always recall past details and may not know specific factual information. For example, asking an adult, "How did you feel about your brother when you were six years old?" is probably worthless. Asking respondents to make a choice about something they know nothing about (e.g., a technical issue in foreign affairs or an internal policy of an organization) may result in an answer, but one that is unreliable and meaningless. When many respondents are unlikely to know about an issue, use a full-filter question form (to be discussed shortly).

   Phrase questions in the terms in which respondents think. For example, few respondents will be able to answer, "How many litres of gasoline did you buy last year for your car?" Yet respondents may be able to answer a question about gasoline purchases for a typical week, which the researcher can multiply by 52 to estimate annual purchases.[2]

9. *Avoid false premises.* Do not begin a question with a premise that respondents may not agree with and then follow it by choices regarding it. Respondents who disagree with the premise will be frustrated and not know how to answer. For example, the question, "The post office is open too many hours. Do you want it to open four hours later or close four hours earlier each day?" leaves those who either oppose the premise or oppose both alternatives without a meaningful choice.

   A better question explicitly asks the respondent to assume a premise is true and then asks for a preference. For example, "Assuming the post office has to cut back its operating hours, which would you find more convenient: opening four hours later or closing four hours earlier each day?" Answers to a hypothetical situation are not very reliable, but being explicit will reduce frustration.

10. *Avoid asking about intentions in the distant future.* Avoid asking people about what they might do under hypothetical circumstances far in the future. Responses are poor predictors of behaviour far removed from the current situation or far in the future. Questions such as, "Suppose a new art gallery opened down the road in three years. Would you attend it?" are usually a waste of time. It is better to ask about current or recent attitudes and behaviour. In general, respondents answer specific, concrete questions that relate to their experiences more reliably than they do those about abstractions that are beyond their immediate experiences.

11. *Avoid double negatives.* Double negatives in ordinary language are grammatically incorrect and confusing. For example, "I ain't got no job" logically means that the respondent does have a job, but the second negative is used for emphasis. Such blatant errors are rare, but more subtle forms of the double negative are also confusing. They arise when respondents are asked to agree or disagree with a statement. For example, respondents who *dis*agree with the statement, "Students should not be required to take a comprehensive exam to graduate" are logically stating a double negative because they *disagree* with *not* doing something.

12. *Avoid overlapping or unbalanced response categories.* Make response categories or choices mutually exclusive, exhaustive, and balanced. *Mutually exclusive* means that response categories do not overlap. Overlapping categories that are numerical ranges (e.g., 5–10, 10–20, 20–30) can easily be corrected (e.g., 5–9, 10–19, 20–29). The ambiguous verbal choice is another type of overlapping response category—for example, "Are you satisfied with your job or are there things you don't like about it?" A person can be satisfied with his or her job but still not like certain things about it. *Exhaustive* means that every respondent has a choice—an answer that represents their position. For example, asking respondents, "Are you working or unemployed?" leaves out respondents who are not working but do not consider themselves unemployed (e.g., full-time

homemakers, people on vacation, students, people with disabilities, retired people, etc.). A researcher first thinks about what he or she wants to measure and then considers the circumstances of respondents. For example, when asking about a respondent's employment, does the researcher want information on the primary job or on all jobs? On full-time work only or both full- and part-time work? On jobs for pay only or on unpaid or volunteer jobs as well?

Keep response categories *balanced*. A case of unbalanced choices is the question, "What kind of job is the mayor doing: outstanding, excellent, very good, or satisfactory?" Another type of unbalanced question omits information—for example, "Which of the five candidates running for mayor do you favour: Eugene Oswego or one of the others?" Researchers can balance responses by offering polar opposites. It is easy to see that the terms *honesty* and *dishonesty* have different meanings and connotations. Asking respondents to rate whether a mayor is *highly honest*, *somewhat honest*, or *not very honest* is not the same as asking them to rate the mayor's level of *dishonesty*. Unless there is a specific purpose for doing otherwise, it is better to offer respondents equal polar opposites at each end of a continuum.[3] For example, ask, "Do you think the mayor is very honest, somewhat honest, neither honest nor dishonest, somewhat dishonest, or very dishonest?" (See Table 8.1.)

Aiding Respondent Recall

Recalling events accurately takes more time and effort than the five seconds that respondents have to answer survey questions. Also, one's ability to recall accurately declines over time. Studies in hospitalization and crime victimization show that although most respondents can recall significant events that occurred in the past several weeks, half are inaccurate a year later.

Survey researchers recognize that memory is less trustworthy than was once assumed. It is affected by many factors—the topic, events occurring simultaneously and subsequently, the significance of an event for a person, situational conditions (question wording and interview style), and the respondent's need to have internal consistency.

The complexity of respondent recall does not mean that survey researchers cannot ask about past events; rather, they need to customize questions and interpret results cautiously. Researchers should provide respondents with special instructions and extra thinking time. They should also provide aids to respondent recall, such as a fixed time frame or location references. Rather than asking, "How often did you attend a sporting event last winter?" they should say, "I want to know how many sporting events you attended last winter. Let's go month by month. Think back to December. Did you attend any sporting events for which you paid admission in December? Now think back to January. Did you attend any sporting events in January?"

LO 3 Give examples of the different types of survey questions that are used.

Types of Questions and Response Categories

Threatening Questions Survey researchers sometimes ask about sensitive issues or issues that respondents may believe threaten their presentation of self, such as questions about sexual behaviour, drug or alcohol use, mental health problems, or deviant behaviour. Respondents may be reluctant to answer the questions or to answer completely and truthfully. Survey researchers who wish to ask such questions must do so with great care and must be extra cautious about the results.[4]

threatening questions: A type of *survey research* question in which respondents are likely to cover up or lie about their true behaviour or beliefs because they fear a loss of self-image or that they may appear to be engaging in undesirable or deviant behaviour.

Threatening questions are part of a larger issue of self-presentation and ego protection. Respondents often try to present a positive image of themselves to others. They may be ashamed, embarrassed, or afraid to give truthful answers, or find it emotionally painful to confront their own actions honestly, let alone admit them to other people. They may

Table 8.1 Summary of Survey Question Writing Pitfalls

Things to Avoid	Not Good	A Possible Improvement
1. Jargon, slang, abbreviations	Did you drown in brew until you were totally wasted last night?	Last night, how many beers did you drink?
2. Vagueness	Do you eat out often?	Last week, how many meals did you eat at a restaurant, cafeteria, or other eating establishment?
3. Emotional language	Millions of our tax dollars are being completely wasted through poor procurement practices, bad management, sloppy bookkeeping, defective contract management, personnel abuses, favouritism, and other wasteful practices. Is cutting pork barrel spending and eliminating government misspending of public funds a top priority for you?"	How important is it to you that the House of Commons adopt measures to reduce government waste? Very important Somewhat important Neither important nor unimportant Somewhat unimportant Not important at all
4. Prestige bias	According to medical experts, tax subsidies would encourage adults to participate in physical fitness. Do you agree?	How likely would you be to take advantage of tax subsidy programs that help with the cost of participating in sports activities? Very likely Somewhat likely Somewhat unlikely Very unlikely
5. Double-barrelled questions	Do you support or oppose raising taxes and increasing spending on the military?	Do you support or oppose raising taxes? Do you support or oppose increasing spending on the military?
6. Beliefs as real	Do you think highly educated people smoke less?	What is your education level? Do you smoke cigarettes?
7. Leading questions	Did you do your patriotic duty and vote in the last federal election?	Did you vote in last month's federal election?
8. Issues beyond respondent capabilities	Two years ago, how many hours of TV did you watch every month?	In the past two weeks, approximately how many hours do you think you watched TV on an average weekday day?
9. False premises	When did you stop beating your girlfriend/boyfriend?	Have you ever slapped, punched, or hit your girlfriend/boyfriend?
10. Distant future intentions	After you graduate from university, get a job, and are settled, will you invest a lot of money in the stock market?	Do you have definite plans to put some money into the stock market within the coming two months?
11. Double negatives	Do you disagree with those who do not want to build a new city swimming pool?	There is a proposal to build a new city swimming pool. Do you agree or disagree with the proposal?
12. Unbalanced responses	Did you find the service at our hotel to be outstanding, excellent, superior, or good?	Please rate the service at our hotel: outstanding, very good, adequate, or poor.

under-report or self-censor reports of behaviour or attitudes they wish to hide or believe to be in violation of social norms. Alternatively, they may over-report positive behaviours or generally accepted beliefs (social desirability bias is discussed later in this chapter).

People are likely to under-report having an illness or disability (e.g., cancer, mental illness, venereal disease), engaging in illegal or deviant behaviour (e.g., evading taxes, taking drugs, consuming alcohol, engaging in uncommon sexual practices), or revealing their financial status (e.g., income, savings, debts). In fact, income questions in surveys often have comparably high nonresponse rates compared with other types of questions because people find them intrusive.

Survey researchers have created several techniques to increase truthful answers to threatening questions. Some techniques involve the context and wording of the question itself. Researchers should ask threatening questions only after a warm-up when an interviewer has developed rapport and trust with the respondents, and they should tell respondents that they want honest answers. They can phrase the question in an "enhanced" way to provide a context that makes it easier for respondents to give honest answers. For example, the following enhanced question was asked of heterosexual males: "In past surveys, many men have reported that at some point in their lives they have had some type of sexual experience with another male. This could have happened before adolescence, during adolescence, or as an adult. Have you ever had a sexual experience with a male at some point in your life?" In contrast, a standard form of the question would have asked, "Have you ever had a sexual experience with another male?"

Also, by embedding a threatening response within more serious activities, it may be made to seem less deviant. For example, respondents might hesitate to admit shoplifting if it is asked first, but after being asked about armed robbery or burglary, they may admit to shoplifting because it appears less serious.

social desirability bias: A bias in *survey research* in which respondents give a "normative" response or a socially acceptable answer rather than giving a truthful answer.

Socially Desirable Questions **Social desirability bias** occurs when respondents distort answers to make their reports conform to social norms. People tend to over-report being cultured (i.e., reading, attending high-culture events), giving money to charity, having a good marriage, loving their children, and so forth. For example, one study found that one third of people who reported in a survey that they gave money to a local charity really did not. Because a norm says that one should vote in elections, many report voting when they did not. In Canada, those under the greatest pressure to vote (i.e., highly educated, politically partisan, highly religious people who had been contacted by an organization that urged them to vote) are the people most likely to over-report voting.

Characteristics of Women with Children Who Divorce in Midlife Compared to Those Who Remain Married

Questionnaire writers try to reduce social desirability bias by phrasing questions in ways that make norm violation appear less objectionable and that present a wider range of behaviour as acceptable. They can also offer multiple response categories that give respondents "face-saving" alternatives. It has also been found that the survey's **mode of delivery** (the means by which a survey is conducted) can affect responses to questions that may be affected by social desirability. Individuals who have less direct personal contact with an interviewer (i.e., doing an online survey compared to a face-to-face interview) may be less swayed to give "desirable" answers (see Table 8.2).

mode of delivery: In *survey research*, this refers to how the data were collected (e.g., by postal survey, telephone interview, in-person interview, or over the internet).

Knowledge Questions Studies suggest that a large majority of the public cannot correctly answer elementary geography questions or identify important political documents (e.g., the Canadian Charter of Rights and Freedoms). Researchers sometimes want to find out whether respondents know about an issue or topic, but knowledge questions can be threatening because respondents do not want to appear ignorant. Surveys may measure opinions better if they first ask about factual information, because many people have inaccurate factual knowledge.

Political Knowledge

Some simple knowledge questions, such as the number of people living in a household, are not always answered accurately in surveys. In some households, a marginal person—the boyfriend who left for a week, the adult daughter who left after an argument about her pregnancy, or the uncle who walked out after a dispute over money—may be reported as not living in a household, but he or she may not have another permanent residence and may consider himself or herself to live there.[5]

A researcher pilot-tests questions so that questions are at an appropriate level of difficulty. Little is gained if 99 percent of respondents cannot answer the question. Knowledge

Table 8.2 Findings from a Study on Social Desirability in a Survey of Recently Graduated University Students by Different Modes of Delivery

	Telephone Interview	Self-Administered Web Survey
Undesirable Characteristics		
GPA less than 2.5	11%	15%
At least one failing grade	61%	62%
Dropped a course	68%	71%
Desirable Characteristics		
GPA higher than 3.5	22%	21%
Honour roll	12%	10%

Source: Kreuter, F., Presser, S., & Tourangeau, R. (2008). Social desirability bias in CAT, IVR and web surveys: The effects of mode and question sensitivity. *Public Opinion Quarterly, 72*(5), 847–865. Reprinted with permission from Oxford University Press.

questions can be worded so that respondents feel comfortable saying they do not know the answer—for example, "How much, if anything, have you heard about. . . ."

Skip or Contingency Questions Researchers avoid asking questions that are irrelevant for a respondent. Yet some questions apply only to specific respondents. A **contingency question** is a two- (or more) part question. The answer to the first part of the question determines which of two different questions a respondent next receives. Contingency questions select respondents for whom a second question is relevant. Sometimes they are called *screen* or *skip questions*. On the basis of the answer to the first question, the respondent or an interviewer is instructed to go to another question or to skip certain questions.

contingency question: A two- (or more) part question in *survey research*. The answer to the first part of the question determines which of two different questions a respondent receives next.

The following example is a contingency question taken from the 2004 Canadian Campus Survey.[6] In this questionnaire, there is a large section that deals with the drinking behaviour of students. A contingency question is used at the beginning of the section on drinking to immediately redirect students who never drink, as the questions that follow on drinking behaviours would not be relevant to them.

1. During the past 12 months, how often, on average, did you consume alcoholic drinks?
   Every day ☐
   4–6 times a week ☐
   2–3 times a week ☐
   Once a week ☐
   1–3 times a month ☐
   Less than once a month ☐
   Never ☐ SKIP TO QUESTION 17
2. During the past 12 months, on the days when you drank, how many drinks did you usually have? (PLEASE WRITE NUMBER OF DRINKS)
   Number of drinks ______________

LO 4 Explain the advantages and disadvantages of open and closed questions.

Open versus Closed Questions

open-ended question: A type of *survey research* question in which respondents are free to offer any answer they wish to the question.

closed-ended question: A type of *survey research* question in which respondents must choose from a fixed set of answers.

There has long been a debate about open versus closed questions in survey research. An **open-ended** (unstructured, free response) **question** asks a question (e.g., "What is your favourite television program?") to which respondents can give any answer. A **closed-ended** (structured, fixed response) **question** both asks a question and gives the respondent fixed responses from which to choose (e.g., "Is the prime minister doing a very good, good, fair, or

Box 8.2 Making It Practical

Closed versus Open Questions

Advantages of Closed Questions

- The answers of different respondents are easier to compare.
- Answers are easier to code and statistically analyze.
- The response choices can clarify question meaning for respondents.
- Respondents are more likely to answer about sensitive topics.
- There are fewer irrelevant or confusing answers to questions.
- Less articulate or less literate respondents are not at a disadvantage.
- Replication is easier.
- It is easier and quicker for respondents to answer.

Disadvantages of Closed Questions

- They can suggest ideas that the respondent would not otherwise have.
- Respondents with no opinion or no knowledge can answer anyway.
- Respondents can be frustrated because their desired answer is not a choice.
- It is confusing if many (e.g., 20) response choices are offered.
- Misinterpretation of a question can go unnoticed.
- Distinctions between respondent answers may be blurred.
- Clerical mistakes or marking the wrong response is possible.
- They force respondents to give simplistic responses to complex issues.
- They force people to make choices they would not make in the real world.

Advantages of Open Questions

- They permit an unlimited number of possible answers.
- Respondents can answer in detail and can qualify and clarify responses.
- Unanticipated findings can be discovered.
- They permit adequate answers to complex issues.
- They permit creativity, self-expression, and richness of detail.
- They reveal a respondent's logic, thinking process, and frame of reference.

Disadvantages of Open Questions

- Different respondents give different degrees of detail in answers.
- Responses may be irrelevant or buried in useless detail.
- Comparisons and statistical analyses become very difficult.
- Coding responses is difficult.
- Articulate and highly literate respondents have an advantage.
- Questions may be too general for respondents who lose direction.
- Responses are written verbatim, which is difficult for interviewers.
- A greater amount of respondent time, thought, and effort is necessary.
- Respondents can be intimidated by questions.
- Answers take up a lot of space in the questionnaire.

poor job, in your opinion?"). Each form has advantages and disadvantages (see Box 8.2). The crucial issue is not which form is best. Rather, it is under what conditions a form is most appropriate.

A researcher's choice to use an open- or closed-ended question depends on the purpose and the practical limitations of a research project. The demands of using open-ended questions, with interviewers writing verbatim answers followed by time-consuming coding, may make them impractical for a specific project.

Large-scale surveys have closed-ended questions because they are quicker and easier for both respondents and researchers. Yet something important may be lost when an individual's beliefs and feelings are forced into a few fixed categories that a researcher created. To learn how a respondent thinks, to discover what is really important to him or her, or to get an answer to a question with many possible answers (e.g., age), open questions may be best. In addition, sensitive topics (e.g., sexual behaviour, liquor consumption) may be more accurately measured with closed questions.

The disadvantages of a question form can be reduced by mixing open-ended and closed-ended questions in a questionnaire. Mixing them also offers a change of pace and helps interviewers establish rapport. Periodic *probes* (i.e., follow-up questions by interviewers) with closed-ended questions can reveal a respondent's reasoning.

Having interviewers periodically use probes to ask about a respondent's thinking is a way to check whether respondents understand the questions as the researcher intended. However, probes are not substitutes for writing clear questions or creating a framework of understanding for the respondent. Unless carefully stated, probes might shape the respondent's answers or force answers when a respondent does not have an opinion or information. Yet flexible or conversational interviewing in which interviewers use many probes can improve accuracy on questions about complex issues on which respondents do not clearly understand basic terms or about which they have difficulty expressing their thoughts. For example, to the question, "Did you do any work for money last week?" a respondent might hesitate, then reply, "Yes." An interviewer asks probingly, "Could you tell me exactly what work you did?" The respondent may reply, "On Tuesday and Wednesday I spent a couple hours helping my buddy John move into his new apartment. For that he gave me $40, but I didn't have any other job or get paid for doing anything else." If the researcher's intention was only to get reports of regular employment, the probe revealed a misunderstanding. Researchers also use **partially open questions** (i.e., a set of fixed choices with a final open choice of "other, please specify"), which allows respondents to offer an answer that the researcher did not include.

partially open question: A type of *survey research* question in which respondents are given a fixed set of answers to choose from, but in addition an "other" category is offered so that they can specify a different answer.

Open-ended questions are especially valuable in early or exploratory stages of research. For large-scale surveys, researchers use open questions in pilot tests, then develop closed-question responses from the answers given to the open questions.

Researchers writing closed questions have to make many decisions. How many response choices should be given? Should they offer a middle or neutral choice? What should be the order of responses? What should be the types of response choices? How will the direction of a response be measured?

Answers to these questions are not easy. For example, two response choices are too few, but more than five response choices are rarely effective. Researchers want to measure meaningful distinctions and not collapse them. More specific responses yield more information, but too many specifics create confusion. For example, rephrasing the question, "Are you satisfied with your dentist?" (which has a yes/no answer) to "How satisfied are you with your dentist: very satisfied, somewhat satisfied, somewhat dissatisfied, or not satisfied at all?" gives the researcher more information and a respondent more choices.

Nonattitudes and the Middle Positions

Survey researchers debate whether to include choices for neutral, middle, and nonattitude positions (e.g., "not sure," "don't know," or "no opinion").[7] Two types of errors can be made: accepting a middle choice or "no attitude" response when respondents hold a non-neutral opinion, or forcing respondents to choose a position on an issue when they have no opinion about it. Many researchers fear that respondents will choose nonattitude choices to avoid making a choice. Yet it is usually best to offer a nonattitude choice, because people will express opinions on fictitious issues, objects, and events. By offering a nonattitude (middle or no opinion) choice, researchers identify those holding middle positions or those without opinions.

The issue of nonattitudes can be approached by distinguishing among three kinds of attitude questions: standard-format, quasi-filter, and full-filter questions (see Box 8.3). The **standard-format question** does not offer a "don't know" choice; a respondent must volunteer

standard-format question: A type of *survey research* question in which the answer categories fail to include "no opinion" or "don't know."

Box 8.3 Making It Practical

Standard-Format, Quasi-Filter, and Full-Filter Questions

Standard-Format Question

Here is a question about another country. Do you agree or disagree with this statement? "The Russian leaders are basically trying to get along with America."

Quasi-Filter Question

Here is a statement about another country: "The Russian leaders are basically trying to get along with America." Do you agree, disagree, or have no opinion on that?

Full-Filter Question

Here is a statement about another country. Not everyone has an opinion on this. If you do not have an opinion, just say so. Here's the statement: "The Russian leaders are basically trying to get along with America." Do you have an opinion on that? If yes, do you agree or disagree?

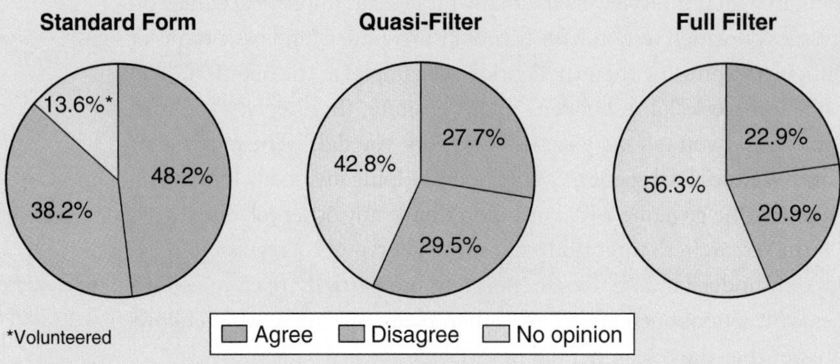

quasi-filter question: A type of *survey research* question including the answer choice "no opinion" or "don't know."

full-filter question: A type of *survey research* question in which respondents are first asked whether they have an opinion or know about a topic, then only the respondents with an opinion or knowledge are asked a specific question on the topic.

floaters: Respondents who lack a belief or opinion but who give an answer anyway if asked in a *survey research* question. Often, their answers are inconsistent.

response set: An effect in *survey research* when respondents tend to agree with every question in a series rather than thinking through their answer to each question.

it. A **quasi-filter question** offers respondents a "don't know" alternative. A **full-filter question** is a special type of contingency question. It first asks if respondents have an opinion, then asks for the opinion of those who state that they do have an opinion.

Many respondents will answer a question if a "no opinion" choice is missing, but they will choose "don't know" when it is offered or say that they do not have an opinion if asked. Such respondents are called **floaters** because they "float" from giving a response to not knowing. Their responses are affected by minor wording changes, so researchers screen them out using quasi-filter or full-filter questions. Filtered questions do not eliminate all answers to nonexistent issues, but they reduce the problem.

Agree/Disagree, Rankings or Ratings? Survey researchers who measure values and attitudes have debated two issues about the responses offered.[8] (1) Should questionnaire items make a statement and ask respondents whether they agree or disagree with it, or should they offer respondents specific alternatives? (2) Should the questionnaire include a set of items and ask respondents to rate them (e.g., approve, disapprove), or should it give them a list of items and force them to rank-order items (e.g., from most favoured to least favoured)?

It is best to offer respondents explicit alternatives. For example, instead of asking, "Do you agree or disagree with the statement, 'Men are better suited to . . . '?" ask, "Do you think men are better suited, women are better suited, or both are equally suited to . . . ?" Less-educated respondents are more likely to agree with a statement, whereas forced-choice alternatives encourage thought and avoid the **response set** bias—a tendency of some respondents to agree and not really decide.

Researchers create bias if question wording gives respondents a reason for choosing one alternative. For example, respondents were asked whether they supported or opposed a law on energy conservation. The results changed when respondents heard, "Do you support the law or do you oppose it because the law would be difficult to enforce?" instead of simply, "Do you support or oppose the law?"

It is better to ask respondents to choose among alternatives by ranking instead of rating items along an imaginary continuum. Respondents can rate several items equally high, but will place them in a hierarchy if asked to rank them.[9]

Wording Issues

Survey researchers face two wording issues. The first issue, discussed earlier, is using simple vocabulary and grammar to minimize confusion. The second issue involves effects of specific words or phrases. This is trickier because it is not possible to know in advance whether a word or phrase affects responses.

The difference between *forbid* and *not allow* illustrates the problem of wording differences. Both terms have the same meaning, but many more people are willing to "not allow" something than to "forbid" it. In general, less-educated respondents are most influenced by minor wording differences.

Certain words seem to trigger an emotional reaction, and researchers are just beginning to learn of them. For example, T. Smith (1987) found large differences (e.g., twice as much support) in U.S. survey responses depending on whether a question asked about spending "to help the poor" or "for welfare." He suggested that the word *welfare* has such strong negative connotations for Americans (lazy people, wasteful and expensive programs) that it is best to avoid it. Research in Canada by Hunter and Miazdyck (2003) has shown that Canadians are somewhat less receptive to "welfare" compared to "help for the poor" as well, but not to the same extent as their American counterparts. Box 8.4 discusses some question wording issues that have been in the popular press recently.

Many respondents are confused by words or their connotations. For example, respondents were asked whether they thought television news was impartial. Researchers later learned that large numbers of respondents had ignored the word *impartial*—a term the middle-class, educated researchers assumed everyone would know. Less than half the respondents had interpreted the word as intended with its proper meaning. Over one quarter ignored it or had no idea of its meaning. Others gave it unusual meanings, and one tenth thought it was directly opposite to its true meaning. Researchers need to be cautious, because some **wording effects** (e.g., the difference between *forbid* and *not allow*) remain the same for decades, while other effects may appear.[12]

wording effect: An effect that occurs when a specific term or word used in a *survey research* question affects how respondents answer the question.

Questionnaire Design Issues

LO 5 Identify major questionnaire design issues.

Length of Survey or Questionnaire How long should a questionnaire be or an interview last? Researchers prefer long questionnaires or interviews because they are more cost effective. The cost for extra questions—once a respondent has been sampled, has been contacted, and has completed other questions—is small. There is no absolute proper length. The length depends on the survey format (to be discussed later in this chapter) and on the respondent's characteristics. A five-minute telephone interview is rarely a problem and may be extended to 20 minutes without issue. National polling organizations and Statistics Canada stretch this to 45 minutes to an hour for major studies. Mail questionnaires are more variable. A short (three- or four-page) questionnaire is appropriate for the general population. Some researchers have had success with questionnaires as long as

Box 8.4 In the News

The Effect of Question Wording on Public Opinion

According to an April 2010 study by Ipsos Reid, (1) 8 percent of Canadians know someone who has been abused by a priest[10] and (2) 58 percent of Canadians believe that Pope Benedict "perpetuated a climate of silence around abuse claims." Of course such results are concerning, but the results of any study are only as good as the questions that were used to arrive at them. Prominent Canadian sociologist Reginald Bibby, who specializes in the sociology of religion, decided to investigate the validity of these results and came up with some rather important points about the design of the survey used to generate such findings.[11] He argued:

> Suppose, for example, that Ipsos-Reid had asked Canadians, "Do you have family members, friends, or acquaintances who have been divorced?" I'd venture to say that the question would have resulted in as many as 90 percent of people across the country saying, "Yes." Contrast this to the number of people who have personally been divorced—my own latest national survey shows this figure is probably around 15 percent.
>
> The first question asks individuals about the people they know—and who doesn't know someone who has been divorced? The other asks individuals about their own experiences. Awareness does not equal incidence. Both are important. But obviously they are two very different things.
>
> Ipsos-Reid probed awareness, not incidence. One person in a neighbourhood or larger community could have been assaulted—and hundreds and maybe thousands of people would be aware of it. No time frame was given, meaning awareness of an incident could span up to 80 or 90 years—not just the post-1950s, for example. In short, the reporting net was an extremely large one.

Bibby went on:

> A second item in the survey that has received considerable media attention is the finding that 58 percent of Canadians believe that Pope Benedict "has perpetuated a climate of silence and cover up around pedophile and hebephile priests."
>
> Now that could be interesting and important information. The problem, however, as George Gallup pointed out some time ago, is that we who poll people for a living have to pose questions that they have a mathematical chance of being able to answer. In this case, I hope that Ipsos-Reid, for starters, defined "hebephile" to respondents. (The word refers to a person attracted to youngsters at the age of puberty.) Furthermore, one cannot assume that everyone from British Columbia to Newfoundland knows who Pope Benedict is, or that abuse has taken place, or that the Pope himself has been linked to a cover-up.
>
> And to the extent respondents can meet those basic information criteria for being able to offer an informed response to the question, what I want to know is this: How on Earth do Canadians have the inside scoop on whether or not the Pope has been a part of the alleged scandal? A follow-up question to the effect of, "On what are you basing your opinion?" may have been extremely telling.
>
> Obviously, most Canadians who offered a take were simply offering views based on information they have received from media and acquaintances. In short, the item doesn't tell us very much—beyond Canadian conjecture.

What this thoughtful analysis from Bibby reminds us of is that even results from well-known and established research groups should be scrutinized and that the knowledge we obtain from such studies cannot be understood independently of how these data were obtained—particularly regarding the questions that were asked of respondents.

Another example of the importance of wording in questionnaires was found in February 2010, when headlines across North America declared that question wording influenced the survey results on a topic of considerable public interest—the issue of gays and lesbians in the United States military. It is not often that methodological issues make headline news!

The *New York Times* and CBS News undertook public opinion polling on the issue of gays and lesbians in the military and the proposal to change the "don't ask, don't tell" policy (where individuals were not asked about their sexual orientation and also did not disclose) to serving "openly." It was found that support of such an idea varied quite remarkably depending on whether the term "homosexual" or "gays and lesbians" was used.

For example, 59 percent of respondents favoured or strongly favoured "homosexuals" serving in the military, compared to 71 percent who favoured or strongly favoured "gay men and lesbians." Similarly, 44 percent supported "homosexuals" serving openly, compared to 58 percent who supported "gay men and lesbians" serving openly.

What is the reason for this difference in opinion based on question wording? It has been suggested that "homosexual" makes people think of a medicalized condition, while "gay men and lesbians" is more socially normalized and acceptable.

Sources: Bibby, R. (2010, April 21). Flawed poll distorts scope of sexual abuse. *Edmonton Journal.* Retrieved from www.edmontonjournal.com/news/Flawed+poll+distorts+scope+sexual+abuse/2932895/story.html; Todd, D. (2010, April 13). Poll: 2 million Canadians know someone abused by priest. Church responds. *Vancouver Sun.* Retrieved from http://communities.canada.com/VANCOUVERSUN/blogs/thesearch/archive/2010/04/13/poll-2-million-canadians-know-someone-abused-by-priest-church-responds.aspx; CBS News/*New York Times* Poll. (2010, February 10). Gays in the military. Press release. Retrieved from www.cbsnews.com/htdocs/pdf/poll_021110_2pm.pdf?tag=contentMain;contentBody. Printed with permission.

10 pages (about 100 items) with the general public, but responses drop significantly for longer questionnaires. For highly educated respondents and a salient topic, using questionnaires of 15 pages may be possible. Face-to-face interviews lasting an hour or more are not uncommon. In special situations, face-to-face interviews as long as three to five hours are conducted.

Question Order or Sequence A survey researcher faces three issues of question sequence: organization of the overall questionnaire, question order effects, and context effects.

Organization of Questionnaire In general, you should sequence questions to minimize the discomfort and confusion of respondents. A questionnaire has opening, middle, and ending questions. After an introduction explaining the survey, it is best to make opening questions pleasant, interesting, and easy to answer to help a respondent feel comfortable about the questionnaire. Avoid asking many tedious background questions or threatening questions first. Organize questions into common topics. Mixing questions on different topics causes confusion. Orient respondents by placing questions on the same topic together and introduce the section with a short introductory statement (e.g., "Now I would like to ask you questions about housing"). Make question topics flow smoothly and logically, and organize them to assist respondents' memory or comfort levels. Do not end with highly threatening questions, and always end with a "thank you."

Order Effects Researchers are concerned that the order in which they present questions may influence respondent answers. Such **order effects** appear to be strongest for people who lack strong views, for less-educated respondents, and for older respondents or those with memory loss.[13] For example, support for an unmarried woman having an abortion rises if the question is preceded by a question about abortion being acceptable when a fetus has serious defects, but not when the question is by itself or comes before a question about fetus defects. An example of order effects is presented in Box 8.5.

order effects: An effect in *survey research* in which respondents hear some specific questions before others and the earlier questions affect their answers to later questions.

Box 8.5 Concepts in Action

Question Order Effects

In order to study how question order affected questionnaire responses, Bassili and Krosnick (2000) administered a telephone survey to a random sample of 621 University of Toronto students. The questionnaire asked the respondents about their opinions on a wide range of topics. The researchers were interested in seeing how the students would respond to the following questions on abortion, depending on which one was presented first:

Question 1

"Would you tell me whether or not you think it should be possible for a pregnant woman to obtain a legal abortion if she is married and does not want any more children?"

Question 2

"Please tell me whether or not you think it should be possible for a pregnant woman to obtain a legal abortion if there is a strong chance of serious defect in the baby."

When Question 1 was asked first, 69 percent of the respondents answered in favour of the woman's right to obtain an abortion. However, when Question 1 was preceded by Question 2, 64 percent reported being in favour of the woman's right to choose an abortion. Upon further examination of the data, the researchers found that people who tended to have more "extreme" attitudes on other questionnaire items were more likely to be affected by question order. The context created by answering the first question affects the answer to the second question.

Source: Adapted from Bassili, J. N., & Krosnick, J. A. (2000). Do strength-related attitude properties determine susceptibility to response effects? New evidence from response latency, attitude extremity, and aggregate indices. *Political Psychology, 21*, 107–132.

Respondents may not perceive each issue of a survey as isolated and separate. They respond to survey questions based on the set of issues and their order of presentation in a questionnaire. Previous questions can influence later ones in two ways: through their content (i.e., the issue) and through the respondent's response. For example, a student respondent is asked, "Do you support or favour an educational contribution for students?" Answers vary depending on the topic of the preceding question. If it comes after "How much tuition does the average Canadian student pay?" respondents interpret "contribution" to mean support for what students will pay. If it comes after "How much does the Swedish government pay to students?" respondents interpret it to mean a contribution that the government will pay. Responses can also be influenced by previous answers because a respondent having already answered one part will assume no overlap. For example, if a person is asked, "How is your spouse?" The next question is, "How is your family?" Most people will assume that the second question means family members other than the spouse because they already gave an answer about the spouse.[14]

funnel sequence: A way to order *survey research* questions in a questionnaire from general to specific.

Context Effects Researchers have found powerful context effects in surveys. As a practical matter, two things can be done regarding context effects. (1) Use a **funnel sequence** of questions—that is, ask more general questions before specific ones (e.g., ask about health in general before asking about specific diseases). (2) Divide the number of respondents in half and give half of the questions in one order and the other half in the alternative order, then examine the results to see whether question order mattered. If question order effects are found, which order tells you what the respondents really think? The answer is that you cannot know for sure.

For example, a few years ago students in one of the authors' (Lawrence Neuman's) classes conducted a telephone survey on two topics: concern about crime and attitudes toward a new anti-drunk-driving law. A random half of the respondents heard questions about the drunk-driving law first; the other half heard about crime first. Neuman examined the results to see whether there was any **context effect**—a difference by topic order. He found that respondents who were asked about the drunk-driving law first expressed less fear about crime than did those who were asked about crime first. Likewise, they were more supportive of the drunk-driving law than were those who first heard about crime. The first topic created a context within which respondents answered questions on the second topic. After they were asked about crime in general and thought about violent crime, drunk driving may have appeared to be a less important issue. By contrast, after they were asked about drunk driving and thought about drunk driving as a crime, they may have expressed less concern about crime in general.

context effect: An effect in *survey research* when an overall tone or set of topics heard by a respondent affects how he or she interprets the meaning of subsequent questions.

Respondents answer all questions based on a context of preceding questions and the interview setting. A researcher needs to remember that the more ambiguous a question's meaning, the stronger the context effects, because respondents will draw on the context to interpret and understand the question. Previous questions on the same topic and heard just before a question can have a large context effect. For example, Sudman, Bradburn, and Schwarz (1996, pp. 90–91) contrasted three ways of asking how much a respondent followed politics. When they asked the question alone, about 21 percent of respondents said they followed politics "now and then" or "hardly at all." When they asked the question after asking what the respondent's elected representative recently did, the percentage who said they did not follow nearly doubled, going to 39 percent. The knowledge question about the representative made many respondents feel that they did not really know much. When a question about the amount of "public relations work" the elected representative provided to the area came between the two questions, 29 percent of respondents said they did not follow politics. This question gave respondents an excuse for not knowing the first question—they could blame their representative for their ignorance. The context of a question can make a difference and researchers need to be aware of it at all times.

Format and Layout There are two format or layout issues: the overall physical layout of the questionnaire and the format of questions and responses.

Questionnaire Layout Layout is important, whether a questionnaire is for an interviewer or for the respondent. Questionnaires should be clear, neat, and easy to follow. Give each question a number and put identifying information (e.g., name of organization) on questionnaires. Never cram questions together or create a confusing appearance. A few cents saved in postage or printing will ultimately cost more in terms of lower validity because of a lower response rate or confusion on the part of interviewers and respondents. Make a **cover sheet** or face sheet for each interview, for administrative use. Put the time and date of interview, the interviewer, the respondent identification number, and the interviewer's comments and observations on it. A professional appearance with high-quality graphics, space between questions, and good layout improves accuracy and completeness and helps the questionnaire flow.

cover sheet: One or more pages at the beginning of a questionnaire with information about an interview or respondent.

Give interviewers or respondents instructions on the questionnaire. Print instructions in a different style from the questions (e.g., in a different colour or font, or in all capitals) to distinguish them. This is so an interviewer can easily distinguish between questions for respondents and instructions intended for the interviewer alone.

Layout is crucial for mail and online surveys because there is no friendly interviewer to interact with the respondent. Instead, the questionnaire's appearance persuades the respondent. In mail and online surveys, include a polite, professional cover letter on letterhead stationery (or an email originating from an organizational address rather than a free email site) identifying the researcher and offering a telephone number and email address for questions. Details matter. Respondents will be turned off if they receive a bulky brown envelope with bulk postage addressed to "Occupant" or an email invitation that looks like spam. Always end with "Thank you for your participation." Interviewers and questionnaires should leave respondents with a positive feeling about the survey and a sense that their participation is appreciated.

Question design matters. One study of university students asked how many hours they studied per day. Some students saw five answer choices ranging from 0.5 hours to more than 2.5 hours; others saw five answer choices ranging from less than 2.5 hours to more than 4.5 hours. Of students who saw the first set, 77 percent said they studied under 2.5 hours versus 31 percent of those receiving the second set. When the mail questionnaire and telephone interview were compared, 58 percent of students hearing the first set said they studied under 2.5 hours, but there was no change among those hearing the second set. More than differences in response categories were involved, because when students were asked about hours of television watching per day with similar response categories and then with the alternative response categories, no differences between the two were found. What can we learn from this? Respondents without clear answers tend to rely on questionnaire response categories for guidance, and more anonymous answering formats tend to yield more honest responses (see Dillman, 2000, pp. 32–39 for more details).

Question Format Survey researchers decide on a format for questions and responses. Should respondents circle responses, check boxes, fill in dots, or put a number in a blank space? The principle is to make responses unambiguous. Boxes or brackets to be checked and numbers to be circled are usually clearest. Also, listing responses down a page rather than across it makes them easier to see (see Box 8.6). As mentioned before, use arrows and instructions for contingency questions (or make sure that the contingency questions operate properly in your online survey). Visual aids are also helpful. For example, hand out thermometer-like drawings to respondents when asking about how warm or cool they feel toward someone. A **matrix question** (or grid question) is a compact way to present a series of questions using the same response categories. It saves space and makes it easier for the respondent or interviewer to note answers for the same response categories.

matrix question: A type of *survey research* question in which a set of questions is listed in a compact form together, all questions sharing the same set of answer categories.

Box 8.6 Making It Practical

Question Format Examples

Example of Horizontal versus Vertical Response Choices

Do you think it is too easy or too difficult to get a divorce, or is it about right?

■ Too Easy ■ Too Difficult ■ About Right

Do you think it is too easy or too difficult to get a divorce, or is it about right?

■ Too Easy
■ Too Difficult
■ About Right

Example of a Matrix Question Format

	Strongly Agree	*Agree*	*Disagree*	*Strongly Disagree*	*Don't Know*
The teacher talks too fast.	■	■	■	■	■
I learned a lot in this class.	■	■	■	■	■
The tests are very easy.	■	■	■	■	■
The teacher tells many jokes.	■	■	■	■	■
The teacher is organized.	■	■	■	■	■

Examples of Some Response Category Choices

Excellent, Good, Fair, Poor
Approve/Disapprove
Favour/Oppose
Strongly Agree, Agree, Somewhat Agree, Somewhat Disagree, Disagree, Strongly Disagree
Too Much, Too Little, About Right
Better, Worse, About the Same
Regularly, Often, Seldom, Never
Always, Most of the Time, Some of the Time, Rarely, Never
More Likely, Less Likely, No Difference
Very Interested, Interested, Not Interested

Nonresponse

The failure to get a valid response from every sampled respondent weakens a survey. The topic of response rates was briefly discussed in Chapter 7 in relation to sampling. Have you ever refused to answer a survey? In addition to research surveys, people are asked to respond to many requests from charities, marketing firms, candidate polls, and so forth. Charities and marketing firms get low response rates, whereas government organizations get much higher cooperation rates. Nonresponse can be a major problem for survey research because if a high proportion of the sampled respondents do not respond, researchers may not be able to generalize results, especially if those who do not respond differ from those who respond.

Public cooperation in survey research has declined over the past 20 to 30 years across many countries.[15] There is both a growing group of "hard core" refusing people and a general decline in participation because many people feel there are too many surveys. Other reasons for refusal include a fear of fraudulent pollsters, a more hectic lifestyle, a loss of privacy, the annoyance of unsolicited calls (and the prevalence of caller ID), and a rising distrust of authority or government. The misuse of the survey to sell products or persuade people, poorly designed questionnaires, and inadequate explanations of surveys to respondents also increase refusals for legitimate surveys.

Survey researchers can improve eligibility rates by careful respondent screening, better sample frame definition, and multilingual interviewers. They can decrease refusals by sending letters in advance of an interview, offering to reschedule interviews, using incentives (i.e., coupons, gifts, cash), adjusting interviewer behaviour and statements (i.e., making eye contact, expressing sincerity, explaining the sampling or survey, emphasizing importance of the interview, clarifying promises of confidentiality). Survey researchers can also use alterna-

Box 8.7 Making It Practical

Ten Ways to Increase Mail and Online Questionnaire Response

1. Address the questionnaire to a specific person.
2. Include a carefully written, dated cover letter on letterhead stationery (if using mail) or a carefully written email originating from an organizational email address (not a free web account). In it, request respondent cooperation, guarantee confidentiality, explain the purpose of the survey, and give the researcher's name, phone number, and email address.
3. *Always* include a postage-paid, addressed return envelope (in the case of the mail questionnaire) or a working link to the online survey.
4. The questionnaire should have a neat, attractive layout and be of reasonable length.
5. The questionnaire should be professionally designed and easy to read with clear instructions.
6. Send two follow-up reminders to those not responding. The first should arrive about one week after sending the questionnaire (or questionnaire request if using email), the second a week later. Gently ask for cooperation again and offer to send another questionnaire.
7. Do not send questionnaires or requests to fill out online surveys during major holiday periods.
8. If using a paper questionnaire, do not put questions on the back page. Instead, leave a blank space and ask the respondent for general comments.
9. Sponsors that are local and are seen as legitimate (e.g., government agencies, universities, large firms) get a better response.
10. Include a small monetary incentive if possible.

tive interviewers (i.e., different demographic characteristics, age, race, gender, or ethnicity), use alternative interview methods (i.e., phone versus face to face), or accept alternative respondents in a household.

A critical area of nonresponse or refusal to participate occurs with the initial contact between an interviewer and a respondent. A face-to-face or telephone interview must overcome resistance and reassure respondents.

Research on the use of incentives found that prepaid incentives appear to increase respondent cooperation in all types of surveys. They do not appear to have negative effects on survey composition or future participation.

There is substantial literature on ways to increase response rates for mail questionnaires, as discussed in Box 8.7.[16]

TYPES OF SURVEYS: ADVANTAGES AND DISADVANTAGES

LO 6 Describe the major types of surveys and identify their advantages and disadvantages.

Mail and Self-Administered Questionnaires

Advantages Researchers can give questionnaires directly to respondents or mail them to respondents who read instructions and questions then record their answers. This type of survey is by far the cheapest, and it can be conducted by a single researcher. A researcher can send questionnaires to a wide geographical area. The respondent can complete the questionnaire when it is convenient and can check personal records if necessary. Mail questionnaires offer anonymity and avoid interviewer bias. They can be effective, and response rates may be high for an educated target population that has a strong interest in the topic or the survey organization.

Disadvantages Since people do not always complete and return questionnaires, the biggest problem with mail questionnaires is a low response rate. Most questionnaires are returned within two weeks, but others trickle in up to two months later. Researchers can raise response rates by sending nonrespondents reminder letters, but this adds to the time and cost of data collection.

A researcher cannot control the conditions under which a mail questionnaire is completed. A questionnaire completed during a drinking party by a dozen laughing people may be returned along with one filled out by an earnest respondent. Also, no one is present to clarify questions or to probe for more information when respondents give incomplete answers.

Someone other than the sampled respondent (e.g., spouse, new resident) may open the mail and complete the questionnaire without the researcher's knowledge. Different respondents can complete the questionnaire weeks apart or answer questions in a different order than that intended by researchers. Incomplete questionnaires can also be a serious problem.

Researchers cannot visually observe the respondent's reactions to questions, physical characteristics, or the setting. For example, an impoverished 70-year-old White woman living alone on a farm could falsely state that she is a prosperous 40-year-old Asian male doctor living in a small town with three children. Such extreme lies are rare, but serious errors can go undetected.

The mail questionnaire format limits the kinds of questions that a researcher can use. Questions requiring visual aids (e.g., look at this picture and tell me what you see), open-ended questions, many contingency questions, and complex questions do poorly in mail questionnaires. Likewise, mail questionnaires are ill suited for the illiterate or near-illiterate in English. Questionnaires mailed to illiterate respondents are not likely to be returned; if they are completed and returned, the questions were probably misunderstood, so the answers are meaningless (see Table 8.3).

Table 8.3 Types of Surveys and Their Features

	Type of Survey			
Features	*Mail Questionnaire*	*Online Survey*	*Telephone Interview*	*Face-to-Face Interview*
Administrative Issues				
Cost	Cheap	Cheapest	Moderate	Expensive
Speed	Slowest	Fastest	Fast	Slow to moderate
Length (number of questions)	Moderate	Moderate	Short	Longest
Response rate	Lowest	Moderate	Moderate	Highest
Research Control				
Probes possible	No	No	Yes	Yes
Specific respondent	No	No	Yes	Yes
Question sequence	No	Yes	Yes	Yes
Only one respondent	No	No	Yes	Yes
Visual observation	No	Yes	No	Yes
Success with Different Questions				
Visual aids	Limited	Yes	None	Yes
Open-ended questions	Limited	Limited	Limited	Yes
Contingency questions	Limited	Yes	Yes	Yes
Complex questions	Limited	Yes	Limited	Yes
Sensitive questions	Some	Yes	Limited	Limited
Sources of Bias				
Social desirability	Some	Some	Some	Most
Interviewer bias	None	None	Some	Most
Respondent's reading skill	Yes	Yes	No	No

Box 8.8 Social Research and the Internet

Making on Online Survey

There are many online services available to help you make your own online survey easily and cheaply (often for free). Various commercial sites (just Google "free online survey") allow researchers to quickly make professional-looking surveys and have pricing structures based on the number of questions asked and the number or respondents who are permitted to answer the survey. Popular websites for survey creation include SurveyMonkey, SurveyGizmo, SoGoSurvey, and Google Forms. Very small surveys with limited numbers of participants are often free to create, even on "pay" sites. Sometimes pay sites even offer free accounts for students and nonprofit organizations. You can also find reviews online about the pros and cons associated with each of the online survey services.

Excellent
Very good
Good
Fair
Poor

Photo Credit: tang90246/Fotolia/LLC

Online Surveys

Online surveys are gaining in popularity and are used by a wide variety of researchers and organizations to obtain data (see Box 8.8). There are, however, specific advantages and disadvantages to using this mode of delivery.

Advantages Online surveys, either over the internet or by email, are very fast and inexpensive. They allow flexible design and can use visual images or even audio or video in some internet versions. Despite great flexibility, the basic principles for question writing and for paper questionnaire design generally apply.

Disadvantages Online surveys have three areas of concern: coverage, privacy and verification, and design issues. The first concern involves sampling and unequal internet access or use. Despite high coverage rates, older, less-educated, lower-income, and more rural people are less likely to have good internet access. In addition, many people have multiple email addresses, which creates problems for sampling. Self-selection is also a potential problem with online surveys. For example, a marketing department could get very distorted results of the population of new car buyers through an online survey. Perhaps half of the new car buyers for a model are over age 55, but 75 percent of respondents to a web survey are under age 32 and only 8 percent are over age 55. Not only would the results be distorted by age, but the relatively small percentage of over-55 respondents may not be representative of all over-55 potential new car buyers (e.g., they may be higher income or more educated).

A second concern is protecting respondent privacy and confidentiality. Researchers should encrypt collected data, use only secure websites, and erase nonessential respondent identification or linking information on a daily or weekly basis. They should develop a system of respondent verification to ensure that only the sampled respondent participates and does so only once. This may involve a system such as giving each respondent a unique personal identification number to access the questionnaire.

A third concern involves the complexity of questionnaire design. Researchers need to check and verify the compatibility of various web software and hardware combinations for respondents using different computers. Researchers are still learning what is most effective for online surveys. It is best to provide screen-by-screen questions and make an entire question visible on the screen at one time in a consistent format with drop-down boxes for answer choices. It is best to include a progress indicator (as motivation), such as a clock or horizontal graphic at the bottom of the survey indicating percentage of survey completed.

Visual appearance of a screen, such as the range of colours and fonts, should be kept simple for easy readability and consistency. Be sure to provide clear instructions for all computer actions (e.g., use of drop-down screens) where they are needed and include "click here" instructions. Also, make it easy for respondents to move back and forth across questions. Researchers using online surveys need to avoid technical glitches at the implementation stage by repeated pretesting, having a dedicated server, and obtaining sufficient broadband to handle high demand.

Telephone Interviews

Use of Black English and Racial Discrimination in Urban Housing Markets

Advantages The telephone interview is a popular survey method because about 95 percent of the population can be reached by telephone. An interviewer calls a respondent (usually at home), asks questions, and records answers. Researchers sample respondents from lists, telephone directories, or random-digit dialing and can quickly reach many people across long distances. A staff of interviewers can interview 1500 respondents across a nation within a few days and, with several callbacks, response rates can reach 90 percent. Although this method is more expensive than a mail or online questionnaire, the telephone interview is a flexible method with most of the strengths of face-to-face interviews but for about half the cost. Interviewers control the sequence of questions and can use some probes. A specific respondent is chosen and is likely to answer all the questions alone. The researcher knows when the questions were answered and can use contingency questions effectively, especially with computer-assisted telephone interviewing (CATI) (to be discussed shortly).

Disadvantages Higher cost and limited interview length are among the disadvantages of telephone interviews. In addition, respondents without telephones are impossible to reach, and the call may come at an inconvenient time. The use of an interviewer reduces anonymity and introduces potential interviewer bias. Open-ended questions are difficult to use, and questions requiring visual aids are impossible. Interviewers can only note serious disruptions (e.g., background noise) and respondent tone of voice (e.g., anger or flippancy) or hesitancy.

Face-to-Face Interviews

Advantages Face-to-face interviews have the highest response rates and permit the longest questionnaires. Interviewers also can observe the surroundings and can use nonverbal communication and visual aids. Well-trained interviewers can ask all types of questions, can ask complex questions, and can use extensive probes.

Disadvantages High cost is the biggest disadvantage of face-to-face interviews. The training, travel, supervision, and personnel costs for interviews can be high. Interviewer bias is also greatest in face-to-face interviews. The appearance, tone of voice, question wording, and so forth of the interviewer may affect the respondent. In addition, interviewer supervision is less than for telephone interviews, which supervisors monitor by listening in.[17]

LO 7 Explain the differences between ordinary conversation and a structured survey interview.

LO 8 Describe the role of the interviewer.

INTERVIEWING

The Role of the Interviewer

Interviews to gather information occur in many settings. Survey research interviewing is a specialized kind of interviewing. As with most interviewing, its goal is to obtain accurate information from another person.[18]

The survey interview is a social relationship. Like other social relationships, it involves social roles, norms, and expectations. The interview is a short-term, secondary social

Table 8.4 Differences between Ordinary Conversations and a Structured Survey Interview

Ordinary Conversation	The Survey Interview
1. Questions and answers from each participant are relatively equally balanced.	1. The interviewer asks and the respondent answers most of the time.
2. There is an open exchange of feelings and opinions.	2. Only the respondent reveals feelings and opinions.
3. Judgments are stated and attempts are made to persuade the other of a particular point of view.	3. The interviewer is nonjudgmental and does not try to change the respondent's opinions or beliefs.
4. A person can reveal deep inner feelings to gain sympathy or as a therapeutic release.	4. The interviewer tries to obtain direct answers to specific questions.
5. Ritual responses are common (e.g., "Uh-huh," shaking head, "How are you?" "Fine").	5. The interviewer avoids making ritual responses that influence a respondent and also seeks genuine answers, not ritual responses.
6. The participants exchange information and correct the factual errors that they are aware of.	6. The respondent provides almost all information. The interviewer does not correct a respondent's factual errors.
7. Topics rise and fall and either person can introduce new topics. The focus can shift directions or digress to less relevant issues.	7. The interviewer controls the topic, direction, and pace. He or she keeps the respondent "on task," and irrelevant diversions are contained.
8. The emotional tone can shift from humour, to joy, to affection, to sadness, to anger, and so on.	8. The interviewer attempts to maintain a consistently warm but serious and objective tone throughout.
9. People can evade or ignore questions and give flippant or noncommittal answers.	9. The respondent should not evade questions and should give truthful, thoughtful answers.

interaction between two strangers with the explicit purpose of one person obtaining specific information from the other. The social roles are those of the interviewer and the interviewee or respondent. Information is obtained in a structured conversation in which the interviewer asks prearranged questions and records answers, and the respondent answers. It differs in several ways from ordinary conversation (see Table 8.4).

An important problem for interviewers is that many respondents are unfamiliar with the survey respondents' role. As a result, they substitute another role that may affect their responses. Some believe the interview is an intimate conversation or therapy session, some see it as a bureaucratic exercise in completing forms, some view it as a citizen referendum on policy choices, some view it as a testing situation, and some consider it as a form of deceit in which interviewers are trying to trick or entrap respondents. Even in a well-designed, professional survey, follow-up research found that only about half the respondents understood questions exactly as intended by researchers. Respondents reinterpreted questions to make them applicable to their idiosyncratic, personal situations or to make them easier to answer.[19]

The role of interviewers is difficult. They obtain cooperation and build rapport, yet they must remain neutral and objective. They encroach on the respondents' time and privacy for information that may not directly benefit the respondents. They try to reduce embarrassment, fear, and suspicion so that respondents feel comfortable revealing information. They may explain the nature of survey research or give hints about social roles in an interview. Good interviewers monitor the pace and direction of the social interaction as well as the content of answers and the behaviour of respondents.

Sexual Infidelity among Married and Cohabiting Americans

Skilled survey interviewers are nonjudgmental and do not reveal their opinions, either verbally or nonverbally (e.g., by a look of shock). If a respondent asks for an interviewer's opinion, he or she politely redirects the respondent and indicates that such questions are inappropriate. For example, if a respondent asks, "What do you think?" the interviewer may answer, "Here, we are interested in what *you* think; what I think doesn't matter." Likewise, if the respondent gives a shocking answer (e.g., "I was arrested three times for beating my infant daughter and burning her with cigarettes"), the interviewer does not show shock, surprise, or disdain but treats the answer in a matter-of-fact manner. He or she helps respondents feel that they can give any truthful answer.

You might ask, "If the survey interviewer must be neutral and objective, why not use a robot or machine?" Machine interviewing has not been successful because it lacks the human warmth, sense of trust, and rapport that an interviewer creates. An interviewer helps define the situation and ensures that respondents have the information sought, understand what is expected, give relevant answers, are motivated to cooperate, and give serious answers.

Interviewers do more than interview respondents. Face-to-face interviewers spend only about 35 percent of their time interviewing. About 40 percent is spent in locating the correct respondent, 15 percent in travelling, and 10 percent in studying survey materials and dealing with administrative and recording details.[20]

Stages of an Interview

The interview proceeds through stages, beginning with an introduction and entry. The interviewer gets "in the door" (literally or figuratively, in the case of telephone interviews), demonstrates legitimate affiliation with a research institution, and reassures and secures cooperation from the respondent. He or she is prepared for reactions such as "How did you pick me?" "What good will this do?" "I don't know about this," and "What's this about, anyway?" The interviewer can explain why the specific respondent is interviewed and not a substitute.

The main part of the interview consists of asking questions and recording answers. The interviewer uses the exact wording on the questionnaire—no added or omitted words and no rephrasing. He or she asks all applicable questions in order, without returning to or skipping questions unless the directions specify to do so. He or she goes at a comfortable pace and gives nondirective feedback to maintain interest.

In addition to asking questions, the interviewer accurately records answers. This is easy for closed-ended questions, where interviewers just mark the correct box. For open-ended questions, the interviewer's job is more difficult. He or she must listen carefully and record what is said verbatim without correcting grammar or slang. More important, the interviewer *never* summarizes or paraphrases. This causes a loss of information or distorts answers. For example, the respondent says, "I'm really concerned about my daughter's heart problem. She's only 10 years old and already she has trouble climbing stairs. I don't know what she'll do when she gets older. Heart surgery is too risky for her and it costs so much. She'll have to learn to live with it." If the interviewer writes "concerned about daughter's health," much is lost.

probe: A follow-up question or action in *survey research* used by an interviewer to have a respondent clarify or elaborate on an incomplete or inappropriate answer.

The interviewer knows how and when to use probes. A **probe** is a neutral request to clarify an ambiguous answer, to complete an incomplete answer, or to obtain a relevant response. Interviewers recognize an irrelevant or inaccurate answer and use probes as needed.[21] There are many types of probes. A three- to five-second pause is often effective. Nonverbal communication (e.g., tilt of head, raised eyebrows, or eye contact) also works well. The interviewer can repeat the question or repeat the reply and then pause. She or he can ask a neutral question, such as, "Any other reasons?" "Can you tell me more about that?" "How do you mean?" or "Could you explain more for me?" (see Box 8.9).

The last stage is the exit, when the interviewer thanks the respondent and leaves. He or she then goes to a quiet, private place to edit the questionnaire and record other details, such as the date, time, and place of the interview; a thumbnail sketch of the respondent and interview situation; the respondent's attitude (e.g., serious, angry, laughing); and any unusual circumstances (e.g., "Telephone rang at question 27 and respondent talked for four

Box 8.9 Making It Practical

Example of Probes and Recording Full Responses to Closed Questions

Interviewer Question: What is your occupation?
Respondent Answer: I work at General Motors.
Probe: What is your job at General Motors? What type of work do you do there?

Interviewer Question: How long have you been unemployed?
Respondent Answer: A long time.
Probe: Could you tell me more specifically when your current period of unemployment began?

Interviewer Question: Considering the country as a whole, do you think we will have good times during the next year, bad times, or what?
Respondent Answer: Maybe good, maybe bad, it depends, who knows?
Probe: What do you expect to happen?

Record Response to a Closed Question

Interviewer Question: On a scale of 1 to 7, how do you feel about capital punishment or the death penalty, where 1 is strongly in favour of the death penalty, and 7 is strongly opposed to it?
(Favour) 1 __ 2 __ 3 __ 4 __ 5 __ 6 __ 7 __ (Oppose)

Respondent Answer: About a 4. I think that all murderers, rapists, and violent criminals should get death, but I don't favour it for minor crimes like stealing a car.

minutes before the interview started again"). He or she notes anything disruptive that happened during the interview (e.g., "Teenage son entered room, sat at opposite end, turned on television with the volume loud, and watched music videos"). The interviewer also records personal feelings and anything that was suspected (e.g., "Respondent became nervous and fidgeted when questioned about his marriage").

Training Interviewers

A large-scale survey requires hiring multiple interviewers. Few people appreciate the difficulty of the interviewer's job. A professional-quality interview requires the careful selection of interviewers and extensive training. As with any employment situation, adequate pay and good supervision are important for consistent high-quality performance. Unfortunately, professional interviewing has not always paid well or provided regular employment. In the past, interviewers were largely drawn from a pool of middle-aged women willing to accept irregular part-time work.

Good interviewers are pleasant, honest, accurate, mature, responsible, stable, and motivated. They have a nonthreatening appearance, have experience with many different types of people, and possess poise and tact. Researchers may consider interviewers' physical appearance, age, race, sex, languages spoken, and even the sound of their voice.

Professional interviewers receive a training course. It includes lectures and reading, observation of expert interviewers, mock interviews in the office and in the field that are recorded and critiqued, many practice interviews, and role-playing. The interviewers learn about survey research and the role of the interviewer. They become familiar with the questionnaire and the purpose of questions.

Although interviewers largely work alone, researchers use an interviewer supervisor in large-scale surveys with several interviewers. Supervisors are familiar with the area, assist with problems, oversee the interviewers, and ensure that work is completed on time. For telephone interviewing, this includes helping with calls, checking when interviewers arrive and leave, and monitoring interview calls. In face-to-face interviews, supervisors check to find out whether the interview actually took place. This means calling back or sending a confirmation postcard to a sample of respondents. They can also check the response rate and incomplete questionnaires to see whether interviewers are obtaining cooperation, and they may re-interview a small subsample, analyze answers, or observe interviews to see whether interviewers are accurately asking questions and recording answers.

Interviewer Bias

Reducing interviewer bias goes beyond reading each question exactly as worded. Ideally, the actions of a particular interviewer will not affect how a respondent answers, and responses will not vary from what they would be if asked by any other interviewer.

Survey researchers know that interviewer expectations can create significant bias. Interviewers who expect difficult interviews have them, and those who expect certain answers are more likely to get them (see Box 8.10). Proper interviewer behaviour and exact question reading may be difficult, but the issue is larger.

The social setting in which the interview occurs, including the presence of other people, can affect answers. For example, students answer differently depending on whether they are asked questions at home or at school. In general, survey researchers do not want others present because they may affect respondent answers. It may not always make a difference, however, especially if the others are small children.[22]

Growing Old in an Arab American Family

An interviewer's visible characteristics, including race and gender, often affect interviews and respondent answers, especially for questions about issues related to race or gender. For example, Black and Asian respondents may express different policy positions on race- or ethnic-related issues depending on the apparent race or ethnicity of the interviewer. This occurs even with telephone interviews when a respondent has clues about the interviewer's race or ethnicity. In general, interviewers of the same ethnic–racial group get more accurate answers.[23] Gender also affects interviews both in terms of obvious issues, such as sexual behaviour, as well as support for gender-related collective action or gender equality.[24] Survey researchers need to note the race and gender of both interviewers and respondents.

Box 8.10 Focus

Interviewer Characteristics Can Affect Responses

Example of Interviewer Expectation Effects

Asked by Female Interviewer Whose Own	***Female Respondent Reports That Husband Buys Most Furniture***
Husband buys most furniture	89%
Husband does not buy most furniture	15%

Example of Race or Ethnic Appearance Effects

	Percentage Answering Yes to:	
Interviewer	*"Do you think there are too many Jews in government jobs?"*	*"Do you think that Jews have too much power?"*
Looked Jewish with Jewish-sounding name	11.7	5.8
Looked Jewish only	15.4	15.6
Non-Jewish appearance	21.2	24.3
Non-Jewish appearance and non-Jewish-sounding name	19.5	21.4

Note: Racial stereotypes held by respondents can affect how they respond in interviews.

Source: Hyman, H. H. (1975). *Interviewing in social research* (pp. 115, 163). Chicago, IL: University of Chicago Press. Printed with permission from University of Chicago Press.

Computer-Assisted Interviewing

Professional survey research organizations by and large all use **computer-assisted telephone interviewing (CATI)** systems.[25] With CATI, the interviewer sits in front of a computer and makes calls. Wearing a headset and microphone, the interviewer reads the questions from a computer screen for the specific respondent who is called, then enters the answer via the keyboard. Once he or she enters an answer, the computer shows the next question on the screen.

computer-assisted telephone interviewing (CATI): *Survey research* in which the interviewer sits in front of a computer screen and keyboard and uses the computer to read questions that are asked in a telephone interview, then enters answers directly into the computer.

Computer-assisted telephone interviewing speeds interviewing and reduces interviewer errors. It also eliminates the separate step of entering information into a computer and speeds up data processing. Of course, CATI requires an investment in computer equipment and some knowledge of computers. The CATI system is valuable for contingency questions because the computer can show the questions appropriate for a specific respondent; interviewers do not have to turn pages looking for the next question. In addition, the computer can check an answer immediately after the interviewer enters it. For example, if an interviewer enters an answer that is impossible or clearly an error (e.g., an *H* instead of an M for "Male"), the computer will request another answer.

Other computer-assisted interviewing techniques exist, including **computer-assisted personal interviewing (CAPI)**, in which the interviewer asks the respondent questions in person and records the answers directly into a computer. As well as the advantages of in-person interviewers discussed earlier, this particular approach has the strength that the interviewer can show the respondent materials on-screen as well.

computer-assisted personal interviewing (CAPI): Like *computer-assisted telephone interviewing,* but used for in-person interviews.

Several companies have developed software programs and websites that help researchers develop questionnaires and analyze survey data. They provide guides for writing questions, recording responses, analyzing data, and producing reports. The programs may speed up the more mechanical aspects of survey research—such as typing questionnaires, organizing layout, and recording responses—but they cannot substitute for a good understanding of the survey method or an appreciation of its limitations. The researcher must still clearly conceptualize variables, prepare well-worded questions, design the sequence and forms of questions and responses, and pilot-test questionnaires. Communicating unambiguously with respondents and eliciting credible responses remain the most important parts of survey research.

THE ETHICAL SURVEY

Like all social research, people can conduct surveys in ethical or unethical ways. A major ethical issue in survey research is the invasion of privacy. Survey researchers can intrude into a respondent's privacy by asking about intimate actions and personal beliefs. People have a right to privacy. Respondents decide when and to whom to reveal personal information. They are likely to provide such information when it is requested in a comfortable context with mutual trust, when they believe serious answers are needed for legitimate research purposes, and when they believe answers will remain confidential. Researchers should treat all respondents with dignity and reduce anxiety or discomfort. They are also responsible for protecting the confidentiality of data.

Risk of Disability Rises in States with Income Inequality

A second issue involves voluntary participation by respondents. Respondents agree to answer questions and can refuse to participate at any time. They give "informed consent" to participate in research. Researchers depend on respondents' voluntary cooperation, so researchers need to ask well-developed questions in a sensitive way, treat respondents with respect, and be very sensitive to confidentiality.

A third ethical issue is the exploitation of surveys and pseudosurveys. Because of the popularity of surveys, some people use surveys to mislead others. A **pseudosurvey** is when someone who has little or no real interest in learning information from a respondent uses

pseudosurvey: When someone who has little or no real interest in learning information from a respondent uses the survey format to try to persuade someone to do something.

the survey format to try to persuade someone to do something. Charlatans use the guise of conducting a survey to invade privacy or gain entry into homes. During elections, you may hear about "suppression polls" or "push polls." These are pseudosurveys that are used to spread negative information about political candidates. Under the guise of conducting a poll, a person is called and asked about his or her political views, such as whom he or she will vote for. If the person favours a candidate other than the one the caller is campaigning for, the interviewer would then ask whether the respondent would still support that candidate if he or she knew that the candidate had an unfavourable characteristic (e.g., had been arrested for drunk driving, used illegal drugs, raised the wages of convicted criminals in prison). The goal of such push polls is not to measure candidate support; rather, it is to identify a candidate's supporters, then attempt to suppress voting. In the 2011 federal election, instances of push polling by the Conservative Party have been acknowledged, including one in which constituents in a Liberal Montreal riding were contacted to be "polled" on their feelings about the current MP's plans to retire after he was reelected. Of course, voters may not want to support a candidate that they knew was intending to retire right after being elected. It was not the case, however, that the MP had indicated any such plans—the push poll was a technique being used by the rival party to sway votes.[26]

A fourth ethical issue is when people misuse survey results or use poorly designed or purposely rigged surveys. Why does this occur? People may demand answers from surveys that surveys cannot provide and may not understand a survey's limitations. Those who design and prepare surveys may lack sufficient training to conduct a legitimate survey. Unfortunately, policy decisions are sometimes made based on careless or poorly designed surveys or surveys designed with biased questions to produce desired "results." They often result in waste or human hardship. This is why legitimate researchers conducting methodologically rigorous survey research are important.

The media report more surveys than other types of social research, yet sloppy reporting of survey results permits abuse.[27] Few people reading survey results may appreciate it, but researchers should include details about the survey (see Box 8.11) to reduce the misuse of survey research and increase questions about surveys that lack such information. Survey researchers urge the media to include such information, but it rarely is. Most of the reporting on surveys in the mass media fails to reveal the researcher who conducted the survey, and only a handful provide details on how the survey was conducted.[28] Currently, there are no quality-control standards to regulate the opinion polls or surveys reported in the Canadian media. The Canadian Broadcasting Corporation claims to have standards, but does not specify exactly what they are.[29] Researchers have made unsuccessful attempts since World War II to require adequate samples, interviewer training

Box 8.11 Making It Practical

Ten Items to Include When Reporting Survey Research

1. The sampling frame used (e.g., membership lists)
2. The dates the survey was conducted
3. The population that the sample represents (e.g., Canadian adults, Australian college students, housewives in Singapore)
4. The size of the sample information was collected for
5. The sampling method (e.g., simple random)
6. The exact wording of the questions asked
7. The method of the survey (e.g., face to face, telephone, online)
8. The organizations that sponsored the survey (paid for it and conducted it)
9. The response rate or percentage of those contacted who actually completed the questionnaire
10. Any missing information or "don't know" responses when results on specific questions are reported

and supervision, satisfactory questionnaire design, public availability of results, and controls on the integrity of survey organizations.[30] As a result, the mass media report both biased and misleading survey results and rigorous, professional survey results without making any distinction. It is not surprising that the public is often confused and distrustful of surveys.

CHAPTER SUMMARY

In this chapter, you learned about survey research. You learned about the six major steps in conducting a survey and the research questions that are appropriate for addressing with this data collection technique. You also learned many principles of writing good survey questions. There are many things to avoid and to include when writing questions. These principles are of the utmost importance in writing meaningful survey items. You were also cautioned about avoiding some of the more common question writing pitfalls. If you make a mistake writing your survey questions, the data you collect will be of compromised quality and utility.

✓ Glossary Flashcards

Questionnaire organization, design, and formatting was also discussed. You learned about the the four types of survey research: mail, online, telephone interviews, and face-to-face interviews. The disadvantages and advantages of each technique were explained. You saw that interviewing, especially face-to-face interviewing, can be difficult. The qualities of a good interviewer were also covered, as training of effective interviewers helps ensure that your study yields high-quality data. Interviewer bias, however, can affect how individuals respond to the people asking the questions and must be considered when questionnaires contain questions that may be sensitive to particular demographic groups, such as race or gender.

Review Questions

✓ Chapter Quiz

1. Identify the six steps involved in conducting a survey.
2. Explain the 12 principles of good question writing.
3. Explain five advantages and five disadvantages of open questions. Do the same for closed questions.
4. Identify six major questionnaire design issues.
5. Describe the four major types of surveys. Identify two advantages and two disadvantages of each.
6. Explain five differences between ordinary conversations and a structured survey interview.
7. Describe three criteria that are important to a person in the role of an interviewer.

Exercises

✓ Research Activities

1. Using EBSCO's ContentSelect, find three studies from within the past five years that used data that were obtained from surveys. For each of the articles, identify the name of the survey that was used by the authors of the articles. How were the survey data collected (telephone interview, in-person interview, etc.)? If the article doesn't explicitly indicate this, do an internet search and see if you can find more detailed information on the study details.
2. Find a free survey design program on the internet and practise making a web survey for your classmates to fill out online. Have your classmates comment on the strengths and weaknesses of your survey.

3. This chapter discussed how nonresponse in surveys is a major concern and how the employment and training of skilled interviewers play a major role in maximizing survey participation. Sometimes, however, people refuse to participate in surveys. On the internet, search for a description of the job of a "refusal converter." What does this person do and why?
4. Go to the Statistics Canada website and find the questionnaire for a major Canadian study like the Labour Force Survey. What is the mode of delivery of this questionnaire, and how can you tell?

Chapter 9
Experimental Research

Photo Credit: Jeffrey Greenberg/ Science Source

LEARNING OBJECTIVES

After reading this chapter, you will be able to

LO 1 Identify research questions appropriate for the experimental method.

LO 2 Explain the process of random assignment.

LO 3 Describe the parts of an experiment.

LO 4 Explain the different types of experimental designs.

LO 5 Identify and define the various threats to internal and external validity.

INTRODUCTION

Experimental research builds on the principles of a positivist approach more directly than do the other research techniques. Researchers in the natural sciences (e.g., chemistry and physics), related applied fields (e.g., agriculture, engineering, and medicine), and the social sciences conduct experiments. The positivist logic that guides an experiment on plant growth in biology or testing a metal in engineering is applied in experiments on human social behaviour. Although the method is most widely used in psychology, the experiment is found in education, criminal justice, journalism, marketing, nursing, political science, social work, and sociology. This chapter focuses first on the experiment conducted in a laboratory under controlled conditions and then looks at experiments conducted in the field.

Experimental Methods Explained

The experiment's basic logic extends common sense thinking. Common sense experiments are less careful or systematic than scientifically based experiments. In common sense language, an *experiment* is when you modify something in a situation and then compare an outcome to what existed without the modification. For example, you try to start your car. To your surprise, it does not start. You "experiment" by cleaning off the battery connections and then try to start it again. You modified something (cleaned the connections) and compared the outcome (whether the car started) to the previous situation (it did not start). You began with an implicit "hypothesis": A buildup of crud on the connections is the reason why the car is not starting, and once the crud is cleaned off the car will start. This illustrates three things researchers do in experiments: (1) begin with a hypothesis, (2) modify something in a situation, and (3) compare outcomes with and without the modification. Like other terms used in previous chapters that are also common in common parlance (e.g. random, valid, reliable), the experiment means something very specific when applied to research.

Compared to the other social research techniques, experimental research is the strongest for testing causal relationships because the three conditions for causality (temporal order, association, and no alternative explanations) are best met in experimental designs. This is the major strength of the experimental method—its ability to demonstrate causation. It is in the experiment that the researcher *can actually observe causation.* In other types of approaches, causation is implied.

LO 1 Identify research questions appropriate for the experimental method.

Research Questions Appropriate for an Experiment

The Issue of an Appropriate Technique The nature of the research question means that some questions are better suited to be answered by certain methodological techniques than others. New researchers often ask, "Which technique (e.g., experiments or surveys) best fits which research question?" There is no easy answer, because the match between a research question and technique is not fixed but depends on informed judgment. You can develop judgment from reading research reports, understanding the strengths and weaknesses of different techniques, assisting more experienced researchers with their research, and gaining practical experience.

Research Tools and Techniques

Research Questions for Experimental Research The experiment allows a researcher to focus sharply on causal relations, and it has practical advantages over other techniques, but it also has limitations. The research questions most appropriate for an experiment fit its strengths and limitations.

The questions appropriate for using an experimental logic confront ethical and practical limitations of intervening in human affairs for research purposes. It is immoral and impossible to manipulate many areas of human life for research purposes. The pure logic of an experiment has an experimenter intervene or induce a change in some focused part of social life and then examine the consequences that result from the change or intervention. This usually means that the experiment is limited to research questions in which a researcher is able to manipulate conditions. Experimental research cannot answer questions such as, "Do people who complete a university education increase their annual income more than people who do not?" "Do children raised with younger siblings develop better leadership skills than children without siblings?" or "Do people who belong to more organizations vote more often in elections?" This is because an experimenter often cannot manipulate conditions or intervene. He or she cannot randomly assign thousands to attend university and prevent others from attending to discover who later earns more income. He or she cannot induce couples to have either many children or a single child so he or she can examine how leadership skills develop in children. He or she cannot compel people to join or quit organizations and then see whether they vote. Experimenters are highly creative in simulating such interventions or conditions, but they cannot manipulate many of the variables of interest to fit the pure experimental logic.

The experiment is usually best for issues that have a narrow scope or scale. This strength allows experimenters to assemble and "run" many experiments with limited resources in a short period of time. Some carefully designed experiments require assembling only 50 or 60 subjects and can be completed in one or two months. In general, the experiment is better suited for micro-level (e.g., individual or small-group phenomena) than for macro-level concerns or questions. Experiments can rarely address questions that require looking at conditions across an entire society or across decades. The experiment also limits one's ability to generalize to larger settings (see "External Validity and Field Experiments" later in this chapter).

Research Methodology

Experiments encourage researchers to isolate and target the impact that arises from one or a few causal variables. This strength in demonstrating causal effects is a limitation in situations where a researcher tries to examine numerous variables simultaneously. The experiment is rarely appropriate for research questions or issues that require a researcher to examine the impact of dozens of diverse variables all together. Although the accumulated knowledge from many individual experiments, each focused on one or two variables, advances understanding, the approach of experimental research differs from doing research on a highly complex situation in which one examines how dozens of variables operate simultaneously.

RANDOM ASSIGNMENT

LO 2 Explain the process of random assignment.

Social researchers frequently want to compare. For example, a researcher has two groups of 15 students and wants to compare the groups on the basis of a key difference between them (e.g., a course that one group completed). Or a researcher has five groups of customers and wants to compare the groups on the basis of one characteristic (e.g., geographic location). The saying, "Compare apples to apples; don't compare apples to oranges," is not about fruit; it is about comparisons. It means that a valid comparison depends on comparing things that are fundamentally alike. Random assignment facilitates comparison in experiments by creating similar groups.

When making comparisons, researchers want to compare cases that do not differ with regard to variables that offer alternative explanations. For example, a researcher compares two groups of students to determine the impact of completing a course. In order to be compared, the two groups must be similar in most respects except for taking the course. If the group that completed the course is also older than the group that did not, for example, the researcher cannot determine whether completing the course or being older accounts for differences between the groups.

Why Randomly Assign?

Random assignment is a method for assigning cases (e.g., individuals, organizations) to groups for the purpose of making comparisons. It is a way to divide or sort a collection of cases into two or more groups to increase one's confidence that the groups do not differ in a systematic way. It is a mechanical method; the assignment is automatic, and the researcher cannot make assignments on the basis of personal preference or the features of specific cases.

random assignment: Dividing subjects into groups at the beginning of *experimental research* using a random process, so the experimenter can treat the groups as equivalent.

Random assignment is random in a statistical or mathematical sense, not in an everyday sense. In everyday speech, *random* means unplanned, haphazard, or accidental, but it has a specialized meaning in mathematics. In probability theory, *random* describes a process in which each case has a known chance of being selected. Random selection lets a researcher calculate the odds that a specific case will be sorted into one group over another. *Random* means a case has an exactly equal chance of ending up in one or the other group. The great thing about a random process is that over many separate random occurrences, predictable things happen, as described in Chapter 8. Although the process itself is entirely due to chance and does not allow predicting a specific outcome at one specific time, it obeys mathematical laws that make very accurate predictions possible when conducted over a large number of situations.

Random assignment or randomization is unbiased because a researcher's desire to confirm a hypothesis or a research subject's personal interests does not enter into the selection process. *Unbiased* does not mean that groups with identical characteristics are selected in each specific situation of random assignment. Instead, it says that the probability of selecting a case can be mathematically determined and, in the long run, the groups will be identical.

From Summer Camps to Glass Ceilings

Sampling and random assignment are processes of selecting cases for inclusion in a study. When a researcher randomly assigns, he or she sorts a collection of cases into two or more groups using a random process. In random sampling, he or she selects a smaller subset of cases from a larger pool of cases (see Figure 9.1). Ideally, a researcher will both randomly sample and randomly assign. He or she can first sample to obtain a smaller set of cases (e.g., 150 people out of 20 000) and then use random assignment to divide the sample into groups (e.g., divide the 150 people into three groups of 50). Unfortunately, few social science experimenters use random samples. Most begin with a convenience sample and then randomly assign. You may have been asked to be part of such an experiment for credit in an undergraduate psychology course, for example (see Box 9.1). There

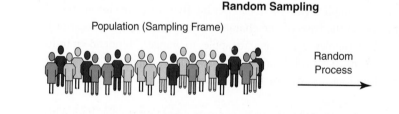

Random Sampling

Population (Sampling Frame)

Random Process

Sample

Random Assignment

Step 1: Begin with a collection of subjects.

Step 2: Devise a method to randomize that is purely mechanical (e.g., flip a coin).

Step 3: Assign subjects with "Heads" to one group and "Tails" to the other group.

Figure 9.1 Random Assignment and Random Sampling

Box 9.1 Focus

Science of the Sophomore

Because a large proportion of research using the experimental method uses undergraduate students, particularly those enrolled in first-year psychology courses, as subjects in data collection, the generalizability of findings of such research has been called into question. It is true that undergraduate psychology students do come from a mixed bag of backgrounds, but if much experimental research is based upon "typical" students, can we really say that these findings are applicable to a wider population? Such concerns about the generalizability of experimental findings based on the undergraduate population have resulted in the rather scathing term **science of the sophomore** (coined by McNemar, 1946), which suggests that disciplines that rely on such sampling techniques are really practising science based on a very narrow population (*sophomore* is an American term referring to a student in the second year of study).

Recently, a Canadian psychologist (Bodner, 2006) argued that this concern may be overstated. After analyzing a random sample of 200 articles appearing in the PsycINFO database, the author stated that experimental designs using only college students appeared in a minority (around 10 percent) of research designs. It should be stressed, however, that the author's data were limited to research articles from a single database, published in English, and published in the year 1999.

is a very important difference between random sampling and random assignment that must be noted. Although both relate to sample selection, they involve different stages of sample selection.

science of the sophomore: A term used to refer to the potentially limited *external validity* of studies based on undergraduate samples, usually using the experimental method.

How to Randomly Assign

Random assignment is very simple in practice. A researcher begins with a collection of cases (individuals, organizations, or whatever the unit of analysis is) and then divides it into two or more groups by a random process, such as asking people to count off, tossing a coin, or throwing dice. For example, a researcher wants to divide 32 people into two groups of 16. A random method is writing each person's name on a slip of paper, putting the slips in a hat, mixing the slips with eyes closed, and then drawing the first 16 names for Group 1 and the second 16 for Group 2.

Matching versus Random Assignment

You might ask, "If the purpose of random assignment is to get two (or more) equivalent groups, would it not be simpler to match the characteristics of cases in each group?" Some researchers match cases in groups on certain characteristics, such as age and sex. Matching is an alternative to random assignment, but it is an infrequently used one.

Matching presents a problem: What are the relevant characteristics to match on, and can one locate exact matches? Individual cases differ in thousands of ways, and the researcher cannot know which might be relevant. For example, a researcher compares two groups of 15 students. There are eight males in one group, which means there should be eight males in the other group. Two males in the first group are only children; one is from a divorced family and the other is from an intact family. One is tall, slender, and Jewish; the other is short, heavy, and Muslim. In order to match groups, does the researcher have to find a tall, Jewish, male only child from a divorced home and a short, Muslim, male only child from an intact home? The tall, slender, Jewish male child is 22 years old and is studying to become a teacher. The short, heavy, Muslim male is 20 years old and wants to be an accountant. Does the researcher also need to match the age and career aspirations of the two males? True matching soon becomes an impossible task.

LO 3 Describe the parts of an experiment.

EXPERIMENTAL DESIGN LOGIC

The Language of Experiments

Experimental research has its own language or set of terms and concepts. You already encountered the basic ideas: random assignment and independent and dependent variables. In experimental research, the cases or people used in research projects and on whom variables are measured are called the **subjects**.

subjects: In *experimental research*, the cases or people used in research projects and on whom *variables* are measured.

Parts of the Experiment We can divide the experiment into seven parts. Not all experiments have all these parts, and some have all seven parts plus others. The following seven, which are discussed in this chapter, make up a true experiment and are illustrated in Figure 9.2:

1. Treatment or independent variable
2. Dependent variable
3. Pretest
4. Post-test
5. Experimental group
6. Control group
7. Random assignment

In most experiments, a researcher creates a situation or enters into an ongoing situation and then modifies it. The **treatment** (or the stimulus or manipulation) is what the researcher modifies. Such independent variables are often denoted with the symbol "X." The term comes from medicine, in which a physician administers a treatment to patients—the physician intervenes in a physical or psychological condition to change it; it is the independent variable or a combination of independent variables. In earlier examples of measurement, a researcher developed a measurement instrument or indicator (e.g., a survey question) and then applied it to a person or case. In experiments, researchers "measure" independent variables by creating a condition or situation. For example, the independent variable is "degree of fear or anxiety"; the levels are high fear and low fear. Instead of asking subjects whether they are fearful, experimenters put subjects into either a high-fear or a low-fear situation. They measure the independent variable by manipulating conditions so that some subjects feel a lot of fear and others feel little fear.

treatment: What the *independent variable* in *experimental research* is called.

Social Psychology Methods for Sociology

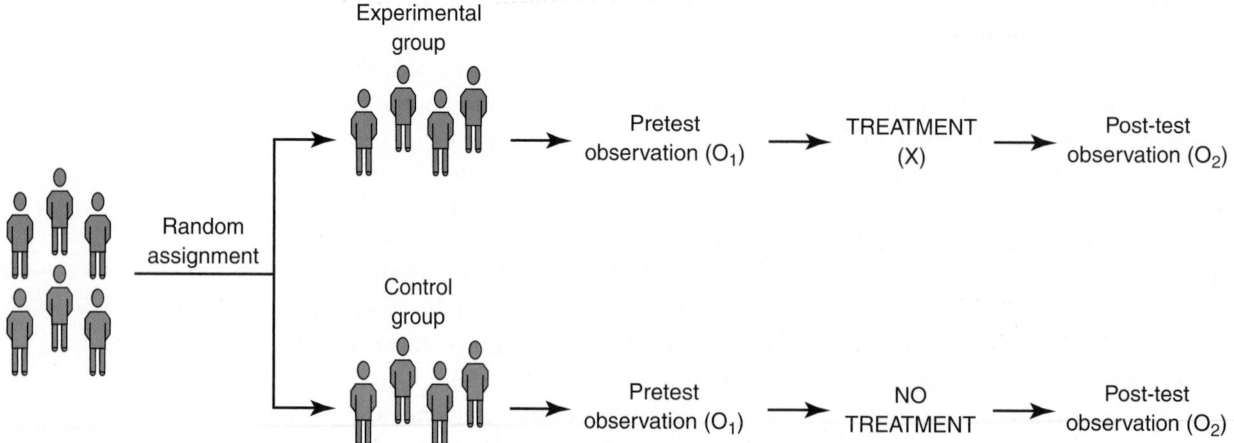

Figure 9.2 General Steps in Classical Experimental Design

Researchers go to great lengths to create treatments. Some are as minor as giving different groups of subjects different instructions. Others can be as complex as putting subjects into situations with elaborate equipment, staged physical settings, or contrived social situations to manipulate what the subjects see or feel. Researchers want the treatment to have an impact and produce specific reactions, feelings, or behaviours.

Dependent variables or outcomes (often denoted as "O" in experimental notation) in experimental research are the physical conditions, social behaviours, attitudes, feelings, or beliefs of subjects that change in response to a treatment. Dependent variables can be measured by paper-and-pencil indicators, observation, interviews, or physiological responses (e.g., heart rate or sweating palms).

Frequently, a researcher measures the dependent variable more than once during an experiment. The **pretest** is the measurement of the dependent variable prior to introduction of the treatment. The **post-test** is the measurement of the dependent variable after the treatment has been introduced into the experimental situation.

pretest: The measurement of the *dependent variable* of an experiment prior to the *treatment.*

post-test: The measurement of the *dependent variable* in *experimental research* after the *treatment.*

Experimental researchers often divide subjects into two or more groups for purposes of comparison. A simple experiment has two groups, only one of which receives the treatment (X). The **experimental group** is the group that receives the treatment or in which the treatment is present. The group that does not receive the treatment is called the **control group**. When the independent variable takes on many different values, more than one experimental group is used.

experimental group: The group that receives the *treatment* in *experimental research.*

control group: The group that does not receive the *treatment* in *experimental research.*

In the study by Hawkes, Senn, and Thorn (2004) on university women with tattoos discussed in Chapter 6, randomly assigned subjects were asked to read one of five scenarios about a 22-year-old female university student who had a tattoo (independent variable). The experimenters then measured the subjects' feelings about the woman and tattoo using various scales (dependent variables).

Steps in Conducting an Experiment Following the basic steps of the research process, experimenters decide on a topic, narrow it into a testable research problem or question, and then develop a hypothesis with variables. Once a researcher has the hypothesis, the steps of experimental research are clear.

A crucial early step is to plan a specific experimental design (to be discussed shortly). The researcher decides on the number of groups to use, how and when to create treatment conditions, the number of times to measure the dependent variable, and what the groups of subjects will experience from beginning to end. He or she also develops measures of the dependent variable and pilot-tests the experiment (see Box 9.2).

The experiment itself begins after a researcher locates subjects and randomly assigns them to groups. Subjects are given precise, preplanned instructions. Next, the researcher measures the dependent variable (Y) in a pretest before the treatment. One group is then exposed to the treatment. Finally, the researcher measures the dependent variable in a post-test. He or she also interviews subjects about the experiment before they leave. The researcher records measures of the dependent variable and examines the results for each group to see whether the hypothesis receives support.

Control in Experiments Control is crucial in experimental research. A researcher wants to control all aspects of the experimental situation to isolate the effects of the treatment and eliminate alternative explanations. Aspects of an experimental situation that are not controlled by the researcher are alternatives to the treatment that cause change in the dependent variable and undermine his or her attempt to establish causality definitively.

Experimental researchers often use deception to control the experimental setting. **Deception** occurs when the researcher intentionally misleads subjects through written or verbal instructions, the actions of others, or aspects of the setting. It may involve the

deception: When an experimenter lies to *subjects* about the true nature of an experiment or creates a false impression through his or her actions or the setting.

Box 9.2 Making It Practical

Steps in Conducting an Experiment

1. Begin with a straightforward hypothesis appropriate to the experimental research design.
2. Decide on an experimental design that will test the hypothesis within practical limitations.
3. Decide how to introduce the treatment or create a situation that induces the independent variable.
4. Develop a valid and reliable measure of the dependent variable.
5. Set up an experimental setting and conduct a pilot test of the treatment and dependent variable measures.
6. Locate appropriate subjects or cases.
7. Randomly assign subjects to groups (if random assignment is used in the chosen research design) and give careful instructions.
8. Gather data for the pretest measure of the dependent variable for all groups (if a pretest is used in the chosen design).
9. Introduce the treatment to the experimental group only (or to relevant groups if there are multiple experimental groups) and monitor all groups.
10. Gather data for post-test measure of the dependent variable.
11. **Debrief** the subjects by informing them of the true purpose and reasons for the experiment. Ask subjects what they thought was occurring. Debriefing is crucial when subjects have been deceived about some aspect of the experiment.
12. Examine data collected and make comparisons between different groups. Where appropriate, use statistics and graphs to determine whether or not the hypothesis is supported.

debrief: When a researcher gives a true explanation of the experiment to *subjects* after using *deception*.

use of *confederates*—people who pretend to be other subjects or bystanders but who actually work for the researcher and deliberately mislead subjects. Through deception, the researcher tries to control what the subjects see and hear and what they believe is occurring. For example, a researcher's instructions falsely lead subjects to believe that they are participating in a study about group cooperation. In fact, the experiment is about male/female verbal interaction, and what subjects say is being secretly tape recorded. Deception lets the researcher control the subjects' definition of the situation. It prevents them from altering their cross-sex verbal behaviour because they are unaware of the true research topic. By focusing their attention on a false topic, the researcher induces the unaware subjects to act "naturally." For realistic deception, researchers may invent false treatments and dependent variable measures to keep subjects unaware of the true ones. The use of deception in experiments raises ethical issues (which are discussed later).

LO 4 Explain the different types of experimental designs.

Types of Design

experimental design: Arranging the parts of an experiment and putting them together.

Researchers combine parts of an experiment (e.g., pretests, control groups) together into an **experimental design**. For example, some designs lack pretests, some do not have control groups, and others have many experimental groups. Certain widely used standard designs have names.

You should learn the standard designs for two reasons. First, in research reports researchers give the name of a standard design instead of describing it. When reading reports, you will be able to understand the design of the experiment if you know the standard designs. Second, the standard designs illustrate common ways to combine design parts. You can use them for experiments you conduct or create your own variations.

The designs are illustrated with a simple example. A researcher wants to learn whether wait staff (waiters and waitresses) receive more in tips if they introduce themselves by first name and return to ask "Is everything fine?" eight to ten minutes after delivering the food. The dependent variable is the size of the tip received. The study occurs in two identical restaurants on different sides of a town that have had the same types of customers and average the same amount in tips.

Classical Experimental Design All designs are variations of the **classical experimental design**, the type of design discussed so far, which has random assignment, a pretest and a post-test, an experimental group, and a control group.

classical experimental design: An *experimental design* that has *random assignment, a control group*, an *experimental group*, and *pretests* and *post-tests* for each group.

Example The experimenter gives 40 newly hired wait staff an identical two-hour training session and instructs them to follow a script in which they are not to introduce themselves by first name and not to return during the meal to check on the customers. They are next randomly assigned into two equal groups of 20 and sent to the two restaurants to begin employment. The experimenter records the amount in tips for all subjects for one month (pretest score). Next, the experimenter "retrains" the 20 subjects at Restaurant 1 (experimental group). The experimenter instructs them henceforth to introduce themselves to customers by first name and to check on the customers, asking, "Is everything fine?" eight to ten minutes after delivering the food (treatment). The group at Restaurant 2 (control group) is "retrained" to continue without an introduction or checking during the meal. Over the second month, the amount of tips for both groups is recorded (post-test score).

Pre-experimental Designs Some designs lack random assignment and are compromises or shortcuts. These **pre-experimental designs** are used in situations where it is difficult to use the classical design. They have weaknesses that make inferring a causal relationship more difficult.

pre-experimental designs: *Experimental designs* that lack *random assignment* or use shortcuts and are much weaker than the *classical experimental design*. They may be substituted in situations where an experimenter cannot use all the features of a *classical experimental design*, but they have weaker *internal validity*.

One-Shot Case Study Design Also called the *one-group post-test–only design*, the **one-shot case study** design has only one group, a treatment, and a post-test. Because there is only one group, there is no random assignment.

one-shot case study: An *experimental design* with only an *experimental group* and a *post-test*, no *pretest*.

Example The experimenter takes a group of 40 newly hired wait staff and gives them all a two-hour training session in which they are instructed to introduce themselves to customers by first name and to check on the customers, asking, "Is everything fine?" eight to ten minutes after delivering the food (treatment). All subjects begin employment, and the experimenter records the amount in tips for all subjects for one month (post-test score).

One-Group Pretest–Post-test Design This design has one group, a pretest, a treatment, and a post-test. It lacks a control group and random assignment.

Example The experimenter takes a group of 40 newly hired wait staff and gives them all a two-hour training session. They are instructed to follow a script in which they are not to introduce themselves by first name and not to return during the meal to check on the customers. All begin employment, and the experimenter records the amount in tips for all subjects for one month (pretest score). Next, the experimenter "retrains" all 40 subjects (experimental group). The experimenter instructs the subjects henceforth to introduce themselves to customers by first name and to check on the customers, asking, "Is everything fine?" eight to ten minutes after delivering the food (treatment). Over the second month, the amount of tips is recorded (post-test score).

This is an improvement over the one-shot case study because the researcher measures the dependent variable both before and after the treatment. But it lacks a control group. The researcher cannot know whether something other than the treatment occurred between the pretest and the post-test to cause the outcome.

Static Group Comparison Also called the *post-test–only nonequivalent group design*, **static group comparison** has two groups, a post-test, and treatment. It lacks random assignment and a pretest. A weakness is that any post-test outcome difference between the groups could be due to group differences prior to the experiment instead of to the treatment.

static group comparison: An *experimental design* with two groups, no *random assignment*, and only a *post-test*.

Example The experimenter gives 40 newly hired wait staff an identical two-hour training session and instructs them to follow a script in which they are not to introduce themselves by first name and not to return during the meal to check on the customers. They can choose one of the two restaurants to work at, so long as each restaurant ends up with 20 people. All begin employment. After one month, the experimenter "retrains" the 20 subjects at Restaurant 1 (experimental group). The experimenter instructs them henceforth to introduce themselves to customers by first name and to check on the customers, asking, "Is everything fine?" eight to ten minutes after delivering the food (treatment). The group at Restaurant 2 (control group) is "retrained" to continue without an introduction or checking during the meal. Over the second month, the amount of tips for both groups is recorded (post-test score).

quasi-experimental designs: *Experimental designs* that are stronger than *pre-experimental designs.* They are variations on the *classical experimental design* that an experimenter uses in special situations or when an experimenter has limited control over the *independent variable.*

Quasi-Experimental and Special Designs

These designs, like the classical design, make identifying a causal relationship more certain than do pre-experimental designs. **Quasi-experimental designs** help researchers test for causal relationships in a variety of situations where the classical design is difficult or inappropriate. They are called *quasi* because they are variations of the classical experimental design. Some have randomization but lack a pretest, some use more than two groups, and others substitute many observations of one group over time for a control group. In general, the researcher has less control over the independent variable than in the classical design (see Table 9.1).

Two-Group Post-test–Only Design This is identical to the static group comparison with one exception: The groups are randomly assigned. It has all the parts of the classical design except a pretest. The random assignment reduces the chance that the groups differed before the treatment, but without a pretest a researcher cannot be as certain that the groups began the same with respect to the dependent variable.

In a study using a two-group post-test–only design with random assignment, Sharpe, Pelletier, and Lévesque (2006) examined how rewards for participation in university psychology experiments affected undergraduates' participation in them. You may have had the experience of being offered course credit for participating in psychology experiments at your university or college if you have taken an introductory psychology course. The researchers in this study were interested to know if participation rates would drop if such incentives (i.e., course credit) were removed, or if participation would increase if incentives were added where they had not existed before. The subjects were psychology undergraduate students from the University of Ottawa and the University of Rochester. The University of Ottawa did not typically offer course credits for study participation, whereas the University of Rochester did. At both universities, students in large undergraduate classes were asked to fill out a questionnaire during class time and were told that

Table 9.1 A Comparison of the Classical Experimental Design with Other Major Designs

Design	Random Assignment	Pretest	Post-test	Control Group	Experimental Group
Classical	Yes	Yes	Yes	Yes	Yes
One-Shot Case Study	No	No	Yes	No	Yes
One-Group Pretest–Post-test	No	Yes	Yes	No	Yes
Static Group Comparison	No	No	Yes	Yes	Yes
Two-Group Post-test–Only	Yes	No	Yes	Yes	Yes
Time Series Designs	No	Yes	Yes	No	Yes

if they wanted to participate in future studies they could fill out a contact sheet at the back of the questionnaire. In each university, classes were randomly chosen so that some classes were told that they would receive course credit if they participated and in the other classes they were told that they would not. The treatment was whether a change in the credit associated with participating in a study would affect participation rates. Would students who were used to receiving credit be less likely to participate when this condition was removed? Would students be more likely to participate if credit was offered where it wasn't before? The results showed that overall participation rates were higher where participants were rewarded and that participation rates fell drastically when previously existing credit opportunity was taken away.

Interrupted Time Series In an **interrupted time series** design, a researcher uses one group and makes multiple pretest measures before and after the treatment. For example, after remaining level for many years, cigarette taxes jumped 35 percent in 1995. Taxes remained relatively constant for the next 10 years. The hypothesis is that an increase in taxes lowers cigarette consumption. A researcher plots the rate of cigarette consumption for 1985 through 2010. The researcher notes that cigarette consumption was level during the 10 years prior to the new taxes and then dropped in 1995 and stayed about the same for the next 15 years.

interrupted time series: An *experimental design* in which the *dependent variable* is measured periodically across many time points, and the *treatment* occurs in the midst of such measures, often only once.

Equivalent Time Series An **equivalent time series design** is another one-group design that extends over a time period. Instead of one treatment, it has a pretest and then a treatment and post-test, followed by treatment and post-test, followed by treatment and post-test, and so on. For example, in the United States people who drive motorcycles were not required to wear helmets before 1985, at which point a law was passed requiring helmets. In 1991, the law was repealed because of pressure from motorcycle clubs. The helmet law was reinstated in 2003. The researcher's hypothesis is that wearing protective helmets lowers the number of head injury deaths in motorcycle accidents. The researcher plots head injury death rates in motorcycle accidents over time. The rate was very high prior to 1985, dropped sharply between 1985 and 1991, returned to pre-1985 levels between 1991 and 2003, and then dropped again from 2003 to the present.

equivalent time-series design: An *experimental design* in which there are several repeated *pretests, post-tests,* and *treatments* for one group often over a period of time.

Latin Square Designs Researchers interested in how several treatments given in different sequences or time orders affect a dependent variable can use a **Latin square design**. For example, a geography teacher has three units to teach students: map reading, using a compass, and the longitude/latitude (LL) system. The units can be taught in any order, but the teacher wants to know which order most helps students learn. In one class, students first learn to read maps, then how to use a compass, and then the LL system. In another class, using a compass comes first, then map reading, and then the LL system. In a third class, the instructor first teaches the LL system, then compass usage, and ends with map reading. The teacher gives tests after each unit, and students take a comprehensive exam at the end of the term. The students were randomly assigned to classes, so the instructor can see whether presenting units in one sequence or another resulted in improved learning.

Latin square design: An *experimental design* used to examine whether the order or sequence in which *subjects* receive multiple versions of the *treatment* has an effect.

Solomon Four-Group Design A researcher may believe that the pretest measure has an influence on the treatment or dependent variable. A pretest can sometimes sensitize subjects to the treatment or improve their performance on the post-test (see the discussion of testing effect to come). Richard L. Solomon developed the **Solomon four-group design** to address the issue of pretest effects. It combines the classical experimental design with the two-group post-test–only design and randomly assigns subjects to one of four groups. For example, a mental health worker wants to determine whether a new training method improves clients' coping skills. The worker measures coping skills with a 20-minute test of reactions to stressful events. Because the clients might learn coping

Solomon four-group design: An *experimental design* in which *subjects* are randomly assigned to two *control groups* and two *experimental groups*. Only one *experimental group* and one *control group* receive a *pretest*. All four groups receive a *post-test*.

skills from taking the test itself, a Solomon four-group design is used. The mental health worker randomly divides clients into four groups. Two groups receive the pretest: One of them gets the new training method and the other gets the old method. Another two groups receive no pretest: One of them gets the new training method and the other the old method. All four groups are given the same post-test and the post-test results are compared. If the two treatment (new method) groups have similar results, and the two control (old method) groups have similar results, then the mental health worker knows pretest learning is not a problem. If the two groups with a pretest (one treatment, one control) differ from the two groups without a pretest, then the worker concludes that the pretest itself may have an effect on the dependent variable.

factorial design: A type of *experimental design* that considers the impact of several *independent variables* simultaneously.

Factorial Designs Sometimes a research question suggests looking at the simultaneous effects of more than one independent variable. A **factorial design** uses two or more independent variables in combination. Every combination of the categories in variables (sometimes called *factors*) is examined. When each variable contains several categories, the number of combinations grows very quickly. The treatment or manipulation is not each independent variable; rather, it is each combination of the categories.

The treatments in a factorial design can have two kinds of effects on the dependent variable: main effects and interaction effects. Only *main effects* are present in one-factor or single-treatment designs. In a factorial design, specific combinations of independent variable categories can also have an effect. They are called **interaction effects** because the categories in a combination interact to produce an effect beyond that of each variable alone.

interaction effect: The effect of two *independent variables* that operate simultaneously. The effect of the variables together is greater than what would occur from a simple addition of the effects from each. The variables operate together on one another to create an extra "boost."

Interaction effects are illustrated in Figure 9.3, which uses data from a study by Ong and Ward (1999). As part of a study of 128 female undergraduates at the National University of Singapore, Ong and Ward measured which of two major ways subjects understood the crime of rape. Some of the women primarily understood it as sex and due to the male sex drive (sex schema); others understood it as primarily an act of male power and domination of a woman (power schema). The researchers asked the subjects to read a realistic scenario about the rape of a student at their university. One randomly selected group of subjects read a scenario in which the victim tried to fight off the rapist. In the other set, she passively submitted. The researchers next asked the subjects to evaluate the degree to which the rape victim was at blame or responsible for the rape.

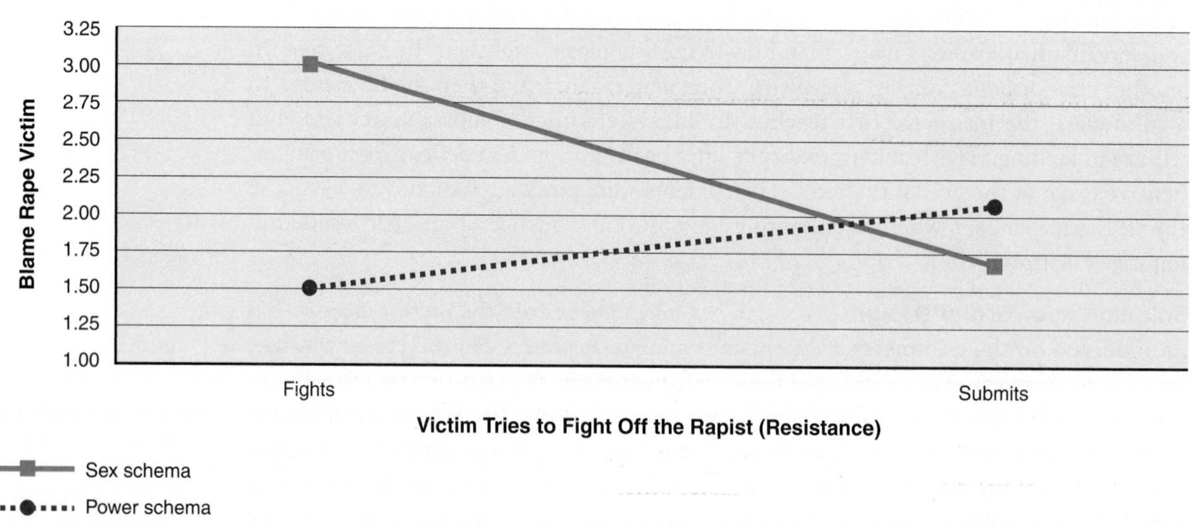

Figure 9.3 Blame, Resistance, and Schema: Interaction Effect

Results showed that the women who held the sex schema (and who also tended to embrace traditionalist gender role beliefs) more strongly blamed the victim when she resisted; blame decreased if she submitted. The women who held a power schema (and who also tended to be nontraditionalists) were less likely to blame the victim if she fought; they blamed her more if she passively submitted. Thus, the subjects' responses to the victim's act of resisting the attack varied by, or interacted with, their understanding of the crime of rape (i.e., the rape schema held by each subject). The researchers found that two rape schemas caused subjects to interpret victim resistance in opposite ways for the purpose of assigning responsibility for the crime.

Researchers discuss factorial design in a shorthand way. A "two by three factorial design" is written "2 × 3." It means that there are two treatments, with two categories in one and three categories in the other. A 2 × 3 × 3 design means that there are three independent variables, one with two categories and two with three categories each.

The previously discussed experiment by Hawkes, Senn, and Thorn (2004) on tattoos among university women used a 3 × 2 factorial design. The experimenters manipulated two independent variables in the descriptions of the tattoo read by subjects. The first related to size of the tattoo and had three possible values: whether the woman had no tattoo, a tattoo smaller than a Canadian $1 coin, or a tattoo larger than a $1 coin. The second independent variable pertained to the visibility of the tattoo and had two possible values: always hidden versus always visible. The study included 268 subjects (122 males and 146 females); 43 subjects (or 16 percent) had a tattoo.

Design Notation

Experiments can be designed in many ways. **Design notation** is a shorthand system for symbolizing the parts of experimental design. Once you learn design notation, you will find it easier to think about and compare designs. For example, design notation expresses a complex, paragraph-long description of the parts of an experiment in five or six symbols arranged in two lines. It uses the following symbols: O = observation of dependent variable; X = treatment, independent variable; R = random assignment. The Os are numbered with subscripts from left to right based on time order. Pretests are O_1, post-tests O_2. When the independent variable has more than two levels, the Xs are numbered with subscripts to distinguish among them. Symbols are in time order from left to right. The R is first, followed by the pretest, the treatment, and then the post-test. Symbols are arranged in rows, with each row representing a group of subjects. For example, an experiment with three groups has an R (if random assignment is used), followed by three rows of Os and Xs. The rows are on top of each other because the pretest, treatment, and post-test occur in each group at about the same time. Table 9.2 gives the notation for many standard experimental designs.

design notation: The name of a symbol system used to discuss the parts of an experiment and to make diagrams of them.

INTERNAL AND EXTERNAL VALIDITY

LO 5 Identify and define the various threats to internal and external validity.

The Logic of Internal Validity

Internal validity means the ability to eliminate alternative explanations of the dependent variable. Variables, other than the treatment, that affect the dependent variable are threats to internal validity. They threaten the researcher's ability to say that the treatment was the true causal factor producing change in the dependent variable. Thus, the logic of internal validity is to rule out variables other than the treatment by controlling experimental conditions and through experimental designs. Next, we examine major threats to internal validity.

Table 9.2 Summary of Experimental Designs with Notation

Name of Design	Design Notation
Classical experimental design	R → O X O R → O O
Pre-experimental designs	
One-shot case study	X O
One-group pretest–post-test	O X O
Static group comparison	X O O
Quasi-experimental designs	
Two-group post-test only	R → X O R → O
Interrupted time series	O O O O X O O O
Equivalent time series	O X O X O X O X O
Latin square designs	R → O X_a O X_b O X_c O R → O X_b O X_a O X_c O R → O X_c O X_b O X_a O R → O X_a O X_c O X_b O R → O X_b O X_c O X_a O R → O X_c O X_a O X_b O
Solomon four-group design	R → O X O R → O O R → X O R → O
Factorial designs	R → X_1 Z_1 O R → X_1 Z_2 O R → X_2 Z_1 O R → X_2 Z_2 O

Threats to Internal Validity

The following are nine common threats to internal validity.[1]

selection bias: A threat to *internal validity* when groups in an experiment are not equivalent at the beginning of the experiment.

Selection Bias **Selection bias** is the threat that research participants will not form equivalent groups. It is a problem in designs without random assignment. It occurs when subjects in one experimental group have a characteristic that affects the dependent variable. For example, in an experiment on physical aggressiveness, the treatment group unintentionally contains subjects who are football, rugby, and hockey players, whereas the control group is made up of musicians, chess players, and painters. Another example is an experiment on the ability of people to dodge heavy traffic. All subjects assigned to one group come from rural areas, and all subjects in the other grew up in large cities. An examination of pretest scores helps a researcher detect this threat because no group differences are expected.

history effects: A threat to *internal validity* due to something that occurs and affects the *dependent variable* during an experiment, but that is unplanned and outside the control of the experimenter.

History Effects This is the threat that an event unrelated to the treatment will occur during the experiment and influence the dependent variable. **History effects** are more likely in experiments that continue over a long time period. For example, halfway through a two-week experiment to evaluate subjects' attitudes toward space travel, a spacecraft explodes on the launch pad, killing the astronauts. The history effect can occur in the cigarette tax example discussed earlier (see the discussion of interrupted time series design). If a public anti-smoking campaign or reduced cigarette advertising also began in 1989, it would be hard to say that higher taxes caused less smoking.

Maturation This is the threat that some biological, psychological, or emotional process within the subjects and separate from the treatment will change over time. **Maturation** is more common in experiments over long time periods. For example, during an experiment on reasoning ability, subjects become bored and sleepy and, as a result, score lower. Another example is an experiment on the styles of children's play between Grade 1 and Grade 6. Play styles are affected by physical, emotional, and maturation changes that occur as the children grow older, instead of or in addition to the effects of a treatment. Designs with a pretest and control group help researchers determine whether maturation or history effects are present, because both experimental and control groups will show similar changes over time.

maturation: A threat to *internal validity* in *experimental research* due to natural processes of growth, boredom, and so on that occur to *subjects* during the experiment and affect the *dependent variable*.

Testing Effect Sometimes, the pretest measure itself affects an experiment. This **testing effect** threatens internal validity because more than the treatment alone affects the dependent variable. The Solomon four-group design helps a researcher detect testing effects. For example, a researcher gives students an examination on the first day of class. The course is the treatment. He or she tests learning by giving the same exam on the last day of class. If subjects remember the pretest questions and this affects what they learned (i.e., what they paid attention to) or how they answered questions on the post-test, a testing effect is present. If testing effects occur, a researcher cannot say that the treatment alone has affected the dependent variable.

testing effect: A *pretest* measure that itself affects an experiment. This testing effect threatens *internal validity* because more than the *treatment* alone affects the *dependent variable*.

Instrumentation This threat is related to reliability. **Instrumentation** occurs when the instrument or dependent variable measure changes during the experiment. For example, in a weight-loss experiment, the springs on the scale weaken during the experiment, giving lower readings in the post-test.

instrumentation: A threat to reliability occurring when the *dependent variable* measure changes during the experiment.

Mortality **Mortality**, or attrition, arises when some subjects do not continue throughout the experiment. Although the word *mortality* means death, it does not necessarily mean that subjects have died. If a subset of subjects leaves partway through an experiment, a researcher cannot know whether the results would have been different had the subjects stayed. For example, a researcher begins a weight-loss program with 50 subjects. At the end of the program 30 remain, each of whom lost five pounds with no side effects. The 20 who left could have differed from the 30 who stayed, changing the results. Maybe the program was effective for those who left, and they withdrew after losing 25 pounds. Or perhaps the program made subjects sick and forced them to quit. Researchers should notice and report the number of subjects in each group during pretests and post-tests to detect this threat to internal validity.

mortality: Threats to *internal validity* due to *subjects* failing to participate through the entire experiment.

Statistical Regression **Statistical regression** is not easy to grasp intuitively. It is a problem of extreme values or a tendency for random errors to move group results toward the average. It can occur in two ways.

statistical regression: A problem of extreme values or a tendency for random errors to move group results toward the average.

One situation arises when subjects are unusual with regard to the dependent variable. Because they begin as unusual or extreme, subjects are unlikely to respond further in the same direction. For example, a researcher wants to see whether violent films make people act violently. He or she chooses a group of violent criminals from a high-security prison, gives them a pretest, shows a violent film, and then administers a post-test. To the researcher's shock, the prisoners are slightly less violent after the film, whereas a control group of prisoners who did not see the film are slightly more violent than before. Because the violent criminals began at an extreme, it is unlikely that a treatment could make

Box 9.3 Concepts in Action

The Mincome Experiment

In the late 1960s and early 1970s, much public policy attention was being given to reducing poverty and implementing programs that would target low-income groups. There was, however, the concern that providing a guaranteed minimum income ("mincome") to individuals would remove their incentive to work. Counterarguments suggested that guaranteed minimum incomes do much more than simply provide money—they also serve to improve various dimensions of individuals' lives (such as health) that tend to fall by the wayside when money concerns dominate one's life.

In the early 1970s, the province of Manitoba selected low-income families in Dauphin and Winnipeg and assigned them randomly to three different Guaranteed Annual Income (GAI) plans for three years. The three "treatments" were $3800, $4800, and $5800 for a family of four and were adjusted for family structure and size, with annual inflationary increases allocated in each year. A control group that did not receive any GAI was also included.

The purpose of the experiment was to see if people reduced their working hours when they received mincome. By and large, they did not. The mincome program ran from 1974 to 1978, when the government then cancelled the program. No final report about the experiment was ever written. Recently, Evelyn Forget, a professor of community health sciences at the University of Manitoba, examined the administrative health records of residents of Dauphin from 1974 to 1978 and found that, compared to a control group, hospitalizations, including those for mental health issues, were significantly lower, suggesting that alleviating poverty also had positive effects in other areas of individual's lives.

Source: Hum, D., & Simpson, W. (2001-01/02). A Guaranteed Annual Income? From Mincome to the Millennium. *Policy Options/Options Politique,* 78–82.

them more violent; by random chance alone, they appear less extreme when measured a second time.[2]

A second situation involves a problem with the measurement instrument. If many research participants score very high (at the ceiling) or very low (at the floor) on a variable, random chance alone will produce a change between the pretest and the post-test. For example, a researcher gives 80 subjects a test, and 75 get perfect scores. He or she then gives a treatment to raise scores. Because so many subjects already had perfect scores, random errors will reduce the group average because those who got perfect scores can randomly move in only one direction—to get some answers wrong. An examination of scores on pretests will help researchers detect this threat to internal validity.

Not all experiments take place at a research laboratory, however. The study in Box 9.3 details an experiment involving low-income families in Manitoba undertaken by the provincial government.

diffusion of treatment: A threat to *internal validity* that occurs when the *treatment* "spills over" from the *experimental group,* and *control group* subjects modify their behaviour because they learn of the *treatment.*

Diffusion of Treatment or Contamination

Diffusion of treatment is the threat that research participants in different groups will communicate with each other and learn about the other's treatment. Researchers avoid it by isolating groups or having subjects promise not to reveal anything to others who will become subjects. For example, subjects participate in a day-long experiment on a new way to memorize words. During a break, treatment-group subjects tell those in the control group about the new way to memorize, which control-group subjects then use. A researcher needs outside information, such as post-experiment interviews with subjects, to detect this threat.

experimenter expectancy: A researcher may threaten *internal validity* not by purposefully unethical behaviour but by indirectly communicating desired findings to the subjects.

Experimenter Expectancy

Although it is not always considered a traditional internal validity problem, the experimenter's behaviour can also threaten causal logic.[3] A researcher may threaten internal validity not by purposefully unethical behaviour but by indirectly communicating **experimenter expectancy** to subjects. Researchers may be highly committed to the hypothesis and indirectly communicate desired findings to the subjects. For example, a researcher studies the effects of memorization training on student learning ability and also sees the grade transcripts of subjects. The researcher believes that students with higher grades tend to do better at the training and will learn more. Through eye contact, tone of voice, pauses, and other nonverbal communication the researcher unconsciously trains the students with higher grades more intensely; the researcher's nonverbal behaviour is the opposite for students with lower grades.

Here is a way to detect experimenter expectancy. A researcher hires assistants and teaches them experimental techniques. The assistants train subjects and test their learning ability. The researcher gives the assistants fake transcripts and records showing that subjects in one group are honour students and the others are failing, although in fact the subjects are identical. Experimenter expectancy is present if the fake honour students, as a group, do much better than the fake failing students.

The **double-blind experiment** is designed to control researcher expectancy. In it, people who have direct contact with subjects do not know the details of the hypothesis or the treatment. It is *double* blind because both the subjects and those in contact with them are blind to details of the experiment (see Figure 9.4). For example, a researcher wants to see if a new drug is effective. Using pills of three colours—green, yellow, and pink—the researcher puts the new drug in the yellow pill, puts an old drug in the pink one, and makes the green pill a **placebo**—a false treatment that appears to be real (e.g., a sugar pill without any physical effects). Assistants who give the pills and record the effects do not know which colour contains the new drug. Only another person who does not deal with subjects directly knows which coloured pill contains the drug and it is he or she who examines the results.

double-blind experiment: A type of *experimental research* in which neither the *subjects* nor the person who directly deals with the subjects knows the specifics of the experiment.

placebo: A false *treatment* or one that has no effect in an experiment. It is sometimes called a "sugar pill" that a *subject* mistakes for a true *treatment*.

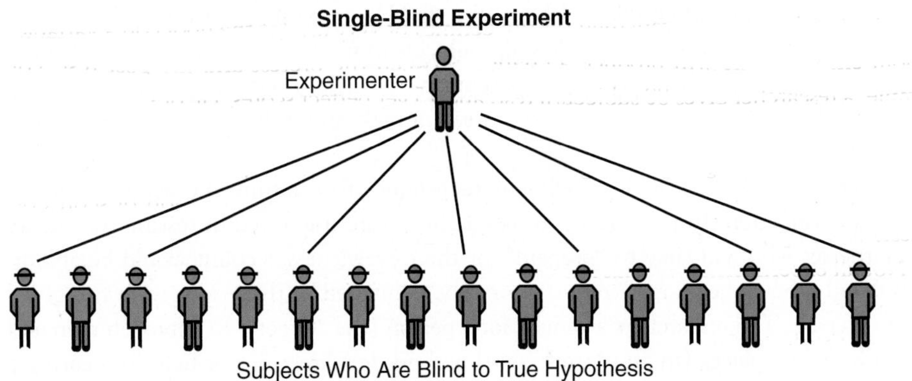

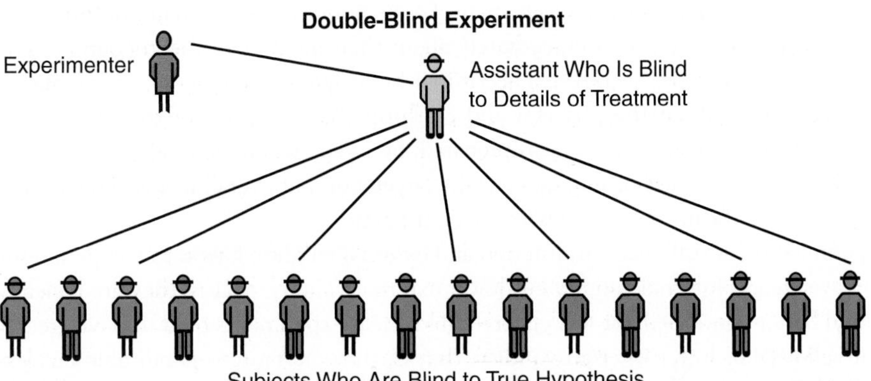

Figure 9.4 Double-Blind Experiments: An Illustration of Single-Blind, or Ordinary, and Double-Blind Experiments

External Validity and Field Experiments

Even if an experimenter eliminates all concerns about internal validity, external validity remains a potential problem. *External validity* is the ability to generalize experimental findings to events and settings outside the experiment itself. If a study lacks external validity, its findings hold true only in experiments, making them useless to both basic and applied science.

reactivity: The general threat to *external validity* that arises because *subjects* are aware that they are in an experiment and being studied.

Hawthorne effect: An effect of *reactivity* named after a famous case in which *subjects* reacted to the fact that they were in an experiment more than they reacted to the *treatment*.

Reactivity

Research participants might react differently in an experiment than they would in real life because they know they are in a study; this is called **reactivity**. The **Hawthorne effect** is a specific kind of reactivity.[4] The name comes from a series of experiments by Elton Mayo at the Hawthorne, Illinois, plant of Westinghouse Electric during the 1920s and 1930s. Researchers modified many aspects of working conditions (e.g., lighting, time for breaks) and measured productivity. They discovered that productivity rose after each modification, no matter what it was. This curious result occurred because the workers did not respond to the treatment but to the additional attention they received from being part of the experiment and knowing that they were being watched. Later research questioned whether this occurred, but the name is used for an effect caused by the attention of researchers. A related effect is the effect of something new, which may wear off over time.

laboratory experiment: *Experimental research* that takes place in an artificial setting over which the experimenter has great control.

field experiment: *Experimental research* that takes place in a natural setting.

Field Experiments

So far, this chapter has focused on experiments conducted under the controlled conditions of a laboratory. Experiments are also conducted in real-life or field settings where a researcher has less control over the experimental conditions. The amount of control varies on a continuum. At one end is the highly controlled **laboratory experiment**, which takes place in a specialized setting or laboratory; at the opposite end is the **field experiment**, which takes place in the "field"—in natural settings such as a subway car, a liquor store, or a public sidewalk. Subjects in field experiments are usually unaware that they are involved in an experiment and react in a natural way. For example, researchers have had a confederate fake a heart attack on a subway car to see how the bystanders react.[5]

Yarmey (2004) used field experiment techniques to examine the accuracy of eye witness identification. In particular, the researchers were interested in testing the theory that witnesses who had time to "prepare" for their eyewitness account would be able to recall details about the "target" more accurately, compared to those who were not given time to prepare. The researchers arranged for a person (the "target") to approach men and women in public places (in an Ontario city) and ask for directions or help in locating a piece of lost jewellery. The targets (those "in" on the experiment) wore dark sunglasses and a baseball cap. After the interaction with the target, the witnesses were approached by a part of the research team and asked to be part of a memory experiment. Half of those that agreed to participate were tested immediately about their memory of the encounter. The other half of the participants was tested about four hours later. The witnesses were asked a variety of questions about the physical and clothing characteristics of the target. The findings revealed that if the witness was prepared, he or she was more likely to give more accurate descriptions of the clothing worn by the target, but that overall witness preparation did not make a significant impact on witness identification.

Experimenter control relates to internal and external validity. Laboratory experiments tend to have greater internal validity but lower external validity; that is, they are logically tighter and better controlled but less generalizable. Field experiments tend to have greater external validity but lower internal validity; that is, they are more generalizable but less controlled. Quasi-experimental designs are common in field experiments. Table 9.3 summarizes threats to internal and external validity. See Box 9.4 for a discussion of how researchers are using the internet to run their experiments,

Table 9.3 Major Internal and External Validity Concerns

Internal Validity	External Validity and Reactivity
Selection bias	Hawthorne effect
History effect	
Maturation	
Testing	
Instrumentation	
Experimental mortality	
Statistical regression	
Diffusion of treatment	
Experimenter expectancy	

Natural Experiments A **natural experiment** is a special type of quasi-experimental design where researchers can take advantage of a "natural" change in a society and measure an outcome before and after such a change takes place. For example, the federal government may implement a law to make Plan B, otherwise known as the "morning after pill," available without prescription. It is envisaged that if this drug is easy to access, fewer unwanted pregnancies will occur. In particular, the government may be targeting a reduction in teenage births. A natural experiment is possible here because a researcher could compare teenage birth rates before the easy availability of Plan B (pre-test) to the teenage birth rates after the easy availability (post-test). If the treatment (making Plan B available without prescription) is effective, one would expect a reduction in the teenage birth rate. See Box 9.5 for a recent example of a natural experiment by Canadian researchers.

natural experiment: A specific type of *quasi-experiment* where a researcher can examine the impact of a policy change or similar change in a social system by comparing an outcome of interest before and after such a change is implemented.

Practical Considerations

Every research technique has informal tricks of the trade. These are pragmatic, common sense ideas that account for the difference between the successful research projects of an experienced researcher and the difficulties a novice researcher faces. Three are discussed here.

Box 9.4 Social Research and the Internet

Web Experiments

While online research is prevalent, often in the form of market research, social researchers have also been moving experimental design to an online format. There are some notable advantages to the online format of an experiment, such as capturing a wider audience, obtaining a larger sample size, and diminishing the effect of experimenter expectancy.

Canadian political scientist Alison Harell and associates (Harell et al., 2012) recently used an online experimental design to examine public support for immigration in Canada and the United States. The data were collected online through a web survey instrument that had various treatments built into it. The researchers used a factorial design (i.e., the simultaneous effects of more than one independent variable), presenting respondents with two vignettes that described an immigrant's circumstances. The respondents were shown a photo of the immigrant and were asked to respond to a series of questions about their support for this individual's work permit and citizenship status. The treatments in the design were the race of person (South Asian, Middle Eastern, and Mexican) in the photo as well as their family status (single, spouse and children). They also varied the skin complexion of the photos, making some darker and some lighter. The job status of the immigrant was also varied. Among their many findings were that Canadians were more supportive of immigrants with higher job statuses than those who were described as doing manual work, regardless of ethnic background or skin colour.

Box 9.5 Concepts in Action

Subsidized Daycare and Women's Labour Market Participation

Occasionally, a "natural" experiment is possible because of public policy changes or a government intervention, and researchers are able to measure, participate in, and learn from it by conducting a natural experiment with high *external validity*. This occurred in Quebec in the late 1990s when the provincial government introduced $5-a-day daycare for children aged four. The coverage spread to all children who were not yet in Kindergarten.

From a social research perspective, such a change in policy lent itself to be studied as a natural experiment. Until the change was implemented, a major barrier for women returning to the labour force after the birth of a child was the cost of child care. If this cost was minimized, however, it should be the case that women would return to the labour force in higher numbers than before the plan was implemented. Therefore, the labour force participation rate for women with young children was measured by Lefebvre and Merrigan (2008) before and after the change in the policy. The labour force participation before the change was the pretest measure and the labour force participation after the change was the post-test measure. The treatment was the new law in Quebec, which highly subsidized child care of pre-kindergarten aged children.

The researchers examined Statistics Canada data from the Survey of Labour and Income Dynamics for the time period 1992 to 2002 and observed a statistically significant increase in the labour market participation of women with preschool children in Quebec, suggesting that the policy had been effective in removing barriers for women returning to the workforce after the birth of a child.

Planning and Pilot Tests All social research requires planning, and most quantitative researchers use pilot tests. During the planning phase of experimental research, a researcher thinks of alternative explanations or threats to internal validity and how to avoid them. The researcher also develops a neat and well-organized system for recording data. In addition, he or she devotes serious effort to pilot-testing any apparatus (e.g., computers, video cameras, tape recorders) that will be used in the treatment situation, and he or she must train and pilot-test confederates. After the pilot tests, the researcher should interview the pilot subjects to uncover aspects of the experiment that need refinement.

Instructions to Subjects Most experiments involve giving instructions to subjects to set the stage. A researcher should word instructions carefully and follow a prepared script so that all subjects hear the same thing. This ensures reliability. The instructions are also important in creating a realistic cover story when deception is used.

Post-experiment Interview At the end of an experiment, the researcher should interview subjects for three reasons. First, if deception was used the researcher needs to debrief the research participants, telling them the true purpose of the experiment and answering questions. Second, he or she can learn what the subjects thought and how their definitions of the situation affected their behaviour. Finally, he or she can explain the importance of not revealing the true nature of the experiment to other potential participants.

RESULTS OF EXPERIMENTAL RESEARCH: MAKING COMPARISONS

Comparison is the key to all research. By carefully examining the results of experimental research, a researcher can learn a great deal about threats to internal validity and whether the treatment has an impact on the dependent variable. For example, in an experiment by Bond and Anderson (1987) on delivering bad news, it took an average of 89.6 seconds in a private setting or 73.1 seconds in a public setting to deliver favourable news, versus 72.5 or 147.2 seconds to deliver unfavourable news in private or public settings, respectively. A comparison shows that delivering bad news in public takes the longest, whereas delivering good news takes a bit longer in private.

	Pretest Weight	Pretest N	Post-Test Weight	Post-Test N	Change in Weight	Change in N
Enrique's Slim Clinic						
Experimental	190	30	140	29	–50	–1
Control	189	30	189	30	0	0
Susan's Scientific Diet Plan						
Experimental	190	30	141	19	–49	–11
Control	189	30	189	28	0	–2
Carol's Calorie Counters						
Experimental	160	30	152	29	–8	–1
Control	191	29	189	29	–2	0
Natalie's Nutrition Centre						
Experimental	190	30	188	29	–2	–1
Control	192	29	190	28	–2	–1
Pauline's Pounds Off						
Experimental	190	30	158	30	–32	0
Control	191	29	159	28	–32	–1

Figure 9.5 **Comparisons of Results, Classical Experimental Design, Weight-Loss Experiments**

A more complex illustration of such comparisons is shown in Figure 9.5 on the results of a series of five weight-loss experiments using the classical experimental design. In the example, the 30 research participants in the experimental group at Enrique's Slim Clinic lost an average of 50 pounds, whereas the 30 in the control group did not lose a single pound. Only one person dropped out during the experiment. Susan's Scientific Diet Plan had equally dramatic results, but 11 people in her experimental group dropped out. This suggests a problem with experimental mortality. People in the experimental group at Carol's Calorie Counters lost eight pounds, compared to two pounds for the control group, but the control group and the experimental group began with an average of 31 pounds' difference in weight. This suggests a problem with selection bias. Natalie's Nutrition Centre had no experimental mortality or selection bias problems, but those in the experimental group lost no more weight than those in the control group. It appears that the treatment was not effective. Pauline's Pounds Off also avoided selection bias and experimental mortality problems. People in her experimental group lost 32 pounds, but so did those in the control group. This suggests that the maturation, history, or diffusion of treatment effects may have occurred. Thus, the treatment at Enrique's Slim Clinic appears to be the most effective one.

A WORD ON ETHICS

Ethical considerations are a significant issue in experimental research because experimental research is intrusive (i.e., it interferes). Treatments may involve placing people in contrived social settings and manipulating their feelings or behaviours. Dependent variables may be what subjects say or do. The amount and type of intrusion is limited by ethical standards.

Researchers must be very careful if they place research participants in physical danger or in embarrassing or anxiety-inducing situations. They must painstakingly monitor events and control what occurs.

Deception is common in social experiments, but it involves misleading or lying to subjects. Such dishonesty is not condoned unconditionally and is acceptable only as the means of achieving a goal that could not be achieved otherwise. Even for a worthy goal, deception can be used only with restrictions. The amount and type of deception should not go beyond what is minimally necessary, and research participants should be debriefed.

CHAPTER SUMMARY

Glossary Flashcards

In this chapter, you learned about experimental research design. The chapter began by explaining the types of research questions that are appropriate for addressing with experiments, pointing to the necessity that such research questions are usually quite narrow in scope, small in scale, and exclude many variables that cannot be manipulated by the researcher. The strength of the experimental method is that it is the only technique in which causality can be directly observed. It is observed through any difference in the observed outcome between the treatment and control group.

Random assignment is a key feature of the experimental method. It is an effective way to create two (or more) groups that can be treated as equivalent and hence compared. It is important to remember that random assignment and random sampling are two distinctly different processes.

This chapter also examined the parts of an experiment and how they can be combined to produce different experimental designs. There are seven parts to the experimental design: the treatment, dependent variable, pretest, post-test, experimental group, control group, and random assignment. In addition to the classical experimental design, you learned about pre-experimental and quasi-experimental designs. You also learned how to express them using design notation.

You learned that internal validity—the internal logical rigour of an experiment—is a key idea in experimental research. Threats to internal validity are possible alternative explanations to the treatment. Nine different threats to internal validity were described: selection bias, history effects, maturation, testing effect, instrumentation, mortality, statistical regression, diffusion of treatment, and experimenter expectancy. You also learned about external validity and how field experiments maximize external validity. Natural experiments, a special type of quasi-experiment, were also introduced as ways that researchers can take advantage of natural changes in society and develop pretest and post-test measures of the change of interest.

Review Questions

1. Give three characteristics of research questions that are appropriate to be tested using the experimental method.
2. Describe the three steps used in the process of random assignment.
3. Describe the seven parts of an experiment.
4. Describe how the experimental method can meet the three criteria of causality.
5. Explain how the classical experimental design compares with the five other major designs in terms of their major components.
6. Explain one similarity and two major differences between experiments conducted in the laboratory versus those conducted in the field.
7. Identify and define the nine threats to internal validity, giving examples of each.

Exercises

1. Using EBSCO's ContentSelect, find three studies within the past five years that used the experimental method. For each of the articles, identify the name of the type of experiment that was used by the authors of the articles. How were the experimental data collected (laboratory experiment, field experiment, etc.)? Identify the pretest and post-test measure in each study, as well as the treatment being used by the researcher.

2. If there is a psychology department in your university or college, visit its website and see what kinds of experiments are currently running. What are the research questions? If possible, participate in one of the experiments as a subject and, when you are finished, identify the elements of an experiment (pretest, post-test, treatment, etc.) as they pertained to your experience.
3. This chapter discussed the experimental method as a technique that did not easily lend itself to many topics examined by social scientists outside of psychology. On the internet, search for experimental sociologists in Canada and see what you can find. What kinds of topics do experimental sociologists examine, and how do they conduct their research?

Chapter 10

Nonreactive Quantitative Research and Secondary Analysis

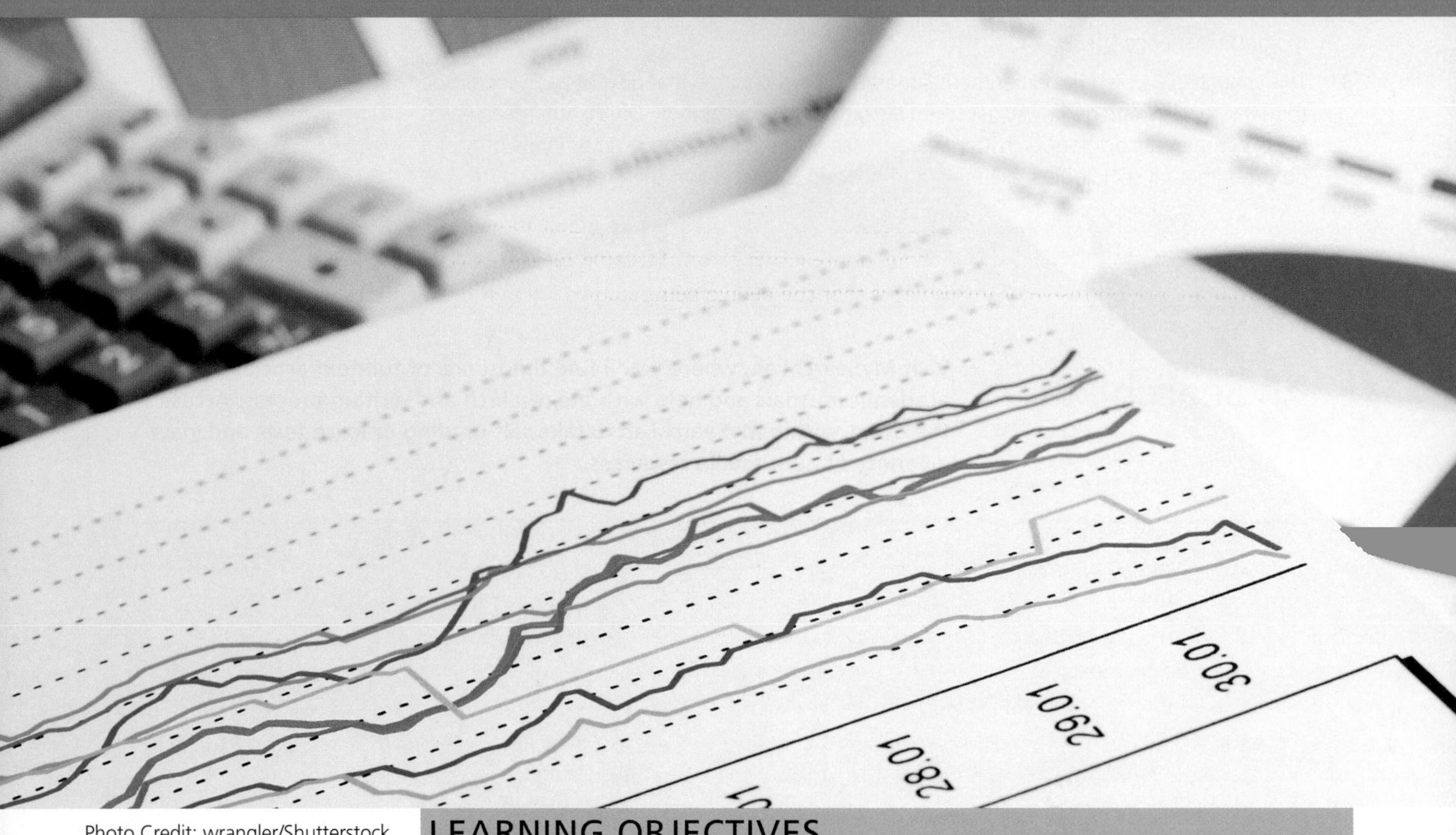

Photo Credit: wrangler/Shutterstock

LEARNING OBJECTIVES

After reading this chapter, you will be able to

- LO 1 Explain the difference between reactive and nonreactive research.
- LO 2 Explain the types of research questions that are appropriate for investigating using nonreactive quantitative techniques.
- LO 3 Describe the different elements and process of a quantitative content analysis.
- LO 4 Differentiate between manifest and latent coding.
- LO 5 Explain how existing statistics and secondary analysis can be used as a nonreactive method.
- LO 6 Identify the advantages and disadvantages of secondary analysis.

LO 1 Explain the difference between reactive and nonreactive research.

nonreactive: Measures in which people being studied are unaware that they are in a study.

INTRODUCTION

Experiments and survey research are both *reactive*; that is, the people being studied are aware of that fact. In this chapter, you will learn about four research techniques that are **nonreactive**—the people being studied are not aware that they are part of a research project.

Nonreactive techniques are largely based on positivist principles but are also used by interpretive and critical researchers.

The first technique we will consider is less a distinct technique than a loose collection of inventive nonreactive measures. It is followed by content analysis, which builds on the fundamentals of quantitative research design and is a well-developed research technique. Existing statistics and secondary analysis, the last two techniques, refer to the collection of already existing information from government documents or previous surveys. Researchers examine the existing data in new ways to address new questions. Although the data may have been reactive when first collected, a researcher can address new questions without reactive effects.

NONREACTIVE MEASUREMENT

The Logic of Nonreactive Research

LO 2 Explain the types of research questions that are appropriate for investigating using nonreactive quantitative techniques.

Nonreactive measurement begins when a researcher notices something that indicates a variable of interest. The critical thing about nonreactive or **unobtrusive measures** (i.e., measures that are not obtrusive or intrusive) is that the people being studied are not aware of it but leave evidence of their social behaviour or actions "naturally." The observant researcher infers from the evidence to behaviour or attitudes without disrupting the people being studied.

unobtrusive measures: Another name for *nonreactive measures*. It emphasizes that the people being studied are not aware of it because the measures do not intrude.

Varieties of Nonreactive or Unobtrusive Observation

Nonreactive measures are varied, and researchers have been creative in inventing indirect ways to measure social behaviour (see Box 10.1). Researchers have examined family portraits in different historical eras to see how gender relations within the family are reflected in seating patterns. Urban anthropologists have examined the contents of garbage dumps to learn about lifestyles from what is thrown away (e.g., liquor bottles indicate level of alcohol consumption; based on garbage, people under-report their liquor consumption by 40 to 60 percent; Rathje & Murphy, 1992, p. 71). Researchers have studied the listening habits of drivers by checking what stations their radios are tuned to when cars are repaired. They have measured interest in different exhibits by noting worn tiles on the floor in different parts of a museum. They have studied differences in graffiti in males' versus females' high school restrooms to show gender differences in themes. Some have examined high school yearbooks to compare the high school activities of those who had psychological problems in later life versus those who did not (see Box 10.2). There are also qualitative nonreactive approaches, but these will not be discussed until Chapter 14.

Qualitative versus Quantitative Research

Box 10.1 Concepts in Action

Finding Data in Birth Announcements

Gonzalez and Koestner (2005) examined the birth announcements on the internet archive sites of *The Gazette* (Montreal) and the *Calgary Herald* between May 2002 and January 2004. They selected about 400 birth announcements to examine. The researchers learned that birth announcements tended to emphasize "pride" when the sex of the baby was a boy, while the emphasis was on "happiness" and "joy" when the child was a girl. The authors interpreted these differences as expressions of the parents' perceptions of their child's worth, with the birth of a boy being tied to heightened social standing.

An additional finding was that parents in Calgary tended to express more "pride" than those in Montreal, while parents in Montreal expressed more "happiness" than parents in Calgary.

Box 10.2 Making It Practical

Examples of Nonreactive Measures

Physical Traces

Erosion: Wear suggests greater use.
Example: A researcher examines children's toys at a daycare that were purchased at the same time. Worn-out toys suggest greater interest by the children.

Accretion: Accumulation of physical evidence suggests behaviour.
Example: A researcher examines the brands of aluminum beverage cans in trash or recycling bins in males' and females' dormitories. This indicates the brands and types of beverages favoured by each sex.

Archives

Running Records: Regularly produced public records may reveal much.
Example: A researcher examines marriage records for the brides' and grooms' ages. Regional differences suggest that the preference for males marrying younger females is greater in certain areas of the country.

Other Records: Irregular or private records can reveal a significant amount of information.
Example: A researcher finds the number of reams of paper purchased by a university dean's office for 10 years when student enrolment was stable. A sizable increase suggests that bureaucratic paperwork has increased.

Observation

External Appearance: How people appear may indicate social factors.
Example: A researcher watches students to see whether they are more likely to wear their school's colours and symbols after the school team won or lost.

Count Behaviours: Counting how many people do something can be informative.
Example: A researcher counts the number of men and women who come to a full stop and those who come to a rolling stop at a stop sign. This suggests gender difference in driving behaviour.

Time Duration: How long people take to do things may indicate their attention.
Example: A researcher measures how long men and women pause in front of a painting of a nude man and in front of a painting of a nude woman. Time may indicate embarrassment or interest in same- or cross-sex nudity by each sex.

Recording and Documentation

Creating nonreactive measures follows the logic of quantitative measurement. A researcher first conceptualizes a construct, then links the construct to nonreactive empirical evidence, which is its measure. The operational definition of the variable includes how the researcher systematically notes and records observations.

Because nonreactive measures indicate a construct indirectly, the researcher needs to rule out reasons for the observation other than the construct of interest. For example, a researcher wants to measure customer walking traffic in a store. The researcher's measure is dirt and wear on floor tiles. He or she first clarifies what the customer traffic means (e.g., Is the floor a path to another department? Does it indicate a good location for a visual display?) Next, he or she systematically measures dirt or wear on the tiles, compares it to that in other locations, and records results on a regular basis (e.g., every month). Finally, the researcher rules out other reasons for the observations (e.g., the floor tile is of lower quality and wears faster, or the location is near an outside entrance).

LO 3 Describe the different elements and process of a quantitative content analysis.

content: Refers to words, meanings, pictures, symbols, ideas, themes, or any message that can be communicated.

text: A general name for symbolic meaning within a communication medium measured in *content analysis.*

QUANTITATIVE CONTENT ANALYSIS

What Is Content Analysis?

Content analysis is a technique for gathering and analyzing the content of text. The **content** refers to words, meanings, pictures, symbols, ideas, themes, or any message that can be communicated. The **text** is anything written, visual, or spoken that serves as a medium for communication. Text is yet another one of those "methods" words that has particular meaning in this context that is different from its everyday meaning. It includes books, newspaper and magazine articles, advertisements, speeches, official documents, films and videotapes, musical lyrics, photographs, articles of clothing, and works of art. It is not restricted to "written text"!

The content analysis researcher uses objective and systematic counting and recording procedures to produce a quantitative description of the symbolic content in a text.[1] There are also qualitative or interpretive versions of content analysis, but in this chapter the emphasis is on quantitative data about a text's content. Nonreactive qualitative techniques, including qualitative approaches to content analysis, are discussed in Chapter 14.

Content analysis is nonreactive because the process of placing words, messages, or symbols in a text to communicate to a reader or receiver occurs without influence from the researcher who analyzes its content. For example, as authors of this book, we wrote words and drew diagrams to communicate research methods content to you, the student. The way the book was written and the way you read it are without any knowledge or intention of its ever being content analyzed.

Content analysis lets a researcher reveal the content (i.e., messages, meanings) in a source of communication (i.e., a book, article, movie). It lets him or her probe into and discover content in a different way from the ordinary way of reading a book or watching a television program.

With content analysis, a researcher can compare content across many texts and analyze it with quantitative techniques (e.g., charts and tables). In addition, he or she can reveal aspects of the text's content that are difficult to see. For example, you might watch television commercials and feel that non-Whites rarely appear in commercials for expensive consumer goods (e.g., luxury cars, furs, jewellery, perfume). Content analysis can document—in objective, quantitative terms—whether your vague feelings based on unsystematic observation are true. It yields repeatable, precise results about the text.

Content analysis involves random sampling, precise measurement, and operational definitions for abstract constructs. **Coding** turns aspects of content that represent variables into numbers. After a content analysis researcher gathers the data, he or she analyzes them with statistics in the same way that an experimenter or survey researcher would.

coding: The process of converting raw information or data into another form for analysis. In *content analysis,* it is a means for determining how to convert symbolic meanings in *text* into another form, usually numbers (see *coding system*); in *quantitative data* analysis, it is a means for assigning numbers; and in *qualitative data* analysis, it is a series of steps for reading raw notes and assigning codes or conceptual terms (see *axial coding, open coding, selective coding*).

Topics Appropriate for Quantitative Content Analysis

Researchers have used content analysis to study many things: themes in popular songs and religious symbols in hymns, trends in the topics that newspapers cover and the ideological tone of newspaper editorials, sex-role stereotypes in textbooks or feature films, how often people of different races appear in television commercials and programs, answers to open-ended survey questions, enemy propaganda during wartime, the covers of popular magazines, personality characteristics from suicide notes, themes in advertising messages, gender differences in conversations, and so on.

Generalizations that researchers make on the basis of content analysis are limited to the cultural communication itself. Content analysis cannot determine the truthfulness of an assertion or evaluate the aesthetic qualities of literature. It reveals the content in text but cannot interpret the content's significance.

Content analysis is useful for three types of research problems. First, it is helpful for problems involving a large volume of text. A researcher can measure large amounts of text (e.g., years of newspaper articles) with sampling and multiple coders. Second, it is helpful when a topic must be studied "at a distance." For example, content analysis can be used to study historical documents, the writings of someone who has died, or broadcasts in a hostile foreign country. Finally, content analysis can reveal messages in a text that are difficult to see with casual observation. The creator of the text or those who read it may not be aware of all its themes, biases, or characteristics. For example, authors of preschool picture books may not consciously intend to portray children in traditional stereotyped sex roles, but a high degree of sex stereotyping has been revealed through content analysis.[2]

LO 4 Differentiate between manifest and latent coding.

Measurement and Coding

General Issues Careful measurement is crucial in content analysis because a researcher converts diffuse and murky symbolic communication into precise, objective, quantitative data. He or she carefully designs and documents procedures for coding to make replication possible. The researcher operationalizes constructs in content analysis with a coding system. A **coding system** is a set of instructions or rules on how to systematically observe and record content from text. A researcher tailors it to the specific type of text or communication medium being studied (e.g., television drama, novels, photos in magazine advertisements). The coding system also depends on the researcher's unit of analysis. For example, in a study by Dowler (2004) on crime reporting on Canadian and American newscasts, the author developed a coding system that included type of crime, region of crime, length of story, reporting of motive, expressions of fear, and presentations of outrage or sympathy.

coding system: A set of instructions or rules used in *content analysis* to explain how to systematically convert the symbolic content from *text* into *quantitative data.*

Units The unit of analysis can vary a great deal in content analysis. It can be a word, a phrase, a theme, a plot, a newspaper article, a character, and so on. In addition to units of analysis, researchers use other units in content analysis that may or may not be the same as units of analysis: recording units, context units, and enumeration units. There are few differences among them and they are easily confused, but each has a distinct role. In simple projects, all three are the same.

What Is Measured? Measurement in content analysis uses **structured observation**: systematic, careful observation based on written rules. The rules explain how to categorize and classify observations. As with other measurement, categories should be mutually exclusive and exhaustive. Written rules make replication possible and improve reliability. Although researchers begin with preliminary coding rules, they often conduct a pilot study and refine coding on the basis of it.

structured observation: A method of watching what is happening in a social setting that is highly organized and that follows systematic rules for observation and documentation.

Coding systems identify four characteristics of text content: frequency, direction, intensity, and space. A researcher measures from one to all four characteristics in a content analysis research project.

Frequency *Frequency* simply means counting whether or not something occurs and, if it occurs, how often. For example, how many elderly people appear on a television program within a given week? What percentage of all characters are they, or in what percentage of programs do they appear?

Direction *Direction* is noting the direction of messages in the content along some continuum (e.g., positive or negative, supporting or opposed). For example, a researcher devises a list of ways an elderly television character can act. Some are positive (e.g., friendly, wise, considerate) and some are negative (e.g., nasty, dull, selfish).

Intensity *Intensity* is the strength or power of a message in a direction. For example, the characteristic of forgetfulness can be minor (e.g., not remembering to take your keys when leaving home, taking time to recall the name of someone you have not seen in years) or major (e.g., not remembering your name, not recognizing your children).

Space A researcher can record the size of a text message or the amount of space or volume allocated to it. *Space* in written text is measured by counting words, sentences, paragraphs, or space on a page (e.g., square inches). For video or audio text, space can be measured by the amount of time allocated. For example, a TV character may be present for a few seconds or continuously in every scene of a two-hour program.

Coding, Validity, and Reliability

Manifest Coding Coding the visible, surface content in a text is called **manifest coding**. For example, a researcher counts the number of times a phrase or word (e.g., *red*) appears in written text, or whether a specific action (e.g., a kiss) appears in a photograph or video scene. The coding system lists terms or actions that are then located in text. A researcher can use a computer program to search for words or phrases in text and have a computer do the counting work. To do this, he or she learns about the computer program, develops a comprehensive list of relevant words or phrases, and puts the text into a form that computers can read.[3]

manifest coding: A type of *content analysis* coding in which a researcher first develops a list of specific words, phrases, or symbols and then finds them in a communication medium.

Manifest coding is highly reliable because the phrase or word either is or is not present. Unfortunately, manifest coding does not take the connotations of words or phrases into account. The same word can take on different meanings depending on the context. The possibility that there are multiple meanings of a word limits the measurement validity of manifest coding.

For example, you read a book with a *red* cover that is a real *red* herring. Unfortunately, its publisher drowned in *red* ink because the editor could not deal with the *red* tape that occurs when a book is *red* hot. The book has a story about a *red* fire truck that stops at *red* lights only after the leaves turn *red*. There is also a group of *Reds* who carry *red* flags to the little *red* schoolhouse. They are opposed by *red*-blooded *red*necks who eat *red* meat. The main character is a *red*-nosed matador who fights *red* foxes, not bulls, with his *red* cape. *Red*-lipped Little *Red* Riding Hood is also in the book. She develops *red* eyes and becomes *red*-faced after eating a lot of *red* peppers in the *red*-light district. She is given a *red* backside by her angry mother, a *red*head.

In the study of crime reporting in Canada and the United States, Dowler (2004) used manifest coding to measure type of crime, stage of crime, region of story, and length of story. These are all fairly objective dimensions from which a coding frame can be developed. A **coding frame** is a list of all possible values that your codes may take. The definitions of the values in your coding frame must be explicitly defined. For example, Dowler had four different possible codes for stage of crime: pre-arrest, arrest, court, or disposition. Therefore, for each of the 1042 crime stories that he examined, Dowler would have to code the stage of the crime. Similarly, with region of story, the researcher had two codes: local or national. He defined local stories as occurring in the local broadcast area (e.g., in Toronto, those stories that originated in the Greater Toronto Area), while those originating from outside of the market area were considered national. Again, each of the 1042 crime stories he examined would have to be coded accordingly.

coding frame: An exhaustive list of all possible values that codes may take in *content analysis*.

Latent Coding A researcher using **latent coding** looks for the underlying, implicit meaning in the content of a text. For example, a researcher reads an entire paragraph and decides whether it contains erotic themes or a romantic mood. The researcher's coding system has general rules to guide his or her interpretation of the text and for determining whether particular themes or moods are present.

latent coding: A type of *content analysis* coding in which a researcher identifies subjective meaning such as general themes or motifs in a communication medium.

Latent coding tends to be less reliable than manifest coding. It depends on a coder's knowledge of language and social meaning.[4] Training, practice, and written rules improve reliability, but still it is difficult to consistently identify themes, moods, and the like. Yet the validity of latent coding can exceed that of manifest coding because people communicate meaning in many implicit ways that depend on context, not just on specific words.

A researcher can use both manifest and latent coding. In the example of crime story reporting in the United States and Canada, Dowler (2004) used latent coding in addition to manifest coding. He used latent coding to assess the reporting of the crime motive, the emotive presentation of the newscast, and the police response to the crime. For example, the researcher had two codes for police response: proactive and nonproactive. The police response was considered proactive if the story contained content about

Box 10.3 Concepts in Action

The Print Media and Content Analysis in Canada

Musso and Wakefield (2009) analyzed Canadian newspaper articles to examine how the media presented the topic of cancer. The researchers chose the *Toronto Star*, the *Globe and Mail*, and the *National Post* as these are the most widely circulating newspapers in Canada.

The researchers used the database Factiva to search the keyword *cancer* in these three newspapers' articles published between January 2003 and December 2004. This yielded an extremely large data set, however, and the researchers decided to limit the pool of possible articles to those that mentioned cancer at least twice and were not obituaries or horoscopes. They then randomly chose six months in the two-year period they originally retrieved articles from and limited the analysis to all articles in these specific six months, yielding 464 articles.

The articles were coded according to the various predetermined criteria, including type of cancer, risk factors, and preventive solutions. They created various tallies that listed the frequency with which each article made mention of these factors and presented numerous summary tables of their numeric findings. Among their findings was that 40 percent of mentions related to breast cancer followed by lung cancer, although lung cancer deaths are more prevalent in Canadian society. They also found much discussion of diet and nutrition and lifestyle as risk factors, with much emphasis across articles given to "risk factors" in general. The authors point out that the emphasis on risk factors also suggested that the management of risk factors was the responsibility of individuals. In the Canadian print media, cancer prevention was generally discussed as though it was easily within the individual's control, with little consideration to the various economic and social factors that act as constraints in Canadian society.

"the police activity seeking the suspect, as verified through adjectives describing the work by police; information about a reward; a police chase; video footage showing an active search, SWAT team activity, or the police actively seeking the public's help" (Dowler, 2004, p. 582). Unlike manifest coding, latent coding requires much more subjective interpretation about the implied meaning of content. Quantitative approaches to content analysis usually focus mostly on manifest codes, while summative qualitative content analysis (discussed in Chapter 14) is a qualitative content analysis technique that gives more attention to latent coding. See Box 10.3 for another example of quantitative content analysis.

Intercoder Reliability Content analysis often involves coding information from a very large number of units. A research project might involve observing the content in dozens of books, hundreds of hours of television programming, or thousands of newspaper articles. In addition to coding the information personally, a researcher may hire assistants to help with the coding. He or she teaches coders the coding system and trains them to fill out a recording sheet. Coders should understand the variables, follow the coding system, and ask about ambiguities. A researcher records all decisions he or she makes about how to treat a new specific coding situation after coding begins so that he or she can be consistent.

A researcher who uses several coders must *always* check for consistency across coders. He or she does this by asking coders to code the same text independently and then checking for consistency across coders. The researcher measures *intercoder reliability* with a statistical coefficient that tells the degree of consistency among coders. The coefficient is *always* reported with the results of content analysis research.

There are several intercoder reliability measures that range from 0 to 1, with 1.0 signifying perfect agreement among coders. An interreliability coefficient of 0.80 or better is generally required, although 0.70 may be acceptable for exploratory research. When the coding process stretches over a considerable time period (e.g., more than three months), the researcher also checks reliability by having each coder independently code samples of text that were previously coded. He or she then checks to see whether the coding is stable or changing. For example, six hours of television episodes are coded in April and coded again in July without the coders' looking at their original coding decisions. Large deviations in coding necessitate retraining and coding the text a second time.

How to Conduct Content Analysis Research

Question Formulation Like other types of research, content analysis researchers always begin with a research question. When the question involves variables that are messages or symbols, content analysis may be appropriate. For example, you want to study how newspapers cover a political campaign. Your construct, "coverage," includes the amount of coverage, the prominence of the coverage, and whether the coverage favours one candidate over another. You could survey people about what they think of the newspaper coverage, but a better strategy is to examine the newspapers directly using content analysis.

Units of Analysis A researcher decides on the units of analysis (i.e., the amount of text that is assigned a code). For example, for a political campaign, each issue (or day) of a newspaper is the unit of analysis.

Sampling Researchers often use random sampling in content analysis. First, they define the population and the sampling element. For example, the population might be all words, all sentences, all paragraphs, or all articles in certain types of documents over a specified time period. Likewise, it could include each conversation, situation, scene, or episode of certain types of television programs over a specified time period. For example, we want to know how women and minorities are portrayed in Canadian weekly newsmagazines. Our unit of analysis is the article. Our population includes all articles published in three weekly newsmagazines from North America—*Time*, *Newsweek*, and *Maclean's*—between 1990 and 2010. We first verify that the three magazines were published in those years and define precisely what is meant by an "article." For instance, do film reviews count as articles? Is there a minimum size (two sentences) for an article? Is a multipart article counted as one or two articles?

Second, we examine the three magazines and find that the average issue of each contains 45 articles and that the magazines are published 52 weeks per year. With a 20-year time frame, our population contains over 140 000 articles (45 × 52 × 20 = 140 400). Our sampling frame is a list of all the articles. Next, we decide on the sample size and design. After looking at our budget and time, we decide to limit the sample size to 1400 articles. Thus, the sampling ratio is 1 percent. We also choose a sampling design. We avoid systematic sampling because magazine issues are published cyclically according to the calendar (e.g., an interval of every 52nd issue results in the same week each year). Because issues from each magazine are important, we use stratified sampling. We stratify by magazine, sampling 1400/3 = 467 articles from each. We want to ensure that articles represent each of the 20 years, so we also stratify by year. This results in about 23 articles per magazine per year.

Finally, we draw the random sample using a random-number table to select 23 numbers for the 23 sample articles for each magazine for each year. We develop a sampling frame worksheet to keep track of the sampling procedure. See Table 10.1 for a sampling frame worksheet in which 1398 sample articles are randomly selected from 140 401 articles.

Variables and Constructing Coding Categories In our example of newsmagazine, we are interested in the construct of an ethnic minority woman portrayed in a significant leadership role. We must define *significant leadership role* in operational terms and

Table 10.1 Excerpt from Sampling Frame Worksheet

Magazine	Issue	Article	Number	Article in Sample?*	Sampled Article ID
Time	January 1–7, 1990	pp. 2–3	000001	No	
Time	"	p. 4, bottom	000002	No	
Time	"	p. 4, top	000003	Yes—1	0001
Time	March 1–7, 2005	pp. 2–5	002101	Yes—10	0454
Time	"	p. 6, right column	002102	No	
Time	"	p. 6, left column	002103	No	
Time	"	p. 7	002104	No	
Time	December 24–31, 2005	pp. 4–5	002201	Yes—22	0467
Time	"	p. 5, bottom	002202	No	
Time	"	p. 5, top	002203	Yes—23	0468
Newsweek	January 1–7, 1990	pp. 1–2	010030	No	
Newsweek	"	p. 3	010031	Yes—1	0469
Maclean's	December 25–31, 2005	p. 62	140401	Yes—23	1389

*"Yes" means the number was chosen from a random-number table. The number after the dash is a count of the number of articles selected for a year.

express it as written rules for classifying people named in an article. For example, if an article discusses the achievements of someone who is now dead, does the dead person have a significant role? What is a significant role—a local Girl Scout leader or a corporate president?

We must also determine the race and sex of people named in the articles. What if the race and sex are not evident in the text or accompanying photographs? How do we decide on the person's race and sex?

Because we are interested in positive leadership roles, our measure indicates whether the role was positive or negative. We can do this with either latent or manifest coding. With manifest coding, we create a list of adjectives and phrases. If someone in a sampled article is referred to with one of the adjectives, then the direction is decided. For example, the terms *brilliant* and *top performer* are positive, whereas *drug kingpin* and *uninspired* are negative. For latent coding, we create rules to guide judgments. For example, we classify stories—about a diplomat resolving a difficult world crisis, a business executive unable to make a firm profitable, or a lawyer winning a case—into positive or negative terms. (Relevant questions for coding each article are in Box 10.4.)

Box 10.4 Making It Practical

Latent Coding Questions

The following questions relate to the magazine articles in the leadership role study.

1. *Characteristics of the article.* What is the magazine? What is the date of the article? How large is the article? What is its topic area? Where does it appear in the issue? Are photographs used?
2. *People in the article.* How many people are named in the article? Of these, how many are significant in the article? What is the race and sex of each person named?
3. *Leadership roles.* For each significant person in the article, which ones have leadership roles? What is the field of leadership or profession of the person?
4. *Positive or negative roles.* For each leadership or professional role, rate how positively or negatively it is shown. For example, 5 = highly positive, 4 = positive, 3 = neutral, 2 = negative, 1 = highly negative, 0 = ambiguous.

Box 10.5 Making It Practical

A Recording Sheet

Blank Example

Coder:_____

Minority/Majority Group Representation in Newsmagazines Project

ARTICLE #_____ MAGAZINE:_____ DATE:_____ SIZE:_____ (in column inches)

Total number of people named: _____ **Number of Photos: _____**

No. people with significant roles: _____ **Article Topic: ________**

Person_____:	Race:_____	Gender:_____	Leader?:_____	Field:_____	Rating:_____
Person_____:	Race:_____	Gender:_____	Leader?:_____	Field:_____	Rating:_____
Person_____:	Race:_____	Gender:_____	Leader?:_____	Field:_____	Rating:_____
Person_____:	Race:_____	Gender:_____	Leader?:_____	Field:_____	Rating:_____
Person_____:	Race:_____	Gender:_____	Leader?:_____	Field:_____	Rating:_____
Person_____:	Race:_____	Gender:_____	Leader?:_____	Field:_____	Rating:_____
Person_____:	Race:_____	Gender:_____	Leader?:_____	Field:_____	Rating:_____
Person_____:	Race:_____	Gender:_____	Leader?:_____	Field:_____	Rating:_____

Example of Completed Recording Sheet for One Article

Coder: Susan J.

Minority/Majority Group Representation in Newsmagazines Project

ARTICLE # 0454 MAGAZINE: Time DATE: March 1–7, 2005 SIZE: 14 col. in.

Total number of people named: 5 **Number of Photos: 0**

No. people with significant roles: 4 **Article Topic: Foreign Affairs**

Person 1:	Race: White	Gender: M	Leader?: Y	Field: Banking	Rating: 5
Person 2:	Race: White	Gender: M	Leader?: N	Field: Government	Rating: NA
Person 3:	Race: Black	Gender: F	Leader?: Y	Field: Minority Rights	Rating: 2
Person 4:	Race: White	Gender: F	Leader?: Y	Field: Government	Rating: 0
Person_____:	Race:_____	Gender:_____	Leader?:_____	Field: _____	Rating:_____
Person_____:	Race:_____	Gender:_____	Leader?:_____	Field: _____	Rating:_____
Person_____:	Race:_____	Gender:_____	Leader?:_____	Field: _____	Rating:_____
Person_____:	Race:_____	Gender:_____	Leader?:_____	Field: _____	Rating:_____

In addition to written rules for coding decisions, a content analysis researcher creates a **recording sheet** (also called a *coding form* or *tally sheet*) on which to record information (see Box 10.5). Each unit should have a separate recording sheet. The sheets do not have to be pieces of paper—they can be file cards or lines in a computer record or file. When a lot of information is recorded for each recording unit, more than one sheet of paper can be used. When planning a project, researchers calculate the work required. For example, during our pilot test, we find that it takes an average of 15 minutes to read and code an article. This

recording sheet: A page on which a researcher writes down what is coded in *content analysis.*

does not include sampling or locating magazine articles. With approximately 1400 articles, that is 350 hours of coding, not counting time to verify the accuracy of coding. Because 350 hours is about nine weeks of nonstop work at 40 hours a week, we should consider hiring assistants as coders.

Each recording sheet has a place to record the identification number of the unit and spaces for information about each variable. We also put identifying information about the research project on the sheet in case we misplace it or it looks similar to other sheets we have. Finally, if we use multiple coders, the sheet reminds the coder to check intercoder reliability and, if necessary, makes it possible to recode information for inaccurate coders. After completing all recording sheets and checking for accuracy, we can begin data analysis.

Inferences

The inferences a researcher can or cannot make on the basis of results are critical in content analysis. Content analysis describes what is in the text. It cannot reveal the intentions of those who created the text or the effects that messages in the text have on those who receive them. For example, content analysis shows that children's books contain sex stereotypes. That does not necessarily mean that children's beliefs or behaviours are influenced by the stereotypes; such an inference requires a separate research project on how children's perceptions develop.

LO 5 Explain how existing statistics and secondary analysis can be used as a nonreactive method.

EXISTING STATISTICS/DOCUMENTS AND SECONDARY ANALYSIS

Appropriate Topics

Document Research

Many types of information about the social world have been collected and are available to the researcher. Some information is in the form of statistical documents (e.g., books, reports) that contain numerical information. Other information is in the form of published compilations available in a library or on computerized records. In either case, the researcher can search through collections of information with a research question and variables in mind, and then reassemble the information in new ways to address the research question.

It is difficult to specify topics that are appropriate for existing statistics research because they are so varied. Any topic on which information has been collected and is publicly available can be studied. In fact, existing statistics projects may not fit neatly into a deductive model of research design. Rather, researchers creatively reorganize the existing information into the variables for a research question after first finding the data that are available.

Immigration

Existing statistics research is best for topics that involve information routinely collected by large bureaucratic organizations. Public or private organizations systematically gather many types of information. Such information is gathered for policy decisions or as a public service. It is rarely collected for purposes directly related to a specific research question. Thus, existing statistics research is appropriate when a researcher wants to test hypotheses involving variables that are also in official reports of social, economic, and political conditions. These include descriptions of organizations or the people in them. Often, such information is collected over long time periods. For example, existing statistics can be used by a researcher who wants to see whether unemployment and crime rates are associated in 150 cities across a 20-year period. See Box 10.6 for a discussion of the Canadian Census.

Hispanics Now Largest Minority

Box 10.6 **Focus**

The Census

Almost every country conducts a census, or a regular count of its population. For example, Australia has done so since 1881, Canada since 1871, and the United States since 1790. Most nations conduct a census every five or ten years. In addition to the number of people, census officials collect information on topics such as housing conditions, ethnicity, religious affiliation, education, and so forth.

The census is a major source of high-quality existing statistical data, but it can be controversial. In Canada, an attempt to count the number of same-sex couples living together evoked public debate about whether the government should document the changes in society. In Great Britain, the Muslim minority welcomed questions about religion in the 2001 census because they felt that they had been officially ignored. In the United States, the measurement of race and ethnicity was hotly debated, so in the 2000 census people could place themselves in multiple racial/ethnic categories.

In 2001, a grassroots email campaign in English-speaking countries suggested that if enough people entered "Jedi" (after the fictitious religious order portrayed in the popular *Star Wars* films) as their religion in the census, the official statisticians would have no choice but to record it as an official religion. The practical joke spread widely, with about 20 000 Canadians, 53 000 New Zealanders, 390 000 English and Welsh, and 70 000 Australians declaring their religion as Jedi. While no country declared "Jedi" as a new official religion, the Office for National Statistics in the United Kingdom stated that, even though information on religion may have been lost due to the joke, the campaign may have increased the participation rate of the census.[5]

Social Indicators

During the 1960s, some social scientists, dissatisfied with the information available to decision makers, spawned the "social indicators movement" to develop indicators of social well-being. Many hoped that information about social well-being could be combined with widely used indicators of economic performance (e.g., gross national product) to better inform government and other policy-making officials. Thus, researchers wanted to measure the quality of social life so that such information could influence public policy.[6]

Today, there are many books, articles, and reports on social indicators, and even a scholarly journal, *Social Indicators Research*, devoted to the creation and evaluation of social indicators. Statistics Canada produces a report, *Canadian Social Trends*, and the United Nations has many measures of social well-being in different nations.

A social indicator is any measure of social well-being used in policy. There are many specific indicators that are operationalizations of well-being. For example, social indicators have been developed for the following areas: population, family, housing, social security and welfare, health and nutrition, public safety, education and training, work, income, culture and leisure, social mobility, and public participation.

Young People are Not Leaving Home

A more specific example of a social indicator is the unemployment rate. It indicates the number of people who are unemployed in Canada (discussed later in this chapter). Social indicators can measure negative aspects of social life, such as the infant mortality rate (the death rate of infants during the first year of life) or alcoholism, or they can indicate positive aspects, such as job satisfaction or the percentage of housing units with indoor plumbing. Social indicators often involve implicit value judgments (e.g., which crimes are serious or what constitutes a good quality of life).

Locating Data

Locating Existing Statistics The main sources of existing statistics are government or international agencies and private sources. An enormous volume and variety of information exists. If you plan to conduct existing statistics research, it is wise to discuss your interests with an information professional—in this case, a reference librarian—who can point you in the direction of possible sources. There are also data libraries or data centres within the library systems of most major Canadian universities that employ specialized data librarians who can help you find the data or statistics that you are looking for.

Many existing documents are "free"—that is, publicly available at libraries—but the time and effort it takes to search for specific information can be substantial. Researchers who conduct existing statistics research spend many hours in libraries or on the internet. After the information is located, it is recorded on cards, graphs, or recording sheets for later analysis. Often, it is already available in a format for computers to read. For example, instead of recording voting data from books, a researcher could use a data library or data centre.

Strong Child Support Enforcement Gets Mixed Reviews

There are so many sources that only a small sample of what is available is discussed here. A valuable source of statistical information about Canada is the *Canada Year Book*, which has been published annually (with a few exceptions) since 1867. The *Canada Year Book* is available in all public and university libraries and can also be ordered online from Statistics Canada. It is a selected compilation of the many official reports and statistical tables produced by Canadian government agencies. It contains statistical information from hundreds of more detailed government reports. There are numerous reports and periodicals published by Statistics Canada.

StatsCan: Gender Pay Gap

Most governments publish similar statistical yearbooks. The United States publishes the *Statistical Abstract*, Australia's Bureau of Statistics produces *Year Book Australia*, New Zealand's Department of Statistics publishes the *New Zealand Official Yearbook*, and in the United Kingdom the Office for National Statistics publishes the *Annual Abstract of Statistics*.[7] Many nations publish books with historical statistics, as well.

Locating government statistical documents is an art in itself. Some publications exist solely to assist the researcher. For example, *Historical Statistics of Canada* is a helpful guide for historical Canadian statistics.[8] The United Nations and international agencies such as the World Bank have their own publications with statistical information for various countries (e.g., literacy rates, percentage of the labour force working in agriculture, birth rates)—for example, the *Demographic Yearbook* and *Statistical Yearbook*, both published by the United Nations, and *UNESCO Statistical Yearbook*.

In addition to government statistical documents, there are dozens of other publications. Many are produced for business purposes and can be obtained, but at a high cost. They include information on consumer spending, the location of high-income neighbourhoods, trends in the economy, and the like.[9] The internet is also a useful source for accessing many existing statistics (see Box 10.7).

A Meta-Analysis of School-Based Social Skills Interventions for Children with Autism Spectrum Disorders

Secondary Survey Data Secondary analysis is a special case of existing statistics; it is the reanalysis of previously collected survey or other data that were originally gathered by others. As opposed to primary research (e.g., experiments, surveys, and content analysis), the focus is on analyzing rather than collecting data. Secondary analysis is increasingly used by researchers. It is relatively inexpensive; it permits comparisons across groups, nations, or time; it facilitates replication; and it permits asking about issues not thought of by the original researchers.

Large-scale data collection is expensive and difficult. The cost and time required for a major national survey that uses rigorous techniques are prohibitive for most researchers. Fortunately, the organization, preservation, and dissemination of major survey data sets have improved. Today, there are archives of past surveys that are open to researchers.

The Inter-University Consortium for Political and Social Research (ICPSR) at the University of Michigan is the world's major archive of social science data. Several Canadian universities are members of this consortium. Over 17 000 survey research and

Box 10.7 Social Research and the Internet

Accessing Existing Statistics and Data Online

Many statistical agencies provide basic statistical information online. For example, the Statistics Canada website provides various summary statistics and tables on a wide range of topics. For example, at the time of writing, the Statistics Canada homepage reported that the population of Canada was 35 002 447, annual inflation was 0.5 percent, the unemployment rate was 7.0 percent, and the monthly GDP growth was –0.2 percent. A menu on the home page allows the user to browse for statistics by subject. Various topics that are of interest to social researchers are provided, such as "Aboriginal peoples," "crime and justice," "education, training, and learning," and "ethnic diversity and immigration." Clicking through the various menus can provide various tables and statistics on a wide range of topics. It is also possible to request "tailored" services from Statistics Canada if the statistic or table you require is more complex than the standard ones provided online. There is, however, often a charge for such services.

Other times, instead of existing statistics, you may want disaggregated data (the data before it is tabulated and presented as overall figures or rates). For example, you may be interested in the individual census records of individuals, or survey data (often called *microdata*) from another national survey. In the case of data held by Statistics Canada, this can be made through a request to the Research Data Centres Program (see Box 10.8) or through accessing "Public Use Micro Files," which are smaller samples of the larger datasets that are available to subscribing institutions, such as university and college libraries.

If you are interested in data from other countries, the statistical agencies there often provide similar services to those of Statistics Canada. In terms of comparing statistics from various countries, the World Bank website (www.worldbank.org) also carries both existing statistics and microdata from a wide variety of countries. The Organisation for Economic and Co-operation and Development (www.oecd.org) also carries a variety of existing statistics free of charge, although access to microdata requires a special subscription.

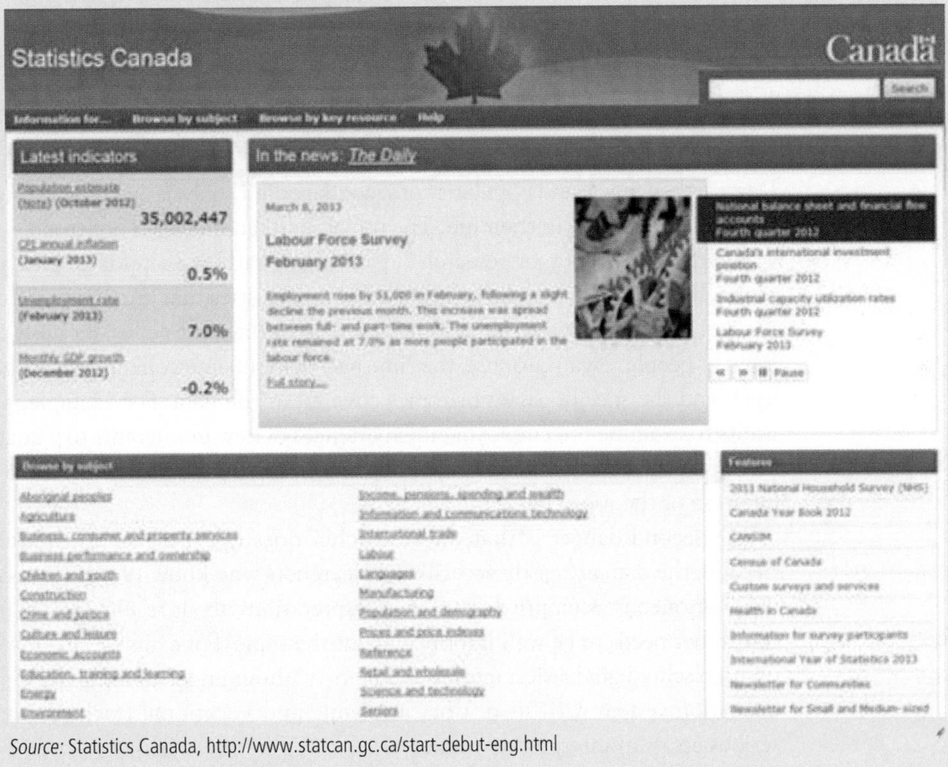

Source: Statistics Canada, http://www.statcan.gc.ca/start-debut-eng.html

related sets of information are stored at the centre in Michigan and made available to researchers at modest costs. Other centres hold survey data in the United States and other nations.[10] It is also possible to access some types of secondary data through data libraries or data centres at university libraries in Canada. As well, Statistics Canada has created Research Data Centres in several Canadian universities to serve the research community (see Box 10.8).

Box 10.8 **Focus**

Research Data Centres and the Data Liberation Initiative

In the 1980s, there was a noticeable increase in the number of Canadian researchers who were using data from other countries, such as the United States and Britain. Two of the major reasons for this shift away from using Canadian data were the problems of data cost and accessibility. Canadian data was costlier to use (to purchase from Statistics Canada for permission to use) and accessibility was very restricted (often requiring travel to Ottawa).

The Data Liberation Initiative (DLI) was created in the mid-1990s, comprising members of the academic community, the Social Sciences and Humanities Research Council, the Federation for the Humanities and Social Sciences, and members of Statistics Canada. The mandate of the DLI was to remove barriers to accessing and analyzing data. This lobby group made significant progress in improving data availability, although limitations on the amount of detail in the data (i.e., exact responses to survey questions) still existed.

In 1998, an evaluation by the Canadian Initiative on Social Statistics on the challenges that faced Canadian academic researchers revealed that there were three main challenges facing the Canadian research community. First, there was a shortage of skilled and trained researchers equipped to undertake data analysis. Second, access to data collected by Statistics Canada was very restricted due to confidentiality laws. Third, there was only limited communication between social researchers, policy-makers, and the wider community.[11] After these shortcomings were identified, several recommendations were made.

One recommendation was to create Research Data Centres, which would improve access to data. The Research Data Centres that are present at several Canadian universities are the product of a cooperative project between the universities and the Government of Canada. The purpose of these centres is to provide low-cost and convenient access to students and researchers who wish to do research on the detailed Statistics Canada microdata files. They are staffed by Statistics Canada employees and are operated under the provisions of the Statistics Act, discussed in Chapter 3. In order to use these centres, prospective users must have their projects approved by Statistics Canada and be sworn in as "deemed employees."

LO 5 Identify the advantages and disadvantages of secondary analysis.

Limitations

Despite the growth and popularity of secondary data analysis and existing statistics research, there are limitations in their use. The use of such techniques is not trouble-free just because a government agency or research organization gathered the data. One danger is that a researcher may use secondary data or existing statistics that are inappropriate for his or her research question. Before proceeding, a researcher needs to consider units in the data (e.g., types of people, organizations), the time and place of data collection, the sampling methods used, and the specific issues or topics covered in the data. For example, a researcher who wants to examine the employment experiences of new immigrants to Canada, but who uses secondary data that includes only rural areas in the prairie provinces, should reconsider the question or the use of data.

A second danger is that the researcher does not understand the substantive topic. Because the data are easily accessible, researchers who know very little about a topic could make erroneous assumptions or false interpretations about results. Before using any data, a researcher needs to be well informed about the topic. For example, if a researcher uses data on high school graduation rates in Germany without understanding the German secondary education system with its distinct academic and vocational tracks, he or she may make serious errors in interpreting results.

fallacy of misplaced concreteness: When a person uses too many digits in a quantitative measure in an attempt to create the impression that the data are accurate or the researcher is highly capable.

A third danger is that a researcher may quote statistics in great detail to give an impression of scientific rigour. This can lead to the **fallacy of misplaced concreteness**, which occurs when someone gives a false impression of precision by quoting statistics in greater detail than warranted and "overloading" the details. For example, existing statistics report that the population of Australia is 19 169 083, but it is better to say that it is a little over 19 million. One might calculate the percentage of divorced people as 15.65495 in a secondary data analysis of the 2005 General Social Survey, but it is better to report that about 15.7 percent of people are divorced.[12]

Units of Analysis and Variable Attributes A common problem in existing statistics is finding the appropriate units of analysis. Many statistics are published for aggregates, not the individual. For example, a table in a government document has information (e.g., unemployment rate, crime rate) for a province, but the unit of analysis for the research question is the individual (e.g., "Are unemployed people more likely to commit property crimes?"). The potential for committing the ecological fallacy is very real in this situation. It is less of a problem for secondary survey analysis because researchers can obtain raw information on each respondent from archives.

A related problem involves the categories of variable attributes used in existing documents or survey questions. This is not a problem if the initial data were gathered in many highly refined categories. The problem arises when the original data were collected in broad categories or ones that do not match the needs of a researcher. For example, a researcher is interested in people of Asian heritage. If the racial and ethnic heritage categories in a document are "White," "Black," and "Other," the researcher has a problem. The "Other" category includes people of Asian and other heritages. Sometimes information was collected in refined categories but is published only in broad categories. It takes special effort to discover whether more refined information was collected or is publicly available.

Validity Validity problems occur when the researcher's theoretical definition does not match that of the government agency or organization that collected the information. Official policies and procedures specify definitions for official statistics. For example, a researcher defines a *work injury* as including minor cuts, bruises, and sprains that occur on the job, but the official definition in government reports only includes injuries that require a visit to a physician or hospital. Many work injuries, as defined by the researcher, would not be in the official statistics. Another example occurs when a researcher defines people as *unemployed* if they would work if a good job were available, if they have to work part time when they want full-time work, and if they have given up looking for work. The official definition, however, includes only those who are now actively seeking work (full or part time) as unemployed. The official statistics exclude those who stopped looking, who work part time out of necessity, or who do not look because they believe no work is available. In both cases, the researcher's definition differs from that in the official statistics (see Box 10.9).

Another validity problem arises when official statistics are a surrogate or proxy for a construct in which a researcher is really interested. This is necessary because the researcher cannot collect original data. For example, the researcher wants to know how many people have been robbed, so he or she uses police statistics on robbery arrests as a proxy. But the measure is not entirely valid because many robberies are not reported to the police, and reported robberies do not always result in an arrest.

A third validity problem arises because the researcher lacks control over how information is collected. All information, even that in official government reports, is originally gathered by people in bureaucracies as part of their jobs. A researcher depends on them for collecting, organizing, reporting, and publishing data accurately. Systematic errors in collecting the initial information (e.g., census enumerators who avoid poor neighbourhoods and make up information, or people who put a false age on a driver's licence), errors in organizing and reporting information (e.g., a police department that is sloppy about filing crime reports and loses some), and errors in publishing information (e.g., a typographical error in a table) all reduce measurement validity. (See Box 10.10 for examples of validity using existing statistics.)

Reliability Problems with reliability can plague existing statistics research. Reliability problems develop when official definitions or the method of collecting information changes

Box 10.9 Focus

Official Unemployment Rates versus the Nonemployed

In most countries, including Canada, the official unemployment rate measures only the unemployed as a percentage of all working people. It would be 50 percent higher if two other categories of nonemployed people were added: involuntary part-time workers and discouraged workers. In some countries (e.g., Sweden and the United States), it would be nearly double if it included these people. This does not consider other nonworking people, transitional self-employed, or the underemployed. What a country measures is a theoretical and conceptual definition issue: What construct should an unemployment rate measure, and why measure it? In Canada, information for calculating the unemployment rate is gathered from the Labour Force Survey, which is a survey of a large sample of the Canadian population. The sample covers all Canadians aged 15 years or older residing in the 10 provinces and three territories. Excluded from the unemployment rate are those residing in the three territories, those living on Firth Nations reservations, members of the Armed Forces, and inmates in institutions. Provincial and territorial unemployment rates are available separately from Statistics Canada, however. By comparison, the target population of the equivalent American survey (the Current Population Survey) is defined as the noninstitutionalized population aged 16 years or older.

An economic policy or labour market perspective says the rate should measure those ready to enter the labour market immediately. It defines nonworking people as a supply of high-quality labour, an input for use in the economy available to employers. By contrast, a social policy or human resource perspective says the rate should measure those who are not currently working to their fullest potential. The rate should represent people who are not or cannot fully use their talents, skills, or time to the fullest. It defines nonworking people as a social problem of individuals unable to realize their capacity to be productive, contributing members of society.

Categories of Nonemployed/Fully Utilized People	
Unemployed people	People who meet three conditions: lack a paying job outside the home, are taking active measures to find work, can begin work immediately if it is offered.
Involuntary part-time workers	People with a job, but work irregularly or fewer hours than they are able and willing to.
Discouraged workers	People able to work and who actively sought it for some time, but being unable to find it, have given up looking.
Other nonworking people	Those not working because they are retired, on vacation, temporarily laid off, semi-disabled, homemakers, full-time students, or in the process of moving.
Transitional self-employed workers	Self-employed workers who are not working full time because they are just starting a business or are going through bankruptcy.
Underemployed people	Individuals with a temporary full-time job for which they are seriously overqualified. They seek a permanent job in which they can fully apply their skills and experience.

Source: Adapted from Counting the jobless: Measuring unemployment is not as simple as it sounds. The Economist, July 22, 1995, p. 74.

Study finds no advantage to prison privatization

over time. Official definitions of work injury, disability, unemployment, and the like change periodically. Even if a researcher learns of such changes, consistent measurement over time is impossible. For example, when police departments computerize their records, there is an apparent increase in crimes reported, not because crime increases but because of improved recordkeeping.

Data Analysis: Crime Study

Researchers often use official statistics for international comparisons, but national governments collect data differently and the quality of data collection varies. For example, in 1994 the official unemployment rate reported for the United States was 7 percent, Japan's was 2.9 percent, and France's was 12 percent. If the nations defined and gathered data the same way, including discouraged workers and involuntary part-time worker rates, the rates would have been 9.3 percent for the United States, 9.6 percent

Box 10.10 Focus

Crime Statistics over Time

Many social scientists are interested in examining crime rates over time, and in Canada official crime statistics are available from Statistics Canada. Crime statistics, much more so than other types of official statistics, have been criticized for their validity over time. Consider a graph depicting prostitution incidents in Canada from 1980 to 1997. You will undoubtedly notice a huge spike in the graph for the year corresponding to 1986. What has happened here? The introduction of Bill C-49, or the "communicating law," in 1985 made it an offence to solicit the services of a prostitute. The spike you see in the graph is the resulting increase in the number of "johns" being arrested for attempting to solicit prostitutes. Without information on this new law, however, the jump in prostitution incidents would be baffling.

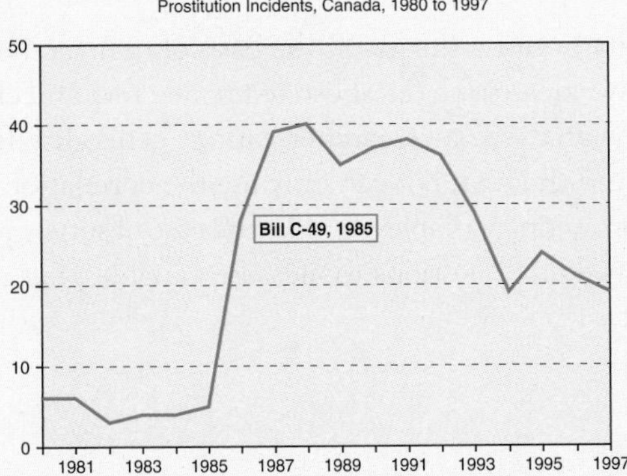

It isn't just changes in the definitions of crimes that can make crime statistics difficult to understand over time. Changes in society can also be reflected in crime statistics. Consider a graph depicting sexual assault incidents in Canada from 1983 to 1997. You will observe a gradual increase that peaks in 1992/1993, followed by a steady decline. Why is this so? The reason here isn't immediately obvious, and it should be emphasized that official statistics on sexual assault only reflect those that are reported to police. A large number of sexual assaults go unreported by victims. One reason for this increase could be that discussion of "date rape" (and other types of sexual assault perpetrated by persons known to the victim) became a topic brought into popular media discussion in the late 1980s and early 1990s. It could be that more assaults were reported because awareness of these types of crimes was heightened and victims were made to feel less ashamed and were strongly encouraged to report such incidents. Also during this time, Canadian researchers conducted the largest, most comprehensive study on violence against women in the world (Violence Against Women Survey of 1993), which is now replicated in many other countries.[13]

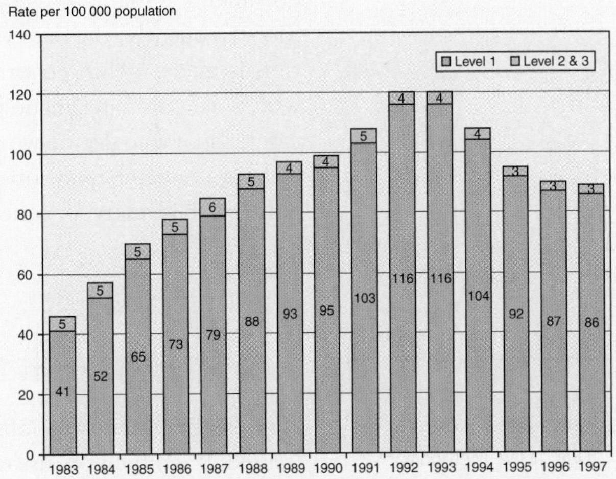

A final point that will be made about crime statistics is in reference to "moral panics." Often, there are issues that society is made acutely aware of—mostly through the media. As discussed in Chapter 1, media myths can make problems seem greater than they actually are. Consider the graph depicting drug incidents in Canada from 1980 to 1997. Notice the line representing cannabis arrests. The rate steadily decreased from 1980 to 1991, and then rose again slightly. It is unlikely that the decrease in incidents corresponds to cannabis *usage* (other studies have found that cannabis use has doubled over the past decade) but more likely reflects policing interests and targeting other illegal drugs, like methamphetamine or crack.

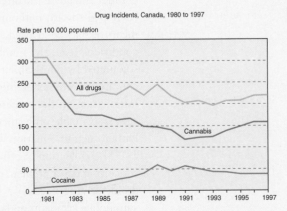

Drug Incidents, Canada, 1980 to 1997

Rate per 100 000 population

All drugs

Cannabis

Cocaine

350 300 250 200 150 100 50 0

1981 1983 1985 1987 1989 1991 1993 1995 1997

Source: Uniform Crime Reporting Survey, Canadian Centre for Justice Statistics, Statistics Canada, 1997. Reproduced and distributed on an "as is" basis with the permission of Statistics Canada.

for Japan, and 13.7 percent for France. To evaluate the quality of official government statistics, *The Economist* magazine asked a team of 20 leading statisticians to evaluate the statistics of 13 nations based on freedom from political interference, reliability, statistical methodology, and coverage of topics. The top five nations in order were Canada, Australia, Holland, France, and Sweden. The United States was tied for sixth with Britain and Germany.[14]

Missing Data One problem that plagues researchers who use existing statistics and documents is that of missing data. Sometimes the data were collected but have been lost. More frequently, the data were never collected. The decision to collect official information is made within government agencies. The decision to ask questions on a survey whose data are later made publicly available is made by a group of researchers. In both cases, those who decide what to collect may not collect what another researcher needs to address a research question. Government agencies start or stop collecting information for political, budgetary, or other reasons.

ISSUES OF INFERENCE AND THEORY TESTING

Inferences from Nonreactive Data

When Can We Use Qualitative Methods?

A researcher's ability to infer causality or test a theory on the basis of nonreactive data is limited. It is difficult to use unobtrusive measures to establish temporal order and eliminate alternative explanations. In content analysis, a researcher cannot generalize from the content to its effects on those who read the text, but can only use the correlation logic of survey research to show an association among variables. Unlike the ease of survey research, a researcher does not ask respondents direct questions to measure variables, but relies on the information available in the text.

ETHICAL CONCERNS

Ethical concerns are not at the forefront of most nonreactive research because the people being studied are not directly involved. The primary ethical concern is the privacy and confidentiality of using information gathered by someone else. Another ethical issue is that official statistics are social and political products. Implicit theories and value assumptions guide which information is collected and the categories used when gathering it. Measures or statistics that are defined as official and collected on a regular basis are objects of political conflict and guide the direction of policy. By defining one measure as official, public policy is shaped toward outcomes that would be different if an alternative but equally valid measure had been used. For example, the collection of information on many social conditions (e.g., the number of patients who died while in public mental hospitals) was stimulated by political activity during the Great Depression of the 1930s. Previously, the conditions were not defined as sufficiently important to warrant public attention. Likewise, information on the percentage of non-White students enrolled in U.S. schools at various ages is available only since 1953 and for specific non-White races only since the 1970s. Earlier, such information was not salient for public policy.

The collection of official statistics stimulates new attention to a problem, and public concern about a problem stimulates the collection of new official statistics. For example, drunk driving became a bigger issue once statistics were collected on the number of automobile accidents and on whether alcohol was a factor in an accident.

Political and social values influence decisions about which existing statistics to collect. Most official statistics are designed for top-down bureaucratic or administrative planning purposes. They may not conform to a researcher's purposes or the purposes of people opposed to bureaucratic decision makers. For example, a government agency measures the number of tonnes of steel produced, kilometres of highway paved, and average number of people in a household. Information on other conditions such as drinking-water quality, time needed to commute to work, stress related to a job, or number of children needing child care may not be collected because officials say it is unimportant. In many countries, the gross national product (GNP) is treated as a critical measure of societal progress. But GNP ignores noneconomic aspects of social life (e.g., time spent playing with one's children) and types of work (e.g., housework) that are not paid. The information available reflects the outcome of political debate and the values of officials who decide which statistics to collect.[15]

CHAPTER SUMMARY

Glossary Flashcards

In this chapter, you have learned about nonreactive research techniques, which are ways to measure or observe aspects of social life without affecting those who are being studied. In particular, quantitative content analysis and the analysis of existing statistics and secondary data were presented as two major nonreactive quantitative approaches.

Quantitative content analysis was presented as a systematic technique for analyzing the content of text. Text was defined as referring to the medium of communication that is being analyzed. Content analysis involves the measurement, coding, and analysis of text. There are various possibilities as to what can be measured: frequency, direction, intensity, and space of content. And researchers can focus on the manifest (obvious) or latent (implicit) content of the text. The researcher must make decisions about how to sample, his or her units of analysis, and the coding categories that he or she will construct. The researcher uses a recording sheet to tally all instances of observing codes.

Researchers also use existing statistics and secondary analysis to answer questions about the social world. A variety of data sources carry information on various features of social life, including social indicators. Many governmental agencies carry official statistics that researchers can use. Secondary survey data can also be analyzed by researchers and can be accessed in a variety of ways, including data libraries.

You should be aware of two potential problems in nonreactive research. First, the availability of existing information restricts the questions that a researcher can address. Second, the nonreactive variables often have weaker validity because they do not measure the construct of interest. Although existing statistics and secondary data analysis are low-cost research techniques, the researcher lacks control over and substantial knowledge of the data collection process. This introduces a potential source of errors about which researchers need to be especially vigilant and cautious.

Review Questions

1. What is the main difference between reactive and nonreactive research? What are two major advantages of nonreactive research?
2. What are the three types of research questions for which content analysis is useful?
3. What is *text* in the context of a content analysis? What are the four characteristics of text content?
4. Identify the main difference between manifest and latent coding, giving an example of each.
5. Define intercoder reliability.
6. What are coding categories? How are they constructed in a content analysis? What is a recording sheet?

7. Where can researchers locate existing statistics? What is meant by secondary survey data? Where can researchers locate secondary survey data?
8. Identify three disadvantages associated with the use of secondary analysis.

Exercises

Research Activities

1. Using EBSCO's ContentSelect, find a quantitative sociology article that uses content analysis. Identify the unit of analysis and the sampling technique used by the researcher. How did the researcher create codes (manifest, latent, or a combination of both)? How did coding take place—was it done by one coder or by many? If the latter, what was the intercoder reliability?
2. Go to the Statistics Canada website and see what is reported in today's *The Daily*. *The Daily* is, as suggested by the name, released daily by Statistics Canada to give up-to-date information on current measures of social and economic conditions. What is the source of the data for *The Daily* report you are reading?
3. Search the Statistics Canada website and find crime statistics that have been reported over a minimum time period of five years. Describe the trend you see in the data. Are there any social factors that might help explain the figures you observe?

Chapter 11

Analysis of Quantitative Data

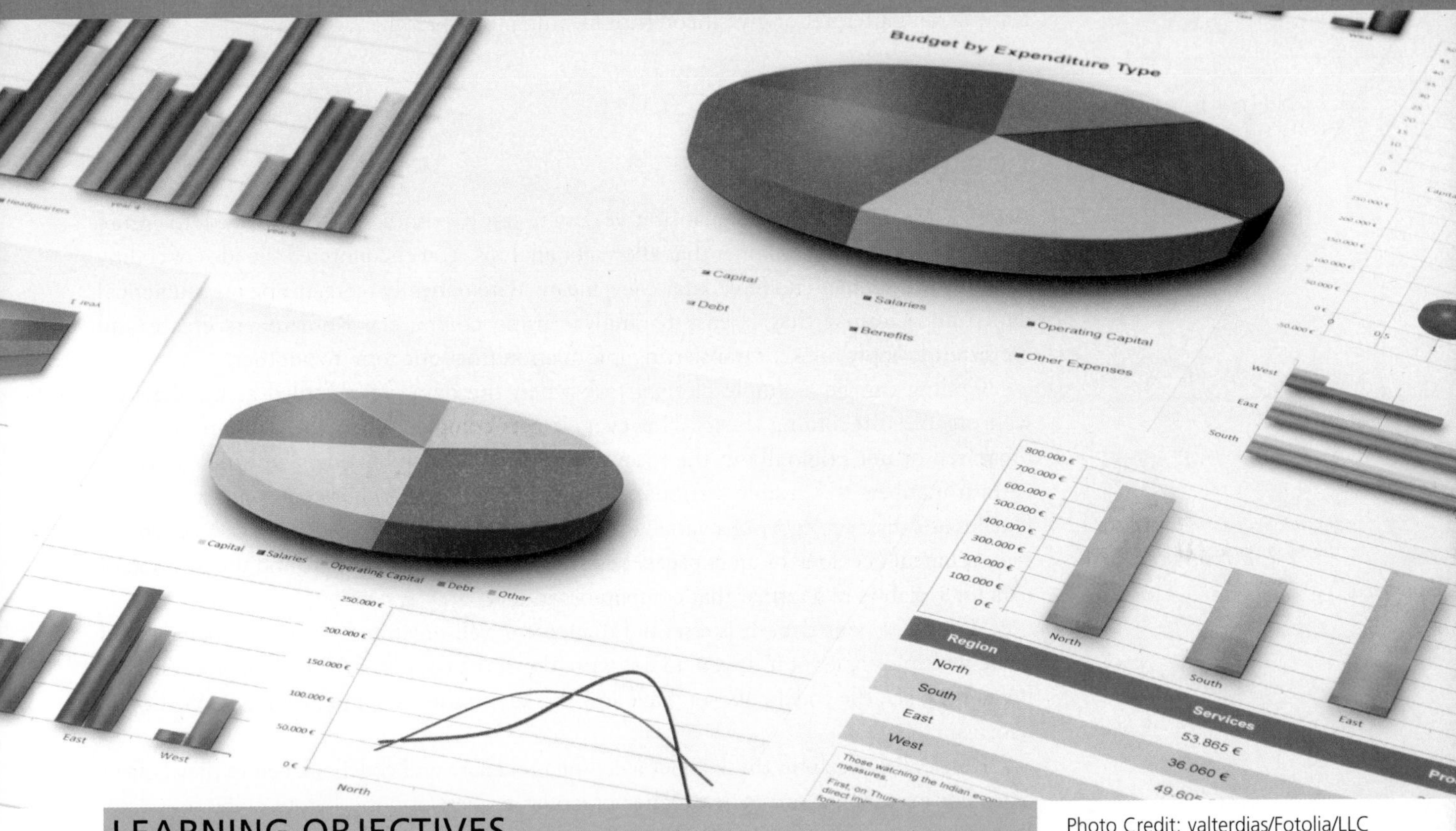

Photo Credit: valterdias/Fotolia/LLC

LEARNING OBJECTIVES

After reading this chapter, you will be able to

- LO 1 Explain what is meant by coding of data.
- LO 2 Define and give examples of univariate analysis.
- LO 3 Explain the techniques of bivariate analysis.
- LO 4 Describe the purpose of multivariate analysis.
- LO 5 Describe the relationship between inferential statistics, levels of significance, and Type I and Type II errors.

INTRODUCTION

One thing that social science students typically regard with fear is the analysis of quantitative data. If you read a research report or article based on quantitative data, you will probably find charts, graphs, and tables full of numbers. A researcher provides the charts, graphs, and tables to give you, the reader, a condensed picture of the data. The charts and tables allow you to see the evidence collected. When you collect your own quantitative data, you will want to use similar techniques to help you see what is inside the data. You will need to organize and manipulate the data so they can summarize characteristics of interest. In this chapter, you will learn the fundamentals of organizing and analyzing quantitative data. The analysis of quantitative data is a complex field of knowledge. This chapter covers only the basic statistical concepts and data-handling techniques necessary to understand social research.

Data collected using the techniques described in the past chapters are in the form of numbers. The numbers represent values of variables, which measure characteristics of subjects, respondents, or other cases. The numbers are in a raw form, on questionnaires, note pads, recording sheets, or paper or computer spreadsheets. Researchers reorganize them into a form suitable for computers, present charts or graphs to summarize their features, and interpret or give theoretical meaning to the results.

LO 1 Explain what is meant by coding of data.

DEALING WITH DATA

Coding Data

Before a researcher examines quantitative data to test hypotheses, he or she needs to ensure they are organized in a manner that allows for analysis. You encountered the idea of coding data in the last chapter. Here, data *coding* means systematically reorganizing raw numerical data into a format that is easy to analyze using computers. Researchers create and consistently apply rules for transferring information from one form to another.

codebook: A document that describes the procedure for *coding variables* and their location in a format for computers.

Coding can be a simple clerical task when the data are recorded as numbers on well-organized recording sheets. However, it gets complex when the data are not well organized or not originally in the form of numbers. Researchers develop rules to assign certain numbers to variable attributes. For example, a researcher codes males as 1 and females as 2. Each category of a variable and missing information needs a code. A **codebook** is a document (i.e., one or more pages) describing the coding procedure and the location of data for variables in a format that computers can use.

When you code data, it is essential to create a well-organized, detailed codebook and make multiple copies of it. If you do not write down the details of the coding procedure, or if you misplace the codebook, you have lost the key to the data and may have to code the data again.

Researchers begin to think about a coding procedure and codebook before they collect data. For example, a survey researcher precodes a questionnaire before collecting data. *Precoding* means placing the code categories (e.g., 1 for male, 2 for female) on the questionnaire.[1] Precoding also takes place in most large-scale telephone interviews, where data are automatically saved in a coded format. If a researcher does not precode, the first step after collecting data is to create a codebook. He or she also gives each case an identification number to keep track of the cases. Next, the researcher transfers the information from each questionnaire into spreadsheet format.

Entering Data

Computer programs designed for statistical analysis need the data in a grid or spreadsheet format. In the grid, each row represents a respondent, subject, or case. A column or a set of columns represents specific variables. It is possible to go from a column and row location (e.g., row 7, column 5) back to the original source of data (e.g., a questionnaire item on marital status for respondent 8).

For example, a researcher codes survey data for three respondents in a format for computers like that presented in Figure 11.1. People cannot easily read it, and without the codebook it is worthless. It condenses answers to 50 survey questions for three respondents into three lines or rows. The raw data for many research projects look like this, except that there may be over 1000 rows and the lines may be over 100 columns long. For example, a 15-minute telephone survey of 250 students produces a grid of data that is 250 rows (one row for each student) by as many columns as survey questions.

Excerpt from Survey Questionnaire

Respondent ID __________ Interviewer Name __________

Note the Respondent's Sex: ____ Male ____ Female

1. The first question is about the prime minister of Canada. Do you Strongly Agree, Agree, Disagree, Strongly Disagree, or Have No Opinion about the following statement:
   The prime minister of Canada is doing a great job.
   ____ Strongly Agree ____ Agree ____ Disagree ____ Strongly Disagree ____ No Opinion
2. How old are you? _______

Excerpt of Coded Data

ID	Interviewer	Sex	Primjob
1	2	1	2
2	2	1	4
3	4	2	3

Excerpt from Codebook

Column	*Variable Name*	*Description*
1–2	ID	Respondent identification number
3	Interviewer	Interviewer who collected the data: 1 = Susan 2 = Xia 3 = Juan 4 = Sophia 5 = Clarence
4	Sex	Interviewer report of respondent's sex 1 = Male, 2 = Female
5	Primjob	The prime minister of Canada is doing a great job. 1 = Strongly Agree 2 = Agree 3 = No Opinion 4 = Disagree 5 = Strongly Disagree Blank = missing information

Figure 11.1 Coded Data for Three Cases and Codebook

The illustrative data set and codebook in Figure 11.1 says that the first column, "ID," is the respondent's identification numbers. Thus, the example data are for the first (1), second (2), and third (3) respondents. The codebook says that the column "Interviewer" tells us that Xia interviewed Cases 1 and 2 and Sophia Case 3. The next column, "Sex," stores the variable "sex": Cases 1 and 2 are male, and Case 3 is female. The last column, "Primjob," records on a Likert scale our respondents' opinions about the prime minister.

There are four ways to get raw quantitative data into a computer:

code sheet: Paper with a printed grid on which a researcher records information so that it can be easily entered into a computer. It is an alternative to the *direct-entry method* and using optical-scan sheets.

1. ***Code sheet.*** Gather the information and then transfer it from the original source onto a grid format (code sheet). Next, type what is on the code sheet into a computer, line by line.

direct-entry method: A method of entering data into a computer by typing data without code or optical-scan sheets.

2. ***Direct-entry method**, including CATI.* As information is being collected, sit at a computer keyboard while listening to/observing the information and enter the information, or have a respondent/subject enter the information himself or herself (such as in an online survey). The computer must be preprogrammed to accept the information.
3. *Optical scan.* Gather the information, then enter it onto optical-scan sheets (or have a respondent/subject enter the information) by filling in the correct "dots." Next, use an optical scanner or reader to transfer the information into a computer.
4. *Bar code.* Gather the information and convert it into different widths of bars that are associated with specific numerical values. Then use a bar code reader to transfer the information into a computer.

Cleaning Data

Accuracy is extremely important when coding data. Errors made when coding or entering data into a computer threaten the validity of measures and cause misleading results. A researcher who has a perfect sample, perfect measures, and no errors in gathering data but who makes errors in the coding process or in entering data into a computer can ruin a whole research project.

possible code cleaning: Cleaning data using a computer in which the researcher looks for responses or answer categories that cannot have cases.

contingency cleaning: Cleaning data using a computer in which the researcher looks at the combination of categories for two *variables* for logically impossible cases.

After careful coding, the researcher verifies the accuracy of coding, or "cleans" the data. After data are entered into a computer, researchers verify coding in two ways. **Possible code cleaning** (or *wild code checking*) involves checking the categories of all variables for impossible codes. For example, respondent sex is coded 1 = Male, 2 = Female. Finding a 4 for a case in the field for the sex variable indicates a coding error. A second method, **contingency cleaning** (or *consistency checking*), involves cross-classifying two variables and looking for logically impossible combinations. For example, education is cross-classified by occupation. If a respondent is recorded as never having finished high school and also is recorded as being a legitimate medical doctor, the researcher checks for a coding error.

A researcher can modify data after they are in the computer. He or she may not use more refined categories than were used when collecting the original data, but may combine or group the information. For example, the researcher may group ratio-level income data into five ordinal categories (levels of measurement were discussed in Chapter 6). Also, he or she can combine information from several indicators to create a new variable or add the responses to several questionnaire items into an index score, such as socio-economic status.

LO 2 Define and give examples of univariate analysis.

RESULTS WITH ONE VARIABLE

Frequency Distributions

descriptive statistics: A general type of simple statistics used by researchers to describe basic patterns in the data.

univariate statistics: Statistical measures that deal with one *variable* only.

frequency distribution: A table that shows the distribution of cases into the categories of one *variable* (i.e., the number or percent of cases in each category).

The word *statistics* can mean a set of collected numbers (e.g., numbers telling how many people live in a city) as well as a branch of applied mathematics used to manipulate and summarize the features of numbers. Social researchers use both types of statistics. Here, we focus on the second type—ways to manipulate and summarize numbers that represent data from a research project.

Descriptive statistics describe numerical data. They can be categorized by the number of variables involved: univariate, bivariate, or multivariate (for one, two, and three or more variables). **Univariate statistics** describe one variable (*uni-* refers to one; *-variate* refers to variable). The easiest way to describe the numerical data of one variable is with a **frequency distribution**. It can be used with nominal-, ordinal-, interval-, or ratio-level data and takes many forms. For example, you have data for 400 respondents. You can summarize the information on the gender of respondents at a glance with a raw count or a percentage frequency distribution (see Figure 11.2). You can present the same information in graphic

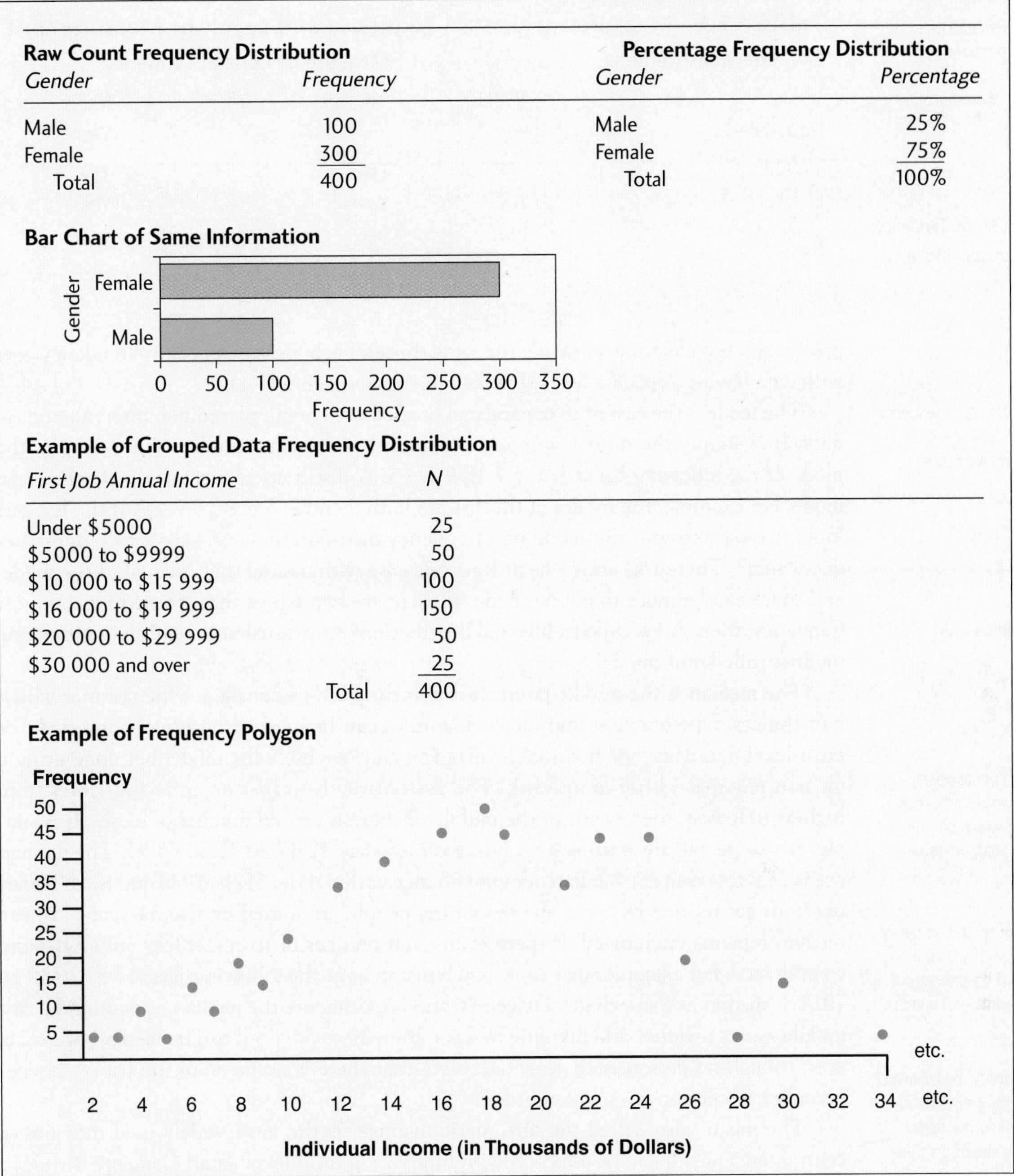

Raw Count Frequency Distribution

Gender	*Frequency*
Male	100
Female	300
Total	400

Percentage Frequency Distribution

Gender	*Percentage*
Male	25%
Female	75%
Total	100%

Example of Grouped Data Frequency Distribution

First Job Annual Income	*N*
Under $5000	25
$5000 to $9999	50
$10 000 to $15 999	100
$16 000 to $19 999	150
$20 000 to $29 999	50
$30 000 and over	25
Total	400

Figure 11.2 Examples of Univariate Statistics

form. Some common types of graphic representations are the **histogram, bar chart**, and **pie chart**. Histograms are a type of bar chart used to visually display the distribution of a continuous variable. Bar charts or graphs are used for discrete variables. They can have a vertical or horizontal orientation with a small space between the bars. The terminology is not exact, but histograms are usually upright bar graphs for interval or ratio data.

histogram: A type of *bar chart* used to visually display the distribution of a continuous *variable.*

bar chart: A display of *quantitative data* for one *variable* in the form of rectangles where longer rectangles indicate more cases in a variable category. Usually, it is used with discrete data and there is a small space between rectangles. Rectangles can have a horizontal or vertical orientation. Also called a bar graph.

Measures of Central Tendency

Researchers often want to summarize the information about one variable into a single number. They use three measures of central tendency, or measures of the centre of the frequency distribution: mean, median, and mode, which are often called *averages* (a less

pie chart: A display of numerical information on one *variable* that divides a circle into fractions by lines representing the proportion of cases in the variable's *attributes*.

Table 11.1 Measures of Central Tendency and Levels of Measurement

Level of Measurement	Measure of Central Tendency			
	Mode	*Median*	*Mean*	*Mode*
Nominal	Yes			Yes
Ordinal	Yes	Yes		Yes
Interval	Yes	Yes	Yes	Yes
Ratio	Yes	Yes	Yes	Yes

Measures of Central Tendency: Mean, Median, and Mode

precise and less clear way of saying the same thing). Each measure of central tendency goes with data having a specific level of measurement (see Table 11.1).

mode: A measure of central tendency for one *variable* that indicates the most frequent or common score.

The **mode** is the easiest to use and can be used with nominal, ordinal, interval, or ratio data. It is simply the most common or frequently occurring number. For example, the mode of the following list is 5: 6 5 7 10 9 5 3 5. A distribution can have more than one mode. For example, the modes of this list are both 5 and 7: 5 6 1 2 5 7 4 7. If the list gets long, it is easy to spot the mode in a frequency distribution—just look for the most frequent score. There will always be at least one case with a score that is equal to the mode, and there can be more than one mode. If there are two scores that are tied for the most frequency, then this is called a **bimodal** distribution. Any distribution with more than one mode is called **multimodal**.

bimodal: A distribution with two *modes*.

multimodal: A distribution with more than one *mode*.

median: A measure of central tendency for one *variable* indicating the point or score at which half the cases are higher and half are lower.

The **median** is the middle point. It is also the 50th percentile, or the point at which half the cases are above it and half below it. It can be used with ordinal-, interval-, or ratio-level data (but not nominal level). You can "eyeball" the mode, but computing a median requires a little more work. The easiest way is to first organize the scores from highest to lowest, then count to the middle. If there is an odd number of scores, it is simple. Seven people are waiting for a bus; their ages are 12 17 20 27 30 55 80. The median age is 27. Note that the median does not change easily. If the 55-year-old and the 80-year-old both get on one bus, and the remaining people are joined by two 31-year-olds, the median remains unchanged. If there is an even number of scores, things are a bit more complicated. For example, six people at a bus stop have the following ages: 17 20 26 30 50 70. The median is somewhere between 26 and 30. Compute the median by adding the two middle scores together and dividing by 2, or 26 + 30 = 56/2 = 28. The median age is 28, even though no person is 28 years old. Note that there is no mode in the list of six ages because each person has a different age.

mean: A measure of central tendency for one *variable* that indicates the arithmetic average (i.e., the sum of all scores divided by the total number of scores).

normal distribution: A "bell-shaped" frequency polygon for a distribution of cases, with a peak in the centre and identical curving slopes on either side of the centre. It is the distribution of many naturally occurring phenomena and is the basis for much statistical theory.

skewed distribution: A distribution of cases among the categories of a variable that is not *normal* (i.e., not a "bell shape"). Instead of an equal number of cases on both ends, more are at one of the extremes.

The **mean**, also called the arithmetic average, is the most widely used measure of central tendency. It can be used *only* with interval- or ratio-level data.[2] Compute the mean by adding up all scores, then divide by the number of scores. For example, the mean age in the previous example is 17 + 20 + 26 + 30 + 50 + 70 = 213; 213/6 = 35.5. No one in the list is 35.5 years old, and the mean does not equal the median.

The mean is strongly affected by changes in extreme values (very large or very small). For example, the 50- and 70-year-old leave and are replaced with two 31-year-olds. The distribution now looks like this: 17 20 26 30 31 31. The median is unchanged: 28. The mean is 17 + 20 + 26 + 30 + 31 + 31 = 155; 155/6 = 25.8. Thus, the mean dropped a great deal when a few extreme values were removed (see Box 11.1).

If the frequency distribution forms a "normal" or bell-shaped curve (**normal distribution**), the three measures of central tendency equal each other. If the distribution is a **skewed distribution** (i.e., more cases are in the upper or lower scores), then the three will not be equal. If most cases have lower scores with a few extreme high scores, the mean will be the highest, the median in the middle, and the mode the lowest. If most cases have higher scores with a few extreme low scores, the mean will be the lowest, the median in the

Box 11.1 Making It Practical

Why Not Always Use the Average?

You may wonder why there are three measures of central tendency when all we ever seem to hear about is "average" wages, "average" prices, or "average" grades. As mentioned earlier, one important weakness of the mean (or what we typically associate with being the average) is that it is sensitive to outliers. Extremely high values or extremely low values influence the average because all values are used in the calculation of the mean. Imagine a very simple example of student ages in an introductory research methods course where there are 10 students who are 19, 10 who are 20, and one mature student who is 65. The modes are 19 and 20, the median is 20, but the mean is 22. The mean is inflated because of the extraordinarily greater age of one student.

There are some everyday examples where the median is reported in favour of the mean, which you may not have noticed before. For example, house prices are often reported in terms of medians. It isn't difficult to imagine why. If you think of a typical neighbourhood, most houses are likely the same or very similar in price. But if there is one house in the neighbourhood that is 20 times the price of the average home, it can inflate the average house price in the neighbourhood. This is why house prices are usually reported in terms of the median house price.

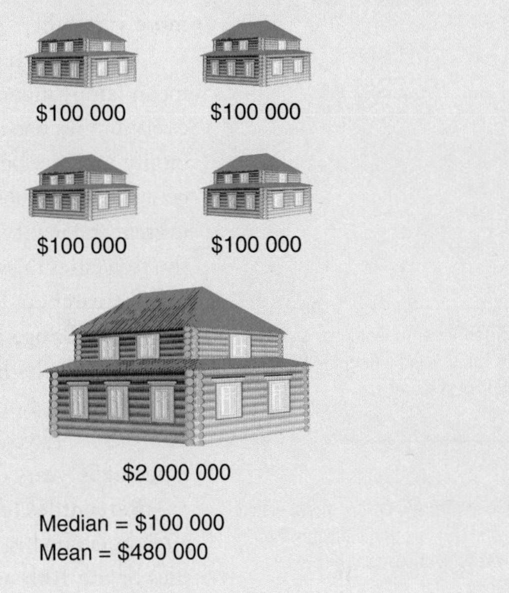

middle, and the mode the highest. In general, the median is best for skewed distributions, although the mean is used in most other statistics (see Figure 11.3).

Measures of Variation

Measures of central tendency are a one-number (univariate) summary of a distribution; however, they give only its *centre*. Another characteristic of a distribution is its spread,

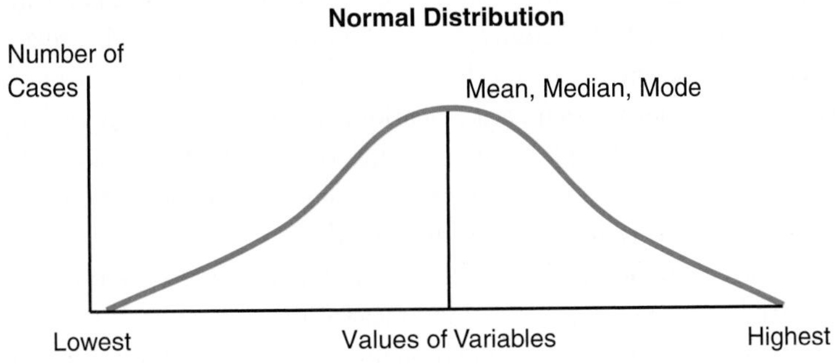

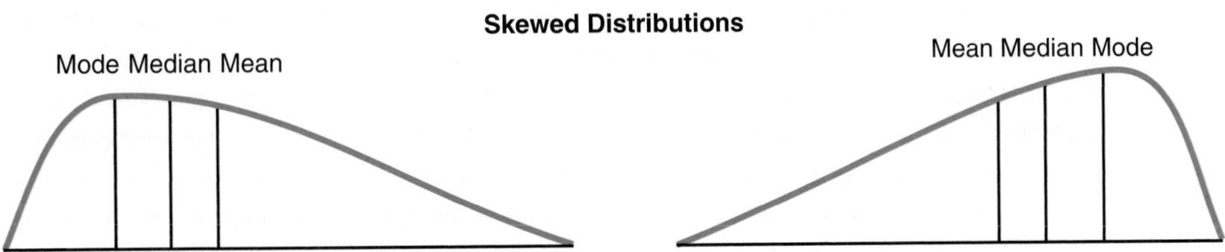

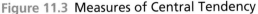

Figure 11.3 Measures of Central Tendency

dispersion, or variability around the centre. Two distributions can have identical measures of central tendency but differ in their spread about the centre. For example, seven people are at a bus stop in front of a bar. Their ages are 25 26 27 30 33 34 35. Both the median and the mean are 30. At a bus stop in front of an ice-cream store, seven people have the identical median and mean, but their ages are 5 10 20 30 40 50 55. The ages of the group in front of the ice-cream store are spread more from the centre, or the distribution has more variability.

Variability has important social implications. For example, in city X the median and mean family income is $35 600 per year, and it has zero variation. *Zero variation* means that every family has an income of exactly $35 600. City Y has the same median and mean family income, but 95 percent of its families have incomes of $12 000 per year and 5 percent have incomes of $300 000 per year. City X has perfect income equality, whereas there is great inequality in city Y. A researcher who does not know the variability of income in the two cities misses very important information.

range: A measure of dispersion for one *variable* indicating the highest and lowest scores.

Researchers can measure variation in three ways: range, percentile, and standard deviation. **Range** is the simplest. It consists of the largest and smallest scores. For example, the range for the bus stop in front of the bar is from 25 to 35, or 35 − 25 = 10 years. If the 35-year-old got onto a bus and was replaced by a 60-year-old, the range would change to 60 − 25 = 45 years. Range has limitations. For example, here are two groups of six with a range of 35 years: 30 30 30 30 30 65 and 20 45 46 48 50 55.

percentile: A measure of dispersion for one *variable* that indicates the percentage of cases at or below a score or point.

Percentiles tell the score at a specific place within the distribution. One percentile you already learned is the median, the 50th percentile. Sometimes the 25th and 75th percentiles or the 10th and 90th percentiles are used to describe a distribution. For example, the 25th percentile is the score at which 25 percent of the items in the distribution have either that score or a lower one. The computation of a percentile follows the same logic as the median. If you have 100 people and want to find the 25th percentile, you rank the scores and count up from the bottom until you reach number 25. If the total is not 100, you simply adjust the distribution to a percentage basis.

standard deviation: A measure of dispersion for one *variable* that indicates an average distance between the scores and the *mean.*

Standard deviation is the measure of dispersion most difficult to compute; it is also the most comprehensive and widely used. The range and percentile are for ordinal-, interval-, and ratio-level data, but the standard deviation requires an interval or ratio level of measurement. The term *standard deviation* sounds hyper-technical, but it doesn't have to be that way. Think about the words *standard* and *deviation*. What does *standard* mean? The average. What does *deviation* mean? Difference. So the standard deviation is the "average difference" between all scores and the mean. The bigger the standard deviation, the bigger the "average difference." The smaller the standard deviation, the more similar the values in a distribution are to one another. People rarely compute the standard deviation by hand for more than a handful of cases because computers and calculators can do it in seconds. The computation isn't difficult—it is more tedious than anything.

Look at the calculation of the standard deviation in Figure 11.4. If you add up the absolute difference between each score and the mean (i.e., subtract each score from the mean), you get zero. This is because the mean is equally distant from all scores. Also, note that the scores that differ the most from the mean have the largest effect on the sum of squares and on the standard deviation.

The standard deviation is used for comparison purposes. For example, the standard deviation for the years of schooling of parents of children in class A is 3.317 years; for class B it is 0.812; and for class C it is 6.239. The standard deviation tells a researcher that the parents of children in class B are very similar, whereas those for class C are very different. In fact, in class B the schooling of an "average" parent is less than a year above or below the mean for all parents, so the parents are very homogeneous. In class C, however, the "average" parent is more than six years above or below the mean, so the parents are very heterogeneous.

Steps in Computing the Standard Deviation

1. Compute the mean.
2. Subtract the mean from each score.
3. Square the resulting difference for each score.
4. Total up the squared differences to get the sum of squares.
5. Divide the sum of squares by the number of cases to get the variance.
6. Take the square root of the variance, which is the standard deviation.

Example of Computing the Standard Deviation

[8 respondents, variable = years of schooling]

Score	*Score – Mean*	*Squared (Score – Mean)*
15	15 – 12.5 = 2.5	6.25
12	12 – 12.5 = –0.5	0.25
12	12 – 12.5 = –0.5	0.25
10	10 – 12.5 = –2.5	6.25
16	16 – 12.5 = 3.5	12.25
18	18 – 12.5 = 5.5	30.25
8	8 – 12.5 = 4.5	20.25
9	9 – 12.5 = –3.5	12.25

Mean = 15 + 12 + 12 + 10 + 16 + 18 + 8 + 9 = 100, 100/8 = 12.5
Sum of squares = 6.25 + .25 + .25 + 6.25 + 12.25 + 30.25 + 20.25 + 12.25 = 88
Variance = Sum of squares/Number of cases-1 = 88/7 = 12.571
Standard deviation = Square root of variance = $\sqrt{12.571}$ = 3.546 years.
Here is the standard deviation in the form of a formula with symbols:

Symbols:
X = SCORE of case — Σ = Sigma (Greek letter) for sum, add together
$\bar{X}$ = MEAN — N = Number of cases

Formula

$$\text{Standard deviation} = \sqrt{\frac{\Sigma(X-\bar{X})^2}{N-1}}$$

Figure 11.4 The Standard Deviation

Another useful comparison of the standard deviation is average grades in classes. You may be taking a research methods course in a large postsecondary institution that has several sections. If you have exams, you may hear the instructor say that the "average" (i.e., mean) was 65 percent. Without information about the standard deviation, however, you don't have a complete picture as to how much dispersion there was, particularly amongst various sections. If the average was the same in two sections, but the standard deviation in Class 1 was 5 and in Class 2 it was 15, that would tell you that the test scores in Class 1 were much more similar to one another than in the other class. In Class 1, most students scored fairly close to the mean grade, but in the other class scores were much more widely distributed. Figure 11.5 displays this example by overlaying two histograms, demonstrating that in Class 1 the scores are more tightly bunched around the mean, while in Class 2 they are much more widely dispersed.

The standard deviation and the mean are used to create *z*-scores. **Z-scores** let a researcher compare two or more distributions or groups. The *z*-score, also called a *standardized score*, expresses points or scores on a frequency distribution in terms of a number of standard deviations from the mean. Scores are in terms of their relative position within a distribution, not as absolute values.

z-score: A way to locate a score in a distribution of scores by determining the number of *standard deviations* it is above or below the *mean* or arithmetic average.

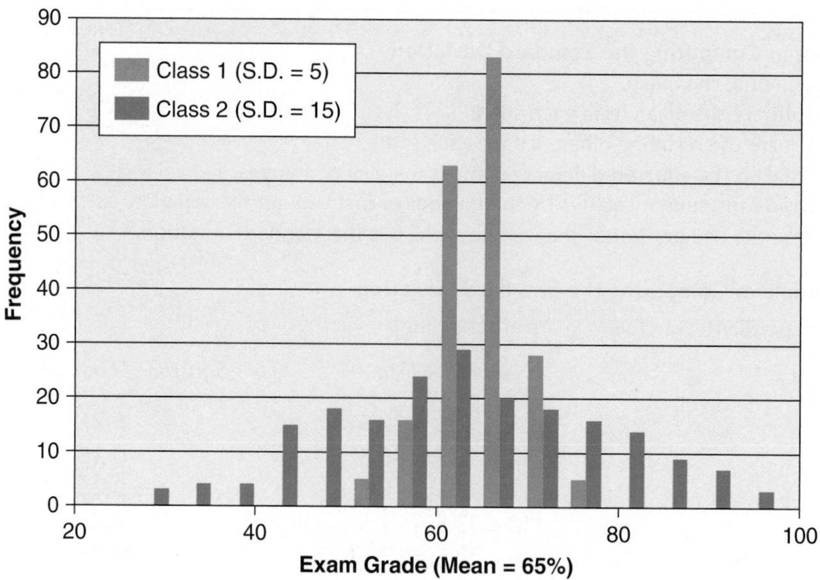

Figure 11.5 Two Classes with an Average Exam Score of 65 Percent, but Very Different Standard Deviations

For example, Katy, a sales manager in firm A, earns \$50 000 per year, whereas Mike in firm B earns \$38 000 per year. Despite the absolute income differences between them, the managers are paid equally relative to others in the same firm. Katy is paid more than two-thirds of other employees in her firm, and Mike is also paid more than two-thirds of the employees in his firm.

Z-scores are easy to calculate from the mean and standard deviation (see Box 11.2). For example, an employer interviews students from Cartier University and Hudson University. She learns that the universities are similar and that both grade on a 4.0 scale. Yet the mean grade point average at Cartier University is 2.62 with a standard deviation of 0.50, whereas

Box 11.2 Making It Practical

Calculating *z*-Scores

The formula for the *z*-score is
z-score = (Score − Mean)/Standard Deviation,
or in symbols:

$$z = \frac{X = \bar{X}}{\delta}$$

where: X = score, $\bar{X}\ \delta$ = mean, δ = standard deviation.

However, you might find it useful to use a simple conceptual diagram that does the same thing and that shows what *z*-scores really do. Consider data on the ages of schoolchildren with a mean of 7 years and a standard deviation of 2 years. How do you compute the *z*-score of five-year-old Miguel, or what if you know that Yashohda's *z*-score is a +2 and you need to know her age in years? First, draw a chart from 3 to +3 with zero in the middle. Put the mean value at zero because a *z*-score of zero is the mean, and *z*-scores measure distance above or below it. Stop at 3 because virtually all cases fall within three standard deviations of the mean in most situations. The chart looks like this:

−3 −2 −1 0 +1 +2 +3

Now label the values of the mean and add or subtract standard deviations from it. One standard deviation above the mean (+1) when the mean is 7 and standard deviation is 2 years is just 7 + 2, or 9 years. For a 2 *z*-score, you put 3 years. This is because it is 2 standard deviations of 2 years each (or 4 years), lower than the mean of 7. Your diagram now looks like this:

1 3 5 7 9 11 13 Age in years

−3 −2 −1 0 +1 +2 +3

It is easy to see that Miguel, who is five years old, has a *z*-score of 1, whereas Yashohda's *z*-score of +2 corresponds to 11 years old. You can read from *z*-score to age, or age to *z*-score. For fractions, such as a *z*-score of 1.5, you just apply the same fraction to age to get 4 years. Likewise, an age of 12 is a *z*-score of +2.5.

the mean grade point average at Hudson University is 3.24 with a standard deviation of 0.40. The employer suspects that grades at Hudson University are inflated. Suzette from Cartier University has a grade point average of 3.62, and Jorge from Hudson University has a grade point average of 3.64. Both students took the same courses. The employer wants to adjust the grades for the grading practices of the two universities (i.e., create standardized scores). She calculates *z*-scores by subtracting each student's score from the mean, then dividing by the standard deviation. For example, Suzette's *z*-score is 3.62 − 2.62 = 1.00/0.50 = 2, whereas Jorge's *z*-score is 3.64 − 3.24 = 0.40/0.40 = 1. Thus, the employer learns that Suzette is two standard deviations above the mean in her university whereas Jorge is only one standard deviation above the mean for his university. Although Suzette's absolute grade point average is lower than Jorge's, relative to the students in each of their universities Suzette's grades are much higher than Jorge's.

RESULTS WITH TWO VARIABLES

LO 3 Explain the techniques of bivariate analysis.

A Bivariate Relationship

Univariate statistics describe a single variable in isolation. **Bivariate statistics** are much more valuable. They let a researcher consider two variables together and describe the relationship between them. Even simple hypotheses require two variables. Bivariate statistical analysis shows a *relationship* between variables—that is, things that appear together.

bivariate statistics: Statistical measures that involve two *variables* only.

Statistical relationships are based on two ideas: correlation and independence. **Correlation** means that things go together or are associated. To be correlated means to vary together; cases with certain values on one variable are likely to have certain values on the other. For example, people with higher values on the income variable are likely to have higher values on the life expectancy variable. Likewise, those with lower incomes have lower life expectancy. This is usually stated in a shorthand way by saying that income and life expectancy are related to each other, or correlated. We could also say that knowing one's income tells us one's probable life expectancy, or that life expectancy depends on income.

correlation: The idea that two *variables* vary together, such that knowing the values in one variable provides information about values found in another variable.

Independence is the opposite of correlation. It means there is no association or relationship between variables. If two variables are independent, cases with certain values on one variable do not have any particular value on the other variable. For example, Rita wants to know whether number of siblings is related to life expectancy. If the variables are independent, then people with many brothers and sisters have the same life expectancy as those who are only children. In other words, knowing how many brothers or sisters someone has tells Rita nothing about the person's life expectancy.

independence: The absence of a statistical relationship between two *variables* (i.e., when knowing the values on one variable provides no information about the values that will be found on another variable). There is no *association* between them.

Most researchers state hypotheses in terms of a causal relationship or expected correlation; if they use the null hypothesis, the hypothesis is that there is independence. It is used in formal hypothesis testing and is frequently found in inferential statistics (to be discussed later in this chapter).

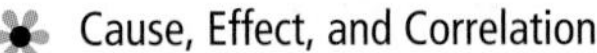

Three techniques help researchers decide whether a relationship exists between two variables: (1) a scattergram, or a graph or plot of the relationship; (2) cross-tabulation, or a percentaged table; and (3) measures of association between two variables expressed as a single number (e.g., correlation coefficient).

Seeing the Relationship: The Scattergram

What Is a Scattergram (or Scatterplot)? A **scattergram** is a graph on which a researcher plots each case or observation, where each axis represents the value of one variable. It is used for variables measured at the interval or ratio level, rarely for ordinal variables, and never if either variable is nominal. Usually the independent variable (symbolized by the letter X) goes on the horizontal axis and the dependent variable (symbolized by Y)

scattergram: A diagram to display the statistical relationship between two *variables* based on plotting each case's values for both of the variables.

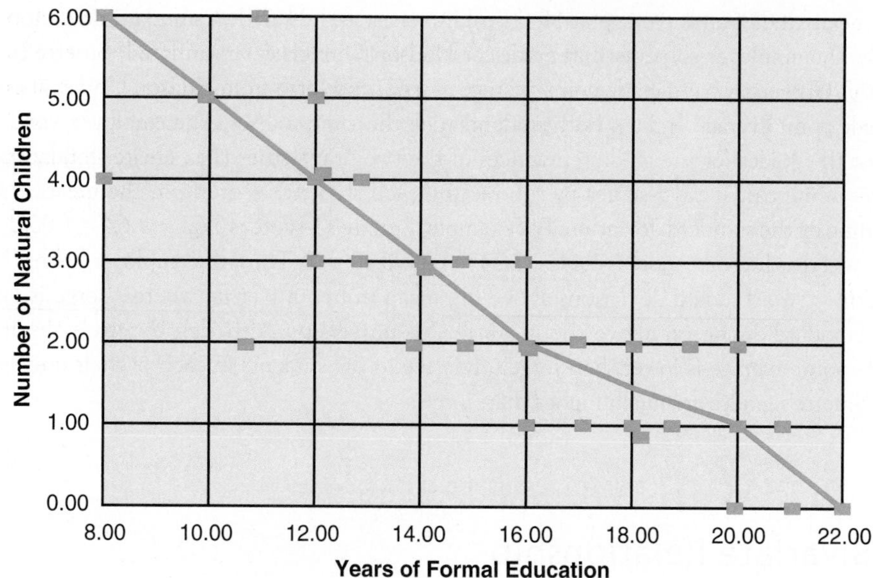

Figure 11.6 Example of a Scattergram: Years of Education by Number of Natural Children for 33 Women

goes on the vertical axis. The lowest value for each should be the lower left corner and the highest value should be at the top or to the right.

How to Construct a Scattergram Begin with the range of the two variables. Draw an axis with the values of each variable marked and write numbers on each axis (graph paper is helpful). Next, label each axis with the variable name and put a title at the top.

You are now ready for the data. For each case, find the value of each variable and mark the graph at a place corresponding to the two values. For example, a researcher makes a scattergram of years of schooling by number of children. He or she looks at the first case to see years of schooling (e.g., 12) and at the number of children (e.g., 3). Then he or she goes to the place on the graph where 12 for the "schooling" variable and 3 for the "number of children" variable intersect and puts a dot for the case.

The scattergram in Figure 11.6 is a plot of data for 33 women. It shows a *negative relationship* between the years of education the woman completed and the number of children she gave birth to.

What Can You Learn from the Scattergram? A researcher can see three aspects of a bivariate relationship in a scattergram: form, direction, and precision.

Form Relationships can take three forms: independent, linear, and curvilinear. *Independence*, or no relationship, is the easiest to see. It looks like a random scatter with no pattern, or a straight line that is exactly parallel to the horizontal or vertical axis. A **linear relationship** means that a straight line can be visualized in the middle of a maze of cases running from one corner to another. A **curvilinear relationship** means that the centre of a maze of cases would form a U curve, right side up or upside down, or an S curve.

linear relationship: An *association* between two *variables* that is positive or negative across the attributes or levels of the variables. When plotted in a *scattergram*, the basic pattern of the association forms a straight line, not a curve or other pattern.

curvilinear relationship: A relationship between two *variables* such that as the values of one variable increase, the values of the second show a changing pattern (e.g., first decrease then increase then decrease). It is not a *linear relationship.*

Direction Linear relationships can have a positive or negative direction. The plot of a *positive* relationship looks like a diagonal line from the lower left to the upper right. Higher values on X tend to go with higher values on Y, and vice versa. The income and life expectancy example described a positive linear relationship.

A *negative* relationship looks like a line from the upper left to the lower right. It means that higher values on one variable go with lower values on the other. For example, people with more education are less likely to have been arrested. If we look at a scattergram of data on a group of males where years of schooling (X axis) are plotted by number of arrests (Y axis) we see that most cases (or men) with many arrests are in the lower right, because most of them completed few years of school. Most cases with few arrests are in the upper left because most have had more schooling. The imaginary line for the relationship can have a shallow or a steep slope. More advanced statistics provide precise numerical measures of the line's slope.

Precision Bivariate relationships differ in their degree of precision. **Precision** is the amount of spread in the points on the graph. A high level of precision occurs when the points hug the line that summarizes the relationship. A low level occurs when the points are widely spread around the line. Researchers can "eyeball" a highly precise relationship. They can also use advanced statistics to measure the precision of a relationship in a way that is analogous to the standard deviation for univariate statistics.

precision: The amount of spread in the points on the graph. A high level of precision occurs when the points hug the line that summarizes the relationship. A low level occurs when the points are widely spread around the line.

Bivariate Tables

What Is a Bivariate Table? The bivariate contingency table is widely used. It presents the same information as a scattergram in a table format. The data can be measured at any level of measurement, although interval and ratio data must be grouped if there are many different values. The table is based on **cross-tabulation**; that is, the cases are organized in the table on the basis of two variables at the same time.

A **contingency table** is formed by cross-tabulating two or more variables. It is contingent because the cases in each category of a variable get distributed into each category of a second (or additional) variable. The table distributes cases into the categories of multiple variables at the same time and shows how the cases, by category of one variable, are "contingent upon" the categories of other variables.

Figure 11.7 is a raw count or frequency table. Its cells contain a count of the cases. It is easy to make, but interpreting a raw count table is difficult because the rows or columns

cross-tabulation: Placing data for two *variables* in a *contingency table* to show the number or percentage of cases at the intersection of categories of the two variables.

contingency table: A table that shows the *cross-tabulation* of two or more *variables*. It usually shows *bivariate quantitative data* for variables in the form of percentages across rows or down columns for the categories of one variable.

Raw Count Table (a)

	Age Group (b)				
Attitude (b)	*Under 30*	*30–45*	*46–60*	*61 and Older*	**Total (c)**
Agree	20	10	4	3	37
No opinion	3 (d)	10	10	2	25
Disagree	3	5	21	10	39
Total (c)	26	25	35	15	101

Missing cases (f) = 8. (e)

The Parts of a Table

(a) Give each table a *title*, which names variables and provides background information.
(b) Label the row and column variable and give a name to each of the variable categories.
(c) Include the totals of the columns and rows. These are called the *marginals*. They equal the univariate frequency distribution for the variable.
(d) Each number or place that corresponds to the intersection of a category for each variable is a *cell of a table*.
(e) The numbers with the labelled variable categories and the totals are called the *body of a table*.
(f) If there is missing information (cases in which a respondent refused to answer, ended interview, said "don't know," etc.), report the number of missing cases near the table to account for all original cases.

Figure 11.7 Age Group by Attitude about Changing the Drinking Age, Raw Count Table

Table 11.2 Age Group by Attitude about Changing the Drinking Age, Percentaged Tables

Column-Percentaged Table			**Age Group**		
Attitude	*Under 30*	*30–45*	*46–60*	*61 and Older*	**Total**
Agree	76.9%	40.0%	11.4%	20.0%	36.6%
No opinion	11.5	40.0	28.6	13.3	24.8
Disagree	11.5	20.0	60.0	66.7	38.6
	___	___	___	___	___
Total	99.9	100.0	100.0	100.0	100.0
(N)	(26)*	(25)*	(35)*	(15)*	(101)*
Missing cases = 8					

Row-Percentaged Table			**Age Group**		
Attitude	*Under 30*	*30–45*	*46–60*	*61 and Older*	**Total**
Agree	54.1%	27%	10.8%	8.1%	100%
No opinion	12.0	40.0	40.0	8.0	100.0
Disagree	7.7	12.8	53.8	25.6	99.9
	___	___	___	___	___
Total	25.7	24.8	34.7	14.9	100.1
Missing cases = 8					

*For percentaged tables, provide the number of cases, or *N*, on which percentages are computed in parentheses near the total of 100%. This makes it possible to go back and forth from a percentaged table to a raw count table.

can have different totals, and what is of real interest is the relative size of cells compared to others.

Researchers convert raw count tables into percentaged tables to see bivariate relationships. There are three ways to percentage a table: by row, by column, and for the total. The first two are often used and show relationships.

Is it best to percentage by row or column? Either can be appropriate. Let's first review the mechanics of percentaging a table. When calculating column percentages, compute the percentage each cell is of the column total. This includes the total column or marginal for the column variable. For example, the first column total is 26 (there are 26 people under age 30), and the first cell of that column is 20 (there are 20 people under age 30 who agree). The percentage is 20/26 = 0.769 or 76.9 percent. Or, for the first number in the marginal, 37/101 = 0.366 = 36.6 percent (see Table 11.2). Except for rounding, the total should equal 100 percent.

marginals: The totals in a *contingency table,* outside the body of a table.

Computing row percentages is similar. Compute the percentage of each cell as a percentage of the row total. For example, using the same cell with 20 in it, we now want to know what percentage it is of the row total of 37, or 20/37 = 0.541 = 54.1 percent. Percentaging by row or column gives different percentages for a cell unless the **marginals** are the same.

The row and column percentages let a researcher address different questions. The row percentage table answers this question: Among those who hold an attitude, what percentage come from each age group? It says of respondents who agree, 54.1 percent are in the under-30 age group. The column percentage table addresses this question: Among those in each age group, what percentage hold different attitudes? It says that among those who are under 30, 76.9 percent agree. From the row percentages, a researcher learns that a little over half of those who agree are under 30 years old, whereas from column percentages the researcher learns that among the under-30 people, over three quarters agree. One way of percentaging tells about people who have specific attitudes; the other tells about people in specific age groups.

Reading a Percentaged Table Once you understand how a table is made, reading it and figuring out what it says are much easier. To read a table, first look at the title, the variable labels, and any background information. Next, look at the direction in which percentages have been computed—in rows or columns. Note that the percentaged tables in Table 11.2 have the same title. This is because the same variables are used. It would have helped to note how the data were percentaged in the title, but this is rarely done. Sometimes researchers present abbreviated tables and omit the 100 percent total or the marginals, which adds to the confusion. It is best to include all the parts of a table and to have clear labels.

Researchers read percentaged tables to make comparisons. Comparisons are made in the opposite direction from that in which percentages are computed. A rule of thumb is to compare across rows if the table is percentaged down (i.e., by column) and to compare up and down in columns if the table is percentaged across (i.e., by row).

For example, in row-percentaged Table 11.2, compare columns or age groups. Most of those who agree are in the youngest group, with the proportion declining as age increases. Most no-opinion people are in the middle-age groups, whereas those who disagree are older, especially in the 46–60 group. When reading column-percentaged Table 11.2, compare across rows. For example, a majority of the youngest group agree, and they are the only group in which most people agree. Only 11.5 percent disagree, compared to a majority in the two oldest groups.

It takes practice to see a relationship in a percentaged table. If there is no relationship in a table, the cell percentages look approximately equal across rows or columns. A linear relationship looks like larger percentages in the diagonal cells. If there is a curvilinear relationship, the largest percentages form a pattern across cells. For example, the largest cells might be the upper right, the bottom middle, and the upper left. It is easiest to see a relationship in a moderate-sized table (9 to 16 cells) where most cells have some cases (at least five cases are recommended) and the relationship is strong and precise.

Principles of reading a scattergram can help you see a relationship in a percentaged table. Imagine a scattergram that has been divided into 12 equal-sized sections. The cases in each section correspond to the number of cases in the cells of a table that is superimposed onto the scattergram. The table is a condensed form of the scattergram. The bivariate relationship line in a scattergram corresponds to the diagonal cells in a percentaged table. Thus, a simple way to see strong relationships is to circle the largest percentage in each row (for row-percentaged tables) or column (for column-percentaged tables) and see if a line appears.

The circle-the-largest-cell rule works—with one important caveat. The categories in the percentages table *must* be ordinal or interval and in the same order as in a scattergram. In scattergrams the lowest variable categories begin at the bottom left. If the categories in a table are not ordered the same way, the rule does not work.

For example, Table 11.3a looks like a positive relationship and Table 11.3b like a negative relationship. Both use the same data and are percentaged by row. The actual relationship is negative. Look closely—Table 11.3b has age categories ordered as in a scattergram. When in doubt, return to the basic difference between positive and negative relationships. A positive relationship means that as one variable increases, so does the other. A negative relationship means that as one variable increases, the other decreases (or vice versa).

Bivariate Tables without Percentages Researchers condense information in another kind of bivariate table with a measure of central tendency (usually the mean) instead of percentages. It is used when one variable is nominal or ordinal and another is

Box 11.4 Making It Practical

The Assumption of Linearity

All statistics have a set of rules under which they perform optimally. This is known as the assumptions. One of the assumptions of many statistical tests, including Pearson's correlation, is that the relationship between the two variables under investigation is linear. This means that the relationship can be drawn in a straight line. This, however, is a huge assumption.

There are many relationships in the social world that are *not linear,* and these require alternative statistical analytic procedures (which are beyond the scope of this book but are covered in introductory statistics courses).

Age is an independent variable that often has nonlinear relationships with other characteristics of interest to social scientists. One of these characteristics is income. In the figure, you can see that income steadily rises as age increases up to around 55, where it levels out and then steadily decreases after retirement. This is a well-known curvilinear relationship. We could not measure this association accurately using rho—the rho reported here would only be 0.51, although we can see that the association is quite clear.

Rho cannot measure curvilinearity, and therefore using it on a relationship such as the one illustrated would be inappropriate and inaccurate as it would misrepresent the relationship between your variables of interest.

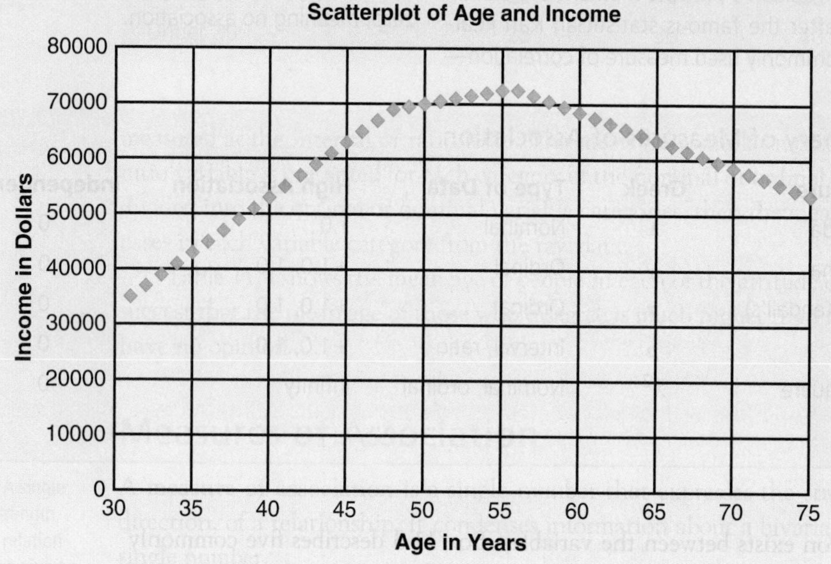

A researcher controls for alternative explanations in multivariate (more than two variables) analysis by introducing a third variable (or sometimes even more). For example, a bivariate table shows that taller teenagers like sports more than shorter ones do. But the bivariate relationship between height and attitude toward sports may be spurious because teenage males are taller than females, and males tend to like sports more than females. To test whether the relationship is actually due to sex, a researcher must *control for* gender; in other words, effects of sex are statistically *removed.* Once this is done, a researcher can see whether the bivariate relationship between height and attitude toward sports remains.

A researcher controls for a third variable by seeing whether the bivariate relationship persists within categories of the control variable. For example, a researcher controls for sex, and the relationship between height and sports attitude persists. This means that tall males and tall females both like sports more than short males and short females do. In other words, the control variable has no effect. When this is so, the bivariate relationship is not spurious.

If the bivariate relationship weakens or disappears after the control variable is considered, it means that tall males are no more likely than short males to like sports, and tall females are no more likely to like sports than short females. It indicates that the initial bivariate relationship is spurious and suggests that the third variable, sex, and not height, is the true cause of differences in attitudes toward sports.

Statistical control is a key idea in advanced statistical techniques. A measure of association like the correlation coefficient only suggests a relationship. Until a researcher considers control variables, the bivariate relationship could be spurious. Researchers are cautious in interpreting bivariate relationships until they have considered control variables.

The Elaboration Model of Percentaged Tables

Constructing Trivariate Tables In order to meet all the conditions needed for causality, researchers want to "control for" or see whether an alternative explanation explains away a causal relationship. If an alternative explanation explains a relationship, then the bivariate relationship is spurious. Alternative explanations are operationalized as third variables, which are called *control variables* because they control for alternative explanations.

One way to take such third variables into consideration and see whether they influence the bivariate relationship is to statistically introduce control variables using trivariate or three-variable tables. Trivariate tables differ slightly from bivariate tables; they consist of multiple bivariate tables.

A trivariate table has a bivariate table of the independent and dependent variable for each category of the control variable. These new tables are called **partials**. The number of partials depends on the number of categories in the control variable. Partial tables look like bivariate tables, but they use a subset of the cases. Only cases with a specific value on the control variable are in the partial. Thus, it is possible to break apart a bivariate table to form partials, or combine the partials to restore the initial bivariate table.

partials: In *contingency tables* for three variables, tables that show the *association* between the *independent* and *dependent variables* for each category of a *control variable.*

Trivariate tables have three limitations. First, they are difficult to interpret if a control variable has numerous categories. Second, control variables can be at any level of measurement, but interval or ratio control variables must be grouped (i.e., converted to an ordinal level), and how cases are grouped can affect the interpretation of effects. Finally, the total number of cases is a limiting factor because the cases are divided among cells in partials. The number of cells in the partials equals the number of cells in the bivariate relationship multiplied by the number of categories in the control variable. For example, a control variable has three categories, and a bivariate table has 12 cells, so the partials have $3 \times 12 = 36$ cells. An average of five cases per cell is recommended, so the researcher will need $5 \times 36 = 180$ cases at minimum.

For three variables, three bivariate tables are logically possible. If we consider the previous example of drinking attitudes and age, we can add the additional variable of gender. The different variable combinations are then (1) gender by attitude, (2) age group by attitude, and (3) gender by age group. The partials are set up on the basis of the initial bivariate relationship. The independent variable in each is "age group" and the dependent variable is "attitude." "Gender" is the control variable. Thus, the trivariate table would consist of a pair of partials, each showing the age/attitude relationship for a given gender.

LINEAR REGRESSION ANALYSIS

Linear or multiple regression is a statistical technique whose calculation is beyond the level of this book. Although it is quickly computed by the appropriate statistics software, a background in statistics is needed to prevent making errors in its calculation and interpretation. It requires interval- or ratio-level data. It is discussed here for two reasons. First, it controls for many alternative explanations and variables simultaneously (it is rarely possible to use more than one control variable at a time using percentaged tables). Second, it is widely used in social science, and you are likely to encounter it when reading research reports or articles.

Linear or multiple regression results tell the reader two things. First, the results have a measure called *R*-squared (R^2), which tells how well a set of variables explains a dependent variable. *Explain* means reduced errors when predicting the dependent variable scores on the basis of information about the independent variables. A good model with several independent variables might account for, or explain, a large percentage of variation in a dependent variable. For example, an R^2 of 0.50 means that knowing the independent and control variables improves the accuracy of predicting the dependent variable by 50 percent, or half as many errors are made as would be made without knowing about the variables.

Second, the regression results measure the direction and size of the effect of each variable on a dependent variable. The effect is measured precisely and given a numerical value. For example, a researcher can see how five independent or control variables simultaneously affect a dependent variable, with all variables controlling for the effects of one another. This is especially valuable for testing theories that state that multiple independent variables cause one dependent variable.

The effect on the dependent variable is measured by a standardized regression coefficient, or the Greek letter beta (β). It is similar to a correlation coefficient. In fact, the beta coefficient for two variables equals the *r* correlation coefficient.

Researchers use the beta regression coefficient to determine whether control variables have an effect. For example, the bivariate correlation between *X* and *Y* is 0.75. Next, the researcher statistically considers four control variables. If the beta remains at 0.75, then the four control variables have no effect. However, if the beta for *X* and *Y* gets smaller (e.g., drops to 0.20), it indicates that the control variables have an effect.

Consider an example of regression analysis with age, income, education, region, and religious attendance as independent variables. The dependent variable is a score on a political ideology index. The multiple regression results show that income and religious attendance have large effects, education and region minor effects, and age virtually no effect. All the independent variables together have a 38 percent accuracy in predicting a person's political ideology (see Table 11.5). The example suggests that high income, frequent religious attendance, and a rural residence are positively associated with conservative opinions, whereas having more education is associated with liberal opinions. The impact of income is more than twice the size of the impact of living in a rural region.

So far we have been examining descriptive statistics (see Table 11.6); next, we look at a different type: inferential statistics.

Table 11.5 Example of Multiple Regression Results

Dependent Variable Is Political Ideology Index (High Score Means Very Liberal)

Independent Variable	**Standardized Regression Coefficients (β)**
Region = rural	2.19
Age	0.01
Income	2.44
Years of education	0.23
Religious attendance	2.39
$R^2 = 0.38$	

Table 11.6 Summary of Major Types of Descriptive Statistics

Type of Technique	Statistical Technique	Purpose
Univariate	Frequency distribution, measure of central tendency, standard deviation, *z*-score	Describe one variable.
Bivariate	Correlation, percentage table, chi-square	Describe a relationship or the association between two variables.
Multivariate		See how several independent variables have an effect on a dependent variable.

INFERENTIAL STATISTICS

LO 5 Describe the relationship between inferential statistics, levels of significance, and Type I and Type II errors.

The Purpose of Inferential Statistics

Researchers often want to do more than describe; they want to test hypotheses, know whether sample results hold true in a population, and decide whether differences in results (e.g., between the mean scores of two groups) are big enough to indicate that a relationship really exists. Inferential statistics use probability theory to test hypotheses formally, permit inferences from a sample to a population, and test whether descriptive results are likely to be due to random factors or to a real relationship.

This section explains the basic ideas of inferential statistics, but it does not deal with them in any detail. This area is more complex than descriptive statistics and requires a background in statistics.

Inferential statistics rely on principles from probability sampling, where a researcher uses a random process (e.g., a random-number table) to select cases from the entire population. Some of these principles were introduced in Chapter 7. Inferential statistics are a precise means of talking about how confident a researcher can be when inferring from the results in a sample to the population. They are called *inferential* statistics because they allow us to make inferences about causal relationships in the population using sample data.

You have already encountered inferential statistics if you have read or heard about "statistical significance" or results "significant at the 0.05 level." Researchers use them to conduct various statistical tests (e.g., a *t*-test or an *F*-test). Statistical significance is also used in formal hypothesis testing, which is a precise way to decide whether to accept or to reject a null hypothesis.[3]

Statistical Significance

statistical significance: A way to discuss the likelihood that a finding or statistical relationship in a *sample* is due to random factors rather than due to the existence of an actual relationship in the entire *population.*

Statistical significance means that results are not likely to be due to chance factors. It indicates the probability of finding a relationship in the sample when there is none in the population. Because probability samples involve a random process, it is always possible that sample results will differ from a population parameter. A researcher wants to estimate the odds that sample results are due to a true population parameter or to chance factors of random sampling. Statistical significance uses probability theory and specific statistical tests to tell a researcher whether the results (e.g., an association, a difference between two means, a regression coefficient) are produced by random error in random sampling.

Statistical significance only tells what is likely; it cannot prove anything with absolute certainty. It states that particular outcomes are more or less probable. Statistical significance is *not* the same as practical, substantive, or theoretical significance. Results can be statistically significant but theoretically meaningless or trivial. For example, two variables can have a statistically significant association because of coincidence, with no logical connection between them (e.g., length of fingernails and ability to speak French).

Levels of Significance

level of statistical significance: A set of numbers researchers use as a simple way to measure the degree to which a statistical relationship results from random factors rather than the existence of a true relationship among *variables*.

Researchers usually express statistical significance in terms of levels (e.g., a test is statistically significant at a specific level) rather than giving the specific probability. The **level of statistical significance** (usually 0.05, 0.01, or 0.001) is a way of talking about the likelihood that results are due to chance factors—that is, that a relationship appears in the sample when there is none in the population. If a researcher says that results are significant at the 0.05 level, this means the following:

- Results like these are due to chance factors only 5 in 100 times.
- There is a 95 percent chance that the sample results are not due to chance factors alone, but reflect the population accurately.
- The odds of such results based on chance alone are 0.05, or 5 percent.
- One can be 95 percent confident that the results are due to a real relationship in the population, not chance factors.

These all say the same thing in different ways. This may sound like the discussion of sampling distributions and the central limit theorem in Chapter 7, which is not an accident. Both are based on probability theory, which researchers use to link sample data to a population. Probability theory lets us predict what happens in the long run over many events when a random process is used. In other words, it allows precise prediction over many situations in the long run, but not for a specific situation. Since we have one sample and we want to infer to the population, probability theory helps us estimate the odds that our particular sample represents the population. We cannot know for certain unless we have the whole population, but probability theory lets us state our confidence—how likely it is that the sample shows one thing while something else is true in the population. For example, a sample shows that male and female university students differ in how many hours they study. Is the result due to an unusual sample and there is really no difference in the population, or does it reflect a true difference between the sexes in the population?

Type I and Type II Errors

The logic of statistical significance is based on stating whether chance factors produce results. You may ask, "Why use the 0.05 level?" It means a 5 percent chance that randomness could cause the results. Why not use a more certain standard—for example, a 1 in 1000 probability of random chance? This gives a smaller chance that randomness versus a true relationship caused the results.

There are two answers. The simple answer is that the scientific community has informally agreed to use 0.05 as a rule of thumb for most purposes. Being 95 percent confident of results is the accepted standard for explaining the social world.

Type I error: The logical error of falsely rejecting the *null hypothesis*.

Type II error: The logical error of falsely accepting the *null hypothesis*.

A second answer involves a tradeoff between making two types of logical errors. A **Type I error** occurs when the researcher says that a relationship exists when in fact none exists. It means falsely rejecting a null hypothesis. A **Type II error** occurs when a researcher says that a relationship does not exist, but in reality it does. It means falsely accepting a null hypothesis (see Table 11.7). Of course, researchers want to avoid both kinds of errors. They want to say that there is a relationship in the data only when it does exist and that there is no relationship only when there really is none. However, they face a dilemma: As the odds of making one type of error decline, the odds of making the opposite error increase.

Table 11.7 Type I and Type II Errors

What the Researcher Says	True Situation in the World	
	No Relationship	*Causal Relationship*
No relationship	No error	Type II error
Causal relationship	Type I error	No error

The idea of Type I and Type II errors may seem difficult at first, but the same logical dilemma appears in many other settings. For example, a judge can err by deciding that an accused person is guilty when in fact he or she is innocent. Or the judge can err by deciding that a person is innocent when in fact he or she is guilty. The judge does not want to make either error—a judge does not want to jail the innocent or to free the guilty. The judge must render a judgment based on limited information and balance the two types of errors. Likewise, a physician has to decide whether to prescribe a new medication for a patient. The physician can err by thinking that the medication will be effective and has no side effects when, in fact, it has a serious side effect, such as causing blindness. Or the physician can err by holding back an effective medication because of fear of serious side effects when in fact there are none. The physician does not want to make either error. By making the first error, the physician causes great harm to the patient and may even face a lawsuit. By making the second error, the physician does not help the patient get better. Again, a judgment must be made that balances the two types of possible errors.

We can put the ideas of statistical significance and the two types of error together. An overly cautious researcher sets a high level of significance. For example, the researcher might use the 0.0001 level. He or she attributes the results to chance unless they are so rare that they would occur by chance only 1 in 10 000 times. Such a high standard means that the researcher is most likely to err by saying results are due to chance when in fact they are not; that is, he or she may falsely accept the null hypothesis when there is a causal relationship (a Type II error). By contrast, a risk-taking researcher sets a low level of significance, such as 0.10. His or her results indicate a relationship would occur by chance 1 in 10 times. He or she is likely to err by saying that a causal relationship exists, when in fact random factors (e.g., random sampling error) actually cause the results. The researcher is likely to falsely reject the null hypothesis (Type I error). In sum, the 0.05 level is a compromise between Type I and Type II errors.

The statistical techniques of inferential statistics are precise and rely on the relationship between sampling error, sample size, and the central limit theorem. The power of inferential statistics is their ability to let a researcher state, with specific degrees of certainty, that specific sample results are likely to be true in a population. For example, a researcher conducts statistical tests and finds that a relationship is statistically significant at the 0.05 level. He or she can state that the sample results are probably not caused by chance factors. Indeed, there is a 95 percent chance that a true relationship exists in the social world.

Tests for inferential statistics are limited. The data must come from a random sample, and tests only take into account sampling errors. Nonsampling errors (e.g., a poor sampling frame or a poorly designed measure) are not considered. Do not be fooled into thinking that such tests offer easy, final answers. Statistical software programs quickly do the calculations for inferential and descriptive statistics (see Box 11.5), but they do not tell you how to interpret your findings or if they are substantially important—they only report the raw statistic. It is up to the researcher to interpret and explain the substantive importance of the findings within a larger context.

Box 11.5 Social Research and the Internet

Online Statistical Analysis Resources

Almost every social researcher who needs to calculate many statistics does so with a computer program, often using a basic spreadsheet program like Excel. Unfortunately, spreadsheets are designed for accounting and bookkeeping functions. They include statistics but are clumsy and limited for that purpose. There are many computer programs designed for calculating general statistics.

In recent years, the software has become less demanding for the user, with all mainstream statistical programs adopting user-friendly interfaces with drop-down windows rather than just the intimidating "syntax boxes" (where the user was required to type in statistical command language) associated with earlier versions of these software programs. The most popular programs in the social sciences are SPSS, Stata, and SAS.

While SPSS has been the market leader in statistical software for the social sciences, other programs are catching up in popularity.

Indeed, some programs like R are being used increasingly in classrooms because they are free and don't have the costly licensing fees associated with other programs. R is probably the most popular free statistical software package among social researchers (www.r-project.org), although some notable others are PSPP (a free "version" of SPSS) (www.gnu.org/software/pspp) and SOFA—Statistics Open For All (www.sofastatistics.com).

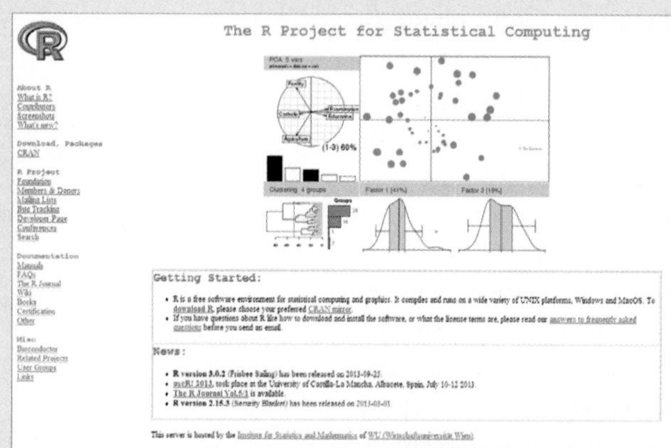

Source: © R Foundation, from http://www.r-project.org.

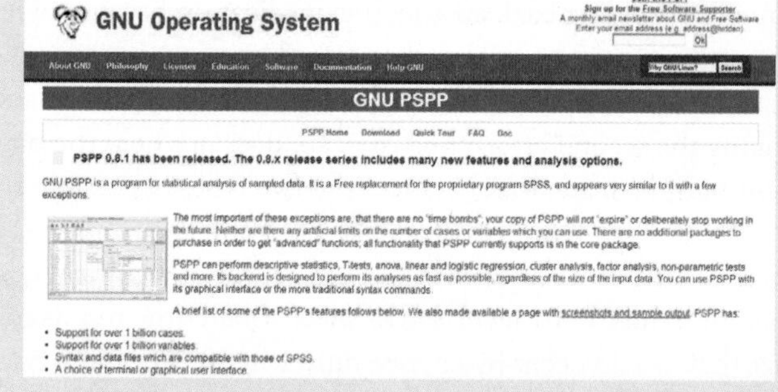

Copyright © 2013 Free Software Foundation, Inc., www.gnu.org/software/pspp.

Printed with permission of www.sofastatics.com.

CHAPTER SUMMARY

In this chapter you learned about the analysis of quantitative data. You learned about organizing quantitative data to prepare them for analysis and about analyzing them (organizing data into charts or tables, or summarizing them with statistical measures). Researchers use statistical analysis to test hypotheses and answer research questions. The chapter began by explaining how data must first be coded so that it may be analyzed using statistical techniques. The process of coding gives a numeric value to each category of a variable so that it can be prepared for statistical analysis.

Glossary Flashcards

Univariate statistics are statistics that focus on the properties of a single variable. In univariate analysis, researchers can use frequency distributions to examine how a variable is distributed across its various categories. Measures of central tendency and measures of variation are the names of two groups of univariate statistical procedures. Measures of central tendency focus on the properties of a variables "centre" or middle values and include the mean, median, and mode. Measures of variation, in contrast, are concerned with how a variable is dispersed across its various categories and include the range, percentile, and standard deviation.

Moving on from univariate analysis is analysis using two variables—or bivariate analysis. Such techniques allow a researcher to consider two variables together and describe their relationship with each other. Bivariate analyses are based on the ideas of correlation and independence. Scattergrams, bivariate tables, and measures of association are ways that the relationship between two variables can be investigated.

Bivariate analyses, however, have the shortcoming they do not allow for the researcher to eliminate possible spurious relationships between the two variables. The introduction of additional variables to control for their effects is the central concern of multivariate analyses—or statistical analysis using more than two variables. Multiple regression analysis is a common technique used to examine the relationship between more than two variables.

The topics of inferential statistics, statistical significance, and error were then introduced, although they had been touched upon in Chapter 7. Inferential statistics allow researchers to take characteristics of samples and generalize them to the wider population using established principles of probability. Statistical significance tells the researcher to what degree his or her findings may be due to chance or to real relationships that exist in the social world. The researcher is always at risk of making errors in his or her interpretations. Type I errors occur when a relationship is perceived to exist when in fact it does not, while a Type II error is the opposite case—when a researcher says a relationship does not exist when in fact it does.

We turn next to qualitative research. The logic and purpose of qualitative research differ from those of the quantitative, positivist approach of the past chapters. It is less concerned with numbers, hypotheses, and causality and more concerned with words, norms and values, and meaning.

Review Questions

Chapter Quiz

1. What are the four ways data can be entered? Define the two types of data cleaning.
2. What is meant by central tendency? What are the three ways of assessing central tendency? How are they calculated?
3. What are measures of variation? What are three techniques of assessing variation? How are they calculated?
4. What is the main purpose of bivariate statistics?
5. Describe the process of constructing a scattergram. What three aspects of a relationship can you see from a scattergram?

6. Describe the components of a bivariate table. What is a contingency table?
7. What is a measure of association? Name three and identify the levels of measurement that are required for its calculation.
8. Describe the purpose of multivariate analysis.
9. What is meant by statistical significance? What are Type I and Type II errors? What is the relationship between statistical significance and these two types of error?

Exercises

✓• Research Activities

1. Using EBSCO's ContentSelect, find a quantitative sociology article that contains a table of descriptive statistics. This type of table is usually found at the beginning of a statistical analysis before the results of a multivariate analysis are reported. Pick three variables from the table and identify their level of measurement. What descriptive statistics are provided for these variables? Interpret the values of the summary statistics reported for each of your three variables.
2. Using EBSCO's ContentSelect, identify a quantitative article that uses a correlation coefficient (rho). What are the variables of interest? What is the value of the correlation coefficient? What does this mean?
3. Using a quantitative journal article identified through EBSCO, find an article that displays statistics in the form of a percentaged table. What are the authors demonstrating in the table? Is any association being implied from the figures in the table?
4. In a quantitative article, you may find reference to a "dummy variable." Use the internet to research what a dummy variable is and how you would interpret one in a table of descriptive statistics.

Chapter 12

Qualitative Interviewing

Photo Credit: Mihai Blanaru/ Fotolia

LEARNING OBJECTIVES

After reading this chapter, you will be able to

LO 1 Identify research questions appropriate for answering using qualitative interviewing, and distinguish between a survey interview and a qualitative interview.

LO 2 Differentiate between a friendly conversation and a qualitative interview.

LO 3 Describe the procedure used to conduct qualitative interviews.

LO 4 Identify and explain the different types of Kvale questions.

LO 5 Describe the advantages and disadvantages of qualitative interviews.

LO 6 Explain the purpose of a focus group and describe the role of the moderator in a focus group.

LO 7 Outline some of the data resources available to qualitative researchers.

INTRODUCTION

This chapter (and much of the remainder of this book) shifts from the quantitative style of the past several chapters to the qualitative research style. As indicated throughout the previous chapters, the qualitative and the quantitative styles can differ a great deal.

We discussed structured interviewing in Chapter 8. Survey researchers also interview study members, but qualitative interviews differ from survey research interviews. This section introduces the qualitative interview.

LO 1 Identify research questions appropriate for answering using qualitative interviewing, and distinguish between a survey interview and a qualitative interview.

Qualitative Methods

Research Questions Appropriate for Qualitative Interviewing

Social science researchers also use less structured, nondirective, in-depth interviews, which differ from formal survey research interviews in many ways (see Table 12.1). The qualitative interview involves asking questions, listening, expressing interest, and recording what was said. It is a joint production of a researcher and an interviewee. Interviewees are active participants whose insights, feelings, and cooperation are essential parts of a discussion process that reveals subjective meanings. For this reason, qualitative interviews are most appropriate for research questions that focus on the subjective (interpretive) meaning that life experiences have for respondents. In general, qualitative interviews are not appropriate for research questions that investigate causal relationships.

When Can We Use Qualitative Methods?

Qualitative interviewing is often used in field research, which is discussed in Chapter 13. It should be noted, however, that qualitative interviewing is a method that is separate from field research and that field researchers use qualitative interviewing often in addition to other data collection techniques. This will be covered in the next chapter.

Qualitative interviews go by many names: unstructured, semi-structured, in depth, ethnographic, open ended, informal, and long. Generally, they involve one or more people being present and are informal and nondirective (i.e., the respondent may take the interview in various directions).

Table 12.1 Survey Interviews versus Qualitative Interviews

Typical Survey Interview	Typical Qualitative Interview
1. It has a clear beginning and end.	1. The beginning and end are not clear. The interview can be picked up later.
2. The same standard questions are asked of all respondents in the same sequence.	2. The questions and the order in which they are asked are tailored to specific people and situations.
3. The interviewer appears neutral at all times.	3. The interviewer shows interest in responses and encourages elaboration.
4. The interviewer asks questions, and the respondent answers.	4. It is like a friendly conversational exchange, but with more interviewer questions.
5. It is almost always conducted with one respondent alone.	5. It can occur in a group setting or with others in an area, but varies.
6. It has a professional tone and businesslike focus; diversions are ignored.	6. It is interspersed with jokes, asides, stories, diversions, and anecdotes, which are recorded.
7. Closed-ended questions are common, and probes are rare.	7. Open-ended questions are common, and probes are frequent.
8. The interviewer alone controls the pace and direction of the interview.	8. The interviewer and member jointly control the pace and direction of the interview.
9. The social context in which the interview occurs is ignored and assumed to make little difference.	9. The social context of the interview is noted and seen as important for interpreting the meaning of responses.
10. The interviewer attempts to mould the framework communication pattern into a standard.	10. The interviewer adjusts to the member's norms and language usage.

Source: Adapted from Briggs, C. L. (1986). *Learning how to ask.* New York, NY: Cambridge University Press; Denzin, N. K. (1989). *The research act* (3rd ed.). Englewood Cliffs, NJ: Prentice-Hall; Douglas, J. D. (1985). *Creative interviewing.* Beverly Hills, CA: Sage; Mishler, E. G. (1986). *Research interviewing.* Cambridge, MA: Harvard University Press; and Spradley, J. P. (1979). *The ethnographic interview.* New York, NY: Holt, Rinehart and Winston.

A qualitative interview involves a mutual sharing of experiences. A researcher might share his or her background to build trust and encourage the informant to open up, but does not force answers or use leading questions. She or he encourages and guides a process of mutual discovery.

In qualitative interviews, study participants express themselves in the forms in which they normally speak, think, and organize reality. A researcher retains members' jokes and narrative stories in their natural form and does not repackage them into a standardized format. The focus is on the members' perspectives and experiences. In order to stay close to a member's experience, the researcher asks questions in terms of concrete examples or situations—for example, "Could you tell me things that led up to your quitting in June?" instead of "Why did you quit your job?"

Social Psychology Methods for Sociology

Qualitative interviews can occur in a series over time. A researcher begins by building rapport and steering conversation away from evaluative or highly sensitive topics. He or she avoids probing inner feelings until intimacy is established, and even then the researcher expects apprehension. After several meetings, he or she may be able to probe more deeply into sensitive issues and seek clarification of less sensitive issues. In later interviews, he or she may return to topics and check past answers by restating them in a nonjudgmental tone and asking for verification—for example, "The last time we talked, you said that you started taking things from the store after they reduced your pay. Is that right?"

Similarities and Differences between Qualitative Interviews and Friendly Conversations

LO 2 Differentiate between a friendly conversation and a qualitative interview.

The qualitative interview is closer to a friendly conversation than the stimulus/response model found in a survey research interview. You are familiar with a friendly conversation. It has its own informal rules and the following elements: (1) a greeting ("Hi, it's good to see you again"); (2) the absence of an explicit goal or purpose (we don't say, "Let's now discuss what we did last weekend"); (3) avoidance of repetition (we don't say, "Could you clarify what you said about . . . "); (4) question asking ("Did you see the game yesterday?"); (5) expressions of interest ("Really? I wish I could have been there!"); (6) expressions of ignorance ("No, I missed it. What happened?"); (7) turn taking, so the encounter is balanced (one person does not always ask questions and the other only answers); (8) abbreviations ("I prefer the CFL, but I'll watch the NFL if it's on TV," not "I prefer the Canadian Football League, but I will watch the American National Football League games if they are on television"); (9) a pause or brief silence when neither person talks is acceptable; (10) a closing (we don't say, "Let's end this conversation"; instead, we give a verbal indicator before physically leaving: "I've got to get back to work now—see you tomorrow").

The qualitative interview differs from a friendly conversation. They are similar in that both involve asking questions. Qualitative interviews, however, have an explicit purpose—to learn about the informant and setting. A researcher includes explanations or requests that diverge from friendly conversations. For example, he or she may say, "I'd like to ask you about . . . " or "Could you look at this and see if I've written it down right?" The qualitative interview is less balanced. A higher proportion of questions come from the researcher, who expresses more ignorance and interest. Also, it includes repetition, and a researcher asks the member to elaborate on unclear abbreviations. Table 12.2 summarizes some important differences between qualitative interviews and friendly conversations.

Using Open and Closed Ended Questions

Albanese (2006) used in-depth interviews in her study of women in Quebec whose children were in provincial child care (discussed in Chapter 7). Interviews lasted about an

Table 12.2 Friendly Conversations versus Qualitative Interviews

Friendly Conversation	Qualitative Interview
1. A casual or friendly greeting often initiates a conversation.	1. Often it begins by obtaining consent from the interviewee.
2. There is no explicit goal or purpose.	2. There is an explicit purpose—to answer the research question.
3. There is avoidance of repetition.	3. Repetition is included to ensure that the researcher's interpretation is correct.
4. Expressions of interest and ignorance can be balanced.	4. The researcher expresses more interest and ignorance.
5. There is turn taking, so the encounter is balanced.	5. There is much less balance—the majority of questions are asked by the interviewer.
6. Abbreviations and jargon familiar to both people is often included.	6. The researcher asks about abbreviations and jargon so that there is no misunderstanding between the interviewer and interviewee.
7. A pause or brief silence when neither person talks is acceptable.	7. Pauses can be used by the interviewer to get the interviewee to elaborate on a previous point.
8. The end of the conversation is a verbal indicator followed by physical departure.	8. There is a formal closing that acknowledges that the interview is over.

hour. Albanese was interested in how the provincial daycare system affected domestic and community life. She asked the women about the school readiness of their children before and after being placed in the daycare program. She also asked the women how they chose the child care facility and what impact the use of these programs had on their relations at home. Open-ended interviewing allowed her to see how the women thought the daycare program had affected their own lives, the lives of their families, and the general quality of life in the wider community.

LO 3 Describe the procedure used to conduct qualitative interviews.

THE PROCEDURE OF QUALITATIVE INTERVIEWING

As with any research method, the researcher should have a clearly defined research question before interviewing participants for his or her study. Unlike quantitative research methods, researchers using qualitative interviewing rarely have hypotheses that they are testing. Rather, they are using an inductive approach to theorizing (see Chapter 2) and will build a theory from the evidence that emerges from the interviews they conduct.

Sampling in Qualitative Interviews

Social scientists typically select interview participants through nonprobability sampling, which was discussed in Chapter 7. With this particular data collection technique, snowball and purposive sampling are often used for recruiting potential interviewees. This is because the topics that researchers are interested in studying through the use of qualitative interviewing do not easily lend themselves to probability sampling. If you recall from Chapter 7, probability sampling requires the use of a sampling frame—the list of all elements in a population. In the examples that follow, there was no official list of all of the members of the target populations. It should be said, however, that not all research that uses qualitative interviewing as a form of data collection uses nonprobability sampling—but the vast majority does.

In Lewis's (2006) study of exotic dancers in southern Ontario, interviewees were selected through purposive sampling so that as much diversity as possible could be incorporated into the sample. The researcher conducted interviews with 30 female dancers, ranging in age from 18 to 38. All but two interviewees were White, but they varied according to educational and marital status. One quarter, for example, were attending some form of schooling. Half of the dancers had partners, while one third of the dancers had children.

Baron (2006), in his study of street youth in Edmonton, used a snowball sampling technique to recruit participants for interviews. Baron approached some street youth and explained the study to them and invited them to participate. Additional participants were recruited through these initial contacts. Baron would visit the same location where he met the original participants daily to initiate contact with more street youth or would be introduced to them through one of the original participants. Albanese (2006) also used snowball sampling in her study of mothers using daycare facilities in Quebec. She knew some mothers using daycare facilities in Quebec and then she asked them for the names of other mothers in similar situations. She also made contact with local child care providers through the names given by the women that she interviewed.

As addressed in Chapter 7, hidden populations refer to people who belong to subcultures whose members are difficult to locate and therefore difficult to study. Many researchers who are interested in studying hidden populations rely on qualitative interviewing as a data collection technique. Clearly, no sampling frame exists for members of hidden populations, such as gangs, members of clandestine religious orders, or illegal drug users, for example. Researchers interested in studying hidden populations often rely on nonprobability sampling techniques, particularly snowball sampling. After making contact with some members of the hidden population, the researchers can then ask members of the hidden population if they would refer them to other potential study participants.

How Many People to Interview?

Research that uses qualitative interviewing as its method of data collection is typically inductive in nature—that is, theory is derived from the data. As discussed in Chapter 7, the process of theoretical sampling goes hand in hand with the grounded theory approach. Theoretical sampling, to recap, means that a researcher does not know in advance how many individuals he or she needs to interview. The researcher continues to interview subjects until the same general themes continue to emerge from the data and no new findings are being revealed. This is known as theoretical saturation.

In reality, however, the number of people interviewed in a study employing qualitative interviewing as the data collection method is usually dictated by the time and resources available to the researcher. Locating suitable interviewees who are willing to participate can be a time-consuming process, especially if you are studying a hidden population or do not know any contacts who can put you in touch with potential subjects. As discussed below, transcribing interview data is also very time demanding, and if a researcher decides to employ a transcriptionist, this can be very costly. A one-hour interview, in the authors' personal experience, takes about six hours to transcribe, but this can vary according to your typing speed, the type of equipment you are working with, and the quality of the interview recording.

Incentives

incentive: A general term for the remuneration given to research participants, often in the form of cash.

Often, because interviews can be time consuming for the interviewee, the researcher offers the potential interviewee an **incentive** for his or her participation. This can be a cash payment, vouchers, being entered into a draw, or simply being offered a copy of the final research report when it is finished. It is important to use an incentive that is appropriate to your target sample. For example, in Baron's (2006) study of street youth he used an incentive for participation—$10 worth of vouchers to a popular fast-food restaurant. It is unlikely that a copy of his final paper would have been much of an incentive for this group of participants.

As well, instead of one-on-one incentives to individual participants, researchers who are doing research in a community or organization may make a gift offering to the entire community or organization at the end of their research project.

Interview Sites

Researchers using qualitative interviews as a form of data collection recognize that the type of conversation that occurs in a private office may not occur in a crowded lunchroom. Often, interviews take place in the member's home environment so that he or she is comfortable. But this is not always best. If a member is preoccupied or there is no privacy, a researcher will move to another setting (e.g., a restaurant or university office). For example, Baron (2006) interviewed street youth in the sheltered and more familiar and comfortable settings of one of the many malls in downtown Edmonton.

The interview's meaning is shaped by its *gestalt*, the whole interaction of a researcher and a member in a specific context. For example, a researcher notes nonverbal forms of communication that add meaning, such as a shrug, a gesture, and so on. The gestalt of an interview is more than just the words that are exchanged between the interviewer and interviewee. The act of the interview is a social process unto itself that is characterized by several factors, including body language, the relationship between the interviewer and interviewee, and the context in which the interview takes place.

Recording and Transcribing

The researcher usually audio-records the interview and jots down notes while the interview takes place. There are many new digital recording devices that have better sound quality, are more dependable, and are more portable than what researchers have had to use in the recent past. Transcribing qualitative interviews is a time-consuming process but should be done as soon as possible after the interview has taken place so that the researcher has a better chance of deciphering audio material that may be difficult to understand. When the interview is "fresh" in the researcher's mind, it is more likely that he or she will have a clearer recollection of the interview and be able to fill in gaps where sound quality might be compromised.

selective transcription: A transcription technique in *qualitative interviews* where only the parts of interviews that the researcher deems most relevant are transcribed.

Sometimes researchers do not transcribe their interviews in full and undertake what is called **selective transcription**. Selective transcription is usually done when the researcher feels it is unnecessary to fully transcribe the interviews to answer his or her research question. Rather than transcribing the entire interview, he or she will opt to only transcribe the parts that are most relevant to the research question that is being asked. As discussed in Chapter 6, in order for qualitative data to be as trustworthy as possible (according to the criteria suggested by Lincoln and Guba [1985]) and to ensure dependability of our findings, we should make our data available for other researchers to examine. Fully transcribed interviews are the best means of ensuring that our findings are dependable and trustworthy.

Informants

An **informant**, or key actor in qualitative research, is a member with whom a researcher develops a relationship and who tells about, or informs on, the aspects of the research setting.[1] Who makes a good informant? The ideal informant has four characteristics:

informant: A general term that is used to refer to individuals who participate in qualitative research projects.

1. The informant is very familiar with the culture and is in a position to witness significant events. He or she lives and breathes the culture and engages in routines in the setting without thinking about them.
2. The individual is currently involved in the culture that the researcher is trying to understand. Ex-members may provide useful insights, but the longer they have been away from direct involvement, the more likely it is that they have reconstructed their recollections.
3. The person can spend time with the researcher. Interviewing may take many hours, and some members are simply not available for extensive interviewing.
4. Nonanalytical individuals make better informants. A nonanalytical informant is familiar with and uses native folk theory or pragmatic common sense. This is in contrast to the analytic member, who pre-analyzes the setting, using categories from the media or education.

A researcher may interview several types of informants. Contrasting types of informants who provide useful perspectives include rookies and old-timers; people in the centre of events and those on the fringes of activity; people who recently changed status (e.g., through promotion) and those who are static; frustrated or needy people and happy or secure people; and the leader in charge and the subordinate who follows. The researcher expects mixed messages when he or she interviews a range of informants.

In Lewis's (2006) study of exotic dancers, three of her key informants worked with her research team as research assistants. Each of her key informants had experience in various positions in strip clubs and was able to give the researchers important information about how these types of organizations operated.

ASKING QUESTIONS IN QUALITATIVE INTERVIEWS

LO 4 Identify and explain the different types of Kvale questions.

Domestic Violence

In Chapter 8, we discussed how structured interviews required trained interviewers to ask the same questions to interviewees, that the questions are asked in the same order, and that the questions are asked in the same way. In qualitative interviewing, the interview takes on much different characteristics.

Kvale Question Types

Kvale (1996) has created a typology of nine different question types that can occur during a qualitative interview. According to Kvale, there are introducing questions, follow-up questions, probing questions, specifying questions, direct questions, indirect questions, structuring questions, interpreting questions, and silence. Box 12.1 provides examples of these question types from an actual interview.

Introducing questions are general opening questions where the interviewee is prompted to give his or her account of a situation or experience. For example, the interviewee might be asked, "Could you tell me about the first time you remember experiencing racism?" or "Do you remember a time when you experienced being treated differently

introducing questions: In *qualitative interviews*, this refers to questions that are general opening questions in which the interviewee is prompted to give his or her account of a situation or experience.

Box 12.1 Concepts in Action

Kvale Question Types in an Actual Interview Transcript

Introducing question

- "I was just wondering how you think of bullying. When you think of it, what kinds of things come to your mind?"

Follow-up questions

- "Okay, during what years in school did you feel this happened to you?"
- "And did they all last for the duration of the school year?"
- "So, when you would tell your teachers, you felt it worsened the situation?"

Probing questions

- "You didn't develop any interests . . . ?"
- "So it was all basically just physical abuse and . . . "
- "You didn't develop any interests . . . computer games or something?"

Specifying questions

- "And did they all last for the duration of the school year?"
- "What kinds of things would they do to you?"
- "What made you decide to start fighting back?"

Direct questions

- "Do you think having been bullied as a child has affected how you are today?"
- "So, when you think about those things, how do you say they affected your experience going to school?"
- "Do you think that having been abused by your peers has any effect on your ability to feel empathy?"

Indirect questions

- "Why do you think they picked you to harass?"

Structuring questions

- "Okay. Do you think that . . . I know we've already talked about this, but do you think that bullying has had any effect on your personal relationships in your adult life?"
- "So, when you think about those things, how do you say they affected your experience going to school?"

Interpreting questions

- "From what you were saying, you weren't really safe at school?"
- "So you kind of take those things and make it into a game, then?"
- "So your closest friends basically weren't in school with you?"
- "So you think you'd outsmart them?"

Silence

- "Wow." (pause)
- "Interesting." (pause)

because of your ethnicity?" It is anticipated that such questions will result in rich, detailed descriptions from the interviewee and will be at the core of answering the research question.

follow-up questions: Refers to questions that are asked in *qualitative interviews* to get additional description about topics just discussed by the interviewee.

Follow-up questions are those that are asked by the interviewer to get additional description about topics just discussed by the interviewee. The goal of follow-up questions is to get additional details of events or experiences. Follow-up questions can simply be the interviewer repeating words that seem important in the interviewee's account. For example, if an interviewee says, "I felt that I was receiving a very negative reaction from the teacher," the interviewer could follow that up by repeating "Negative reaction?"—at which point the interviewee would more than likely elaborate on what he or she meant by this.

probing questions: In *qualitative interviews*, refers to types of questions used by an interviewer to expand on incomplete points an interviewee has raised.

Probing questions are very much like *probes* used by structured interviewers. Sometimes, an interviewee will respond to a question with a yes or no answer, for example. Or the interviewee may give a very brief description of an event or experience. An interviewer can probe such answers by asking if the interviewee could give more details about the event or if there are any other examples that he or she could share. Probing questions are different from follow-up questions. With follow-up questions, the interviewer asks the interviewee to expand on a particular point; with probing questions, the interviewer asks for general expansion without indicating which part of the answer he or she is interested in getting more information about. A general probing question would be, "Could you tell me more about that?" or "Do you have any other examples?"

Specifying questions are those that the researcher asks to get more detailed descriptions about specific aspects of the interviewee's descriptions. In response to a statement, the interviewer may ask, "How did you react then?" Additionally, a simple probe of "uh-huh" can be used to encourage the interviewee to continue speaking.

specifying questions: In *qualitative interviews*, questions that the researcher asks to get more detailed descriptions about specific aspects of the interviewee's descriptions.

Direct questions are usually introduced by the interviewer toward the end of the interview to address specific topics that may not have been covered yet—for example, "Have you ever left a job due to perceived racist treatment?"

direct questions: In *qualitative interviewing*, questions introduced by the interviewer usually toward the end of the interview to address specific topics that may not have been covered.

Indirect questions are those that the interviewer asks to get a sense of how the interviewee believes other people think, behave, or feel. The researcher must be careful in his or her interpretation of such answers because it must be clear whether the opinion expressed through indirect questioning is actually that of the interviewee or what she or he thinks that other people think. An example of an indirect question is, "How do you think other employees regard racist behaviours in the workplace?"

indirect questions: In *qualitative interviews*, questions that the interviewer asks to get a sense of how the interviewee believes other people think, behave, or feel.

Structuring questions are used by the interviewer to keep the interview on track if it has gone off topic, or if he or she believes the answer to a question has been fully exhausted. Structuring questions are also used to keep the interview moving along. An example of a structuring question is, "I would now like to discuss another issue . . ."

structuring questions: Questions used in *qualitative interviews* to keep the interview on track if it has gone off topic or to keep the interview moving along.

How we interpret our interview data is at the heart of how we answer our research question. We listen to the interviewee, and his or her answers to our questions are filtered through our own minds. **Interpreting questions** help us to ensure that we are interpreting what the interviewee is saying as correctly as possible. We can ask the interviewee if our own interpretations are accurate by asking questions that begin, "From what I understand, you mean that . . . " or "From what you've told me, your experience can be summed up like . . . ."

interpreting questions: In *qualitative interviewing*, questions that are asked to ensure that the researcher is interpreting what the interviewee is saying as correctly as possible.

You may also ask your interviewee to make connections between different pieces of information that he or she has disclosed to you in the interview. For example, "Do you see a connection between how you were bullied at school and the racism you experienced in the workplace?"

Using Reflective Questions

While "silence" is not technically a question, using **silence** can encourage interviewees to continue talking. You've probably noticed that among people whom you do not know very well, there is a tendency for pauses in conversation to feel rather awkward. Typically, people try to fill in these gaps in the conversation. If researchers use the technique of allowing for pauses, it is likely that interviewees will continue talking and will elaborate on their answers.

silence: In *qualitative interviews*, a technique used by researchers (not saying anything) to get interviewees to continue speaking.

Interview Guide

Keeping the research question in mind, the researcher should develop an **interview guide**. An interview guide is a list of questions that the researcher wants to ensure are covered during the course of the interview. It does not have to be followed chronologically but serves as a guide for the interviewer during the course of the interview. He or she can refer to the guide to introduce a structuring question, for example. When the interview is nearing its end, the researcher can also refer to the guide to make sure all topics have been covered. In Box 12.2, the interview used for the bullying study undertaken by one of the authors (Robson) is presented.

interview guide: A list of questions that a researcher wishes to address in the course of a *qualitative interview*.

Box 12.2 Concepts in Action

Interview Guide for Research on the Long-Term Effects of Childhood Bullying

1. As you know, when I was looking for participants to volunteer for this project, I indicated that I was interested in talking to adults who had experienced bullying as children. You identified yourself to me as someone who had experienced this. In this interview, I am going to ask you some questions about your experiences as a child.

   To begin, could you just start by telling me what "bullying" means to you, as someone who experienced it?
2. During what years in school did you feel that your peers abused you?
3. How long did this last?
4. Why do you think you were picked on?
5. Who were the people that bullied you? Was there some kind of bullying group? A leader of it? What was your relationship to it?
6. Many people find talking about these events very difficult, but if you could, do you think you could tell me some of the things that occurred to you in general?
7. Where did this bullying occur?
8. How did these events affect your overall school experience?
9. Did you ever do something to prevent these things from happening? Did you ever skip classes, stay home from school, or hide?
10. Did you ever do other things to help you forget about these experiences? What were they? Did it help?
11. Did you ever participate in bullying anyone? If so, what did you do? Why?
12. Did you ever have a "safe" environment of peers you could turn to? (i.e., If bullying occurred at school, did you have neighbourhood friends, for example?)
13. Did your parents or teachers ever try to intervene? If so, how? Did it help the situation?
14. Do you feel that parents or teachers improved or worsened the situation?
15. When did you begin to feel like you were no longer a victim of bullying?
16. What did you do during the time between being a victim and a nonvictim? How did you make the transition?
17. Was there a specific moment when you finally felt free of the bullies?
18. Did you receive any help from others in freeing yourself of them?
19. Now that you are an adult, do you think about your experiences as a victim of bullying?
20. Do you think that being bullied as a child has shaped who you are today? How?
21. Have you been able to recover feelings of self-worth? If not, do you think you ever will?
22. What kinds of effects has it had on your personal relationships?
23. Do you think that being bullied has influenced your ability to feel empathy toward others? Has it improved your ability to understand how others feel? If so, why do you think this is so?
24. Are there things that you do or have done in order to cope with the memories that resulted from being bullied as a child? What kinds of things? Have they helped?
25. Have you been able to forgive your bullies?
26. What would you do if your children were bullied?
27. What would you do if your child was a bully?
28. Is there anything you would like to add?

LO 5 Describe the advantages and disadvantages of qualitative interviews.

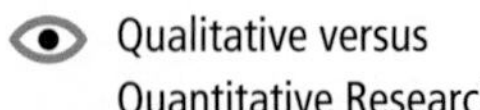

ADVANTAGES AND LIMITATIONS OF QUALITATIVE INTERVIEWS

Just like any data collection technique, there are advantages and limitations of qualitative interviews. The discussion below, while not an exhaustive list of the pluses and minuses of this approach, summarizes some of the more compelling arguments for and against this particular data collection technique.

From the Perspective of the Interviewee

One of the major advantages of qualitative interviews is that they allow the researcher to see the world from the perspective of his or her interviewees. The differences between the types of data a person collects in survey research methods and qualitative interviewing are very pronounced. While survey respondents are often required to answer from a fixed set of possible answers, the types of responses possible in qualitative interviewing are much more varied and allow the "voice" of the interviewee to be heard. Qualitative interviewees are free to respond in whatever way they wish, using whatever words they feel best express their accounts of experiences, feelings, or opinions. Reading research reports that use qualitative interviewing as a data collection method is very engaging and creates a sense of intimacy between the researcher, interviewees, and reader that cannot be captured in research reports full of statistics and graphs.

Data Rich with Description

Field Research

The types of data collected in qualitative interviews are often rich with descriptive detail. Indeed, the more descriptive detail that is available in the data, the better. This is what qualitative interviewers are seeking when conducting an interview of this sort—that the interviewee will give plenty of description and explanation around the events, experiences, opinions, or feelings that he or she is describing. As a result, qualitative interview transcripts can be very long and the amount of data that needs to be analyzed even in a small study of 10 people can be rather overwhelming.

The techniques involved in the analysis of qualitative interview data are very different from those used in structured survey interviews (where answers are converted to numbers and then analyzed statistically) and can be very time consuming. We will return to the topic of qualitative data analysis in Chapter 15.

Development of New Theories

Because researchers using qualitative interviewing usually have an inductive approach to theory (theory emerges from data), it is through qualitative interviewing (and other qualitative approaches) that new theories are developed using the grounded theory approach. Researchers look for themes to emerge from their interview data to create theories of social behaviour. While quantitative research is primarily concerned with testing and refining existing theories, data from qualitative interviews can contribute to the development of new theories where none had previously existed. This is particularly true in the case of studying hidden or marginalized groups on which there has been very little previous research (see Chapter 7).

Development of New Avenues of Research

As mentioned above, qualitative interviewing is a particularly valuable research method for studying understudied or previously unstudied populations. In addition to learning about groups for which very little information exists, qualitative interviewing data can create theories that can feed into the future research of other social scientists, including those who use quantitative techniques. Theories that are developed through the grounded theory approach can be used later to develop structured interview questions (i.e., surveys) where greater numbers of individuals from these populations can be studied, which can lead to a greater understanding of these individuals and more generalizable research findings.

Problems with Validity and Reliability

One of the biggest criticisms launched against qualitative interviewing as a method of data collection is that it encounters unique problems in relation to data validity and reliability. Sample sizes are usually small in comparison to those used in quantitative work, and therefore members of the research community question whether the results of such studies are actually applicable to a wider population beyond those in the interview sample.

The archiving of qualitative interview data so that it is available for scrutiny and further analysis by other members of the research community has been very rare. This is steadily changing, with more and more researchers depositing their data with established data banks (discussed below).

In Chapter 6, the alternative criteria for the validity and reliability of qualitative data were discussed. Lincoln and Guba (1985) have suggested that qualitative data be evaluated according to their trustworthiness. To increase the trustworthiness of qualitative interview data, researchers can ensure that their data are made available to other interested researchers who may want to reanalyze it. Researchers using qualitative interviews can also maximize the transferability (or generalizability) of their findings to populations beyond their immediate sample by selecting participants who are not entirely homogeneous. For example, in Lewis's (2006) study of exotic dancers, interviewees were chosen who were from a variety of ages and dance clubs. The interviewees also represented a variety of marital and motherhood statuses. The topic of validity and reliability in qualitative data is revisited in the next chapter when we discuss techniques for establishing trustworthiness.

LO 6 Explain the purpose of a focus group and describe the role of the moderator in a focus group.

FOCUS GROUPS

The *focus group* is a special qualitative research technique in which people are informally "interviewed" in a group-discussion setting.[2] Sometimes focus groups are called *group interviews*. Focus group research has grown over the past 20 years. It is also a particularly popular way for market researchers to test their products, although social scientists use the technique extensively. Many students in our methods courses have told us that they have been part of focus group research, often for market research purposes. Focus group topics might include public attitudes (e.g., race relations, workplace equality), personal behaviours (e.g., avoiding sexually transmitted infections), a new product (e.g., breakfast cereal), a political candidate, and so on.

The Focus Group Procedure

moderator: Refers to a trained facilitator used in *focus group* research who guides the focus group discussion.

In very general terms, a researcher gathers together 6 to 12 people in a room with a **moderator** to discuss a few issues. The moderator is the person who leads the focus group and asks questions to prompt group discussion. Most focus groups last about 90 minutes. Often, focus groups are held in rooms equipped with audio and video recording facilities so that the sessions can be accurately transcribed afterward.

The Role of the Moderator

The moderator is trained to be nondirective and to facilitate free, open discussion by all group members. Moderators are also called facilitators. The moderator does not typically interfere in the discussion but starts the group off with the general topic. As in regular qualitative interviewing, the moderator follows an interview guide to make sure that all the topics related to answering the research question are answered. (See Box 12.3 for an example of an interview guide used in focus group research.)

The moderator's job is also to ensure that the conversation stays on track and does not veer too far off the topic determined by the research question. Moderating a focus group is a special skill that should not be underestimated. Effective moderators have extensive

Box 12.3 Concepts in Action

The Interview Guide for a Focus Group

In this example, high school students in a suburban community near Toronto were studied part of a research project that was concerned with various topics, including the experience of racialized students and their perceptions of their school, community, and future plans.

Focus groups were done in groups of 4–5 students of the same gender, with a moderator (graduate student) of the same gender. Each focus group was 90 minutes long, which was the length of the class. These focus groups were completed as part of the larger research project and following interviews where each student interviewed their parents. The parental interview focused on the parents' own schooling experiences, their understandings of their childrens' educational experiences, and their life in a suburban community.

Interview Guide

Focus Group Questions

1. In the interviews, almost all of the parents said that they like this community, and they think it's a good place to live. Specifically, they talked about community safety, and also about multiculturalism, as some of the reasons the community is 'good'. Do you agree with them—is this a 'safe' community? Is multiculturalism 'good'?

   (Prompts: What does 'multiculturalism' mean? Are there any racial/ethnic tensions or stereotypes in the community?)
2. What, if any, are the challenges of growing up in this community?
3. What is the best and worst thing about this school?
4. What were the most important skills, habits or ideas that you have gained, in or out of school, in the past few years?
5. In the interviews, there were some clear differences between the boys and the girls in their responses. We observed that the girls are more likely to be applying themselves in their school work, they are more likely to obey their parents, and they are more likely to apply to college/university. What do you think are the reasons that the boys are not doing the same?

   (Prompts: in terms of academic achievement, behaviour, contribution to the community, social relations)
6. How well do you think your parents understand your life at school?

   (Prompts: do parents understand the way schools operate, social life in school? If they lack knowledge, what do you think they're misinformed or under-informed about? Where do they get their information from? How often do they come to the school? How often do you talk about school with them?)
7. Where do you see yourself in 5 years? In 10 years?

   (Prompts: job, living situation, family life, social life, economic stability, career)

Source: Danielle Kwan-Lafond

experience and are able to gently control several people at one time. The moderator is always aware in advance of the problems that might occur in the focus group and is trained to intervene in specific circumstances. For example, the moderator ensures that a single person does not dominate the discussion, and conversely can "probe" quieter individuals for their opinions. The moderator will also know how to effectively defuse arguments between people. Because there are several people to manage concurrently, there are more possibilities for problems that the moderator will have to handle compared to one-on-one interviews.

Composition of Focus Groups

Who is in a focus group is largely determined by the research question at hand. In general, group members should be homogeneous but not include close friends or relatives. If researchers have reason to believe that opinions will vary by some kind of demographic factor, for example sex or ethnicity, then additional groups should be included where these characteristics are represented.

In a study of adolescents' perceptions of abuse in heterosexual dating relationships, Sears and associates (2006) recruited adolescents from four francophone and three anglophone schools in New Brunswick. The students were in Grades 9 and 11 and were predominantly White. The researchers used a total of 26 focus groups and divided them by sex so that 13 comprised only males and 13 comprised only females. In half of the groups, the focus of the discussion was on psychological abuse, while for the other half of the groups the focus was on physical abuse. It is reasonable to think that perceptions of inappropriate behaviour in dating relationships would vary according to sex, so this division of participants by sex could identify whether this was the case. Focus groups also included only individuals who were in the same grade. Again, perception of appropriate dating behaviour among adolescents likely varies by age, so by keeping the participants in different groups according to grade, the researchers would be able to investigate if any differences in opinions emerged that could be attributed to maturity.

The Number of Groups in a Focus Group Study

There is no set number of groups that a researcher interviews to answer his or her research question. The number of groups has a lot to do with the number of demographic factors that he or she wants to "control" or account for. In the example above, the researchers used a total of 26 groups, but this is atypical. In a typical study, a researcher uses four to six separate groups. The researchers studying adolescent attitudes to appropriate dating behaviour, however, had a number of characteristics by which they wanted to make their groups as homogeneous as possible: age, sex, and language. As well, they also had two research questions that they were investigating (psychological abuse and physical abuse), which essentially doubled the number of groups they required.

As with qualitative interviewing, time and money often dictate the number of interviews that a researcher can undertake. The grounded theory approach discussed in Chapter 7, however, should ideally be the yardstick by which researchers decide on their number of focus groups. Recall that theoretical sampling requires that the researcher continue to collect and analyze data until he or she reaches theoretical saturation—that is, the point at which the same themes and concepts keep emerging from the data. In other words, if similar themes appear after four groups, then data collection is complete. However, for some research questions, the number of groups may be much higher; it cannot be known in advance and the researcher must continue running focus group sessions until saturation is achieved. As will be discussed in more detail in Chapter 15, the analysis of both qualitative interview data and focus group data often follows the principles of grounded theory, where theory is developed from analysis of the data.

Researchers often combine focus groups with quantitative research, and the procedure has its own specific strengths and weaknesses (see Box 12.4). Several years ago, one of the authors (Neuman) conducted an applied study on why parents and students chose a private high school. In addition to collecting quantitative survey data, he formed six focus groups, each with 8 to 10 students from the high school. A trained university student moderator asked questions, elicited comments from group members, and prevented one person from dominating discussions. The six groups were mixed sex and contained members of either one grade level or two adjacent grades (e.g., Grade 10 and Grade 11). Students discussed their reasons for attending the high school and whether specific factors were important. The author tape-recorded the discussions, which lasted about 45 minutes, then analyzed the tapes to understand what the students saw as important to their decisions. In addition, the data helped when interpreting the survey data.

Focus Groups as Social Groups

Unlike individual qualitative interviews, focus groups have the additional characteristic of being a group, and as social scientists, we know that groups have their own social dynamics. The impact of the focus group itself on opinions expressed within it has become a topic of

Box 12.4 Focus

Advantages and Limitations of Focus Groups

Advantages

- The natural setting allows people to express opinions/ideas freely.
- Open expression among members of marginalized social groups is encouraged.
- People tend to feel empowered, especially in action-oriented research projects.
- Survey researchers are provided with a window into how people talk about survey topics.
- The interpretation of quantitative survey results is facilitated.
- Participants may query one another and explain their answers to each other.

Limitations

- A "polarization effect" exists (attitudes become more extreme after group discussion).
- Only one or a few topics can be discussed in a focus group session.
- A moderator may unknowingly limit open, free expression of group members.
- Focus groups produce the possibility of groupthink.
- It is not clear whom the members of the focus group are representing—themselves, social groups, or their membership to the focus group.
- Focus group participants produce fewer ideas than individual interviews do.
- Focus group studies rarely report all the details of study design/procedure.
- Researchers cannot reconcile the differences that arise between individual-only and focus group-context responses.

study in its own right. There are a number of concerns about focus groups that relate to their characteristic of using the group interview.

The first is whether or not the opinions expressed during the focus group are actually representative of any definable population. Hydén and Bülow (2003, p. 306) ask, "Do the participants represent various groups outside the focus group, like professional or social groups; or do they just represent themselves as individuals; or do they act as members of the focus group? Further, do they talk and act as the same type of representatives throughout the entire focus group session, or is it possible that they shift positions?"

Researching these questions themselves, the researchers concluded that focus group participants speak from many "voices," depending on how other members of the focus group are contributing and how they are being instructed by the moderator.

A related topic of concern about focus groups is tied to the notion of **groupthink**. The term *groupthink* was coined by prominent American sociologist William H. Whyte, who first used the term in *Fortune* magazine (March 1952, p. 114). The term generally refers to a person's natural desire to avoid conflict and lean toward group consensus, even when the opinion of the group does not reflect his or her own personal opinions. Obviously, this can be a major problem for the validity of focus group data. But how do we tackle the problem of groupthink if it is caused by human nature? MacDougall and Baum (1997) have recommended that researchers using focus groups employ the selective use of a devil's advocate to prevent groupthink from occurring. The term **devil's advocate** generally refers to a person whose role it is to argue against a dominant idea. MacDougall and Baum suggest that the role of the devil's advocate in a focus group would be someone who could introduce new questions and new ways of thinking into the group so as to prevent the tendency toward group conformity. The devil's advocate is not played by the moderator but rather by a pretrained member of the focus group who is identified at the outset as having this particular role.

groupthink: In *focus group* research, refers to people's natural desire to avoid conflict and lean toward group consensus, even when the opinion of the group does not reflect their own personal opinions.

devil's advocate: In *focus group* research, refers to a person whose role it is to argue against a dominant idea and who could introduce new questions and new ways of thinking into the group so as to prevent the tendency toward group conformity.

Box 12.5 Social Research and the Internet

Online Sources of Qualitative Data

As noted below, the UK Data Archive is the most extensive qualitative data archive in the world. It can been explored by going to http://data-archive.ac.uk. Other notable qualitative data archives include the following:

- The Inter-University Consortium for Political and Social Research (ICPSR) at the University of Michigan, which was mentioned in Chapter 10 as being a resource for quantitative data, also has a limited number of qualitative data sources. www.icpsr.umich.edu
- The Center for Oral History and Cultural Heritage at the University of Mississippi has over 1000 transcripts of interviews with individuals about the history of Mississippi. Oral histories are discussed more in Chapter 14 but are very much like qualitative interviews, although their focus is on accounts of history—either cultural history or personal history. www.usm.edu/oral-history
- The First Black Women at Virginia Tech History Project publishes its transcript data online. As the name suggests, the project chronicles the experiences of the first Black women to study, work, or teach at Virginia Tech, which highlights the role of race and gender in the mid-1960s. http://spec.lib.vt.edu/blackwom
- The Online Archive of California also has a searchable catalogue with links to transcribed oral histories. Major topics at this archive include oral histories of Japanese Americans interned during World War II and Black history in California. www.oac.cdlib.org
- Texas Tech University has an online archive of oral histories associated with the Oral History Project of The Vietnam War. The interviews are fully transcribed and available online and often have associated streaming audio files to accompany them. www.vietnam.ttu.edu/oralhistory
- Rutgers University has a large collection of interviews available online as part of the Oral History Archives. http://oralhistory.rutgers.edu

As this list of resources suggests, there is no one body that organizes the archiving of qualitative data in Canada. As technological innovations increase the ease with which these data can be digitized, however, the numbers of secondary sources available online are increasing. It is just a matter of time before major North American data archives initiate an effort in archiving these materials.

LO 7 Outline some of the data resources available to qualitative researchers.

QUALITATIVE DATA RESOURCES

In Chapter 10, we discussed the data archives and data centres that store quantitative data, which are available for researchers to analyze. There are also similar resources for researchers interested in analyzing previously collected qualitative data. In the United Kingdom, qualitative data are archived by the UK Data Archive, which is home to many quantitative data sources as well. Adding qualitative data has been a major project for this archive for the past several years, and it continues to encourage qualitative researchers to archive their research materials there.

In recent years the efforts to archive qualitative data have really begun to materialize into publicly accessible archives, many of which are accessible online (see Box 12.5). The amount of work that has to go into converting qualitative material into archivable materials is appreciable: Audio materials must be digitized, notes scanned, and interviews fully transcribed.

QUALITATIVE RESEARCH RESOURCES

The Qualitative Research and Resource Centre at York University (affiliated with the Department of Sociology) was created to promote the practice of qualitative research methods. The centre has a range of research facilities available, including focus group facilities (with audio- and videotaping capabilities), transcription equipment, qualitative data analysis software, expert consultation, and an extensive collection of reference materials.

The International Institute for Qualitative Methodology is an interdisciplinary institute affiliated with the Faculty of Nursing at the University of Alberta. It has on-site facilities for individuals to use and also hosts a number of workshops and seminars over the course of the year. The institute also has an extensive on-site library.

CHAPTER SUMMARY

Glossary Flashcards

In this chapter, you learned about qualitative interviewing and the qualitative interviewing process (finding interviewees, preparing an interview guide, asking questions). The chapter began by identifying research questions that were appropriate for investigation through qualitative interviewing—namely those that focus on the subjective meaning of events and experiences by informants. Because structured survey interviewing was covered in a previous chapter, major differences between the survey interview and typical qualitative interview were highlighted. While qualitative interviews can resemble friendly conversations insofar as they are usually far less formal and rigid, several additional distinctions between the two were also considered.

The procedure of qualitative interviewing begins as all data collection techniques do: with sampling. Qualitative interviews are typically sampled using nonprobability techniques because sampling frames of the population of interest are generally unavailable. Incentives and interview sites were considered, as both are critical to maximizing the likelihood of cooperation and data quality.

There are nine types of questions that were identified by Kvale as being important to the qualitative interview: introducing, follow-up, probing, specifying, direct, indirect, structuring, interpreting, and silence. Definitions and examples of each were given. The interview guide as a tool to remind the researcher of key questions to ask informants during the process of the qualitative interview was also highlighted.

You also learned about the group interview, or focus group. Qualitative interviews are almost always done on an individual basis. When a group interview takes place, however, it is called a focus group. You learned about how the composition of groups is decided, how the number of groups is determined, and the moderator's role within the group. Both qualitative interviewers and focus group researchers begin data analysis and theorizing during the data collection phase. The advantages and disadvantages of qualitative interviews and focus groups were also considered.

Review Questions

Chapter Quiz

1. What kind of research question is appropriate for answering using qualitative interviews? What kind of research question is inappropriate for answering using qualitative interviews?
2. Name five differences between a typical survey interview and a typical qualitative interview.
3. Name five differences between a friendly conversation and a typical qualitative interview.
4. Define *informant* and *incentives*.
5. What is the purpose of an interview guide?
6. Identify and explain the nine different types of Kvale questions.
7. Describe four advantages and one disadvantage of qualitative interviews.
8. Explain the purpose of a focus group.
9. Describe two roles of the moderator in a focus group.
10. Explain what is meant by *devil's advocate* and *groupthink*.
11. Describe four advantages and four disadvantages of focus groups.

Exercises

1. Using one of the online sources for qualitative interview transcripts identified earlier in the chapter, select a qualitative interview transcript of interest to you and print it out. Now go through the transcript and identify the Kvale question types in the interview transcript.
2. Using EBSCO's ContentSelect, identify a research article that obtained data using qualitative interviewing. How did the researcher recruit people for his or her study? How many people were interviewed? What kinds of questions were the interviewees asked? How long did the interviews take?
3. Using EBSCO's ContentSelect, identify a research article that obtained data using focus groups. How did the researcher recruit people for his or her study? How many people were in the focus group? Demographically, how were the focus groups comprised? What kinds of questions did the moderator ask? How many focus groups were conducted?

Chapter 13

Field Research

Photo Credit: Polka Dot Images/ Thinkstock

LEARNING OBJECTIVES

After reading this chapter, you will be able to

LO 1 Identify research questions appropriate for answering with field research.

LO 2 Define *ethnography* and explain how it is different from field research.

LO 3 Explain what a field researcher does.

LO 4 Explain the steps in a field research project.

LO 5 Identify the levels of involvement of a field researcher.

LO 6 Explain how a field researcher collects data.

LO 7 Describe how data quality are ensured in field research.

LO 8 Explain the different types of ethical issues that the field researcher may face.

INTRODUCTION

This chapter describes field research, also called *participant-observation research*. It is a qualitative style in which a researcher directly observes and (usually) participates in small-scale social settings. The researcher also often uses qualitative interviewing in the process of doing field research, although field research is a method that is distinct from pure qualitative interviewing.

Box 13.1 Making It Practical

What Does a Field Researcher Do?

A field researcher does the following:

1. Observes ordinary events and everyday activities as they happen in natural settings, in addition to any unusual occurrences
2. Becomes directly involved with the people being studied and personally experiences the process of daily social life in the field setting
3. Acquires an insider's point of view while maintaining the analytic perspective or distance of an outsider
4. Uses a variety of techniques and social skills in a flexible manner as the situation demands
5. Produces data in the form of extensive written notes, as well as diagrams, maps, or pictures to provide very detailed descriptions
6. Sees events holistically (e.g., as a whole unit, not in pieces) and individually in their social context
7. Understands and develops empathy for members in a field setting, and does not just record "cold" objective facts
8. Notices both explicit (recognized, conscious, spoken) and tacit (less recognized, implicit, unspoken) aspects of culture
9. Observes ongoing social processes without upsetting, disrupting, or imposing an outside point of view
10. Copes with high levels of personal stress, uncertainty, ethical dilemmas, and ambiguity

In field research, the individual researcher directly talks with and observes the people being studied (see Box 13.1). Through interaction over months or years, the researcher learns about them, their life histories, their hobbies and interests, and their habits, hopes, fears, and dreams. Meeting new people, developing friendships, and discovering new social worlds can be fun. It is also time consuming, emotionally draining, and sometimes even physically dangerous.

LO 1 Identify research questions appropriate for answering with field research.

QUESTIONS APPROPRIATE FOR FIELD RESEARCH

Field research is appropriate when the research question involves learning about, understanding, or describing a group of interacting people. It is usually best when the question is, "How do people do Y in the social world?" or "What is the social world of X like?" It can be used when other methods (e.g., survey, experiments) are not feasible, as in a study of street gangs.

Field researchers study people in a location or setting. The technique has also been used to study entire communities. Beginning field researchers should start with a relatively small group (30 or fewer) who interact with each other on a regular basis in a relatively fixed setting (e.g., a street corner, place of worship, pub, café, recreation centre). Studying a smaller group allows the beginner to get acquainted with all of the many necessary steps involved in this data collection experience without getting overwhelmed by the even greater complexity of a large group study.

In order to use consistent terminology, we can call the people who are studied in a field setting *members*. They are insiders or "natives" in the field and belong to a group, subculture, or social setting that the "outsider" field researcher wants to penetrate and learn about.

Field researchers have explored a wide variety of social settings, subcultures, and aspects of social life[1] (see Figure 13.1). Places where our students have conducted successful short-term, small-scale field research studies include a beauty salon, daycare centre, bakery, bingo parlour, bowling alley, church, coffee shop, laundromat, police dispatch office, nursing home, tattoo parlour, and weight room.

Small-Scale Settings	Door-to-door salespersons
Passengers in an airplane	Factory workers
Bars or taverns	Gamblers
Battered women's shelters	Medical students
Camera clubs	Female exotic dancers
Laundromats	Police officers
Social movement organizations	Restaurant chefs
Social welfare offices	Social workers
Television stations	Taxi drivers
Waiting rooms	
	Deviance and Criminal Activity
Community Settings	Body/genital piercing and branding
Retirement communities	Drug dealers and addicts
Small towns	Cults
Urban ethnic communities	Hippies
Working-class neighbourhoods	Nude beaches
Children's Activities	Occult groups
Children's playgrounds	Sex workers
Minor baseball leagues	Street gangs, motorcycle gangs
Youth in schools	Street people, homeless shelters
Middle school girl groups	
	Medical Settings and Medical Events
Occupations	Death
Airline attendants	Emergency rooms
Artists	Intensive care units
Cocktail servers	Pregnancy and abortio Support groups for
Dog catchers	Alzheimer's caregivers

Figure 13.1 Examples of Field Research Sites/Topics

ETHNOGRAPHY

LO 2 Define *ethnography* and explain how it is different from field research.

You may have heard of a research approach called *ethnography* that sounds a lot like field research in many respects. Ethnography, however, uses field research as just one technique, often combined with qualitative interviews. The term *ethnography* comes from cultural anthropology. *Ethno-* means people or folk, and *-graphy* refers to describing something. Thus, **ethnography** means describing a culture and understanding another way of life from the native point of view. Ethnographies are a particular approach to doing fieldwork. *Doing field research is a core part of ethnography, but field research is usually just one part of an ethnographic study*. An ethnographer usually obtains and analyzes other forms of data as well, like qualitative interviews and archival documents. Ethnography is often considered a **methodology** rather than a method, which means it is a collection of methods that are tied together by an underlying theoretical orientation.

ethnography: An approach to *field research* that emphasizes providing a very detailed description of a different culture from the viewpoint of an insider in that culture to permit a greater understanding of it.

methodology: A collection of data collection and analysis approaches that are linked together through an overarching theoretical orientation.

Ethnography assumes that people make inferences—that is, go beyond what is explicitly seen or said to what is meant or implied. People display their culture (what people think, ponder, or believe) through behaviour (e.g., speech and actions) in specific social contexts. Displays of behaviour do not give meaning; rather, meaning is inferred, or someone figures out meaning. Moving from what is heard or observed to what is actually meant is at the centre of ethnography. For example, when a student is invited to a "kegger," the student infers that it is an informal party with other student-aged people at which beer will be served, based on his or her cultural knowledge. Cultural knowledge includes symbols, songs, sayings, facts, ways of behaving, and objects (e.g., telephones, newspapers). We learn the culture by watching television, listening to parents, observing others, and the like.

The Promise and Pitfalls of Going Into the Field

Cultural knowledge includes both explicit knowledge (what we know and talk about) and tacit knowledge (what we rarely acknowledge). For example, *explicit knowledge* includes the social event (e.g., a "kegger"). Most people can easily describe what

Box 13.2 Concepts in Action

Ethnography of Canadian Parkour Enthusiasts

Canadian sociologist Michael Atkinson (2009) conducted an ethnographic study of individuals who participated in parkour—which is a kind of "urban gymnastics" in which individuals run in a freestyle form, using elements of the urban landscape as their running course.

Atkinson describes his first time participating in one of the runs: "The 8 miles saw us hurtling through alleys and across low roof tops, vaulting over fences, scrambling underneath bridges and hop-scotching down city streets, and weaving our way between cars" (p. 169).

Over a period of two years, Atkinson studied a group of individuals who practised parkour (who are known as traceurs), both spending time in the field with them as a participant observer and conducting individual qualitative interviews. Among his findings are that most traceurs are urban middle-class White males who view themselves as anarcho-environmentalists.

When Can We Use Qualitative Methods?

happens at one. *Tacit knowledge* includes the unspoken cultural norm for the proper distance at which to stand from others. People are generally unaware that they use this norm. They feel unease or discomfort when the norm is violated, but it is difficult to pinpoint the source of discomfort. Ethnographers describe the explicit and tacit cultural knowledge that members use. Their detailed descriptions and careful analysis take apart what is described and put it back together.[2] See Box 13.2 for an example of an ethnographic study.

LO 3 Explain what a field researcher does.

THE LOGIC OF FIELD RESEARCH

What Is Field Research?

Qualitative versus Quantitative Research

It is difficult to pin down a specific definition of *field research* because it is more of an orientation toward research than a fixed set of techniques to apply.[3] A field researcher uses various methods to obtain information. A *field researcher* is a resourceful, talented individual who has ingenuity and an ability to think quickly while in the field.

naturalism: The principle that researchers should examine events as they occur in natural, everyday, ongoing social settings.

Field research is based on naturalism, which is also used to study other phenomena (e.g., oceans, animals, plants). **Naturalism** involves observing ordinary events in natural settings, not in contrived, invented, or researcher-created settings. Research occurs in the field and outside the safe settings of an office, laboratory, or classroom.

A field researcher's goal is to examine social meanings and grasp multiple perspectives in natural social settings. He or she wants to get inside the meaning system of members and then return to an outside or research viewpoint. To do this, the researcher switches perspectives and looks at the setting from multiple points of view simultaneously.

Field research is usually conducted by a single individual, although small teams have been effective. The researcher is directly involved in and part of the social world studied, so his or her personal characteristics are relevant in research. The researcher's direct involvement in the field often has an emotional impact. Field research can be fun and exciting, but it can also disrupt one's personal life, physical security, or mental well-being. More than other types of social research, it can reshape friendships, family life, self-identity, and personal values.

LO 4 Explain the steps in a field research project.

STEPS IN A FIELD RESEARCH PROJECT

Naturalism and direct involvement mean that field research is less structured than quantitative research. This makes it essential for a researcher to be well organized and prepared for the field. It also means that the steps of a project are not entirely predetermined but

Box 13.3 Making It Practical

General Steps in Field Research

1. Prepare yourself, read the literature, and defocus.
2. Select a field site and gain access to it.
3. Enter the field and establish social relations with members.
4. Adopt a social role, learn the ropes, and get along with members.
5. Watch, listen, and collect quality data.
6. Begin to analyze data and to generate and evaluate working hypotheses.
7. Focus on specific aspects of the setting and use theoretical sampling.
8. Conduct field interviews with member informants.
9. Disengage and physically leave the setting.
10. Complete the analyses and write the research report.

Note: There is no fixed percentage of time needed for each step. For a rough approximation, Junker (1960, p. 12) suggested that, once in the field, the researcher should expect to spend approximately one sixth of his or her time observing, one third recording data, one third analyzing data, and one sixth reporting results. Also see Denzin (1989, p. 176) for eight steps of field research.

serve as an approximate guide or road map (see Box 13.3). Field researchers rarely follow rigidly fixed steps. In fact, flexibility is a key advantage of field research, as it lets a researcher shift direction and follow leads. Good field researchers recognize and seize opportunities, "play it by ear," and rapidly adjust to fluid social situations.

Preparing, Reading, and Defocusing

Human and personal factors can play a role in any research project, but they are crucial in field research. Field projects often begin with chance occurrences or a personal interest. Field researchers can begin with their own experiences, such as working at a job, having a hobby, or being a patient or an activist.

Field researchers use the skills of careful looking and listening, short-term memorizing, and regular writing. Before entering the field, a new researcher practises observing the ordinary details of situations and writing them down. Attention to details and short-term memory can improve with practice. Likewise, keeping a daily diary or personal journal is good practice for writing field notes.

As with all social research, reading the scholarly literature helps the researcher learn about concepts, potential pitfalls, data collection methods, and techniques for resolving conflicts. In addition, a field researcher finds diaries, novels, journalists' accounts, and autobiographies useful for gaining familiarity with the field and preparing emotionally for it.

Field research begins with a general topic, not specific hypotheses. A researcher does not get locked into any initial misconceptions. He or she needs to be well informed but open to discovering new ideas. Finding the right questions to ask about the field takes time.

A researcher first empties his or her mind of preconceptions. The researcher should move outside his or her comfortable social niche to experience as much as possible in the field without betraying a primary commitment to being a researcher.

Field researchers need to know themselves and reflect on personal experiences. They can expect anxiety, self-doubt, frustration, and uncertainty in the field. Especially in the beginning, researchers may feel that they are collecting the wrong data and may suffer emotional turmoil, isolation, and confusion. They often feel doubly marginal: an outsider in the field setting and also distant from friends, family, and other researchers.[4] The relevance of a researcher's emotional makeup, personal biography, and cultural experiences makes it important to be aware of his or her personal commitments and

Box 13.4 Concepts in Action

Field Research on Tattoo Enthusiasts

Often, field researchers are motivated to study topics in which they have a very personal interest. Atkinson (2004) spent three years studying tattoo enthusiasts in Calgary and Toronto. Atkinson explains his data collection strategy as one of "hanging out." As a researcher who was personally interested in tattoos, he immersed himself in the tattooing "subculture." Below, he describes how he entered the field:

> The nature of my participation in tattooing considerably influenced the sampling process. As a person who immersed himself in a tattoo-enthusiast role and as a researcher who spent copious amounts of time hanging around tattoo enthusiasts, I interacted with a substantial diversity of individuals during the field work process. At first, I interacted with a core group of enthusiasts in Calgary but progressively "branched out" by hanging around with their tattooed friends in various social locales. By tactically "doing nothing" . . . with them in everyday life (i.e., going to restaurants, running routine errands, watching television, sitting in tattoo studios, or simply "shooting the breeze" over drinks), I casually inquired about their tattooing experiences, perspectives, and stories. (p. 128)

inner conflicts (see Box 13.4). Fieldwork can have a strong impact on a researcher's identity and outlook. Researchers may be personally transformed by the field experience. Some adopt new values, interests, and moral commitments, or change their religion or political ideology.[5]

Although a field research project does not proceed by fixed steps, some common concerns arise in the early stages. These include selecting a site and gaining access to it, entering the field, learning the ropes, and developing rapport with members in the field.

Selecting a Field Site and Gaining Access to It

field site: The one or more natural locations where a researcher conducts *field research*.

Field researchers talk about doing research on a setting, or **field site**, but this term is misleading. A site is the context in which events or activities occur; a socially defined territory with shifting boundaries. A social group may interact across several physical sites. For example, a university hockey team may interact on the ice, in the locker room, in student residence, at a training camp, or at a local hangout. The team's field site includes all five locations.

The field site and research question are bound together, but choosing a site is not the same as focusing on a case for study. A *case* is a social relationship or activity; it can extend beyond the boundaries of the site and have links to other social settings. A researcher selects a site, then identifies cases to examine within it—for example, how football team members relate to authority figures. And sites are no longer restricted to the physical world, as discussed in Box 13.5.

Selecting a field site is an important decision, and researchers take notes on the site selection processes. Three factors are relevant when choosing a field research site: richness of data, unfamiliarity, and suitability.[6] Some sites are more likely than others to provide rich data. Sites that present a web of social relations, a variety of activities, and diverse events over time provide richer, more interesting data. Beginning field researchers should choose an unfamiliar setting. It is easier to see cultural events and social relations in a new site. It is not impossible for researchers to examine familiar sites, but for new researchers, an unfamiliar site will provide them with the environment to develop their observation skills. In a very familiar site (such as a sports club that you've been going to for years), much of the experiences of the group under study may be taken for granted, or assumed to be "normal." As researchers, we can train ourselves to "see" things in a familiar or "home" environment, but this does take some degree of experience. When "casing" possible field sites, one must consider such practical issues as the researcher's time and skills, serious

Box 13.5 Social Research and the Internet

Online Field Research and "Netnography"

As discussed above, field research can occur at a plethora of possible research sites. The growth of the online world in the past two decades has also expanded the number of "places" that field research can occur. Internet technologies have permeated modern day living extensively, with the interactions in online contexts having the ability to have influence well beyond the subjects directly involved in the online interaction (Markham, 2005).

Online field research, sometimes called *netnography*, also comes with similar types of challenges as those faced by doing field research in the conventional manner. For example, to what extent does the researcher participate in the online culture, and therefore contribute to the shape it takes? However, online research, as pointed out by Markham (2005), also has its own unique sets of questions that the researcher must consider. Online communication, for example, relies almost exclusively on the written word. What can we say about our subjects when our entire knowledge of them exists through the exchange of messages? How can we understand the "real" social relationship when we are limited to interacting with subjects who may never have any physical interaction with each other? Can we simply "observe" and truly understand the culture we are trying to study?

As discussed in Chapter 3, Whitehead (2010) undertook field research of online eating disorder (pro-ED) communities. Whitehead describes her study as a "virtual ethnography." After using Google to search for the terms "pro-ana" (pro-anorexia) and "pro-mia" (pro-bulimia), she identified a major communication hub, where she covertly conducted her field research for one to three hours a day for six months. She describes her online ethnographic approach:

> Visiting the sites on a daily basis . . . approximated the visiting habits of individuals most involved in the sites' production and maintenance. Much like individuals who check their email every day, Pro-ED adherents check the Pro-ED sites on a daily basis, and often have free email accounts associated with the websites. My daily visits made use of links on the site to keep track of the changes and updates that occurred. In the first two weeks of my analysis I explored all sections of the website to get a sense of the overall online environment; however, not all my visits over the course of the six-month period explored every section of the website. Instead I kept an archive on the data on the site in a separate document in the event that the website content was modified or taken offline. I took descriptive fieldnotes in the process of visiting the sites in order to maintain a record of my observations." (p. 600)

conflicts among people in the site, the researcher's personal characteristics and feelings, and access to parts of a site.

A researcher's ascriptive characteristics (e.g., age, gender, race) can limit or enhance access. Physical access to a site can be an issue. Sites are on a continuum, with open and public areas (e.g., public restaurants, airport waiting areas) at one end and closed and private settings (e.g., private firms, clubs, activities in a person's home) at the other. A researcher may find that he or she is not welcome or not allowed on the site, or there are legal and political barriers to access. Laws and regulations in institutions (e.g., public schools, hospitals, prisons) restrict access. In addition, institutional ethics review boards may limit field research on ethical grounds.

Entering the Field and Establishing Social Relations with Members

LO 5 Identify the levels of involvement of a field researcher.

Once the site has been selected and is accessible, the researcher needs to consider the appropriate level of involvement and a strategy for entering the field.

Level of Involvement Field roles can be arranged on a continuum by the degree of detachment or involvement a researcher has with members. At one extreme is a complete observer; at the other extreme is complete participant (see Figure 13.2).

The field researcher's level of involvement depends on negotiations with members, specifics of the field setting, the researcher's personal comfort, and the particular role adopted in the field. Many move from observer to semi-participant levels with more time in the field. Each level has its advantages and disadvantages. Different field researchers advocate different levels of involvement.

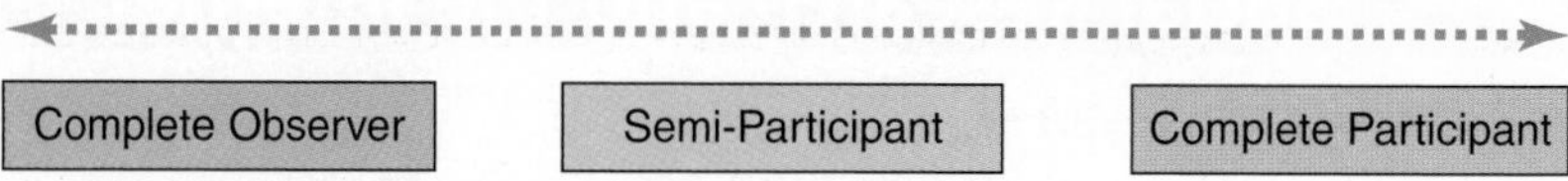

Figure 13.2 Levels of Involvement in Field Research

complete observer: In *field research*, when a researcher only observes the study group without participating in their activities.

complete participant: In *field research*, when a researcher fully participates in all aspects of the study group's activities as though a member of the group.

semi-participant: Refers to the role of the researcher in *field research* when he or she participates to some degree in group activities, but not as much as a full member.

gatekeeper: Someone with the formal or informal authority to control access to a site.

As a **complete observer,** the researcher's role is limited to simple observation, without any participation in the activities of his or her study group. This type of role reduces the time needed for acceptance, makes over-rapport less of an issue, and can sometimes help members open up. It can facilitate detachment and protect the researcher's self-identity. A researcher feels marginal. Although there is less risk of "going native," he or she is also less likely to know an insider's experience and misinterpretation is more likely. To really understand social meaning for those being studied, the field researcher must participate in the setting to some extent, as others do.

By contrast, roles at the **complete participant** end of the continuum facilitate empathy and sharing of a member's experience. The goal of fully experiencing the intimate social world of a member is achieved. Nevertheless, a lack of distance from, too much sympathy for, or over-involvement with members is likely. A researcher's reports may be questioned, data gathering is difficult, there can be a dramatic impact on the researcher's self, and the distance needed for analysis may be hard to attain.

Often, researchers adopt a "middle of the road" approach to involvement. They are not complete participants (or full members) of the group they study, nor are they complete observers. The term **semi-participant** is given to researchers who participate to some extent with the activities of the group but who do not immerse themselves completely in the group's culture, giving priority to their role as a social researcher.

Strategy for Entering Entering a field site requires having a flexible strategy or plan of action, negotiating access and relations with members, and deciding how much to disclose about the research to field members or gatekeepers.

Planning Entering and gaining access to a field site is a process that depends on common sense judgment and social skills. Field sites usually have different levels or areas, and entry is an issue for each. Entry is more analogous to peeling the layers of an onion than to opening a door. Moreover, bargains and promises of entry may not remain stable over time. A researcher needs fallback plans or may have to return later for renegotiation. Because the specific focus of research may not emerge until later in the research process or may change, it is best to avoid being locked into specifics by gatekeepers. A **gatekeeper** is someone with the formal or informal authority to control access to a site.[7] It can be the gang leader on the corner, an administrator of a hospital, or the owner of a business. Informal public areas (e.g., sidewalks, public waiting rooms) rarely have gatekeepers; formal organizations have authorities from whom permission must be obtained.

Field researchers expect to negotiate with gatekeepers and bargain for access. The gatekeepers may not appreciate the need for conceptual distance or ethical balance. The researcher must set nonnegotiable limits to protect research integrity. If there are many restrictions initially, a researcher can often reopen negotiations later, and gatekeepers may forget their initial demands as trust develops. It is ethically and politically astute to call on gatekeepers. Researchers do not expect them to listen to research concerns or care about the findings, except insofar as these findings might provide evidence for someone to criticize them.

Dealing with gatekeepers is a recurrent issue as a researcher enters new levels or areas. In addition, a gatekeeper can shape the direction of research. In some sites, gatekeeper approval creates a stigma that inhibits the cooperation of members. For example, prisoners may not be cooperative if they know that the prison warden gave approval to the researcher.

Negotiating Social relations are negotiated and formed throughout the process of fieldwork.[8] Negotiation occurs with each new member until a stable relationship develops to gain access, develop trust, obtain information, and reduce hostile reactions. The researcher expects to negotiate and explain what he or she is doing over and over in the field (see "Normalizing Social Research" later in the chapter).

Deviant groups and elites often require special negotiations for gaining access. To gain access to deviant subcultures, field researchers have used contacts from the researchers' private lives, gone to social welfare or law enforcement agencies where the deviants are processed, advertised for volunteers, offered a service (e.g., counselling) in exchange for access, or gone to a location where deviants hang out and joined a group.

Disclosing A researcher must decide how much to reveal about himself or herself and the research project. Disclosing one's personal life, hobbies, interests, and background can build trust and close relationships, but the researcher will also lose privacy, and he or she needs to ensure that the focus remains on events in the field.

A researcher also decides how much to disclose about the research project. Disclosure ranges on a continuum from being a fully **covert observer**, in which no one in the field is aware that research is taking place, to the opposite end, as an **overt observer**, where everyone knows the specifics of the research project. The degree and timing of disclosure depends on a researcher's judgment and particulars in the setting. Disclosure may unfold over time as the researcher feels more secure. See Box 13.6 for examples of both types of approaches.

covert observer: In *field research*, refers to a researcher who is secretly studying a group without the group members knowing that they are being studied.

overt observer: In *field research*, refers to a researcher who is studying the group members with their full knowledge.

Researchers disclose the project to gatekeepers and others unless there is a good reason for not doing so, such as the presence of gatekeepers who would seriously limit or inhibit research for illegitimate reasons (e.g., to hide graft or corruption). Even in these cases, a researcher may disclose his or her identity as a researcher, but may pose as one who seems submissive, harmless, and interested in nonthreatening issues.

Adopting a Social Role and Learning the Ropes

Researchers must next adopt a role in the setting, learn the ropes, develop rapport with members, and maintain social relations. Before confronting such issues, the researcher should ask, "How will I present myself?" "What does it mean for me to be a measurement instrument?" "How can I assume an attitude of strangeness?"

Presentation of Self People explicitly and implicitly present themselves to others. We display who we are—the type of person we are or would like to be—through our physical appearance, what we say, and how we act. The presentation of self sends a symbolic message. It may be "I'm a serious, hard-working student," "I'm a warm and caring person," "I'm a cool jock," or "I'm a rebel and a party animal." Many selves are possible, and presentations of selves can differ depending on the occasion.

A field researcher is conscious of the presentation of self in the field. For example, how should he or she dress in the field? The best guide is to respect both yourself and those you are studying. Do not overdress so as to offend or stand out, but copying the dress of those being studied is not always necessary. A professor who studies street people does not have to dress or act like one; dressing and acting informally is sufficient. Likewise, more

Box 13.6 Concepts in Action

Overt and Covert Field Research

There are two distinct roles that a researcher can take in the field—overt or covert. As discussed earlier in this book, the ethics surrounding research on human participants requires that participants, where possible, give their informed consent to being studied. This, however, is not always possible, as letting some groups know you want to study them makes them inaccessible or causes them to change their behaviour so drastically that little can be learned from studying them in this manner. This is particularly the case with deviant or controversial groups.

Lauder (2007) was interested in studying a racial nationalist group (otherwise known as a "White supremacist" group) in Canada called the Heritage Front. Lauder originally began his study as an overt researcher. That is, his role as a researcher was openly known to all members. He did not pretend to be interested in the mandates of the group—he made it clear that he was just there to study them. For several months he maintained this role and reflected upon it as follows:

> Over the following months I met with a number of members and conducted semi-formal and formal interviews. Although the majority of the participants were extremely friendly and courteous, I found that the interviews produced little useful information about the anti-Semitic and religious character of the organisation's ideology. Inquiries, whether direct or indirect, regarding Jews, Judaism, or a general discussion regarding religion and worship were often answered ambiguously or were simply avoided. On one occasion, the interviewee responded with an outburst of hostility: "What the hell, are you a Jew? Is that it, you're a Jew, right? What do you want to hear from me, that all of us evil Nazis hate Jews, that we want to kill all of them? You've been brainwashed by the media." A few respondents even accused me of being a police officer or a government agent. "C'mon, admit it, you're a cop," said one long-time member. "I don't care, I'll still talk to you. You can tell me, I promise I won't tell anyone." Further complicating research endeavours, the respondents refused to sign consent forms or complete a formal questionnaire (regardless of guarantees of anonymity) for fear of criminal prosecution. I later discovered that many of the participants were specifically selected (by the group leader) for their experience in dealing with the media and were instructed to treat the interviews as if I was a reporter. These instructions, along with the level of paranoia that naturally exists in the white supremacist movement, resulted in answers that were contrived and superficial and generally lacking in honesty, authenticity, and spontaneity. Overall, responses were devalued because participants were self-conscious and anxious. (p. 190)

It was after six months of such disappointing results that Lauder decided to change his strategy to become a covert observer. He decided to use deception and tell the group that he had become a convert. He stopped bringing pads of paper and pens to the meetings, instead opting to record his field notes after the encounters using memorization. He bought the group's books and pretended to have adopted their worldview in discussions with them. He did not, however, hide his role as a researcher, but told them that he had been convinced by their arguments:

> One of the methods employed to convince participants that I had converted relied on meeting with several participants in coffee shops and pubs for informal discussions about politics, government, and everyday personal interests, such as sports, gradually increasing my "support" of the movement and indicating that I was disillusioned with both school and the policies of the government. When asked about my research, I simply told the respondents that I altered the emphasis of the project to focus on "unfair media representations of the racialist movement," that the end product was going to be "very controversial." It was a project they appreciated and were eager to assist. (p. 191)

Lauder was not a true covert observer, as he began as an overt researcher and then used deception as a technique to extract more natural interactions from group members.

Kemple and Huey (2005) used covert field observations in their study of surveillance in "skid row" areas of Vancouver. They were interested in seeing how local area residents and street people were monitored by surveillance strategies, such as the police and privately hired security guards. They accomplished part of their research through covert observation by secretly observing security guards at "fixed vantage points (sidewalk benches, café seats, bus stops, etc.) or [the security guards] were discreetly followed while on patrol" (p. 146). The researchers explain that because much of the observation took place in tourist areas of the city, the researchers dressed in shorts and carried cameras to "blend in."

formal dress and professional demeanor are required when studying corporate executives or top officials.

A researcher must be aware that self-presentation will influence field relations to some degree. It is difficult to present a highly deceptive front or to present oneself in a way that deviates sharply from the person one is ordinarily.

Researcher as Instrument The researcher is the instrument for measuring field data. This has two implications. First, it puts pressure on the researcher to be alert and sensitive to what happens in the field and to be disciplined about recording data. Second, it has personal consequences. Fieldwork involves social relationships and personal feelings. Field researchers are flexible about what to include as data and admit their own subjective insights and feelings. Personal, subjective experiences are part of field data. They are valuable both in themselves and for interpreting events in the field. Instead of trying to be objective and eliminate personal reactions, field researchers treat their feelings toward field events as data.

Field research can heighten a researcher's awareness of personal feelings. For example, a researcher may not be fully aware of personal feelings about nudity until he or she is in a nudist colony, or about personal possessions until he or she is in a setting where others "borrow" many items. The researcher's own surprise, indignation, or questioning then may become an opportunity for reflection and insight.

An Attitude of Strangeness It is hard to recognize what we are very close to. The everyday world we inhabit is filled with thousands of details. If we paid attention to everything all the time, we would suffer from severe information overload. We manage by ignoring much of what is around us and by engaging in habitual thinking. Unfortunately, we fail to see the familiar as distinctive and assume that others experience reality just as we do. We tend to treat our own way of living as natural or normal.

Field research in familiar surroundings is difficult because of a tendency to be blinded by the familiar. By studying other cultures, researchers encounter dramatically different assumptions about what is important and how things are done. This confrontation of cultures, or *culture shock*, has two benefits: It makes it easier to see cultural elements and it facilitates self-discovery. Researchers adopt the attitude of strangeness to gain these benefits. An **attitude of strangeness** involves questioning and noticing ordinary details or looking at the ordinary through the eyes of a stranger. Strangeness helps a researcher overcome the boredom of observing ordinary details. It helps him or her see the ordinary in a new way, one that reveals aspects of the setting of which members are not consciously aware. A field researcher adopts both a stranger's and an insider's point of view.

attitude of strangeness: A technique in *field research* in which researchers study a *field site* by mentally adjusting to "see" it for the first time or as an outsider.

People rarely recognize customs they take for granted. For example, when someone gives us a gift, we say thank you and praise the gift. By contrast, gift-giving customs in some cultures include complaining that the gift is inadequate. The attitude of strangeness helps make the tacit culture visible—for example, that gift givers expect to hear "Thank you" and "The gift is nice," and become upset otherwise.

Strangeness also encourages a researcher to reconsider his or her own social world. Immersion in a different setting breaks old habits of thought and action. He or she finds reflection and introspection easier and more intense when encountering the unfamiliar, whether it is a different culture or a familiar culture seen through a stranger's eyes.

Building Rapport A field researcher builds rapport by getting along with members in the field. He or she forges a friendly relationship, shares the same language, and laughs and cries with members. This is a step toward obtaining an understanding of members and moving beyond understanding to empathy—that is, seeing and feeling events from another's perspective.

It is not always easy to build rapport. The social world is not all in harmony, with warm, friendly people. A setting may contain fear, tension, and conflict. Members may be unpleasant, untrustworthy, or untruthful; they may do things that disturb or disgust a researcher. An experienced researcher is prepared for a range of events and relationships. He or she may find, however, that it is impossible to penetrate a setting or get really close to members. Settings where cooperation, sympathy, and collaboration are impossible require different techniques.[9]

Charm and Trust A field researcher needs social skills and personal charm to build rapport. Trust, friendly feelings, and being well liked facilitate communication and help him or her to understand the inner feelings of others. There is no magical way to do this. Showing a genuine concern for and interest in others, being honest, and sharing feelings are good strategies, but they are not foolproof. Much depends on the specific setting and members.

Many factors affect trust and rapport: how a researcher presents himself or herself; the role he or she chooses for the field; and the events that encourage, limit, or make it impossible to achieve trust. Trust is not gained once and for all. It is a developmental process built up over time through many social nuances (e.g., sharing of personal experiences, storytelling, gestures, hints, facial expressions). It is constantly re-created and seems easier to lose once it has been built up than to gain in the first place.

Establishing trust is important, but it does not ensure that all information will be revealed. It may be limited to specific areas. For example, trust can be built up regarding financial matters but not regarding intimate dating behaviour. Trust may have to be created anew in each area of inquiry; it requires constant reaffirmation.

Understanding Rapport helps field researchers understand members, but understanding is a precondition for greater depth, not an end in itself. It slowly develops in the field as the researcher overcomes an initial bewilderment with a new or unusual language and system of social meaning. Once he or she attains an understanding of the member's point of view, the next step is to learn how to think and act within a member's perspective. This is *empathy*, or adopting another's perspective. Empathy does not necessarily mean sympathy, agreement, or approval; it means feeling things as another person does. Rapport helps create understanding and ultimately empathy, and the development of empathy facilitates greater rapport.

RELATIONS IN THE FIELD

You play many social roles in daily life—daughter/son, student, customer, sports fan—and maintain social relations with others. You choose some roles and others are structured for you (e.g., few have a choice but to play the role of son or daughter). Some roles are formal (e.g., bank teller, police chief), while others are informal (flirt, elder statesperson, buddy). You can switch roles, play multiple roles, and play a role in a particular way. Field researchers play roles in the field. In addition, they learn the ropes and maintain relations with members.

Roles in the Field

Pre-existing versus Created Roles At times, a researcher adopts an existing role. Some existing roles provide access to all areas of the site, the ability to observe and interact with all members, the freedom to move around, and a way to balance the requirements of researcher and member. At other times, a researcher creates a new role or modifies an existing one. Sometimes, to gain acceptance into groups, a researcher may have to do favours for group members, or take an active role in the group as a member.

Limits on the Role Chosen The field roles open to a researcher are affected by ascriptive factors and physical appearance. He or she can change some aspects of appearance, such as dress or hairstyle, but not ascriptive features such as age, race, gender, and attractiveness. Nevertheless, such factors can be important in gaining access and can restrict the available roles. For example, Kusow (2003) reported that being a Somali immigrant required extra negotiations and hassles, even when studying other Somali immigrants in Canada. Nevertheless, his ethnicity provided insights and created situations that would have been absent with a researcher from outside this immigrant community.

Since many roles are sex-typed, gender is an important consideration. Female researchers often have more difficulty when the setting is perceived as dangerous or seamy and where males are in control (e.g., police work, firefighting). They may be shunned or pushed into limiting gender stereotypes (e.g., "sweet kid," "mascot," "loud mouth").

Maintaining a "marginal" status is stressful; it is difficult to be an outsider who is not fully involved, especially when studying settings full of intense feelings (e.g., political campaigns, religious conversions). The loneliness and isolation of fieldwork may combine with the desire to develop rapport and empathy to cause over-involvement. A researcher may **go native** and drop the professional researcher's role to become a full member of the group being studied. Or the researcher may feel guilt about learning intimate details as members drop their guard, and may come to over-identify with members.

go native: What happens when a researcher in *field research* gets overly involved, loses all distance or objectivity, and becomes like the people being studied.

Normalizing Social Research

A field researcher not only observes and investigates members in the field but is observed and investigated by members as well. In overt field research, members are usually initially uncomfortable with the presence of a researcher. Most are unfamiliar with field research and fail to distinguish between sociologists, psychologists, counsellors, and social workers. They may see the researcher as an outside critic or spy, or as a saviour or all-knowing expert.

An overt field researcher must **normalize social research**—that is, help members redefine social research from something unknown and threatening to something normal and predictable. He or she can help members manage research by presenting his or her own biography, explaining field research a little at a time, appearing nonthreatening, or accepting minor deviance in the setting (e.g., minor violations of official rules).

normalize social research: Techniques in *field research* used by researchers to make the people being studied feel more comfortable with the research process and to help them accept the researcher's presence.

Maintaining Relations

Qualitative Methods

Social Relations

With time, a field researcher develops and modifies social relationships. Members who are cool at first may warm up later. Or they may put on a front of initial friendliness, and their fears and suspicions surface only later. A researcher is in a delicate position. Early in a project, when not yet fully aware of everything about a field site, the researcher does not form close relationships because circumstances may change. Yet if he or she does develop close friends, they can become allies who will defend the researcher's presence and help him or her gain access.

A field researcher monitors how his or her actions and appearance affect members. For example, a physically attractive researcher who interacts with members of the opposite sex may encounter crushes, flirting, and jealousy. He or she develops an awareness of these field relations and learns to manage them.

In addition to developing social relationships, a field researcher must be able to break or withdraw from relationships as well. Ties with one member may have to be broken to forge ties with others or to explore other aspects of the setting. As with the end of any friendly relationship, the emotional pain of social withdrawal can affect both the researcher and the member. The researcher must balance social sensitivity and the research goals.

Small Favours

Exchange relationships develop in the field, in which small tokens or favours, including deference and respect, are exchanged. A researcher may gain acceptance by helping out in small ways. Exchange helps when access to sensitive issues is limited. A researcher may offer small favours but not burden members by asking for return favours. As the researcher and members share experiences and see each other again, members recall the favours and reciprocate by allowing access.

exchange relationships: Relationships that develop in the field, in which small tokens or favours, including deference and respect, are exchanged.

Conflicts in the Field

Fights, conflict, and disagreements can erupt in the field, or a researcher may study groups with opposing positions. In such situations, the researcher will feel pressure to take sides and will be tested to see if he or she can be trusted. On such occasions, a researcher usually stays on the neutral sidelines and walks a tightrope between opposing sides. This is because by becoming aligned with one side, the researcher will cut off access to the other side. In addition, he or she will see the situation from only one point of view.

Other types of conflicts that can occur are those that relate to researcher participation. If the group that the researcher is studying is involved in illegal acts, to what extent should the researcher participate? It may seem obvious to say "Not at all," but trust between researchers and group members may be at stake if the researcher does not participate in activities that are core to the group's identity. Obviously, the risks that are involved must be weighed against the benefits of participating in such acts. But such conflicts are not limited simply to issues of legality. Sometimes a group may be involved in morally tenuous activities that are harmful or exploitative to others. Clearly, there are ethical issues surrounding the participation of a researcher in such acts. Again, complete detachment from "core" activities of a group may result in the researcher's being ethically conscious, but it also may serve to distance the researcher from the group members and make the group members less likely to trust the intentions of the researcher. (You can get a sense of Lauder's struggle with the issue of participating in morally tenuous activities in Box 13.6.)

appearance of interest: A technique in *field research* in which researchers maintain relations in a *field site* by pretending to be interested and excited by the activities of those studied, even though they are actually uninterested or very bored.

Appearing Interested Field researchers maintain an **appearance of interest** in the field. An experienced researcher appears to be interested in and involved with field events by statements and behaviours (e.g., facial expression, going for coffee, organizing a party) even if he or she is not truly interested. This is because field relations may be disrupted if the researcher appears to be bored or distracted. Putting up such a temporary front of involvement is a common small deception in daily life and is part of being polite.

Of course, selective inattention (i.e., not staring or appearing not to notice) is also part of acting polite. If a person makes a social mistake (e.g., accidentally uses an incorrect word, passes gas), the polite thing to do is to ignore it. Selective inattention is used in fieldwork, as well. It gives an alert researcher an opportunity to learn by casually eavesdropping on conversations or observing events not meant to be public.

LO 6 Explain how a field researcher collects data.

OBSERVING AND COLLECTING DATA

This section looks at how to get good qualitative field data. Field data are what the researcher experiences and remembers and what are recorded in field notes and become available for systematic analysis.

Watching and Listening

Research Tools and Techniques

Observing In the field, researchers pay attention, watch, and listen carefully. They use all the senses, noticing what is seen, heard, smelled, tasted, or touched. The researcher becomes an instrument that absorbs all sources of information.

A field researcher carefully scrutinizes the physical setting to capture its atmosphere. He or she asks, "What is the colour of the floor, walls, ceiling? How large is the room? Where are the windows and doors? How is the furniture arranged, and what is its condition (e.g., new or old and worn, dirty or clean)? What type of lighting is there? Are there signs, paintings, plants? What are the sounds or smells?"

Why bother with such details? You may have noticed that stores and restaurants often plan lighting, colours, and piped-in music to create a certain atmosphere. Maybe you know that used-car salespeople spray a new-car scent into used cars, or that stores in shopping malls intentionally send out the odour of freshly made cookies. These subtle, unconscious signals influence human behaviour.

Observation in field research is often detailed, tedious work. Instead of the quick flash, motivation arises out of a deep curiosity about the details. Good field researchers are intrigued about details that reveal "what's going on here" through careful listening and watching. Field researchers believe that the core of social life is communicated through the mundane, trivial, everyday minutiae. This is what people often overlook, but field researchers need to learn how to notice.

In addition to physical surroundings, a field researcher observes people and their actions, noting each person's observable physical characteristics: age, sex, race, and stature. People socially interact differently depending on whether another person is 18, 40, or 70 years old; male or female; short and frail or tall, heavyset, and muscular. When noting such characteristics, the researcher is included.

The researcher records such details because something of significance *might* be revealed. It is better to err by including everything than to ignore potentially significant details. For example, "The tall, White, muscular 19-year-old male sprinted into the brightly lit room just as the short, overweight Black woman in her sixties eased into a battered chair" says much more than "One person entered, and another sat down."

A field researcher notes aspects of physical appearance such as neatness, dress, and hairstyle because they express messages that can affect social interactions. People spend a great deal of time and money selecting clothes, styling and combing hair, grooming with makeup, shaving, ironing clothes, and using deodorant or perfumes. These are part of their presentation of self. Even people who do not groom, shave, or wear deodorant present themselves and send a symbolic message by their appearance. No one dresses or looks "normal." Such a statement suggests that a researcher is not seeing the social world through the eyes of a stranger or is insensitive to social signals.

Behaviour is also significant. A field researcher notices where people sit or stand, the pace at which they walk, and their nonverbal communication. People express social information, feelings, and attitudes through nonverbal communication, including gestures, facial expressions, and how one stands or sits (e.g., standing stiffly, sitting in a slouched position). People express relationships by how they position themselves in a group and through eye contact. A researcher may read the social communication of people by noting that they are standing close together, looking relaxed, and making eye contact.

A field researcher also notices the context in which events occur: Who was present? Who just arrived or left the scene? Was the room hot and stuffy? Such details may help the researcher assign meaning and understand why an event occurred. If they are not noticed, the details are lost, as is a full understanding of the event.

Serendipity is important in field research. Many times, a field researcher does not know the relevance of what he or she is observing until later. This has two implications. First is the importance of keen observation and excellent notes at all times, even when nothing seems to be happening. Second is the importance of looking back over time and learning to appreciate wait time. Most field researchers say that they spend a lot of time "waiting." Novice field researchers get frustrated with the amount of time they seem to "waste," either waiting for other people or waiting for events to occur.

A field researcher must be attuned to the rhythms of the setting, operate on other people's schedules, and observe how events occur within their own flow of time. Wait time is not always wasted time. Wait time is time for reflection, for observing details, for developing social relations, for building rapport, and for becoming a familiar sight to people in the field setting. Wait time also displays that a researcher is committed and serious; perseverance is a significant trait field researchers need to cultivate. The researcher may be impatient to get in, get the research over with, and get on with his or her "real life," but for the people in the field site, this *is* real life. The researcher should subordinate his or her personal wants to the demands of the field site.

Listening A field researcher listens carefully to phrases, accents, and incorrect grammar, listening both to *what* is said and *how* it is said or what was implied. For example, people often use phrases such as "you know" or "of course" or "et cetera." A field researcher knows the meaning behind such phrases. He or she can try to hear everything, but listening is difficult when many conversations occur at once or when eavesdropping. Luckily, significant events and themes usually recur.

Taking Notes

Field Research

Most field research data are in the form of field notes. Full field notes can contain maps, diagrams, photographs, tape recordings, videotapes, memos, artifacts or objects from the field, notes jotted in the field, and detailed notes written away from the field. A field researcher expects to fill many notebooks or the equivalent in computer memory. He or she may spend more time writing notes than being in the field. Some researchers produce 40 single-spaced pages of notes for three hours of observation. With practice, even a new field researcher can produce several pages of notes for each hour in the field.

Writing notes is often boring, tedious work that requires self-discipline. The notes contain extensive descriptive detail drawn from memory. A researcher makes it a daily habit or compulsion to write notes immediately after leaving the field. The notes must be neat and organized because the researcher will return to them over and over again. Once written, the notes are private and valuable. A researcher treats them with care and protects confidentiality. Field notes may be of interest to hostile parties, blackmailers, or legal officials, so some researchers write field notes in code.

A researcher's state of mind, level of attention, and conditions in the field affect note taking. He or she will usually begin with relatively short one- to three-hour periods in the field before writing notes.

Types of Field Notes Field researchers take notes in many ways.[10] The recommendations here (also see Box 13.7) are suggestions. Full field notes have several types or levels. Five levels will be described here. It is usually best to keep all the notes for an observation period together and to distinguish types of notes by separate pages. Some researchers include inferences with direct observations if they are set off by a visible device, such as brackets or coloured ink. The quantity of notes varies across types. For example, six hours in the field might result in one page of jotted notes, 40 pages of direct observation, five pages of researcher inference, and two pages total for methodological, theoretical, and personal notes. It is nearly impossible to take good notes in the field. Even a known observer in a public setting looks strange when furiously writing. More important, when looking down and writing, the researcher cannot see and hear what is happening. The attention given to note writing is taken away from field observation, where it belongs. The specific setting determines whether any notes can be taken in the field. The researcher may be able to write and members may expect it, or he or she may have to be secretive (e.g., go to the bathroom).

jotted notes: In *field research*, what a researcher inconspicuously writes while in the *field site* on whatever is convenient to "jog the memory" later.

Jotted Notes Jotted notes are written in the field. They are short, temporary memory triggers, such as words, phrases, or drawings taken inconspicuously, often scribbled on any convenient item (e.g., napkin, matchbook). They are incorporated into direct observation notes but are never substituted for them.

Direct Observation Notes The basic sources of field data are notes a researcher writes immediately after leaving the field, which he or she can add to later; these are

Box 13.7 Making It Practical

Recommendations for Taking Field Notes

- Record notes as soon as possible after each period in the field.
- Begin the record of each field visit with a new page, with the date and time noted.
- Use jotted notes only as a temporary memory aid, with keywords or terms or the first and last things said.
- Use wide margins to make it easy to add to notes at any time. Go back and add to the notes if you remember something later.
- Plan to type notes and keep each level of notes separate so it will be easy to go back to them later.
- Record events in the order in which they occurred, and note how long they last (e.g., a 15-minute wait, a one-hour ride).
- Make notes as concrete, complete, and comprehensible as possible.
- Use frequent paragraph breaks and quotation marks. Exact recall of phrases is best, with double quotes; use single quotes for paraphrasing.
- Record small talk or routines that do not appear to be significant at the time; they may become important later.
- Let your feelings flow and write quickly without worrying about spelling or "wild ideas." Assume that no one else will see the notes, but use pseudonyms.
- Never substitute tape recordings completely for field notes.
- Include diagrams or maps of the setting, and outline your own movements and those of others during the period of observation.
- Include the researcher's own words and behaviour in the notes. Also record emotional feelings and private thoughts in a separate section.
- Avoid evaluative summarizing words. Instead of "The sink looked disgusting," say, "The sink was rust-stained and looked as if it had not been cleaned in a long time. Pieces of food and dirty dishes looked as if they had been piled in it for several days."
- Reread notes periodically and record ideas generated by the rereading.
- Always make one or more backup copies, keep them in a locked location, and store the copies in different places in case of fire or theft.

called **direct observation notes**. The notes should be ordered chronologically with the date, time, and place on each entry. They serve as a detailed description of what the researcher heard and saw in concrete, specific terms. To the extent possible, they are an exact recording of the particular words, phrases, or actions.

direct observation notes: Notes taken in *field research* that attempt to include all details and specifics of what the researcher heard or saw in a *field site*. They are written in a way that permits multiple interpretations later.

A researcher's memory improves with practice. A new researcher can soon remember exact phrases from the field. Verbatim statements should be written with double quotation marks to distinguish them from paraphrases. Dialogue accessories (nonverbal communication, props, tone, speed, volume, gestures) should be recorded as well. A researcher records what was actually said and does not clean it up; notes include ungrammatical speech, slang, and misstatements (e.g., write, "Uh, I'm goin' home, Sal," not, "I am going home, Sally").

A researcher puts concrete details, not summaries, in notes. For example, instead of, "We talked about sports," he or she writes, "Anthony argued with Sam and Jason. He said that the Cubs would win next week because they traded for a new shortstop, Chiappetta. He also said that the team was better than the Mets, who he thought had inferior infielders. He cited last week's game where the Cubs won against Boston by 8 to 3." A researcher would note who was present, what happened, where it occurred, when, and under what circumstances. New researchers may not take notes because "nothing important happened." An experienced researcher knows that events when "nothing happened" can reveal a lot. For example, members may express feelings and organize experience into folk categories even in trivial conversations.

Researcher Inference Notes A field researcher listens to members to "climb into their skin" or "walk in their shoes." This involves a three-step process. The researcher listens without applying analytical categories; he or she compares what is heard to what was heard at other times and to what others say; then the researcher applies his or her own interpretation to infer or figure out what it means. In ordinary interaction, we do all three steps simultaneously and jump quickly to our own inferences. A field researcher learns to look and listen without inferring or imposing an interpretation. His or her observations without inferences go into direct observation notes.

A researcher records inferences in a separate section that is keyed to direct observations. People never see social relationships, emotions, or meaning; they see specific physical actions and hear words, then use background cultural knowledge, clues from the context, and what is done or said to assign social meaning. For example, one does not see *love* or *anger*; one sees and hears specific actions (red face, loud voice, wild gestures, obscenities) and draw inferences from them (the person is angry).

Sociological Perspective on Gender

People constantly infer social meaning on the basis of what they see and hear, but not always correctly. A researcher keeps inferred meaning separate from direct observation because the meaning of actions is not always self-evident. Sometimes people try to deceive others. For example, an unrelated couple register at a motel as Mr. and Mrs. Smith. More frequently, social behaviour is ambiguous or multiple meanings are possible. For example, you see a male and female, both in their late twenties, get out of a car and enter a restaurant together. They sit at a table, order a meal, and talk with serious expressions in hushed tones, sometimes leaning forward to hear each other. As they get up to leave, the woman, who has a sad facial expression and appears ready to cry, is briefly hugged by the male. They then leave together. Did you witness a couple breaking up, two friends discussing a third, two people trying to decide what to do because they have discovered that their spouses are having an affair with each other, or a brother and sister whose father just died?

Analytic Notes Researchers make many decisions about how to proceed while in the field. Some acts are planned (e.g., to conduct an interview, to observe a particular activity) and others seem to occur almost out of thin air. Field researchers keep methodological ideas in analytic notes to record their plans, tactics, ethical and procedural decisions, and self-critiques of tactics.

Theory emerges in field research during data collection and is clarified when a researcher reviews field notes. Analytic notes have a running account of a researcher's attempts to give meaning to field events. He or she "thinks out loud" in the notes by suggesting links between ideas, creating hypotheses, proposing conjectures, and developing new concepts.

analytical memos: The written notes a qualitative researcher takes during data collection and afterward to develop concepts, themes, or preliminary generalizations.

Analytical memos are part of the theoretical notes. They are systematic digressions into theory, where a researcher elaborates on ideas in depth, expands on ideas while still in the field, and modifies or develops more complex theory by rereading and thinking about the memos.

Personal Notes As discussed earlier, personal feelings and emotional reactions become part of the data and colour what a researcher sees or hears in the field. A researcher keeps a section of notes that is like a personal diary. He or she records personal life events and feelings in it ("I'm tense today. I wonder if it's because of the fight I had yesterday with Chris," or "I've got a headache on this gloomy, overcast day").

Personal notes serve three functions: They provide an outlet for a researcher and a way to cope with stress; they are a source of data about personal reactions; and they give him or her a way to evaluate direct observation or inference notes when the notes are later reread. For example, if the researcher was in a good mood during observations, it might colour what he or she observed (see Figure 13.3).

Maps and Diagrams Field researchers often make maps and draw diagrams or pictures of the features of a field site. This serves two purposes: It helps a researcher organize

Direct Observation	Inference	Analytic	Personal Journal
Sunday, October 4. Kay's Kafé 3:00 p.m. Large White male in mid-40s, overweight, enters. He wears worn brown suit. He is alone; sits at booth #2. Kay comes by, asks, "What'll it be?" Man says, "Coffee, black for now." She leaves and he lights cigarette and reads menu. 3:15 p.m. Kay turns on radio.	Kay seems friendly today, humming. She becomes solemn and watchful. I think she puts on the radio when nervous.	Women are afraid of men who come in alone since the robbery.	It is raining. I am feeling comfortable with Kay but am bored today.

Figure 13.3 Types of Field Notes

events in the field and it helps convey a field site to others. For example, a researcher observing a bar with 15 stools may draw and number 15 circles to simplify recording (e.g., "Yosuke came in and sat on stool 12; Phoebe was already on stool 10"). Field researchers find three types of maps helpful: spatial, social, and temporal. The first helps orient the data; the latter two are preliminary forms of data analysis. A *spatial map* locates people, equipment, and the like in terms of geographical, physical space to show where activities occur (Figure 13.4a). A *social map* shows the number or variety of people and the arrangements among them of power, influence, friendship, division of labour, and so on. These types of maps can also be done with families to show relationships to one another (Figure 13.4b). A *temporal map* shows the ebb and flow of people, goods, services, and communications, or schedules (Figure 13.4c).

Machine Recordings to Supplement Memory Tape recorders and videotapes can be helpful supplements in field research. They never substitute for field notes or a researcher's presence in the field. They cannot be introduced into all field sites and can be used only after a researcher develops rapport. Recorders and videotapes provide a close approximation to what occurred and a permanent record that others can review. They serve as "jotted notes" to help a researcher recall events and observe what is easy to miss. Nevertheless, these items can create disruption and an increased awareness of surveillance. Researchers who rely on them must address associated problems (e.g., ensure that batteries are fresh and there are enough blank tapes). Also, relistening to or viewing tapes can be time consuming. For example, it may take over 100 hours to listen to 50 hours recorded in the field. Transcriptions of tape are expensive and not always accurate; they do not always convey subtle contextual meanings or mumbled words.

Data Quality

LO 7 Describe how data quality are ensured in field research.

Trustworthiness of Data The reliability and validity of quantitative data have been addressed in earlier chapters. It was, however, briefly mentioned (in Chapter 6) that the techniques used to assess reliability and validity in quantitative research are not directly applicable to qualitative research. This is because the nature of the research and the data are so different. It would be unreasonable, for example, to expect the results of field research to have replication of results in the same way an experiment or a survey item may.

Lincoln and Guba (1985) suggested a set of alternative criteria by which qualitative studies could be assessed that generally correspond to the quantitative concerns of reliability, validity, objectivity, and generalizability. These are credibility, confirmability, dependability, and transferability.

a Spatial Map

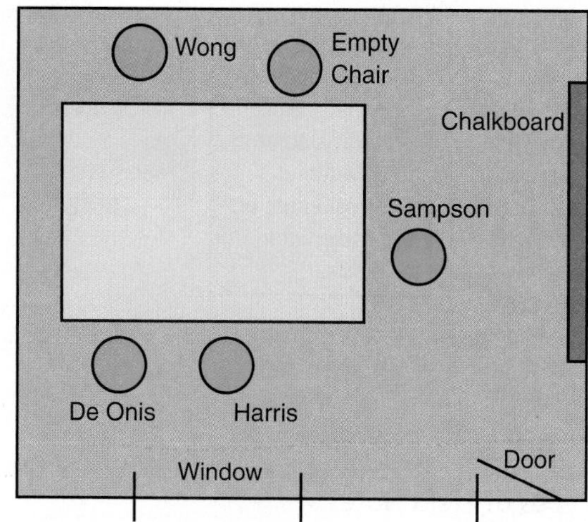

b Social Map

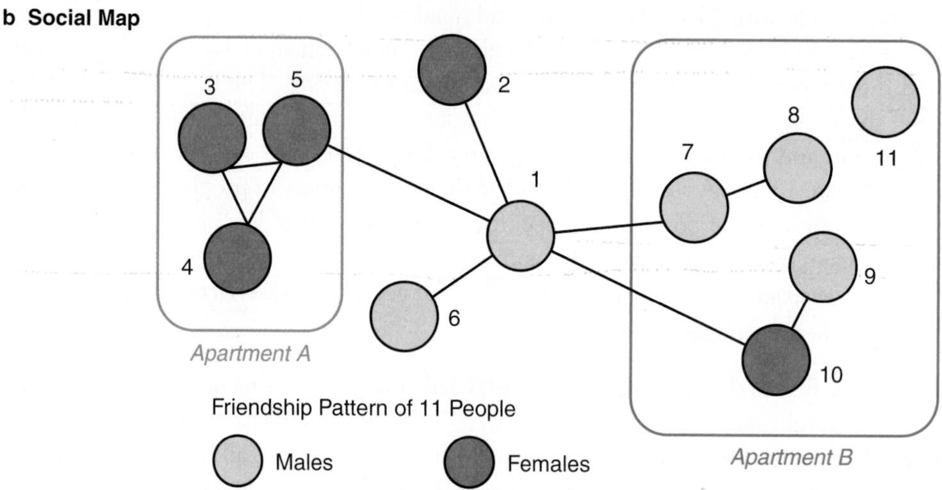

c Temporal Map

Day of Week, Buzz's Bar

	Mon	Tue	Wed	Thr	Fri	Sat
Open 10:00 – 5:00	Old Drunks	Old Drunks	Old Drunks	Old Drunks	Skip Work or Leave Early	Going to Fish
5:00 – Close 1:00	Football Watchers	Neighbours and Bridge Players	Softball Team (All-Male Night)	Young Crowd	Loud Music, Mixed Crowd	Loners and No Dates

Figure 13.4 Types of Maps Used in Field Research

credibility: One aspect of *trustworthiness*, which relates to how much truth value the results of a qualitative study have.

member checking: A way of establishing the *trustworthiness* criterion of *credibility*, where members of the study group are consulted about whether they agree with the researcher's conclusions and interpretations.

Credibility **Credibility** is concerned with how much truth value the results of our qualitative study have. It is most comparable with the notion of validity in quantitative social research. There are several techniques a researcher can use to establish credibility. One technique is through **member checking**, which means that we ask members of the group we are studying if they agree with our interpretations and conclusions. (See

Box 13.8 Focus

Participatory Action Research

Participatory action research (PAR) is an approach to research that questions the authority and power of the researcher in relation to what he or she is studying. *It is not a specific technique* like field research or qualitative interviewing—*it is an orientation to research*. Most of the techniques in this book come from the underlying assumption that the researcher is the expert who will gather and analyze the data for his or her respondents, subjects, or research participants. PAR questions this assumption and challenges the taken-for-granted structure of power relations that acknowledge the researcher as the sole "expert" on the topic.

In PAR approaches, the people who are being studied are included as active members of the research process. They are involved in aspects of research design, data collection, and interpretation of results. The objectives of the research are also motivated by a desire for social change. It is anticipated that the findings of PAR will be related to "action" that will help facilitate what is perceived by members as a necessary change.

Simich, Maiter, and Ochocka (2009) report on the process and outcomes of a participatory action research project called *Taking Culture Seriously in Community Mental Health*. This study was concerned with the psychological and social processes surrounding immigrant mental well-being. There was an objective of understanding immigrant strategies for adapting from a wide variety of cultural perspectives. To achieve this objective of understanding adaptation strategies within a context of cultural diversity, the researchers targeted participants from Somali, Punjabi-Sikh, Polish, Mandarin-speaking Chinese, and Spanish-speaking Latin Americans in Toronto. To foster the voice of the community in the shaping of the research process, the authors explain:

> An example of this participatory approach was the hiring and 5-month training of community researchers, who, as enthusiastic agents of change and "ambassadors" of the study, met bi-monthly for mutual support, organized and conducted the focus groups and contributed to data interpretation and to the validity of findings . . . A total of 10 people were hired, one from each of the five cultural linguistic communities in both study sites. (p. 256)

Thus, a key component for this particular PAR study was the hiring of co-investigators who were members of the ethno-linguistic groups being studied. These individuals had multiple roles that weren't limited to being a research assistant, but were key members of the research group who helped shape the process of the research as well as the end product. After the data were analyzed by the team, the authors also report that:

> Team members, including community researchers, discussed and received feedback on initial study findings from participants at a conference attended by over 150 participants held for this purpose in December 2006. (p. 257)

This demonstrates not only that the research team comprised members of the community under study, but also how after initial data analyses the wider community was invited to listen to the findings and offer feedback, an example of member checking as discussed above. The study authors also comment that PAR was beneficial in addressing their research question in that it fostered a new trust between the immigrants and their host society that would benefit their mental health and also allowed immigrants to discuss mental health problems among their peers, which in many communities is not openly done.

Box 13.8 for a special case of member checking within participatory action research.) Another technique is through **prolonged engagement** such that a researcher stays in the field long enough to be able to make informed conclusions and interpretations about what he or she is studying. Through prolonged engagement, the researcher will be exposed to a variety of different settings and group interactions, and develop rapport with members. A final way of establishing credibility that will be considered here is through the use of **negative case analysis**, which involves identifying data or cases that differ from the general pattern of findings and making attempts to explain these contradictory cases.

Transferability **Transferability** concerns the extent to which the findings of the study can be applied to other contexts. It is comparable to the idea of external validity (generalizability) in qualitative research. According to Lincoln and Guba (1985), transferability of a study can be established through **thick description**, which means that the researcher keeps very detailed accounts of his or her study. If sufficient detail is provided, it is possible to speculate with more certainty how the findings may be applicable to other settings or situations.

participatory action research: An approach to research that removes the researcher from the centre of power and involves community members and research participants in the design, implementation, and interpretation of the research process.

prolonged engagement: When a researcher remains in the field long enough to make informed conclusions about what he or she is studying. Also used so that the researcher can be exposed to a variety of different settings and develop a rapport with members of the study group.

negative case analysis: A way of establishing the *trustworthiness* criterion of *credibility* where the researcher closely examines cases that deviate from the dominant pattern.

Components of Trustworthiness

Credibility Established through . . .	Transferability	Dependability	Confirmability
Member-checking Prolonged engagement Negative case analysis	Thick description	External audit	External audit Audit trail Reflexivity

Figure 13.5 Components of Trustworthiness

transferability: The component of establishing *trustworthiness* in *qualitative research* that is concerned with how generalizable the findings are.

thick description: Used to establish the *transferability* of a qualitative study through the detailed notes of a researcher.

dependability: An aspect of establishing *trustworthiness* of *qualitative data* in which data are assessed in terms of how likely it is that similar results would be obtained if the study were repeated.

external audit: A technique for establishing *dependability* and *confirmability* in qualitative research wherein researchers outside of the study examine *qualitative data* to see if they would have come to the same results as the original researcher.

trustworthiness: An alternative set of criteria by which to assess the *validity* and *reliability* of qualitative research.

confirmability: A component of establishing *trustworthiness* that relates to the extent to which the findings of a qualitative study are value free.

audit trail: A technique for establishing the *trustworthiness* criterion of *confirmability* by collecting detailed and transparent *qualitative data*.

reflexivity: A technique for establishing *confirmability* in qualitative research where the researcher is self-aware of his or her influence and potential bias.

Dependability **Dependability** is most closely associated with the quantitative idea of reliability, as it concerns how consistent our results would be if the study were repeated under similar conditions. Dependability is established through what is known as an **external audit**, which involves having the research materials (field notes, interview transcripts, and other research materials) examined by an external evaluator to see if he or she would draw the same conclusions from the data as the original researcher did.

Confirmability The **trustworthiness** aspect of **confirmability** concerns the extent to which the research is neutral and is not simply the product of the researcher's biases or motivations. Like with dependability, confirmability can be established through an *external audit*. Researchers external to the project can examine the data sources and search for evidence of bias. Similarly, to be able to answer the questions concerning confirmability, a researcher should be transparent about his or her research techniques, keeping detailed notes and fully transcribed interviews. This process of transparent record-keeping is known as keeping an **audit trail**. **Reflexivity**, or being self-aware of the researcher's role in the process of knowledge construction, is also a technique for establishing confirmability. Throughout the research process, researchers must be aware of how they may be influencing the behaviour of the group they are studying, and be alert to how their own biases may influence how they perceive events or the group members themselves.

Figure 13.5 summarizes the various components of trustworthiness.

Focusing and Sampling

Focusing The field researcher first gets a general picture, then focuses on a few specific problems or issues (see Figure 13.6). A researcher decides on specific research questions and develops hypotheses only after being in the field and experiencing it firsthand. At first, everything seems relevant; later, however, selective attention focuses on specific questions and themes.

Sampling Field researchers often use nonprobability samples, such as snowball sampling. Many times the field research is sampling different types of units. A field researcher may take a smaller, selective set of observations from all possible observations, or sample

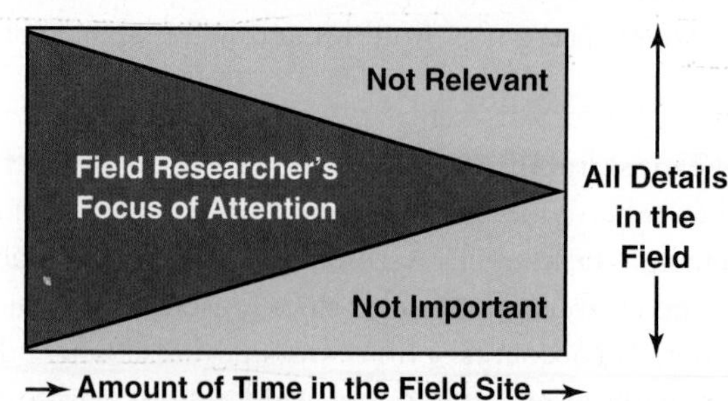

Figure 13.6 Focusing in Field Research

times, situations, types of events, locations, types of people, or contexts of interest. For example, a researcher samples time by observing a setting at different times. He or she observes at all times of the day, on every day of the week, and in all seasons to get a full sense of how the field site stays the same or changes. It is often best to overlap when sampling (e.g., to have sampling times from 7:00 a.m. to 9:00 a.m., from 8:00 a.m. to 10:00 a.m., and from 9:00 a.m. to 11:00 a.m.).

A researcher often samples locations because one location may give depth, but a narrow perspective. Sitting or standing in different locations helps the researcher get a sense of the whole site. For example, the peer-to-peer behaviour of schoolteachers usually occurs in a faculty lounge, but it also occurs at a local bar when teachers gather or in a classroom temporarily used for a teacher meeting. In addition, researchers trace the paths of members to various field locations.

Field researchers sample people by focusing their attention on different kinds of people (old-timers and newcomers, old and young, males and females, leaders and followers). As a researcher identifies types of people, or people with opposing outlooks, he or she tries to interact with and learn about all types. A field researcher also samples various kinds of events, such as routine, special, and unanticipated. Routine events (e.g., opening up a store for business) happen every day but should not be considered unimportant simply because they are routine. Special events (e.g., the annual office party) are announced and planned in advance. They focus member attention and reveal aspects of social life not otherwise visible. Unanticipated events are those that just happen to occur while a researcher is present (e.g., the actions of unsupervised workers when the manager gets sick and cannot oversee workers at a store for a day). In this case, the researcher sees something unusual, unplanned, or rare by chance.

LEAVING THE FIELD

Work in the field can last for a few weeks or several years. In either case, at some point work in the field ends. Some researchers (e.g., Schatzman & Strauss, 1973) suggest that the end comes naturally when theory building ceases or reaches a closure; others feel that fieldwork could go on without end and that a firm decision to cut off relations is needed.

Experienced field researchers anticipate a process of disengaging and exiting the field. Depending on the intensity of involvement and the length of time in the field, the process can be disruptive or emotionally painful for both the researcher and the members. A researcher may experience the emotional pain of breaking intimate friendships when leaving the field. He or she may feel guilty and depressed immediately before and after leaving. He or she may find it difficult to let go because of personal and emotional entanglements. If the involvement in the field was intense and long, and the field site differed from his or her native culture, the researcher may need months of adjustment before feeling at home with his or her original cultural surroundings.

Once a researcher decides to leave—because the project reaches a natural end and little new is being learned, or because external factors force it to end (e.g., end of a job, gatekeepers order the researcher out, research funding runs out)—he or she chooses a method of exiting. The researcher can leave by a quick exit (simply not return one day) or slowly withdraw, reducing his or her involvement over weeks. He or she also needs to decide how to tell members and how much advance warning to give.

The exit process depends on the specific field setting and the relationships developed. In general, a researcher lets members know a short period ahead of time. He or she fulfills any bargains or commitments that were made and leaves with a clean slate. Sometimes, a ritual or ceremony, such as a going-away party or shaking hands with everyone, helps signal the break for members. Maintaining friendships with members is also possible and is preferred by researchers into feminist issues.

A field researcher is aware that leaving affects members. Some members may feel hurt or rejected because a close social relationship is ending. They may react by trying to pull a researcher back into the field and make him or her more of a member, or they may become angry and resentful. They may grow cool and distant because of an awareness that the researcher is really an outsider. In any case, fieldwork is not finished until the process of disengagement and exiting is complete.

LO 8 Explain the different types of ethical issues that the field researcher may face.

ETHICAL DILEMMAS OF FIELD RESEARCH

The direct personal involvement of a field researcher in the social lives of other people raises many ethical dilemmas. The dilemmas arise when a researcher is alone in the field and has little time to make moral decisions. Although he or she may be aware of general ethical issues beforehand, they arise unexpectedly in the course of observing and interacting in the field. We will look at four ethical issues in field research: deception, confidentiality, involvement with deviants, and publishing reports.[11]

Deception

Deception arises in several ways in field research: The research may be covert; the researcher may assume a false role, name, or identity; or it may involve misleading members in some way. The most hotly debated of the ethical issues arising from deception is that of covert versus overt field research. Some support covert research and see it as necessary for entering into and gaining a full knowledge of many areas of social life. Others oppose it and argue that it undermines a trust between researchers and society. Although its moral status is questionable, there are some field sites or activities that can only be studied covertly, as highlighted in Box 13.6. Covert research is never preferable and never easier than overt research because of the difficulties of maintaining a front and the constant fear of getting caught.

Confidentiality

A researcher learns intimate knowledge that is given in confidence. He or she has a moral obligation to uphold the confidentiality of data. This includes keeping information confidential from others in the field and disguising members' names in field notes. Sometimes a field researcher cannot directly quote a person. One strategy is that, instead of reporting the source as an informant, the researcher can find documentary evidence that says the same thing and use the document (e.g., an old memo, a newspaper article) as if it were the source of the information.

Involvement with Deviants

guilty knowledge: When a researcher in *field research* learns of illegal, unethical, or immoral actions by the people in the *field site* that is not widely known.

Researchers who conduct field research on deviants who engage in illegal behaviour face additional dilemmas. They know of and may sometimes be involved in illegal activity. This **guilty knowledge** is of interest not only to law-enforcement officials but also to other deviants.[12] The researcher faces a dilemma of building trust and rapport with the deviants, yet not becoming so involved as to violate his or her basic personal moral standards. Usually, the researcher makes an explicit arrangement with the deviant members.

Publishing Field Reports

The intimate knowledge that a researcher obtains and reports creates a dilemma between the right to privacy and the right to know. A researcher does not publicize member secrets, violate privacy, or harm reputations. Yet if he or she cannot publish anything that might offend or harm someone, part of what the researcher learned will remain hidden, and it may be difficult for others to believe the report if a researcher omits critical details. Some researchers ask members to look at a report to verify its accuracy and to approve their portrayal in print. For marginal groups (e.g., addicts, sex workers, crack users), this may not be possible, but researchers must respect member privacy. On the other hand, censorship or self-censorship can be a danger. A compromise position is for a researcher to publish truthful but unflattering material after consideration and only if it is essential to the researcher's arguments.

CHAPTER SUMMARY

In this chapter, you learned about field research and the field research process (choosing a site and gaining access, relations in the field, and observing and collecting data). The chapter began by identifying the types of research questions appropriate for field research. The most appropriate types of questions for this mode of inquiry are those that involve understanding or describing a group of people. The various steps of field research were then considered. The selection of a field and gaining access was considered, highlighting various factors that can enable or constrain potential researchers. Field researchers also must decide on their level of involvement in field research, which can range from complete observer to complete participant. All levels of involvement have their advantages and disadvantages.

Field research involves adopting a role in the field and managing the presentation of self. Part of the research process involves "learning the ropes," which requires understanding the group being studied and gaining their trust. Establishing and maintaining roles in the field are also an integral part of field research, and like all social relationships can be complex.

The data obtained through field research are the product of careful watching and listening. The field researcher makes careful field notes, which can have various forms. In addition to direct observation notes, the researcher also records jotted notes, inference notes, analytic notes, personal notes, as well as maps and diagrams of field sites. Qualitative data are assessed for their "trustworthiness" through a variety of techniques that ensure that the data exhibit credibility, transferability, dependability and confirmability. These criteria are somewhat similar to the concepts of reliability and validity that were discussed in an earlier chapter, but are more appropriate for qualitative data.

The chapter ended by addressing the issue of how to sample in field research, pointing to the complexity of the sampling problem in this type of research. The researcher must decide what to sample: times, situations, contexts, or settings. Leaving the field also presents its own set of issues, as complex personal relationships may have been established over the course of the research. Finally several ethical issues are possible given the placement of the researcher in the social lives of other people. Field researchers must be aware of how their research practices have ethical implications.

Review Questions

1. Identify two different types of research questions appropriate for addressing with field research.
2. Describe five activities in which a field researcher engages.
3. Explain the 10 major steps in a field research project.
4. Explain the three different levels of involvement that a field researcher may adopt.

5. Explain how a field researcher collects data. What are the seven different types of notes that a field researcher can collect?
6. Describe how data quality is ensured in field research, identifying the four components of trustworthiness and at least one way that each can be established.
7. What are four possible ethical dilemmas that the field researcher may encounter?

Exercises

Research Activities

1. Using EBSCO's ContentSelect, identify a research article that obtained data using field research. What kind of group was the researcher studying? What kind of participant was he or she? If the researcher was overt, how did he or she negotiate access to the group being studied? How long did the researcher study the group? What kinds of difficulties of studying the group does the researcher report about?
2. Using EBSCO's ContentSelect, identify a research article that obtained data using participatory action research. How did the researcher include the study participants in the research process?
3. Looking at the two research studies you used to answer the previous two questions, now explain what aspects of trustworthiness the researchers attempted to establish. What methods did they use to establish trustworthiness?

MySearchLab

Visit MySearchLab, where you'll find thousands of full-text articles from academic journals and help with the research and writing process. Access the eText within MySearchLab to take self-grading practice tests and view a variety of multimedia resources.

Chapter 14

Nonreactive Qualitative Research

Photo Credit: Hemeroskopion/Fotolia/LLC

LEARNING OBJECTIVES

After reading this chapter, you will be able to

LO 1 Identify research questions appropriate for historical research.

LO 2 Explain the distinctive features of historical research and describe how it is similar to field research.

LO 3 Describe the steps in a historical research project.

LO 4 Identify the types of data used in historical research.

LO 5 Define *equivalence* and explain why it is important in historical research

LO 6 Define qualitative content analysis and describe how it is different from quantitative content analysis.

LO 7 Differentiate between the various approaches to content analysis.

LO 8 Distinguish between content analysis and discourse analysis, and describe the stages of a discourse analysis.

INTRODUCTION

In this chapter, we focus on nonreactive qualitative techniques. The three major ones that we concentrate on are appropriate for the analysis of historical phenomena and the analysis of text. In Chapter 10, we discussed the analysis of text using content analysis—but our treatment there was from a quantitative perspective. There are many users of textual analysis who approach it from a distinctly qualitative orientation where the focus is uncovering meanings in the text, rather than the quantitative approach of tallying frequencies of predetermined categories observed in the text. These types of qualitative approaches have many advantages, with one being that the texts that researchers examine in this type of inquiry do not suffer from potential problems with reactivity (i.e., research participants who act differently because they know they are being studied).

LO 1 Identify research questions appropriate for historical research.

HISTORICAL RESEARCH

The classical social thinkers of the nineteenth century—such as Émile Durkheim, Karl Marx, and Max Weber, who founded the social sciences—used a historical method. This method is used extensively in a few areas of sociology (e.g., social change, political sociology, social movements, and social stratification) and has been applied in many others as well (e.g., religion, criminology, sex roles, race relations, and family). Although much social research focuses on current social life in one country, historical or comparative studies have become more common in recent years.

The Way We Weren't: The Myth and Reality of the "Traditional" Family

Historical and archival social research is a collection of techniques and approaches. Some blend in to traditional history; others extend quantitative social research. The focus of this chapter is on the distinct type of social research that puts historical time (and often cross-cultural variation) at the centre of research—that is, the type of research that treats what is studied as part of the flow of history, situated in a cultural context.

Research Questions Appropriate for Historical Research

Women Entering the Workforce

Historical research is a powerful method for addressing big questions: "How did major societal change take place?" "What fundamental features are common to most societies?" "Why did current social arrangements take a certain form in some societies but not in others?" For example, historical researchers have addressed the questions of how major social institutions, like medicine, have developed and changed over two centuries (Starr, 1982); how basic social relationships, such as feelings about the value of children, change (Zelizer, 1985); and how recent changes in major cities, such as New York, London, and Tokyo, reveal the rise of a new global urban system (Sassen, 2001).[1]

History of Religion in America

Historical research is suited for examining the combinations of social factors that produce a specific outcome (e.g., civil war). It is also appropriate for comparing entire social systems to see what is common across societies and what is unique. A historical researcher may apply a theory to specific cases to illustrate its usefulness. He or she brings out or reveals the connections between divergent social factors or groups, and he or she compares the same social processes and concepts in different historical contexts.

Historical research can strengthen conceptualization and theory building. By looking at historical events, a researcher can generate new concepts and broaden his or her perspective. Concepts are less likely to be restricted to a single historical time or to a single culture; they can be grounded in the experiences of people living in specific cultural and historical contexts.[2]

A difficulty in reading historical studies is that one needs knowledge of the past or other cultures to fully understand them. Readers who are familiar with only their own cultures or contemporary times may find it difficult to understand historical studies or classical theorists. For example, it is difficult to understand Karl Marx's *The Communist Manifesto* without knowledge of the conditions of feudal Europe and the world in which Marx was writing. In that time and place, serfs lived under severe oppression. Feudal society included caste-based dress codes in cities and a system of peonage that forced serfs to give a large percentage of their product to landlords. The one and only Church had extensive landholdings, and tight familial ties existed among the aristocracy, landlords, and Church. Modern readers might ask why the serfs did not flee if conditions were so bad. The answer requires an understanding of the conditions at the time. The serfs had little chance of surviving in European forests living on roots, berries, and hunting. Also, no one would aid a fleeing serf refugee because the traditional societies did not embrace strangers but feared them.

The Logic of Historical Research and Quantitative Research

Quantitative versus Historical Research One source of the confusion around historical methods can arise because both positivist, quantitatively oriented researchers and interpretive (or critical), qualitatively oriented researchers study historical issues. Positivist researchers may reject the idea that there is a distinct historical method. They measure variables, test hypotheses, analyze quantitative data, and replicate research to discover generalizable laws that hold across time and societies. They see no fundamental difference between quantitative social research and historical research.

Most social research examines social life in the present in a single nation—that of the researcher. Historical research can be organized along three dimensions: (1) Is the focus on what occurs in one nation, a small set of nations, or many nations? (2) Is the focus on a single time period in the past, across many years, or a recent time period? (3) Is the analysis based primarily on quantitative or qualitative data?

The Logic of Historical Research and Interpretive Research

A distinct, qualitative historical type of social research differs from the positivist approach and from an extreme interpretive approach. Historical researchers who use case studies and qualitative data may depart from positivist principles. Their research is an intensive examination of a limited number of cases in which social meaning and context are critical. Case studies, even on one nation, can be very important. Case studies can elaborate on historical processes and specify concrete historical details (see Box 14.1).

Scholars who adopt the positivist approach to social science criticize the historical approach for using a small number of cases. They believe that historical research is inadequate because it rarely produces probabilistic causal generalizations that they take as indicating a "true" (i.e., positivist) science.

Like interpretive field researchers, historical researchers focus on culture, try to see through the eyes of those being studied, reconstruct the lives of the people studied, and examine particular individuals or groups. An extremist interpretive position says that an empathic understanding of the people being studied is the sole goal of social research. It takes a strict, idiographic, descriptive approach and rejects causal statements, systematic concepts, or abstract theoretical models. In the extremist interpretive approach, each social setting is unique and comparisons are impossible.

Box 14.1 Concepts in Action

Male Mental Patients at Colquitz, British Columbia

In "I Do Not Care for a Lunatic's Role: Modes of Regulation and Resistance Inside the Colquitz Mental Home, British Columbia, 1919–33," Robert Menzies (1999) used historical psychiatric records to chronicle the experience of the male patients held there between 1919 and 1933. The Colquitz facility was a psychiatric institution that housed both criminal and civilian patients until 1964. Menzies described the facility as one that resembled a prison more than a hospital and that was very much preoccupied with security.

The psychiatric institute, located in British Columbia, treated more than 68 000 patients from the time it opened in 1872 until it was closed in the mid-1960s. After a refurbishment in the mid-1980s, the facility reopened and now serves as a correctional facility.

The data for Menzies's analysis came from historical clinical case files of patients, which included

> legal documents pertaining to commitment, confinement conditions, and release; records of patient belongings and personal visits; ward notations; nursing notes; charts monitoring physical health; transcripts of interviews with medical staff; family, personal, and medical histories; social work and psychological reports; case conference proceedings where these were held; reports on special incidents (assaults, escapes, etc.); letters from patients to staff; death registries when applicable; and correspondence between the hospital and interested parties outside the institution. (Menzies, 1999, p. 184)

Menzies analyzed the records of 100 male patients who were held in the facility between 1919 and 1933. These 100 men represented 26.7 percent of the 375 patients who were recorded as being in the facility during those years. The researcher was able to obtain these records at the British Columbia Archives in Victoria as well as East Lawn Clinical Records of Riverview Hospital (located in Coquitlam, British Columbia). Provinces and municipalities often have their own archives in which they store historical documents that are available for viewing by the public. Organizations also often have archives, but they may be more difficult for researchers to access for reasons of confidentiality.

Menzies was interested in examining the power relationships that existed within the facility, noting the ways in which officials tried to uphold the regimen of the institution, while the patients engaged in various techniques aimed at resisting authority and overcoming their oppressive surroundings. He highlights the stark contrasts between the officials' desire to impose authority and the patients' attempts to contest that authority.

LO 2 Explain the distinctive features of historical research and describe how it is similar to field research.

A Distinct Historical Approach

The following discussion describes similarities between historical research and field research, and six more unique features of historical research (see Table 14.1).

Similarities to Field Research First, both historical research and field research recognize that the researcher's point of view is an unavoidable part of research. Both involve interpretation, which introduces the interpreter's location in time, place, and worldview. Historical research does not try to produce a single, unequivocal set of objective facts. Rather, it is a confrontation of old with new or of different worldviews. It recognizes that a researcher's reading of historical evidence is influenced by an awareness of the past and by living in the present.

Second, both field and historical research examine a great diversity of data. In both, the researcher becomes immersed in data to gain an empathic understanding of events and people. Both capture subjective feelings and note how everyday, ordinary activities signify important social meaning. The researcher inquires, selects, and focuses on specific aspects of social life from the vast array of events, actions, symbols, and words. A historical researcher organizes data and focuses attention on the basis of evolving concepts. He or she examines rituals and symbols that dramatize culture (e.g., parades, clothing, placement of objects) and investigates the motives, reasons, and justifications for behaviours.

Third, both field and historical researchers use *grounded theory*. Theory usually emerges during the process of data collection. (Grounded theory was discussed in Chapters 2, 5, and 7.)

Fourth, in both field and historical research, the researcher's meaning system frequently differs from that of the people he or she studies, but he or she tries to penetrate and understand their point of view. Once the life, language, and perspective of the people

Table 14.1 Summary of a Comparison of Approaches to Research: The Qualitative versus Quantitative Distinction

Topic	Both Field and Historical	Quantitative
Researcher's perspective	Include as an integral part of the research process	Remove from the research process
Approach to data	Immersed in many details to acquire understanding	Precisely operationalize variables
Theory and data	Grounded theory, dialogue between data and concepts	Deductive theory compared with empirical data
Present findings	Translate a meaning system	Test hypotheses
Action/structure	People construct meaning but within structures	Social forces shape behaviour
Laws/generalization	Limited generalizations that depend on context	Discover universal, context-free laws

Features of a Distinct Historical Research Approach

Topic	Historical Researcher's Approach
Evidence	Reconstructs from fragments and incomplete evidence
Distortion	Guards against using own awareness of factors outside the social or historical context
Human role	Includes the consciousness of people in a context and uses their motives as causal factors
Causes	Sees cause as contingent on conditions, beneath the surface, and due to a combination of elements
Micro/macro	Compares whole cases and links the micro- to macro-levels or layers of social reality
Cross-contexts	Moves between concrete specifics in a context and across contexts for more abstract comparisons

being studied have been mastered, the researcher "translates" them for others who read his or her report.

Fifth, both field and historical researchers focus on process and sequence. They see the passage of time and process as essential to how people construct social reality. This is related to how both are sensitive to an ever-present tension between agency (the active, moving, fluid side of people changing social reality) and structure (the fixed regularities and patterns that shape social life). For both types of research, social reality simultaneously is what people create and something that imposes restrictions on human choice.[3]

Sixth, generalization and theory are limited in field and historical research. Historical knowledge is incomplete and provisional, based on selective facts and limited questions. Neither deduces propositions or tests hypotheses to uncover fixed laws. Likewise, replication is unrealistic because each researcher has a unique perspective and assembles a unique body of evidence. Instead, researchers offer plausible accounts and limited generalizations.

Unique Features of Historical Research Despite its many similarities to field research, some important differences distinguish historical research. Research on the past and on an alien culture share much in common, and what they share distinguishes them from other approaches.

Historical research usually relies on limited and indirect evidence. Direct observation or involvement by a researcher is often impossible. A historical researcher reconstructs what occurred from the evidence but cannot have absolute confidence in the reconstruction. Historical evidence depends on the survival of data from the past, usually in the form of documents (e.g., letters and newspapers). The researcher is limited to what has not been destroyed and what leaves a trace, record, or other evidence behind.

Defining Families

Historical researchers must also interpret the evidence. Different people looking at the same evidence often ascribe different meanings to it, so a researcher must reflect on evidence. An understanding based on a first glance is rarely possible; to gain understanding, a researcher becomes immersed in and absorbs details about a context. For example, a researcher examining the family in the past or a distant country needs to be aware of the full social context (e.g., the nature of work, forms of communication, transportation technology). He or she looks at maps and gets a feel for the laws in effect, the condition of medical care, and common social practices. For example, the meaning of "a visit by a family member" is affected by conditions such as roads of dirt and mud, the inability to call ahead of time, and the lives of people who work on a farm with animals that need constant care.

A reconstruction of the past or another culture is easily distorted. Compared to the people being studied, a researcher is usually more aware of events occurring prior to the time studied, events occurring in places other than the location studied, and events that occurred after the period studied. This awareness gives the researcher a greater sense of coherence than was experienced by those living in the past or in an isolated social setting that the researcher guards against in a reconstruction.

Historical researchers recognize the capacity of people to learn, make decisions, and act on what they learn to modify the course of events. For example, if a group of people are aware of or gain consciousness of their own past history and avoid the mistakes of the past, they may act consciously to alter the course of future events. Of course, people will not necessarily learn or act on what they have learned, and if they do act they will not necessarily be successful. Nevertheless, people's capacity to learn introduces indeterminacy into historical explanations.

A historical researcher wants to find out whether people viewed various courses of action as plausible. Thus, the worldview and knowledge of the people under study shaped what they saw as possible or impossible ways to achieve goals. The researcher asks whether people were conscious of certain things. For example, if an army knew an enemy attack was coming and so decided to cross a river in the middle of the night, the action "crossing the river" would have a different meaning than in the situation where the army did not know the enemy was approaching.

A historical researcher integrates the micro- (small-scale, face-to-face interaction) and macro- (large-scale social structures) levels. The historical researcher describes both levels or layers of reality and links them to each other. For example, a historical researcher examines the details of individual biographies by reading diaries or letters to get a feel for the individuals: the food they ate, their recreational pursuits, their clothing, their sicknesses, their relations with friends, and so on. He or she links this micro-level view to macro-level processes: increased immigration, mechanization of production, proletarianization, tightened labour markets, and the like.

Historical researchers shift between details of specific context and making general comparisons. A researcher examines specific contexts, notes similarities and differences, then generalizes. Historical researchers investigate past contexts, usually in one culture (e.g., periods, epochs, ages, eras), for sequence and comparison. Of course, a researcher can combine both to investigate multiple cultural contexts in one or more historical contexts. Yet each period or society has its unique causal processes, meaning systems, and social relations, which may lack equivalent elements across the units. This produces a creative tension between the concrete specifics in a context and the abstract ideas a researcher uses to make links across contexts.

STEPS IN A HISTORICAL RESEARCH PROJECT

LO 3 Describe the steps in a historical research project.

In this section, we turn to the process of doing historical research. Conducting historical research does not involve a rigid set of steps and, with only a few exceptions, it does not use complex or specialized techniques.

Conceptualizing the Object of Inquiry

A historical researcher begins by becoming familiar with the setting and conceptualizing what is being studied. He or she may start with a loose model or a set of preliminary concepts and apply them to a specific setting. The provisional concepts contain implicit assumptions or organizing categories to "package" observations and guide a search through evidence.

If a researcher is not already familiar with the historical era or comparative settings, he or she conducts an orientation reading (reading several general works). This will help the researcher grasp the specific setting, assemble organizing concepts, subdivide the main issue, and develop lists of questions to ask. It is impossible to begin serious research without a framework of assumptions, concepts, and theory. Concepts and evidence interact to stimulate research.

Locating Evidence

Next, a researcher locates and gathers evidence through extensive bibliographic work. A researcher uses many indexes, catalogues, and reference works that list what libraries contain. For comparative research, this means focusing on specific nations or units and on particular kinds of evidence within each. The researcher frequently spends many weeks searching for sources in libraries, travels to several different specialized research libraries or archives, and reads dozens (if not hundreds) of books and articles.

As the researcher masters the literature and takes numerous detailed notes, he or she completes many specific tasks: creating a bibliography list (on cards or computer) with complete citations; taking notes that are neither too skimpy nor too extensive (i.e., more than one sentence but less than dozens of pages of quotations); leaving margins on note cards for adding themes later on; taking all notes in the same format (e.g., on cards, paper); and developing a file on themes or working hypotheses. A researcher adjusts initial concepts, questions, or focus on the basis of what he or she discovers in the evidence and considers a range of research reports at different levels of analysis (e.g., general context and detailed narratives on specific topics).

Evaluating Quality of Evidence

The historical researcher gathers evidence with two questions in mind: (1) How relevant is the evidence to emerging research questions and evolving concepts? (2) How accurate and strong is the evidence?

As the focus of research shifts, evidence that was not relevant can become relevant. Likewise, some evidence may stimulate new avenues of inquiry and a search for additional confirming evidence. A historical researcher reads evidence for three things: the implicit conceptual frameworks, particular details, and empirical generalizations. He or she evaluates alternative interpretations of evidence and looks for "silences" or cases where the evidence fails to address an event, topic, or issue. For example, when examining a group of leading male merchants in the 1890s, a researcher finds that the evidence and documents about them ignore the roles of their wives and many servants.

Organizing Evidence

As a researcher gathers evidence and locates new sources, he or she begins to organize the data. Obviously, it is unwise to take notes madly and let them pile up haphazardly. A researcher begins a preliminary analysis by noting low-level generalizations or themes. Next, a researcher organizes evidence using theoretical insights to stimulate new ways to organize data and new questions to ask of evidence.

The interaction of data and theory means that a researcher goes beyond a surface examination of the evidence to develop new concepts by critically evaluating the evidence based on theory. For example, a researcher reads a mass of evidence about a protest movement. The preliminary analysis organizes the evidence into a theme: People who are active in protest interact with each other and develop shared cultural meanings. He or she examines theories of culture and movements and then formulates a new concept: "oppositional movement subculture." The researcher then uses this concept to reexamine the evidence.

Synthesizing

The next step is to synthesize evidence. Once most of the evidence is in, the researcher refines concepts, creates new ones, and moves toward a general explanatory model. Concrete events in the evidence give meaning to new concepts. The researcher looks for patterns across time or units and draws out similarities and differences with analogies. He or she organizes divergent events into sequences and groups them together to create a larger picture. Plausible explanations are then developed that subsume both concepts and evidence into a coherent whole. The researcher reads and rereads notes and sorts and resorts them into piles or files on the basis of organizing schemes. He or she looks for links or connections while looking at the evidence in different ways.

Synthesis links specific evidence with an abstract model of underlying relations or causal mechanisms. Researchers may use metaphors. For example, mass frustration leading to a revolution is "an emotional rollercoaster drop" in which things seem to be getting better but then there is a sudden letdown after expectations have risen very quickly. The models are sensitizing devices.

Writing a Report

Assembling evidence, arguments, and conclusions into a report is always a crucial step, but more than in quantitative approaches, the careful crafting of evidence and explanation makes or breaks historical research. A researcher distills mountains of evidence into exposition and prepares extensive footnotes. She or he must also weave together the evidence and arguments to communicate a coherent, convincing picture to "tell a story" to readers.

LO 4 Identify the types of data used in historical research.

DATA AND EVIDENCE IN HISTORICAL CONTEXT

Types of Historical Evidence

First, some terms need clarification. *History* means the events of the past (e.g., it is *history* that the French withdrew troops from Vietnam), a record of the past (e.g., a *history* of French involvement in Vietnam), and a discipline that studies the past (e.g., a department of *history*). *Historiography* is the method of doing historical research or of gathering and analyzing historical evidence. Historical social science is a part of historical research.

Researchers draw on four types of historical evidence or data: primary sources, secondary sources, running records, and recollections.[4] Traditional historians rely heavily on primary sources. Historical researchers often use secondary sources or the different data types in combination.

Primary Sources The letters, diaries, newspapers, movies, novels, articles of clothing, photographs, and so forth of those who lived in the past that have survived to the present are **primary sources**. They are found in archives (a place where documents are stored, see Box 14.2), in private collections, in family closets, and in museums. Today's documents and objects (our letters, television programs, commercials, clothing, automobiles) will be primary sources for future historians. An example of a classic primary source is a bundle of yellowed letters, written by a husband away at war to his wife, found in an attic by a researcher.

primary sources: *Qualitative data* or *quantitative data* used in *historical research*. It is evidence about past social life or events that was created and used by the individuals who actually lived in the historical period.

Published and unpublished written documents are the most important type of primary source. Researchers find them in their original form or preserved in microfiche or on film. They are often the only surviving record of the words, thoughts, and feelings of people in the past. Written documents are helpful for studying societies and historical periods with writing and literate people. A frequent criticism of written sources is that they were largely written by the elite or those in official organizations; thus, the views of the illiterate, the poor, or those outside official social institutions may be overlooked. For example, the history of First Nations people in Canada has been passed down through oral tradition (discussed shortly), and thus written sources on their experiences and histories have been indirect or difficult to find.

The written word on paper was the main medium of communication prior to the widespread use of telecommunications, computers, and video technology to record events and ideas. In fact, the spread of forms of communication that do not leave a permanent physical record (e.g., telephone conversations, computer records, and television or radio broadcasts), and which have largely replaced letters, written ledgers, and newspapers, may make the work of future historians more difficult.

Secondary Sources Primary sources have realism and authenticity, but the practical limitation of time can restrict research on many primary sources to a narrow time frame or location. To get a broader picture, many historical researchers use **secondary sources**, the writings of specialist historians who have spent years studying primary sources.

secondary sources: *Qualitative data* and *quantitative data* used in *historical research*, where information about events or settings is documented or written later by historians or others who did not directly participate in the events or setting.

Running Records **Running records** consist of files or existing statistical documents maintained by organizations. An example of a running record is a file in a country church that contains a record of every marriage and every death from 1910 to the present.

A major project was recently undertaken to reconstruct historical running records from Canada's past. The Canadian Century Research Infrastructure is a collaborative effort of many researchers (from many disciplines) at several Canadian universities to create databases that draw on the Canadian censuses of 1911, 1921, 1931, 1941, and 1951, which will be joined to other databases to create a set of historical data that spans from 1871 to 2001. Details about the project can be found at www.canada.uottawa.ca/ccri/CCRI/index.htm.

running records: A special type of *existing statistics research* used in *historical research* because the files, records, or documents are maintained in a relatively consistent manner over a period of time.

Recollections The words or writings of individuals about their past lives or experiences based on memory are **recollections**. These can be in the form of memoirs, autobiographies, or interviews. Because memory is imperfect, recollections are often distorted in ways that primary sources are not.

recollections: The words or writings of people about their life experiences after some time has passed. The writings are based on a memory of the past, but may be stimulated by a review of past objects, photos, personal notes, or belongings.

In Canadian Aboriginal cultures, knowledge has traditionally been passed from one generation to the next through **oral histories** rather than through written documents. Skills necessary for survival, such as those related to hunting and healing, were passed on by telling others how to do them. Histories and stories related to their ancestors were also passed on through the oral tradition. In gathering oral history, a researcher conducts unstructured interviews with people about their lives or events in the past. This approach is especially valuable for groups who do not have a tradition of written recorded documents,

oral history: A type of *recollection* in which a researcher interviews a person about the events, beliefs, or feelings in the past that were directly experienced.

Box 14.2 Social Research and the Internet

Using Archival Data and Online Archives

Doing historical research requires the use of archival material, and the archive is the main source for primary historical materials. Archives are accumulations of documentary materials (e.g., papers, photos, letters) in private collections, museums, libraries, or formal archives. Material held in archives is fundamentally different from the holdings of a library. In a library, you can access books that many of the libraries around the world will have identical copies of. In archival research, you are looking at documents and records that are unique. They are only held in a particular location and are usually not reproduced in mass quantities, like books. Archival records are one-of-a-kind and therefore tracking down exactly what you need can feel quite a bit like detective work.

Library and Archives Canada has an extensive collection and excellent online resources at www.collectionscanada.gc.ca. While an increasing number of records at this national archives are being digitized, the vast majority of materials are still in hard format and cannot be accessed online. Cities and towns usually have their own historical archives that are open to the public. Provincial archives are usually housed in government buildings that are also open to the public. Most university libraries have their own archives as well.

Another valuable source of Canadian archival material that has been considerably digitized can be found at www.canadiana.ca. Through their "memory portal," users have access to over 65 million pages of digitized archival material from museums, libraries, and archives that has been collected from 40 member institutions.

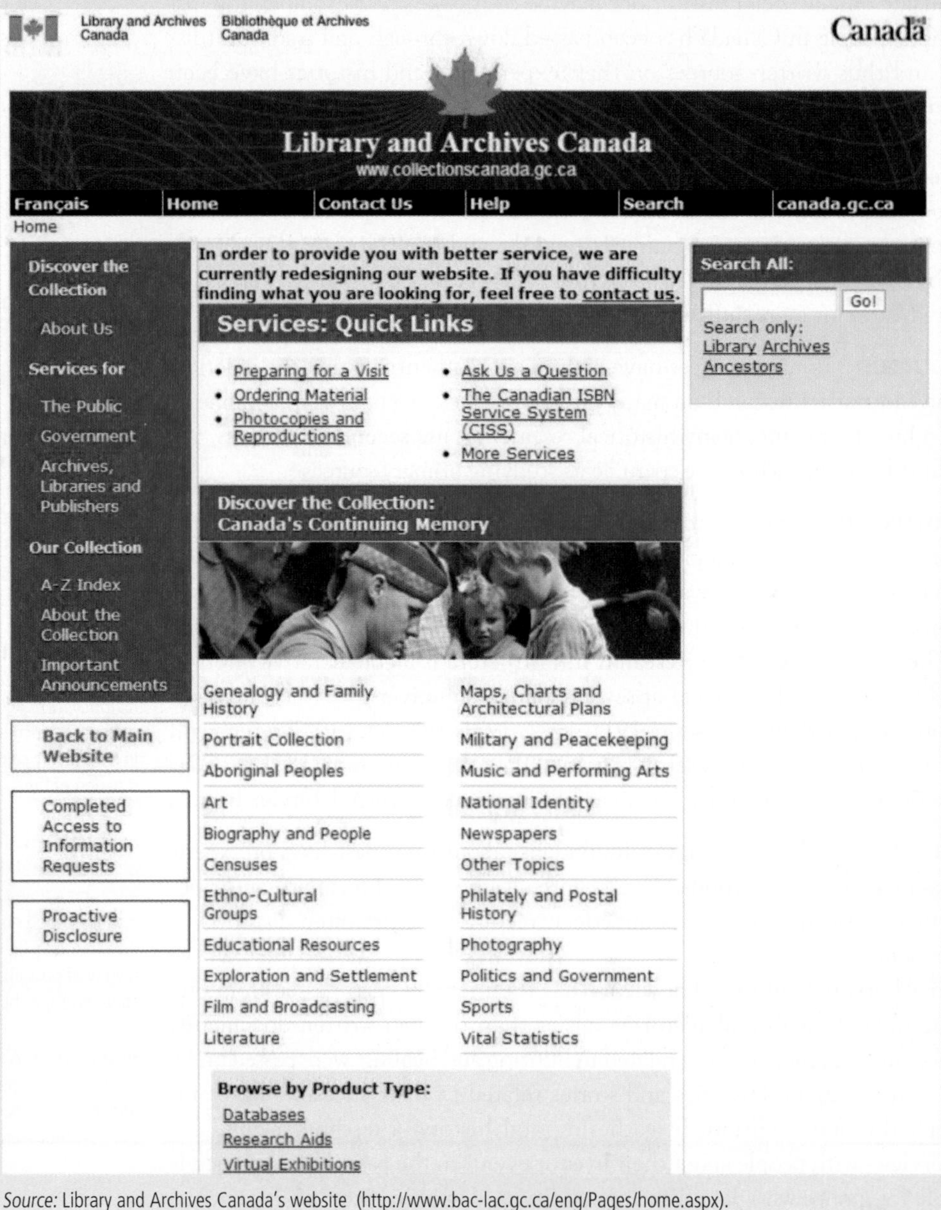

Source: Library and Archives Canada's website (http://www.bac-lac.gc.ca/eng/Pages/home.aspx).

Box 14.2 *(continued)*

Location and Access

Finding whether a collection exists on a topic, organization, or individual can be a long, frustrating task consisting of many emails, phone calls, and referrals. If the material on a person or topic does exist, it may be scattered in multiple locations. Gaining access may depend on appealing to a family member's kindness for private collections or travelling to distant libraries and verifying one's reason for examining many dusty boxes of old letters. Also, the researcher may discover limited hours (e.g., an archive is open only four days a week from 10 a.m. to 5 p.m., but the researcher needs to inspect the material for 40 hours).

Sorting and Organization

Archival material may be unsorted or organized in a variety of ways. The organization may reflect criteria that are unrelated to the researcher's interests. For example, letters and papers may be in chronological order, but the researcher is interested only in letters to four professional colleagues over three decades, not daily bills, family correspondence, and so on.

Technology and Control

Archival materials may be in their original form, on microforms, or increasingly in a digitized form. Researchers may be allowed only to take notes, not make copies, or they may be allowed only to see select parts of the whole collection. Researchers become frustrated with the limitations of having to read dusty papers in one specific room and being allowed only to take notes by pencil for the few hours a day the archive is open to the public.

Tracking and Tracing

One of the most difficult tasks in archival research is tracing common events or persons through the materials. Even if all material is in one location, the same event or relationship may appear in several places in many forms. Researchers sort through mounds of paper to find bits of evidence here and there.

Drudgery, Luck, and Serendipity

Archival research is often painstakingly slow. Spending many hours poring over partially legible documents can be very tedious. Also, researchers will often discover holes in collections, gaps in a series of papers, or destroyed documents. Yet careful reading and inspection of previously untouched material can yield startling new connections or ideas. The researcher may discover unexpected evidence that opens new lines of inquiry (see Elder, Pavalko, & Clipp, 1993, and Hill, 1993).

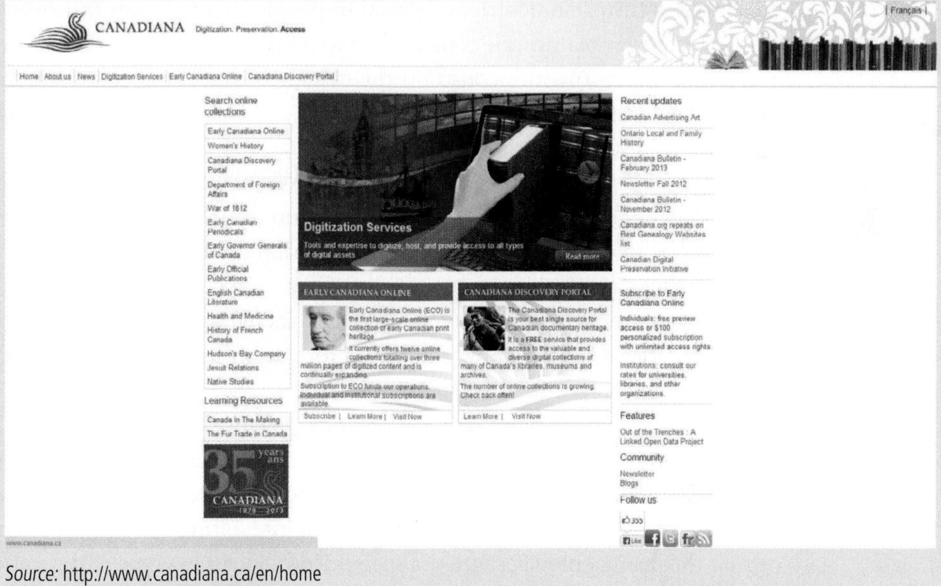

Source: http://www.canadiana.ca/en/home

as well as nonelite groups and those who cannot read or write. The oral history research technique began in the 1930s and now has a professional association and a scholarly journal devoted to it.

Miller (1998) collected the *adawx* of Tsimshian of the North Pacific Coast of Canada, who insisted that this term be translated as "history." Through the oral tradition, Miller collected rich and complex cultural epics, which were all nested within the distinct social structure of this particular First Nations group. The author illustrates that despite the adversities experienced by the Tsimshian in the face of depopulation and outside pressures, they have kept their *adawx*, spanning 10 000 years, through the use of the oral tradition.

Research with Secondary Sources

Uses and Limitations Social researchers often use secondary sources, the books and articles written by historians, as evidence of past conditions.[5] Secondary sources have limitations and need to be used with caution, though.

Limitations of secondary historical evidence include problems of inaccurate historical accounts and a lack of studies in areas of interest. Such sources cannot be used to test hypotheses. *Post facto* (after-the-fact) explanations cannot meet positivist criteria of falsifiability, because few statistical controls can be used and replication is impossible. Yet historical research by others plays an important role in developing general explanations, among its other uses. For example, such research substantiates the emergence and evolution of tendencies over time.

Potential Problems The many volumes of secondary sources present a maze of details and interpretations for a historical researcher. He or she must transform the mass of descriptive studies into an intelligible picture that is consistent with the richness of the evidence. It also must bridge the many specific time periods or locales. The researcher faces potential problems with secondary sources.

One problem is that historians rarely present theory-free, objective "facts." They implicitly frame raw data, categorize information, and shape evidence using concepts. The historian's concepts are a mixture drawn from journalism, the language of historical actors, ideologies, philosophy, everyday language in the present, and social science. Most are vague, applied inconsistently, and neither mutually exclusive nor exhaustive. For example, a historian describes a group of people in a nineteenth-century town as upper class, but never defines the term and fails to link it to any theory of social class. The historian's implicit theories constrain the evidence, and the social researcher may be looking for evidence for explanations that are contrary to ones implicitly being used by historians in secondary sources.

Historians also choose some information from all possible evidence, but the historical researcher does not know how this was done. Without knowing the selection process, a historical researcher must rely on the historian's judgments, which can contain biases.[6] For example, a historian reads 10 000 pages of newspapers, letters, and diaries, then boils this information down into summaries and selected quotes in a 100-page book. A historical researcher does not know whether information that the historian left out is relevant for his or her purposes.

The typical historian's research practice also introduces an individualist bias. A heavy reliance on primary sources and surviving artifacts combines with an atheoretical orientation to produce a narrow focus on the actions of specific people. This particularistic, micro-level view directs attention away from integrating themes or patterns. This emphasis on the documented activities of specific individuals is a type of theoretical orientation.[7]

narrative history: A type of writing about a historical setting in which the writer attempts to "tell a story" by following chronological order, describing particular people and events, and focusing on many colourful details.

Another problem is in the organization of the evidence. Traditional historians organize evidence as a **narrative history**. This compounds problems of undefined concepts and the selection of evidence. In the historical narrative, material is chronologically organized around a single coherent "story." Each part of the story is connected to each other part by its place in the time order of events. Together, all the parts form a unity or whole. Conjuncture and contingency are key elements of the narrative form—that is, if X (or X plus Z) occurred, then Y would occur, and if X (or X plus Z) had not occurred, something else would have followed. The contingency creates a logical interdependency between earlier and later events.

A difficulty of the narrative is that the primary organizing tool—time order or position in a sequence of events—does not denote theoretical or historical causality. In other words, the narrative meets only one of the three criteria for establishing causality—that of temporal order. Moreover, narrative writing frequently obscures causal processes. This occurs when a historian includes events in the narrative to enrich the background or context to add colour, but the events have no causal significance. Likewise, he or she presents events with a delayed causal impact, or events that are temporarily "on hold" with a causal impact occurring at some unspecified later time.

Also, narratives rarely explicitly indicate how combination or interaction effects operate or the relative sizes of different factors. For example, the historian discusses three conditions as causing an event. Yet rarely do readers know which is most important or whether all three conditions must operate together to have a causal impact, but no two conditions or single condition alone could create the same impact.[8]

The narrative organization creates difficulties for the researcher using secondary sources and creates conflicting findings. The historical researcher must read though weak concepts, unknown selection criteria, and unclear causal logic. Theory may reside beneath the narrative but it remains implicit and hidden.

Two final problems with secondary sources are concerned with historiographic schools and with the influences on a historian when he or she is writing. Various schools of historiography (e.g., diplomatic, demographic, ecological, psychological, Marxist, intellectual) have their own rules for seeking evidence and asking questions, and they give priority to certain types of explanatory factors. Likewise, a historian writing today will examine primary materials differently from how those writing in the past, such as in the 1920s, did.

Research with Primary Sources

The historian is the major issue when using secondary sources. When using primary sources, however, the biggest concern is that only a fraction of everything written or used in the past has survived into the present. Moreover, what survived is a nonrandom sample of what once existed.

Historical researchers attempt to read primary sources with the eyes and assumptions of a contemporary who lived in the past. This means "bracketing," or holding back knowledge of subsequent events and modern values. For example, when reading a source produced by a slave holder, moralizing against slavery or faulting the author for not seeing its evil is not worthwhile. The historical researcher holds back moral judgments and becomes a moral relativist while reading primary sources.

Another problem is that locating primary documents is a time-consuming task. A researcher must search through specialized indexes and travel to archives or specialized libraries. Primary sources are often located in dusty, out-of-the-way rooms full of stacked cardboard boxes containing masses of fading documents. These may be incomplete, unorganized, and in various stages of decay. Once the documents or other primary sources are located, the researcher evaluates them by subjecting them to external and internal criticism (see Figure 14.1).

External criticism means evaluating the authenticity of a document itself to be certain that it is not a fake or a forgery. Criticism involves asking questions: "Was the document created when it is claimed to have been, in the place where it was supposed to be, and by the person who claims to be its author?" "Why was the document produced to begin with, and how did it survive?"

external criticism: In *historical research*, a way to check the authenticity of *primary sources* by accurately locating the place and time of its creation (i.e., ensuring it is not a forgery).

Once the document passes as being authentic, a researcher uses **internal criticism**, an examination of the document's contents, to establish credibility. A researcher evaluates whether what is recorded was based on what the author directly witnessed or is secondhand information. This requires examining both the literal meaning of what is recorded and the

internal criticism: How historical researchers establish the authenticity and credibility of *primary sources* and determine their accuracy as an account of what occurred.

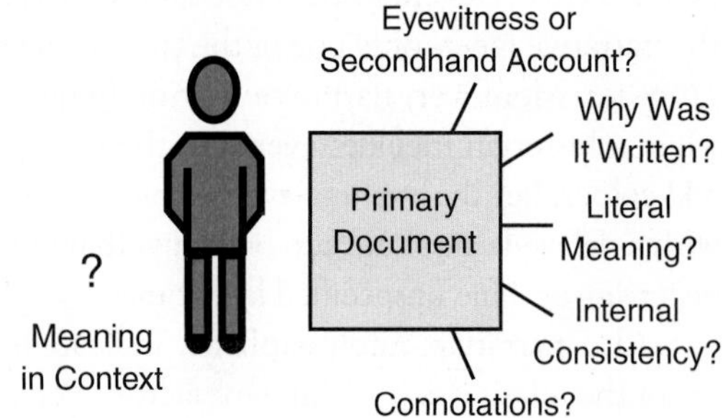

Figure 14.1 Internal and External Criticism

subtle connotations or intentions. The researcher notes other events, sources, or people mentioned in the document and asks whether they can be verified. He or she examines implicit assumptions or value positions, and the relevant conditions under which the document was produced are noted (e.g., during wartime or under a totalitarian regime). The researcher also considers language usage at the time and the context of statements within the document to distill meaning.

In a historical study of immigration policy toward Blacks in Canada, the United Kingdom, and the United States, Bashi (2004) used both primary and secondary historical sources and running records. He considered writings that spanned over two centuries of history and in three nations and included everything from major international events and national laws to newspaper articles. He relied on secondary sources for major national or international events. Although his study was primarily historical and qualitative, he also examined quantitative data from running records and statistics on immigration numbers and visas issued. His evidence also included quotations from official government documents, original newspaper reports, and selections from enacted laws of the time. By comparing Black immigration over a long historical period and in different socio-cultural settings, he could trace the formation of strategies to keep Black immigrants out of Canada, the UK, and the United States.

LO 5 Define *equivalence* and explain why it is important in historical research.

EQUIVALENCE IN HISTORICAL RESEARCH

The Importance of Equivalence

equivalence: The issue of making comparisons across divergent contexts, or whether a researcher, living in a specific time period and culture, correctly reads, understands, or conceptualizes data about people from a different historical era or culture.

Equivalence is a critical issue in all research. It is the issue of making comparisons across divergent contexts, or whether a researcher, living in a specific time period and culture, correctly reads, understands, or conceptualizes data about people from a different historical era or culture. Without equivalence, a researcher cannot use the same concepts or measures in different cultures or historical periods, and this makes comparison difficult, if not impossible. It is similar to the problems that arise with measurement validity in quantitative research.

contextual equivalence: The issue in *historical research* of whether social roles, norms, or situations across different cultures or historical periods are equivalent or can be compared.

Contextual Equivalence **Contextual equivalence** is the correct application of terms or concepts in different social or historical contexts. It is an attempt to achieve equivalence within specific contexts. For example, in cultures with different dominant religions, a religious leader (e.g., priest, minister, or rabbi) can have different roles, training, and authority. In some contexts, priests are full-time male professionals who are wealthy, highly esteemed, well-educated community leaders and also wield political power. In other contexts, a priest is anyone who rises above others in a congregation on a temporary basis but is without power or standing in the community. Priests in such a context may be less educated, have low incomes, and be viewed as foolish but harmless people. A researcher who asks about "priests" without noticing the context could make serious errors in interpretations.

Context also applies across historical eras. For example, *attending university* has a different meaning today than in a historical context in which only the richest 1 percent of the population attended university, most universities had fewer than 500 students, all were private all-male institutions that did not require a high school diploma for entry, and university curriculum consisted of classical languages and moral training. Attending university 100 years ago was not the same as it is today: The historical context has altered the meaning of attending university.

The Persistence of Religion in America

Conceptual Equivalence The ability to use the same concept across divergent cultures or historical eras is **conceptual equivalence**. Researchers live within specific cultures and historical eras. Their concepts are based on their experiences and knowledge from their own culture and era. Researchers may try to stretch their concepts by learning about other cultures or eras, but their views are coloured by their current life situations. This creates a persistent tension and raises the question: Can a researcher create concepts that are simultaneously true reflections of life experiences in different cultures or eras and that also make sense to him or her?

conceptual equivalence: In *historical research,* the issue of whether the same ideas or concepts occur or can be used to represent phenomena across divergent cultural or historical settings.

THE QUALITATIVE ANALYSIS OF TEXT

LO 6 Define qualitative content analysis and describe how it is different from quantitative content analysis.

When Can We Use Qualitative Methods?

We now turn to qualitative techniques for the analysis of text. Here, we focus specifically on qualitative content analysis and discourse analysis. If you recall from Chapter 10, the word *text* can refer to a variety of written and recorded forms: books, newspaper articles, magazine articles, photographs, movies, commercials, television programs, and advertisements, to name a few. In qualitative content analysis, the text can also include interview transcripts and related types of qualitative data. In Chapter 10, we discussed how to analyze these texts from a quantitative perspective, but here we turn to alternative approaches that are rooted in interpretivism rather than positivism.

You might find it odd that a method like content analysis can be both quantitative and qualitative. But think of it this way: Earlier in the book (Chapter 8) we talked about interviews in the form of surveys, which is a distinctly quantitative approach. In Chapter 12 we discussed qualitative interviewing. Both the structured form of survey interviewing and the semi-structured qualitative interview are *types of interviews*—they just have very different ways of being undertaken. The same goes for content analysis—both quantitative and qualitative content analyses analyze the content of text, but each technique uses a different approach for going about the task.

Research Problems Appropriate for Qualitative Content Analysis

Document Research

Chapter 10 showed that research problems appropriate for quantitative content analysis were those that concerned a large volume of text, topics that needed to be studied at a distance, or when a search for messages embedded in text (not easily seen with casual observation) was desired. Quantitative content analysis can answer questions about "how much" or "how often" certain instances of a code are observed. But it cannot tell you much about "why" or the deeper meanings behind such observed frequencies.

Qualitative content analysis, to contrast, is concerned with going beyond counting instances of codes to classifying large amounts of text into a manageable number of categories that reflect either explicit or inferred meaning. This is much like the process of manifest and latent coding in quantitative content analysis, with much more attention being given to the latent aspects of implied meaning. The codes in a qualitative content analysis are usually concerned, however, with broader issues. In quantitative content analysis, one might examine *how often* illicit drug use is portrayed in primetime television, while in qualitative content analysis the focus would shift to a broader issue such as the *meanings* attributed to illicit drug use on television (i.e., if it is portrayed as fun, forbidden, deviant, shameful, etc.).

The Major Differences between Qualitative and Quantitative Content Analyses

qualitative content analysis: An approach to analyzing text that involves the coding of themes, their patterns, and linkages.

The biggest differences between qualitative approaches to content analysis and the quantitative approach are in the approach to coding and how the codes are interpreted. In both approaches, a researcher uses a systematic set of codes that are allocated to data segments of text. But how the researcher arrives at these codes in quantitative and **qualitative content analysis** is quite different.

In quantitative approaches to content analysis, manifest (or clearly observable) content is usually the focus, while in qualitative approaches, attention shifts to revealing implied meanings and motives. Similarly, quantitative content analysis uses segments of text to identify instances of a code (i.e., how many times it appears), while qualitative content analysts are more likely to examine *entire texts* at once for their meaning. As mentioned before, both approaches use coding procedures, but quantitative content analysis focuses on the counting of various instances of a code, while in qualitative content analysis the data analysis techniques are quite different. (We turn to qualitative data analysis in the next chapter, where we discuss how these types of data are examined for themes and general codes.) In qualitative content analysis, the task at hand is not to count the codes, but to identify general themes that run through the different texts and to organize and link these general themes into a coherent theory about social life. Both approaches look for patterns, but quantitative content analysis often finds them by using statistical techniques, while patterns and linkages between codes in qualitative content analysis are discovered through the coding process. A final major difference between the two approaches is how the data are presented. Quantitative content analysis is usually presented through the use of statistical tables and graphs, while qualitative content analysis usually provides evidence of themes and their linkages through extensive quotation and the development of a narrative around the themes that explains their connectedness.[9] See Table 14.2 for a summary of the differences between quantitative and qualitative content analyses.

LO 7 Differentiate between the various approaches to content analysis.

The Different Types of Qualitative Content Analyses

summative content analysis: A type of *qualitative content analysis* that uses both *manifest* and *latent codes* and is most closely related to *quantitative content analysis.*

conventional content analysis: A type of *qualitative content analysis* in which the researcher develops themes during the *coding* process.

There is not one standardized way of doing a qualitative content analysis. In fact, Hsiu-Fang and Shannon (2005) have identified at least three different approaches that researchers use when undertaking this method of social research (see Table 14.3). **Summative content analysis** most closely resembles the type of content analysis described in Chapter 10 in the sense that there is a focus on manifest and latent content. The appearance of words or particular content in textual material is recorded for frequency, and these codes are determined before data analysis occurs. However, what sets this method apart from quantitative content analysis is the equal attention paid to latent (or implied) meaning and the development of codes in the data analysis process (as opposed to exclusively *a priori*).

A second type of qualitative content analysis is known as **conventional content analysis**. In this approach, codes are developed only during data analysis and are derived from the data. There are often several stages in the coding process, which are covered in more detail in Chapter 15. After codes are developed, patterns are detected and linkages among the

Table 14.2 Major Differences between Qualitative and Quantitative Content Analyses

Aspect of Inquiry	Quantitative Approach	Qualitative Approach
What is being observed?	Most manifest content, the counting of sequences and mentionings	Largely latent content; observing motives, purpose, and meaning
What is the unit of analysis?	Segments of text	Entire texts
What is the coding procedure?	Tabulation of counts	Identifying themes and tagging them
How are patterns discovered?	Statistically calculated during data analysis	Linked and developed through coding process
How are data presented?	Figures, tables, graphs, statistics	Quotes that are exemplars of particular themes, conceptual maps, narratives

Source: Adapted from Wesley, J. (2009). *Building bridges in content analysis: Quantitative and qualitative traditions*. Paper presented at the Annual Meeting of the Canadian Political Science Association, May 29, 2009, Carleton University, Ottawa, Ontario, Canada.

codes are identified to generate a theory. This approach to content analysis is associated with the grounded theory approach that has been discussed in earlier chapters.

The third type of qualitative content analysis is known as **directed content analysis**. What makes this particular approach distinct is that it has a deductive approach to theory. If you recall from earlier chapters, the inductive approach tests theory rather than generating it. Researchers using the directed approach to content analysis use predetermined codes that are derived from theory. During the data analysis, however, additional codes are added if they do not fit into the pre-existing coding frame that is suggested by the theoretical framework that is being tested. See Box 14.3 for examples of different types of qualitative content analyses.

directed content analysis: A type of *qualitative content analysis* that begins with predetermined codes derived from theory.

Qualitative content analysis techniques, while varied, are just one approach to the analysis of text. There are many more ways that social researchers examine text, including discourse analysis.

Table 14.3 Major Differences between the Different Approaches to Content Analysis

Type of Content Analysis	Extent of inductive reasoning	Process Begins With	When Codes Are Defined	Where Codes Come From
Summative	Weak/Medium	Keywords	Before and during data analysis	Derived from literature review or researcher's interest
Directed	Medium	Theory	Before and during data analysis	Derived from theory
Conventional	Strong	Observation	During data analysis	Derived from data

Source: Adapted from Hsiu-Fang, H., & Shannon, S. E. (2005). Three approaches to qualitative content analysis. *Qualitative Health Research, 15*(9), 1277–1288.

Box 14.3 Concepts in Action

Examples of Qualitative Content Analysis

Using a *summative* approach, Clarke, Friedman, and Hoffman-Goetz (2004) examined 14 English-language Aboriginal print newspapers to examine Aboriginal people's experiences with HIV/AIDS. After searching the publications, the researchers found that there were 167 articles on HIV/AIDS. The researchers decided to keep all of the stories that were "anecdotal" or reflected personal experiences with HIV/AIDS (34 stories) and a 25 percent random sample of the remaining "scientific" or "fact-based" articles (32 stories). *Manifest codes* that were recorded were the socio-demographic characteristics of the individuals who were featured in the articles, such as sex and age. *Latent codes* that were examined included the role of Aboriginal culture and spirituality, fear of both the disease and other people's finding out, and risk factors. After a short discussion of the manifest codes, the authors explored the emergent latent codes and their significance. Among the findings were that women and young people were under-represented in this medium and that there was a focus on contextualizing HIV/AIDS within Aboriginal culture and concerns, rather than within the dominant medical framework found in the mainstream media.

Abdelmutti and Hoffman-Goetz (2009) used a *directed* approach to qualitative content analysis when they examined Canadian and U.S. newspaper articles on cervical cancer, human papillomavirus (HPV), and the HPV vaccine Gardasil. For the Canadian sample, the authors searched the *Globe and Mail* and the *National Post* for articles written on these topics between 2006 and 2007. They also examined two national newspapers in the United States: the *Wall Street Journal* and *USA Today*. The researchers used a directed approach, which means they had a theory that they wanted to test, which guided how they constructed their coding categories. Their initial coding was based on previous research that suggested there are "fright factors" that influence the public's perception of health risks. These fright factors include the looming threat of death or illness, the idea that the disease is inescapable, and that the disease is poorly understood by scientists. The researchers coded the articles according to these fright factors, but also noted emergent themes that appeared (and did not fit into any of the predetermined fright-factor categories). These themes included reference to pharmaceutical lobbying and sexual promiscuity.

To contrast, Rutherford (2009) used a *conventional* approach to qualitative content analysis to examine child-rearing advice articles from *Parents* magazine from 1929 to 2006. Using a systematic random sample (see Chapter 7), the author identified 34 issues and analyzed the content of these issues. The researcher was particularly interested in the topic of children's autonomy and choices, and thus this guided the creation of the categories that emerged from the data. She found that forms of autonomy were discussed in reference to children's daily lives, their leisure activities, their responsibilities, their expressions, and their consumption habits. Her analysis demonstrates a shift to more restricted freedom of children's movements and delays in children's being given meaningful responsibilities, which she attributes to larger social and cultural changes in American society.

LO 8 Distinguish between content analysis and discourse analysis, and describe the stages of a discourse analysis.

discourse analysis: A type of qualitative analysis of texts that focuses on how knowledge and meaning are created through the use of language.

Similarities and Differences Between Men and Women

DISCOURSE ANALYSIS

Sometimes you may hear people use the terms *qualitative content analysis* and **discourse analysis** interchangeably, but this can add to the confusion around what makes discourse analysis unique. Many students find the discussion of discourse analysis to be intimidating and difficult, often because the meaning of "discourse" can be rather vague. It is useful to think about discourse in terms of "how a certain topic is being talked about." This is what discourse analysis accomplishes—it examines how a particular topic is being discussed in some text (e.g., books, newspaper articles, television shows, conversations) and focuses on the language that is being used to frame these discussions. What makes discourse analysis unique is that it focuses on how language itself is used. Discourse analysts in general study how knowledge and meaning are created through the use of language.

As with qualitative content analysis, there are several different approaches to doing discourse analysis.[10] One approach often used by social scientists is called *critical discourse analysis*, which is informed by the work of French philosopher, historian, and sociologist Michel Foucault, among others. Foucault analyzed language and demonstrated how the concepts of madness, sexuality, and criminality (and several other topics) over history have been shaped by language usage, and how those in positions of power used language to define social problems and ultimately to control certain people and how certain types of social phenomena are understood.[11]

Box 14.4 Focus

General Steps in a Critical Discourse Analysis

- The researcher must decide on the general topic area that he or she is interested in studying.
- The researcher must then engage in extensive background reading on discourse analysis as well as the topic that he or she wants to study. This reading should span disciplines. For example, if you are a sociology student, you should read in your topic area outside of sociology, such as in psychology, history, economics, health research, or wherever writings on your general topic appear.
- You should seek the support and mentorship of a researcher who has expertise in discourse analysis. In some ways, you can think of this as an apprenticeship in learning the ropes in discourse analysis.
- Move from a general topic area into a more narrowly defined research question.
- Identify the data you wish to study (i.e., the form of your text) and collect that data.
- Read your data numerous times to familiarize yourself with its content. This process of repeated readings will allow you to begin to ask questions of the data, such as the particular context in which the text was created. It is at this stage you will start noticing the interesting and subtle features of the text that were at the foundation of its creation.
- Keep notes around any themes you see emerging.
- Continue to keep rereading your data, making detailed notes of any discursive practices you see emerging. Follow up any "hunches" you may have through careful rereadings.
- Discuss your emerging themes with colleagues.
- Begin writing your initial analyses, cycling between reading, writing, and continued analysis.
- Redraft your written analysis as required.

Source: Adapted from Billig, M. (1997). Rhetorical and discursive analysis: How families talk about the royal family. In N. Hayes (Ed.), *Doing qualitative analysis in psychology* (pp. 39–54). Hove, UK: Psychology Press, p. 54. Adapted with permission from Taylor & Francis Books Ltd.

The End of Welfare as We Know It: An Overview of the PRWORA*

What makes critical discourse analysis unique is that it looks at how power is created (and recreated) through the use of language. Critical discourse analysis is better thought of as a *methodology* rather than a specific method, however, as it is really a collection of techniques that are guided by an overarching Foucauldian theoretical set of concerns and assumptions rather than a firm set of "steps" to follow. For novices, however, this absence of steps to follow can be confusing and intimidating. Scholars of discourse analysis have suggested that there are some general stages in a critical discourse analysis that need to be followed, as summarized in Box 14.4.

Zimmerman (2007) undertook a critical discourse analysis when she analyzed published medical journal articles on the topic of palliative care (care given to those at the end of their life when no further medical treatment will prevent their dying from a terminal illness). She was interested in understanding how attitudes toward death influenced the clinical research discourse around the topic of palliative care. Her general research area began as an interest in "death attitudes" in palliative care settings. In the process of conducting her discourse analysis, she focused on medical journal articles that used the words *denial* or *deny* along with the subject headings "terminal care," "palliative care," or "hospice care," identifying 57 articles that met these criteria. Zimmerman was interested in examining how denial of death was discussed as an "obstacle" to palliative care. After carefully reading, rereading, and coding the articles, Zimmerman found several themes around denial, such as how it prevented open discussions about death, prevented people from dying at home, encouraged futile treatments, and impeded advance planning. She further analyzed how this orientation to understanding palliative care as fraught with "obstacles" influences how the medical establishment promotes a "proper way to die" and sees itself as having to manage the "dying process."

CHAPTER SUMMARY

Glossary Flashcards

In this chapter, you learned about three nonreactive qualitative techniques. The first general technique discussed was historical research. You learned that research questions appropriate for historical research are focused on the "big questions" in social research, such as how and under what circumstances social change took place. Historical research aligns itself most strongly with the interpretivist approach, as intensive examination of meaning around a limited number of cases is often undertaken. While historical research has many similarities with field research, it also has its own distinct approach that guides its process. You learned about the conceptualizing of the object of inquiry, locating evidence, evaluating the quality of that evidence, organizing evidence, synthesizing evidence, and writing the report. You also learned the various sources of historical evidence that are possible for such research. Finally, the importance of equivalence was emphasized as researchers, whatever their method, must be aware of the risks of making comparisons across contexts and time periods.

Qualitative content analysis was the second nonreactive qualitative approach to analyzing text discussed. Three distinct approaches were discussed, highlighting the definition of codes and coding procedures unique to each. Compared to quantitative content analysis, qualitative approaches are more concerned with implied meanings and messages being conveyed by a text, rather than simply counting up instances of the appearance of manifest coding categories. Each approach, however, has its own strengths and weaknesses and what type of content analysis a researcher should use is contingent on the type of research question he or she is trying to answer.

Finally, discourse analysis was discussed. Although discourse analysis is also the nonreactive analysis of text, it differs from qualitative content analysis in significant ways. Discourse analysts are interested in determining how a subject is being discussed and how larger social processes are contextualized within the use of language. While there are various approaches to discourse analysis, this chapter focused on critical discourse analysis, which is heavily influenced by the theoretical contributions of Michel Foucault.

Review Questions

1. What kind of research questions are appropriate for investigation through historical methods?
2. Describe four ways that historical research is similar to field research.
3. Explain five features of a distinctive historical research approach.
4. Describe the six steps in a historical research project.
5. Identify the four types of data used in historical research.
6. Define what is meant by *equivalence*.
7. Define *qualitative content analysis* and describe five ways it is different from quantitative content analysis.
8. Name the three different approaches to qualitative content analysis. For each type, explain what the process begins with, when codes are defined, and where the codes come from.
9. What is one way that qualitative content analysis and discourse analysis are similar? In what way do they differ from each other?
10. Describe the general stages of a discourse analysis.

Exercises

Research Activities

1. Using EBSCO's ContentSelect, identify a research article that uses a historical approach. What is the time period being studied? Summarize the research question and the findings of this article.

2. Using EBSCO's ContentSelect, identify three different studies that use qualitative content analysis. What type of qualitative content analytic approach does each study use? How do you know? Describe the process of how codes were decided upon in each of the articles. What kinds of text are the researchers analyzing in each of the articles? How were those texts sampled?
3. Using EBSCO's ContentSelect, find a study that employs a critical discourse analysis. What is the discourse of interest to the author(s) of the study? How does he or she go about determining the discourses? What types of text does the study author use?

Chapter 15
Analysis of Qualitative Data

Photo Credit: Scott Griessel/Fotolia LLC

LEARNING OBJECTIVES

After reading this chapter, you will be able to

LO 1 Explain the similarities and differences between qualitative and quantitative data analysis.
LO 2 Describe the process of coding qualitative data.
LO 3 Identify the different types of files generated in qualitative data analysis.
LO 4 Describe the four different strategies of qualitative data analysis.
LO 5 Describe other techniques researchers can use for qualitative data analysis.

INTRODUCTION

Qualitative data come in the form of written words, phrases, photos, symbols, images, or sounds describing or representing people, actions, and events in social life. Qualitative research rarely uses statistical analysis, but this does not mean that qualitative data analysis is based on vague impressions. It can be systematic and logically rigorous, although in a different way from quantitative or statistical analysis. Over time, qualitative data analysis has become more explicit, although no single qualitative data analysis approach is widely accepted.

This chapter is divided into four parts. First, we discuss the similarities and differences between qualitative and quantitative data analysis. Second, we look at how researchers use coding and concept/theory building in the process of analyzing qualitative data. Third, we review some of the major analytical strategies researchers deploy and ways they think about linking qualitative data with theory. Finally, we briefly review other techniques that researchers use to manage and examine patterns in the qualitative data they have collected.

COMPARING METHODS OF DATA ANALYSIS

LO 1 Explain the similarities and differences between qualitative and quantitative data analysis.

Similarities

Both qualitative and quantitative styles of research involve inferring from the empirical details of social life. To *infer* means to pass a judgment, to use reasoning, and to reach a conclusion based on evidence. In both forms of data analysis, the researcher carefully examines empirical information to reach a conclusion. The conclusion is reached by reasoning, simplifying the complexity in the data, and abstracting from the data, but this varies by the style of research. Both forms of data analysis anchor statements about the social world and are faithful to the data.

Qualitative as well as quantitative analysis involves a public method or process. Researchers systematically record or gather data and in so doing make accessible to others what they did. Both types of researchers collect large amounts of data, describe the data, and document how they collected and examined it. The degree to which the method is standardized and visible may vary, but all researchers reveal their study design in some way.

Research Tools and Techniques

All data analysis is based on comparison. Social researchers compare features of the evidence they have gathered internally or with related evidence. Researchers identify multiple processes, causes, properties, or mechanisms within the evidence. They then look for patterns—similarities and differences, aspects that are alike and unlike. Both qualitative and quantitative researchers strive to avoid errors, false conclusions, and misleading inferences. Researchers are also alert for possible fallacies or illusions. They sort through various explanations, discussions, and descriptions, and evaluate merits of rivals, seeking the more trustworthy among them.

Differences

Qualitative data analysis differs from quantitative analysis in four ways. First, there are different types and numbers of analysis techniques. Quantitative researchers choose from a specialized, standardized set of data analysis techniques. Hypothesis testing and statistical methods vary little across different social research projects. Quantitative analysis is highly developed and builds on applied mathematics. By contrast, qualitative data analysis is less standardized. The wide variety in qualitative research is matched by the many approaches to data analysis.

Second, there are different starting points for data analysis. Quantitative researchers do not begin data analysis until they have collected all of the data and condensed them into numbers. They then manipulate the numbers to see patterns or relationships. Qualitative researchers can look for patterns or relationships, but they begin analysis early in a research project, while they are still collecting data. The results of early data analysis guide subsequent data collection. The grounded theory approach, which involves the iterative relationship between data collection, analysis, and theory development, has been discussed in earlier chapters. Thus, qualitative analysis is less a distinct final stage of research than a dimension of research that stretches across all stages.

Third, there are different relationships between data and social theory. Quantitative researchers manipulate numbers that represent empirical facts to test theoretical hypotheses. By contrast, qualitative researchers create new concepts and theory by blending together empirical evidence and abstract concepts. Instead of testing a hypothesis, a qualitative analyst may illustrate or colour in evidence showing that a theory, generalization, or interpretation is plausible.

Fourth, there are different degrees of abstraction or distance from the details of social life. In all data analysis, a researcher places raw data into categories that he or she manipulates to identify patterns. Quantitative researchers assume that social life can be represented by using numbers. When they manipulate the numbers according to the laws of statistics, the numbers reveal features of social life. Qualitative analysis does not draw on a large, well-established body of formal knowledge from mathematics and statistics. The data are in the form of words, which are relatively imprecise, diffuse, and context based and can have more than one meaning.

Explanations and Qualitative Data

When Can We Use Qualitative Methods?

Qualitative explanations take many forms. A qualitative researcher does not have to choose between a rigid idiographic/nomothetic dichotomy—that is, between describing specifics and verifying universal laws. Instead, a researcher develops explanations or generalizations that are close to concrete data and contexts but are more than simple descriptions. He or she usually uses a lower-level, less abstract theory, which is grounded in concrete details presented in the data. He or she may build new theory to create a realistic picture of social life and stimulate understanding more than to test a causal hypothesis. Explanations tend to be rich in detail, sensitive to context, and capable of showing the complex processes or sequences of social life. The explanations may be causal, but this is not always the case. The researcher's goal is to organize specific details into a coherent picture, model, or set of interlocked concepts.

A qualitative researcher divides explanations into two categories: highly unlikely and plausible. The researcher is satisfied by building a case or supplying supportive evidence. He or she may eliminate some theoretical explanations from consideration while increasing the plausibility of others because only a few explanations will be consistent with a pattern in the data. Qualitative analysis can eliminate an explanation by showing that a wide array of evidence contradicts it. The data might support more than one explanation, but *all* explanations will not be consistent with it. In addition to eliminating less plausible explanations, qualitative data analysis helps to verify a sequence of events or the steps of a process. This temporal ordering is the basis of finding associations among variables, and it is useful in supporting causal arguments.

LO 2 Describe the process of coding qualitative data.

CODING AND CONCEPT FORMATION

Qualitative researchers often use general ideas, themes, or concepts as analytical tools for making generalizations.

Conceptualization

Quantitative researchers conceptualize and refine variables in a process that comes before data collection or analysis. By contrast, qualitative researchers form new concepts or refine concepts that are grounded in the data. Concept formation is integral to data analysis and begins during data collection. Conceptualization is how a qualitative researcher organizes and makes sense of the data.

"Night to His Day": The Social Construction of Gender

A qualitative researcher organizes data into categories on the basis of themes, concepts, or similar features. He or she develops new concepts, formulates conceptual definitions, and examines the relationships among concepts. Eventually, he or she links concepts to each other in terms of a sequence, as oppositional sets (*X* is the opposite of *Y*), or as sets of similar categories that he or she interweaves into theoretical statements. Qualitative researchers conceptualize, or form concepts, as they read through and ask critical questions of data (e.g., field notes, historical documents, secondary sources). The questions can come from the abstract vocabulary of a discipline such as sociology—for example, "Is this a case of class conflict?" "Was role conflict present in that situation?" "Is this a social movement?" Questions can also be logical—for example, "What was the sequence of events?" "How does the way it happened here compare to over there?" "Are these the same or different, general or specific cases?" Researchers often conceptualize as they code qualitative data.

In qualitative data analysis, ideas and evidence are mutually interdependent. This applies particularly to case study analysis. Cases are not given pre-established empirical units or theoretical categories apart from data; they are defined by data and theory. By analyzing a situation, the researcher organizes data and applies ideas simultaneously to create or specify a case. Making or creating a case, called *casing*, brings the data and theory together. Determining what to treat as a case resolves a tension or strain between what the researcher observes and his or her ideas about it.

Coding Qualitative Data

A quantitative researcher codes after all the data have been collected. He or she arranges measures of variables, which are in the form of numbers, into a machine-readable form for statistical analysis.

Coding data has a different meaning in qualitative research. A researcher codes by organizing the raw data into conceptual categories and creates themes or concepts. Instead of a simple clerical task, coding is an integral part of data analysis guided by the research question. Coding encourages higher-level thinking about the data, and in the case of grounded theory, moves a researcher toward theoretical generalizations.

Using Multiple Data

Coding is two simultaneous activities: mechanical data reduction and analytical data categorization. Coding data is the hard work of reducing mountains of raw data into manageable piles. In addition to making a large mass of data manageable, it is how a researcher imposes order on the data. Coding also allows a researcher to quickly retrieve relevant parts of the data. Between the moments of thrill and inspiration, coding qualitative data, or filework, can be wearisome and tedious.

The data that are coded in a qualitative project include various types of texts, which are not limited to field notes, interview transcripts, and historical documents. The coding of all these data types involves the same general technique: organizing the data into themes and then refining and drawing links between the themes. A researcher can code more than one type of data source during a single research project. In other words, interview transcripts and field notes can be coded to look for themes that relate to a single research question. In the examples that follow, however, the case of a single data type (i.e., interview only or field notes only) is considered.

Qualitative Methods

There is not one correct way of coding qualitative data. Next, we discuss open, axial, and selective coding, which are the three main steps that have been recommended by advocates of the grounded theory approach (Strauss & Corbin, 1990).

Open Coding

Open coding is performed during a first pass through recently collected data. The researcher locates ideas in the data and assigns initial codes. He or she slowly reads field notes, historical sources, or other data, looking for critical terms, key events, or themes, which are then noted. Next, he or she writes a preliminary concept or label at the edge of a note card or computer record and highlights it with brightly coloured ink or in some similar way. The researcher is open to creating new themes and to changing these initial codes in subsequent analysis. A theoretical framework helps if it is used in a flexible manner.

open coding: A first *coding* of *qualitative data* in which a researcher examines the data to condense them into preliminary analytical categories or codes for analyzing the data.

Open coding brings themes to the surface from deep inside the data. The themes are at a low level of abstraction and come from the researcher's initial research question, concepts in the literature, terms used by members in the social setting, or new thoughts

Pew Study Report on Globalization

stimulated by immersion in the data. In open coding, a researcher can develop literally hundreds of codes. It is the ones with the most evidence (i.e., the most interview quotes or excerpts from field notes) that are usually considered the strongest codes or themes.

One of the authors (Robson) was interested in studying the long-term effects of being bullied in childhood and interviewed a sample of adults who had been bullied as children. When she open coded the interview transcripts, she saw three themes emerge: *distrusting of intimate relationships in adulthood*, *empathetic toward people*, and *awkward in social settings*.

Following are examples of actual interviews that were open coded with the theme *awkward in social settings:*

- Interviewee 1 (male, mid-20s): "I try to avoid group situations out of habit . . . Not that I fear anymore that I am going to get teased or harassed or fucked with, but I just have these habits that are hard to break. Avoiding groups, avoiding being the centre of attention, because when I was the centre of attention when I was growing up, it was for bad things, so now it's hard to be the centre of attention even though it might be for something positive."
- Interviewee 2 (female, mid-20s): "It's only been since I've been married that I've started to form good solid relationships with women . . . I'm still not really confident in social situations around people that I don't know very well. I'm not confident . . . I think that the friends I do have are a lot more deeper and more meaningful because I knew how to form those when I was a kid—deeper, more meaningful relationships."

Men and Women: Together and Apart in the Later Years

Qualitative researchers vary in the units they code. Some code every line or every few words; others code paragraphs and argue that much of the data are not coded and are dross or left over. The degree of detail in coding depends on the research question, the "richness" of the data, and the researcher's purposes. See Box 15.1 for some practical tips on open coding.

Open-ended coding extends to analytical notes or memos that a researcher writes to himself or herself while collecting data. Researchers should write memos on their codes (see the later discussion in "Analytical Memo Writing").

axial coding: A second *coding* of *qualitative data* after *open coding*. The researcher organizes the codes, develops linkages among them, and discovers key analytical categories.

Axial Coding This is a "second pass" through the data. During open coding, a researcher focuses on the actual data and assigns code labels for themes. There is no concern about making connections among themes or elaborating the concepts that the themes represent. By contrast, in **axial coding**, the researcher begins with an organized set of initial codes or preliminary concepts. In this second pass, he or she focuses on the initial coded themes more than on the data. Additional codes or new ideas may emerge during

Box 15.1 Making It Practical

Tips on Open Coding in Qualitative Research

Students new to qualitative research often worry about how to code "correctly." If the student has started his or her methods training with the quantitative techniques described earlier in this book, it can be difficult to make the transition to the idea that there is no one objectively correct way to do coding. This does not mean that "anything goes"—just that even if two highly skilled and experienced qualitative researchers coded the same piece of data, their coding systems will look different. The example that follows shows how two researchers have open coded the same piece of data. Both are "right," but you will notice that they are quite dissimilar to one another. The new qualitative researcher must keep in mind that the merit of the qualitative research will be assessed through the final outcome of the coding process—that is, being able to demonstrate a coherent theory that is embedded in the data (assuming one is using the grounded theory approach).

Below are two transcripts from people who were asked about their experiences of "coming out" as gay or lesbian to their families. Both researchers were asked to open code the transcripts, bearing in mind the range of emotions that were experienced by each of the interviewees. As you can see, each researcher did the task in his or her own way. One is not more correct than the other.

Box 15.1 *(continued)*

Researcher 1	Researcher 2
Coming out to my family was a huge deal, yeah. I hid my sexuality from my parents until I was 19, because that's when I moved out. I was starting university so I thought I needed to be true to myself and them. All my friends knew I was gay and I'd had a few boyfriends and I guess I just kind of hoped they'd figure it out and I wouldn't have to say anything. I was scared and nervous to actually say it out loud to them. I knew they wouldn't stop loving me or anything. I'd always had a good relationship with them both. I just didn't want to disappoint them. I mean it's stupid, right, it's not my fault that I'm gay and I'm not gay to disappoint anyone, but you know, it isn't easy to come out and say because you don't know how things are going to change. I just decided to tell them one day. I just said it to them when I was visiting home a little while after I moved out. Yeah it was awkward but I felt better right away like a huge weight was lifted. They didn't know how to react, they just kind of looked at each other and me. Yeah it was pretty uncomfortable and I'm not sure they even accept it, but they haven't made me feel bad about myself or anything. (Carl, 21)	Coming out to my family was a huge deal, yeah. I hid my sexuality from my parents until I was 19, because that's when I moved out. I was starting university so I thought I needed to be true to myself and them. All my friends knew I was gay and I'd had a few boyfriends and I guess I just kind of hoped they'd figure it out and I wouldn't have to say anything. I was scared and nervous to actually say it out loud to them. I knew they wouldn't stop loving me or anything. I'd always had a good relationship with them both. I just didn't want to disappoint them. I mean it's stupid, right, it's not my fault that I'm gay and I'm not gay to disappoint anyone, but you know, it isn't easy to come out and say because you don't know how things are going to change. I just decided to tell them one day. I just said it to them when I was visiting home a little while after I moved out. Yeah it was awkward but I felt better right away like a huge weight was lifted. They didn't know how to react, they just kind of looked at each other and me. Yeah it was pretty uncomfortable and I'm not sure they even accept it, but they haven't made me feel bad about myself or anything. (Carl, 21)
Well my mom is super-religious so I knew it wasn't going to go down well, telling her I am a lesbian. Then one day she actually saw me once with my girlfriend – we were holding hands downtown and my mom she saw us. I was like 19 or something I think. She asked me about it when I got home. I didn't know she saw me and when she brought it up I felt sick and panicked. Like she caught me. I just started crying. It was so weird, she was silent, I was crying and I just said something like 'I'm sorry I'm a lesbian' and she said nothing. It was awkward for a few days and we basically avoided each other and then she just said a few days later to me that she didn't understand but that I'm her daughter and she'd always love me. She doesn't accept it and I guess I don't 'flaunt' it or whatever. I've never introduced her to any of my girlfriends. Maybe that will change one day, I don't know. (Shana, 22)	Well my mom is super-religious so I knew it wasn't going to go down well, telling her I am a lesbian. Then one day she actually saw me once with my girlfriend – we were holding hands downtown and my mom she saw us. I was like 19 or something I think. She asked me about it when I got home. I didn't know she saw me and when she brought it up I felt sick and panicked. Like she caught me. I just started crying. It was so weird, she was silent, I was crying and I just said something like 'I'm sorry I'm a lesbian' and she said nothing. It was awkward for a few days and we basically avoided each other and then she just said a few days later to me that she didn't understand but that I'm her daughter and she'd always love me. She doesn't accept it and I guess I don't 'flaunt' it or whatever. I've never introduced her to any of my girlfriends. Maybe that will change one day, I don't know. (Shana, 22)

Researcher 1 codes (left margin): avoidance; true to self and to others; avoidance; 'double life'; scared to disappoint; fear of change; awkward; relief; doesn't feel bad about self; not sure of acceptance; fear; found out; was asked about it; sick/panicked; awkward; love unconditionally; doesn't accept; avoidance of introducing girlfriends

Researcher 2 codes (right margin): major event; hiding; true to self; hoping they'd know; wouldn't stop loving; good relationship; disappoint; not easy; when decided; relief; uncomfortable; not sure they accept; not feeling bad about self; religious; not going to go well; found out; confrontation; stress; weird; awkward; avoided; didn't understand; always love her; avoidance; hope will change

this pass, and the researcher notes them, but his or her primary task is to review and examine initial codes and create linkages between them. The researcher looks at relationships between open codes to see how they may cluster together into larger theses or categories.

During axial coding, a researcher asks about causes and consequences, conditions and interactions, and strategies and processes and looks for categories or concepts that cluster together. He or she asks questions such as, "Can I divide existing concepts into subdimensions or subcategories?" "Can I combine several closely related concepts into one more general one?" "Can I organize categories into a causal sequence (i.e., A, then B, then C), or by their physical location (i.e., where they occur) or their relationship to a major topic of interest?"

For example, a researcher compiled field notes from a field study on a marijuana legalization group in Western Canada. Three of the themes that emerged were *distrust*, *partying*, and *marginalized people*. *Distrust* reflected the attitude of the group members that institutions and many aspects of mainstream culture were corrupt and could not be trusted. The theme of *partying* referred to the tendency of the group members to want to smoke marijuana and focus on recreational activities rather than plan and carry out acts of protest. The theme of *marginalized people* reflected the alternative lifestyle of most group members. During axial coding, the researcher tried to develop linkages between these three major themes. She thought about what these themes had in common and then grouped these three themes into the larger theme of *avoidance*, which she thought explained the number of different ways that the open codes reflected the group members' ways of hiding or avoiding normative contact with the larger society.

Axial coding not only stimulates thinking about linkages between concepts or themes, it also raises new questions. It can suggest dropping some themes or examining others in more depth. In addition, it reinforces the connections between evidence and

Box 15.2 Making It Practical

Tips for Axial Coding

Let's revisit Researcher 1 and Researcher 2, discussed in Box 15.1. Both researchers open coded two transcript excerpts on "coming out" stories. If we make lists of both researchers' open codes, they are as follows:

Researcher 1:

Avoidance
True to self and to others
"Double life"
Scared to disappoint
Fear of change
Awkward
Relief
Doesn't feel bad about self
Not sure of acceptance
Fear
Found out
Was asked about
Sick/panicked
Love unconditionally
Doesn't accept
Avoiding of introducing girlfriends

Researcher 2:

Major event
Hiding
True to self
Hoping they'd know
Wouldn't stop loving
Good relationship
Disappoint
Not easy
When decided
Relief
Uncomfortable
Not sure they accept
Not feeling bad about self
Religious
Not going to go well
Found out
Confrontation
Stress
Weird
Awkward
Avoided
Didn't understand
Always love her
Avoidance
Hope will change

(continued)

Box 15.2 (*continued*)

You can see that both researchers' codes are similar, but not exactly the same, and that is to be expected.

An important part of axial coding is reorganizing codes to see if any of them fit together. Again, there is not any one "right" way to do this. Axial coding helps to manage the enormous amounts of codes you will have achieved in open coding.

If we look at Researcher 1's codes, we might regroup them like this into four major themes around *deception*, *fears*, *motivation*, and *outcomes* (with subgroups for positive and negative):

Deception
- Avoidance
- "Double life"

Fears
- Fear of change
- Scared to disappoint
- Asked about

Motivation
- True to self and to others
- Outcomes
- *Positive:*
- Doesn't feel bad about self
- Love unconditionally
- Relief
- *Negative:*
- Awkward
- Avoiding of introducing girlfriends
- Not sure of acceptance
- Sick/panicked
- Doesn't accept

If we look at Researcher 2's codes, we could also regroup them into the themes of *anxieties, avoidance, family characteristics, good outcomes, negative outcomes, true to self*, and *when decided*. You can also see that the theme *anxieties* has several subcategories while *true to self* and *when decided* are stand-alone categories.

Anxieties
- Disappoint
- Not easy
- Not going to go well
- Stress
- Weird
- Awkward
- Major event

Avoidance
- Not sure they accept
- Hiding
- Hoping they'd know

Family characteristics
- Good relationship
  - Wouldn't stop loving
- Religious

Good outcomes
- Relief
- Not feeling bad about self
- Always love her

Negative outcomes
- Found out
- Confrontation
- Didn't understand
- Uncomfortable
- Hope will change

True to self

When decided

Researcher 1 and Researcher 2 have different codes and have arrived at somewhat different axial codes as well, but they are not tremendously different in substantive terms. It is in the third and final step of coding—where you build relationships between your codes and engage in theory construction—that your skills as a qualitative researcher are put to the task.

concepts. As a researcher consolidates codes and locates evidence, he or she finds evidence in many places for core themes and builds a dense web of support for them in the qualitative data. This is analogous to the idea of multiple indicators described with regard to reliability and measuring variables. The connection between a theme and data is strengthened by multiple instances of empirical evidence.

See Box 15.2 for some practical tips on axial coding.

Selective Coding By the time a researcher is ready for this last pass through the data, he or she has identified the major themes of the research project. **Selective coding** involves scanning data and previous codes and determining a core category around which the remaining categories all "fit." This can be easier in some cases than in others. For example, in the example of the research on the marijuana legalization group, the researcher decided to make *marginalized people* a major theme. After axial coding, she noticed that the themes of *distrust* and *partying* and *marginalized people* could be grouped

selective coding: A last pass at *coding qualitative data* in which a researcher examines previous codes to identify a core theme around which the remaining codes will fit.

into a larger code she called *avoidance*. It therefore appeared that *avoidance* was the major, core theme of the research, around which the other codes could arranged. In selective coding, the researcher went through her field notes, looking for how the other themes she identified fit into the major theme of *avoidance*. She noted that in her code of *distrust*, group members talked about their encounters with police, their views on conspiracy theories, clashes with family members over their beliefs, and their experiences being harassed by members of the public. She found that the marginalization was both an outcome of the distrust and reason for the distrust, while the linkage between *partying* and *marginalized people* had a similar relationship. It was an outcome of their marginalization, but also served to keep them marginalized.

concept map: A visual illustration of the relationship among themes that emerge from *qualitative data*.

See Box 15.3 for some practical tips on selective coding.

Box 15.3 Making It Practical

Tips for Selective Coding

In Boxes 15.1 and 15.2, we worked through open and axial coding done by two researchers. The final step is selective coding. You typically would not begin selective coding with only two interview excerpts, so to make this worked example more typical of the path that real-world research would take, it is necessary to suppose that our researchers have done several more interviews and further refined their codes based on evidence from their additional data. We will focus on only one of the researchers in this final step.

After doing several more interviews with young adults who have "come out," Researcher 2 further refined her codes to these (which added additional subcategories and deleted weaker, lesser substantiated codes):

Fears
- Fear of disappointment
- Fear of being caught
- Stress
- Fear of outcome
- Guilt

Identity
- True to self
- Tired of lying
- Nothing to be ashamed about

Avoidance
- Not sure they accept
- Hoping they'd figure it out

Family characteristics
- Good relationship
- Wouldn't stop loving
- Religious

Positive outcomes
- Relief
- Not feeling bad about self
- Unconditional love
- Better relationship with parents

Negative outcomes
- Found out
- Confrontation
- Didn't understand
- Uncomfortable
- Alienated from parents

In order to make sense of the relationship among the codes, Researcher 1 made a **concept map** of them (shown below), visually illustrating the themes' relationships with each other. At the centre of the concept map was the theme *identity*, which seemed to feed into all the other themes. Family characteristics led to fear of coming out, while fear led to avoidance. Researcher 1 also found that avoidance made those who resisted coming out question their identity. Depending on the nature of the family, the outcomes could be either positive or negative. The nature of the outcome (whether positive or negative) also feeds back into the identity of the interviewee. These are the first steps that the researcher would take to explain the theory emerging from his or her data and create statements (or propositions) on how the concepts work together.

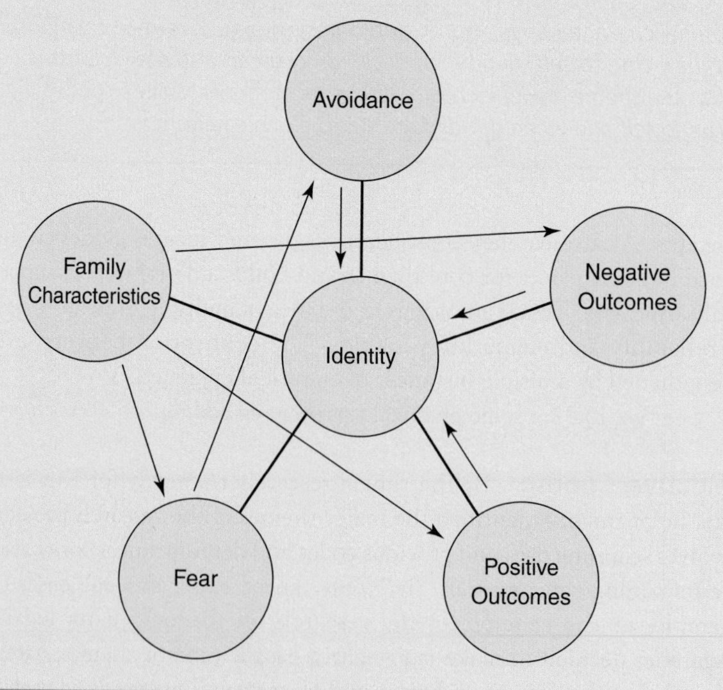

Step 1: Open Coding

Carefully read and review all data notes, then create a code that captures the idea, process, or theme in the data.

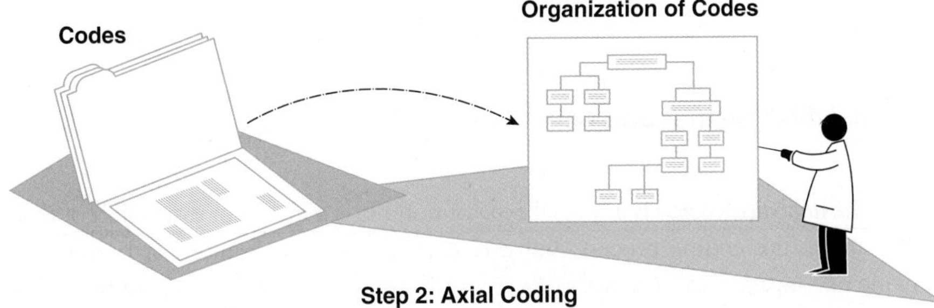

Step 2: Axial Coding

Organize all the codes created during open coding into a structure by separating them into major or minor levels and showing relations among the codes.

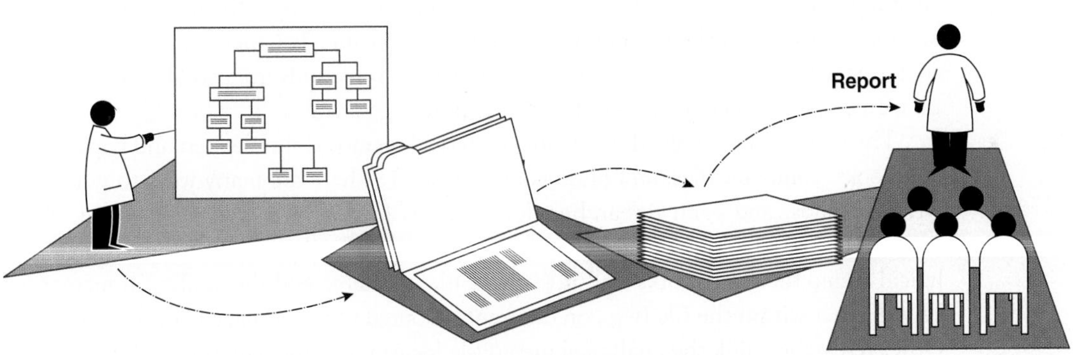

Step 3: Selective Coding

Take the organized codes from the axial coding process and review the codes in the original data notes to select the best illustrations for entering them into a final report.

Figure 15.1 The Coding Process for Qualitative Data Analysis

Figure 15.1 provides a visual summary of what we've discussed about the coding process with qualitative data.

Analytical Memo Writing

LO 3 Identify the different types of files generated in qualitative data analysis.

Qualitative researchers are compulsive note takers. Their data are recorded in notes, they write comments on their research strategy in notes, and so on. They keep their notes organized in files and often have many files with different kinds of notes: a file on methodological issues (e.g., locations of sources or ethical issues), a file of maps or diagrams, a file on possible overall outlines of a final report or chapter, a file on specific people or events, and so on.

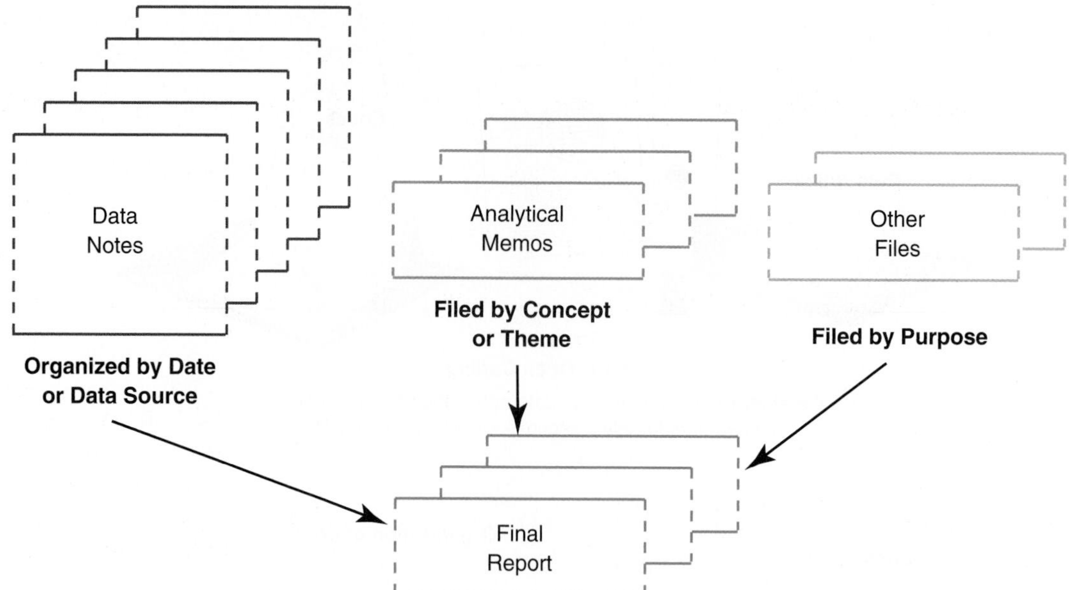

Figure 15.2 Analytical Memos and Other Files

Field Research

The *analytical memo* is a special type of note. It is a memo or discussion of thoughts and ideas about the coding process that a researcher writes to himself or herself. Each coded theme or concept forms the basis of a separate memo, and the memo contains a discussion of the concept or theme. The rough theoretical notes form the beginning of analytical memos.

The analytical memo forges a link between the concrete data or raw evidence and more abstract, theoretical thinking (see Figure 15.2). It contains a researcher's reflections on and thinking about the data and coding. The researcher adds to the memo and uses it as he or she passes through the data with each type of coding. The memos form the basis for analyzing data in the research report. In fact, rewritten sections from good-quality analytical memos can become sections of the final report.

The technology involved in writing analytical memos is simple: pen and paper, a few notebooks, computer files, and photocopies of notes. There are many ways to write analytical memos, and each researcher develops his or her own style or method. Some researchers make multiple copies of notes, then cut them and place selections into an analytical memo file. This works well if the data files are large and the analytical memos are kept distinct within the file (e.g., on different-coloured paper or placed at the beginning). Other researchers link the analytical memo file locations to the data notes where a theme appears. Then it is easy to move between the analytical memo and the data. Because data notes contain links or marked themes, it is easy to locate specific sections in the data. An intermediate strategy is to keep a running list of locations where a major theme appears in the raw data.

As a researcher reviews and modifies analytical memos, he or she discusses ideas with colleagues and returns to the literature with a focus on new issues. Analytical memos may help to generate potential hypotheses, which can be added and dropped as needed, and to develop new themes or coding systems.

LO 4 Describe the four different strategies of qualitative data analysis.

ANALYTICAL STRATEGIES FOR QUALITATIVE DATA

Techniques of coding and memo writing are approaches to the analysis of qualitative data. Most qualitative researchers use these techniques to some degree, often combined with a more specific strategy for the analysis of qualitative data. In this section you will learn about

Box 15.4 Social Research and the Internet

Computer-Assisted Qualitative Data Analysis

Increasingly, researchers analyzing qualitative data are using software programs to assist them in the process. Some qualitative data analysis software programs perform searches of text documents. What they do is similar to the searching function available in most word processing software. The specialized text retrieval programs are faster and have the capability of finding close matches, slight misspellings, similar-sounding words, and synonyms.

Most programs show the keyword or phrase and the surrounding text—this is where the researcher can then place his or her codes. The programs may also permit a researcher to write separate memos or add short notes to the text. Some programs count the keywords found and give their location. Most programs create a specific index for the text, based only on the terms of interest to the researcher.

There are a couple of popular software packages that qualitative researchers tend to use, particularly NVivo and ATLAS. There are, however, a number of open-access software packages that also handle qualitative data analysis and are free to download. For instance, the University Center for Social and Urban Research at the University of Pittsburgh and QDAP-UMass in the College of Social and Behavioral Sciences at the University of Massachusetts Amherst host a Coding Analysis Toolkit website, http://cat.ucsur.pitt.edu, which is a freely downloadable program. Other freeware includes QDA Miner Lite and Weft QDA. Before committing to any freeware, however, you should research the pros and cons of these programs and investigate what kind of user support is available.

four strategies researchers use to analyze qualitative data: the narrative, ideal types, successive approximation, and the illustrative method.

Qualitative versus Quantitative Research

Compared to the analysis of quantitative data, strategies for qualitative data are more diverse, less standardized, and less explicitly outlined by researchers. Only in the past decade have researchers started to explain and outline exactly how they analyze qualitative data.

In general, *data analysis* means a search for patterns in data—recurrent behaviours, objects, or a body of knowledge. Once a pattern is identified, it is interpreted in terms of a social theory or the setting in which it occurred. The qualitative researcher moves from the description of a historical event or social setting to a more general interpretation of its meaning. Some researchers employ the assistance of software in analyzing their qualitative data (Box 15.4).

Political Knowledge

The Narrative

Injury, Gender, and Trouble

You encountered the narrative in the last chapter on historical research. In field research, it is also called a *natural history* or *realist tale approach*. The narrative is largely a theoretical description. The researcher–author "disappears" from the analysis and presents the concrete details in chronological order as if they were the product of a unique and naturally unfolding sequence of events. He or she simply tells a story of what occurred.

Some argue that the narrative approach is a presentation of data without analysis. There can be analysis in a narrative, but it is "light" and subtle. In the narrative method, a researcher assembles the data into a descriptive picture or account of what occurred, but he or she largely leaves the data to speak for themselves. He or she interjects little in the form of new systematic concepts, external theories, or abstract models. The explanation resides not in abstract concepts and theories, but in a combination of specific, concrete details. The researcher presents or reveals the social reality as members in a field setting experience it, or as the worldview of specific historical actors at a particular point in time. By using little commentary, a researcher tries to convey an authentic feel for life's complexity as experienced by particular people in specific circumstances and does not derive abstract principles or identify generalizable analytical patterns.

In the narrative, data are analyzed or "explained" in the terminology and concepts of the people being studied. The analysis appears in how a researcher organizes the data for

Box 15.5 Focus

The Narrative

Many qualitative researchers, especially feminist researchers, use the narrative because they believe it best enables them to retain a richness and authenticity from their original data sources (i.e., individual personal stories or events in ethnographies, or specific historical events). In simple terms, the narrative is storytelling. In it, an author presents two or more events in temporal and causal sequences. Some narratives are complex, with elements such as (1) a summary statement of the entire story; (2) an orientation that identifies specific times, places, persons, and situations; (3) complicating actions or twists in the plot of "what happened"; (4) an evaluation or emotional assessment of the narrative's meaning or significance; (5) a resolution or what occurred after a dramatic high point that resolves a suspenseful climactic event; and (6) a coda or signal that the narrative is ending.

People frequently tell one another stories in daily life. They usually structure or organize their narratives into one of several recognized patterns, often recounting them with visual clues, gestures, or voice intonations for dramatic emphasis. The structure may include plot lines, core metaphors, and rhetorical devices that draw on familiar cultural and personal models to effectively communicate meaning to others. The narrative is found in literature, artistic expressions, types of therapy, judicial inquiries, social or political histories, biography and autobiography, medical case histories, and journalistic accounts.

As a way to organize, analyze, and present qualitative social science data, the narrative shares many features with other academic and cultural communication forms, but it differs from the positivist model for organizing and reporting on data. The positivist model emphasizes using impersonal, abstract, "neutral" language and a standardized analytical approach. Many qualitative researchers argue that researchers who adopt the positivist model are simply using an alternative form of narrative, one with specialized conventions. These conventions encourage formal analytical models and abstract theories, but such models or theories are not necessarily superior to a storytelling narrative. Positivist data analysis and reporting conventions have two negative effects. First, they make it easier for researchers to lose sight of the concrete actual events and personal experiences that compose social science data. Second, they make it more difficult for researchers to express ideas and build social theories in a format that most people are familiar and comfortable with.

presentation and tells the story. It appears in a greater attention to particular people, events, or facts, and it relies on literary devices—the creative selection of particular words to tell a story, describe a setting, show character development, and present dramatic emphasis, intrigue, or suspense.

Researchers debate the usefulness of the narrative strategy. On the one hand, it provides rich concrete detail and clearly demonstrates the temporal ordering of processes or specific events. It captures a high degree of complexity and conveys a nuanced understanding of how particular events or factors mutually affect each other. The narrative allows the researcher to assemble very specific concrete details (i.e., the names, actions, and words of specific people and the detailed descriptions of particular events at specific times) that may be idiosyncratic but that contribute to a complete explanation. On the other hand, many researchers criticize the narrative approach for being too complex, particular, and idiosyncratic. It does not provide generalizations. The narrative may present an overwhelming array of particular details but not provide a general explanation that researchers can apply to other people, situations, or time periods (see Box 15.5).

Ideal Types

ideal type: A pure model about an idea, process, or event. One develops it to think about it more clearly and systematically. It is used both as a method of *qualitative data* analysis and in *social theory* building.

Max Weber's ideal type[1] is used by many qualitative researchers. **Ideal types** are models or mental abstractions of social relations or processes. They are pure standards against which the data or "reality" can be compared. An ideal type is a device used for comparison because no reality ever fits an ideal type. For example, a researcher develops a mental model of the ideal democracy or an ideal university beer party. These abstractions, with lists of characteristics, do not describe any specific democracy or beer party; nevertheless, they are useful when applied to many specific cases to see how well each case measures up to the ideal. This stage can be used with the illustrative method, which will be described shortly.

Weber's method of ideal types also complements John Stuart Mill's method of agreement. With the method of agreement, a researcher's attention is focused on what is common across cases, and he or she looks for common causes in cases with a common outcome. By itself, the method of agreement implies a comparison against actual cases. This comparison of cases could also be made against an idealized model. A researcher could develop an ideal type of a social process or relationship and then compare specific cases to it.

Qualitative researchers have used ideal types in two ways: to contrast the impact of contexts and as analogy.

Contrast Contexts Researchers who adopt a strongly interpretive approach may use ideal types to interpret data in a way that is sensitive to the context and cultural meanings of members. They do not test hypotheses or create a generalizable theory but use the ideal type to bring out the specifics of each case and to emphasize the impact of the unique context.

Researchers making contrasts between contexts often choose cases with dramatic contrasts or distinctive features.

When comparing contexts, researchers do not use the ideal type to illustrate a theory in different cases or to discover regularities. Instead, they accentuate the specific and the unique. Other methods of analysis focus on the general and ignore peculiarities. By contrast, a researcher who uses ideal types can show how unique features shape the operation of general processes.

Analogies Ideal types are used as analogies to organize qualitative data. An **analogy** is a statement that two objects, processes, or events are similar to each other. Researchers use analogies to communicate ideas and to facilitate logical comparisons. Analogies transmit information about patterns in data by referring to something that is already known or an experience familiar to the reader. They can describe relationships buried deep within many details and are a shorthand method for seeing patterns in a maze of specific events. They also make it easier to compare social processes across different cases or settings. For example, a researcher says that a room went silent after person X spoke: "A chill like a cold gust of air" spread through the room. This does not mean that the room temperature dropped or that a breeze was felt, but it succinctly expresses a rapid change in emotional tone. Likewise, a researcher reports that gender relations in society Y were such that women were "viewed like property and treated like slaves." This does not mean that the legal and social relations between genders were identical to those of slave owner and slave. It implies that an ideal type of a slave-and-master relationship would show major similarities to the evidence on relations between men and women if applied to society Y.

analogy: A statement that two objects, processes, or events are similar to each other.

The use of analogies to analyze qualitative data serves as a heuristic device (i.e., a device that helps one learn or see). It can represent something that is unknown and is especially valuable when researchers attempt to make sense of or explain data by referring to a deep structure or an underlying mechanism. Ideal types do not provide a definitive test of an explanation. Rather, they guide the conceptual reconstruction of the mass of details into a systematic format.

Successive Approximation

Successive approximation involves repeated iterations or cycling through steps, moving toward a final analysis. Over time, or after several iterations, a researcher moves from vague ideas and concrete details in the data toward a comprehensive analysis with generalizations. This is similar to the three kinds of coding discussed earlier.

successive approximation: A method of *qualitative data* analysis in which the researcher repeatedly moves back and forth between the empirical data and the abstract concepts, theories, or models.

A researcher begins with research questions and a framework of assumptions and concepts. He or she then probes into the data, asking questions of the evidence to see how well the concepts fit the evidence and reveal features of the data. He or she also creates new concepts by abstracting from the evidence, and adjusts concepts to fit the evidence better. The researcher then collects additional evidence to address unresolved issues that appeared in the first stage, and repeats the process. At each stage, the evidence and the theory shape each other. This is called *successive approximation* because the modified concepts and the model approximate the full evidence and are modified over and over to become successively more accurate.

Each pass through the evidence is provisional or incomplete. The concepts are abstract, but they are rooted in the concrete evidence and reflect the context. As the analysis moves toward generalizations that are subject to conditions and contingencies, the researcher refines generalizations and linkages to reflect the evidence better. For example, a historical researcher believes that historical reality is not even or linear; rather, it has discontinuous stages or steps. He or she may divide 100 years of history into periods by breaking continuous time into discrete units or periods and define the periods theoretically. Theory helps the researcher identify what is significant and what is common within periods or between different periods.

The researcher cannot determine the number and size of periods and the breaks between them until after the evidence has been examined. He or she may begin with a general idea of how many periods to create and what distinguishes them but will adjust the number and size of the periods and the location of the breaks after reviewing the evidence. The researcher then reexamines the evidence with added data, readjusts the periodization, and so forth. After several cycles, he or she approximates a set of periods in 100 years on the basis of successively theorizing and looking at evidence.

The Illustrative Method

illustrative method: A method of *qualitative data* analysis in which a researcher takes the concepts of a *social theory* or explanation and treats them as *empty boxes* to be filled with empirical examples and descriptions.

empty boxes: A name for conceptual categories in an explanation that a researcher uses as part of the *illustrative method* of *qualitative data* analysis.

Another method of analysis uses empirical evidence to illustrate or anchor a theory. With the **illustrative method**, a researcher applies theory to a concrete historical situation or social setting, or organizes data on the basis of prior theory. Pre-existing theory provides the **empty boxes**; the researcher sees whether evidence can be gathered to fill them. The evidence in the boxes confirms or rejects the theory, which he or she treats as a useful device for interpreting the social world. The theory can be in the form of a general model, an analogy, or a sequence of steps.

There are two variations of the illustrative method. One is to show that the theoretical model illuminates or clarifies a specific case or single situation. A second is the parallel demonstration of a model in which a researcher juxtaposes multiple cases (i.e., units or time periods) to show that the theory can be applied in multiple cases. In other cases, the researcher illustrates theory with specific material from multiple cases. An example of parallel demonstration is found in Paige's (1975) study of rural class conflict. Paige first developed an elaborate model of conditions that cause class conflict and then provided evidence to illustrate it from Peru, Angola, and Vietnam. This demonstrated the applicability of the model in several cases.

See Box 15.6 for a summary of types of qualitative data analysis.

Box 15.6 **Focus**

A Summary of Four Strategies for Qualitative Data Analysis

1. *The narrative.* Tell a detailed story about a particular slice of social life.
2. *Ideal types.* Compare qualitative data with a pure model of social life.
3. *Successive approximation.* Repeatedly move back and forth between data and theory until the gap between them shrinks or disappears.
4. *The illustrative method.* Fill the "empty boxes" of theory with qualitative data.

OTHER TECHNIQUES

LO 5 Describe other techniques researchers can use for qualitative data analysis.

Qualitative researchers use many analysis techniques. Here is a brief look at other techniques to illustrate the variety.

Flowchart and Time Sequence

In addition to the amount of time devoted to various activities, researchers analyze the order of events or decisions. Historical researchers have traditionally focused on documenting the sequence of events, but comparative and field researchers also look at flow or sequence. In addition to when events occur, researchers use the idea of a decision tree or flowchart to outline the order of decisions and to understand how one event or decision is related to others. For example, an activity as simple as making a cake can be outlined (see Figure 15.3). The idea of mapping out steps, decisions, or events and looking at their interrelationship has been applied to many settings.

Multiple Sorting Procedure

Multiple sorting is a technique similar to domain analysis that a researcher can use in field research or oral history. Its purpose is to discover how people categorize their experiences or classify items into systems of "similar" and "different." The multiple sorting procedure has been adopted by cognitive anthropologists and psychologists. It can be used to collect, verify, or analyze data. The researcher gives those being studied a list of terms, photos, places, names of people, and so on and asks them to organize the lists into categories or piles. The subjects or members use categories of their own devising. Once sorted, the researcher asks about the criteria used. The subjects are then given the items again and asked to sort them in other ways. For example (Canter, Brown, & Goat, 1985, p. 90), a gambler sorts a list of eight gambling establishments five times. Each sort has three to four categories. One of the sorts organized them based on "class of casino" (high to low). Other sorts were based on "frills," "size of stake," "make me money," and "personal preference." By examining the sorts, the researcher sees how others organize their worlds.

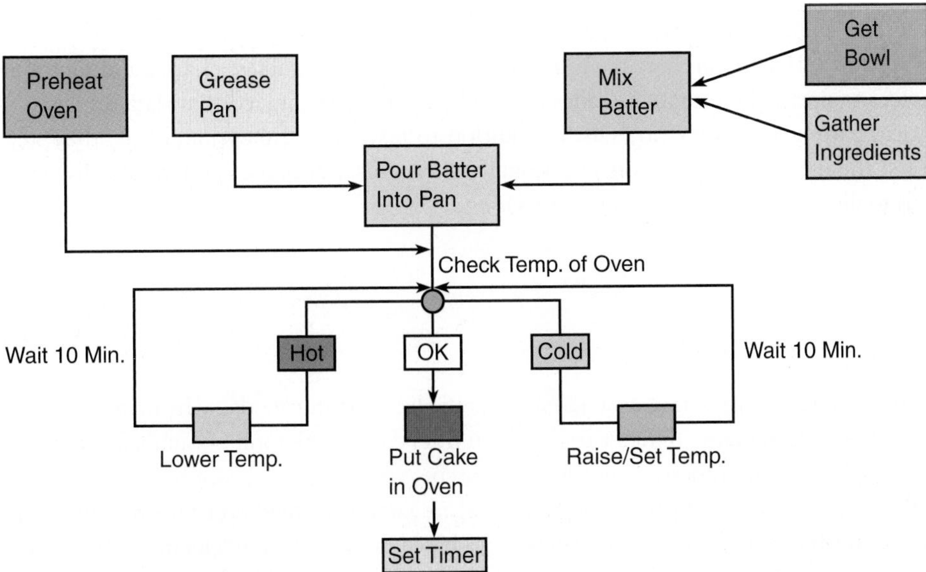

Figure 15.3 Partial Flowchart of Cake Making

		Example 1		
Person	Worked Before University	Part-Time Job in University	Pregnant Now	Had Own Car
John	Yes	Yes	N/A	No
Mary	Yes	DK	No	Yes
Martin	No	Yes	N/A	Yes
Yoshi	Yes	No	Yes	Yes

DK = don't know, N/A = not applicables

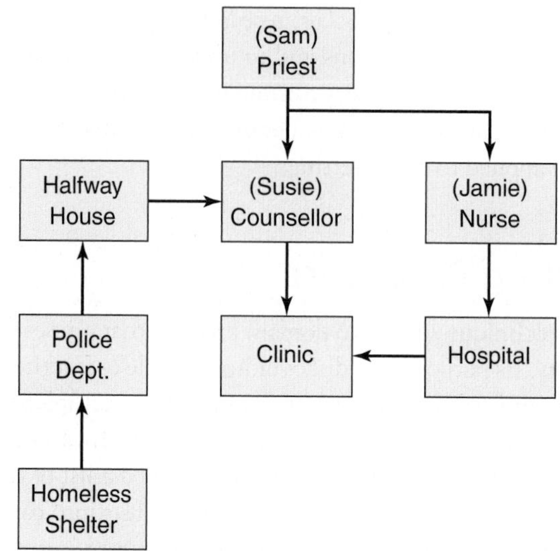

Figure 15.4 Examples of the Use of Diagrams in Qualitative Analysis

Diagrams

Qualitative researchers have moved toward presenting their data analysis in the form of diagrams and charts. Diagrams and charts help them organize ideas and systematically investigate relations in the data as well as communicate results to readers. Researchers use spatial or temporal maps, typologies, or sociograms.

Quantitative researchers have developed many graphs, tables, charts, and pictorial devices to present information. Miles and Huberman (1994) argued that data display is a critical part of qualitative analysis. In addition to taxonomies, maps, and lists, they suggested the use of flowcharts, organizational charts, causal diagrams, and various lists and grids to illustrate analysis (see Figure 15.4).

CHAPTER SUMMARY

In this chapter, you learned how researchers analyze qualitative data. In many respects, qualitative data are more difficult to deal with than data in the form of numbers. Numbers have mathematical properties that let a researcher use statistical procedures. Qualitative analysis requires more effort by an individual researcher to read and reread data notes, reflect on what is read, and make comparisons based on logic and judgment. In the beginning of the chapter, we detailed the major differences and similarities between quantitative and qualitative data analysis

Most forms of qualitative data analysis involve coding and writing analytical memos. The different stages of moving from conceptualization to the three stages of coding—open, axial, and selective—were explained, using a worked example. You learned that the stages of coding data help reduce the masses of data collected in qualitative research into more manageable and organized evidence that can be used to describe social processes. You also learned that there is no "objectively correct" way of coding—your codes will not be identical to another researcher coding the same material. How you build the analysis and the logic you demonstrate and employ in the process as well as the various aspects of "trustworthiness" of your data will be the criteria upon which your analyses will be judged. Four different analytic strategies were also considered—the narrative, ideal types, successive approximation, and the illustrative methods. All of these require searching for patterns in the data, although the specific techniques of each approach do vary.

Review Questions

Chapter Quiz

1. Explain the four differences between qualitative and quantitative data analysis.
2. Describe the three stages of coding qualitative data.
3. Identify the different types of files generated in qualitative data analysis.
4. Describe and differentiate between the four different strategies of qualitative data analysis.

Exercises

Research Activities

1. Using one of the online sources for qualitative interview transcripts in Chapter 12, select a qualitative interview transcript of interest to you and print it out. Think of a research question that is relevant to the topic being addressed in the interview. Practise open, axial, and selective coding on this transcript.
2. Using EBSCO's ContentSelect, identify a research article that obtained data using qualitative interviewing. How do the researchers describe how they analyzed their data? What steps did they undertake and how did they code their transcripts?
3. The coding of qualitative data extends beyond only qualitative interview transcripts to various forms of text. Go to EBSCO's ContentSelect and type in "open coding" and "axial coding" as search terms. Pick three articles that come up in your search. What methods did the researchers use in data collection? What kind of data did the researchers analyze?
4. Discuss how the coding techniques addressed in this chapter apply to qualitative content analysis (Chapter 14). What type of qualitative content analysis are they most relevant to?

Chapter 16

Combining Methods in Social Science Research

Photo Credit: mariocigic/Fotolia

LEARNING OBJECTIVES

After reading this chapter, you will be able to

LO 1 Explain the overall advantages and disadvantages of the quantitative approaches.

LO 2 Describe the advantages and disadvantages of specific quantitative approaches.

LO 3 Explain the overall advantages and disadvantages of the qualitative approaches.

LO 4 Describe the advantages and disadvantages of specific qualitative approaches.

LO 5 Identify the stages of mixed methods research.

LO 6 List the strengths and weaknesses of mixed methods research.

INTRODUCTION

In the last several chapters, we talked about the various forms of data collection methods and techniques associated with social research. You may have gotten the impression that a researcher picks a single method to carry out his or her research. While this is true in the vast majority of cases, social science researchers are combining methods in an increasing number of cases; that is, they are picking two or more methods to better carry out their data collection and analysis. The term **triangulation** refers to the use of more than one

triangulation: A general term that refers to *mixed methods* research.

method to answer a research question and is synonymous with the **mixed methods** approach. For example, a researcher may choose to do a survey as well as carry out qualitative interviews, thereby combining a quantitative and a qualitative approach. Or a researcher may decide to use more than one qualitative or quantitative technique. For example, he or she may decide to do focus groups while doing field research. Or, in addition to carrying out an analysis of secondary data, a researcher may decide to do a quantitative content analysis of relevant documents. A major motivation behind using multiple methods is to allow the researcher to compensate for the weaknesses of any one individual method by combining them with the strengths of others.

mixed methods: In general, when more than one research method is used to address a research question. Also often refers specifically to when qualitative and quantitative methods are used together in a single project.

In this chapter, we begin by discussing the strengths and weaknesses of the various methodological approaches that we have discussed in this textbook. We argue that the weaknesses of some methodological approaches can be enhanced by the strengths of other approaches. While quantitative and qualitative research may seem to be almost opposite in their natures and philosophical underpinnings, in actual practice these two general approaches to research can be very *complementary* to one another. The focus of this chapter is to highlight the possible ways in which methods can be combined to answer research questions, and to illustrate the benefits of using such techniques.

Overall Advantages and Disadvantages of the Quantitative Approaches

LO 1 Explain the overall advantages and disadvantages of the quantitative approaches.

In Chapter 2, we made the distinction between *positivist* and *interpretive* approaches to social science research. If you recall, positivism is rooted in the belief that the study of social science should follow the same principles as that of the natural sciences: There are objective facts to be collected by value-free researchers, and the pursuit of truth is achieved through the testing of causal hypotheses. Positivism is most closely linked to quantitative methods of inquiry, such as survey research, experimental design, the analysis of existing statistics or secondary data sources, and quantitative approaches to content analysis.

One perceived shortcoming of all the general approaches linked to positivism is the belief that the topics of social science are not appropriate for purely "scientific" inquiry. Human beings do not behave the same way as atoms, and although we have biological properties, social interactions are far more complex. In particular, critics of positivism argue that understanding the social world requires an in-depth understanding of the meaning that individuals attribute to their interactions and their surroundings—something that cannot be achieved by effectively reducing human behaviour to a series of "laws" and properties to be unearthed.

Qualitative versus Quantitative Research

As suggested above, one of the major advantages of all the quantitative techniques is the possibility that they can be used while employing probability sampling. If you recall from Chapter 7, the advantage of using probability sampling is that you can determine the exact probability of a unit (e.g., a person, a family, a newspaper article) being included in the sample. If done correctly, probability sampling allows you to have a representative snapshot of the population that you are trying to study. The nature of probability sampling also allows the researcher to confidently state that his or her findings are generalizable to the wider population. That is, the sample that the researcher reports on is actually representative of the general population from which this sample is drawn so the findings are representative of a population wider than just those who participated (or were included) in the study.

Another advantage of quantitative methods is that the researcher reduces the concepts he or she is trying to study to measurable and quantifiable items, thereby making them as "objective" as possible. Variables are created to measure concepts as uniformly across sample members as possible. The rationale behind this exercise in quantification is that researchers are then able to measure characteristics about their samples in a standardized manner. If a concept is measured in a precise way across all members of the sample, then the conclusions that the researcher makes about his or her data are more valid. For example, if we measured ethnicity by just asking respondents if they were "White" or "Other" in half our sample, and then in the other half of our sample we allowed sample members to describe their ethnicity in their own words, we would have a very difficult time comparing the results across both halves. In the first half we would have just two categories; in the second half, possibly hundreds! Thus, the standardization of concepts is at the heart of quantitative approaches.

A final overall advantage of quantitative approaches is that the results can often be replicated because the techniques lend themselves to checks of reliability and validity. Researchers can replicate experiments on different subjects to see if they get the same results as other researchers. Researchers can reanalyze secondary data sources to check the results obtained by their peers. Surveys can be administered to other samples if it is suspected that the results are unusual.

Sense and Nonsense About Surveys

Funnily enough, the major disadvantages of quantitative methods are closely related to their advantages. While probability sampling is often possible when undertaking quantitative research, one disadvantage of studying large, representative samples is that often only fairly superficial information can be obtained. The ways that data are collected, such as through surveys or experiments, often do not permit the researcher to be certain that the sample members understand the standardized questions in the way that was intended.

As well, the types of concepts that quantitative approaches tend to quantify often do not reveal much information about the deeper meanings that individuals may attribute to social life. For example, members of a sample or subjects in an experiment may be asked a series of questions about their feelings on a particular topic. But merely answering these standardized items does not ensure that we know other crucial pieces of information that would allow us, as researchers, to have a broader understanding of the social phenomena we are trying to study. Thus, a major criticism of quantitative approaches is that it can seem that people's opinions and beliefs are forced to fit into "tick boxes" when the reality of social life may be much more complicated than that!

LO 2 Describe the advantages and disadvantages of specific quantitative approaches.

Advantages and Disadvantages of Specific Quantitative Approaches

In the previous section, we considered the general advantages and disadvantages of quantitative approaches. Now, more attention is given to the strengths and weaknesses of specific methods that are generally considered to be quantitative in their orientation. Table 16.1 summarizes some of the main advantages and disadvantages associated with the methodological approaches that have been discussed in this book.

Examining the Historical Relationship of Native Americans and Child Welfare Agencies

Survey Research Survey research was covered in Chapter 8. One major advantage of survey research is that, unlike many other data collection techniques, the samples used in survey research tend to be quite large. Using structured interviewing, it is possible to administer the survey to a large number of people, particularly when the data are collected over the telephone. Survey research can also collect a large amount of information on individuals, and because questions are asked in the same way to each respondent, the results can be compared across respondents.

There are shortcomings associated with surveys, however. It is not possible to know, for example, if everyone who is asked a specific survey question understands it in the same way. Even if the question is asked to sample members in the same way, if it is not *understood* in the same way making comparisons across sample members is not meaningful. Survey research can also be impersonal. Long interviews done over the telephone can

Table 16.1 Advantages and Disadvantages of the Different Methodological Approaches

	Quantitative Approaches				Qualitative Approaches				
Technique	*Survey Research*	*Experimental Research*	*Quantitative Content Analysis*	*Existing Statistics/ Documents and Secondary Analysis*	*Qualitative Interviews*	*Focus Groups*	*Field Research*	*Historical Research*	*Qualitative Content Analysis*
Major Advantages	• possible to cover large populations • can cover a large range of topics • questions from respondent to respondent are comparable because they are asked in the same way and same order	• the only technique that allows causation to be demonstrated	• nonreactive • possible to use probability sampling techniques • data can be rechecked and reanalyzed to check for accuracy • often inexpensive	• data are often free and fairly easy to access • using existing sources frees up the immense amount of time that the data collection procedure can take • many better known, nationally represented data sets (i.e., NLSCY, GSS, Labour Force Survey) are highly reputable and are unlikely to have serious flaws	• allow participants to give accounts in their own words and allow for unexpected responses • possible to explore "meaning" of events, experiences, etc., in much detail	• people tend to feel empowered and opinions are expressed freely • participants can query one another and explain answers to one another	• collection of data in the field allows researcher to formulate a deep understanding of a group and its members • possibility of studying hidden or deviant groups about which there is little public knowledge	• nonreactive when using documents • possible to make comparisons across time/ cultures	• nonreactive • can use probability sampling techniques • inexpensive • can reveal implied meanings in texts

(continued)

Table 16.1 *(continued)*

	Quantitative Approaches				Qualitative Approaches				
Technique	*Survey Research*	*Experimental Research*	*Quantitative Content Analysis*	*Existing Statistics/ Documents and Secondary Analysis*	*Qualitative Interviews*	*Focus Groups*	*Field Research*	*Historical Research*	*Qualitative Content Analysis*
Major Disadvantages	• respondents may understand questions differently • not suitable for some topics (sensitive issues) • can be impersonal • interviewer effect (if in person or on the telephone) • social desirability	• many of the questions social scientists are interested in cannot be tested using experiments • experimental conditions are often rather artificial • sample is often limited to university undergraduates	• fairly limited range of research questions can be addressed with this technique • latent coding open to interpretation issues • if not clearly linked to theory, can be merely a word count	• researcher may use secondary data that is not appropriate for his or her research question • can take considerable time to get acquainted with data • data collected by someone else, so unlikely all the concepts the researcher is interested in will be included, or they may be measured in a less than ideal manner • definitions of concepts (especially in official statistics) may change over time	• interviewer effect	• possibility of groupthink • a polarization effect exists • only a few topics can be addressed in a focus group session • moderator may affect outcome • produces fewer ideas than individual interviews	• group may change behaviour if members know they are being studied • accessing some groups may be difficult	• limited by the availability and quality of documents and data • sources may be biased • context of meanings within times in history must be taken into account	• fairly limited range of research questions can be addressed with this technique • qualitative coding technique subject to interpretations • coding procedures subject to interpretation

be unappealing to potential respondents, particularly if there is nothing in it for them. And survey research is not appropriate for all topics. Some sensitive topics, such as research on sexual abuse for example, would be difficult (and likely undesirable) to study using surveys, given the nature of the topic and the generally impersonal nature of structured interviewing. However, surveys *have* been used by previous researchers to collect data on sensitive issues. For example, spousal abuse has been studied by Statistics Canada's Violence Against Women Survey.[1]

While survey researchers strive to create the best measurements for their concepts, problems associated with administering surveys can affect these efforts. For example, characteristics of the interviewer (e.g., race or gender) may influence how a person responds to survey questions, which is known as the *interviewer effect*; thus, a person may respond differently to questions about attitudes toward immigrants if he or she detects an accent in the interviewer's voice. Respondents may also respond to questions in a way that they feel is socially desirable or expected of them, rather than in ways that honestly reflect their own opinions or beliefs. For example, a person might say he or she drinks less alcohol than he or she actually does because to answer truthfully might be embarrassing.

Experiments In Chapter 9, a major advantage of the experimental method was identified as its ability to demonstrate causality (i.e., that an independent variable caused a change in a dependent variable). Although the overall goal of most research questions asked in social science is to demonstrate some kind of association between concepts, it is only in experimental design that a condition is manipulated so that its impact on an outcome of interest can be observed. In a classic experimental design, a researcher collects information from two groups (an experimental group and a control group) at one period in time. The experimental group is then exposed to some kind of treatment (e.g., receiving training or being involved in some kind of activity). Data are then collected again from both the experimental group and the control group. If a change is observed in the experimental group and not the control group, then the change can be attributed to the treatment, and hence causality has been demonstrated.

From Summer Camps to Glass Ceilings: The Power of Experiments

While experiments are widely considered to be the best demonstration of causal relationships, a major disadvantage of this approach is that it is only useful for a limited range of research questions. Many of the topics that social scientists are interested in have to do with fixed characteristics and how these characteristics impact on individuals' experience of life. For example, many social scientists are interested in topics related to gender and ethnicity. Obviously, it is not possible to change conditions in an experiment to see how life would turn out for people if they were of the opposite gender or a different ethnicity.

Experimental Methods Explained

Related to this shortcoming is the criticism that experimental designs are often artificial and do not mimic social life closely enough for their results to be generalized to life in the real world. People may not behave naturally in these artificial settings, which may mean that research findings do not reflect what would happen in the natural social world.

Another potential criticism of experiments that has been identified (see, for example, Dobbins, Lane, & Steiner, 1988) is that a vast majority of knowledge that the social science community has gleaned from experiments is from studies on undergraduate students. For example, many universities offer courses where participation in experiments results in course credit. The potential problem with so many studies based on this population is the extent to which results from research on undergraduate students is generalizable to the wider population. Are undergraduate students—or more precisely, undergraduate students enrolled in psychology courses—representative of the large population? Or is there something about this group that makes them fundamentally different from the general population?

Nonreactive Methods The last two quantitative approaches that will be considered are content analysis and the analysis of existing statistics and secondary data, both of which were addressed in Chapter 10. Both quantitative content analysis and the analysis of existing statistics/secondary data share the advantage that they are nonreactive approaches. This means that the data are not altered because they are being studied. If you recall, the responses of people taking surveys or involved in experiments may be influenced by the fact that they are in these types of unnatural situations. Survey respondents may feel that they must answer in socially desirable ways, for example. Experimental subjects may be affected by the artificial nature of the experimental environment. The data used in content analysis and the analysis of existing statistics/secondary data are not affected by reactivity—the data (e.g., documents, spreadsheets of numbers, official crime rates) are fixed and will not change as a result of being analyzed. Both approaches also share the advantage that they are often relatively inexpensive to collect.

Another advantage of quantitative content analysis is that results can be checked and rechecked. It is always possible to go back to the documents being coded and reanalyze them if errors are suspected. In the analysis of secondary data and existing statistics, an additional advantage is that the researcher can save an immense amount of time and resources on data collection. Many sources of existing statistics and secondary data are government agencies or professional survey research organizations, whose data are well known and reputable. The data that these organizations collect are often from very large samples and cover a wide range of topics that would be very costly (and likely impossible) for an individual researcher to collect alone.

In terms of disadvantages, content analyses can be quite limited in the types of research questions that they can answer. They are best suited to questions that are interested in how often a sentiment is expressed in a text. Questions that ask "How many . . . ?" or "How often . . . ?" are the most suitable for quantitative content analysis. For example, "How often is racism discussed in major Canadian newspapers?" and "How many instances of gendered roles are observable in popular situation comedies?" Questions that ask "How . . . ?" are not suitable for content analyses because this technique simply is not designed to answer them. We cannot investigate questions like "How do recent immigrants experience racism?" or "How do official policies result in racial profiling?" because these questions cannot be answered by examining the types of data used in quantitative content analyses (e.g., most typically written texts and recorded media).

Because quantitative content analyses are most suited to answering questions that are associated with "How many . . . ?" or "How often . . . ?", there is the danger that such analyses can be reduced to simple word counts if the research question is not firmly rooted in the testing of theory. The importance of linking theory and social research was covered in Chapter 2.

A final disadvantage of quantitative content analysis that will be considered here is that when latent coding is used, it is subject to the interpretation of the researcher. Unlike manifest coding, which is the recording of fairly objective instances of a word or phrase, latent coding is based on searching for underlying content within a text. The identification of implied meaning is reliant upon the researcher's interpretation of the content, which can be less reliable than the coding of manifest content.

With regard to the analysis of secondary data sources and existing statistics, there are two further disadvantages that will be considered here. The first is that the researcher must rely on data that were collected by someone else who probably did not have the same research question(s) in mind. This means that the concepts that the researcher is interested in studying may not be ideally represented in the data, or that not all the concepts that the researcher wants to measure are available. For example, a secondary data set may have variables that measure sex, age, occupation, and years of education, but may not have any variables that measure ethnicity. If measuring ethnicity is an important part of a researcher's study, then he or she will have to either compromise or seek out a different source of data. It also takes considerable time for a researcher to get acquainted with such data sources, so although time is saved in collecting data, learning the nuances of the new source of data (e.g., the sampling strategy and the way concepts were measured) can be time consuming.

As discussed in Chapter 10, existing statistics can be problematic if the definition of a crime (for example) has changed over time. Researchers using existing statistics must be sure to take the time to understand how the official statistics they are analyzing have been defined and collected and if there have been any changes to these definitions during the time period they are studying.

Overall Advantages and Disadvantages of Qualitative Approaches

LO 3 Explain the overall advantages and disadvantages of the qualitative approaches.

As mentioned earlier, Chapter 2 dealt with the differences between positivist and interpretive approaches to social science. Interpretivism is most closely linked to the qualitative approaches because it focuses on the investigation of how members of the social world understand and interpret their surroundings and social experiences. The qualitative approaches considered in this book were qualitative interviews, focus groups, field research, historical methods, and qualitative content analysis.

When Can We Use Qualitative Methods

Only one advantage of qualitative methods in general will be considered here—but it is a *very important* advantage and it is at the heart of qualitative approaches. This advantage is that qualitative approaches give a voice to research participants in a way that is not possible in quantitative studies. Participants are invited to give their own answers and interpretation of their social worlds and are not constrained by categories as they can be in quantitative approaches like surveys. This personalized voice and in-depth understanding of the experiences of members of the social world, which can only be achieved through qualitative investigations, makes these approaches a fundamentally important tool for studying the social world.

Before discussing criticisms of qualitative methods, it should be noted that the criticisms that will be considered here are largely based on assumptions associated with the positivistic approaches of what research is meant to entail. (It was also the case that the criticisms of quantitative approaches discussed above were largely based on assumptions of what interpretivist researchers believe research is meant to be.) It is important to note that the shortcomings are not objective shortcomings in their own right, but reflect differences in opinion about what social research "should" be. Quantitative researchers tend to believe that social research should be as objective and as scientific as possible, while qualitative researchers are more concerned with understanding meaning and are skeptical that objectivity is truly possible. Qualitative researchers and the interpretivist approach assume that all research is subjective. If you recall from Chapter 6, Lincoln and Guba (1985) suggest that qualitative research be appraised on different criteria than those that are used to assess quantitative research.

A general criticism that is often launched against qualitative methods is with regard to their validity and reliability. Because of the close linkage between interpretivism and qualitative approaches, they are subject to scrutiny about their inherent subjectivity, difficulty (or impossibility) of replication, researcher bias, and lack of transparency.

Hanging Tongues: A Social Encounter with the Assembly Line

Because qualitative research is concerned with understanding the meaning that individuals and groups attribute to their social experiences, researchers need to gain an in-depth understanding of how their group of interest sees and understands the social world and their place within it. A disadvantage of using qualitative approaches is that the researcher must often become immersed in the people and situations that he or she is studying. This may lead to problems of subjectivity, as it may be difficult for the researcher to take a strictly objective position when he or she is so closely involved with research participants. The translation of how the research participants interpret their surroundings must necessarily be translated back through the interpretation of the researcher. In other words, the accounts (interpretations) of the research participants also must be interpreted by the researcher. This can lead to unintentional subjectivity and bias on the part of the researcher.

As discussed in Chapter 6, qualitative research is not replicable in the same way that quantitative research often is. As such, it can be questionable whether the results of these studies are valid and reliable. Related to this criticism is that these studies can be very limited in their scope. For example, are the results of interviews with 30 individuals recruited through snowball sampling representative of a larger population? Or are the results limited to the specific sample that was studied? It was highlighted in Chapters 6 and 13 that alternative criteria for validity and reliability might be considered in qualitative studies. In particular, Lincoln and Guba (1985) have suggested that such studies be evaluated based on their trustworthiness, a criterion that is more appropriate to these types of studies. And the principles of grounded theory provide guidelines for purposive sampling to increase the possibility of the sample being representative of the general population.

The final criticism of qualitative methods in general that will be considered here is that they tend to be very labour intensive. Recruiting participants for interviews or focus groups, transcribing individual and focus group interviews, and spending time in the field can take months or even years. These approaches tend to require a time investment in data collection and analysis that far exceeds that of the quantitative approaches. This is not necessarily a bad thing, but often in the "real world" of research, researchers are constrained by money and deadlines.

LO 4 Describe the advantages and disadvantages of specific qualitative approaches.

Advantages and Disadvantages of Specific Qualitative Approaches

After considering the general advantages and disadvantages of qualitative approaches, we now give attention to the strengths and weaknesses of specific methods that are generally considered to be qualitative in their orientation. Again, Table 16.1 summarizes some of the main advantages and disadvantages associated with these methods.

Qualitative Methods

Qualitative Interviews Qualitative interviewing was discussed at length in Chapter 12. A major advantage of qualitative interviews is that they allow for unexpected answers. Structured interviews (i.e., those used in survey research) often use closed questions, where the interviewee must select an answer from a series of fixed categories. In contrast, semi-structured interviews, such as those conducted in qualitative interviewing, allow the interviewee to answer using his or her own words. This allows the researcher to understand how the interviewee has experienced a situation or how the interviewee attributes meaning to particular events. As suggested above with regard to the general advantages of qualitative approaches, qualitative interviews allow for rich and detailed accounts that use the respondents' own words and give research participants their own unique voice in the study.

Discussion of Methodology

A disadvantage of qualitative interviewing is that, similar to structured interviewing, results might be influenced by the interviewer effect. That is, characteristics of the interviewer may affect how the research participant answers questions.

Focus Groups In Chapter 12, focus groups were introduced as group interviews. An advantage of focus groups is that qualitative interview data can be collected from numerous individuals at once. Participants tend to feel empowered and are encouraged to express their ideas freely. They may also ask each other questions to get to more detailed information on opinions that have been expressed.

A disadvantage of focus groups that was mentioned in Chapter 12 is the possibility of groupthink. Related to this disadvantage is that focus group interviews produce very different data and fewer ideas than what tend to be expressed in individual interviews. The nature of focus groups can also result in "polarization effects" in which only extreme opinions become expressed. Opinions "for" and "against" a topic are expressed very vocally, but little "middle-of-the-road" opinion is shared.

Finally, like structured and qualitative interviewing, the data can be affected by an interviewer effect. If you recall, the person leading the focus group is called a *moderator*. Characteristics or behaviours of the moderator may affect how the focus group is conducted, how people express their opinions, or the general atmosphere of the focus group itself.

Gender, Objectivity, and Bias in Research

Field Research Field research was discussed Chapter 13. One of the major strengths of this data collection approach is that the prolonged engagement of the researcher in the field allows him or her to develop an intimate understanding of the group and its members. Field research often studies marginalized or deviant groups about which little is known.

The Promise and Pitfalls of Going Into the Field

The major disadvantage of this approach is that group members may change their behaviour if they know they are being studied. Researchers also sometimes have difficulty accessing some groups, particularly if the groups are secretive in nature or involved in illegal activities. To overcome these disadvantages, researchers sometimes adopt a covert role, as discussed in Chapter 13.

Field Research

Historical Research Historical research was discussed in Chapter 14. This technique can involve a wide variety of data sources that can broadly be divided into two groups: historical documents and oral histories. An advantage of historical research is that when the researcher focuses on historical documents, the method is nonreactive. Also, comparisons can be made across time and cultures in a way that cannot be achieved with other techniques.

The Way We Weren't: The Myth and Reality of the "Traditional" Family

Disadvantages of this research include that the organization of the evidence can be difficult to interpret. The accuracy of historical documents and historical accounts must also be interpreted with caution. History is often not written in value-free terms, so distinguishing fact from opinion must be taken seriously by the individual researcher. For example, historical documents written by elite members of a society may not accurately reflect (or even include) the experiences of the poor at that particular time period. Language usage at earlier times in history was also different, so interpreting the meaning of historic documents can be tricky.

Qualitative Content Analysis In Chapter 14, qualitative content analysis was presented as a set of approaches to the analysis of texts that differed from quantitative content analysis in two important ways: the coding process and how codes were developed. An advantage to qualitative content analysis is that it does not only focus on obvious observable messages in text, but seeks to reveal hidden meanings and messages. This means that the analysis does not run the risk of being simply a word count, but can reveal important ways in which language is used to convey subtle meanings and ways of thinking about social phenomena. Like quantitative content analysis, qualitative content analysis also shares the advantage of being a nonreactive technique.

Document Research

Qualitative content analysis, however, also shares a disadvantage with quantitative content analysis in that the scope of the types of research questions that are asked using this method is rather limited. As well, as with all methods that rely on the interpretation of codes that emerge from data, there is always the risk that a researcher's biases may influence the way he or she sees the emergent themes.

LO 5 Identify the stages of mixed methods research.

MIXING METHODS IN QUALITATIVE-ONLY AND QUANTITATIVE-ONLY ANALYSES

monostrand design: A research design using a single research method. The opposite of *mixed methods* design.

multi-method research: An approach of using more than one quantitative method or more than one qualitative method in a single research project.

As has been discussed in the preceding sections, each particular method of social science inquiry has its own set of strengths and weaknesses. Until now, we have mostly used examples that illustrate the use of a single research method, otherwise known as **monostrand design**.[2] While mixed methods research typically refers to the combining of quantitative and qualitative methods, we first visit the possibility of mixing quantitative methods with quantitative methods and qualitative with qualitative. This approach of mixing "like with like" is referred to as **multi-method research**. (See Morse [2003] for further discussion of multi-method research.)

Mixing Quantitative Methods with Quantitative Methods

As discussed earlier in this chapter, each quantitative method examined in this textbook has its own set of strengths and weaknesses. Sometimes researchers combine different quantitative approaches together to offset the shortcomings of a particular approach or to get at a different angle of a research question.

For example, Jenkins (1999) used mixed quantitative methods to study the media coverage and popular support for the Reform Party in the early 1990s. The Reform Party was founded in the late 1980s as an Alberta-based "protest" party, which quickly rose in popularity (largely due to the dissatisfaction of Western Canadians with the Progressive Conservative government of the early 1990s). Jenkins conducted secondary analysis of survey data from the 1993 Canadian Election Study[3] and also conducted secondary analysis on content analysis data of the Reform Party's media coverage, which was originally collected by the Fraser Institute (in Vancouver). From the media coverage data, Jenkins was interested in determining what proportion of media coverage made a reference to the Reform Party. Jenkins wanted to see if there was a connection between media coverage and how people voted. The data from the survey of voters told him how people intended to vote and the reasons that they gave for their decision. Jenkins, however, suspected that media coverage would influence how people voted, and by analyzing how much coverage the Reform Party received (relative to other parties) he could determine if there was indeed an association between how much the Reform Party was mentioned in the media and its popularity with voters. Jenkins did find support for his hypothesis: Reform did get a disproportionate amount of media attention when it gained popularity. He also argued that the great unpopularity of the government at the time also had to be taken into consideration and that his results were not strictly causal (i.e., the media attention received by the Reform Party was not the only reason that it became so popular).

Mixing Qualitative Methods with Qualitative Methods

Apart from field research and ethnography (covered in Chapter 13), which routinely mix observation with interviews, other forms of mixing qualitative methods are possible. For

Box 16.1 Focus

Institutional Ethnography as a Multi-Method Research Approach

Institutional ethnography (IE) is strongly associated with the work of prominent Canadian sociologist Dorothy Smith (1986, 1987, 1990, 2005). Rather than being a specific social research method, it is more appropriate to describe IE as a methodological approach. In other words, there is no precise set of steps to follow when doing an IE, but rather there is more of an adherence to a particular way of thinking about the social world and how it should be investigated.

Institutional ethnography is situated in a Marxist orientation, where political and economic relations are viewed as a problematic source of power relations. It is important to note that this type of methodological approach is firmly rooted in a specific theoretical affiliation and, although qualitative in its underlying methods, it does not practise grounded theory.

In IE, linkages are made among situations of everyday life and the places in which they occur with attention given to professional practices and policy-making. The method is ethnographic and relies on fieldwork and interviews, but because the orientation of the approach is very much geared toward political and economic concerns, much attention is also given to the discursive analysis of texts (discourse analysis is addressed briefly in Chapter 14) and how they shape dimensions of social life. In particular, how *texts* function in institutional settings to produce "ruling relations" that shape the experiences of individuals is of central concern to IE researchers.

In sum, practitioners of IE use ethnographic methods combined with discourse analysis—through a Marxist lens—to examine their research questions. For example, Nichols (2008) used an institutional ethnography to examine the experiences of homeless youth trying to find shelter. She shows how homeless youth must navigate a complex maze of bureaucracy to access services and how benefits are denied because they do not have the correct identification. Young homeless people trying to access services are subjected to a politically motivated administrative regime, which can be intimidating and frustrating and ultimately hinder them from actually getting the help they need.

example, Smith (2006) was interested in studying Native peoples' involvement with evangelical race reconciliation movements in the United States. She wanted to understand the rise of Native people as prominent members of these "charismatic" Christian Right movements. Smith analyzed archival documents (historical methods) and conducted qualitative interviews with 30 members of a Christian Right group, the Promise Keepers. In particular, Smith was interested in how the concept of "race reconciliation" played out with Native peoples' participation in these groups. On one hand, Smith noted that the doctrines and texts of these movements emphasize political quietness, male dominance, and the dominance of Whites over Aboriginal people. On the other hand, Smith noted that "race reconciliation"—the position of the Christian Right to advocate for the inclusion of racial minorities in its groups and distance itself from racist stereotypes—had been used by Native evangelicals to promote treaty rights and other sovereignty issues. Her data highlight the inherent struggle of the Christian Right's race reconciliation approach and the use of these policies to further the interests of racial minority groups. See also Box 16.1 for an example of an institutional ethnography, which mixed various qualitative methods.

institutional ethnography (IE): A specific methodological approach where, from a Marxist perspective, the discourse of key texts is analyzed along with ethnographic techniques to examine how relatively powerless people are "structured" by organizations.

MIXING QUANTITATIVE AND QUALITATIVE METHODS

When researchers refer to "mixed methods," they are probably talking about mixing quantitative and qualitative techniques. There are many books that are dedicated solely to the discussion of mixed methods approaches, and these approaches are growing in popularity within the social sciences. As stated earlier, the driving force behind mixed methods research is that using a variety of methods can take advantage of the strengths of particular approaches, which can serve to not only offset the weaknesses of other approaches but also to acquire a larger swathe of data from which to answer the research questions under investigation. Figure 16.1 illustrates how the properties of qualitative and quantitative research methods can be combined to produce a stronger piece of research.

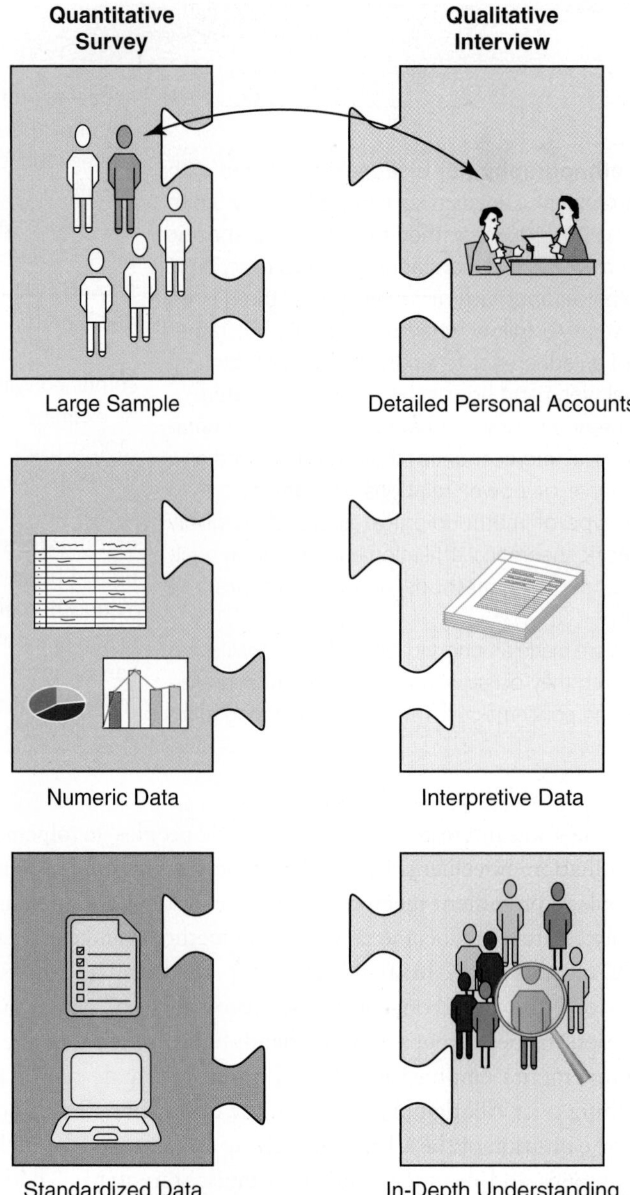

Figure 16.1 How Mixing Methods Can Strengthen a Research Project: Example of a Quantitative Survey and Qualitative Interviews

The Stages of Mixed Methods Research

Just as when you plan for a monostrand analysis, analyses involving mixed methods require you to plan all stages of each qualitative and quantitative portion(s) of your study with the same type of attention given to theory testing, sampling, data collection, and data analysis. Figure 16.2 illustrates the different steps that need to be followed when undertaking a mixed methods research project. As you can see from the figure, many decisions need to be made *before* you actually start collecting and analyzing data.

priority: In *mixed methods* research, refers to when a researcher has a preference for a quantitative or qualitative method to be considered the primary technique, with others used as supplementary methods.

Priority and Sequence in Data Collection There are, however, two main properties of a mixed methods study that need to be considered. When designing a mixed methods study, the researcher needs to decide which approach will take **priority** (if any)

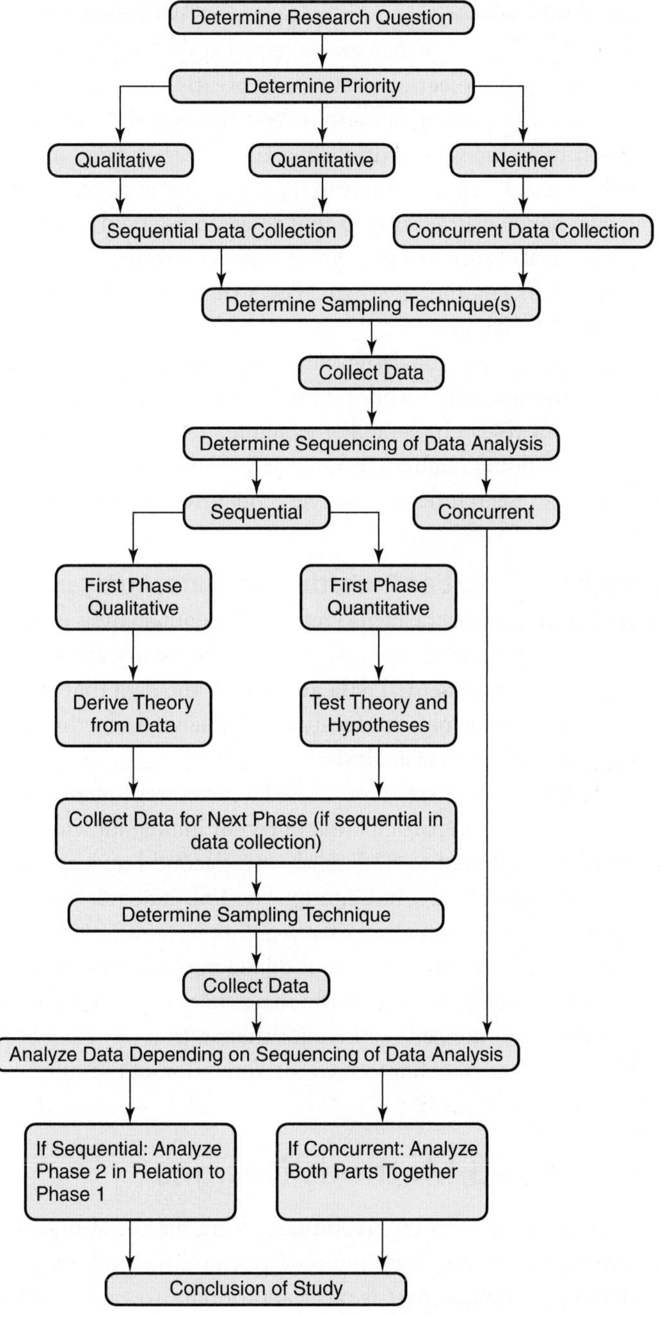

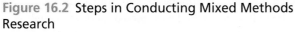

Figure 16.2 Steps in Conducting Mixed Methods Research

and the **sequence** in which the mixed methods approach will be carried out on the data analyzed.[4]

sequence: In *mixed methods* research, refers to the order in which a researcher prefers to carry out analysis on data.

If a researcher has a preference for either quantitative or qualitative methods to take priority, the preferred method will *often* occur first. This is because it is the primary data collection technique. The researcher would view the purpose of mixing methods as enhancing any weaknesses or limitations of the prioritized method. When a qualitative/quantitative preference does exist, the ordering of the research methods used in the study is called **sequential data collection.**[5] A study giving priority to qualitative methods would use a *sequential qualitative then quantitative design*, while a study giving priority to quantitative methods would use a *sequential quantitative then qualitative design*. Research designs that give

sequential data collection: Refers to when data for different parts of a *mixed methods* project are collected in stages (i.e., not at the same time).

concurrent data collection: In *mixed methods* research, refers to when *qualitative* and *quantitative data* are collected at the same time.

no priority to either qualitative or quantitative approaches use **concurrent data collection.**[6] That is, qualitative and quantitative data are collected at the same time.

Mixed methods research projects, however, vary greatly from one to another and therefore the terms discussed here are generalizations. You may actually find in some studies that quantitative research techniques were prioritized (i.e., deemed more important), but that they occurred as the second step in the research project. For example, qualitative exploration of the topic may have occurred first so that researchers could better understand their research topic when creating the questionnaire they were going to use. There are many ways in which researchers combine methods. For a thorough overview of this topic, see Creswell and Plano Clark (2007).

Usually mixed methods research designs are sequential in their data collection, particularly if there is just one researcher working on the study. This is because it is extremely difficult to do concurrent research alone. For example, designing and administering a survey at the same time as doing qualitative interviews would be a lot of work for just one person. When there is a research team, however, concurrent mixed methods are less difficult to undertake.

Sequential and Concurrent as Procedure in Data Analysis It should also be noted that *sequential* and *concurrent* can also refer to the data analysis procedure. If the first part of a mixed methods project is analyzed prior to the next stage of a mixed methods study, this approach is called **sequential data analysis**. If the data that are collected during the quantitative and qualitative phases of a study are analyzed together at the same time, this is referred to as **concurrent data analysis**.[7]

sequential data analysis: Refers to when the first part of a *mixed methods* project is analyzed prior to the next stage of the study.

concurrent data analysis: In *mixed methods* research, refers to when *qualitative* and *quantitative data* are analyzed at the same time.

For example, Taylor and Doherty (2005) used a concurrent mixed methods approach to study the sports and recreation participation of recent immigrant adolescents in Canada. Questionnaires were administered to 87 English as a Second Language (ESL) students at three high schools in a mid-sized city in Ontario. The ESL students were also asked to participate in focus groups, and eight single-sex focus groups were run (with four to six students per group). In Taylor and Doherty's concurrent mixed method data analysis, both qualitative and quantitative data were analyzed at the same time. Descriptive statistics about the ESL students' attitudes were "merged" with major themes that came out of the focus group interviews. Data from each approach informed interpretation of the other.

Sampling in Mixed Methods Designs

Qualitative and quantitative sampling techniques were discussed in Chapter 7. As you might imagine, when you decide to use multiple research methods in your research, you must use the sampling technique that is most appropriate to each method that you are going to use. The different sampling techniques required at the quantitative and qualitative stages of mixed methods studies are referred to as **mixed methods sampling.**[8]

mixed methods sampling: Refers to the sampling decisions that must be made at the qualitative and quantitative portions of a *mixed methods* study.

In Kidd's (2004, 2006) studies of homeless youth (see Box 16.2), different samples were used in each stage of the research. In the qualitative portion, for example, the researcher used a snowball sample of 80 homeless youth from Vancouver and Toronto. In the second stage of his research, questionnaires were administered to 208 homeless youth in New York City and Toronto. In both cases, purposive sampling was used. In this case, similar sampling techniques were used, but different samples were drawn. It is usually the case that quantitative portions of mixed methods studies have higher sample sizes, as filling out questionnaires and processing the data from them is less time consuming than transcribing and analyzing qualitative interview data.

In their study of immigrant adolescents' participation in sports discussed earlier in this chapter, Taylor and Doherty (2005) approached students in ESL classes in three Ontario high schools. Of the 133 students who fit the criteria for inclusion (i.e., they were recent

Box 16.2 Concepts in Action

Using Mixed Methods to Study Homeless Street Youth and Suicide: Qualitative Methods Followed by Quantitative Methods

Kidd (2004, 2006) used a mixed methods approach to examine suicide among street youth in Canada. His approach was *sequential* in that he conducted the qualitative portion of his study first, and then followed up these analyses using quantitative methods.

In the first stage of the study (Kidd, 2004), 80 street youth (under 24 years of age) were interviewed using open-ended, semi-structured qualitative interviews. Forty youth were interviewed in Vancouver and a further 40 were interviewed in Toronto. These cities were chosen because of their large homeless populations. Interviews lasted between 30 and 90 minutes, and interviewees were given $5 in food vouchers in exchange for their cooperation. The participants were asked about suicide among street youth and the meanings that they associated with suicide.

After coding the data, Kidd found that four major themes emerged: being trapped, hopelessness, feeling worthless, and loneliness. For illustrative purposes, for the theme of "hopelessness," Kidd (2004, p. 39) gives the following quotations and examples:

> [*Re: suicide*]: You get feeling stuck, like kind of hopeless. I think a lot of people become hopeless and think about it. Especially young people. (Woman, 18)
>
> Suicide on the streets is . . . the last way out basically. I've thought of suicide but I haven't actually tried it while I was on the streets but that was my own reasons . . . the only way out. There is nowhere left to turn. You don't have foster care. You don't have the government to turn to. You can't turn back to your parents. You don't have anyone to turn to. And basically . . . after a while of living on the streets your dreams begin to fade, and you can't see yourself . . . like when you are younger you can actually visualize yourself doing all this stuff 30 years from now but when you are on the streets for a while you begin to lose that. You can't visualize yourself any further than a day or two away. That's usually where the drugs come in, and the suicide usually comes after the drugs because they have found that they are hopeless and have nowhere left to go. And then when they are on the drugs they realize "I am still wandering around in a circle but now I am addicted to drugs so I can't get off." That is usually when it happens. (Man, 18)

Using a grounded theory approach, Kidd concluded from this study that homeless youth were at a high risk of attempting suicide. In fact, in his interviews with the 80 youth, he found that almost half had attempted suicide at least once. The researcher concluded that the feelings of being trapped, worthless, lonely, and hopeless acted as "mediators" between life events and suicidal ideas. In other words, difficult life events (e.g., abuse by a family member), which led to the youth's leaving home, are related to the feelings of being trapped, worthless, lonely, and hopeless that he or she may have. These feelings can lead the youth to contemplate suicide.

After discovering this inductively derived theory in his qualitative data, Kidd went on to undertake quantitative analyses to confirm and add to the transferability of his findings. (Recall that *transferability* was discussed in Chapter 6 as a criterion of Lincoln and Guba's (1985) "trustworthiness.") In general, the idea of transferability is to demonstrate that the findings can be applied to a wider population than just those people who were included in the study.

In the quantitative portion of his study, Kidd (2006) recruited 208 street youth (again, 24 years of age or younger) to fill in questionnaires. The youth were approached and recruited on the street and through youth agencies in both Toronto and New York City. In total, 100 youth were recruited from New York City and 108 were recruited from Toronto. As an incentive, participants were given $20 in food vouchers for their participation in the study.

Items in the questionnaire asked respondents about difficulties in their past (e.g., dysfunctional families), their experience of street life (e.g., if they had exchanged sex for money), their physical health, their drug use, aspects of their psychological well-being, and their "suicidality."

Kidd undertook statistical analysis of the survey results, testing the theory that he had derived from the qualitative portion of his study—that feelings of being trapped, worthlessness, lonely, and hopeless acted as "mediators" between life events and suicidal ideas. Like the qualitative study he undertook earlier on Toronto and Vancouver street youth, he found that almost half of the youth in his quantitative study had attempted suicide at least once. The results of the statistical analyses confirmed the findings of the previous study. In other words, the quantitative portion of the analyses supported the theory derived from the qualitative portion of the study. Further evidence was found that street youth with abusive family histories and drug dependence experienced loneliness and low self-esteem, which led to feelings of being "trapped." Feeling "trapped" then led to ideas about committing suicide.

immigrants with a command of English adequate to complete the questionnaire), 87 agreed to fill in the survey. Focus group participants were recruited from the questionnaire sample, and 40 of these students agreed to participate. In this particular example, nonprobability purposive sampling was undertaken at both stages, although the questionnaire sample was considerably larger.

Box 16.3 Concepts in Action

Using Mixed Methods to Study Immigrant Settlement Patterns in Ontario: Quantitative Methods Followed by Qualitative Methods

When people think about immigrant settlement in Canada, they usually think of this phenomenon occurring in large, urban centres, not in small towns and rural areas. Di Biase and Bauder (2005) used a mixed methods approach to examine immigrant settlement patterns in Ontario, giving special attention to nonurban areas.

The first portion of their analysis was quantitative. The researchers analyzed the 2001 Canadian Census data maps to identify the rural and urban areas across Ontario in which immigrants had settled. They found that while the majority of immigrants settled in Toronto and surrounding areas, high concentrations were found in the townships of Plummer Additional, Dawn-Euphemia, and Bayham, as well as Westport (a village). However, over three quarters of immigrants who arrived in Canada between 1996 and 2001 settled in Toronto and surrounding urban areas (Markham, Richmond Hill, Mississauga, and Brampton).

The researchers then carried out statistical analyses on the Census data to determine the relationship between settlement location (dependent variable) and the labour market and housing characteristics of the region (independent variables). For Ontario as a whole, the researchers found associations between settlement patterns and housing prices. That is, immigrants tended to settle in regions with higher housing prices. However, no associations were found between labour market conditions and concentration of immigrants. These surprising findings led the researchers to speculate that reasons other than labour market conditions, such as friends and family, prompted immigration settlement decisions more so than labour market conditions.

To make more sense out of their statistical analyses, the researchers conducted 19 qualitative interviews: 13 were undertaken with immigrants and a further 6 were conducted with settlement and employment counsellors. All immigrants who were interviewed expressed a desire to live in a large suburban home, supporting the findings of their statistical analyses. The researchers also found that many interviewees made a decision to live in an area based on their premigration perceptions of places and the lifestyles associated with them. Many did not want to settle in an area with large concentrations of immigrants as they felt it would limit their job opportunities.

Using qualitative interviewing allowed the researchers to more fully understand reasons for settlement patterns among immigrants in Ontario. While the Census data allowed for certain hypotheses to be tested, the data did not have any measurements for the various social reasons that immigrants may have had for choosing their settlement location. Through using these triangulation techniques, the researchers were able to elaborate on their quantitative findings with explanations for settlement decisions in the words of those with first-hand experience—the immigrants themselves.

To contrast, Di Biase and Bauder's (2005) study of immigrant settlement in Ontario (see Box 16.3) began with the secondary analysis of Canadian Census data. A census, as you will recall from Chapter 7, is a survey of everyone in a population. Therefore, the Canadian Census data contains literally millions of records. The qualitative portion of their mixed methods study, however, was a snowball sample of 19 immigrants and settlement counsellors.

It is important for researchers to put careful thought into the sampling strategies chosen for each method that they plan to use. Where possible, probability sampling is preferable for the quantitative portion of mixed methods studies as it increases the generalizability of the findings. In the case of Kidd's study (see Box 16.2), the nature of his population (homeless youth) meant that a sampling frame (a list of all members of a population) could not be used to create a random sample. He opted for a considerably larger purposive sample than the one used in the qualitative portion of his study, which is a good option when probability sampling is not possible.

The Role of Theory in Mixed Methods Research

In Chapter 2, the relationship between theory and social research was discussed. In general, quantitative methods are more closely related to deductive theorizing, while qualitative methods are associated with inductive theorizing. If you recall, deductive theorizing involves testing previously existing theories. This is done through hypothesis testing. This approach sharply contrasts with the inductive approach, where theory is generated out of the data (also known as grounded theorizing).

Theory in Sequential Mixed Methods Studies So what happens when you use both quantitative and qualitative research methods in your mixed methods research? If you begin a sequential mixed methods study with a qualitative investigation, you have the opportunity to generate a theory that is grounded within your data. In Kidd's (2004) study (see Box 16.2) using interview data from homeless youth in Vancouver and Toronto, he developed a theory that hinged on the four themes of feeling trapped, lonely, worthless, and hopeless. He theorized that these feelings "mediated" the experiences that led the youth to becoming homeless in the first place (family problems, drug dependency) and to their suicidal ideas.

After generating this theory from his qualitative interviews, Kidd (2006) conducted additional research to confirm that the theory was accurate. Using questionnaire data from 208 street youth, he quantified these concepts and tested them statistically, which revealed support for his earlier research findings.

In the same vein, if your sequential mixed methods study gives priority to quantitative methods, then you should begin with a theory to test. If the theory is supported in your quantitative analyses, the qualitative portion of your study can be used to elaborate upon parts of the theory that perhaps were not fully tested using the quantitative techniques you chose. If the theory was not supported by your quantitative analysis, you could use qualitative techniques to refine the theory. This is the approach that was used by Di Biase and Bauder (2005) in their study of immigrant settlers in Ontario (see Box 16.3). The original theory that they tested was that new immigrants' decisions about where to settle within Ontario were economically motivated by labour market and housing conditions. When they found only partial support for this theory, they explored other reasons for settlement patterns by conducting qualitative interviews with immigrants and counsellors.

Theory in Concurrent Mixed Methods Studies How do we deal with theory in concurrent mixed methods studies? If you are using qualitative and quantitative methods at the same time, one approach is oriented toward deductive theorizing and the other to inductive theorizing. How do you resolve this? There is no one right answer to this apparent conundrum. In Taylor and Doherty's (2005) study on the sports participation of immigrant youth, these researchers began their study with a theoretical framework about ethnicity and recreation participation, but their data analysis was undertaken concurrently so that themes from the focus group interviews could elaborate on findings from the statistics generated from the questionnaires (and vice versa). Their findings generally supported the theory that they had tested, although details from the focus group data allowed the researchers to somewhat modify the theory, which previously did not account for gender differences.

Obtaining Conflicting Results

It may seem that mixed methods research will produce results in the quantitative portions and qualitative portions that will, by and large, agree with one another. This is, however, sometimes not the case. Sometimes, in the process of doing qualitative and quantitative investigations on a research topic, contradictory findings are produced. For example, in a mixed methods study of social scientists' relationships with the mass media, Deacon, Bryman, and Fenton (1998) found that the results of the quantitative and qualitative portions of their study appeared to contradict each other. The quantitative data that they collected through questionnaires seemed to suggest that the relationships between social scientists (from the perspective of the social scientists) and journalists (from the perspective of the social scientists) were amiable. Data collected from the qualitative parts of their study, however, suggested that there was actually a considerable rift between the values and priorities of journalists and social scientists.

epistemic prioritization: When the results of quantitative findings are given priority in *mixed methods* research, particularly when contradictory findings are discovered between the qualitative and quantitative portions of the study.

There is a temptation, when such apparently contradictory results appear, to prioritize one approach over the other. In other words, more attention may be paid to the questionnaire results than the focus groups. Prioritizing one method over another to "resolve" conflicting results is referred to as **epistemic prioritization**, and resorting to this manages to erase many of the good intentions the social scientists using mixed methods research started their research projects with![9]

Deacon and colleagues opted to reanalyze their data and found that the social scientists answering the survey questions about the coverage of their research by the press tended to express that the experiences weren't as bad as they had expected them to be. But in the interviews, the social scientists tended to focus on particularly bad experiences that they had had with the media. In other words, the social scientists were generally satisfied with how their research was covered in the media, but in interviews tended to focus on particularly negative experiences.

The best approach to take when you obtain apparently contradictory findings in the qualitative and quantitative parts of a mixed methods study is to carefully reanalyze the data to investigate the reasons behind the contradictions. As in the example just discussed, it is likely that you will have overlooked some important explanation that acts to resolve the contradictions. If this still does not help, it is useful to ask other researchers to look at your data and see if they can offer any insights. Sometimes a new "set of eyes" on your data can be particularly helpful in seeing things that you had overlooked.

LO 6 List the strengths and weaknesses of mixed methods research.

ARGUMENTS AGAINST MIXING METHODS

The benefits of mixing methods have been emphasized throughout this chapter. There are, however, some weaknesses that are associated with the use of mixed methods in social science research and these are presented (along with the strengths) in Box 16.4.

Box 16.4 Focus

Strengths and Weaknesses of Mixed Methods Research

Strengths

- Rich text, narrative, and images can add meaning to numbers.
- Numbers can add precision to text, narrative, and images.
- The strengths of both quantitative and qualitative methods can be combined.
- Grounded theory can be both generated and tested.
- Broader researcher questions can be answered.
- Strengths of one approach can offset the weaknesses of another.
- More insights may be generated than if only a single approach is used; a more complete picture of social life may be revealed.
- Generalizability of findings can increase.

Weaknesses

- It is very labour intensive, particularly for a single researcher.
- The researcher may have to learn about research methods with which he or she is not familiar to practise them effectively.
- It can be very expensive.
- Some "purists" argue that a researcher should work with either qualitative methods or quantitative methods and that mixing them violates the philosophical underpinnings of these approaches.
- Conflicting results from quantitative and qualitative components can be difficult to resolve—the researcher may be tempted to resort to epistemic prioritization.

Source: Adapted from Burke, J., & Christensen, L. B. (2004). *Educational research: Quantitative, qualitative, and mixed approaches* (2nd ed.). Boston, MA: Allyn and Bacon. Adapted with permission from Pearson Education.

A reality about mixed methods research is that while social scientists tend to agree that this is the ideal way to approach research questions, in practice very few do! Why is this? Most likely it is because mixed methods research is very time consuming, labour intensive, and expensive. In addition, it is often the case that social scientists consider themselves predominantly "quantitative" or "qualitative" researchers and that to undertake mixed methods requires them either to master a new technique or to step outside their own comfort zones.

Another reason for not undertaking mixed methods research comes from what can be considered philosophical arguments. Because quantitative research is closely associated with positivism and deductive theorizing, and qualitative research is associated with interpretivism and inductive theorizing, critics argue that combining these techniques is logically impossible and any attempts to do so will succeed at only a superficial level.[10] In other words, critics believe that there are fundamental embedded philosophies that are associated with the quantitative and qualitative approaches, and that these are violated if the methods are combined.

CHAPTER SUMMARY

Glossary Flashcards

In this chapter, you learned about the strengths and weaknesses of the research methods that were covered in this book and how using qualitative and quantitative methods together in a single research project is possible.

The chapter began by addressing the general strengths and weaknesses of quantitative methods and then moved on to the specific strengths and weaknesses of each quantitative approach. Similarly, the general strengths and weakness of qualitative methods were discussed before moving on to the pros and cons of each individual qualitative approach discussed in this book.

A major motivation for doing mixed methods research is that the qualitative and quantitative investigations can be complementary to one another, inform one another, and provide additional information for answering a research question that would not be possible by using a single approach. The weaknesses of one approach can be offset by the strengths of another. Because all approaches have their good and bad aspects, combining methods to create an overall stronger research product makes obvious sense.

Using mixed methods requires the researcher to follow the same procedures that are required of the individual methods that he or she is going to use. A mixed methods study requires several decisions be made by the researcher before and during the course of the study, including decisions about the priority given to qualitative or quantitative methods, the sequencing of data collection and data analysis, sampling, and the approach to theorizing.

Doing good mixed methods research means that the qualitative and quantitative parts of the study are integrated well with one another and do not stand apart as separate studies. The quantitative portion(s) should complement the findings of the qualitative portion(s) and vice versa. Researchers planning to do mixed methods research should be prepared that they may arrive at results in their quantitative and qualitative analyses that seem contradictory. Careful reanalysis of the data might be required to make sense out of apparently contradictory findings.

We want to end this chapter and this book by urging you, as a consumer of social research or a new social researcher, to be self-aware. Be aware of the place of the social researcher in society and of the social context of social research itself. Social researchers bring a unique perspective to the larger society. Be curious (and critical) about how "facts" from research are reported in the media. You have the skills in your methodological toolkit—now use them not only in your research, but in your day-to-day life!

Review Questions

Chapter Quiz

1. Identify two advantages and two disadvantages of quantitative approaches in general.
2. Describe one advantage and one disadvantage of each specific quantitative approach discussed in this chapter.
3. Identify one major advantage and two disadvantages of the qualitative approaches in general.
4. Describe one advantage and one disadvantage of each specific qualitative approach discussed in this chapter.
5. What do *priority* and *sequence* mean in mixed methods research?
6. What are the two approaches to data analysis as procedure in mixed methods research?
7. How is sampling decided upon in a mixed methods project?
8. What is the role of theory in mixed methods research?
9. List five strengths and five weaknesses of mixed methods research.

Exercises

Research Activities

1. Using EBSCO's ContentSelect, identify a research article that obtained data using a multi-method research design. Describe if it was a quantitative or qualitative multi-method design and what specific techniques were used in all phases of the study.
2. Using EBSCO's ContentSelect, identify three research articles that used a mixed methods design. What kinds of methods were used in the articles? Are the studies sequential or concurrent? Does any method have priority? Explain the methods for all parts of the study.
3. In the articles identified for the previous question, determine which sampling techniques were used in all phases of the research. What was the researchers' approach to theory? Critique and identify limitations of the study.

MySearchLab

Visit MySearchLab, where you'll find thousands of full-text articles from academic journals and help with the research and writing process. Access the eText within MySearchLab to take self-grading practice tests and view a variety of multimedia resources.

Appendix

Doing a Research Project

Photo Credit: stokkete/Fotolia

INTRODUCTION

In the 16 chapters of this book, we have addressed the various components involved in doing social research. After Chapter 1, in which the reasons for and importance of social research were discussed, we moved to an overview of sociological theory in Chapter 2. It was stressed that the interconnection of theory and research methods was of paramount importance—in fact, these two things are the building blocks upon which sociology and other related social sciences were founded. Then, in Chapter 3, various issues around ethics were raised, giving you guidelines as to how to ensure that your proposed research meets the various ethics standards required by professional bodies and research ethics boards. It was shown that, in keeping with ethical requirements, your proposed research may have to be altered from what you had originally envisaged to abide by numerous ethical considerations that place the well-being of research subjects front and centre. Chapter 4 then showed you how to do a thorough overview of the current "state of the art" by reviewing published studies related to your research question. Being familiar with findings in your research area is a key step in ensuring that your proposed project will make a meaningful contribution to knowledge and that you have noted the strengths and weaknesses of the attempts of previous researchers. We then moved to other important aspects of a research project: design

(Chapter 5), measurement (Chapter 6), and sampling (Chapter 7). The remaining chapters of the book (Chapters 8 to 16) were devoted to specific data collection and analytic techniques and were divided broadly into quantitative and qualitative approaches.

Having a mastery of the topics covered in this book gives you the tools required for undertaking a social research project. The contents of each chapter can be thought of as an essential part of your research methods toolkit. And like any building project, tools must be used together and in the proper sequence. Undertaking your own research project for the first time will likely seem like a daunting and even overwhelming task, and the purpose of this appendix is to give you some basic structure to follow to carry one out.

As discussed throughout the book, qualitative and quantitative research projects follow similar trajectories, yet each has their own distinct characteristics. For example, it has been stressed that quantitative projects are much more likely to follow a *linear* trajectory, following a set series of steps in a precise order. In contrast, qualitative projects are much less likely be committed to following a strict series of stages, instead adopting a *nonlinear* trajectory wherein the researcher moves back and forth between crucial steps in the research process. Similarly, the relationship that quantitative and qualitative approaches have with theory and hypothesis testing is quite distinct, with the former favouring testing existing theory with clearly articulated hypotheses and the latter often developing theory and working with emergent research questions (rather than a set of hypotheses).

Because the stages in qualitative and quantitative research projects can be so different from one another, they will be presented as such in the following examples. The reader should note that the steps here are guidelines and not "hard and fast" rules. As well, the examples used will be the most "typical" approaches used in the bulk of social research. In terms of a quantitative research project, the key exemplar will be *secondary data analysis*, while for the qualitative project *qualitative interviews* will be the data collection tool used. It should be noted that other methods will of course require slightly different steps, but that the purpose of the stages presented here is to give the novice researcher guidance on how to tackle their first major project from start to finish.

STEP 1: PICKING A TOPIC AND NARROWING IT TO A RESEARCH QUESTION

The obvious first step in any research project is picking a topic. This is usually motivated by what interests you. Unsurprisingly, many of the topics that researchers pick are often spawned by their own personal interests and biographies. Some personal characteristic or experience of your own may be the starting point of your topic selection. Perhaps you are an immigrant or a child of an immigrant and you are interested in the experience of immigrants in Canada. Perhaps you are a visible minority and you are interested in the life experiences of other visible minorities. Or how do sexual minorities experience bullying? Or how do people with particular medical conditions cope? The list goes on. People's choices for research topics are not always biographically motivated, of course, but often people's interests are intrinsically driven by aspects of their lives for which they want more information. Your choice of topics, however, may be confined by what your instructors require, the topic of a course, or what a granting agency mandates.

Let's say that the topic we are interested in is the experience of visible minorities in Canada. In Canada, "visible minority" is the term given by Statistics Canada to refer to individuals who are not visibly the same as the majority group. This is a pretty broad topic and can take many directions. This topic now needs to be further refined into a research question. What is it about the experiences of visible minorities in Canada that we are interested in? There are many subtopics we can focus on: employment, education, experiences of discrimination, to name a few. In the particular example that follows, we use the subtopic

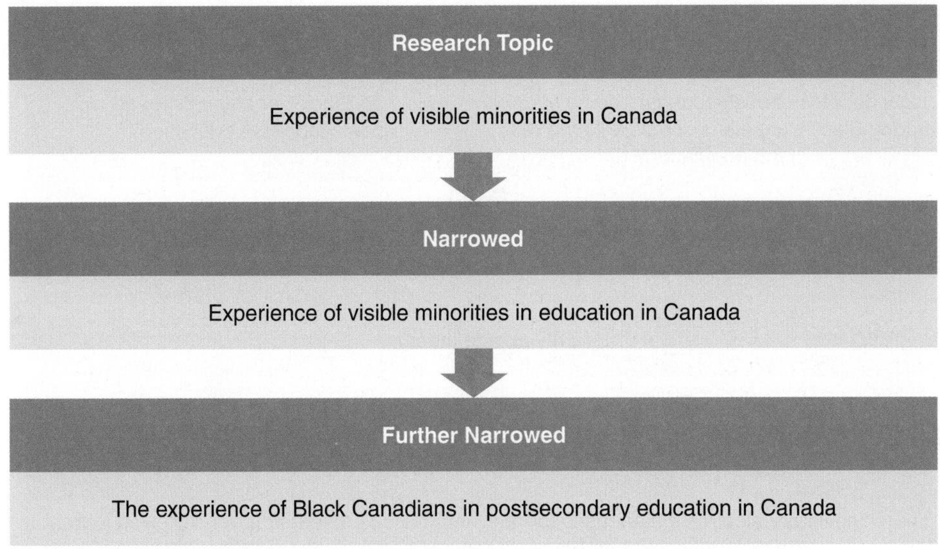

Figure A.1 Narrowing a Research Topic into a Research Question

of education. Therefore, we have narrowed our topic to the experience of visible minorities in education in Canada. We may even want to narrow our topic of "visible minority" into a specific minority group, such as South Asians, Blacks, or Latin Americans. And because education in Canada has various forms (early childhood, primary, secondary, postsecondary, and continuing education), we will want to be specific about the type of education in which we are interested. In the following example, we will examine the topic of Black Canadians and postsecondary education (Figure A.1).

Now that we've narrowed our topic, it is necessary to refine our topic into a researchable research question. The topic of "the experience of Black Canadians in postsecondary education in Canada" is still rather broad. What specifically about this experience are we interested in? One possible direction may be "How do rates of postsecondary completion among Black Canadians compare to the rest of the population?" Or you may be interested, more generally, in how Black Canadians experience postsecondary education.

For the purposes of the worked example, we will explore both of these research questions because one lends itself to quantitative research and the other to qualitative research. It is your research question that should determine your selected approach.

STEP 2: THEORETICAL CONSIDERATIONS

After you have narrowed your research question, you should start thinking about the theoretical framework that will inform your work. It is sometimes useful to examine how previous researchers in your general topic area have approached choosing a theory. While there are several major theorists with whom you have likely become familiar in your studies, you may or may not see an obvious linkage between your topic area and theory. If you do not, it is useful to look at previous research and see which theorists other researchers have appealed to. This can give you ideas about what theorists are most relevant for your area of research. It may also give you a new way of thinking about a theory you are already familiar with.

In the previous step, we narrowed our research questions to two general ones that will be pursued for the remainder of this example. The first lends itself to quantitative research approaches (it is very specific, focusing on "rates") and the second to qualitative research approaches (it is more general, asking about "how" a process works). In terms of choosing a theory, however, whether you are doing a qualitative or quantitative project does not matter (Figure A.2). All social theories can be incorporated into qualitative or quantitative

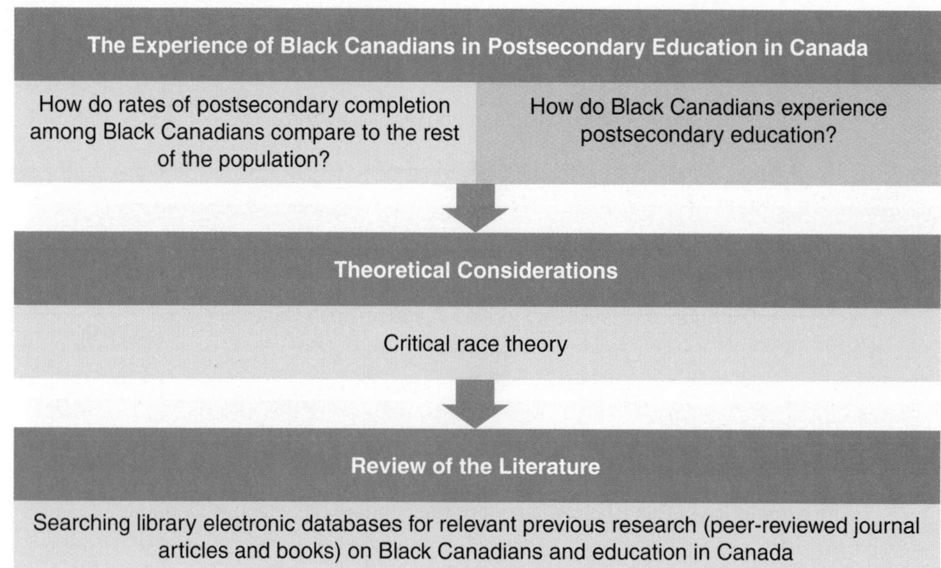
The Experience of Black Canadians in Postsecondary Education in Canada
How do rates of postsecondary completion among Black Canadians compare to the rest of the population?
How do Black Canadians experience postsecondary education?
Theoretical Considerations
Critical race theory
Review of the Literature
Searching library electronic databases for relevant previous research (peer-reviewed journal articles and books) on Black Canadians and education in Canada

Figure A.2 Theoretical Considerations and Reviewing the Literature

projects. In the particular topic area we are focusing on, it seems most appropriate to use critical race theory, which was discussed in Chapter 2.

STEP 3: REVIEWING THE LITERATURE

A crucial step in the process of undertaking a research project is to thoroughly familiarize yourself with related research in your topic area (see Figure A.2). You can use information from previous research to understand what is already known about a topic area, and more importantly what remains to be known. You can also get ideas for how you might construct your own research project based on how seasoned experts in peer-reviewed academic journals have done theirs. You can build on the strengths of their conceptualizations of concepts or try to improve upon any apparent weaknesses in the various components of their research.

It is not enough to simply "Google" a topic and see what a search engine provides. The internet can be a valuable resource for your research topic, but you must review *high-quality peer-reviewed research* (see Chapter 4) in your area, and this is often only possible to find in electronic academic databases that your library subscribes to. You can access these databases through your library's online resources and search a subject-appropriate database by keywords. For the research topic being considered in this example, we could go to the electronic database *Sociological Abstracts* and enter the keywords "Black Canadians" and "postsecondary education." If this does not yield enough results, you will want to use broader search terms such as "Black Canadians" and "education." Such a search will likely produce several results; you can then review the abstracts and decide which ones you want to read more closely. Such a search will reveal papers (among others!) such as "Revisiting the Notion of a 'Recast' Vertical Mosaic in Canada: Does a Post Secondary Education Make a Difference?" by Kevin Gosine, published in 2000 in the journal *Canadian Ethnic Studies*, and "Schooling as Community: Race, Schooling, and the Education of African Youth" by George Dei, published in 2008 in the *Journal of Black Studies*.

New researchers often want to know how long their literature review "should" be. The simplest reply to this is "until it is complete." The length of a literature review depends on your research question and the amount of research already published in your topic area. If there is a lot of research in your area, you will need to carefully review it and synthesize the findings—and this will, of course, be a loftier project than reviewing the literature for which only a handful of studies exist. If the existing research is very extensive, you may want to limit the time period (e.g., the past 10 years) and/or the geographic area (e.g., North America) in which you are searching. As explained in Chapter 4, it is important to synthesize the literature rather than producing an article-by-article summary. The latter is an annotated bibliography, which may be a useful first step in constructing your literature review, but is not itself the same thing as a literature review.

STEP 4: DESIGNING YOUR STUDY AND SELECTING YOUR DATA COLLECTION METHOD

After you have narrowed your research topic into a research question and reviewed the literature in your topic area, it is time to design your study and select the type of method you will use to collect your data. Your method is driven by the research question you are asking. *You must pick the method most appropriate to your research question.* Above, two questions were decided upon: "How do rates of postsecondary completion among Black Canadians compare to the rest of the population?" and "How do Black Canadians experience postsecondary education?" The first question is very specific and addresses the differences between postsecondary completion rates between two groups; this question lends itself to quantitative research approaches. The second question is more general and asks about subjective experiences; this type of question lends itself to more interpretive forms of data collection (i.e., qualitative methods).

In quantitative research, hypotheses are often formulated before data collection or analysis occurs, and these hypotheses are usually informed by the theory that the researcher is testing (Figure A.3). Earlier, we identified critical race theory as the theory of interest, so based on this we can test the hypothesis that Black Canadians will have lower rates of postsecondary completion rates than White Canadians. Recall that this is the deductive approach to theory. In contrast, qualitative projects rarely test hypotheses. Often, researchers using such approaches try to enhance or develop theory. Therefore, they start with more general questions that become more focused over time.

In terms of data collection techniques, many were covered in this book. For answering the hypothesis that Black Canadians have lower rates of postsecondary completion

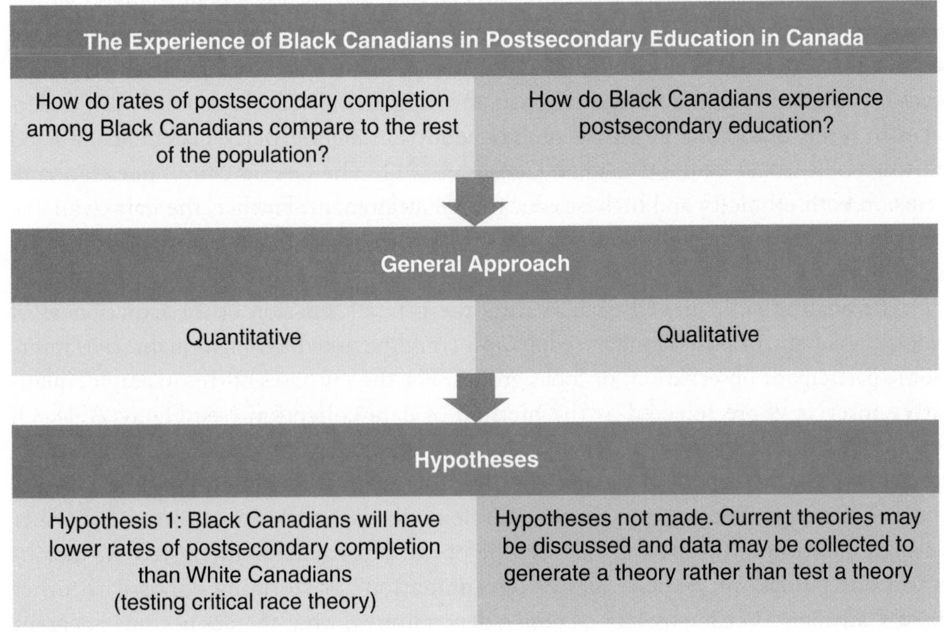
The Experience of Black Canadians in Postsecondary Education in Canada
How do rates of postsecondary completion among Black Canadians compare to the rest of the population?
How do Black Canadians experience postsecondary education?
General Approach
Quantitative
Qualitative
Hypotheses
Hypothesis 1: Black Canadians will have lower rates of postsecondary completion than White Canadians (testing critical race theory)
Hypotheses not made. Current theories may be discussed and data may be collected to generate a theory rather than test a theory

Figure A.3 Generating Hypotheses

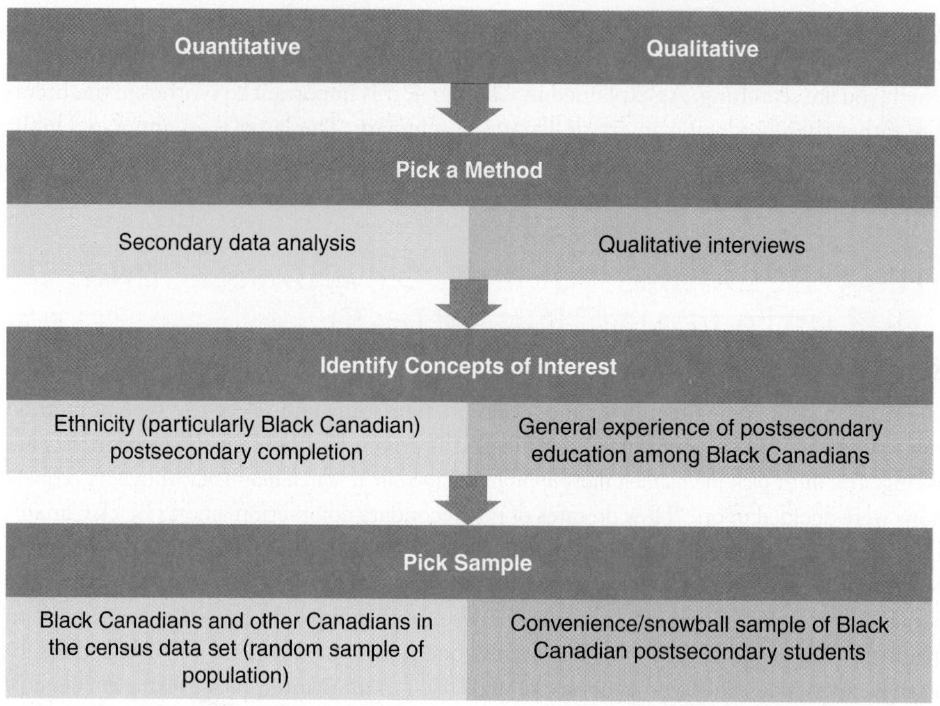

Figure A.4 Choosing Data Collection Techniques and Sampling Procedures

than White Canadians, there are two clear alternatives: *secondary data analysis* or a *survey*. There are two distinct concepts that need to be measured in your data: *ethnicity* and *educational attainment*. While a novice researcher may be keen to launch his or her own survey, it is also worth investigating whether or not comparable surveys on your topic have already been completed. Using secondary data analysis is a common way of answering hypotheses by social researchers for various reasons (see Figure A.4). First and foremost, the survey data you will be able to analyze will likely be far more extensive than anything you can manage to organize on your own. Secondary data collected by Statistics Canada or other official agencies will have been collected by experts in the field with a very large budget. Thousands, perhaps tens of thousands or hundreds of thousands, of respondents will have been contacted. The breadth of coverage of population and topic areas is going to be far more extensive than anything an individual researcher can undertake. In terms of looking at postsecondary education among Black Canadians, a good starting point would be the Canadian Census of 2011. The Census carries questionnaire items on both ethnicity and highest educational attainment. Further, the data available for public use are often available through most libraries at postsecondary institutions (ask your librarian).

The qualitative approach to answering the general question of the experiences of Black Canadians in postsecondary education could be asked through qualitative interviews, participant observation, or focus groups. For the purposes of this example, qualitative interviews are selected as the method of data collection (see Figure A.4). Of central importance to the researcher would be to design an interview guide that asks a variety of questions around the experiences of the respondents in terms of their postsecondary education. Through successive interviews, the researcher may narrow his or her research question further and decide that he or she is particularly interested in "racialization on campus" or "experiences of discrimination" or "forming bonds with other Black Canadians on campus," for example, depending on what themes become apparent in the emergent data.

STEP 5: SELECTING YOUR SAMPLE

Sampling was addressed in Chapter 7. If you are using secondary data, you have little choice around your sample and you should read the official documents (i.e., the "documentation") that accompany your data set. In the documentation, there will be extensive details on the sampling technique used by the primary collectors of the data. When you use secondary data, you may also wish to examine only a subset of the data. For example, for the particular question under consideration it would not make sense to include individuals who are not old enough to have had the chance to pursue postsecondary education. You may also want to exclude older individuals because they represent postsecondary choices made decades ago rather than in recent times. You may want to limit your sample to individuals aged 21–35, for example. Whatever you choose—and there is no "objectively right way" to do this—your choice of subsample should logically match your research question, and you must explain and rationalize your choice when you write up your findings.

In terms of sampling for qualitative interviews, nonprobability sampling techniques would be used. You may consider a snowball sampling technique if you know any individuals that fit your target population (i.e., Black Canadians in postsecondary education). Individuals who agree to be in your study can then recommend other friends and acquaintances who they think may be interested. You may also consider putting up posters around campus, contacting campus groups, or using email listservs to solicit participation in your study. The size of your snowball sample should be big enough to adequately answer your research question, although the practical concerns of time and money (particularly if you are offering your participants incentives) can also be strong determinants. Ideally, you will continue interviewing subjects until you reach the saturation point in your emerging data—that is, interviewing additional cases would be unlikely to add any new insights.

STEP 6: PREPARING YOUR INSTRUMENT

Before you collect any data, you must ensure that your instruments for collecting data are in place (see Figure A.5). In the case of secondary data analysis, you are not actually engaging in the collection of data as the data have already been collected, so preparing an instrument (such as a survey) is not required. It is, of course, of central importance that the secondary data source you select must have operationalizations of your key concepts. However, if you were embarking on your own quantitative data collection, this would be the point at which you would design your survey (or develop your coding frame, or design your experiment). Your review of the previous research will give you an idea of how other researchers before you approached this step and will allow you to build on the strengths (and address the weaknesses) of your academic predecessors. If you are undertaking a project that requires you to develop a survey, looking at what other researchers have done to operationalize your concepts in the form of questionnaire items will be useful. Using previously tested measures is a recommended way of ensuring that your items display various properties of reliability and validity.

In a qualitative study using qualitative interviews, it is important to develop your interview guide. While generally not a strict list of questions that you must follow during the interviews, it does serve as a guide and reminder of the questions that you want to make sure you ask your study participants during the course of an interview. You will likely find that the interview guide changes as you interview more people and new questions arise that you had not thought of before. The qualitative interview guide is flexible, and enhancing it during the course of your research is to be expected. Regardless of the instrument you use to collect your data, it is always a good idea to "pilot" your instrument on friends or colleagues to identify any errors or problems in wording that may be present.

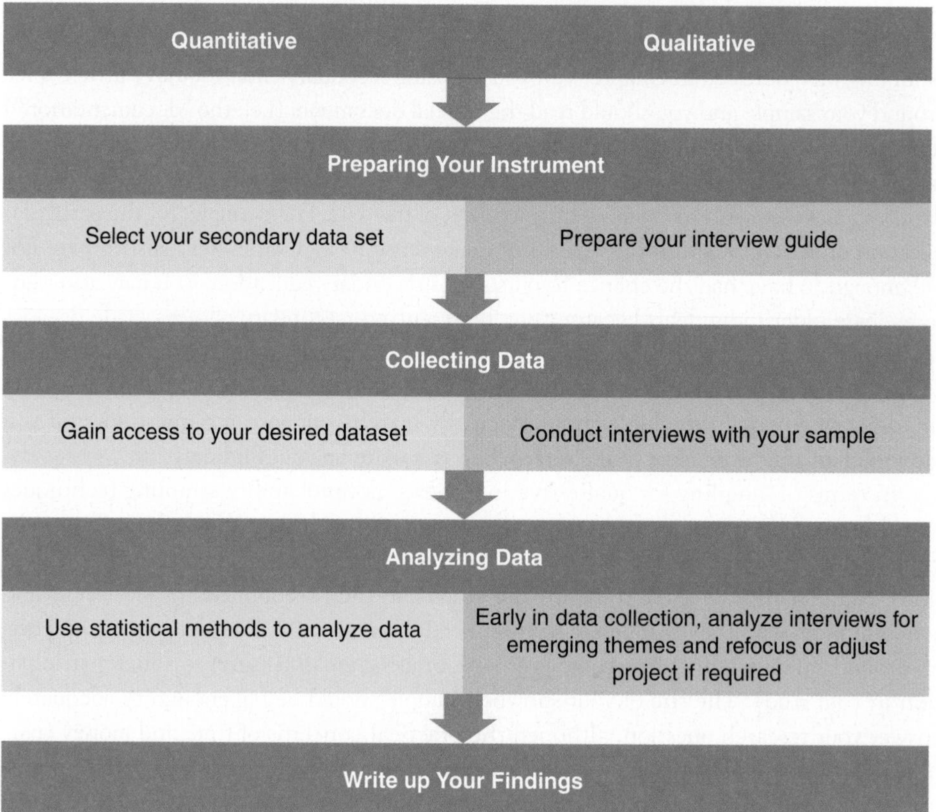

Figure A.5 The Final Steps in a Research Project

STEP 7: COLLECTING YOUR DATA

The next step in your research project is to collect your data (see Figure A.5). Many of the chapters in this book have been devoted to different data collection techniques. After you have chosen your sample, you must administer your instrument—such as a survey—to your sample. You would administer the study instrument in a way that is appropriate to your chosen method. In the case of secondary data analysis, this step is not required because your data have already been collected. You must, however, engage in the process of gaining access to your desired data set—which can be a lengthy process! If you are using data housed by the Statistics Canada Research Data Centres (RDCs), you are required to submit a formal application and proposal. Once your proposal is approved, you must meet with RDC staff to sign documents and swear an oath that you will not use the data in unauthorized ways. If your data are owned by a private organization, you may have to engage in negotiations to get permission for access. Data access can be a time-consuming part of your research project and you should not underestimate the time it will take to acquire your data. Some Statistics Canada data—the Public Use Microdata Files (PUMF)—are quite a bit easier to access because they are a much smaller sample of cases and variables (and therefore less accurate and detailed). If you opt for a PUMF, make sure that your key concepts are adequately operationalized in the data set. The data librarian in your college or university library can assist you in getting access to these data.

A qualitative project precedes in much the same manner. In the case of qualitative interviews, you begin interviewing your study participants. In qualitative projects, however, the focus of the general topic may shift as successive interviews occur, and there may be slight changes to the interview guide. Unlike quantitative projects, this process of data collection is more fluid and less of an absolute stage with firm boundaries. The researcher may go back to revise the interview guide and refocus the research questions, unlike in a quantitative project.

STEP 8: ANALYZING YOUR DATA

The analysis of quantitative data necessitates the use of statistical analysis, which occurs at the end of data collection. Whether you are using secondary data or your own survey data, you must first familiarize yourself with the data set. If you have collected a survey, you will need to ensure that numeric codes for your questionnaire items have been entered into a spreadsheet that can be read by a statistical software program. You should analyze your data for possible keypunch errors (they do exist in secondary data sets) by looking at frequency distributions for all your nominal and ordinal variables of interest. For example, if someone is recorded as 234 years of age, it is clearly a mistake. You should look at the measures of central tendency and dispersion of all the continuous and interval level variables in your data. The second step in general is to undertaken bivariate analyses between your independent (race) and dependent variables (postsecondary completion rates) of interest. Your final step is to use multivariate techniques to control for spurious relationships between your independent and dependent variables of interest. While we are interested in the relationship between being Black Canadian and completing postsecondary education, we would also want to ensure that family socio-economic background, parental education, and years of age are also "controlled for" so that we do not overstate the relationship between race and postsecondary completion rates. The statistical techniques you will use depend on the level of measurement of your variables and your technical skills in this area.

The analysis of qualitative data does not necessarily begin when all interviews are complete. Often, researchers begin analyzing their data early in the data collection process to identify emerging themes. Identification of themes may cause the focus of the research to somewhat shift or narrow, or it may result in adding new questions to the interview guide and revisiting previous interviewees for more information. There are several approaches to the analysis of qualitative data, which were covered in Chapter 15. In general, however, a researcher goes through his or her data looking for themes that are identified through open coding and further refined during axial coding. Many qualitative researchers do this by hand on printed transcripts, although many also use qualitative data analysis software that greatly assists in the organization of codes.

STEP 9: WRITING UP YOUR FINDINGS

Writing up your research paper will probably seem like a daunting task at first. It is a good idea to look at the structure of peer-reviewed academic articles in your subject area to get an idea of how to "model" your paper. Learning by positive example is the best way of becoming a skilled writer, whatever your subject area or discipline.

In most social research, peer-reviewed articles begin with an abstract. The abstract is a summary of the research paper that is usually around 250 words. The structure of the paper, whether quantitative or qualitative, usually follows this general structure (although the titles of these sections may vary): Introduction, Review of the Literature, Study Objectives, Data and Methods, Results, Discussion, and Conclusion. The introduction of the paper introduces the problem to be investigated and highlights its social importance; there is often also a summary of the structure of the paper. The review of the literature is precisely that—the overview and synthesis of the literature related to your topic area, usually highlighting gaps that your study proposes to fill. The study objectives indicate what is to be accomplished in the remainder of the paper and any hypotheses that will be tested (in the case of quantitative work). The data and methods section carefully describes the sample and the manner in which the data were collected and analyzed. In the results section, the findings of the data analysis are described, while in the discussion section the results are revisited, often with reference to previous research. Authors may note similarities and differences with the findings of previous research or explain how their research contributes to theory. Finally, in the conclusion section, the findings are summarized, potential weaknesses of the study are considered, and suggestions for future research are offered.

The art of executing a research project and writing it up is certainly a skill that develops over time. Looking to previous research for guidance and to more experienced researchers for mentorship is essential in developing your own talents in these areas. Practice will not make you a perfect researcher, but it will certainly make you a better researcher and social scientist.

Glossary

Following the definition, the number in parentheses indicates the page number where the term first appears in boldface in the text. Italicized words refer to terms defined elsewhere in this glossary.

Abstract: A term with two meanings in literature reviews: a short summary of a scholarly journal article that usually appears at its beginning, and a reference tool for locating scholarly journal articles. (69)

Academic social research: Research designed to advance fundamental knowledge about the social world. (10)

Action research: A type of *applied social research* in which a researcher treats knowledge as a form of power and abolishes the division between creating knowledge and using knowledge to engage in political action. (12)

Agency: Refers to the individual's ability to act and make independent choices. (28)

Aggregate: Collection of many individuals, cases, or other units. (24)

Alternative hypothesis: A *hypothesis* paired with a *null hypothesis* stating that the *independent variable* has an effect on a *dependent variable*. (90)

Analogy: A statement that two objects, processes, or events are similar to each other. (341)

Analytical memos: The written notes a qualitative researcher takes during data collection and afterward to develop concepts, themes, or preliminary generalizations. (298)

Annotated bibliography: A list of sources pertaining to a specific topic, which includes full citation information, a summary of the article (including research methods employed) and its findings, as well as evaluative comments about the quality of the research. (74)

Anonymity: Research participants remain anonymous or nameless. (54)

Appearance of interest: A technique in *field research* in which researchers maintain relations in a *field site* by pretending to be interested and excited by the activities of those studied, even though they are actually uninterested or very bored. (294)

Applied social research: Research that attempts to solve a concrete problem or address a specific policy question and that has a direct, practical application. (10)

Association: A co-occurrence of two events, factors, characteristics, or activities such that when one happens, the other is likely to occur as well. Many statistics measure this. (37)

Assumption: A part of a social theory that is not tested but acts as a starting point or basic belief about the world. These are necessary to make other theoretical statements and to build *social theory*. (27)

Attitude of strangeness: A technique in *field research* in which researchers study a *field site* by mentally adjusting to "see" it for the first time or as an outsider. (291)

Attributes: The categories or levels of a *variable*. (87)

Audit trail: A technique for establishing the *trustworthiness* criterion of *confirmability* by collecting detailed and transparent *qualitative data*. (302)

Axial coding: A second *coding* of *qualitative data* after *open coding*. The researcher organizes the codes, develops linkages among them, and discovers key analytic categories. (332)

Bar chart: A display of *quantitative data* for one *variable* in the form of rectangles where longer rectangles indicate more cases in a variable category. Usually, it is used with discrete data and there is a small space between rectangles. Rectangles can have a horizontal or vertical orientation. Also called a bar graph. (241)

Bimodal: A distribution with two *modes*. (242)

Bivariate statistics: Statistical measures that involve two *variables* only. (247)

Case-study research: Research, usually qualitative, on one or a small number of cases in which a researcher carefully examines a large number of details about each case. (18)

Causal explanation: A statement in social theory about why events occur that is expressed in terms of causes and effects. They correspond to associations in the empirical world. (36)

Census: An attempt to count everyone in a target population. (134)

Central limit theorem: A law-like mathematical relationship stating that whenever many *random samples* are drawn from a *population* and plotted, a *normal distribution* is formed, and the centre of such a distribution for a variable is equal to its *population parameter*. (147)

Citation: Details of a scholarly journal article's location that help people find it quickly. (68)

Classical experimental design: An *experimental design* that has *random assignment*, a *control group*, an *experimental group*, and *pretests* and *post-tests* for each group. (201)

Closed-ended question: A type of *survey research* question in which respondents must choose from a fixed set of answers. (171)

Cluster sampling: A type of *random sample* that uses multiple stages and is often used to cover wide geographic areas in which aggregated units are randomly selected; *samples* are then drawn from the sampled aggregated units, or clusters. (152)

Codebook: A document that describes the procedure for *coding variables* and their location in a format for computers. (238)

Coding: The process of converting raw information or data into another form for analysis. In *content analysis*, it is a means for determining how to convert symbolic meanings in *text* into another form, usually numbers (see *coding system*); in *quantitative data* analysis, it is a means for assigning numbers; and in *qualitative data* analysis, it is a series of steps for reading raw notes and assigning codes or conceptual terms (see *axial coding, open coding, selective coding*). (219)

Coding frame: An exhaustive list of all possible values that codes may take in *content analysis*. (221)

Coding system: A set of instructions or rules used in *content analysis* to explain how to systematically convert the symbolic content from *text* into *quantitative data*. (220)

Code sheet: Paper with a printed grid on which a researcher records information so that it can be easily entered into a computer. It is an alternative to the *direct-entry method* and using optical-scan sheets. (239)

Cohort study: A type of *longitudinal research* in which a researcher focuses on a category of people who share a similar life experience in a specified time period. (17)

Complete observer: In *field research*, when a researcher only observes the study group without participating in their activities. (288)

Complete participant: In *field research*, when a researcher fully participates in all aspects of the study group's activities as though a member of the group. (288)

Computer-assisted personal interviewing (CAPI): Like *computer-assisted telephone interviewing*, but used for in-person interviews. (189)

Computer-assisted telephone interviewing (CATI): *Survey research* in which the interviewer sits in front of a computer screen and keyboard and uses the computer to read questions that are asked in a telephone interview, then enters answers directly into the computer. (189)

Concept: An idea expressed as a symbol or in words. (27)

Concept cluster: A collection of interrelated ideas that share common *assumptions*, belong to the same larger *social theory*, and refer to one another. (27)

Concept map: A visual illustration of the relationship among themes that emerge from *qualitative data*. (336)

Conceptual definition: A careful, systematic definition of a construct that is explicitly written to clarify one's thinking. It is often linked to other concepts or theoretical statements. (108)

Conceptual equivalence: In *historical research*, the issue of whether the same ideas or concepts occur or can be used to represent phenomena across divergent cultural or historical settings. (321)

Conceptual hypothesis: A type of *hypothesis* in which the researcher expresses variables in abstract, conceptual terms and expresses the relationship among variables in a theoretical way. (111)

Conceptualization: The process of developing clear, rigorous, systematic *conceptual definitions* for abstract ideas or concepts. (108)

Concurrent data analysis: In *mixed methods* research, refers to when *qualitative* and *quantitative data* are analyzed at the same time. (360)

Concurrent data collection: In *mixed methods* research, refers to when *qualitative* and *quantitative data* are collected at the same time. (360)

Concurrent validity: *Measurement validity* that relies on a preexisting and already accepted measure to verify the indicator of a construct. (116)

Confidence interval: A range of values, usually a little higher and lower than a specific value found in a *sample*, within which a researcher has a specified and high degree of confidence that the *population parameter* lies. (147)

Confidentiality: Information has participant names attached, but the researcher holds it in confidence or keeps it secret from the public. (55)

Confirmability: A component of establishing *trustworthiness* that relates to the extent to which the findings of a qualitative study are value free. (302)

Content: Refers to words, meanings, pictures, symbols, ideas, themes, or any message that can be communicated. (218)

Content analysis: Research in which one examines patterns of symbolic meaning within written text, audio, visual, or other communication medium. (19)

Content validity: *Measurement validity* that requires that a measure represent all the aspects of the *conceptual definition* of a construct. (115)

Context effect: An effect in *survey research* when an overall tone or set of topics heard by a respondent affects how he or she interprets the meaning of subsequent questions. (178)

Contextual equivalence: The issue in *historical research* of whether social roles, norms, or situations across different cultures or historical periods are equivalent or can be compared. (320)

Contingency cleaning: Cleaning data using a computer in which the researcher looks at the combination of categories for two *variables* for logically impossible cases. (240)

Contingency question: A two- (or more) part question in *survey research*. The answer to the first part of the question determines which of two different questions a respondent receives next. (171)

Contingency table: A table that shows the *cross-tabulation* of two or more *variables*. It usually shows *bivariate quantitative data* for variables in the form of percentages across rows or down columns for the categories of one variable. (249)

Continuous variables: Variables measured on a continuum in which an infinite number of finer gradations between variable *attributes* are possible. (120)

Control group: The group that does not receive the *treatment* in *experimental research*. (199)

Control variable: A "third" *variable* that shows whether a bivariate relationship holds up to alternative explanations. It can occur before or between other variables. (253)

Conventional content analysis: A type of *qualitative content analysis* in which the researcher develops themes during the *coding* process. (322)

Correlation: The idea that two *variables* vary together, such that knowing the values in one variable provides information about values found in another variable. (247)

Cover sheet: One or more pages at the beginning of a questionnaire with information about an interview or respondent. (179)

Covert observer: In *field research*, refers to a researcher who is secretly studying a group without the group members knowing that they are being studied. (289)

Credibility: One aspect of *trustworthiness*, which relates to how much truth value the results of a qualitative study have. (300)

Criterion validity: *Measurement validity* that relies on some independent, outside verification. (116)

Cross-sectional research: Research in which a researcher examines a single point in time or takes a one-time snapshot approach. (17)

Cross-tabulation: Placing data for two *variables* in a *contingency table* to show the number or percentage of cases at the intersection of categories of the two variables. (249)

Curvilinear relationship: A relationship between two *variables* such that as the values of one variable increase, the values of the second show a changing pattern (e.g., first decrease, then increase, and then decrease). It is not a *linear relationship*. (248)

Data: The *empirical evidence* or information that a person gathers carefully according to established rules or procedures; it can be qualitative or quantitative. (7)

Debrief: When a researcher gives a true explanation of the experiment to *subjects* after using *deception*. (200)

Deception: When an experimenter lies to *subjects* about the true nature of an experiment or creates a false impression through his or her actions or the setting. (199)

Deductive approach: An approach to inquiry or social theory in which one begins with abstract ideas and principles then works toward concrete, *empirical evidence* to test the ideas. (34)

Dependability: An aspect of establishing *trustworthiness* of *qualitative data* in which data are assessed in terms of how likely it is that similar results would be obtained if the study were repeated. (302)

Dependent variable: The effect variable that is last and results from the causal variable(s) in a *causal explanation*. Also the variable that is measured in the *pretest* and *post-test* and that is the result of the *treatment* in *experimental research*. (87)

Descriptive research: Research in which one "paints a picture" with words or numbers, presents a profile, outlines stages, or classifies types. (14)

Descriptive statistics: A general type of simple statistics used by researchers to describe basic patterns in the data. (240)

Design notation: The name of a symbol system used to discuss the parts of an experiment and to make diagrams of them. (205)

Deviant case sampling: A type of *nonrandom sample* in which a researcher selects unusual or nonconforming cases purposely as a way to provide greater insight into social processes or a setting; especially used by qualitative researchers. (136)

Devil's advocate: In *focus group* research, refers to a person whose role it is to argue against a dominant idea and who could introduce new questions and new ways of thinking into the group so as to prevent the tendency toward group conformity. (277)

Diffusion of treatment: A threat to *internal validity* that occurs when the *treatment* "spills over" from the *experimental group*, and *control group* subjects modify their behaviour because they learn of the *treatment*. (208)

Direct-entry method: A method of entering data into a computer by typing data without code or optical-scan sheets. (240)

Direct observation notes: Notes taken in *field research* that attempt to include all details and specifics of what the researcher heard or saw in a *field site*. They are written in a way that permits multiple interpretations later. (297)

Direct questions: In *qualitative interviewing*, questions introduced by the interviewer usually toward the end of the interview to address specific topics that may not have been covered. (271)

Directed content analysis: A type of *qualitative content analysis* that begins with predetermined codes derived from theory. (323)

Discourse analysis: A type of qualitative analysis of texts that focuses on how knowledge and meaning are created through the use of language. (324)

Discrete variables: Variables in which the *attributes* can be measured only with a limited number of distinct, separate categories. (120)

Double-barrelled question: A problem in *survey research* question wording that occurs when two ideas are combined into one question and it is unclear whether the answer is for the combination of both or one or the other question. (166)

Double-blind experiment: A type of *experimental research* in which neither the *subjects* nor the person who directly deals with the subjects knows the specifics of the experiment. (209)

Ecological fallacy: Something that appears to be a *causal explanation* but is not. It occurs because of confusion about *units of analysis*. A researcher has *empirical evidence* about an *association* for large-scale units or huge aggregates, but *overgeneralizes* to make theoretical statements about an *association* among small-scale units or individuals. (92)

Empirical evidence: The observations that people experience through their senses—touch, sight, hearing, smell, and taste; these can be direct or indirect. (7)

Empirical generalization: A quasi-theoretical statement that summarizes findings or regularities in *empirical evidence*. It uses few, if any, abstract concepts and only makes a statement about a recurring pattern that researchers observe. (26)

Empirical hypothesis: A type of *hypothesis* in which the researcher expresses variables in specific terms and expresses the *association* among the measured indicators of observable, *empirical evidence*. (111)

Empty boxes: A name for conceptual categories in an explanation that a researcher uses as part of the *illustrative method* of *qualitative data* analysis. (342)

Epistemic prioritization: When the results of quantitative findings are given priority in *mixed methods* research, particularly when contradictory findings are discovered between the qualitative and quantitative portions of the study. (364)

Epistemology: A branch of philosophy that studies knowledge, including how we pursue knowledge. (28)

Equivalence: The issue of making comparisons across divergent contexts, or whether a researcher, living in a specific time period and culture, correctly reads, understands, or conceptualizes data about people from a different historical era or culture. (320)

Equivalent time series design: An *experimental design* in which there are several repeated *pretests*, *post-tests*, and *treatments* for one group often over a period of time. (203)

Ethnography: An approach to *field research* that emphasizes providing a very detailed description of a different culture from the viewpoint of an insider in that culture to permit a greater understanding of it. (283)

Evaluation research study: A type of *applied social research* in which one tries to determine how well a program or policy is working or reaching its goals and objectives. (12)

Exchange relationships: Relationships that develop in the field, in which small tokens or favours, including deference and respect, are exchanged. (293)

Exhaustive attributes: The principle that response categories in a *scale* or other measure should provide a category for all possible responses (i.e., every possible response fits into some category). (122)

Existing statistics research: Research in which one examines numerical information from government documents or official reports to address new research questions. (19)

Experimental design: Arranging the parts of an experiment and putting them together. (200)

Experimental group: The group that receives the *treatment* in *experimental research*. (199)

Experimental research: Research in which one intervenes or does something to one group of people but not to another and then compares the results for the two groups. (18)

Experimenter expectancy: A researcher may threaten *internal validity* not by purposefully unethical behaviour but by indirectly communicating desired findings to the subjects. (208)

Explanatory research: Research that focuses on why events occur or tries to test and build social theory. (15)

Exploratory research: Research into an area that has not been studied and in which a researcher wants to develop initial ideas and a more focused research question. (13)

External criticism: In *historical research*, a way to check the authenticity of *primary sources* by accurately locating the place and time of its creation (i.e., ensuring it is not a forgery). (319)

External audit: A technique for establishing *dependability* and *confirmability* in qualitative research wherein researchers outside of the study examine *qualitative data* to see if they would have come to the same results as the original researcher. (302)

External validity: The ability to generalize from *experimental research* to settings or people that differ from the specific conditions of the study. (119)

Face validity: A type of *measurement validity* in which an indicator "makes sense" as a measure of a construct in the judgment of others, especially those in the scientific community. (115)

Factorial design: A type of *experimental design* that considers the impact of several *independent variables* simultaneously. (204)

Fallacy of misplaced concreteness: When a person uses too many digits in a quantitative measure in an attempt to create the impression that the data are accurate or the researcher is highly capable. (230)

Field experiment: *Experimental research* that takes place in a natural setting. (210)

Field research: A type of qualitative research in which a researcher directly observes the people being studied in a natural setting for an extended period. Often, the researcher combines intense observation with participation in the people's social activities. (19)

Field site: The one or more natural locations where a researcher conducts *field research*. (286)

Floaters: Respondents who lack a belief or opinion but who give an answer anyway if asked in a *survey research* question. Often, their answers are inconsistent. (174)

Focus group: A type of group interview in which an interviewer asks questions to the group and answers are given in an open discussion among the group members. (19)

Follow-up questions: Refers to questions that are asked in *qualitative interviews* to get additional description about topics just discussed by the interviewee. (270)

Frequency distribution: A table that shows the distribution of cases into the categories of one *variable* (i.e., the number or percent of cases in each category). (240)

Full-filter question: A type of *survey research* question in which respondents are first asked whether they have an opinion or know about a topic, then only the respondents with an opinion or knowledge are asked a specific question on the topic. (174)

Funnel sequence: A way to order *survey research* questions in a questionnaire from general to specific. (178)

Gatekeeper: Someone with the formal or informal authority to control access to a site. (288)

Go native: What happens when a researcher in *field research* gets overly involved, loses all distance or objectivity, and becomes like the people being studied. (293)

Grounded theory: Social theory that is rooted in observations of specific, concrete details. (34)

Groupthink: In *focus group* research, refers to people's natural desire to avoid conflict and lean toward group consensus, even when the opinion of the group does not reflect their own personal opinions. (277)

Guilty knowledge: When a researcher in *field research* learns of illegal, unethical, or immoral actions by the people in the *field site* that is not widely known. (304)

Halo effect: An error often made when people use personal experience as an alternative to science for acquiring knowledge. It is when a person overgeneralizes from what he or she accepts as being highly positive or prestigious and lets its strong reputation or prestige "rub off" onto other areas. (6)

Haphazard sampling: A type of *nonrandom sample* in which the researcher selects anyone he or she happens to come across. (135)

Hawthorne effect: An effect of *reactivity* named after a famous case in which *subjects* reacted to the fact that they were in an experiment more than they reacted to the *treatment*. (210)

Hidden populations: People who engage in clandestine, deviant, or concealed activities and who are difficult to locate and study. (155)

Histogram: A type of *bar chart* used to visually display the distribution of a continuous *variable*. (241)

Historical research: Research in which one examines different cultures or periods to better understand the social world. (20)

History effects: A threat to *internal validity* due to something that occurs and affects the *dependent variable* during an experiment, but which is unplanned and outside the control of the experimenter. (206)

Hypothesis: The statement from a *causal explanation* or a proposition that has at least one *independent* and one *dependent variable*, but it has yet to be empirically tested. (89)

Ideal type: A pure model about an idea, process, or event. One develops it to think about it more clearly and systematically. It is used both as a method of *qualitative data* analysis and in *social theory* building. (340)

Idiographic: An approach that focuses on creating detailed descriptions of specific events in particular time periods and settings. It rarely goes beyond *empirical generalizations* to abstract social theory or causal laws. (31)

Illustrative method: A method of *qualitative data* analysis in which a researcher takes the concepts of a *social theory* or explanation and treats them as *empty boxes* to be filled with empirical examples and descriptions. (342)

Incentive: A general term for the remuneration given to research participants, often in the form of cash. (268)

Independence: The absence of a statistical relationship between two *variables* (i.e., when knowing the values on one variable provides no information about the values that will be found on another variable). There is no *association* between them. (247)

Independent variable: The first variable that causes or produces the effect in a *causal explanation*. (87)

Index: The summing or combining of many separate measures of a construct or variable. (123)

Indirect questions: In *qualitative interviews*, questions that the interviewer asks to get a sense of how the interviewee believes other people think, behave, or feel. (271)

Inductive approach: An approach to inquiry or social theory in which one begins with concrete empirical details then works toward abstract ideas or general principles. (34)

Inferential statistics: A branch of applied mathematics or statistics based on a *random sample*. It lets a researcher make precise statements about the level of confidence he or she has in the results of a *sample* being equal to the *population parameter*. (157)

Informant: A general term that is used to refer to individuals who participate in qualitative research projects. (269)

Informed consent: An agreement by participants stating they are willing to be in a study after they learn something about what the research procedure will involve. (50)

Institutional ethnography (IE): A specific methodological approach where, from a Marxist perspective, the discourse of key texts is analyzed along with ethnographic techniques to examine how relatively powerless people are "structured" by organizations. (357)

Instrumentation: A threat to reliability occurring when the *dependent variable* measure changes during the experiment. (207)

Interaction effect: The effect of two *independent variables* that operate simultaneously. The effect of the variables together is greater than what would occur from a simple addition of the effects from each. The variables operate together on one another to create an extra "boost." (204)

Internal criticism: How historical researchers establish the authenticity and credibility of *primary sources* and determine their accuracy as an account of what occurred. (319)

Internal validity: The ability of experimenters to strengthen a *causal explanation's* logical rigour by eliminating potential alternative explanations for an *association* between the *treatment* and the *dependent variable* through an *experimental design*. (119)

Interpreting questions: In *qualitative interviewing*, questions that are asked to ensure that the researcher is interpreting what the interviewee is saying as correctly as possible. (271)

Interpretivism: The philosophical orientation that the study of society requires research techniques specific to understanding the interpretation of meaning. (28)

Interrupted time series: An *experimental design* in which the *dependent variable* is measured periodically across many time points, and the *treatment* occurs in the midst of such measures, often only once. (203)

Interval measures: A *level of measurement* that identifies differences among variable *attributes*, ranks, and categories and that measures distance between categories, but there is no true zero. (121)

Intervening variable: A variable that is between the initial causal variable and the final effect variable in a *causal explanation*. (87)

Interview guide: A list of questions that a researcher wishes to address in the course of a *qualitative interview*. (271)

Interview schedule: The name of a survey research questionnaire when a telephone or face-to-face interview is used. (163)

Introducing questions: In *qualitative interviews*, this refers to questions that are general opening questions in which the interviewee is prompted to give his or her account of a situation or experience. (269)

Jotted notes: In *field research*, what a researcher inconspicuously writes while in the *field site* on whatever is convenient to "jog the memory" later. (296)

Laboratory experiment: *Experimental research* that takes place in an artificial setting over which the experimenter has great control. (210)

Latent coding: A type of *content analysis* coding in which a researcher identifies subjective meaning such as general themes or motifs in a communication medium. (221)

Latin square design: An *experimental design* used to examine whether the order or sequence in which *subjects* receive multiple versions of the *treatment* has an effect. (203)

Leading (or loaded) question: A question that leads the respondent to choose one response over another by its wording. (166)

Level of analysis: A way to talk about the scope of a *social theory*, *causal explanation*, proposition, *hypothesis*, or theoretical statement. The range of phenomena it covers, or to which it applies, goes from social psychological (micro-level) to organizational (meso-level) to large-scale social structure (macro-level). (91)

Levels of measurement: A system that organizes the information in the measurement of variables into four general levels, from the *nominal level* to the *ratio level*. (120)

Level of statistical significance: A set of numbers researchers use as a simple way to measure the degree to which a statistical relationship results from random factors rather than the existence of a true relationship among *variables*. (258)

Likert scale: A *scale* often used in *survey research* in which people express attitudes or other responses in terms of several *ordinal-level* categories (e.g., agree, disagree) that are ranked along a continuum. (127)

Linear relationship: An *association* between two *variables* that is positive or negative across the attributes or levels of the variables. When plotted in a *scattergram*, the basic pattern of the association forms a straight line, not a curve or other pattern. (248)

Linear research path: Research that proceeds in a clear, logical, step-by-step straight line. It is more characteristic of a quantitative than a qualitative approach to social research. (81)

Literature review: A systematic examination of previously published studies on a research question, issue, or method that a researcher undertakes and integrates together to prepare for conducting a study or to bring together and summarize the "state of the field." (65)

Longitudinal research: Research in which the researcher examines the features of people or other units at multiple points in time. (17)

Macrosocial theory: Social theories and explanations about abstract, large-scale, and broad-scope aspects of social reality, such as social change in major institutions (e.g., the family, education) in a whole nation across several decades. (25)

Manifest coding: A type of *content analysis* coding in which a researcher first develops a list of specific words, phrases, or symbols, then finds them in a communication medium. (221)

Margin of error: An estimate about the amount of *sampling error* that exists in a survey's results. (141)

Marginals: The totals in a *contingency table*, outside the body of a table. (250)

Matrix question: A type of *survey research* question in which a set of questions is listed in a compact form together, all questions sharing the same set of answer categories. (179)

Maturation: A threat to *internal validity* in *experimental research* due to natural processes of growth, boredom, and so on that occur to *subjects* during the experiment and affect the *dependent variable*. (207)

Mean: A measure of central tendency for one *variable* that indicates the arithmetic average (i.e., the sum of all scores divided by the total number of scores). (242)

Measure of association: A single number that expresses the strength, and often the direction, of a relationship. It condenses information about a bivariate relationship into a single number. (252)

Measurement validity: How well an empirical indicator and the *conceptual definition* of the concept that the indicator is supposed to measure "fit" together. (115)

Median: A measure of central tendency for one *variable* indicating the point or score at which half the cases are higher and half are lower. (242)

Member checking: A way of establishing the *trustworthiness* criterion of *credibility*, where members of the study group are consulted about whether they agree with the researcher's conclusions and interpretations. (300)

Mesosocial theory: Social theories and explanations about the middle level of social reality between a broad and narrow scope, such as the development and operation of social organizations, communities, or social movements over a five-year period. (25)

Meta-analysis: A quantitative overview of existing evidence on a particular topic. (69)

Methodology: A collection of data collection and analysis approaches that are linked together through an overarching theoretical orientation. (283)

Microsocial theory: Social theories and explanations about the concrete, small-scale, and narrow level of reality, such as face-to-face interaction in small groups during a two-month period. (25)

Middle-range theory: A theory that focuses on specific aspects of social life and sociological topics that can be tested with empirical hypotheses. (26)

Mixed methods: In general, when more than one research method is used to address a research question. Also often refers specifically to when qualitative and quantitative methods are used together in a single project. (347)

Mixed methods sampling: Refers to the sampling decisions that must be made at the qualitative and quantitative portions of a *mixed methods* study. (360)

Mode: A measure of central tendency for one *variable* that indicates the most frequent or common score. (242)

Mode of delivery: In *survey research*, this refers to how the data were collected (e.g., by postal survey, telephone interview, in-person interview, or over the internet). (170)

Moderator: Refers to a trained facilitator used in *focus group* research who guides the focus group discussion. (274)

Monostrand design: A research design using a single research method. The opposite of *mixed methods* design. (356)

Mortality: Threats to *internal validity* due to *subjects* failing to participate through the entire experiment. (207)

Multi-method research: An approach of using more than one quantitative method or more than one qualitative method in a single research project. (356)

Multimodal: A distribution with more than one *mode*. (242)

Multiple indicators: Many procedures or instruments that indicate or provide evidence of the presence or level of a variable using *empirical evidence*. Researchers use the combination of several indicators together to measure a variable. (114)

Mutually exclusive attributes: The principle that response categories in a *scale* or other measure should be organized so that a person's responses fit into only one category (i.e., categories should not overlap). (122)

Narrative history: A type of writing about a historical setting in which the writer attempts to "tell a story" by following chronological order, describing particular people and events, and focusing on many colourful details. (318)

Natural experiment: A specific type of *quasi-experiment* where a researcher can examine the impact of a policy change or similar change in a social system by comparing an outcome of interest before and after such a change is implemented. (211)

Naturalism: The principle that researchers should examine events as they occur in natural, everyday, ongoing social settings. (284)

Negative case analysis: A way of establishing the *trustworthiness* criterion of *credibility* where the researcher closely examines cases that deviate from the dominant pattern. (301)

Negative relationship: An *association* between two variables such that as values on one variable increase, values on the other variable fall or decrease. (39)

Nominal measures: The lowest, least precise *level of measurement* for which there is only a difference in type among the categories of a variable. (120)

Nomothetic: An approach based on laws or one that operates according to a system of laws. (30)

Nonlinear research path: Research that proceeds in a circular, back-and-forth manner. It is more characteristic of a qualitative than a quantitative style to social research. (81)

Nonrandom sample: A type of *sample* in which the *sampling elements* are selected using something other than a mathematically random process. (134)

Nonreactive: Measures in which people being studied are unaware that they are in a study. (216)

Normal distribution: A "bell-shaped" frequency polygon for a distribution of cases, with a peak in the centre and identical curving slopes on either side of the centre. It is the distribution of many naturally occurring phenomena and is the basis for much statistical theory. (242)

Normalize social research: Techniques in *field research* used by researchers to make the people being studied feel more comfortable with the research process and to help them accept the researcher's presence. (293)

Null hypothesis: A *hypothesis* that says there is no relationship or *association* between two variables, or no effect. (90)

One-shot case study: An *experimental design* with only an *experimental group* and a *post-test*, no *pretest*. (201)

Ontology: A branch of philosophy that considers the way we understand the nature of reality. (28)

Open coding: A first *coding* of *qualitative data* in which a researcher examines the data to condense them into preliminary analytic categories or codes for analyzing the data. (331)

Open-ended question: A type of *survey research* question in which respondents are free to offer any answer they wish to the question. (171)

Operational definition: The definition of a variable in terms of the specific activities to measure or indicate it with *empirical evidence*. (109)

Operationalization: The process of moving from the *conceptual definition* of a *concept* to a set of specific activities or measures that allow a researcher to observe it empirically (i.e., its *operational definition*). (109)

Oral history: A type of *recollection* in which a researcher interviews a person about the events, beliefs, or feelings in the past that were directly experienced. (315)

Order effects: An effect in *survey research* in which respondents hear some specific questions before others and the earlier questions affect their answers to later questions. (177)

Ordinal measures: A *level of measurement* that identifies a difference among categories of a variable and allows the categories to be rank ordered. (120)

Overgeneralization: An error that people often make when using personal experience as an alternative to science for acquiring knowledge. It occurs when some evidence supports a belief, but a person falsely assumes that it applies to many other situations, too. (6)

Overt observer: In *field research*, refers to a researcher who is studying the group members with their full knowledge. (289)

Panel study: A powerful type of *longitudinal research* in which a researcher observes exactly the same people, group, or organization across multiple time points. (17)

Paradigm: A general organizing framework for *social theory* and empirical research. It includes basic *assumptions*, major questions to be answered, models of good research practice and theory, and methods for finding the answers to questions. (28)

Parameter: A characteristic of the entire *population* that is estimated from a *sample*. (140)

Partially open question: A type of *survey research* question in which respondents are given a fixed set of answers to choose from, but in addition an "other" category is offered so that they can specify a different answer. (173)

Partials: In *contingency tables* for three variables, tables that show the *association* between the *independent* and *dependent variables* for each category of a *control variable*. (255)

Participatory action research: An approach to research that removes the researcher from the centre of power and involves community members and research participants in the design, implementation, and interpretation of the research process. (301)

Percentile: A measure of dispersion for one *variable* that indicates the percentage of cases at or below a score or point. (244)

Pie chart: A display of numerical information on one *variable* that divides a circle into fractions by lines representing the proportion of cases in the variable's *attributes*. (242)

Placebo: A false *treatment* or one that has no effect in an experiment. It is sometimes called a "sugar pill" that a *subject* mistakes for a true *treatment*. (209)

Plagiarism: A type of unethical behaviour in which one uses the writings or ideas of another without giving proper credit. It is "stealing ideas." (44)

Population: The name for the large general group of many cases from which a researcher draws a *sample* and which is usually stated in theoretical terms. (138)

Positive relationship: An *association* between two variables such that as values on one increase, values on the other also increase. (39)

Positivism: The philosophical orientation that the social world should be studied in a similar manner to the natural world. (28)

Possible code cleaning: Cleaning data using a computer in which the researcher looks for responses or answer categories that cannot have cases. (240)

Post-test: The measurement of the *dependent variable* in *experimental research* after the *treatment*. (199)

Precision: The amount of spread in the points on the graph. A high level of precision occurs when the points hug the line that summarizes the relationship. A low level occurs when the points are widely spread around the line. (249)

Prediction: A statement about something that is likely to occur in the future. (35)

Predictive validity: *Measurement validity* that relies on the occurrence of a future event or behaviour that is logically consistent to verify the indicator of a concept. (116)

Pre-experimental designs: *Experimental designs* that lack *random assignment* or use shortcuts and are much weaker than the *classical experimental design*. They may be substituted in situations where an experimenter cannot use all the features of a *classical experimental design*, but they have weaker *internal validity*. (201)

Premature closure: An error that is often made when using personal experience as an alternative to science for acquiring knowledge. It occurs when a person feels he or she has the answers and does not need to listen, seek information, or raise questions any longer. (6)

Prestige bias: A problem in *survey research* question writing that occurs when a highly respected group or individual is linked to one of the answers. (165)

Pretest: The measurement of the *dependent variable* of an experiment prior to the *treatment*. (199)

Primary sources: *Qualitative data* or *quantitative data* used in *historical research*. It is evidence about past social life or events that was created and used by the individuals who actually lived in the historical period. (315)

Principle of voluntary consent: An ethical principle of social research that people should never participate in research unless they first explicitly agree to do so. (49)

Priority: In *mixed methods* research, refers to when a researcher has a preference for a quantitative or qualitative method to be considered the primary technique, with others used as supplementary methods. (358)

Probability proportionate to size (PPS): An adjustment made in *cluster sampling* when each cluster does not have the same number of *sampling elements*. (154)

Probe: A follow-up question or action in *survey research* used by an interviewer to have a respondent clarify or elaborate on an incomplete or inappropriate answer. (186)

Probing questions: In *qualitative interviews*, refers to types of questions used by an interviewer to expand on incomplete points an interviewee has raised. (270)

Prolonged engagement: When a researcher remains in the field long enough to make informed conclusions about what he or she is studying. Also used so the researcher can be exposed to a variety of different settings and develop a rapport with members of the study group. (301)

Pseudosurvey: When someone who has little or no real interest in learning information from a respondent uses the survey format to try to persuade someone to do something. (189)

Purposive sampling: A type of *nonrandom sample* in which the researcher uses a wide range of methods to locate all possible cases of a highly specific and difficult-to-reach *population*. (136)

Qualitative content analysis: An approach to analyzing text that involves the coding of themes, their patterns, and linkages. (322)

Qualitative data: Information in the form of words, pictures, sounds, visual images, or objects. (7)

Qualitative interview: A one-on-one interview between a researcher and an interviewee that is usually characterized by being semi-structured and open ended. (19)

Quantitative data: Information in the form of numbers. (7)

Quasi-experimental designs: *Experimental designs* that are stronger than *pre-experimental designs*. They are variations on the *classical experimental design* that an experimenter uses in special situations or when an experimenter has limited control over the *independent variable*. (202)

Quasi-filter question: A type of *survey research* question including the answer choice "no opinion" or "don't know." (174)

Quota sampling: A type of *nonrandom sample* in which the researcher first identifies general categories into which cases or people will be selected, then he or she selects a predetermined number of cases in each category. (135)

Random assignment: Dividing subjects into groups at the beginning of *experimental research* using a random process, so the experimenter can treat the groups as equivalent. (195)

Random-digit dialing (RDD): A method of randomly selecting cases for telephone interviews that uses all possible telephone numbers as a *sampling frame*. (154)

Random-number table: A list of numbers that has no pattern in it and that is used to create a random process for selecting cases and other randomization purposes. (142)

Random sample: A type of *sample* in which the researcher uses a *random-number table* or similar mathematical random process so that each *sampling element* in the *population* will have an equal probability of being selected. (141)

Range: A measure of dispersion for one *variable* indicating the highest and lowest scores. (244)

Ratio measures: The highest, most precise *level of measurement* for which variable *attributes* can be rank ordered, the distance between the *attributes* precisely measured, and an absolute zero exists. (121)

Reactivity: The general threat to *external validity* that arises because *subjects* are aware that they are in an experiment and being studied. (210)

Recollections: The words or writings of people about their life experiences after some time has passed. The writings are based on a memory of the past, but may be stimulated by a review of past objects, photos, personal notes, or belongings. (315)

Recording sheet: A page on which a researcher writes down what is coded in *content analysis*. (225)

Reductionism: Something that appears to be a *causal explanation* but is not, because of confusion about *units of analysis*. A researcher has *empirical evidence* for an *association* at the level of individual behaviour or very small-scale units, but *overgeneralizes* to make theoretical statements about very large-scale units. (93)

Reflexivity: A technique for establishing *confirmability* in qualitative research where the researcher is self-aware of his or her influence and potential bias. (302)

Reliability: The dependability or consistency of the measure of a *variable*. (113)

Replication: The principle that researchers must be able to repeat scientific findings in multiple studies to have a high level of confidence that the findings are true. (29)

Research fatigue: The perception by a community that has been extensively researched that they have experienced no measurable gains from participating in the research and is therefore uninterested in further participation. (53)

Research fraud: A type of unethical behaviour in which a researcher fakes or invents data that he or she did not really collect or fails to honestly and fully report how he or she conducted a study. (44)

Response set: An effect in *survey research* when respondents tend to agree with every question in a series rather than thinking through their answer to each question. (174)

Running records: A special type of *existing statistics research* used in *historical research* because the files, records, or documents are maintained in a relatively consistent manner over a period of time. (315)

Sample: A smaller set of cases a researcher selects from a larger pool and generalizes to the *population*. (133)

Sampling distribution: A distribution created by drawing many *random samples* from the same *population*. (143)

Sampling distribution of sample means: A distribution of sample means created by drawing many *random samples* from the same *population*. (146)

Sampling element: The name for a case or single unit to be selected. (138)

Sampling error: How much a *sample* deviates from being representative of the *population*. (141)

Sampling frame: A list of cases in a *population*, or the best approximation of it. (139)

Sampling interval: The inverse of the *sampling ratio*, which is used in *systematic sampling* to select cases. The sampling interval (i.e., 1 in k, where k is some number) tells the researcher how to select elements from a *sampling frame* by skipping elements in the frame before selecting one for the sample. (147)

Sampling ratio: The number of cases in the *sample* divided by the number of cases in the *population* or the *sampling frame*, or the proportion of the *population* in the *sample*. (139)

Scale: A type of *quantitative data* measure often used in *survey research* that captures the intensity, direction, level, or potency of a variable construct along a continuum. Most are at the *ordinal level* of measurement. (126)

Scattergram: A diagram to display the statistical relationship between two *variables* based on plotting each case's values for both of the variables. (247)

Science of the sophomore: A term used to refer to the potentially limited *external validity* of studies based on undergraduate samples, usually using the experimental method. (197)

Scientific community: A collection of people who share a system of rules and attitudes that sustain the process of producing scientific knowledge. (7)

Scientific method: The process of creating new knowledge using the ideas, techniques, and rules of the *scientific community*. (8)

Scientific misconduct: When someone engages in *research fraud*, *plagiarism*, or other unethical conduct that significantly deviates from the accepted practice for conducting and reporting research within the *scientific community*. (43)

Secondary sources: *Qualitative data* and *quantitative data* used in *historical research*, where information about events or settings is documented or written later by historians or others who did not directly participate in the events or setting. (315)

Selection bias: A threat to *internal validity* when groups in an experiment are not equivalent at the beginning of the experiment. (206)

Selective coding: A last pass at *coding qualitative data* in which a researcher examines previous codes to identify a core theme around which the remaining codes will fit. (335)

Selective observation: The tendency to take notice of certain people or events based on past experience or attitudes. (6)

Selective transcription: A transcription technique in *qualitative interviews* where only the parts of interviews that the researcher deems most relevant are transcribed. (268)

Semantic differential: A *scale* in which people are presented with a topic or object and a list of many polar opposite adjectives or adverbs. They are to indicate their feelings by marking one of several spaces between two adjectives or adverbs. (130)

Semi-participant: Refers to the role of the researcher in *field research* when he or she participates to some degree in group activities, but not as much as a full member. (288)

Sequence: In *mixed methods* research, refers to the order in which a researcher prefers to carry out analysis on data. (359)

Sequential data analysis: Refers to when the first part of a *mixed methods* project is analyzed prior to the next stage of the study. (360)

Sequential data collection: Refers to when data for different parts of a *mixed methods* project are collected in stages (i.e., not at the same time). (359)

Sequential sampling: A type of *nonrandom sample* in which a researcher tries to find as many relevant cases as possible until there is no new information or diversity from the cases. (138)

Silence: In *qualitative interviews*, a technique used by researchers (not saying anything) to get interviewees to continue speaking. (271)

Simple random sampling: A type of *random sample* in which a researcher creates a *sampling frame* and uses a pure random process to select cases. Each *sampling element* in the *population* will have an equal probability of being selected. (141)

Simpson's paradox: An error in explanation where apparent differences between groups tend to reverse or disappear when groups are combined. (96)

Skewed distribution: A distribution of cases among the categories of a variable that is not *normal* (i.e., not a "bell shape"). Instead of an equal number of cases on both ends, more are at one of the extremes. (242)

Snowball sampling: A type of *nonrandom sample* in which the researcher begins with one case then, based on information about interrelationships from that case, identifies other cases, and then repeats the process again and again. (137)

Social desirability bias: A bias in *survey research* in which respondents give a "normative" response or a socially acceptable answer rather than giving a truthful answer. (170)

Social impact assessment (SIA): A type of *applied social research* in which a researcher estimates the likely consequences or outcome of a planned intervention or intentional change to occur in the future. (12)

Social research: A process in which a researcher combines a set of principles, outlooks, and ideas with a collection of specific practices, techniques, and strategies to produce knowledge. (2)

Social theory: A system of interconnected abstractions or ideas that condenses and organizes knowledge about the social world. (24)

Sociogram: A diagram or "map" that shows the network of social relationships, influence patterns, or communication paths among a group of people or units. (137)

Solomon four-group design: An *experimental design* in which *subjects* are randomly assigned to two *control groups* and two *experimental groups*. Only one *experimental group* and one *control group* receive a *pretest*. All four groups receive a *post-test*. (203)

Special populations: People who lack the necessary cognitive competency to give real *informed consent*, people in a weak position who might compromise their freedom to refuse to participate in a study, or groups who have been historically exploited and oppressed. (52)

Specifying questions: In *qualitative interviews*, questions that the researcher asks to get more detailed descriptions about specific aspects of the interviewee's descriptions. (271)

Spuriousness: A statement that appears to be a *causal explanation* but is not, because of a hidden, unmeasured, or initially unseen variable. The unseen variable comes earlier in the temporal order, and it has a causal impact on what was initially posited to be the *independent variable* as well as the *dependent variable*. (95)

Standard deviation: A measure of dispersion for one *variable* that indicates an average distance between the scores and the *mean*. (244)

Standard-format question: A type of *survey research* question in which the answer categories fail to include "no opinion" or "don't know." (173)

Standardization: The procedure to statistically adjust measures to permit making an honest comparison by giving a common basis to measures of different units. (125)

Static group comparison: An *experimental design* with two groups, no *random assignment*, and only a *post-test*. (201)

Statistic: A numerical estimate of a *population parameter* computed from a *sample*. (140)

Statistical regression: A problem of extreme values or a tendency for random errors to move group results toward the average. (207)

Statistical significance: A way to discuss the likelihood that a finding or statistical relationship in a *sample* is due to random factors rather than due to the existence of an actual relationship in the entire *population*. (257)

Statistical validity: This is achieved when an appropriate statistical procedure is selected and the assumptions of the procedure are fully met. (119)

Stratified sampling: A type of *random sample* in which the researcher first identifies a set of *mutually exclusive* and *exhaustive* categories, then uses a random selection method to select cases for each category. (150)

Structure: Refers to aspects of the social landscape that appear to limit or influence the choices made by individuals. (28)

Structured observation: A method of watching what is happening in a social setting that is highly organized and that follows systematic rules for observation and documentation. (220)

Structuring questions: Questions used in *qualitative interviews* to keep the interview on track if it has gone off topic or to keep the interview moving along. (271)

Subjects: In *experimental research*, the cases or people used in research projects and on whom *variables* are measured. (198)

Successive approximation: A method of *qualitative data* analysis in which the researcher repeatedly moves back and forth between the empirical data and the abstract concepts, theories, or models. (341)

Summative content analysis: A type of *qualitative content analysis* that uses both *manifest* and *latent codes* and is most closely related to *quantitative content analysis*. (322)

Survey research: A quantitative social research technique in which one systematically asks many people the same questions, then records and analyzes their answers. (19)

Systematic sampling: A type of *random sample* in which a researcher selects every *k*th (e.g., 12th) case in the *sampling frame* using a *sampling interval*. (147)

Target population: The name for the large general group of many cases from which a *sample* is drawn and which is specified in very concrete terms. (139)

Tautology: An error in explanation that rests on circular reasoning. (98)

Temporal order: In establishing causation, the cause must come before the effect. (36)

Teleology: An error in explanation that relies on the fulfillment of an ultimate purpose. (98)

Testing effect: A *pretest* measure that itself affects an experiment. This testing effect threatens *internal validity* because more than the *treatment* alone affects the *dependent variable*. (207)

Text: A general name for symbolic meaning within a communication medium measured in *content analysis*. (218)

Theoretical sampling: An iterative sampling technique associated with the *grounded theory* approach in which the sample size is determined when the data reach *theoretical saturation*. (138)

Theoretical saturation: A term associated with the *grounded theory* approach that refers to the point at which no new themes emerge from the data and sampling is considered complete. (138)

Thick description: Used to establish the *transferability* of a qualitative study through the detailed notes of a researcher. (302)

Threatening questions: A type of *survey research* question in which respondents are likely to cover up or lie about their true behaviour or beliefs because they fear a loss of self-image or that they may appear to be engaging in undesirable or deviant behaviour. (168)

Time-series study: Any research that takes place over time, in which different people or cases may be looked at in each time period. (17)

Transferability: The component of establishing *trustworthiness* in qualitative research that is concerned with how generalizable the findings are. (302)

Treatment: What the *independent variable* in *experimental research* is called. (198)

Triangulation: A general term that refers to *mixed methods* research. (346)

Trustworthiness: An alternative set of criteria by which to assess the *validity* and *reliability* of qualitative research. (302)

Type I error: The logical error of falsely rejecting the *null hypothesis*. (258)

Type II error: The logical error of falsely accepting the *null hypothesis*. (258)

Unidimensionality: The principle that when using *multiple indicators* to measure a construct, all the indicators should consistently fit together and indicate a single construct. (123)

Unit of analysis: The kind of empirical case or unit that a researcher observes, measures, and analyzes in a study. (91)

Univariate statistics: Statistical measures that deal with one *variable* only. (240)

Unobtrusive measures: Another name for *nonreactive measures*. It emphasizes that the people being studied are not aware of it because the measures do not intrude. (217)

Validity: A term meaning "truth" that can be applied to the logical tightness of *experimental design*, the ability to generalize findings outside a study, the quality of measurement, and the proper use of procedures. (113)

Variable: A concept or its *empirical* measure that can take on multiple values. (86)

***Verstehen*:** A German word that translates as "understanding"; specifically, it means an empathic understanding of another's worldview. (31)

Whistle-blower: A person who sees ethical wrongdoing, tries unsuccessfully to correct it internally, and then informs an external audience, agency, or the media. (58)

Wording effect: An effect that occurs when a specific term or word used in a *survey research* question affects how respondents answer the question. (175)

***z*-score:** A way to locate a score in a distribution of scores by determining the number of *standard deviations* it is above or below the *mean* or arithmetic average. (245)

Endnotes

Chapter 1

1. See Rampton and Stauber (2001, pp. 247–277, 305–306).
2. See Best (2001, p. 15) on advocates and media.
3. An Ipsos-Reid (Canada) poll of Canadians conducted in 2006 revealed a wide range of beliefs that Canadians had about the paranormal. The study results can be accessed on the Ipsos Reid website: www.ipsos.ca.
4. Schacter (2001) provides a summary of memory issues.
5. See Harvey and Lui (2003) for a detailed discussion of how the data were reanalyzed.
6. Beck (1995) provides a useful overview.
7. See Statistics Canada (2007), *Perspectives on Labour and Income: Gambling*.
8. See Statistics Canada (2006), *The Daily*.

Chapter 2

1. For more detailed discussions of concepts, see Chafetz (1978, pp. 45–61), Hage (1972, pp. 9–85), Kaplan (1964, pp. 34–80), Mullins (1971, pp. 7–18), Reynolds (1971), and Stinchcombe (1968, 1973).
2. Introductions to alternative theoretical frameworks and social theories are provided in Craib (1984), Phillips (1985, pp. 44–59), and Skidmore (1979).

Chapter 3

1. For a discussion of research fraud, see Broad and Wade (1982), Diener and Crandall (1978), and Weinstein (1979). Hearnshaw (1979) and Wade (1976) discuss the Cyril Burt case. Kusserow (1989) discusses the concept of scientific misconduct.
2. See Tibbetts (2006) and Armstrong (2006) for news coverage of this event.
3. See Blum (1989) and D'Antonio (1989) for details on this case. Also see Goldner (1998) on legal versus scientific views of misconduct. Gibelman (2001) discusses several cases and the changing definition of misconduct.
4. See Lifton (1986) for information on Nazi experiments, and Williams and Wallace (1989) discuss Japanese experiments. Harris (2002) argues that the Japanese experiments were more horrific, but the United States did not prosecute the Japanese scientists as they did the Germans because the U.S. military wanted the results to develop its own biological warfare program.
5. See Jones (1981) and Mitchell (1997) on bad blood.
6. Diener and Crandall (1978, p. 128) discuss examples.
7. A discussion of physical harm to research participants can be found in Kelman (1982), Reynolds (1979, 1982), and Warwick (1982).
8. For a discussion, see Diener and Crandall (1978, pp. 21–22) and Kidder and Judd (1986, pp. 481–484).
9. Information on the Statistics Act can be found on the Statistics Canada website: www.statcan.gc.ca/about-apercu/act-loi-eng.htm
10. Newer censuses (i.e., 2006 and on) obtain consent from the respondents to use their data after 92 years if the respondent agrees to this. The Statistics Canada website has additional information on Historical Access to Census Records: http://www12.statcan.gc.ca/census-recensement/2011/ref/about-apropos/personal-personnels-eng.cfm
11. See Lowman and Palys (2000) for further discussion of the Ogden case.
12. See Todd, 2008. http://communities.canada.com/vancouversun/blogs/thesearch/archive/2008/07/03/noted-assisted-suicide-researcher-runs-into-barrier.aspx
13. See Olivieri (2003) for a discussion.
14. See McIlroy (2001).
15. See Adler and Adler (1993).

Chapter 4

1. See Neylon (2012).

Chapter 5

1. For a discussion of the "logic of the disconfirming hypothesis," see Singleton Straits, Straits, and McAllister (1988, pp. 456–460).
2. See Kottak (2003) for a discussion of the definition of race.
3. See Pope (2007) for a news report on the Church of the Flying Spaghetti Monster.

Chapter 6

1. See the Statistics Canada website for more information on the LICO: www.statcan.gc.ca
2. See Rose and Pevalin (2002) for a discussion of the different ways of measuring social class in the United Kingdom.
3. For an example of the use of the feeling thermometer in recent Canadian political science research, see Clarke, Kornberg, Ellis, and Rapkin (2000).
4. Cronbach's alpha is a statistic that reports on the inter-item reliability of several measures at once. It ranges from 0 to 1, with values closer to 1 indicating better internal reliability.

Chapter 8

1. Sudman and Bradburn (1983, p. 39) suggested that even simple questions (e.g., "What brand of soft drink do you usually buy?") can cause problems. Respondents who are highly loyal to one brand of traditional carbonated sodas can answer the question easily. Other respondents must implicitly address the following questions to answer the question as it was asked: (a) What time period is involved—the past month, the past year, the past 10 years? (b) What conditions count—at home, at restaurants, at sporting events? (c) Does this refer to buying for oneself alone or for other family members? (d) What is a "soft drink"? Do lemonade, iced tea, mineral water, or fruit juices count? (e) Does "usually" mean a brand purchased as 51 percent or more of all soft drink purchases, or the brand purchased more frequently than any other? Respondents rarely stop and ask for clarification; they make assumptions about what the researcher means.
2. See Dykema and Schaeffer (2000) and Sudman, Bradburn, and Schwarz (1996, pp. 197–226).
3. See Ostrom and Gannon (1996).
4. See Bradburn (1983), Bradburn and Sudman (1980), and Sudman and Bradburn (1983) on threatening or sensitive questions. Backstrom and Hursh-Cesar (1981, p. 219) and Warwick and Lininger (1975, pp. 150–151) provide useful suggestions as well.
5. For more on how the question "Who knows who lives here?" can be complicated, see Martin (1999) and Tourangeau et al. (1997).
6. The questionnaire from the Canadian Campus Survey can be downloaded from the CAMH website at www.camh.ca/en/research/research_areas/community_and_population_health/Documents/CCS_2004_report.pdf.
7. For a discussion of the "don't know," "no opinion," and middle positions in response categories see Backstrom and Hursh-Cesar (1981, pp. 148–149), Bishop (1987), Bradburn and Sudman (1988, p. 154), Brody (1986), Converse and Presser (1986, pp. 35–37), Duncan and Stenbeck (1988), and Sudman and Bradburn (1983, pp. 140–141).

8. The disagree/agree versus specific alternatives debate can be found in Sudman and Bradburn (1983, pp. 149–151), Converse and Presser (1986, pp. 38–39), and Schuman and Presser (1981, pp. 179–223).
9. The ranking versus ratings issue is discussed in Alwin and Krosnick (1985) and Krosnick and Alwin (1988). Also see Backstrom and Hursh-Cesar (1981, pp. 132–134) and Sudman and Bradburn (1983, pp. 156–165) for formats of asking rating and ranking questions.
10. See Todd (2010).
11. See Bibby (2010).
12. See Foddy (1993) and Presser (1990).
13. Studies by Krosnick (1992) and Narayan and Krosnick (1996) show that education reduces response-order (primacy or recency) effects, but Knäuper (1999) found that age is strongly associated with response-order effects.
14. This example comes from Strack (1992).
15. For a discussion, see Couper, Singer, et al. (1998), de Heer (1999), Keeter et al. (2000), Sudman and Bradburn (1983, p. 11), and Rothenberg (1990). T. Smith (1995) and Sudman (1976, pp. 114–116) also discuss refusal rates.
16. Bailey (1987, pp. 153–168), Church (1993), Dillman (1978, 1983), Fox, Crask, and Kim (1988), Goyder (1982), Hubbard and Little (1988), Jones (1979), and Willimack, Schuman, Pennell, and Lepkowski (1995) discuss increasing return rates in surveys.
17. For a comparison among types of surveys, see Backstrom and Hursh-Cesar (1981, pp. 16–23), Bradburn and Sudman (1988, pp. 94–110), Dillman (1978, pp. 39–78), and Frey (1983, pp. 27–55).
18. For more on survey research interviewing, see Brenner, Brown, and Canter (1985), Cannell and Kahn (1968), Converse and Schuman (1974), Dijkstra and van der Zouwen (1982), Foddy (1993), Gorden (1980), Hyman (1975), and Moser and Kalton (1972, pp. 270–302).
19. See Turner and Martin (1984, pp. 262–269, 282).
20. From Moser and Kalton (1972, p. 273).
21. The use of probes is discussed in Backstrom and Hursh-Cesar (1981, pp. 266–273), Gorden (1980, pp. 368–390), and Hyman (1975, pp. 236–241).
22. See Bradburn and Sudman (1980), Pollner and Adams (1997), and Zane and Matsoukas (1979).
23. The race or ethnicity of interviewers is discussed in Anderson, Silver, and Abramson (1988), Bradburn (1983), Cotter, Cohen, and Coulter (1982), Davis (1997), Finkel, Guterbock, and Borg (1991), Gorden (1980, pp. 168–172), Reese, Danielson, Shoemaker, Chang, and Hsu (1986), Schaffer (1980), Schuman and Converse (1971), and Weeks and Moore (1981).
24. See Catania and associates (1996) and Kane and MacAulay (1993).
25. CATI is discussed in Bailey (1987, pp. 201–202), Bradburn and Sudman (1988, pp. 100–101), Frey (1983, pp. 24–25, 143–149), Groves and Kahn (1979, p. 226), Groves and Mathiowetz (1984), and Karweit and Meyers (1983).
26. See Cheadle (2013).
27. On reporting survey results in the media, see Channels (1993) and MacKeun (1984).
28. See Singer (1988).
29. According to www.cbc.radio-canada.ca/accountability/journalistic/surveys.shtml, "To ensure the validity and reliability of their results, surveys of public opinion must be conducted according to tested methods and recognized standards. Any departure from methods or standards and other relevant information on the techniques or funding of such research should be known to the public."
30. From Turner and Martin (1984, p. 62).

Chapter 9

1. For additional discussions of threats to internal validity, see Cook and Campbell (1979, pp. 51–68), Kercher (1992), Smith and Glass (1987), Spector (1981, pp. 24–27), and Suls and Rosnow (1988).
2. This example is borrowed from Mitchell and Jolley (1988, p. 97).
3. Experimenter expectancy is discussed in Aronson and Carlsmith (1968, pp. 66–70), Dooley (1984, pp. 151–153), and Mitchell and Jolley (1988, pp. 327–329).
4. The Hawthorne effect is described in Roethlisberger and Dickenson (1939), Franke and Kaul (1978), and Lang (1992). Also see the discussion in Cook and Campbell (1979, pp. 123–125) and Dooley (1984, pp. 155–156). Gillespie (1988, 1991) discusses the political context of the experiments.
5. See Piliavin, Rodin, & Piliavin (1969).

Chapter 10

1. For definitions of content analysis, see Holsti (1968, p. 597), Krippendorff (1980, pp. 21–24), Markoff, Shapiro, and Weitman (1974, pp. 5–6), Stone and Weber (1992), and Weber (1983, 1984, 1985, p. 81, note 1).
2. Weitzman, Eifler, Hokada, and Ross (1972) provides a classic example of this type of research.
3. Stone and Weber (1992) and Weber (1984, 1985) summarize computerized content analysis techniques.
4. See Andren (1981, pp. 58–66) for a discussion of reliability. Coding categorization in content analysis is discussed in Holsti (1969, pp. 94–126).
5. See Perrott (2002), Canadian Press (2003), Australian Bureau of Statistics (2001), and Office of National Statistics (2001).
6. A discussion of social indicators can be found in Carley (1981). Also see Bauer (1966), Duncan (1984, pp. 233–235), Juster and Land (1981), Land (1992), and Rossi and Gilmartin (1980).
7. Many non-English yearbooks are also produced; for example, *Statistisches Jahrbuch* for Germany, *Annuaire statistique de la France* for France, and Denmark's *Statistisk Ti Arsoversigt*. Japan produces an English version of its yearbook, called the *Statistical Handbook of Japan*.
8. Guides exist for the publications of various governments—for example, the Guide to British Government Publications, Australian Official Publications, and Irish Official Publications. Similar publications exist for most nations.
9. See Churchill (1983, pp. 140–167) and Stewart (1984) for lists of business information sources.
10. Other major U.S. archives of survey data include the National Opinion Research Center, University of Chicago; the Survey Research Center, University of California–Berkeley; the Behavioral Sciences Laboratory, University of Cincinnati; Data and Program Library Service, University of Wisconsin–Madison; the Roper Center, University of Connecticut–Storrs; and the Institute for Research in Social Science, University of North Carolina–Chapel Hill. Also see Kiecolt and Nathan (1985) and Parcel (1992).
11. See SSHRC and Statistics Canada (2002).
12. For a discussion of these issues, see Dale, Arber, and Procter (1988, pp. 27–31), Maier (1991), and Parcel (1992). Horn (1993, p. 138) gives a good discussion with examples of the fallacy of misplaced concreteness.
13. You can find out more about the Violence Against Women Survey on Health Canada's website at www.hc-sc.gc.ca/hl-vs/pubs/women-femmes/violence_e.html.
14. See *The Economist*, "The Good Statistics Guide" (September 11, 1993), "The Overlooked Housekeeper" (February 5, 1994), and "Fewer Damned Lies?" (March 30, 1996).
15. See Block and Burns (1986), Carr-Hill (1984), Hindess (1973), Horn (1993), Maier (1991), and Van den Berg and Van der Veer (1985).

Chapter 11

1. Note that coding sex as 1 = Male, 2 = Female, or as 0 = Male, 1 = Female, or reversing the numbers for sex is arbitrary. The

only reason numbers are used instead of letters (e.g., M and F) is because many computer programs work best with numbers. Sometimes coding data as a zero can create confusion, so the number 1 is usually the lowest value.

2. There are other statistics to measure a special kind of mean for ordinal data and for other special situations, which are beyond the level of discussion in this book.
3. In formal hypothesis testing, researchers test the *null hypothesis*. They usually want to reject the null because rejection of the null indirectly supports the alternative hypothesis to the null, the one they deduced from theory as a tentative explanation.

Chapter 12

1. Field research informants are discussed in Dean, Eichhorn, and Dean (1969), Kemp and Ellen (1984), Schatzman and Strauss (1973), Spradley (1979a, pp. 46–54), and Whyte (1982).
2. For a discussion of focus groups, see Bischoping and Dykema (1999), Churchill (1983, pp. 179–184), Krueger (1988), Labaw (1980, pp. 54–58), and Morgan (1996).

Chapter 13

1. For studies of these sites or topics, see Neuman (2000, 2003). For studies of children or schools, see Corsaro (1994), Corsaro and Molinari (2000), Eder (1995), Eder and Kinney (1995), Kelle (2000), and Merten (1999). For studies of homeless people, see Lankenau (1999), and for studies of female exotic dancers, see Wood (2000).
2. Ethnography is described in Agar (1986), Franke (1983), Hammersley and Atkinson (1983), Sanday (1983), and Spradley (1979a, pp. 3–12; 1979b, pp. 3–16).
3. For a general discussion of field research and naturalism, see Adler and Adler (1994), Georges and Jones (1980), Holy (1984), and Pearsall (1970). For discussions of contrasting types of field research, see Clammer (1984), Gonor (1977), Holstein and Gubrium (1994), Morse (1994), Schwandt (1994), and Strauss and Corbin (1994).
4. See Lofland (1976, pp. 13–23) and Shaffir, Stebbins, and Turowetz (1980, pp. 18–20) on feeling marginal.
5. See Adler and Adler (1993).
6. See Hammersley and Atkinson (1983, pp. 42–45) and Lofland and Lofland (1995, pp. 16–30).
7. For more on gatekeepers and access, see Beck (1970, pp. 11–29) and Bogdan and Taylor (1975, pp. 30–32).
8. Negotiation in the field is discussed in Gans (1982), Johnson (1975, pp. 58–59, 76–77), and Schatzman and Strauss (1973, pp. 22–23).
9. See Douglas (1976), Emerson (1981, pp. 367–368), and Johnson (1975, pp. 124–129) on the question of whether the researcher should always be patient, polite, and considerate.
10. For more on ways to record and organize field data, see Bogdan and Taylor (1975, pp. 60–73), Hammersley and Atkinson (1983, pp. 144–173), and Kirk and Miller (1986, pp. 49–59).
11. See Lofland and Lofland (1995, pp. 26, 63, 75, 168–177), Miles and Huberman (1994, pp. 288–297), and Punch (1986).
12. Fetterman (1989) discusses the idea of guilty knowledge.

Chapter 14

1. See Mahoney (1999) for major works of historical–comparative research.
2. See Calhoun (1996), McDaniel (1978), Przeworski and Teune (1970), and Stinchcombe (1978) for additional discussion.
3. For additional discussion, see Sewell (1987).
4. See Lowenthal (1985, p. 187).
5. Bendix (1978, p. 16) distinguished between the *judgments* of historians and the *selections* of sociologists.
6. Bonnell (1980, p. 161), Finley (1977, p. 132), and Goldthorpe (1977, pp. 189–190) discuss how historians use concepts. Selection in this context is discussed by Abrams (1982, p. 194) and Ben-Yehuda (1983).
7. For introductions to how historians see their method, see Barzun and Graff (1970), Braudel (1980), Cantor and Schneider (1967), Novick (1988), or Shafer (1980).
8. The narrative is discussed in Abbott (1992), Gallie (1963), Gotham and Staples (1996), Griffin (1993), McLennan (1981, p. 76–87), Runciman (1980), and Stone (1987, pp. 74–96).
9. See Wesley (2009) for a fuller discussion of the differences between quantitative and qualitative content analysis.
10. See Gee (2005), Johnstone (2002), and Renkema (2004) for more detail on the different approaches to discourse analysis.
11. See Foucault (1973, 1979, 1990) and Foucault, Khalfa, and Murphy (2006).

Chapter 15

1. *Ideal type* is a typological term invented by German sociologist Max Weber (1864–1920).

Chapter 16

1. For information on Statistics Canada's Violence Against Women Survey from 1993, see http://www23.statcan.gc.ca/imdb/p2SV.pl?Function=getSurvey&SDDS=3896&lang=en&db=imdb&adm=8&dis=2.
2. See Tashakkori and Teddlie (2003).
3. The Canadian Election Study is a large-scale survey that collects data on why Canadians vote the way that they do and why some political parties are more successful than others. It is a collaborative project involving researchers from three universities, Montreal, Toronto, and McGill. For additional information on the study, see www.ces-eec.ca.
4. See Creswell and Plano Clark (2007).
5. See Creswell and Plano Clark (2007).
6. See Creswell and Plano Clark (2007).
7. See Creswell and Plano Clark (2007).
8. A detailed discussion of sampling in mixed methods can be found in Kemper, Stringfield, and Teddlie (2003).
9. See Deacon, Bryman, and Fenton (1998) for more discussion of epistemic prioritization and other inappropriate "fixes" (methodological purism) for contradictory mixed methods findings.
10. See Tashakkori and Teddlie (2003) for an in-depth discussion of the controversies surrounding the use of mixed methods in the social sciences.

References

Abbott, A. (1992). From causes to events. *Sociological Methods and Research, 20*, 428–455.

Abdelmutti, N., & Hoffman-Goetz. L. (2009). Risk messages about HPV, cervical cancer, and the HPV vaccine Gardasil: A content analysis of Canadian and U.S. national newspaper articles. *Women and Health, 49*, 422–440.

Abrams, P. (1982). *Historical sociology*. Ithaca, NY: Cornell University Press.

Adler, P. A., & Adler, P. (1993). Ethical issues in self-censorship. In C. Renzetti & R. Lee (Eds.), *Research on sensitive topics* (pp. 249–266). Thousand Oaks, CA: Sage.

Adler, P. A., & Adler, P. (1994). Observational techniques. In N. Denzin & Y. Lincoln (Eds.), *Handbook of qualitative research* (pp. 377–392). Thousand Oaks, CA: Sage.

Agar, M. (1986). *Speaking of ethnography*. Beverly Hills, CA: Sage.

Albanese, P. (2006). Small town, big benefits: The ripple effect of $7/day child care. *Canadian Review of Sociology and Anthropology, 43*, 125–140.

Alwin, D. F., & Krosnick, J. A. (1985). The measurement of values in surveys. *Public Opinion Quarterly, 49*, 535–552.

Anderson, B. A., Silver, B. D., & Abramson, P. R. (1988). The effects of the race of the interviewer on race-related attitudes of black respondents in SRC/CPS national election studies. *Public Opinion Quarterly, 52*, 289–324.

Andren, G. (1981). Reliability and content analysis. In K. Rosengren (Ed.), *Advances in content analysis* (pp. 43–67). Beverly Hills, CA: Sage.

Anisef, P., Brown, R., Phythian, K., Sweet, R., & Walters, D. (2010). Early school leaving among immigrants in Toronto secondary schools. *Canadian Review of Sociology, 47*(2), 103–128.

Armstrong, J. (2006, January 28). Falsely accused of abuse, woman wins case. *The Globe and Mail*, p. A5. Retrieved June 30, 2007, from Canadian Newsstand Major Dailies database (document ID: 1056339681).

Aronson, E., & Carlsmith, J. M. (1968). Experimentation in social psychology. In G. Lindzey & E. Aronson (Eds.), *The handbook of social psychology, Vol. 2: Research methods* (pp. 1–78). Reading, MA: Addison-Wesley.

Atkinson, M. (2004). Tattooing and civilizing processes: Body modification as self-control. *Canadian Review of Sociology and Anthropology, 41*, 125–146.

Atkinson, M. (2009). Parkour, anarcho-environmentalism, and poiesis. *Journal of Sport & Social Issues, 33*(2), 169–194.

Austin, P. C., Mamdani, M. M., Juurlink, D. N., & Hux, J. E. (2006). Testing multiple statistical hypotheses resulted in spurious associations: A study of astrological signs and health. *Journal of Clinical Epidemiology, 59*(9), 964–969.

Australian Bureau of Statistics. (2001, May 2). Census of population and housing—The 2001 Census, religion and the Jedi. Retrieved from www.abs.gov.au/websitedbs/d3110124.nsf/24e5997b9bf2ef35ca2567fb00299c59/86429d11c45d4e73ca256a400006af80!OpenDocument

Backstrom, C. H., & Hursh-Cesar, G. (1981). *Survey research* (2nd ed.). New York, NY: Wiley.

Bailey, K. D. (1987). *Methods of social research* (3rd ed.). New York, NY: Free Press.

Baron, S. W. (2006). Street youth, strain theory and crime. *Journal of Criminal Justice, 34*(2), 209–223.

Barzun, J., & Graff, H. F. (1970). *The modern researcher* (Rev. ed.). New York, NY: Harcourt, Brace and World.

Bashi, V. (2004). Globalized anti-blackness: Transnationalizing Western immigration law, policy, and practice. *Ethnic and Racial Studies, 27*, 584–606.

Bassili, J. N., & Krosnick, J. A. (2000). Do strength-related attitude properties determine susceptibility to response effects? New evidence from response latency, attitude extremity, and aggregate indices. *Political Psychology, 21*, 107–132.

Bauer, R. (Ed.). (1966). *Social indicators*. Cambridge, MA: MIT Press.

Beck, B. (1970). Cooking welfare stew. In R. W. Habenstein (Ed.), *Pathways to data* (pp. 7–29). Chicago, IL: Aldine.

Beck, R. A. (1995). Publishing evaluation research. *Contemporary Sociology, 24*, 9–12.

Ben-Yehuda, N. (1983). History, selection and randomness—towards an analysis of social historical explanations. *Quality and Quantity, 17*, 347–367.

Bendix, R. (1978). *Kings or people? Power and the mandate to rule*. Berkeley, CA: University of California Press.

Best, J. (2001). *Damned lies and statistics: Untangling numbers from the media, politicians, and activists*. Berkeley, CA: University of California Press.

Bibby, R. (2010, April 21). Flawed poll distorts scope of sexual abuse. *Edmonton Journal*. Retrieved from www.edmontonjournal.com/news/Flawed+poll+distorts+scope+sexual+abuse/2932895/sftory.html

Billig, M. (1997). Rhetorical and discursive analysis: How families talk about the royal family. In N. Hayes (Ed.), *Doing qualitative analysis in psychology* (pp. 39–54). Hove, UK: Psychology Press.

Bischoping, K., & Dykema, J. (1999). Toward a social psychological programme for improving focus group methods of developing questionnaires. *Journal of Official Statistics, 15*, 495–516.

Bishop, G. F. (1987). Experiments with the middle response alternative in survey questions. *Public Opinion Quarterly, 51*, 220–232.

Blishen, B. R. (1967). A socio-economic index of occupations in Canada. *Canadian Review of Sociology and Anthropology, 4*, 41–53.

Block, F., & Burns, G. A. (1986). Productivity as a social problem: The uses and misuses of social indicators. *American Sociological Review, 51*, 767–780.

Blum, D. E. (1989). Dean charged with plagiarizing a dissertation for his book on Muzak. *Chronicle of Higher Education, 35*, A17.

Bodner, T. E. (2006). Design, participants, and measurement methods in psychological research. *Canadian Psychology, 47*(4), 262–272.

Bogdan, R., & Taylor, S. J. (1975). *Introduction to qualitative research methods: A phenomenological approach to the social sciences*. New York, NY: Wiley.

Bond, C. F., Jr., & Anderson, E. L. (1987). The reluctance to transmit bad news: Private discomfort or public display? *Journal of Experimental Social Psychology, 23*, 176–187.

Bonnell, V. E. (1980). The uses of theory, concepts and comparison in historical sociology. *Comparative Studies in Society and History, 22*, 156–173.

Bos, N., Karahalios, K., Musgrove-Chavez, M., Poole, E., Thomas, J. C., & Yardi, S. (2009). Research ethics in the Facebook era: Privacy, anonymity, and oversight. *27th International Conference's Extended Abstracts on Human Factors in Computing*. ACM Conference on Human Factors in Computing Systems, New York, NY.

Bradburn, N. M. (1983). Response effects. In P. Rossi, J. Wright, & A. Anderson (Eds.), *Handbook of survey research* (pp. 289–328). Orlando, FL: Academic.

Bradburn, N. M., & Sudman, S. (1980). *Improving interview method and questionnaire design*. San Francisco, CA: Jossey-Bass.

Bradburn, N. M., & Sudman, S. (1988). *Polls and surveys*. San Francisco, CA: Jossey-Bass.

Brant Castellano, M. (2004). Ethics of Aboriginal research. *Journal of Aboriginal Health, 1*(1), 98–114.

Braudel, F. (1980). *On history*. (S. Matthews, Trans.). Chicago, IL: University of Chicago Press.

Brenner, M., Brown, J., & Canter, D. (Eds.). (1985). *The research interview: Uses and approaches*. Orlando, FL: Academic Press.

Broad, W. J., & Wade, N. (1982). *Betrayers of the truth*. New York, NY: Simon and Schuster.

Brody, C. J. (1986). Things are rarely black or white. *American Journal of Sociology, 92*, 657–677.

Calhoun, C. (1996). The rise and domestication of historical sociology. In T. J. McDonald (Ed.), *The historical turn in the human sciences* (pp. 305–337). Ann Arbor, MI: University of Michigan Press.

Canadian Institutes of Health Research, Natural Sciences and Engineering Research Council of Canada, & Social Sciences and Humanities Research Council of Canada. (2010). *Tri-Council Policy Statement: Ethical Conduct for Research Involving Humans*. www.ethics.gc.ca/pdf/eng/tcps2/TCPS_2_FINAL_Web.pdf

Canadian Press. (2003, May 13). Some 20,000 Canadians worship at the altar of Yoda. Retrieved from www.jedichurch.org/webapps/i/4448/5930/32311

Cannell, C. F., & Kahn, R. L. (1968). Interviewing. In G. Lindzey & E. Aronson (Eds.), *Handbook of social psychology* (2nd ed.). (Vol. 2). (pp. 526–595). Reading, MA: Addison-Wesley.

Canter, D., Brown, J., & Goat, L. (1985). Multiple sorting procedure for studying conceptual systems. In M. Brenner, J. Brown, & D. Canter (Eds.), *The research interview: Uses and approaches* (pp. 79–114). New York, NY: Academic Press.

Cantor, N. F., & Schneider, R. I. (1967). *How to study history*. New York, NY: Thomas Y. Crowell.

Carley, M. (1981). *Social measurement and social indicators*. London, UK: George Allen and Unwin.

Carr-Hill, R. A. (1984). The political choice of social indicators. *Quality and Quantity, 18*, 173–191.

Castleden, H., Garvin, T., & Huu-ay-aht First Nation. (2008). Modifying photovoice for community-based participatory indigenous research. *Social Science and Medicine, 66*(6), 1393–1405.

Catania, J., Dinson, D., Canahola, J., Pollack, L., Hauck, W., & Coates, T. (1996). Effects of interviewer gender, interviewer choice and item wording on responses to questions concerning sexual behavior. *Public Opinion Quarterly, 60*, 345–375.

C.D. Howe Institute. (2010). Picking up savings: The benefits of competition in municipal waste services. *Urban Issues Series, 308*. www.cdhowe.org/pdf/commentary_308.pdf

Chafetz, J. S. (1978). *A primer on the construction and testing of theories in sociology*. Itasca, IL: Peacock.

Channels, N. L. (1993). Anticipating media coverage. In C. Renzetti & R. Lee (Eds.), *Research on sensitive topics* (pp. 267–280). Thousand Oaks, CA: Sage.

Chapple, S. (2009). Child well-being and sole-parent family structure in the OECD: An analysis. *OECD social, employment, and migration working papers No. 82*. Paris, FR: OECD. Retrieved from www.oecd.org/els/workingpapers

Cheadle, B. (2013, February 5). Federal Conservatives acknowledge they're behind Saskatchewan "push poll." Retrieved from http://globalnews.ca/news/388963/federal-conservatives-acknowledge-theyre-behind-saskatchewan-push-poll-2/

Church, A. H. (1993). Estimating the effect of incentives on mail survey response rates: A meta analysis. *Public Opinion Quarterly, 57*, 62–80.

Churchill, G. A., Jr. (1983). *Marketing research* (3rd ed.). New York, NY: Dryden.

Clammer, J. (1984). Approaches to ethnographic research. In R. F. Ellen (Ed.), *Ethnographic research: A guide to general conduct* (pp. 63–85). Orlando, FL: Academic Press.

Clarke, H. D., Kornberg, A., Ellis, F., & Rapkin, J. (2000). Not for fame or fortune: A note on membership and activity in the Canadian Reform Party. *Party Politics, 6*, 51–70.

Clarke, J. N., Friedman, D. B., & Hoffman-Goetz, L. (2004). Canadian Aboriginal people's experiences with HIV/AIDS as portrayed in selected English language Aboriginal media (1996–2000). *Social Science and Medicine, 60*, 2169–2180.

Converse, J. M., & Presser, S. (1986). *Survey questions*. Beverly Hills, CA: Sage.

Converse, J. M., & Schuman, H. (1974). *Conversations at random*. New York, NY: Wiley.

Cook, T. D., & Campbell, D. T. (1979). *Quasi-experimentation*. Chicago, IL: Rand McNally.

Cooke, M. (2009). A welfare trap? The duration and dynamics of social assistance use among lone mothers in Canada. *Canadian Review of Sociology, 46*, 179–206.

Corsaro, W. (1994). Discussion, debate, and friendship processes. *Sociology of Education, 67*, 1–26.

Corsaro, W., & Molinari, L. (2000). Priming events and Italian children's transition from preschool to elementary school: Representations and action. *Social Psychology Quarterly, 63*, 16–33.

Cotter, P. R., Cohen, J., & Coulter, P. B. (1982). Race of interviewer effects in telephone interviews. *Public Opinion Quarterly, 46*, 278–286.

Couper, M. P., Singer, E., et al. (1998). Participation in the 1990 decennial census. *American Politics Quarterly*, *26*, 59–81.

Craib, I. (1984). *Modern social theory: From Parsons to Habermas*. New York, NY: St. Martin's Press.

Creswell, J. W., & Plano Clark, V. L. (2007). *Designing and conducting mixed methods research*. Thousand Oaks, CA: Sage.

Croll, J. & Lee, P. (2008). *Report of the French Second Language Commission*. Fredericton, NB: Department of Education.

Dale, A., Arber, S., & Procter, M. (1988). *Doing secondary analysis*. Boston, MA: Unwin Hyman.

D'Antonio, W. (1989, August). Executive Office Report: Sociology on the move. *ASA Footnotes*, *17*, p. 2.

Davis, D. W. (1997). The direction of race of interviewer effects among African-Americans: Donning the black mask. *American Journal of Political Science*, *41*, 309–322.

Deacon, D., Bryman, A., & Fenton, N. (1998). Collision or collusion? A discussion and case study of the unplanned triangulation of quantitative and qualitative research methods. *International Journal of Social Research Methodology*, *1*, 47–63.

Dean, J. P., Eichhorn, R. L., & Dean, L. R. (1969). Fruitful informants for intensive interviewing. In G. McCall & J. L. Simmons (Eds.), *Issues in participant observation* (pp. 142–144). Reading, MA: Addison-Wesley.

de Heer, W. (1999). International response trends: Results from an international survey. *Journal of Official Statistics*, *15*, 129–142.

Denzin, N. K. (1989). *The research act* (3rd ed.). Englewood Cliffs, NJ: Prentice-Hall.

Di Biase, S., & Bauder, H. (2005). Immigrant settlement in Ontario: Location and local labour markets. *Canadian Ethnic Studies*, *37*, 114–135.

Diener, E., & Crandall, R. (1978). *Ethics in social and behavioral research*. Chicago, IL: University of Chicago Press.

Dijkstra, W., & van der Zouwen, J. (Eds.). (1982). *Response behavior in the survey interview*. New York, NY: Academic Press.

Dillman, D. A. (1978). *Mail and telephone surveys: The total design method*. New York, NY: Wiley.

Dillman, D. A. (1983). Mail and other self-administered questionnaires. In P. Rossi, J. Wright, & A. Anderson (Eds.), *Handbook of survey research* (pp. 359–377). Orlando, FL: Academic Press.

Dillman, D. A. (2000). *Mail and Internet surveys* (2nd ed.). New York, NY: Wiley.

Dobbins, G. H., Lane, I. M., & Steiner, D. D. (1988). A note on the role of laboratory methodologies in applied behavioral research: Don't throw out the baby with the bath water. *Journal of Organizational Behavior*, 9, 281–286.

Doob, A. N., & Sprott, J. B. (2007). The sentencing of Aboriginal and non-Aboriginal youth: Understanding local variation. *Canadian Journal of Criminology and Criminal Justice*, 49(1), 109–123

Dooley, D. (1984). *Social research methods*. Englewood Cliffs, NJ: Prentice-Hall.

Douglas, J. D. (1976). *Investigative social research*. Beverly Hills, CA: Sage.

Dowler, K. (2004). Comparing American and Canadian local television crime stories: A content analysis. *Canadian Journal of Criminology and Criminal Justice*, 46(5), 573–596.

Duncan, O. D. (1984). *Notes on social measurement*. New York, NY: Russell Sage Foundation.

Duncan, O. D., & Stenbeck, M. (1988). No opinion or not sure? *Public Opinion Quarterly*, *52*, 513–525.

Durkheim, É. (1951). *Suicide*. (J. A. Spalding & G. Simpson, Trans.). New York, NY: Free Press.

Dykema, J., & Schaeffer, N. C. (2000). Events, instruments, and reporting errors. *American Sociological Review*, *65*, 619–629.

Eder, D. (1995). *School talk*. New Brunswick, NJ: Rutgers University Press.

Eder, D., & Kinney, D. (1995). The effect of middle school extracurricular activities on adolescents' popularity and peer status. *Youth and Society*, *26*, 298–325.

Elder, G. H., Jr., Pavalko, E., & Clipp, E. (1993). *Working with archival data*. Thousand Oaks, CA: Sage.

Emerson, R. M. (1981). Observational field work. *Annual Review of Sociology*, *7*, 351–378.

Fetterman, D. M. (1989). *Ethnography: Step by step*. Newbury Park, CA: Sage.

Finkel, S. E., Guterbock, T. M., & Borg, M. J. (1991). Race-of-interviewer effects in a preelection poll: Virginia 1989. *Public Opinion Quarterly*, *55*, 313–330.

Finley, M. I. (1977, Summer). Progress in historiography. *Daedalus*, 125–142.

Foddy, W. (1993). *Constructing questions for interviews and questionnaires*. New York, NY: Cambridge University Press.

Foucault, M. (1973). *The birth of the clinic: An archaeology of medical perception*. New York, NY: Vintage.

Foucault, M. (1979). *Discipline and punish*. New York, NY: Vintage.

Foucault, M. (1990). *The history of sexuality: An introduction* (Vol. 1). New York, NY: Vintage.

Foucault, M., Khalfa, J., & Murphy, J. (2006). *The history of madness*. New York, NY: Routledge.

Fox, R., Crask, M. R., & Kim, J. (1988). Mail survey response rate. *Public Opinion Quarterly*, *52*, 467–491.

Franke, C. O. (1983). Ethnography. In R. M. Emerson (Ed.), *Contemporary field research* (pp. 60–67). Boston, MA: Little, Brown.

Franke, R. H., & Kaul, J. D. (1978). The Hawthorne experiments. *American Sociological Review*, *43*, 623–643.

Frey, J. H. (1983). *Survey research by telephone*. Beverly Hills, CA: Sage.

Funk, L. (2010). Prioritizing parental autonomy: Adult children's accounts of feeling responsible and supporting aging parents. *Journal of Aging Studies*, *24*, 57–64.

Funk, L. M. (2012). 'Returning the love,' not 'balancing the books': Talk about delayed reciprocity in supporting ageing parents. *Ageing and Society*, *32*(4), 634–654.

Funk, L. M., & Kobayashi, K. M. (2009). 'Choice' in filial care work: Moving beyond a dichotomy. *Canadian Review of Sociology*, *46*, 235–252.

Gallie, W. B. (1963). The historical understanding. *History and Theory*, *3*, 149–202.

Gans, H. J. (1982). The participant observer as a human being: Observations on the personal aspects of fieldwork. In R. G. Burgess (Ed.), *Field research* (pp. 53–61). Boston, MA: George Allen and Unwin.

Gee, J. P. (2005). *An introduction to discourse analysis: Theory and method*. London, UK: Routledge.

Georges, R. A., & Jones, M. O. (1980). *People studying people*. Berkeley, CA: University of California Press.

Gibelman, M. (2001). Learning from the mistakes of others. *Journal of Social Work Education, 37*, 241–255.

Gillespie, R. (1988). The Hawthorne experiments and the politics of experimentation. In J. Morawski (Ed.), *The rise of experimentation in American psychology* (pp. 114–137). New Haven, CT: Yale University Press.

Gillespie, R. (1991). *Manufacturing knowledge*. New York, NY: Cambridge University Press.

Godlee, F., Smith, J., & Marcovitch, H. (2011). Wakefield's article linking MMR vaccine and autism was fraudulent. *BMJ, 342*, c7452.

Goldner, J. A. (1998). The unending saga of legal controls over scientific misconduct. *American Journal of Law & Medicine, 24*, 293–344.

Goldthorpe, J. (1977). The relevance of history to sociology. In M. Bulmer (Ed.), *Sociological research methods* (pp. 178–191). London, UK: Macmillan.

Gonor, G. (1977). "Situation" versus "frame": The "interactionist" and the "structuralist" analysis of everyday life. *American Sociological Review, 42*, 854–867.

Gonzalez, A. Q., & Koestner R. (2005). Parental preference for sex of newborn as reflected in positive affect in birth announcements. *Sex Roles, 52*, 407–411.

Gorden, R. (1980). *Interviewing: Strategy, techniques and tactics* (3rd ed.). Homewood, IL: Dorsey Press.

Gotham, K. F., & Staples, W. G. (1996). Narrative analysis and the new historical sociology. *Sociological Quarterly, 37*, 481–502.

Goyder, J. C. (1982). Factors affecting response rates to mailed questionnaires. *American Sociological Review, 47*, 550–554.

Griffin, L. J. (1993). Comparative–historical analysis. In E. Borgatta & M. Borgatta (Eds.), *Encyclopedia of sociology* (Vol. 1) (pp. 263–271). New York, NY: Macmillan.

Groves, R. M., & Kahn, R. L. (1979). *Surveys by telephone*. New York, NY: Academic Press.

Groves, R. M., & Mathiowetz, N. (1984). Computer assisted telephone interviewing: Effects on interviewers and respondents. *Public Opinion Quarterly, 48*, 356–369.

Hage, J. (1972). *Techniques and problems of theory construction in sociology*. New York, NY: Wiley.

Hammersley, M., & Atkinson, P. (1983). *Ethnography: Principles in practice*. London, UK: Tavistock.

Harris, S. H. (2002). *Factories of death*. New York, NY: Taylor & Francis.

Harvey, E. B., & Lui, R. (2003, March). An independent review of the *Toronto Star* analysis of Criminal Information Processing System (CIPS) data provided by the Toronto Police Services (TPS). Toronto, ON: Toronto Police Service. www.torontopolice.on.ca

Hawkes, D., Senn, C., & Thorn, C. (2004). Factors that influence attitudes toward women with tattoos. *Sex Roles, 50*, 593–604.

Hearnshaw, L. S. (1979). *Cyril Burt: Psychologist*. London, UK: Hodder and Stoughten.

Hill, M. R. (1993). *Archival strategies and techniques*. Thousand Oaks, CA: Sage.

Hindess, B. (1973). *The use of official statistics in sociology: A critique of positivism and ethnomethodology*. New York, NY: Macmillan.

Hirschman, A. O. (1970). *Exit, voice, and loyalty: Response to decline in firms, organizations and states*. Cambridge, MA: Harvard University Press.

Holstein, J. A., & Gubrium, J. F. (1994). Phenomenology, ethnomethodology and interpretative practice. In N. Denzin & Y. Lincoln (Eds.), *Handbook of qualitative research* (pp. 262–272). Thousand Oaks, CA: Sage.

Holsti, O. R. (1968). Content analysis. In G. Lindzey & E. Aronson (Eds.), *Handbook of social psychology* (2nd ed.). (Vol. 2). (pp. 596–692). Reading, MA: Addison-Wesley.

Holsti, O. R. (1969). *Content analysis for the social sciences and humanities*. Reading, MA: Addison-Wesley.

Holy, L. (1984). Theory, methodology and the research process. In R. F. Ellen (Ed.), *Ethnographic research: A guide to general conduct* (pp. 13–34). Orlando, FL: Academic Press.

Horn, R. V. (1993). *Statistical indicators for the economic and social sciences*. Cambridge UK: Cambridge University Press.

Hsiu-Fang, H., & Shannon, S. E. (2005). Three approaches to qualitative content analysis. *Qualitative Health Research, 15*(9), 1277–1288.

Hubbard, R., & Little, E. (1988). Promised contributions to charity and mail survey responses: Replication with extension. *Public Opinion Quarterly, 52*, 223–230.

Humphreys, L. (1975). *Tearoom trade: Impersonal sex in public places*. Chicago, IL: Aldine.

Hunter, G., & Miazdyck, D. (2003). Question wording and public opinion about social assistance, Social Policy Research Unit, Faculty of Social Work, University of Regina. An occasional paper published by the Parkland Institute, University of Alberta.

Hydén, L.-C., & Bülow, P. H. (2003). Who's talking? Drawing conclusions from focus groups—some methodological considerations. *International Journal of Social Research Methodology*, 6, 305–321.

Hyman, H. H. (1975). *Interviewing in social research*. Chicago, IL: University of Chicago Press.

Jenkins, R. W. (1999). How much is too much? Media attention and popular support for an insurgent party. *Political Communication, 16*, 429–445.

Johnson, J. M. (1975). *Doing field research*. New York, NY: Free Press.

Johnstone, B. (2002). *Discourse analysis*. Oxford, UK: Blackwell.

Jones, J. H. (1981). *Bad blood: The Tuskegee syphilis experiment*. New York, NY: Free Press.

Jones, W. H. (1979). Generalizing mail survey inducement methods: Populations' interactions with anonymity and sponsorship. *Public Opinion Quarterly, 43*, 102–111.

Junker, B. H. (1960). *Field work*. Chicago, IL: University of Chicago Press.

Juster, F. T., & Land, K. C. (Eds.). (1981). *Social accounting systems: Essays on the state of the art*. New York, NY: Academic Press.

Kane, E. W., & MacAulay, L. J. (1993). Interview gender and gender attitudes. *Public Opinion Quarterly, 57*, 1–28.

Kaplan, A. (1964). *The conduct of inquiry: Methodology for behavioral science*. New York, NY: Harper & Row.

Karweit, N., & Meyers, E. D., Jr. (1983). Computers in survey research. In P. Rossi, J. Wright, & A. Anderson (Eds.), *Handbook of survey research* (pp. 379–414). Orlando, FL: Academic Press.

Keeter, S., et al. (2000). Consequences of reducing non-response in a national telephone survey. *Public Opinion Quarterly, 64*, 125–148.

Kelle, H. (2000). Gender and territoriality in games played by nine to twelve-year-old schoolchildren. *Journal of Contemporary Ethnography, 29*, 164–197.

Kelman, H. (1982). Ethical issues in different social science methods. In T. Beauchamp, R. Faden, R. J. Wallace, & L. Walters (Eds.), *Ethical issues in social science research* (pp. 40–99). Baltimore, MD: Johns Hopkins University Press.

Kemp, J., & Ellen, R. F. (1984). Informants. In R. F. Ellen (Ed.), *Ethnographic research: A guide to general conduct* (pp. 224–236). Orlando, FL: Academic Press.

Kemper, E. A., Stringfield, S., & Teddlie, C. (2003). Mixed methods sampling strategies in social science research. In A. Tashakkori & C. Teddlie (Eds.), *Handbook of mixed methods in social & behavioral research* (pp. 273–296). Thousand Oaks, CA: Sage.

Kemple, T & Huey, L. (2005) Observing the observers: Researching surveillance and counter-surveillance on "skid row." *Surveillance & Society*, 3(2/3), 139–157.

Kercher, K. (1992). Quasi-experimental research designs. In E. Borgatta & M. Borgatta, *Encyclopedia of sociology* (Vol. 3) (pp. 1595–1613). New York, NY: Macmillan.

Kidd, S. A. (2004). "The walls were closing in, and we were trapped": A qualitative analysis of street youth suicide. *Youth & Society, 36*, 30–55.

Kidd, S. A. (2006). Factors precipitating suicidality among homeless youth: A quantitative follow-up. *Youth & Society, 37*, 393–422.

Kidder, L. H., & Judd, C. M. (1986). *Research methods in social relations* (5th ed.). New York, NY: Holt, Rinehart and Winston.

Kiecolt, K. J., & Nathan, L. E. (1985). *Secondary analysis of survey data*. Beverly Hills, CA: Sage.

Kirk, J., & Miller, M. L. (1986). *Reliability and validity in qualitative research*. Beverly Hills, CA: Sage.

Knäuper, B. (1999). The impact of age and education on response order effects in attitude measurement. *Public Opinion Quarterly, 63*, 347–370.

Kottak, C. (2003). *Cultural Anthropology* (10th ed.). Boston, MA: McGraw-Hill.

Krahn, H. (n.d.) School–work transition project (SWT). University of Alberta, Edmonton, Canada. www.artsrn.ualberta.ca/transition/SWT_Overview.html

Krippendorff, K. (1980). *Content analysis: An introduction to its methodology*. Beverly Hills, CA: Sage.

Krosnick, J. (1992). The impact of cognitive sophistication and attitude importance on response-order and question-order effects. In N. Schwarz & S. Sudman (Eds.), *Context effects* (pp. 203–218). New York, NY: Springer-Verlag.

Krosnick, J., & Alwin, D. (1988). A test of the form-resistant correlation hypothesis: Ratings, rankings, and the measurement of values. *Public Opinion Quarterly, 52*, 526–538.

Krueger, R. A. (1988). *Focus groups: A practical guide for applied research*. Beverly Hills, CA: Sage.

Kusow, A. M. (2003). Beyond indigenous authenticity: Reflections on the insider/outsider debate in immigration research. *Symbolic Interaction, 26*, 591–599.

Kusserow, R. P. (1989, March). *Misconduct in scientific research*. Report of the Inspector General of the US Department of Health and Human Services. Washington, DC: Department of Health and Human Services.

Kvale, S. (1996). *InterViews: An introduction to qualitative research interviewing*. Thousand Oaks, CA: Sage.

Labaw, P. J. (1980). *Advanced questionnaire design*. Cambridge, MA: Abt Books.

Lamba, N. K. (2003). The employment experiences of Canadian refugees: Measuring the impact of human and social capital on employment outcomes. *Canadian Review of Sociology and Anthropology, 40*, 45–64.

Land, K. (1992). Social indicators. In E. Borgatta & M. Borgatta (Eds.), *Encyclopedia of sociology* (Vol. 4). (pp. 1844–1850). New York, NY: Macmillan.

Lang, E. (1992). Hawthorne effect. In E. Borgatta & M. Borgatta (Eds.), *Encyclopedia of sociology* (Vol. 2). (pp. 793–794). New York, NY: Macmillan.

Lankenau, S. E. (1999). Stronger than dirt. *Journal of Contemporary Ethnography, 28*, 288–318.

Latimer, J., & Foss, L. C. (2005). The sentencing of Aboriginal and non-Aboriginal youth under the Young Offenders Act: A multivariate analysis. *Canadian Journal of Criminology and Criminal Justice, 47*, 481–499.

Lauder, M. A. (2007). Covert participant observation of a deviant community: Justifying the use of deception. *Journal of Contemporary Religion, 18*, 185–196.

Lee, O. J., & Brotman, S. (2011). Identity, refugeeness, belonging: Experiences of sexual minority refugees in Canada. *Canadian Review of Sociology*, 48(3), 241–274.

Lefebvre, P., & Merrigan, P. (2008). Child-care policy and the labor supply of mothers with young children: A natural experiment from Canada. *Journal of Labor Economics*, 26(3), 519–548.

Lehmann, W. (2009). University as vocational education: Working-class students' expectations for university. *British Journal of Sociology of Education*, 30(2), 137–149.

Lewis, J. (2006). "I'll scratch your back if you'll scratch mine": The role of reciprocity, power and autonomy in the strip club. *Canadian Review of Sociology and Anthropology, 43*, 297–311.

Lifton, R. J. (1986). *Nazi doctors*. New York, NY: Basic Books.

Lincoln, Y. S., & Guba, E. G. (1985). *Naturalistic inquiry*. Newbury Park, CA: Sage.

Lofland, J. (1976). *Doing social life*. New York, NY: Wiley.

Lofland, J., & Lofland, L. H. (1995). *Analyzing social settings* (3rd ed.). Belmont, CA: Wadsworth.

Lowenthal, D. (1985). *The past is a foreign country*. New York, NY: Cambridge University Press.

Lowman, J., & Palys, T. (2000). Ethics and institutional conflict of interest: The research confidentiality controversy at Simon Fraser University. *Sociological Practice: A Journal of Clinical and Applied Sociology, 2*, 245–264.

MacDougall, C., & Baum, F. (1997). The devil's advocate: A strategy to avoid groupthink and stimulate discussion in focus groups. *Qualitative Health Research, 7*, 532–541.

MacKeun, M. B. (1984). Reality, the press and citizens' political agendas. In C. Turner & E. Martin (Eds.), *Surveying subjective phenomena* (Vol. 2). (pp. 443–473). New York, NY: Russell Sage Foundation.

Mahoney, J. (1999). Nominal, ordinal, and narrative appraisal in macrocausal analysis. *American Journal of Sociology, 104*, 1154–1196.

Maier, M. H. (1991). *The data game*. Armonk, NY: M. E. Sharpe.

Malacrida, C. (2007). Negotiating the dependency/nurturance tightrope: Dilemmas of motherhood and disability. *Canadian Review of Sociology, 46*(3), 235–252.

Manzoni, P., Brochu, S., Fischer, B., & Rehm, J. (2006). Determinants of property crime among illicit opiate users outside of treatment across Canada. *Deviant Behavior, 27*, 351–376.

Markham, A. (2005). The politics, ethics, and methods of representation in online ethnography. In N. Denzin & Y. Lincoln (Eds.), *Handbook of qualitative research* (3rd ed.) (pp. 793–820). Thousand Oaks CA: Sage.

Markoff, J., Shapiro, G., & Weitman, S. R. (1974). Toward the integration of content analysis and general methodology. In D. Heise (Ed.), *Sociological methodology* (pp. 1–58). San Francisco, CA: Jossey-Bass.

Martin, E. (1999). Who knows who lives here? *Public Opinion Quarterly, 63*, 200–236.

McDaniel, T. (1978). Meaning and comparative concepts. *Theory and Society, 6*, 93–118.

McIlroy, A. (2001, September 18). Under siege in the ivory tower. *Globe and Mail*. Retrieved from www.theglobeandmail.com/incoming/under-siege-in-the-ivory-tower/article4152276/?page=all

McLennan, G. (1981). *Marxism and the methodologies of history*. London, UK: Verso.

McNemar, Q. (1946). Opinion–attitude methodology. *Psychological Bulletin, 43*(4), 289–374.

Menzies, R. (1999). "I do not care for a lunatic's role": Modes of regulation and resistance inside the Colquitz Mental Home, British Columbia, 1919–33. *Canadian Bulletin of Medical History, 16*, 181–213.

Merten, D. E. (1999). Enculturation into secrecy among junior high school girls. *Journal of Contemporary Ethnography, 28*, 107–138.

Merton, R. K. (1967). *On theoretical sociology*. New York, NY: Free Press.

Miles, M. B., & Huberman, A. M. (1994). *Qualitative data analysis* (2nd ed.). Thousand Oaks, CA: Sage.

Milgram, S. (1963). Behavioral study of obedience. *Journal of Abnormal and Social Psychology, 6*, 371–378.

Milgram, S. (1965). Some conditions of obedience and disobedience to authority. *Human Relations, 18*, 57–76.

Milgram, S. (1974). *Obedience to authority*. New York, NY: Harper & Row.

Miller, J. (1998). Tsimshian ethno-ethnohistory: A "real" indigenous chronology. *Ethnohistory, 45*, 657–674.

Mitchell, A. (1997, May 17). Survivors of Tuskegee study get apology from Clinton. *New York Times*.

Mitchell, M., & Jolley, J. (1988). *Research design explained*. New York, NY: Holt, Rinehart and Winston.

Morgan, D. L. (1996). Focus groups. *Annual Review of Sociology, 22*, 129–152.

Morse, J. M. (1994). Designing funded qualitative research. In N. Denzin & Y. Lincoln (Eds.), *Handbook of qualitative research* (pp. 220–235). Thousand Oaks, CA: Sage.

Morse, J. M. (2003). Principles of mixed methods and multimethod research design. In A. Tashakkori & C. Teddlie (Eds.), *Handbook of mixed methods in social and behavioral research* (pp. 289–308). Thousand Oaks, CA: Sage.

Moser, C. A., & G. Kalton. (1972). *Survey methods in social investigation*. New York, NY: Basic Books.

Mullins, N. C. (1971). *The art of theory: Construction and use*. New York, NY: Harper & Row.

Murch, S. H., Anthony, A., Casson, D. H., et al. (2004). Retraction of an interpretation, *The Lancet, 363*(9411), 750.

Musso, E., & Wakefield, S. E. L. (2009). 'Tales of mind over cancer': Cancer risk and prevention in the Canadian print media. *Health Risk and Society, 11*(1), 17–38.

Nakhaie, M. R., & Brym, R. J. (2011). The ideological orientations of Canadian university professors. *Canadian Journal of Higher Education, 41*(1), 18–33.

Narayan, S., & Krosnick, J. A. (1996). Education moderates some response effects in attitude measurement. *Public Opinion Quarterly, 60*, 58–88.

National Aboriginal Health Organization. (2005). *Ownership, control, access, and possession (OCAP) or self-determination applied to research: A critical analysis of contemporary First Nations research and some options for First Nations communities*. Ottawa, ON: First Nations Centre.

Neuman, W. L. (2000). *Social research methods* (4th ed.). Boston, MA: Allyn and Bacon.

Neuman, W. L. (2003). *Social research methods* (5th ed.). Boston, MA: Allyn and Bacon.

Neylon, T. (2012, April 24). Life after Elsevier: Making open access to scientific knowledge a reality [Web log message]. *The Guardian*. Retrieved from www.guardian.co.uk/science/blog/2012/apr/24/life-elsevier-open-access-scientific-knowledge

Nichols, N. E. (2008). Gimme shelter! Investigating the social service interface from the standpoint of youth. *Journal of Youth Studies, 11*(6), 685–699.

Novick, P. (1988). *That noble dream*. New York, NY: Cambridge University Press.

Office of National Statistics. (2001). *Ethnicity and religion: Jedi*. Retrieved from www.statistics.gov.uk/census2001/profiles/rank/jedi.asp

Olivieri, N. F. (2003). Patients' health or company profits? The commercialisation of academic research. *Science and Engineering Ethics, 9*, 29–41.

Ong, A. S. J., & Ward, C. A. (1999). The effects of sex and power schemas, attitudes toward women, and victim resistance on rape attributions. *Journal of Applied Social Psychology, 29*, 362–376.

Ostrom, T. M., & Gannon, K. M. (1996). Exemplar generation. In N. Schwarz & S. Sudman, *Answering questions* (pp. 293–318). San Francisco, CA: Jossey-Bass.

Paige, J. M. (1975). *Agrarian revolution*. New York, NY: Free Press.

Parcel, T. L. (1992). Secondary data analysis and data archives. In E. Borgatta & M. Borgatta, *Encyclopedia of sociology* (Vol. 4). (pp. 1720–1728). New York, NY: Macmillan.

Pearce, M. E., Christian, W. M., Patterson, K., Norris, K., Moniruzzaman, A., Craib, K. J., Schechter, M. T., & Spittal, P. M. (2008). The Cedar Project: Historical trauma, sexual abuse and HIV risk among young Aboriginal people who use injection and non-injection drugs in two Canadian cities. *Social Science and Medicine, 66*, 2185–2194.

Pearsall, M. (1970). Participant observation as role and method in behavioral research. In W. J. Filstead (Ed.), *Qualitative methodology* (pp. 340–352). Chicago, IL: Markham.

Perrott, A. (2002, August 31). Jedi order lures 53,000 disciples. *New Zealand Herald*. Retrieved from www.nzherald.co.nz/nz/news/article.cfm?c_id=1&objectid=2352142

Phillips, B. (1985). *Sociological research methods: An introduction*. Homewood, IL: Dorsey.

Piliavin, I. M., Rodin, J., & Piliavin, J. A. (1969). Good Samaritanism: An underground phenomenon? *Journal of Personality and Social Psychology, 13*, 289–299.

Pineo, P. C., & Porter, J. (1967). Occupational prestige in Canada. *Canadian Review of Sociology and Anthropology, 4*, 24–40.

Pollner, M., & Adams, R. (1997). The effect of spouse presence on appraisals of emotional support and household strain. *Public Opinion Quarterly, 61*, 615–626.

Pope, J. (2007, November 16). Pasta monster gets academic attention. Associated Press (MSNBC). Retrieved from www.msnbc.msn.com/id/21837499//

Presser, S. (1990). Measurement issues in the study of social change. *Social Forces, 68*, 856–868.

Przeworski, A., & Teune, H. (1970). *The logic of comparative inquiry*. New York, NY: Wiley.

Punch, M. (1986). *The politics and ethics of fieldwork*. Beverly Hills, CA: Sage.

Ragin, C. C. (1992). Introduction: Cases of "what is a case?" In C. Ragin & H. Becker (Eds.), *What is a case?* (pp. 1–18). New York, NY: Cambridge University Press.

Rampton, S., & Stauber, J. (2001). *Trust us, we're experts*. New York, NY: Putnam.

Rathje, W., & Murphy, C. (1992). *Rubbish: The archaeology of garbage*. New York, NY: Vintage.

Reese, S., Danielson, W., Shoemaker, P., Chang, T., & Hsu, H. (1986). Ethnicity of interview effects among Mexican Americans and Anglos. *Public Opinion Quarterly, 50*, 563–572.

Renkema, J. (2004). *Introduction to discourse studies*. Amsterdam, NL: Benjamins.

Reynolds, P. D. (1971). *A primer in theory construction*. Indianapolis, IN: Bobbs-Merrill.

Reynolds, P. D. (1979). *Ethical dilemmas and social science research*. San Francisco, CA: Jossey-Bass.

Reynolds, P. D. (1982). *Ethics and social science research*. Englewood Cliffs, NJ: Prentice-Hall.

Robson, K., & Berthoud, R. (2003). Teenage motherhood in Europe: A multi-country analysis of socioeconomic outcomes. *European Sociological Review, 19*, 451–466.

Robson, K., & Pevalin, D. (2007). Gender differences in the predictors and outcomes of young parenthood. *Research in Social Stratification and Mobility, 25*, 205–218.

Roethlisberger, F. J., & Dickenson, W. J. (1939). *Management and the worker*. Cambridge, MA: Harvard University Press.

Rose, D., & Pevalin, D. J. (2002) The National Statistics Socio-economic Classification: Unifying official and sociological approaches to the conceptualisation and measurement of social class in the United Kingdom. *Sociétés Contemporaines, 45*, 75–106.

Rossi, R. J., & Gilmartin, K. J. (1980). *The handbook of social indicators*. New York, NY: Garland STPM Press.

Rothenberg, R. (1990, October 5). Surveys proliferate, but answers dwindle, *New York Times*, p. 1.

Rubenson, D., Blais, A., Gidengil, E., Nevitte, N., & Fournier, P. (2007). Does low turnout matter? Evidence from the 2000 Canadian federal election. *Electoral Studies, 26*(3), 589–597.

Runciman, W. G. (1980). Comparative sociology or narrative history. *European Journal of Sociology, 21*, 162–178.

Rutherford, M. B. (2009). Children's autonomy and responsibility: An analysis of childrearing advice. *Qualitative Sociology, 32*, 337–353.

Sanday, P. R. (1983). The ethnographic paradigm(s). In J. Van Maanen (Ed.), *Qualitative methodology* (pp. 19–36). Beverly Hills, CA: Sage.

Sassen, S. (2001). *The global city*. New York, NY: Princeton University Press.

Schacter, D. L. (2001). *The seven deadly sins of memory*. Boston, MA: Houghton Mifflin.

Schaffer, N. C. (1980). Evaluating race-of-interviewer effects in a national survey. *Sociological Methods and Research, 8*, 400–419.

Schatzman, L., & Strauss, A. L. (1973). *Field research*. Englewood Cliffs, NJ: Prentice-Hall.

Schuman, H., & Converse, J. M. (1971). Effects of black and white interviewers on black response in 1968. *Public Opinion Quarterly, 65*, 44–68.

Schuman, H., & Presser, S. (1981). *Questions and answers in attitude surveys: Experiments on question form, wording and content*. New York, NY: Academic Press.

Schwandt, T. A. (1994). Constructivist, interpretivist approaches to human inquiry. In N. Denzin & Y. Lincoln (Eds.) *Handbook of qualitative research* (pp. 118–137). Thousand Oaks, CA: Sage.

Sears, H. A., Byers, S. E., Whelan, J. J., & Saint-Pierre, M. (2006). "If it hurts you, then it is not a joke": Adolescents' ideas about girls' and boys' use and experience of abusive behavior in dating relationships. *Journal of Interpersonal Violence, 21*, 1191–1207.

Sewell, W. H., Jr. (1987). Theory of action, dialectic, and history. *American Journal of Sociology, 93*, 166–171.

Shafer, R. J. (1980). *A guide to historical method* (3rd ed.). Homewood, IL: Dorsey.

Shaffir, W. B., Stebbins, R. A., & Turowetz, A. (1980). Introduction. In W. B. Shaffir, R. Stebbins, & A. Turowetz (Eds.), *Fieldwork experience* (pp. 3–22). New York, NY: St. Martin's Press.

Sharpe, E. C., Pelletier, L. G., & Lévesque, C. (2006). Double-edged sword of rewards for participation in psychology experiments. *Canadian Journal of Behavioural Science, 38*, 269–277.

Sheuer, K. (2011, March 18). Privatization seen as the answer. *Town Crier*. Retrieved from www.mytowncrier.ca/privatization-seen-as-the-answer.html

Simich, L., Maiter, S., & Ochocka, J. (2009). From social liminality to cultural negotiation: Transformative processes in immigrant mental wellbeing. *Anthropology & Medicine, 16*(3), 253–266.

Singer, E. (1988). Surveys in the mass media. In H. O'Gorman (Ed.), *Surveying social life: Papers in honor of Herbert H. Hyman* (pp. 413–436). Middletown, CT: Wesleyan University Press.

Singleton, R., Jr., Straits, B., Straits, M., & McAllister, R. (1988). *Approaches to social research*. New York, NY: Oxford University Press.

Skidmore, W. (1979). *Theoretical thinking in sociology* (2nd ed.). New York, NY: Cambridge University Press.

Smith, A. (2006). "The one who did not break his promises": Native Americans in the evangelical race reconciliation movement. *American Behavioral Scientist, 50*, 478–509.

Smith, D. E. (1986). Institutional ethnography: A feminist method. *Resource for Feminist Research, 15*, 6–13.

Smith, D. E. (1987). *The everyday world as problematic: A feminist sociology*. Boston, MA: Northeastern University Press.

Smith, D. E. (1990). *The conceptual practices of power: A feminist sociology of knowledge*. Boston, MA: Northeastern University Press.

Smith, D. E. (2005). *Institutional ethnography: A sociology for people*. Toronto, ON: AltaMira Press.

Smith, G. J., & Wynne, H. J. (2002). *Final report: Using the Canadian Problem Gambling Index (C.P.G.I.)*. Prepared for the Alberta Gaming Research Institute.

Smith, M. L., & Glass, G. V. (1987). *Research and evaluation in education and the social sciences*. Englewood Cliffs, NJ: Prentice-Hall.

Smith, T. W. (1987). That which we call welfare by any other name would smell sweeter. *Public Opinion Quarterly, 51*, 75–83.

Smith, T. W. (1995). Trends in non-response rates. *International Journal of Public Opinion Research, 7*, 156–171.

Spector, P. E. (1981). *Research designs*. Beverly Hills, CA: Sage.

Spradley, J. P. (1979a). *The ethnographic interview*. New York, NY: Holt, Rinehart and Winston.

Spradley, J. P. (1979b). *Participant observation*. New York, NY: Holt, Rinehart and Winston.

SSHRC and Statistics Canada. (2002). *Final Report: Joint Working Group on the Advancement of Research Using Social Statistics*. Retrieved from www.sshrc-crsh.gc.ca/about-au_sujet/publications/stats_can_e.pdf

Starr, P. (1982). *The social transformation of American medicine*. New York, NY: Basic Books.

Statistics Canada. (2007, May). *Perspectives on labour and income*.

Statistics Canada. (2007, July 12). *The Daily*.

Stewart, D. W. (1984). *Secondary research: Information sources and methods*. Beverly Hills, CA: Sage.

Stinchcombe, A. L. (1968). *Constructing social theories*. New York, NY: Harcourt, Brace and World.

Stinchcombe, A. L. (1973). Theoretical domains and measurement, Part 1. *Acta Sociologica, 16*, 3–12.

Stinchcombe, A. L. (1978). *Theoretical methods in social history*. New York, NY: Academic Press.

Stone, L. (1987). *The past and present revisited*. Boston, MA: Routledge and Kegan Paul.

Stone, P. J., & Weber, R. P. (1992). Content analysis. In E. Borgatta & M. Borgatta (Eds.), *Encyclopedia of sociology* (Vol. 1). (pp. 290–295). New York, NY: Macmillan.

Strack, F. (1992). "Order effects" in survey research. In N. Schwarz & S. Sudman (Eds.), *Context effects in social and psychological research* (pp. 23–24). New York, NY: Springer-Verlag.

Strauss, A., & Corbin, J. (1990). *Basics of qualitative research*. Newbury Park, CA: Sage.

Strauss, A., & Corbin, J. (1994). Grounding theory methodology. In N. Denzin & Y. Lincoln (Eds.), *Handbook of qualitative research* (pp. 273–285). Thousand Oaks, CA: Sage.

Sudman, S. (1976). Sample surveys. *Annual Review of Sociology, 2*, 107–120.

Sudman, S., & Bradburn, N. M. (1983). *Asking questions*. San Francisco, CA: Jossey-Bass.

Sudman, S., Bradburn, N. M., & Schwarz, N. (1996). *Thinking about answers*. San Francisco, CA: Jossey-Bass.

Suls, J. M., & Rosnow, R. L. (1988). Concerns about artifacts in psychological experiments. In J. Morawski (Ed.), *The rise of experimentation in American psychology* (pp. 153–187). New Haven, CT: Yale University Press.

Tashakkori, A., & Teddlie, C. (2003). Major issues and controversies in the use of mixed methods in the social and behavioral sciences. In A. Tashakkori & C. Teddlie (Eds.), *Handbook of mixed methods in social & behavioral research* (pp. 3–50). Thousand Oaks, CA: Sage.

Taylor, S. (1987). Observing abuse. *Qualitative Sociology, 10*, 288–302.

Taylor, T., & Doherty, A. (2005). Adolescent sport, recreation, and physical education: Experiences of recent arrivals to Canada. *Sport, Education, and Society, 10*, 211–238.

Tibbetts, J. (2006, January 28). Child-abuse allegations earn $1-million award. *The Gazette*, p. A16. Retrieved June 30, 2007, from Canadian Newsstand Major Dailies database (document ID: 977934891).

Todd, D. (2008, July 3). Noted assisted suicide researcher runs into barrier. *Vancouver Sun*. Retrieved from http://blogs.vancouversun.com/2008/07/03/noted-assisted-suicide-researcher-runs-into-barrier

Todd, D. (2010, April 13). Poll: 2 million Canadians know someone abused by priest. Church responds. *Vancouver Sun*. Retrieved from http://communities.canada.com/VANCOUVERSUN/blogs/thesearch/archive/2010/04/13/poll-2-million-canadians-know-someone-abused-by-priest-church-responds.aspx

Tourangeau, R., et al. (1997). Who lives here? *Journal of Official Statistics, 13*, 1–18.

Turner, C., & Martin, E. (Eds.) (1984). *Surveying subjective phenomena* (Vol. 1). New York, NY: Russell Sage Foundation.

Van den Berg, H., & Van der Veer, C. (1985). Measuring ideological frames of references. *Quality and Quantity, 19*, 105–118.

van Laar, C., Levin, S., Sinclair, S., & Sidanius, J. (2005). The effect of university roommate contact on ethnic attitudes and behavior. *Journal of Experimental Social Psychology, 41*, 329–345.

Van Maanen, J. (1988). *Tales of the field*. Chicago, IL: University of Chicago Press.

van Poppel, F., & Day, L. (1996). A test of Durkheim's theory of suicide—without committing the "ecological fallacy." *American Sociological Review, 61*, 500–507.

van Rhijn, T. M., Smit Quosai, T., & Lero, D. S. (2011). A profile of undergraduate student parents in Canada. *Canadian Journal of Higher Education, 41*(3), 59–80.

Veenstra, G. (2007). Who the heck is Don Bradman? Sport culture and social class in British Columbia, Canada. *Canadian Review of Sociology, 44*(3), 319–344.

Vidich, A. J., & Bensman, J. (1968). *Small town in mass society* (Rev. ed.). Princeton, NJ: Princeton University Press.

Wade, N. (1976). IQ and heredity. *Science, 194*, 916–919.

Wakefield, A. J., Murch, S. H., Anthony, A., Linnell, J., Casson, D. M., Malik, M., et al. (1998). Ileal-lymphoid-nodular hyperplasia, non-specific colitis, and pervasive developmental disorder in children. *Lancet, 351*(9103), 637–641.

Warwick, D. P. (1982). Types of harm in social science research. In T. Beauchamp, R. Faden, R. J. Wallace, & L. Walters (Eds.), *Ethical issues in social science research* (pp. 101–123). Baltimore, MD: Johns Hopkins University Press.

Warwick, D. P., & Lininger, C. A. (1975). *The sample survey*. New York, NY: McGraw-Hill.

Weber, R. P. (1983). Measurement models for content analysis. *Quality and Quantity, 17*, 127–149.

Weber, R. P. (1984). Computer assisted content analysis: A short primer. *Qualitative Sociology, 7*, 126–149.

Weber, R. P. (1985). *Basic content analysis*. Beverly Hills, CA: Sage.

Weeks, M. F., & Moore, R. P. (1981). Ethnicity of interviewer effects on ethnic respondents. *Public Opinion Quarterly, 45*, 245–249.

Weinstein, D. (1979). Fraud in science. *Social Science Quarterly, 59*, 639–652.

Weitzer, R., & Tuch, S. (2004). Race and perceptions of police misconduct. *Social Problems, 51*, 305–325.

Weitzman, L., Eifler, D., Hokada, E., & Ross, C. (1972). Sex role socialization in picture books for preschool children. *American Journal of Sociology, 77*, 1125–1150.

Wesley, J. (2009). *Building bridges in content analysis: Quantitative and qualitative traditions*. Paper presented at the Annual Meeting of the Canadian Political Science Association, May 29, 2009, Carleton University, Ottawa, Ontario, Canada.

Whitehead, K. (2010). "Hunger hurts but starving works": A case study of gendered practices in the online pro-eating disorder community. *Canadian Journal of Sociology, 35*(4), 595–626.

Whyte, W. F. (1982). Interviewing in field research. In R. G. Burgess (Ed.), *Field research* (pp. 111–122). Boston, MA: George Allen and Unwin.

Whyte, W. H. (1952, March). Groupthink. *Fortune*, 114.

Wilkinson, L. (2008). Labour market transitions of immigrant-born, refugee-born, and Canadian-born youth. *Canadian Review of Sociology, 45*(2), 151–176.

Williams, P., & Wallace, D. (1989). *Unit 731: Japan's secret biological warfare in World War II*. New York, NY: Free Press.

Williams, R. J., Rehm, J., & Stevens, M. G. (2011). *The social and economic impacts of gambling: Final report*. The Canadian Consortium for Gambling Research. Retrieved from www.gamblingresearch.org/download.php?docid=11322

Willimack, D. K., Schuman, H., Pennell, B., & Lepkowski, J. M. (1995). Effects of prepaid non-monetary incentives on response rates and response quality in face-to-face survey. *Public Opinion Quarterly, 59*, 78–92.

Wood, E. A. (2000). Working in the fantasy factory. *Journal of Contemporary Ethnography, 29*, 5–32.

Yarmey, A. D. (2004). Eyewitness recall and photo identification: A field experiment. *Psychology, Crime, and Law, 10*, 53–68.

Zane, A., & Matsoukas, E. (1979). Different settings, different results? A comparison of school and home responses. *Public Opinion Quarterly, 43*, 550–557.

Zelizer, V. A. (1985). *Pricing the priceless child*. New York, NY: Basic Books.

Zimbardo, P. G. (1972). Pathology of imprisonment. *Society, 9*, 4–6.

Zimbardo, P. G. (1973). On the ethics of intervention in human psychological research. *Cognition, 2*, 243–256.

Zimbardo, P. G., et al. (1973, April 8). The mind is a formidable jailer. *New York Times Magazine, 122*, 38–60.

Zimbardo, P. G., et al. (1974). The psychology of imprisonment: Privation, power and pathology. In Z. Rubin (Ed.), *Doing unto others*. Englewood Cliffs, NJ: Prentice-Hall.

Zimmermann, C. (2007). Death denial: Obstacle or instrument for palliative care? An analysis of clinical literature. *Sociology of Health & Illness, 29*(2), 297–314.

Name Index

Page numbers followed by "*b*" indicate boxes.

Subject Index

Page numbers followed by "*b*" and "*f*" indicate boxes and figures respectively; and those followed by "*t*" indicate table.

D

E

F

G

H

I

J

K

L

M

N

O

P

Q

T

U

V

W

Y

Z